United States History to 1865

Saint Leo University

HTY 121

Carol Berkin | Christopher L. Miller | Robert W. Cherny |
James L. Gormly

CENGAGE
Learning·

Australia · Brazil · Japan · Korea · Mexico · Singapore · Spain · United Kingdom · United States

CENGAGE
Learning·

United States History to 1865: Saint Leo University, HTY 121

Making America: A History of the United States, Volume 1: To 1877, Seventh Edition
Carol Berkin | Christopher L. Miller | Robert W. Cherny | James L. Gormly

© 2015 Cengage Learning. All rights reserved.

A Brief Primary Reader for U.S. History, Volume 1
Editor Michael Bellesiles

© 2007 Cengage Learning. All rights reserved.

Senior Manager, Student Engagement:

Linda deStefano

Janey Moeller

Manager, Student Engagement:

Julie Dierig

Marketing Manager:

Rachael Kloos

Manager, Production Editorial:

Kim Fry

Manager, Intellectual Property Project Manager:

Brian Methe

Senior Manager, Production and Manufacturing:

Donna M. Brown

Manager, Production:

Terri Daley

For product information and technology assistance, contact us at
Cengage Learning Customer & Sales Support, 1-800-354-9706

For permission to use material from this text or product,
submit all requests online at **cengage.com/permissions**
Further permissions questions can be emailed to
permissionrequest@cengage.com

This book contains select works from existing Cengage Learning resources and was produced by Cengage Learning Custom Solutions for collegiate use. As such, those adopting and/or contributing to this work are responsible for editorial content accuracy, continuity and completeness.

Compilation © 2014 Cengage Learning

ISBN-13: 9781305318281

ISBN-10: 1305318285

WCN: 01-100-101

Cengage Learning

5191 Natorp Boulevard
Mason, Ohio 45040
USA

Cengage Learning is a leading provider of customized learning solutions with office locations around the globe, including Singapore, the United Kingdom, Australia, Mexico, Brazil, and Japan. Locate your local office at:
international.cengage.com/region.

Cengage Learning products are represented in Canada by Nelson Education, Ltd.
For your lifelong learning solutions, visit **www.cengage.com/custom.**
Visit our corporate website at **www.cengage.com.**

Printed in the United States of America

Brief Contents

Contents

Contents **xi**

Maps

Features

The authors of this book were once students themselves. We remember groaning when we opened a textbook, our heads filled with images of underlining, highlighting, memorizing facts and dates—at least until the exam was over. Because these memories are still vivid for us, we have worked hard to produce a history book that is different. We wanted it to convey the excitement, the drama, the surprising twists and turns, the individual and collective tales of success and failure that are the real story of our American past. It is a complex story, of course, and it introduces us to women and men we have never met, to a world very different from the one we live in today, and to ideas and behaviors that may strike us as odd or foolish or simply wrong. We have found this story endlessly interesting and we hope to stimulate that interest in others.

Many of the textbooks we read only allowed us to be passive recipients of history. We were told what happened but never how the authors knew what happened. We decided therefore to invite students to "do history," as well as simply read it, by including special features that ask our readers to consider where evidence can be found, why some stories are easier to tell than others, and what questions we might never be able to answer fully. Providing a textbook that both challenges students to try new ways of thinking and sparks curiosity about the past has been, and remains, the guiding principle behind *Making America*.

Our own teaching experience has played a role in shaping this book. Three of us teach in large public universities located on our nation's borders—the Pacific Ocean, the Atlantic, and the Rio Grande—while one teaches in a small college in Pennsylvania. We know that every student body today is culturally diverse, with a mix of recent immigrants and U.S.-born students. For some, English is a first language but for others it is a second or even a third tongue. Many of our serious-minded students do not have the formal skills to match their enthusiasm for learning. Thus, from its first edition to this, its seventh, we have made certain that our textbook meets the needs of the modern student.

For example, *Making America* offers a chronological narrative that does not assume or demand a lot of prior knowledge about the American past. It does not rely solely on words to tell this story, for we know that people, places, and events can be brought to life through maps, paintings, photos, and cartoons as well as the written word. Above all, our book speaks in a voice intended to communicate with rather than impress. We want to encourage our readers to draw their own conclusions about the causes and consequences of individual choices, public policies, political decisions, protest, and reform, and we provide them with primary source materials on which to build their own interpretations. Finally, our book offers a full array of integrated and supportive learning aids to help students at every level of preparedness comprehend what they read.

Over the years we have remained learners as well as teachers. In each edition of *Making America* we have listened to readers, both professors and students, and made changes to improve the book. Thus, this seventh edition has eliminated elements that did not prove effective and added features that we believe will help us convey the pleasure and value of understanding the people of the past and their role in making America.

The Approach

Professors and students who have used the previous editions of *Making America* will recognize immediately that we have preserved many of its central features. We have again set the nation's complex story within an explicitly political chronology, relying on a basic and familiar structure that is nevertheless broad enough to accommodate generous attention to social, economic, and diplomatic aspects of our national history. Because our own scholarly research often focuses on the experiences of women, working people, immigrants, African Americans, and Native Americans, we would not have been content with a framework that marginalized their history. *Making America* continues to be built on the premise that *all* Americans have been historically active figures, playing significant roles in creating the history of our nation's development. We have also continued the tradition in *Making America* of providing pedagogical tools for students that allow them to master complex material and enable them to develop analytical skills.

Themes

The seventh edition continues to weave five central themes through the narrative. The first of these themes, the political development of the nation, is evident in the text's coverage of the creation and revision of the federal and local governments, the contests waged over domestic and diplomatic policies, the internal and external crises faced by the United States and its political institutions, and the history of political parties and elections.

The second theme is the diversity of a national citizenry created by both Native Americans and immigrants. To do justice to this theme, *Making America* explores the full array of groups that have immigrated to the North American continent. The text attends to the tensions and conflicts that arise in a diverse population, but it also examines the shared values and aspirations that define middle-class and working-class American lives.

Making America's third theme is the significance of regional subcultures and economies. This regional theme is developed for societies in North America before European colonization and for the colonial settlements of the seventeenth and eighteenth centuries. It can be seen in our attention to the striking social and cultural divergences that existed between the American Southwest and the Atlantic coastal regions and between the antebellum South and North, as well as significant differences in social and economic patterns in the West.

A fourth theme is the rise and impact of large social movements, from the Great Awakening in the 1740s to the rise of youth cultures in the post–World War II generations, movements prompted by changing material conditions or by new ideas challenging the status quo.

The fifth theme is the relationship of the United States to other nations. In *Making America* we explore in depth the causes and consequences of this nation's role in world conflict and diplomacy, whether in the era of colonization of the Americas, the eighteenth-century independence movement, the removal of Indian nations from their traditional lands, the rhetoric of manifest destiny, American policies of isolationism and interventionism, or the modern role of the United States as a dominant player in world affairs. Viewing American history in a global context, we point out the parallels and the contrasts between our society and those of other nations.

Learning Features

Making America provides students with several ways to engage with the content. Each chapter begins with an absorbing story, **Individual Choices,** which spotlights a woman or man whose experiences provide a window on the major events and themes of the chapter and whose own words or deeds, whether public or private, are part of the record of the era relied on by historians. Whether historical figures or lesser-known individuals, these people demonstrate the importance of individual agency, or the ability to make choices and act on them. At the end of the chapter, **Individual Voices** offers a primary source related to that person with thought-provoking questions and comments about that source. The primary sources allow the individuals profiled to speak for themselves and encourage students to engage directly in historical analysis. An introduction to each source explains how the source can aid historians in understanding the era and its events.

Each chapter concludes with a **Study Tools** section, which includes a summary that reinforces the most important themes and information covered in the chapter; a chronology that lists key events discussed in the chapter; a restatement of the focus questions; a list of the glossary terms that are highlighted as key study terms in the on-page glossary, with page numbers provided for review; and a group of annotated suggested resources. These tools can help students gain a firmer understanding of the material they have just read.

Within each chapter students will encounter several distinctive features that will help them get the most out of their reading. To help students focus on the broad questions and themes throughout the text, we provide **focus questions** at the beginning of each major chapter section. Students can use these critical thinking questions as guideposts to prepare for reading and also as review prompts to help remember the important points to take from a section. *Making America* provides a unique on-page glossary that defines two types of words for students. The first type is basic vocabulary—words that might trip up some students. The glossary defines words such as "allegory," "impeach," and "dividend" and each provides the word's historical context to ensure that students understand the full meaning of a discussion. The second type of term highlighted and defined includes major historical events, people, phrases, and documents. These historical key terms appear with a color bullet to emphasize their importance to the historical narrative. We believe that this approach will help students simultaneously build their vocabularies and review for tests; it reflects our concern about communicating fully with student readers without sacrificing the complexity of the history we are relating.

The seventh edition also retains the popular feature **It Matters Today,** which points out critical connections between current events and past ones. This feature includes discussion and reflection questions that challenge students to examine and evaluate these connections. We hope that these brief essays will also stimulate faculty and students to generate their own additional "It Matters Today" discussions on other key issues within the chapter. We have also retained the **In the Wider World** feature, which introduces a global perspective on the era covered in each chapter. It reminds students that, no matter how significant or how unique to American society an event or development may be, it always exists within the context of a world in motion around it.

Finally, the illustrations in each chapter were chosen carefully to provide a visual connection to the past that is useful rather than simply decorative. The captions that accompany these illustrations analyze the subject of the painting, photograph, or artifact—and relate it to the narrative. For this edition we have selected many new illustrations to reinforce or illustrate the themes of the narrative.

New to This Edition

In this new edition we have preserved what our colleagues and their students considered the best and most useful aspects of *Making America*, including the strong narrative voice, the respect for chronology, and features such as Individual Choices, Individual Voices, and focus questions. We have replaced what was less successful, revised what could be improved, and added new elements to strengthen the book.

The seventh edition includes two new features. The first, **A Deeper Understanding of History,** introduces students to the processes historians use as they work, actively engaging students in methods of historical investigation and critical thinking. Each of these features includes a visual component, and many of them make use of graphs and maps to help students learn how to read and interpret visual data as well as primary sources. Following are selected examples of the content in this new feature:

Chapter 2
- "Cowboy and Indian Movies Got It All Wrong": Explains the importance of cross-disciplinary study in understanding the true complexity and sophistication of Native American societies.

Chapter 3
- "Who's Telling the Story? And Whose Voice Is Silent?": Guides students in interpreting a primary source, in this case, an artifact from Jamestown.

Chapter 7
- "The Maze of History": Walks students through analysis of how historical actors arrived at a particular choice (the Electoral College).

Chapter 9
- "Charting the Growth of Cotton and Slavery": Explains that there are various ways to visualize historical information and shows how different methods (a graph and a county map) can answer different questions.

Chapter 11
- "Immigration: Visualizing the Numbers": Shows how use of a graph-enhanced map can make historical information manageable.

Chapter 15
- "When Historians Disagree": Explains the process of historical interpretation, using the contrasting assumptions and conclusions of W. E. B. Du Bois and William A. Dunning to illustrate.

Chapter 17
- "Reconstructing Past Social Patterns": Walks students through analysis of an excerpt from the 1880 manuscript census and one from the Sanborn insurance maps of the late 1890s to make conclusions about the life of individuals featured in the chapter's Individual Choices/Voices features.

Chapter 20
- "A History Detective at Work": As an example of the need to approach sources critically, we give a step-by-step account of how historian Jerald Auerbach arrived at his persuasive argument that a widely cited conversation between Woodrow Wilson and *New York World* editor Frank Cobb never took place.

Chapter 25
- "Television Pictures the American Family": Guides students in analyzing a primary source, in this case a Motorola television ad picturing the "typical" American family.

Chapter 28
- "Immigration Since 1965: Unintended Consequences": Leads students into an analysis of immigration since the Immigration Act of 1965, illustrated by a graph showing country of origin, as an example of an unintended consequence.

The second new feature, **Toward a More Perfect Union,** appears in most chapters of Volume 1 and all chapters of Volume 2. Each instance of this feature briefly explains how a constitutional issue was addressed by an amendment or a Supreme Court decision. In pre-Constitution chapters where the feature appears, it offers background on matters related to the Constitution, such as the Magna Carta (Chapter 1) and direct versus virtual representation (Chapter 5). Following are some other examples of the content in this new feature:

Chapter 3
- "The Case of the Vanishing Women," on coverture

Chapter 10
- "Establishing Federal Supremacy over Commerce" (*Gibbons v. Ogden,* etc.)

Chapter 13
- "*Dred Scott v. Sandford*"

Chapter 16
- "Corporate Personhood," on the Supreme Court's endorsement of this concept

Chapter 22
- "The 'Judicial Revolution' of 1937," on Harlan Fiske Stone's footnote in the *U.S. v. Carolene Products* opinion

Chapter 25
- "Desegregation and the Supreme Court" (*Brown, Cooper,* and circuit court *Gayle v. Browder* decisions).

We have also introduced several new Individual Choices and Individual Voices profiles and primary sources. Selected examples are Charles Cotesworth Pinckney and the XYZ affair, in Chapter 8; Jarena Lee, an African American woman who became a licensed preacher, in Chapter 11; Mary Ashton Rice Livermore, a reformer who became a Sanitary Commission leader and feminist activist, in Chapter 14; the middle-class Chinese American family of Mary Tape, who challenged the San Francisco School Board on segregated schools for Chinese American children, in Chapter 17; reformer and settlement house leader Jane Addams in Chapter 19; Alan Freed, rock 'n' roll's "Moondog," in Chapter 25; and STOP-ERA leader Phyllis Schlafly in Chapter 28.

In addition, a new element, **Suggested Resources**, has been added to the Study Tools section at the end of each chapter and directs students to Internet, print, and film sources where they can gain further insight into topics in each chapter and conduct research on their own.

We have also made important changes in the text itself. Many are based on feedback from instructors, and all reflect our commitment to incorporating the newest scholarship and producing a coherent narrative, rather than an oversimplified one. Selected examples follow:

Chapter 1
- Expanded discussion of slavery in West Africa and how slavery worked there among Africans. Reorganized treatment of the Columbian Exchange.

Chapters 3 and 4
- An explanation and discussion of mercantilism has been added. An addition has been made on the Carolina-Barbados connection. The section on colonial politics has been revised, with examples added, to liven up the discussion.

Chapter 7
- The Articles of Confederation section has been reworked and expanded, with more analysis of why the Articles were framed as they were.

Chapter 10
- Coverage of the Peggy Easton affair has been added. Coverage of Denmark Vesey has been moved into this chapter from Chapter 9 for better chronology.

Chapter 12
- Two new subsections have been created, one on labor and one on slavery, and all information on each topic has been consolidated in its new section.

Chapter 13
- For better chronology, the subsection "Politicizing Slavery in the 1840s" has been moved to precede the section on the Mexican war, and the discussion of the Gold Rush has been moved from Chapter 11 to the wrap-up discussion of the Mexican war.

Chapter 18
- Coverage of the political landscape after the 1896 election has been reorganized to improve flow.

Chapter 21
- Coverage of Frederick W. Taylor has been added in the discussion of manufacturing efficiency.

Chapter 22
- Significantly reorganized to bring more attention to some topics and to consolidate coverage of closely related topics.

Chapter 23
- Added details on the coverage of Latin America and the Good Neighbor Policy. Additions on the patriotism of Japanese American internees and on Higgins Industries (Louisiana) and Higgins Boats.

Chapter 26
- Coverage of Young Americans for Freedom and of *Baker v. Carr* has been added.

Chapter 28
- Expanded discussion of Reagan's first budget to add emphasis on the deficit. Coverage of immigration has been expanded.

Chapter 29
- Fully updated with new material on the Obama administration, Afghanistan, the Affordable Care Act and Court decision, the 2012 election, and the fiscal crises.

We, the authors of *Making America,* believe that this new edition will be effective in the history classroom. Please let us know what you think.

Making America Versions and Platforms

Making America is available in a number of different versions and formats, so you can choose the version and format that makes the most sense for you and your students. The options include eBooks, Aplia™ online homework, and MindTap™, a personalized, fully online digital learning platform that contains the eBook and homework all in one product. In addition, a number of useful teaching and learning aids are available to help you with course management/presentation and to help students get the most from their course studies.

eBook for *Making America* An eBook version of *Making America* in pdf format and individual eChapters are availablurchase at www.cengagebrain.com. Students can also purchase the eBook from our partner, CourseSmart, at www.CourseSmart.com.

MindTap Reader for *Making America* This eBook is specifically designed to e for paddress the ways students assimilate content and media assets. The MindTap Reader for *Making America* combines thoughtful navigation, advanced student annotation, note-taking, search tools, embedded media assets such as video and MP3 chapter summaries, primary source documents with critical thinking questions, and interactive (zoomable) maps. Students can use the eBook as their primary text or as a multimedia companion to their printed book. The MindTap Reader eBook is available within the MindTap and Aplia online offerings found at www.cengagebrain.com.

MindTap™: The Personal Learning Experience MindTap for Berkin's *Making America* is a personalized, online digital learning platform providing students with the *Making America* content and related interactive assignments and app services—while giving you a choice in the configuration of coursework and curriculum enhancement. Through a carefully designed chapter-based learning path, students can access the *Making America* eBook (**MindTap Reader**, see description below); Aplia™ assignments developed for the most important concepts in each chapter (see **Aplia** description below); brief quizzes written by Trent Booker of Northwest Mississippi Community College; and a set of Web applications known as MindApps to help you create the most engaging course for your students. The MindApps range from ReadSpeaker (which reads the text out loud to students) to Kaltura (allowing you to insert inline video and audio into your curriculum) to ConnectYard (allowing you to create digital "yards" through social media—all without "friending" your students). To learn more, ask your Cengage Learning sales representative to demo it for you—or go to www.Cengage.com/MindTap.

Aplia™ This online homework product improves comprehension and outcomes by increasing student effort and engagement. Founded by a professor to enhance his own courses, Aplia provides automatically graded assignments with detailed, immediate explanations on every question. The assignments developed for *Making America* address the major concepts in each chapter and are designed to promote critical thinking and engage students more fully in their learning. Question types include questions built around animated maps, primary sources such as newspaper extracts and cartoons, or imagined scenarios, like engaging in a conversation with Benjamin Franklin; images, video clips, and audio clips are incorporated into many of the questions. More in-depth primary source question sets built around larger topics, such as "Native American and European Encounters" or "The Cultural Cold War," promote deeper analysis of historical evidence. Students get immediate feedback on their work (not only what they got right or wrong, but *why*), and they can choose to see another set of related questions if they want to practice further. A searchable **MindTap Reader eBook** (see description below) is available inside the course as well, so that students can easily reference it as they are working. Aplia's simple-to-use course management interface allows you to post announcements, upload course materials, and manage the gradebook. Personalized support from a knowledgeable and friendly support team also offers assistance in customizing assignments to the instructor's course schedule. For a more comprehensive, all-in-one course solution, Aplia assignments may be found within the **MindTap Personal Learning platform** (see above). To learn more, ask your Cengage Learning sales representative to provide a demo—or view a specific demo for this book, at www.aplia.com.

Instructor Resources

Instructor Companion Site Instructors will find here all the tools they need to teach a rich and successful U.S. history survey course. The protected teaching materials include the Test Bank and Cognero® online testing program, Instructor's Resource Manual, and customizable Microsoft® PowerPoint® slides of both lecture outlines and images from the text. Go to login.cengage.com to access this site.

Instructor's Resource Manual Prepared by Kelly Woestman of Pittsburg State University, this manual includes instructional objectives, chapter outlines and summaries, lecture suggestions, suggested debate and research topics, cooperative learning activities, and suggested readings and resources. Available on the instructor's companion website.

CourseReader CourseReader lets you create a customized electronic reader in minutes. With our easy-to-use interface and assessment tool, you can choose exactly what your students will be assigned—simply search or browse Cengage Learning's extensive document database to preview and select your customized collection of readings.

Once you've made your choices, students will always receive the pedagogical support they need to succeed with the materials you've chosen: each source document includes a descriptive head note that puts the reading into context, and every selection is further supported by both critical thinking and multiple-choice questions designed to reinforce key points. Contact your local Cengage Learning sales representative for more information and packaging options.

Test Bank and Cognero Online Testing. The Test Bank for *Making America*, authored by Steven J. Rauch of Georgia Regents University and Trent Booker of Northwest Mississippi Community College, includes between 65 and 75 multiple-choice questions plus five essay questions with model responses for each chapter. It is available in Word format on the instructor's companion site and through Cognero®, a flexible online system that allows you to author, edit, and manage the content. You can create multiple test versions instantly and deliver them through your learning management system from your classroom, or wherever you may be, with no special installations or downloads required.

Student Resources

cengagebrain.com Save your students time and money. Direct them to www.cengagebrain. com for choices of formats and savings and a better chance to succeed in class. Students have the freedom to purchase or rent à la carte exactly what they need when they need it, including a downloadable eBook or access to MindTap and Aplia course products. Here students will also be able to access study and review tools developed specifically for *Making America* and additional U.S. history study materials such as eAudio modules from *The History Handbook* (see below). Students can save 50 percent on the electronic textbook and can pay as little as $1.99 for an individual eChapter.

The History Handbook, **2e** [ISBN: 9780495906766] Written by Carol Berkin of Baruch College, City University of New York, and Betty Anderson of Boston University, this book teaches students both basic and history-specific study skills such as how to take notes, get the most out of lectures and readings, read primary sources, research historical topics, and correctly cite sources. Substantially less expensive than comparable skill-building texts, *The History Handbook* also offers tips for Internet research and evaluating online sources. Additionally, students can purchase and download the **eAudio** version of *The History Handbook* or any of its eighteen individual units at www.cengagebrain.com to listen to on the go.

Doing History: Research and Writing in the Digital Age, **2e** [ISBN: 9781133587880] Prepared by Michael J. Galgano, J. Chris Arndt, and Raymond M. Hyser of James Madison University. This text's "soup to nuts" approach to researching and writing about history addresses every step of the process, from locating sources and gathering information, to writing clearly and making proper use of various citation styles to avoid plagiarism.

Rand McNally Atlas of American History, **2e** [ISBN: 9780618842018] This comprehensive atlas features more than eighty maps, with new content covering global perspectives, including events in the Middle East from 1945 to 2005, as well as population trends in the United States and around the world. Additional maps document voyages of discovery; the settling of the colonies; major U.S. military engagements, including the American Revolution and World Wars I and II; and sources of immigrations, ethnic populations, and patterns of economic change.

Reader Program Cengage Learning publishes a number of readers, some containing only primary sources, some with essays only, and others with a combination of primary and secondary sources; all are designed to guide students through the process of historical inquiry. Visit www.Cengage.com/history for a complete list of readers or ask your sales representative to recommend a reader that would work well for your specific needs.

Custom Options

Nobody knows your students like you, so why not give them a text that is tailor-fit to their needs? Cengage Learning offers custom solutions for your course—whether it's making a small modification to *Making America* to match your syllabus or combining multiple sources to create something truly unique. You can pick and choose chapters, include your own material, and add additional map exercises along with the Rand McNally Atlas (including questions developed around the maps in the atlas) to create a text that fits the way you teach. Ensure that your students get the most out of their textbook dollar by giving them exactly what they need. Contact your Cengage Learning representative to explore custom solutions for your course.

Acknowledgments

The authors of *Making America* have benefited greatly from the critical reading of this edition of the book by instructors from across the country. We would like to thank these scholars and teachers who provided feedback for this current revision:

Tom Angle, Metropolitan Community College
Anthony Beninati, Valencia Community College
Martha Bonte, Clinton Community College, Eastern Iowa
    Community College District
Trent Booker, Northwest Mississippi Community College
Scott Buchanan, South Plains College
Thomas Clarkin, San Antonio College
Robert Cray, Montclair State University
Latangela Crossfield, Paine College
Mary Ellen Curtin, American University
Jeffrey Davis, Bloomsburg University of Pennsylvania
Julian DelGaudio, Long Beach City College
Gretchen Eick, Friends University
Ronald Feinman, Florida Atlantic University
George Frode, Mass. Bay Community College
Jennifer Fry, King's College
Michael Gabriel, Kutztown University
John Glen, St. Louis Community College
Leah Hagedorn, Tidewater Community College
Jillian Hartley, Arkansas Northeastern College
Stephen Katz, Community College of Philadelphia
Eileen Kerr, Modesto Junior College
Kurt Kortenhof, Saint Paul College
Mark Kuss, Our Lady of Holy Cross College
Margaret Lowe, Bridgewater State College
Mark McCarthy, Southern New Hampshire
    University Online
Richard McCaslin, University of North Texas
Suzanne McCormack, Community College of Rhode Island
Todd Menzing, Saddleback College
Rebecca Montgomery, Texas State University
Bryant Morrison, South Texas College
David Parker, California State University–Northridge
Laura Perry, The University of Memphis
Mark Quintanilla, Hannibal-LaGrange University
Steven Rauch, Augusta State University
Kathryn Rokitski, Old Dominion University
James Seaman, Saddleback College
Carey Shellman, Armstrong Atlantic State University
Bruce Way, University of Toledo

Carol Berkin, who is responsible for Chapters 3 through 7, wants to acknowledge the colleagues and students who suggested interesting new Individual Choices subjects and primary sources for her chapters. She thanks the many teachers she met through Teaching American History grant programs for their excellent ideas about what makes a textbook useful in the classroom. She has gained valuable insights from her work as editor of the online journal for teachers, *History Now,* and through her Gilder Lehrman Summer Institutes with teachers from across the country. Finally she thanks the wonderful team of historians, editors, and Cengage staff who make working on this book such a pleasure.

Christopher L. Miller, who is responsible for Chapters 1 and 2 and 8 through 14, is indebted to the community at the University of Texas–Pan American for providing the constant inspiration to innovate. Colleagues, including Tamer Balci, Robert Hoppins, and Kristine Wirts, were particularly helpful in identifying events to include in the In the Wider World features. Colleagues on various H-Net discussion lists as always were generous with advice, guidance, and often abstruse points of information. As in each of our collaborative projects, thanks are owed to Carol Berkin, Bob Cherny, and Jim Gormly, and to Kelly Woestman and Doug Egerton.

Robert W. Cherny, who is responsible for Chapters 15 through 22, wishes to thank his students who, over the years, have provided the testing ground for much that is included in these chapters, and especially to thank his colleagues and research assistants who have helped with the previous editions. The staff of the Leonard Library at San Francisco State has always been most helpful. Rebecca Marshall Cherny, Sarah Cherny, and Lena Hobbs Kracht Cherny have been unfailing in their encouragement, inspiration, and support.

James L. Gormly, who is responsible for Chapters 23 through 30, would like to acknowledge the support and encouragement he received from Washington and Jefferson College. He wants to gives a special thanks to Sharon Gormly, whose support, ideas, advice, and critical eye have helped to shape and refine his chapters.

Kelly Woestman has been involved with *Making America* from the First Edition and has continued her substantive role in the seventh edition. We suspect that no other supplements author has been so well integrated into the author team as Kelly has been with our team, and we know that this adds significantly to the value of these resources.

As always, this book is a collaborative effort between authors and the editorial staff of Wadsworth, Cengage Learning. We would like to thank Ann West, senior product manager; Megan Chrisman, associate content developer: Carol Newman, senior content project manager; Pembroke Herbert and Reba Fredericks, who helped us fill this edition with remarkable illustrations, portraits, and photographs; and Charlotte Miller, who helped us improve the maps in the book. Finally, but far from least, we thank Jan Fitter, our always patient and tactful text editor, who made our prose clearer and more concise in every chapter. These talented, committed members of the publishing world encouraged us and generously assisted us every step of the way.

☆ Your Guide to *Making America* ☆

Dear Student:

History is about people—brilliant and insane, brave and treacherous, lovable and hateful, murderers and princesses, daredevils and visionaries, rule breakers and rule makers. It has exciting events, major crises, turning points, battles, and scientific breakthroughs. We, the authors of *Making America*, believe that knowing about the past is critical for anyone who hopes to understand the present and chart the future. In this book, we want to tell you the story of America from its earliest settlement to the present and to tell it in a language and format that helps you enjoy learning that history.

This book is organized and designed to help you master your American History course. The narrative is chronological, telling the story as it happened, decade by decade or era by era. We have developed special tools to help you learn. Here, we'll introduce you to the unique features of this book that will not only help you understand the complex and fascinating story of American history but also provide you the tools to "do" history yourself.

At the back of the book, you will find some additional resources. The Appendix provides reprints of three of the most important documents in American history: the Declaration of Independence, the Articles of Confederation, and the Constitution. Here, too, a table gives you quick access to important data on presidential elections. Finally, you will see the index, which will help you locate a subject quickly if you want to read about it. Terms that appear in the on-page glossary are boldfaced in the index.

In addition, you will find a number of useful study tools on the *Making America* companion website. Go to cengagebrain.com to access these tools. If your instructor has adopted one of the digital products available with *Making America* (for instance, Aplia or MindTap) be sure to take advantage of all they have to offer! These products offer numerous avenues for engaging with the content in meaningful ways, and they can provide not just additional opportunity for further study and practice, but multiple opportunities to make your learning deeper and longer lasting. Here, now, is some additional advice on how to approach your learning experience.

How to Succeed in Your History Course

We know that, at first glance, a history textbook can seem overwhelming. There is so much to learn, so much to remember, so much to think about. The features of *Making America* are all designed to help you conquer your anxiety and enjoy your journey through the American past. Here are a few tips to make this a smoother trip:

☆ *Follow all the clues the authors provide.*

What are the important issues raised in the Individual Choices story? How many of the key topics in the chapter outline are familiar to you—and which ones are new? Don't just pay attention to the unfamiliar material; read carefully how the authors describe those events you have encountered before. Surprises may be in store. Use the focus questions as your guide to each major section of the chapter. Don't highlight everything. Read the whole section once; then read it again to find the answers to the focus questions. They are there because they point to the most important issues in the section.

☆ *Don't skip over unfamiliar words in the text.*

Use the glossary to help you understand the reading—and to increase your vocabulary. That vocabulary will come in handy if you are asked to write an exam essay.

☆ *Use the study tools feature to test your own strengths and weaknesses as you prepare for an exam.*

Would your own summary of the chapter be similar to the summary the authors provide? Can you remember the context for the events that appear in the chapter chronology? Can you answer the focus questions now that you have read and taken notes on the chapter? Would you be able to identify and explain the significance of the key terms if your professor required you to do so? If not, page numbers will help you review and strengthen your command of the material.

Working with Primary Sources

This book gives you multiple opportunities to practice doing what historians do. The Deeper Understanding of History feature inside each chapter, gives you a chance to see historical investigation in action, showing you how to read and interpret primary sources and visual data, including graphs and maps.

The Individual Voices feature at the end of each chapter lets you try your hand at doing the work of a historian. This feature gives you a primary source document that we have annotated to show you what kinds of questions historians hope the source can answer. We call this process "interrogating the source," much as a detective interrogates a witness. Often the questions historians ask cannot be answered by a single source, and so we turn to other sources to help us piece together the puzzle of the past. Any public, official, or private document, any illustration or portrait, even any artifact that was created during the era we are examining is a primary source. You can find them in books, in historical societies, in libraries, and sometimes in your own attic.

In addition to those in the book, *Making America* offers a wealth of primary sources online and inside its digital products. Your professor may distribute some in class or point you to others online. Practice analyzing some primary sources, asking questions such as: Who was the person who created this source? Under what circumstances was it created? What prompted this person to write this document or to paint this portrait or to build this house or make this piece of clothing or this tool or weapon? Was the author a reliable witness or was he or she a participant in the event being described? Does this source agree with or contradict other sources you have found? Does it challenge the interpretations you have read in history books?

This type of analysis is not only useful for success in a history class. It will also benefit you as you read the newspaper, watch today's news on the Web or TV, or listen to the critical arguments of your own day. It will help you form your own independent judgments about the world around you.

We hope that our textbook conveys to you our own fascination with the American past and sparks your curiosity about the nation's history. We invite you to share your feedback with your instructor and with us.

CAROL BERKIN, CHRIS MILLER,
BOB CHERNY, *and* JIM GORMLY

Carol Berkin

Born in Mobile, Alabama, Carol Berkin received her undergraduate degree from Barnard College and her Ph.D. from Columbia University. Her dissertation won the Bancroft Award. She is now Presidential Professor of history at Baruch College and the Graduate Center of City University of New York. She has written *First Generations: Women in Colonial America* (1996); *A Brilliant Solution: Inventing the American Constitution* (2002); *Revolutionary Mothers: Women in the Struggle for America's Independence* (2005); *Civil War Wives: The Lives and Times of Angelina Grimke Weld, Varina Howell Davis, and Julia Dent Grant* (2009); and *Wondrous Beauty: The Extraordinary Life of Elizabeth Patterson Bonaparte* (2014). She has edited *Women of America: A History* (with Mary Beth Norton, 1979); *Women, War and Revolution* (with Clara M. Lovett, 1980); *Women's Voices, Women's Lives: Documents in Early American History* (with Leslie Horowitz, 1998); *Looking Forward/Looking Back: A Women's Studies Reader* (with Judith Pinch and Carole Appel, 2005); and *Clio in the Classroom: A Guide to Teaching U.S. Women's History* (with Margaret Crocco and Barbara Winslow, 2009). Professor Berkin edits *History Now,* an online journal for teachers sponsored by the Gilder Lehrman Institute of American History. She has appeared in the PBS series *Liberty! The American Revolution; Ben Franklin;* and *Alexander Hamilton;* and The History Channel's *Founding Fathers.* She has served on the Planning Committee for the U.S. Department of Education's National Assessment of Educational Progress, and chaired the CLEP Committee for Educational Testing Service. She currently serves on the Board of Trustees of the Gilder Lehrman Institute of American History and is an elected member of the American Antiquarian Society and the Society of American Historians.

Christopher L. Miller

Born and raised in Portland, Oregon, Christopher L. Miller received his bachelor of science degree from Lewis and Clark College and his Ph.D. from the University of California, Santa Barbara. He is currently associate professor of history at the University of Texas–Pan American. He is the author of *Prophetic Worlds: Indians and Whites on the Columbia Plateau* (1985), which was republished (2003) as part of the Columbia Northwest Classics Series by the University of Washington Press and co-editor with Tamer Balci of *The Gülen Hizmet Movement: Circumspect Activism in Faith-Based Reform* (2012). His articles and reviews have appeared in numerous scholarly journals and anthologies as well as standard reference works. He has been a research fellow at the Charles Warren Center for Studies in American History at Harvard University and was the Nikolay V. Sivachev Distinguished Chair in American History at Lomonosov Moscow State University (Russia).

Robert W. Cherny

Born in Marysville, Kansas, and raised in Beatrice, Nebraska, Robert W. Cherny received his B.A. from the University of Nebraska and his M.A. and Ph.D. from Columbia University. He is professor of history at San Francisco State University. His books include *Competing Visions: A History of California* (with Richard Griswold del Castillo and Gretchen Lemke Santangelo, 2005, 2014); *American Politics in the Gilded Age, 1868–1900* (1997); *San Francisco, 1865–1932: Politics, Power, and Urban Development* (with William Issel, 1986); *A Righteous Cause: The Life of William Jennings Bryan* (1985, 1994); and *Populism, Progressivism, and the Transformation of Nebraska Politics, 1885–1915* (1981). He is co-editor of *California Women and Politics from the Gold Rush to the Great Depression* (with Mary Ann Irwin and Ann Marie Wilson, 2011) and of *American Labor and the Cold War: Unions, Politics, and Postwar Political Culture* (with William Issel and Keiran Taylor, 2004). In 2000, he and Ellen Du Bois co-edited a special issue of the *Pacific Historical Review* that surveyed woman suffrage movements in nine locations around the Pacific Rim. Most of his thirty-some articles in journals and anthologies have dealt with politics and labor in the late nineteenth and early twentieth centuries and with California and the West. He has been an NEH Fellow, Distinguished Fulbright Lecturer at Lomonosov Moscow State University (Russia), Visiting Research Scholar at the University of Melbourne (Australia), and Senior Fulbright Scholar at the Heidelberg Center for American Studies, University of Heidelberg (Germany). He has served as president of H-Net (an association of more than one hundred electronic networks for scholars in the humanities and social sciences), the Society for Historians of the Gilded Age and Progressive Era, and the Southwest Labor Studies Association; as treasurer of the Organization of American Historians; and as a member of the council of the American Historical Association, Pacific Coast Branch.

JAMES L. GORMLY

Born in Riverside, California, James L. Gormly received a B.A. from the University of Arizona and his M.A. and Ph.D. from the University of Connecticut. He is now professor of history at Washington and Jefferson College. He has written *The Collapse of the Grand Alliance* (1970) and *From Potsdam to the Cold War* (1979). His articles and reviews have appeared in *Diplomatic History, The Journal of American History, The American Historical Review, The Historian, The History Teacher,* and *The Journal of Interdisciplinary History.*

Making America

1

Making a "New" World, to 1588

INDIVIDUAL CHOICES

Wahunsunacock (The Powhatan)

Things were bad, and getting worse, for the people who lived along North America's eastern shore. For generations they had lived peacefully in their largely self-sufficient villages on the corn that the women grew and the game that the men hunted. Warfare was infrequent, and famine all but unknown. But around six hundred years ago a long-lasting change in the weather made corn production less dependable, and the people were forced to hunt and gather more wild foods. As hunters from individual villages roamed deeper into the forests looking for food, they encountered others who, like themselves, were desperate to harvest the diminishing resources. Conflicts became common.

The Powhatan people decided that collaboration with neighbors for both defense and expansion of resources was the best solution. Oral testimony suggests that in around 1550,

Wahunsunacock (The Powhatan)

six village-based groups whose territories occupied about 25 square miles near what is now Richmond, Virginia, formed an alliance and placed a hereditary chieftain (*weroance*) in charge of coordinating their mutual efforts. At about the same time, a child was born in one of those villages who would become a great figure in the confederation's future. We do not know what his childhood name was, but as an adult he was called Wahunsunacock or sometimes just The Powhatan.

Throughout Wahunsunacock's life, conditions for the people got continuously worse. In addition to the bad weather, other neighboring groups had also begun to consolidate into local confederacies and brushfire conflicts were common. But what was more troubling was the increasingly frequent appearance of odd-looking strangers who arrived in ever greater numbers along their shores. Most times these strangers seemed just to be looking around, exploring the coastline and various river inlets. Other times they seemed interested in trading often wonderful things for items that the Indians traditionally traded among themselves. But sometimes they took away women and children never to be seen again. And even worse, shortly after each time these strangers appeared, people in the villages became sick and a great many died.

When Wahunsunacock reached adulthood, he became the *weroance* of the six-village confederacy into which he had been born. He decided that, in light of worsening conditions, the limited scope of his little alliance system was not adequate to ensure the continued safety and prosperity of his people. He then made a consequential decision: his political state must either expand or die. Calling upon support from the five to six hundred fighting men who lived in the six villages, Wahunsunacock launched an effort to restructure the region's political makeup.

Over a period of twenty years or so, Wahunsunacock and his followers used a combination of diplomacy, intermarriage, and brute force to pull other little confederacies and isolated villages into a larger confederation, as depicted on Powhatan's Mantle, shown in the Individual Voices feature at the end of this chapter. Eventually the six-village alliance grew to nearly thirty villages that occupied some 8,000 square miles and could field between fifteen hundred and two thousand armed soldiers.

As remarkable as Wahunsunacock's story is, his experience was not entirely unique. Faced with changing conditions, natural ones at first and then those brought by invading Europeans, Indians throughout the Americas struggled valiantly and creatively to restructure their societies and their lives. Sometimes the effort brought success, but often at the cost of war and great sacrifice. Wahunsunacock and his contemporary visionaries succeeded in reshaping America, crafting what Europeans naively—but in this one sense quite correctly—called the New World. And in the process, they helped shape the entire Atlantic world, where the making of America would soon take center stage.

For nearly a thousand years before the Powhatans formed their confederacy, a combination of natural and human forces truly global in scope was having a profound impact throughout the Atlantic world. For example, in 632, a vibrant new religion swept out of the Arabian Peninsula to conquer much of the Mediterranean world. At the same time, climatic changes encouraged expansion by Viking warlords out of Scandinavia southward into the European mainland and westward to Iceland and Greenland. Together these expansive societies introduced new technologies and knowledge of distant and mysterious worlds that would engender an air of restlessness throughout Europe.

One of those mysterious worlds lay to the south of the forbidding Sahara Desert in Africa. There, as in both America and Europe, people had been dealing with changing conditions by crafting societies and economies that made the most of varying environments. When trading caravans began penetrating this region in the eighth century, they found highly developed cities that could draw on massive populations and natural resources to produce goods that were in great demand throughout the evolving Atlantic world. Like Native Americans, Africans too would be drawn into the restlessness that characterized this dynamic age.

A mere fifty or so years before the Powhatans united, Christopher Columbus, a Genoese navigator in Spain's employ, rediscovered the Western Hemisphere while trying to find the hidden and distant worlds known to Islamic traders. Columbus's accident brought two historical streams together, and from that point onward, the history of each helped to form the future of both. On a global scale, this event launched a new era in human history. On a more local scale, it began a process we call *Making America*.

individuals began looking for ways to profit by supplying such luxuries to European consumers. At the same time, northern European Vikings were extending their holdings throughout many parts of Europe. Then after Columbus, millennia of relative isolation for the Western Hemisphere ended, and the natural and human environments in America were opened to the flow of people, animals, and goods already circulating in this dynamic new system.

American Origins

It might be said that the process of Making America actually began about 2.5 million years ago with the onset of the Great Ice Ages. During the height of the Ice Ages, gigantic glaciers advanced and withdrew across the world's continents. During periods of glacial advancement, so much water was frozen into the glaciers that sea levels dropped as much as 450 feet. Migratory animals found vast regions closed to them by the imposing ice fields and ventured into areas exposed by the receding sea. One such region, Beringia, lay between present-day Siberia on the Asian continent and Alaska in North America (see Map 1.1). Now covered by the waters of the Bering Sea and Arctic Ocean, Beringia during the Ice Ages was a dry, frigid grassland—most recently between seventy thousand and ten thousand years ago, it was a perfect grazing ground for animals such as giant bison and huge-tusked woolly mammoths. Hosts of predators, including large wolves and saber-toothed cats, followed them.

What was true for other species may also have been true for humans. Each of the indigenous peoples who continue to occupy this hemisphere has its own account of its origins. Some of those origin stories involve migration, others do not. The most recent biological evidence suggests that the majority

---

A WORLD OF CHANGE

☆ How did environmental changes influence the development of various societies in North America during the millennia before the emergence of the Atlantic world?

☆ What forces came into play in the centuries before 1500 that would launch Europeans on a program of outward exploration?

☆ What factors in sub-Saharan African history helped lead to the development of the slave trade?

Christopher Columbus's accidental encounter with the Western Hemisphere came after nearly a thousand years of increasing restlessness and dramatic change that affected all of the areas surrounding the Atlantic Ocean. As Muslims gained a foothold in southern Europe, word spread of the finery they obtained through trade with Africa and Asia and enterprising

□ **Western Hemisphere** When discussing the world longitudinally (lengthwise), geographers often divide the globe into two halves (hemispheres). The **Western Hemisphere** includes North America, Mexico, Central America, and South America; the **Eastern Hemisphere** includes Europe, Asia, and Africa.

□ **Muslims** People who practice the religion of Islam, a monotheistic faith that accepts Mohammed as the chief and last prophet of God; born ca. 570 on the Arabian Peninsula, around 610 Mohammed began having religious visions, which were recorded as the Qur'an, the sacred text that is the foundation for the Islamic religion.

□ **Vikings** Medieval Danish, Swedish, and Norwegian groups who responded to land shortages and climatic conditions in Scandinavia by taking to the sea and establishing communities in various parts of western Europe, Iceland, Greenland, and North America.

millennia The plural of *millennium*, a period of one thousand years.

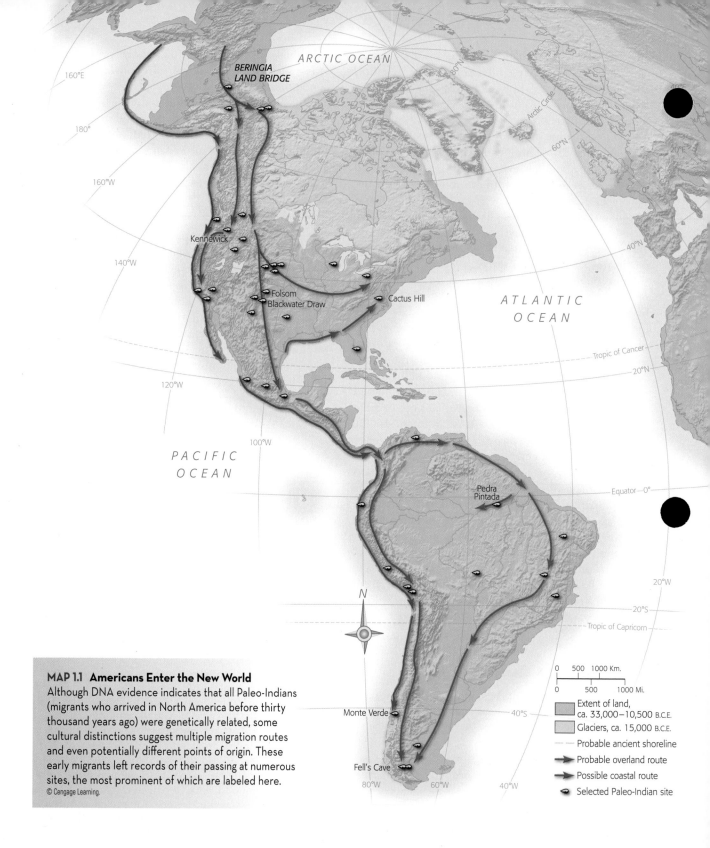

MAP 1.1 Americans Enter the New World
Although DNA evidence indicates that all Paleo-Indians (migrants who arrived in North America before thirty thousand years ago) were genetically related, some cultural distinctions suggest multiple migration routes and even potentially different points of origin. These early migrants left records of their passing at numerous sites, the most prominent of which are labeled here.
© Cengage Learning.

□ **Paleo-Indian** The first group of migrants from Asia to the Western Hemisphere, presumed to have begun arriving before thirty thousand years ago.

of Native Americans did migrate here and are descended from three genetic lines. The first of these, so-called **Paleo-Indians**, probably made the migration more than thirty thousand years ago and their population spread throughout North and South America

Paleo-Indians left a wide variety of tools as evidence of their movements throughout the Americas. These spear points are but a few examples of the materials they used in their various economic activities and speak to these people's craft skills and aesthetic values.

This sixteenth-century engraving illustrates the variety, abundance, and importance of agriculture in pre-Columbian and post-contact America. The product of centuries of genetic engineering, crops like corn, squashes, and other vegetables supported large settled communities in much of North America.

(see Map 1.1). Then for a period stretching to about sixteen thousand years ago, a sheet of ice more than 8,000 feet thick covered the northern half of North America and prevented further migration. After that a second migration of what are called the Na-Dene people began arriving, to be followed ten thousand or so years later by a third group, the Eskimo-Aleut people. DNA evidence indicates that these three groups intermingled, creating the variety of Indians that Europeans encountered when they arrived many millennia later.

Beginning about nine thousand years ago, temperatures warmed, leading to the extinction of the large Ice Age animals. As these staple meat sources disappeared, people everywhere in North America abandoned big-game hunting and began to explore newly emerging local environments for new sources of food, clothing, shelter, and tools. In the forests that grew up to cover the eastern half of the continent, they developed finely polished stone tools, which they used to make functional and beautiful implements out of wood, bone, shell, and other materials. There and along the Pacific shore, people hollowed out massive tree trunks, making boats from which they could harvest food from inland waterways and from the sea. During this time incoming migrants brought domesticated dogs into North America. With boats for river transportation and dogs to help carry loads on land, Native American people were able to make the best use of their local environments by moving around to different spots during different seasons of the year, following an annual round of movement from camp to camp—perhaps collecting shellfish for several weeks at the mouth of a river, then moving on to where wild strawberries were ripening, and later in the summer relocating to fields where they could harvest maturing wild onions or sunflower seeds.

Although these ancestors of modern Native Americans believed in and celebrated the animating spirits of the plants and animals they depended on for survival, they nonetheless engaged in large-scale environmental engineering. They used fire to clear forests of unwanted scrub and to encourage the growth of berries and other plants they found valuable. In this way they produced vegetables for themselves and also provided food for browsing animals such as deer, which increased in number while other species, less useful to people, declined. They also engaged in genetic engineering. A highly significant example comes from north-central Mexico where, beginning perhaps seven thousand years ago, human intervention helped a wild strain of grass develop bigger seedpods with more nutritious seeds. Such intervention eventually

◻ **Na-Dene** The second group of migrants from Asia to the Western Hemisphere, presumed to have begun arriving around fifteen thousand years ago.

◻ **Eskimo-Aleut** The last major group of migrants from Asia to the Western Hemisphere, who probably began arriving around five thousand years ago.

staple A basic and reliable food source.

It Matters Today

Native Americans Shape a New World

It may be hard to imagine why understanding the original peopling of North America and how native cultures evolved during the millennia before Columbus could possibly matter to the history of the United States or, more specifically, to how we live our lives today. But without this chapter in our history, there likely would have been no U.S. history at all. Europeans in the fifteenth century lacked the tools, the organization, the discipline, and the economic resources to conquer a true wilderness—such a feat would have been the equivalent of our establishing a successful colony on the moon today. But the environmental and genetic engineering conducted through the millennia of North American history created a hospitable environment into which European crops, animals, and people could easily transplant themselves. And while the descendants of those Europeans may often suppose that they constructed an entirely new world in North America, the fact is that they simply grafted new growth onto ancient rootstock, creating the unique hybrid that is today's America.

- As an exercise in "counter-factual" history, describe what life would have been like for European colonists in the New World if no Indians had been present. For example, what if Columbus had found no gold or French fishermen had found no one to trade with? What if there had been no tobacco or corn for colonists to grow and market?
- In what ways are the Indian heritages of America still visible in our society today?

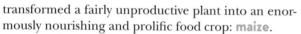

transformed a fairly unproductive plant into an enormously nourishing and prolific food crop: maize.

Maize (corn), along with other engineered plants like beans, squash, and chilies, formed the basis for an agricultural revolution in North America, allowing many people to settle in larger villages for longer periods. Successful adaptation—including plant cultivation and eventually agriculture—along with population growth and the constructive use of spare

maize Corn; the word *maize* comes from an Indian word for this plant.

◻ **mound builder** Name applied to a number of Native American societies—including the Adena, Hopewell, and Mississippian cultures—that constructed massive earthen mounds as monuments and building foundations.

◻ **Moors** Natives of northern Africa who converted to Islam in the eighth century and carried the Islamic religion and culture both to southern Africa and to the Iberian Peninsula (Spain and Portugal), which they conquered in the eighth century.

◻ **Reconquista** The campaign undertaken by European Christians to recapture the Iberian Peninsula from the Moors, accomplished in 1492.

◻ **Ferdinand and Isabella** Joint rulers of Spain (r. 1469–1504); their marriage in 1469 brought together the rival kingdoms of Aragon and Castile and united Spain.

time allowed some Indians in North America to build large, ornate cities. The map of ancient America is dotted with such centers. Beginning about three thousand years ago, the Ohio and Mississippi Valleys became the home for a number of mound builder societies whose cities became trading and ceremonial centers that had enormous economic and social outreach. Large quantities of both practical and purely decorative artifacts from all over North America have been found at these sites. Then, about eight hundred years ago, midwestern mound builder sites fell into decline, and the people who once had congregated there withdrew to separated villages or bands. No single satisfactory explanation accounts for why this happened.

Change and Restlessness in the Atlantic World

During the few centuries following the death of the prophet Mohammed in 632, Muslim Arabs, Turks, and Moors made major inroads into western Asia and northern Africa, eventually encroaching on Europe's southern and eastern frontiers (see Map 1.2). During these same years, Scandinavian Vikings, who controlled the northern frontiers of Europe, began expanding southward. They also began colonizing Iceland and Greenland. Over the decades that followed, Vikings established several outposts on the North American coast from present-day Maine to Newfoundland.

By about the year 1000, then, the heartland of Europe was surrounded by dynamic societies that served as conduits to a much broader world. Although Europeans resented and resisted both Viking and Islamic invasion, the newcomers brought with them tempting new technologies, food items, and expansive knowledge. These contributions not only enriched European culture but also improved the quality of life. For example, new farming methods increased food production so much that Europe began to experience a population explosion. Soon Europeans would begin turning this new knowledge and these new tools against the people who brought them.

Iberians launched a Reconquista, an effort to break Islamic rule on the peninsula. Portugal attained independence in 1147, and by 1380 Portugal's King John I had united that country's various principalities under his rule. In Spain, unification took much longer, but in 1469 Ferdinand and Isabella, heirs to the rival thrones of Aragon and Castile, married and created a united Spain. Twenty-three years later, in 1492, the Spanish subdued the last Moorish stronghold on the peninsula, completing the Reconquista.

Dealings with the Vikings in the north took a somewhat different turn. Although experts disagree about the exact timing, it appears that at some time between 1350 and 1450 a significant climatic shift called the Little Ice Age began to affect the entire world. In the Arctic and subarctic, temperatures fell, snowfall increased, and sea ice became a major hazard to navigation. This shift made it impossible for the Vikings to practice the herding, farming, and trading that supported their economy in the North Atlantic. Finding themselves cut off from a vibrant North Atlantic empire, Viking

MAP 1.2 Europe and Its Neighbors, ca. 1000
During medieval times, Viking and Islamic empires surrounded western Europe, and their trade routes crisscrossed the region. © Cengage Learning.

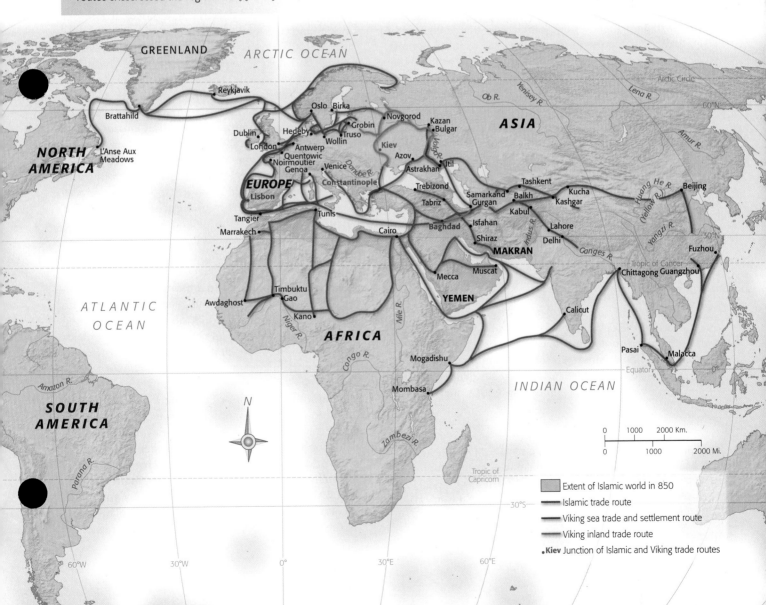

In the Wider World

Polynesians Populate the Pacific

At the same time that the American populations were settling into their new environments, another great migration was taking place on the opposite side of the world. Some six thousand years ago, from a starting point somewhere near the modern island nation of Taiwan, people in sail-rigged canoes began taking well-planned voyages toward the Philippine Islands. Setting up residence there, they continued to island hop until around 1200 B.C.E., by which time they had established populations in a chain all the way to the Solomon Islands, east of New Guinea. From there, they continued moving eastward, setting up residence in Fiji, Samoa, and Tonga. During the next thousand years, such voyages continued until these Polynesian people occupied, in the words of Jared Diamond, "every habitable scrap of land in the vast watery triangle of ocean whose apexes are Hawaii, New Zealand, and Easter Island." And while there is little physical evidence of their voyaging to the west coast of the Americas, it was certainly within their technical and navigational abilities, and some speculate that they may well have.

settlements in the British Isles, Russia, France, and elsewhere merged with local populations.

Like Native Americans at the same time, these Viking refugees often joined with their neighbors in recognizing the value of large-scale political organization. Consolidation began in France in around 1480, when Louis XI took control of five rival provinces to create a unified kingdom. Five years later in England, Henry Tudor and the House of Lancaster defeated the rival House of York, ending nearly a hundred years of civil war. Tudor, now styling himself King Henry VII, cemented this victory by marrying into the rival house, wedding Elizabeth of York to finally unify the English throne. As in Spain and Portugal, the formation of unified states in France and England opened the way to new expansion activities that would accelerate the creation of an Atlantic world.

The Complex World of Indian America

The world into which Vikings first sailed at the beginning of the second millennium and into which other Europeans would intrude half a millennium later was not some static realm stuck in the Stone Age. Native American societies were every bit as progressive, adaptable, and historically dynamic as those that would invade their homes. In fact, adaptive flexibility characterized Indian life throughout North America. Scholars have tried to make the extremely complicated cultural map of North America understandable by dividing the continent into a series of culture areas—regions where the similarities among native societies were greater than the differences (see Map 1.3).

In the southeastern region of North America, peoples speaking Siouan, Caddoan, and Muskogean languages formed vibrant agricultural and urban societies with ties to exchange centers farther north as well as to traders from Mexico. At places like Natchez, fortified cities housed gigantic pyramids, and farmland radiating outward provided food for large residential populations. These were true cities and, like their counterparts in Europe and Asia, were magnets that attracted ideas, technologies, and religious notions from the entire continent.

Farther north, in the region called the Eastern Woodlands, people lived in smaller villages and combined agriculture with hunting and gathering. The Iroquois, for example, lived in towns numbering three thousand or more people, changing locations only as soil fertility, firewood, and game became exhausted. Each town was made up of a group of longhouses, structures often 60 feet or more in length.

A tradition that may go back to the time when the Iroquois lived as nomadic hunters and gatherers dictated that men and women occupy different spheres of existence. The women's world was the world of plants, healing, nurturing, and order. The men's was the world of animals, hunting, and war. By late pre-Columbian times, the Iroquois had become strongly agricultural, and because plants were in the women's sphere, women occupied places of

longhouses Communal dwellings, usually built of poles and bark and having a central hallway with family apartments on either side.

pre-Columbian Existing in the Americas before the arrival of Columbus.

It's the Weather, Stupid: Climate and Culture

History is often written as though it happens in a vacuum, ignoring that our species, like all others, lives in a dynamic physical environment: the earth under our feet changes (geology), the water that supports all life changes (hydrology), and vast changes in climate also affect us (climatology). And these changes all interact in complicated ways. History, in part, must study how we have responded to this physical world in our constant quest to survive. The graph below shows the average of various reconstructions of global average temperatures between 1000 and 1800.

Noting that the zero line on this graph represents the normal modern temperature, it is apparent that during the time period covered by this and several of the chapters that follow, things were a lot colder than usual. There is no consensus among climatologists as to why this happened. Different theories suggest orbital cycles, decreased solar activity, increased volcanic activity, and altered ocean current flows or some combination of these. Some even think that inadvertent human contributions may have been responsible for the changes: that population declines due to medieval plagues may have led to increased forestation, which in turn decreased carbon dioxide in the atmosphere.

This four-hundred-year cooling trend had different impacts on different societies. Hunting/gathering societies, like many in North America, found that they had to expand their territories to compensate for diminished resources. Agricultural societies often found that usually reliable crops could no longer sustain local populations. In both the Old and New Worlds, there was a tendency to create larger and more complicated political organizations to even out the ill effects. Interest grew in new technologies that might help people to compensate for the changes they were experiencing. Europeans expanded trading networks into the Middle East and Asia. From there they borrowed navigational tools that permitted them to expand even more, finally all the way to North America. There, Native Americans borrowed European technologies to enhance survival. And side by side with these trends, conflict, war, and subjugation of populations increased as self-interested societies sought to improve their own conditions irrespective of the impact on others.

It is easy, then, to look back at this period in human history and point fingers at the nearly unremitting violence and selfishness that seems to characterize it, but taking a rapid, radical, and sustained change of climate into consideration forces us to reassess and perhaps temper our judgments. It also forces us to think a little more broadly about what causes history to happen the way it does.

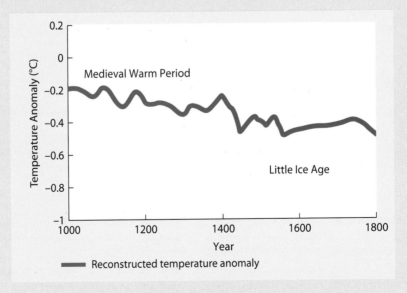

Source: Based on Robert A. Rohde, Global Warming Art project.

MAP 1.3 Indian Culture Areas in North America
Social scientists who study Native American societies have divided them into a complex of "culture areas": regions in which cultural similarities outnumber differences between resident groups. While there is some disagreement among scholars about the exact number, historical timing, and extent of the specific areas shown, this map provides a representative view of the various culture areas in North America. © Cengage Learning.

high social and economic status in Iroquois society, ruling over domestic politics. Families were matrilineal, meaning that they traced their descent through the mother's line, and matrilocal, meaning that a man left his home to move in with his wife's family upon marriage. Women distributed the rights to cultivate specific fields and controlled the harvest.

Variations on the Iroquois economic and social pattern were typical throughout the Eastern Woodlands and in the neighboring Great Plains and Southwest.

Having strong ties with agriculturalists in the east, Plains groups such as the Mandans began settling on bluffs overlooking the many streams that eventually drain into the Missouri River. Living in substantial houses insulated against the cold winters, these people divided their time among hunting, crop raising, and trade. By 1300, such villages could be found along every stream ranging southward from North Dakota into present-day Kansas.

In the Southwest, groups with strong ties to Mexico began growing corn as early as 3,200 years ago, but they continued to follow a migratory life until about 400 C.E., when they began building larger and more substantial houses and limiting their migrations. The greatest change, however, came during the eighth century, when a shift in climate made the region drier and a pattern of late-summer thunderstorms triggered dangerous and erosive flash floods.

There seem to have been two quite different responses to this change in climate. A group called the Anasazi expanded their agricultural ways, cooperating to build flood-control dams and irrigation canals. The need for cooperative labor meant forming larger communities, and between about 900 and 1300 the Anasazi built whole cities of multi-story apartment houses along the high cliffs, safe from flooding but near their irrigated fields. In these densely populated towns, Anasazi craft specialists manufactured goods such as pots, textiles, and baskets for the community, while farmers tended fields and priests attended to the spiritual needs of the society.

Another contingent of southwestern Indians abandoned the region, moving southward into Mexico. One of these groups, the **Aztecs**, arrived in the Valley of Mexico soon after 1200, settling on a small island in the middle of a brackish lake. From this unappealing center, a series of strong leaders used a combination of diplomacy and brutal warfare to establish a **tributary empire** that eventually ruled as many as 6 million people.

Other major changes occurred in the Southwest after 1300. During the last quarter of the thirteenth century, a long string of summer droughts and bitterly cold winters forced the Anasazi to abandon their cities. They disappeared as a people, splitting

In the American Southwest, the Anasazi Indians built monumental cities of multi-story buildings housing hundreds, sometimes thousands of people. This community, called Cliff Palace on Mesa Verde in Colorado, is but one example. The name "Palace," by the way, is misleading; there was no royalty among the Anasazi, and this was a dwelling for everyday farmers and craft workers.

into smaller communities that eventually became the various Pueblo groups. At the same time, an entirely new population entered the region. These hunter-gatherers brought new technologies, including the bow and arrow, into the Southwest. About half of them continued to be hunter-gatherers, while the rest borrowed cultivating and home-building techniques from the Pueblos. Europeans who later entered the area called the hunter-gatherers Apaches and the settled agriculturalists Navajos.

In other regions agriculture was practiced only marginally, if at all. In areas like the Great Basin, desert conditions made agriculture too risky, and in California, the Northwest Coast, and the Intermountain Plateau (see Map 1.3), the bounty of available wild foods made it unnecessary. In these regions, hunting and gathering remained the chief occupations. For example, the Nez Perces and their neighbors living in the Plateau region occupied permanent village sites in the winter but did not stay together in a single group all year. Rather, they formed task groups—temporary

□ **Aztecs** An Indian group living in central Mexico; the Aztecs used military force to dominate nearby tribes; their civilization was at its peak at the time of the Spanish conquest.

tributary empire An empire in which subjects rule themselves but are required to contribute goods and labor, called tribute, to an imperial government in return for protection and services.

villages that came together to share the labor required to harvest a particular resource—and then went their separate ways. These task groups brought together not only people who lived in different winter villages but often people from different tribes and even different language groups. In such groups, political authority passed among those who were best qualified to supervise particular activities. If the task group was hunting, the best and most senior hunters—almost always men—exercised political authority. If the task group was gathering roots, then the best and most senior diggers—almost always women—ruled. Thus among such hunting-gathering people, political organization changed from season to season, and social status depended on what activities were most important to the group at a particular time.

After being separated from the rest of Africa by the formation of the Sahara Desert, the Bantu people—aided perhaps by their mastery of iron-smelting technology—expanded throughout the sub-Saharan portion of the continent. This painting, rendered by non-Bantu Bushmen, records a battle between themselves and Bantus. Note the relatively huge size and menacing quality of the Bantus compared with the retreating Bushmen, an indication of how the newly dominant group was perceived by its neighbors. Individuals captured in such encounters might well be adopted into the captor's kin group as a slave.

As these examples illustrate, variations in daily life and social arrangements in pre-Columbian North America reflected variations in climate, soil conditions, food supplies, and cultural heritages from place to place across the vast continent. But despite the enormous size of the continent and the amazing variety of cultures spread across it, economic and social connections within and between ecological regions tied the people together in complex ways. For example, varieties of shell found only along the northwestern Pacific Coast were traded to settlements as far away as Florida, having been passed from hand to hand over thousands of miles of social and physical space.

A World of Change in Africa

Like North America, Africa was home to an array of societies that developed in response to varying natural and historical conditions. But unlike contemporary Indian groups, Africans maintained continual if perhaps only sporadic contacts with societies in Europe and Asia.

In ancient times tendrils of trade tied the Mediterranean and **sub-Saharan Africa** together, but during the past five thousand years increasing desertification cut off most of Africa from the fertile areas of the Mediterranean coast. The people living south of the desert were forced to largely reinvent civilization in response to changing conditions. They abandoned the wheat and other grain crops that had dominated in earlier economies, domesticating new staples such as **millet**. They also abandoned the cattle and horses that had been common in earlier times, adopting sheep and goats, which were better suited to arid environments. Depending on immediate conditions, groups could establish large villages and live on a balance of vegetables, meat, and milk or, if necessary, shift over to a purely nomadic lifestyle following their herds.

Social organization tended to follow a similar adaptive strategy. The most common social structure was based on the belief that large geographically and linguistically related groups were descended from a common **fictive ancestor**. These larger organizations were then subdivided into smaller and smaller groups, each independent—as a modern nuclear family might be—but tied through an elaborate family tree to hundreds or even thousands of other similar groups.

sub-Saharan Africa The region of Africa south of the Sahara Desert.

millet A large family of grain grasses that produce nutritious, carbohydrate-rich seeds used for both human and animal food.

fictive ancestor A mythical figure believed by a social group to be its founder, from whom all members are biologically descended.

The status of each group was determined by seniority in the line of descent—those descended from the oldest offspring of the common ancestor were socially and politically superior to those descended from younger branches. This fundamental hierarchy created an organizational structure that permitted large-group cooperation and management when appropriate but also permitted each small band to function independently when conditions required. Within each group, seniority also determined political and social status: the eldest descendant of the common ancestor within each group held superior power.

Like many Native American societies, traditional African groups practiced various forms of bonded labor. Most often slaves in these societies were war captives, debtors, or criminals, and they frequently were treated like junior members of the fictive family into which they were adopted. It was not unheard of for such subordinates to earn their freedom or even to attain positions of honor and leadership.

Sometime between two and three thousand years ago, sub-Saharan groups appear to have discovered iron smelting. Craftsmen were able to make use of abundant raw iron deposits in southern Africa to produce tools, vessels, and weapons. Often, large cities with elaborate social hierarchies grew in neighborhoods where iron and other ores were particularly abundant. These would then become centers for trade as well as political hubs, the seeds from which later kingdoms and empires would sprout.

These trading centers became particularly important when Islamic expansion brought new, outside sources for trade into the sub-Saharan world. The first mention of trade between Islamic adventurers and African communities stems from the eighth century, and it seems to have developed slowly over the next several hundred years. Increasingly after 1100, iron, gold, precious gems, and slaves were carried across the desert by Muslim traders, who gave African middlemen silks, spices, and other foreign goods in exchange. This trade tended to enhance the power of African elites, leading to ever larger and more elaborate states.

EXPLOITING ATLANTIC OPPORTUNITIES

☆ *How did the Atlantic world change as a result of efforts to exploit new discoveries leading up to and following 1492?*

☆ *How did Native Americans and Africans respond initially to European expansion?*

Dynamic forces in America, Europe, Africa, and beyond were drawing the disparate societies that occupied the Atlantic shore into a complex world of mutual

Introducing camels as draft animals made it possible for Arab and other traders to penetrate the forbidding Sahara Desert to open up a highly profitable trade with sub-Saharan states that were rich with gold, ivory, and other valuable commodities. This gold and diamond miniature (the sculpture is only about two-and-a-half inches tall) celebrates the riches that these animals carried out of Africa. *Indian, Mughal period, ca. 1800. Camel: gold enamel, diamond chips, ivory. Gr. H. 2 5/8 in. (6.7 cm.). L. 2 3/4 in. (7.0 cm.). Diam. 1 3/16 in. (3.0 cm.). The Metropolitan Museum of Art, New York, NY, U.S.A. Gift of The Shaw Foundation, Inc., 1959 (59.44.1). Photograph © 1996 The Metropolitan Museum of Art/Art Resource, New York.*

experience. Generally seeking profits for themselves and advancement for their own nations, tribes, or classes, those who sought to exploit the emerging New World nonetheless had an enormous impact on the lives of all who occupied it. The process of outreach and historical evolution that helped launch the American experience grew directly from these efforts at exploitation.

The Portuguese, Africa, and Plantation Slavery

The first of the European states to pull itself together was also the first to challenge Islamic dominance in both the Asian and African trade. Portugal's John I encouraged exploration by establishing a school of navigation on his kingdom's southwestern shore; the school sent numerous expeditions in search of new sources of wealth. By the 1430s, the Portuguese had discovered and taken control of islands off the western shore of Africa, and within thirty years had pushed their way to Africa itself, opening relations with various states. For centuries, traders in these states had shipped valuable trade goods across the Sahara by means of caravans (see Map 1.4). The Portuguese, however, offered speedier shipment and higher profits by carrying trade goods directly to Europe by sea.

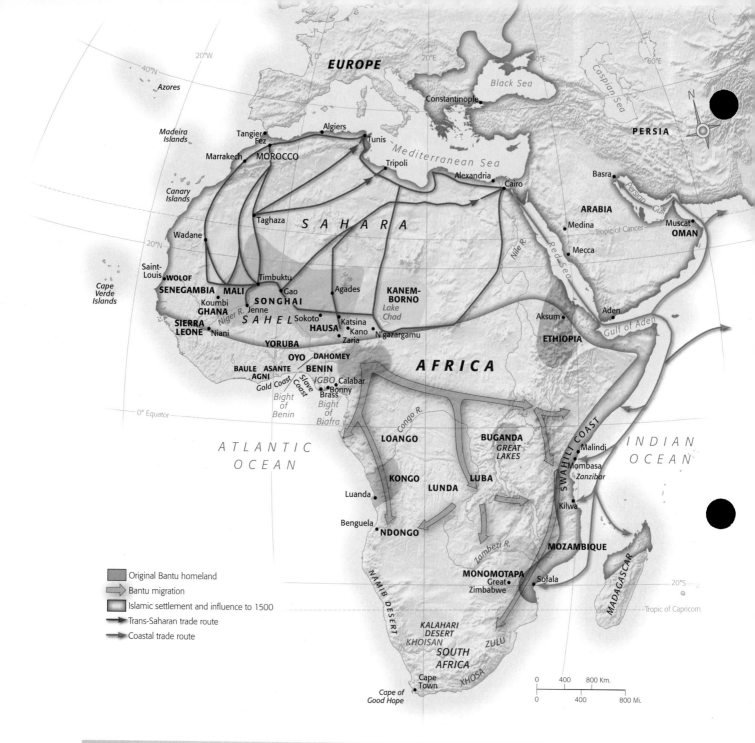

MAP 1.4 Sub-Saharan Africa Before Sustained European Contact
During the many centuries that followed the formation of the Sahara Desert, Bantu people expanded throughout the southern half of Africa. They and other groups established a number of powerful kingdoms, the capitals of which served as major trading centers among these kingdoms and for Islamic traders, who finally penetrated the desert after the year 750. © Cengage Learning.

Legend:
- Original Bantu homeland
- Bantu migration
- Islamic settlement and influence to 1500
- Trans-Saharan trade route
- Coastal trade route

By the end of the fifteenth century, Portuguese navigators had gained control over the flow of prized items such as gold, ivory, and spices out of West Africa, and Portuguese colonizers were growing sugar and other crops on the newly conquered Azores and Canary Islands. Increasing contact with African societies led to growing awareness among Europeans of the traditional forms of slavery practiced by these groups. As early as the fourteenth century, African slaves began to be seen in Southern Europe, but they remained largely a novelty. From the beginning of the sixteenth century onward, however, the Portuguese became increasingly involved in slave trafficking as the demand for labor on their Atlantic plantation islands increased. Having no sense of kinship, even fictive kinship, with Africans led to much harsher conditions for slaves under European ownership, though there is no indication that those African merchants who sold their slaves to the Portuguese understood what horrors these men and women would experience. And as plantations expanded throughout the Americas, the demand for labor led to an ever-increasing traffic in such unfortunates, which in their ignorance—or indifference—African merchants were more than willing to provide. By 1550, Portuguese ships were carrying African slaves throughout the world.

The Continued Quest for Asian Trade

Meanwhile, the Portuguese continued to venture outward. In 1487 Bartolomeu Dias became the first European to reach the Cape of Good Hope at the southern tip of Africa. Ten years later Vasco da Gama sailed around the cape and launched the Portuguese exploration of eastern Africa and the Indian Ocean. Because of its early head start, Portugal remained fairly cautious in its explorations, hugging the coast around Africa before crossing the ocean to India. As latecomers, other European nations could not afford to take such a conservative approach to exploration. Voyagers from those countries took advantage of borrowed technologies to expand their horizons. From China, Europeans acquired the magnetic compass, which allowed mariners to determine direction even when out of sight of land. An Arab invention, the astrolabe, allowed seafarers to calculate the positions of heavenly bodies and determine their latitude (their distance north or south of the equator). These inventions, together with improvements in steering mechanisms and hull design, made voyages much less risky.

A number of visionary navigators longed for the opportunity to seek new routes. One, an ambitious sailor from the Italian port city of Genoa, Christopher Columbus, approached several European governments to support a voyage westward from Europe across the Atlantic to the East Indies, but found no one willing to fund him. Finally, in 1492, Ferdinand

Astrolabes were one of the navigational tools that Europeans imported, in this case from Arabs, which helped them to find their way even very far from land. This example is from sixteenth century Spain and demonstrates clearly how complicated, and often beautiful, these devices were.

and Isabella's defeat of the Moors provided Columbus with an opportunity.

Eager to break into overseas trading, dominated in the east by the Arabs and in the south and west by the Portuguese, Ferdinand and Isabella agreed to equip three ships in exchange for a short, safe route to the Orient. On August 3, 1492, Columbus and some ninety sailors departed on the *Niña*, *Pinta*, and *Santa Maria* for the uncharted waters of the Atlantic. More than three months later, they finally made landfall. Columbus thought he had arrived at the East Indies, but in fact he had reached the islands we now call the Bahamas.

Cape of Good Hope A point of land at the southern tip of Africa around which European mariners had to sail to reach the Indian Ocean and trade with Asia.

◻ **Christopher Columbus** (Cristoforo Colombo) Italian explorer in the service of Spain who attempted to reach Asia by sailing west from Europe, thereby arriving in America in 1492.

Bahamas A group of islands in the Atlantic Ocean east of Florida and Cuba.

Over the next ten weeks, Columbus explored the mysteries of the Caribbean, making landfalls on the islands now known as Cuba and Hispaniola. He collected spices, coconuts, bits of gold, and some native captives. Columbus then returned to Spain, where he was welcomed with great celebration and rewarded with backing for three more voyages. Over the next several years, the Spanish gained a permanent foothold in the region that Columbus had discovered and became aware that the area was a world entirely new to them.

England, like Spain, was jealous of Portugal's trade monopoly, and in 1497 Henry VII commissioned another Italian mariner, Giovanni Caboto, to search for a sea route to India. John Cabot, as the English called him, succeeded in crossing the North Atlantic. Shortly thereafter, another Italian, **Amerigo Vespucci**, sailing under the Spanish flag, sighted the northeastern shore of South America and sailed northward into the Caribbean in search of a passage to the East. Finally, in 1524, Giovanni da Verrazano, sailing for France, explored the Atlantic coast of North America, quite possibly becoming the first of the strangers to visit Wahunsunacock's land.

A New Transatlantic World

At first, European monarchs greeted the discovery of a new world as bad news: they wanted access to the riches of Asia, not contact with some undiscovered place. As knowledge of the New World spread, the primary goal of exploration became finding a route around or through it. Yet even before Verrazano, ambitious adventurers from western Europe began exploring the fertile fishing grounds off the northern shores of North America. By 1506, such voyages became so common that the king of Portugal placed a 10 percent tax on fish imported from North America. But these voyages did more than feed the European imagination and the continent's appetite for seafood. Europeans, even relatively poor fishermen, had many things that the Indians lacked: copper pots, jewelry, woolen blankets, and hundreds of other novelties. For their part, the Indians provided firewood, food, ivory, and furs. Apparently the trade grew quickly. By 1534, when Jacques Cartier made the first official exploration of the Canadian coast for the French government, he was approached by party after party of

Indians offering to trade furs for the goods he carried. He could only conclude that many other Europeans had come before him.

The presence of explorers such as Verrazano and Cartier and of unknown numbers of anonymous fishermen and part-time traders had several effects on the native population. The Mi'kmaqs, Hurons, and other northeastern Indian groups approached the invading Europeans in friendship, eager to trade and to learn more about the strangers. In part this response was a sign of natural curiosity, but it also reflected some serious changes taking place in the native world of North America.

As we have noted, the onset of the Little Ice Age had far-reaching effects. The deteriorating climate made it more difficult for groups like Wahunsunacock's villages to depend on their corn crops for food. Forced to rely more on hunting and gathering, they had to expand their territory, and in doing so came into conflict with their neighbors. As warfare became more common, groups increasingly formed alliances for mutual defense—systems like the Powhatan Confederacy. And Indians often found it beneficial to welcome European newcomers into their midst—as trading partners bearing new tools, as allies in the evolving conflicts with neighboring Indian groups, and as powerful magicians whose **shamans** might provide explanations and remedies for the hard times that had befallen them.

THE CHALLENGES OF MUTUAL DISCOVERY

☆ How did Native Americans and Europeans respond to increasing contact with each other?

☆ What global changes occurred through the process called the Columbian Exchange?

Europeans approached the New World with certain ideas in mind and defined what they found there in terms that reflected what they already believed. American Indians approached Europeans in the same way. Both of these groups—as well as Africans—were thrown into a new world of understanding that challenged many of their fundamental assumptions. They also exchanged material goods that affected their physical well-being profoundly.

A Meeting of Minds in America

Most Europeans had a firm sense of how the world was arranged, who occupied it, and how they had come to be where they were. The existence of America—and even more the presence there of American Indians—challenged that secure knowledge. In the first stages of mutual discovery in America, most Europeans were

□ **Amerigo Vespucci** Italian explorer of the South American coast; Europeans named America after him.

shamans People who act as a link between the visible material world and an invisible spirit world; a shaman's duties include healing, conducting religious ceremonies, and foretelling the future.

Scala/White Images / Art Resource, NY.

Bridgeman-Giraudon/Art Resource, NY.

Europeans had trouble fitting American Indians into their preconceived ideas about the world. Native Americans were sometimes cast as noble savages and other times as devils. The Brazilian Indian shown in these two works illustrates the conflicting views. In one, the feather-clad Indian is shown as a wise magus paying homage to the Christ child; in the other, an Indian devil wears the same costume while presiding over the tortures of Hell.

content mentally to reshape what they found in the New World to fit with what they expected to find. Columbus expected to find India and Indians, and he believed that was precisely what he had found. Other Europeans understood that America was a new land and that the Indians were a new people, but they attempted to fit both into the cosmic map outlined in the Bible.

In some ways, Europeans may have been easier for American Indians to understand than the existence of American Indians was for Europeans. To Indians, the world was alive, animated by a spiritual force that was both universal and intelligent. This force took on many forms. Some of these forms were visible in the everyday world of experience, some were visible only at special times, and some were never visible. Social ties based on fictive kinship and **reciprocal trade** linked all creatures—human and nonhuman— together into a common cosmos. These connections were chronicled in myth, maintained through ritual, and graphically recorded in forms like the Powhatan Mantle. Their formation and continuity often involved the exchange of ceremonial items believed to have spiritual value. In the pre-Columbian trading world, such prized goods passed from society to

society, establishing a spiritual bond between the initial givers and the eventual receivers, even though the two groups might never meet.

Europeans and European goods slipped easily into this ceremonial trading system. The trade items that the Europeans generally offered to American Indians on first contact—glass beads, mirrors, brass bells— resembled closely the items that the Indians traditionally used to establish friendly spiritual and economic relations with strangers. The perceived similarity of the trade goods offered by the Europeans led Indians to accept the newcomers as simply another new group in the complex social cosmos uniting the spiritual and material worlds.

On the other hand, Europeans perceived such items as worthless trinkets, valuing instead Indian

reciprocal trade A system of trading in which the objective is equal exchange of commodities rather than profit; Native Americans easily incorporated Europeans into this system of trade and personal connection. Europeans, however, viewed trade as a transfer of ownership without obligation.

furs and Indian land. This difference in perception became a major source of misunderstanding and conflict. To the Indians, neither the furs nor the land was of much value because by their understanding they did not "own" either. According to their beliefs, all things had innate spirits and belonged to themselves. Thus passing animal pelts along to Europeans was simply extending the social connection that had brought the furs into Indian hands in the first place. Similarly, according to Indian belief, land was seen as a living being—a mother—who feeds, clothes, and houses people as long as she receives proper respect. The idea of buying or selling land was therefore unthinkable. When Europeans offered spiritually significant objects in exchange for land on which to build, farm, or hunt, Indians perceived the offer as an effort to join an already existing relationship, and not as a contract transferring ownership.

The Columbian Exchange

Even though Europeans and American Indians saw some similarities in each other, their worlds differed greatly, sometimes in ways hidden to both groups. The natural environments of these worlds were different, and the passage of people, plants, and animals among Europe, Africa, and North America wrought profound changes in all three continents. Historians call this process the Columbian Exchange.

The introduction of plants into the New World extended a process that had been taking place for centuries in the Old World. Trade with Asia had carried exotic plants such as bananas, sugar cane, and rice into Africa as early as 2,300 years ago. From Africa, these plants were imported to Iberian-claimed islands such as the Canaries and eventually to America, where, along with cotton, indigo, coffee, and other imports, they would become cash crops on European-controlled plantations. From both Africa and Europe, grains such as wheat, barley, and millet were readily transplanted to some areas in North America, as were grazing grasses and various vegetables, including turnips, spinach, and cabbage.

North American plants also traveled from west to east in the Columbian Exchange. Leading the way in economic importance was tobacco, a stimulant used widely in North America for ceremonial purposes and broadly adopted by Europeans and Africans as a recreational drug. In addition, New World vegetables helped to revolutionize world food supplies. Remarkably easy to grow, maize thrived virtually everywhere. In addition, the white-fleshed potato, tomato, manioc, squash, and beans native to the Western Hemisphere were soon cultivated throughout the world. Animals also moved in the Columbian Exchange. Europeans brought horses, pigs, cattle, oxen, sheep, goats, and domesticated fowl to America, where their numbers soared.

The transplanting of European grain crops and domesticated animals reshaped the American landscape. The contours of the land were changed by clearing trees and undergrowth and by plowing and fencing, which altered the flow of water, the distribution of seeds, the nesting of birds, and the movement of native animals. Gradually, imported livestock pushed aside native species, and imported plants choked out indigenous ones.

Perhaps the most tragic trade among the three continents came about as the direct and unavoidable consequence of human contact. During the period leading up to the age of exploration, many Europeans lost their lives to epidemic diseases. The Black Death of the fourteenth century, for example, wiped out more than a third of Europe's population. Exposure to smallpox, measles, typhus, and other serious diseases often had devastating results, but Europeans gradually developed resistance to infection. In contrast, the Indian peoples encountered by Columbus and other European explorers lived in an environment in which contagious diseases were never a serious threat until the Europeans arrived. They had no acquired immunity to the various bacteria and viruses that Europeans carried. As a result, the new diseases spread very rapidly and were much more deadly among the native peoples than they were among Europeans.

Controversy rages over the number of Indians killed by imported European diseases. Estimates of how many people lived in America north of Mexico in 1492 run from a high of 25 million to a low of 1 million. At the moment, most scholars accept a range of from 3 to 10 million. Even if the most conservative estimate is correct, the raw numbers of people who died of imported diseases were enormous. Between 90 and 95 percent of the native population appears to have died of disease during the first century of contact. Although the percentage was probably lower in areas where contact was infrequent and where native

□ **Columbian Exchange** The exchange of people, plants, animals, and diseases among Europe, Africa, and North America that occurred after Columbus's arrival in the New World.

□ **cash crops** A crop raised in large quantities for sale rather than for local or home consumption.

□ **manioc** Also called *cassava* and *tapioca*, a root vegetable native to South America that became a staple food source throughout the tropical world after 1500.

□ **acquired immunity** Resistance or partial resistance to a disease; acquired immunity develops in a population over time as a result of exposure to harmful bacteria or viruses. Indians lacked acquired immunity to European diseases, which decimated Indian populations.

populations were sparse, disease took a terrible toll as it followed the lines of kinship and trade that held native North America together.

Although exchanged diseases killed many millions of Indians and lesser numbers of Africans and Europeans, the transplantation of North American plants significantly expanded food production in what had been marginal areas of Europe and Africa. At the same time, the environmental changes that Europeans wrought along the Atlantic shore of North America permitted the region to support many more people than it had sustained under Indian cultivation. The overall result in Europe and Africa was a population explosion that eventually spilled over to repopulate a devastated North America.

New Worlds in Africa and America

As the Columbian Exchange redistributed plants, animals, and populations among Europe, Africa, and North America, it permanently altered the history of both hemispheres. In North America, for example, the combination of disease, environmental transformation, and immigrant population pressure changed American Indian life and culture in profound ways.

Clearly, imported disease had the most ruinous influence on the lives of Indians. Cooperative labor was required for hunting and gathering, and native groups faced extinction if disease caused a shortage of labor. Also, most societies in North America were **nonliterate** and wholesale death by disease wiped out the elders and storytellers who preserved practical, religious, and cultural knowledge, resulting in confusion and disorientation among survivors. In an effort to avert extinction, remnant groups banded together to share labor and lore. Members of formerly self-sustaining kinship groups joined together in composite villages or, in some cases, intertribal leagues or confederacies. And the devastation that European diseases wrought eased the way for the deeper penetration of Europeans into North America as Indians sought alliances with the newcomers to gain new tools, new sources of information, and new military partners, pushing Indians into increasingly tangled relationships with Europeans.

The Columbian Exchange also severely disrupted life in Africa. Africa had supplied labor in the Old World. Perhaps as many as 4 million slaves

The Granger Collection, NYC.

Although slavery began as a benign practice in traditional African societies—an extension of the hierarchical fictive kin system—at the height of the Atlantic slave trade in the sixteenth through eighteenth centuries, it had devolved into a highly malignant enterprise. As depicted here, slave drivers were heavily influenced by outside contact. One of those shown here is wearing an Arab-influenced turban, while the clothing of the other is more European. Note, too, that the latter carries both a gun and a traditional African spear.

were carried across the desert by Muslim traders between 800 and the time the Portuguese redirected the trade in the sixteenth century. From that time forward, European technology, wealth, and ideas fostered the development of aggressive centralized states along the Slave Coast on the shore of West Africa's Gulf of Guinea (see Map 1.5). Armed with European

nonliterate Lacking a system of reading and writing, relying instead on storytelling and mnemonic (memory-assisting) devices such as pictures.

☐ **Slave Coast** A region of coastal West Africa adjacent to the Gold Coast; it was the principal source of the slaves taken out of West Africa from the sixteenth to the early nineteenth centuries.

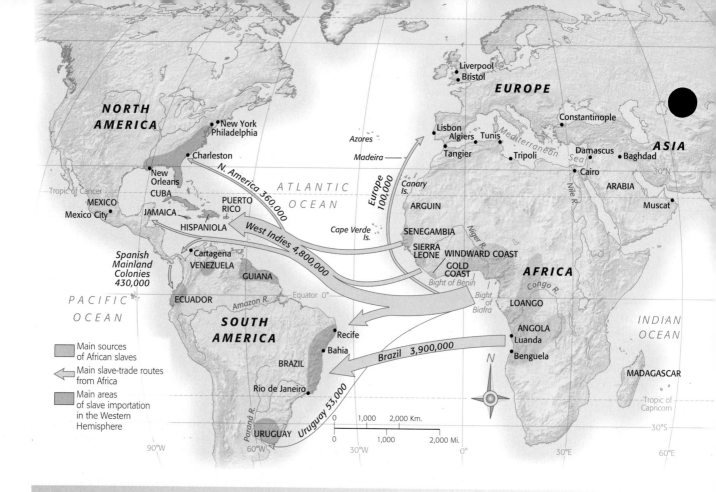

MAP 1.5 Western Africa and the Atlantic Slave Trade
Africa's western shore was the major source for slaves who were transported to European colonies on the Atlantic islands, the Caribbean islands, and mainland North and South America. Powerful coastal kingdoms mounted organized raids into many inland areas to capture people who were then marched to the coast for shipment to the New World. This map shows the several regions from which slaves were taken, and the approximate numbers of people exported to different destinations. © Cengage Learning.

firearms, aggressive tribes engaged in large-scale raiding deep into the Niger and Congo River regions. These raiders captured millions of prisoners, whom they herded back to the coast and sold to Portuguese, Spanish, Dutch, and other European traders to supply labor for mines and plantations in the New World.

The most recent estimates suggest that more than 9.5 million enslaved Africans arrived in the New World between 1500 and 1800. And they were only a small portion of the total number of Africans victimized by the system. On average, between 10 and 20 percent of the slaves shipped to the Americas died in transit. Adding in the numbers who were shipped to other locations in the Eastern Hemisphere, who were kept in slavery

within Africa, and who died during the raids and on the marches to the coast yields a staggering total.

A New World in Europe

The discovery of America and the Columbian Exchange also had staggering repercussions on life in Europe. New economic opportunities and new ideas demanded new kinds of political and economic organization. The discovery of the New World clearly forced a new and more modern society onto Europeans.

Europe's population was already rising when potatoes, maize, and other New World crops began to revolutionize food production. Populations then began to soar despite nearly continuous wars and a flood of migration to the New World. European rulers and their advisers saw that centralized states offered the most promising device for harnessing the riches of the New World while controlling ever-increasing numbers of people at home. The sons and daughters of Europe's first generation of absolute monarchs chose to continue the consolidation of authority begun by their parents.

absolute monarch The ruler of a kingdom who practices absolutism, a political form in which every aspect of national life—including politics, religion, the economy, and social affairs—comes under royal authority.

As Europeans responded to social, political, and economic changes, traditional patterns of authority broke down, especially in the realm of religion. A generation of theologians who were dissatisfied with the perceived corruption and superstition they found in the medieval Catholic Church launched the period known as the Reformation. Known as Protestantism, the doctrines adopted by these reformers launched an ideology that appealed to a broad audience in the rapidly changing European world of the sixteenth century. Ever critical of entrenched authority, the new doctrines attracted lawyers, bureaucrats, merchants, and manufacturers, whose economic and political status was on the rise thanks to increased prosperity generated by the Columbian Exchange. But many in the ruling classes also found aspects of the new theology attractive. Henry VIII of England, at one time a critic of Protestant ideas, found Protestantism convenient when he wanted to resist the authority of the pope and expand English national power.

Henry VIII, the son of Henry VII and Elizabeth of York, was the first undisputed heir to the English throne in several generations, and he was consumed with the desire to avoid renewed civil war. When his wife, Catherine of Aragon, failed to bear a son who might inherit the throne, Henry demanded in 1527 that Pope Clement VII grant him an annulment and permission to marry someone else. Clement refused, and in desperation, Henry seized control of the church in England. While the idea of unifying religious and civil authority under his personal control was appealing, Henry needed Protestant support in his war against the pope's authority, so he reluctantly opened the door to Protestant practices in his newly created Church of England.

After Henry's death, his very young son ascended the throne as Edward VI. In the absence of a strong king, Protestants had virtual free rein, and the pace of reform quickened. Edward, however, died after ruling for only six years, and Mary, his oldest sister, succeeded him. Married to Philip II of Spain and a devout Roman Catholic, Mary attempted to reverse the reforming trend, but her brutality only drove the movement underground and made it more militant. By the time her half-sister Elizabeth, who was born and raised a Protestant, inherited the crown in 1558, the Protestant underground had become powerful and highly motivated. In fact, Elizabeth I spent her entire half-century reign trying to reach a workable settlement with Protestant dissenters that would permit them free worship without endangering her political authority.

TOWARD A MORE PERFECT UNION

Limiting English Absolutism

Although absolutism became the norm in European governing, various legal instruments prevented it from depriving citizens of all rights. One of the most important of these instruments in England was the Magna Carta. Originally forced upon King John in 1215, it was renewed a number of times and finally entered into the official statute rolls in 1297, forming the key prop for the creation of an English Constitution. Among other things, this document placed the king under the authority of an assembly of "five and twenty barons of the kingdom" who were empowered to hear petitions for redress of grievances against the king, entitling them to "distress us [the king] in all possible ways, namely, by seizing our castles, lands, possessions, and in any other way they can, until redress has been obtained as they deem fit." It also proclaimed that "No freeman shall be taken, imprisoned, disseised [dispossessed], outlawed, banished, or in any way destroyed, nor will We proceed against or prosecute him, except by the lawful judgment of his peers and by the law of the land." As Americans later sought to make a more perfect union, the principles of the Magna Carta loomed large in their designs.

□ **Reformation** A religious movement beginning in the sixteenth century that began as an internal attempt to reform the Roman Catholic Church, but soon led to the breakup of the Church into competing denominations.

□ **Protestantism** The beliefs and practices of Christians who broke with the Roman Catholic Church during the Reformation; rejecting church authority and the necessity of the priesthood, Protestants accepted the Bible as the only source of revelation, salvation as God's gift to the faithful, and a direct, personal relationship with God as available to every believer.

□ **Henry VIII** King of England (r. 1509–1547); his desire for an annulment from his first wife led him to break with Catholicism and establish the Church of England.

□ **Elizabeth I** Queen of England (r. 1558–1603); she succeeded the Catholic Mary I and reestablished Protestantism in England; her reign was a time of domestic prosperity and cultural achievement.

dissenters People who do not accept the doctrines of an established or national church.

NATIVE AMERICANS'
View of the World: "Powhatan's Mantle"

Though we usually do not think of maps as "voices," they do give voice to particular views of the world held by particular people in particular places and they are designed for particular purposes. A case in point is a map referred to as Powhatan's Mantle. Though it may not have been an actual cloak worn by Wahunsunacock, experts agree that it is from that time and that place. This map depicts the alliance system constructed by Wahunsunacock during his lifetime, with him in the center and the various confederation villages, as beaded disks, surrounding him.

The Granger Collection, NYC.

❶ This is an example of what geographers call an "egocentric" map. What makes the map effective in symbolizing the importance of the central figure?

❷ Given its location and size, what can you say about the village represented by this disk?

❸ Or this one?

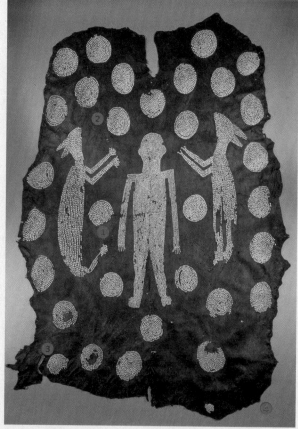

Chief Powhatan's Mantle, North American Indian, from Virginia, late 16th–early 17th century (deerskin with shell patterns), American School/Ashmolean Museum, University of Oxford, UK/The Bridgeman Art Library.

❹ Taken in its entirety, how does this map differ from what we think of as conventional maps? What might that tell us about how Wahunsunacock and his people thought about relationships in their world? How might their view differ from that of Europeans?

SUMMARY

Making America began many thousands of years ago. Over millennia the continent's residents continually crafted economic strategies, social arrangements, and political systems to preserve and enhance their lives. The result was a rich and flourishing world of different cultures, linked by common religious and economic bonds.

At first, the arrival of Europeans only added another society to an already cosmopolitan sphere. Ultimately, though, the dynamic European society that arose after the onset of the Little Ice Age became more intrusive. As a result, Native Americans faced challenges that they had never imagined: economic crises, disease, war, and the unfolding environmental changes wrought by the Europeans who followed Columbus.

In addition, influences from the New World reached out to accelerate processes that were already affecting the Old. The flow of wealth and food out of the West was increasing populations, and this growth, with the accompanying rise of powerful kings and unified nations, led to continuing conflict over newfound resources. In Africa, strong coastal states raided weaker neighboring groups, more than doubling the flow of slaves out of Africa. This, in turn, influenced further developments in America. As disease destroyed millions of Indians, newcomers from the entire Atlantic rim poured in to replace them. These newcomers came from very different physical environments and had distinctly foreign ideas about nature. Their novel practices and ideas helped to create a new America on top of the old, rendering drastic changes to the landscape. Continuing interactions among these various newcomers, and between them and the survivors of America's original people, would launch the process of Making America.

CHRONOLOGY
The New World

ca. 70,000–8000 B.C.E.	Human migration from Asia into Beringia
ca. 7000 B.C.E.	Plant cultivation begins in North America
ca. 34 C.E.	Death of Jesus of Nazareth and beginning of Christianity
632	Death of Mohammed and beginning of Islamic expansion
ca. 750	Islamic caravans travel to West Africa; African slave trade begins
ca. 500–1000	Rise of Hopewell culture
ca. 800–1700	Rise of Mississippian culture
ca. 1000–1400	Vikings in North America
1096–1291	The Crusades
ca. 1200	Aztecs arrive in the Valley of Mexico
ca. 1400	Beginning of Little Ice Age
1492	Reconquista completed; Columbus's first voyage
1500	Portuguese begin to transport and trade African slaves
1527–1535	Henry VIII initiates English Reformation
ca. 1550	Formation of the Powhatan Confederacy
1558	Elizabeth I becomes queen of England

Note: B.C.E. means "before the common era."

Study Tools

FOCUS QUESTIONS

If you have mastered this chapter, you should be able to answer these questions and to identify the terms that follow the questions.

1. How did environmental changes influence the development of various societies in North America during the millennia before the emergence of the Atlantic world?

2. What forces came into play in the centuries before 1500 that would launch Europeans on a program of outward exploration?

3. What factors in sub-Saharan African history helped lead to the development of the slave trade?

4. How did the Atlantic world change as a result of efforts to exploit new discoveries leading up to and following 1492?

5. How did Native Americans and Africans respond initially to European expansion?

6. How did Native Americans and Europeans respond to increasing contact with each other?

7. What global changes occurred through the process called the Columbian Exchange?

KEY TERMS

Western Hemisphere *p. 3*

Muslims *p. 3*

Vikings *p. 3*

Paleo-Indian *p. 4*

Na-Dene *p. 5*

Eskimo-Aleut *p. 5*

mound builder *p. 6*

Moors *p. 6*

Reconquista *p. 7*

Ferdinand and Isabella *p. 7*

Aztecs *p. 11*

Christopher Columbus *p. 15*

Amerigo Vespucci *p. 16*

Columbian Exchange *p. 18*

cash crops *p. 18*

manioc *p. 18*

acquired immunity *p. 18*

Slave Coast *p. 19*

Reformation *p. 21*

Protestantism *p. 21*

Henry VIII *p. 21*

Elizabeth I *p. 21*

SUGGESTED RESOURCES

Alfred W. Crosby. *The Columbian Exchange: Biological and Cultural Consequences of 1492* (1972). The landmark book that brought the impact of the Columbian Exchange into focus for the first time. Parts of the book are technical, but the explanations are clear and exciting.

Alvin M. Josephy. *America in 1492: The World of the Indian Peoples Before the Arrival of Columbus* (1992). An overview of American civilizations prior to Columbus's and subsequent European intrusions. Nicely written, comprehensive, and engaging.

Roland Oliver and J. D. Fage. *A Short History of Africa* (1988). The most concise and understandably written comprehensive history of Africa available.

David Reich et al. "Reconstructing Native American Population History," *Nature* 488 (July 11, 2012), 370–374. doi:10.1038/nature11258. The most up-to-date and exhaustive study of DNA records tracing Native American origins and population distribution in the Western Hemisphere.

Merry E. Wiesner. *Early Modern Europe, 1450–1789* (2006). In total, this covers European history from the invention of the printing press to the French Revolution; however, the first seven chapters provide an accessible and engaging account of people's lives between 1450 and 1600.

A Continent on the Move, 1400–1725

INDIVIDUAL CHOICES

Bartolomé de Las Casas

In 1550 Spanish church officials ordered a council of learned theologians to assemble in the city of Valladolid to hear a debate over an issue so important that it challenged the entire underpinning of Spain's New World empire. At issue was the question of whether Native American Indians were human beings. Arguing that they were not was the well-respected scholar Juan Ginés de Sepúlveda. Arguing on the Indians' behalf was a former conquistador and *encomendero* named Bartolomé de Las Casas.

Las Casas embarked for the West Indies in 1502 and once there became a successful **conquistador** earning an imperial land grant with a full complement of Indian laborers. Meeting the demands of both church and king, he taught the Indians Catholicism while he exploited their labor. Unlike many of his neighbors, Las Casas took his religious duty to them seriously.

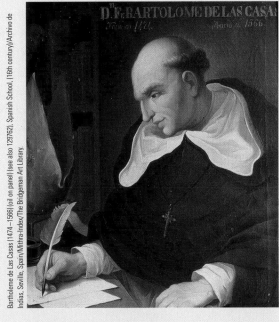

Bartolomé de Las Casas (1474–1566) (oil on panel) (see also 129762), Spanish School, (16th century)/Archivo de Indias, Seville, Spain/Mithra-Index/The Bridgeman Art Library.

Bartolomé de Las Casas

Finally, after a decade as a soldier and land baron, he took the vows to become a priest, joining the Dominican order in 1523. With their support, he began writing a history of the Spanish Empire in America. As an outgrowth, he sent a series of long letters to the Council of the Indies exposing the harsh exploitation of the natives throughout Spanish America. Las Casas then took his case personally to Spain. In 1540 he petitioned for an audience with King Charles V. As he waited for Charles to respond, he wrote a report summarizing his experiences and views.

By the time he finally met with Charles V, Las Casas was well prepared to argue for wholesale reform of Spanish Indian policy in America. And Charles was convinced. He signed a series of new laws in 1542—the *Leyes Nuevas*—reforming the *encomienda* system and placing Indian relations under church authority. To ensure that these reforms would be carried out, Las Casas was appointed bishop of Chiapas and sent back to the New World with forty fellow Dominicans to oversee the enforcement of the laws.

Las Casas served as bishop until 1547, when hostility from landowners in America and growing opposition to humane colonization at home prompted him to return to Spain. Sepúlveda, a well-respected scholar whose star was rising in court circles, was the chief spokesman for that growing opposition. Las Casas's return prompted demands for a face-off between the two, leading to the Council of Valladolid.

The debate went on for a year, extending through 1550 into 1551. Speaking for Spanish investors and court-based politicians who, like himself, had never been to the Western Hemisphere, Sepúlveda argued that it was impossible for Indians in the Americas to be descendants of Adam and Eve; hence, they were, in his words, "as apes are to men." As such, Indians did not deserve protection from the church. Las Casas countered with firsthand evidence, drawing on his varied experiences as priest, historian, conquistador, and *encomendero* in an attempt to prove that Indians truly were human beings. (See the Individual Voices feature at the end of this chapter.)

Despite Sepúlveda's great learning and his influence at court, he lost the debate: his writings were denied official recognition by the church, whereas Las Casas's were accepted. But this official victory for Las Casas made little immediate difference. Though Sepúlveda's views were rejected by the church, they were embraced by conquistadores as justification for the continuing conquest and enslavement of the native population. In arguing effectively for the recognition of Indians as human beings, however, Las Casas established an undercurrent of official disapproval that served as a braking mechanism against more extreme abuse of the native population. The resulting three-way tension—between those who would exploit the Indians, those who sought to protect them, and the Indians themselves—would shape the colonial process and would punctuate life in the Americas for generations to come.

▫ **encomendero** A landowner/proprietor in the *encomienda* system, Spain's system of bonded labor in which Indians were assigned to Spanish plantation and mine owners in exchange for a tax payment and an agreement to "civilize" and convert them to Catholicism.

▫ **conquistadores** Spanish soldiers who conquered Indian civilizations in the New World.

The debate in the Council of Valladolid in 1550 focused early attention on a situation that all European colonizers would have to face. Despite Sepúlveda's claims, the population native to the Americas *was* human. Of course, changing natural conditions and the influx of new forces such as epidemic disease had weakened them, but for centuries successful European settlement continued to require Indian cooperation. Court-based scholars like Sepúlveda might fool themselves into thinking that the Indians did not matter, but experienced veterans like Las Casas knew better. Conflicts with the Indians could spell disaster for vulnerable overseas colonies.

Conflicts with other imperial powers could lead to disaster as well. It was virtually inevitable that other nations would join Spain in seeking a share of the wealth promised by the New World. Forced into a defensive posture and unable to fend off the ambitions of numerous European rivals, Spain had to watch as the Dutch and the French carved out substantial inroads into North America.

The presence of many Europeans presented both challenges and opportunities for Indians. In areas where a single European power was asserting dominance, Indians could often do little but bear up under relentless economic and religious pressures. Sometimes the encounter facilitated friendship, intermarriage, and the formation of complex composite societies; sometimes it led to open hostilities and even war. But in areas where two or more European powers were contesting for control, Indians could take advantage of their pivotal position and play one side off against the other in seeking their own ends.

The constant interplay among different European traditions, a novel physical environment, and a dynamic Indian presence forged a series of new societies across the North American continent. Throughout the colonial era and beyond, these hybrid societies continued to influence historical development and to color the life of the people and the nation.

THE NEW EUROPE AND THE ATLANTIC WORLD

☆ *Why did European rulers promote exploration and colonization in North America?*

☆ *How did religious and political rivalries influence each European power's approach to New World colonization?*

Expansion into the New World and the subsequent economic and political pressures of colonization aggravated the crisis of authority in Europe. Eager to enlist political allies against Protestants, popes during this era used land grants in the New World as rewards to faithful monarchs. At the same time, Henry VIII and Elizabeth I, constantly fearful of being outflanked by Catholic adversaries, promoted the development of a powerful English navy and geographical exploration as defensive measures.

The differences between European and Native American styles and conceptions of warfare were often striking. This scene, from the *Codex Durán*, illustrates a Spanish force besieged by Aztec warriors. Note the contrast in clothing, for example. For most Indian groups, warfare was a highly spiritual affair surrounded by ceremony, often involving colorful and fanciful costumes. The European battle dress, however, bespeaks a very different conception of warfare: practical and deadly.

Codex Duran: Pedro de Alvarado (c. 1485–1541) companion-at-arms of Hernando Cortes (1485–1547) besieged by Aztec warriors (vellum), Duran, Diego (16th century)/Biblioteca Nacional, Madrid, Spain/The Bridgeman Art Library.

Acting on information collected from Indians on Mexico's frontiers, in 1540 Francisco Vásquez de Coronado set out with an armed party to find seven cities of gold rumored to exist in the northern wilderness. Though the party crisscrossed much of the American Southwest, venturing as far as modern-day Kansas, they found no golden cities. Such search parties, however, increased the Spaniards' knowledge of America and, through numerous encounters, increased Americans' knowledge of the new invaders in their land.

Spanish Expansion in America

Spain was in an enviable position when it came to New World colonization. In the year following Columbus's entry into the Americas, Pope Alexander VI decreed that all new lands found in this region of the world would belong exclusively to Spain, granting that nation a monopoly on exploration, at least in the eyes of Roman Catholics. Over the next several decades Spanish monarchs recruited hardened veterans of the Reconquista to lead their New World colonization efforts. Hernán Cortés was one such figure. In 1519 Cortés landed on the mainland of Mexico with an army of six hundred soldiers. Within three years he and his small force had conquered the mighty Aztec Empire. Crucially, smallpox and other European germs weakened the Aztecs during the two years in which Cortés maintained strained but peaceful relations with them. However, good relations with Indians who were subjects of the Aztec Empire also proved critical to the effort. An Indian woman whom he called Doña Marina served as his translator and cultural adviser, and with her help the conquistadores gained military support from numerous tribes of Mexican Indians who resented the Aztecs' power and their continuous demands for tribute.

The Spanish Crown supported many other exploratory ventures designed to bring new regions under Spain's control. In 1513 and again in 1521, Juan Ponce de León led expeditions to Florida. Following up on these voyages, Pánfilo de Narváez embarked on a colonizing mission to Florida in 1527. The stories such pioneers told upon returning to Mexico led the Spanish to send Hernando de Soto to claim the Mississippi River, and he penetrated into the heart of the mound builders' territory in present-day Louisiana and Mississippi. One year later, Francisco Vásquez de Coronado left Mexico to look for seven cities that were rumored to glitter with gold. Coronado eventually crossed what are now the states of New Mexico, Arizona, Colorado, Oklahoma, and Kansas. These explorations were but a few of the ambitious adventures undertaken by Spanish conquistadores.

◻ **Hernán Cortés** Spanish soldier and explorer who conquered the Aztecs and claimed Mexico for Spain.

◻ **Francisco Vásquez de Coronado** Spanish soldier and explorer who led an expedition northward from Mexico in search of fabled cities of gold; his explorations gave Spain a claim to most of the American Southwest.

Coronado never found "cities of gold," but other Spaniards did locate enormous sources of mineral wealth. Enslaving local Indians for labor, Spanish officials everywhere in the New World quickly moved to rip precious metals both out of the ground and out of what they characterized as "heathen temples." Between 1545 and 1660, Indian and later African slaves extracted over 7 million pounds of silver from Spanish-controlled areas, twice the volume of silver held by all of Europe before 1492. In the process, Spain became the richest nation in Europe, perhaps in the world.

Dreams of an English Eden

Given the stormy political and religious climate that prevailed during the sixteenth century, it is not surprising that Spain's early successes in the New World stirred up conflict with the other emerging states in Europe. To England, France, and other European countries, the massive flow of wealth made Spanish power a growing threat that had to be checked. The continuing religious controversies that accompanied the Reformation worsened the situation. Economic, religious, and political warfare was the rule throughout the century. One of the most celebrated of these early conflicts involved Spain and England.

Tension between Spain and England had been running high ever since Henry VIII had divorced his Spanish wife, Catherine of Aragon. That he quit the Catholic Church to do so and began permitting Protestant reforms in England added to the affront. Firmly wedded to the Catholic Church politically and religiously, Spain was aggressive in denouncing England. For his part, Henry was concerned primarily with domestic issues and steered away from direct confrontations with Spain or any of the other outraged Catholic countries.

Henry did, however, move to bring Ireland firmly under his control through colonization and land confiscation. During the years to come, England's rulers continued a systematic policy of colonization in Ireland. In the process, British authorities instituted a new set of colonial offices and encouraged generations of military adventurers, both of which would shape and advance later ventures in North America.

During the reign of Henry's younger daughter, Elizabeth, the continuing flow of New World wealth into Spain and that nation's anti-Protestant aggression led to an upturn in hostile activity. When Philip II of Spain, Elizabeth's brother-in-law and most vehement critic, sent an army of twenty thousand soldiers to root out Protestantism in the nearby Netherlands, the English queen began providing covert aid to the Dutch rebels. Elizabeth also struck at Philip's most valuable and vulnerable possession: his New World empire. In 1577 Elizabeth secretly authorized English privateer

and explorer Francis Drake to attack Spanish ships. Drake carried out his task with enthusiasm, seizing tons of gold and silver during a three-year cruise around the world.

Elizabeth was open to virtually any venture that might vex her troublesome brother-in-law. New World colonizing efforts promised to do that and had the potential to enrich the kingdom as well. Although Elizabeth's father had confiscated and redistributed large tracts of church-owned land during his reign, farmland was becoming extremely scarce, and members of both the traditional nobility and the gentry—a class that was becoming increasingly important because of its investments in manufacturing and trading ventures—wanted more space for expansion. A relatively small island, England could acquire more territory only by carving it out of the New World.

Thus in 1578, Elizabeth granted Sir Humphrey Gilbert permission to settle two hundred colonists south of the St. Lawrence River in what is now Newfoundland. One disaster after another plagued the effort, and Gilbert himself died at sea while trying to return to England. Thereafter, Gilbert's half-brother, Sir Walter Raleigh, took over the colonizing effort. This time, Elizabeth commanded Raleigh to locate farther south on the border of Spanish Florida, where an English base would facilitate raids on Philip's treasure fleets. Raleigh chose an island off the coast of present-day North Carolina. He advertised Roanoke Island as an "American Eden," where "the earth bringeth forth all things in abundance, as in the first Creation, without toile or labour." To honor his benefactor, he decided to call this paradise Virginia, tribute to the unwed, and thus officially virgin, queen.

In 1585 Elizabeth further angered the Spanish king by openly sending an army of six thousand troops to aid the Dutch rebels. In the meantime, Philip was supporting various Catholic plots within England, as well as in Scotland and Ireland, to subvert Elizabeth's authority and bring down the Protestant state. As tensions increased, so did English piracy. In 1586 Drake

Netherlands/Holland/Dutch The first two terms, often used interchangeably, refer to the low-lying area in western Europe on the coast north of France and Belgium; the Dutch are the inhabitants of the Netherlands.

privateer A ship captain who owned his own boat, hired his own crew, and was authorized by his government to attack and capture enemy ships.

gentry The class of English landowners ranking just below the nobility.

□ **Sir Walter Raleigh** English courtier, soldier, and adventurer who attempted to establish the Virginia Colony.

□ **Roanoke Island** Island off North Carolina that Raleigh sought to colonize beginning in 1585.

Queen Elizabeth I used her charm and intelligence to turn England into a major world power and restored order to a kingdom shaken by religious and political turmoil following the death of her father. This portrait, painted around 1588, shows the queen at the peak of her power, a fact depicted by the artist in the scenes visible through the windows in the background. Through the left window, we can see Elizabeth's naval fleet; through the right one, we witness the Spanish Armada sinking in the stormy Atlantic.

Woburn Abbey, Bedfordshire, UK/The Bridgeman Art Library.

intensified his campaign, not only raiding Spanish ships at sea but attacking settlements in the Caribbean. By 1586, war between the two powers loomed.

The Decline of Spanish Power

The enormous inflow of wealth from the New World brought Spain power that no European country since the Roman Empire had enjoyed, but such rapid enrichment was a mixed blessing. Starting in Spain and radiating outward, prices began to climb as the growth of the money supply outpaced the growth of European economies. Too much money was chasing too few goods. Between 1550 and 1600, prices doubled in much of Europe, and inflation continued to soar for another half-century.

In addition, the social impact of the new wealth was forcing European monarchs to expand geographically and crack down domestically. As prices rose, the traditional landholding classes earned enormous profits from the sale of food and other necessities. Other groups fared less well. Artisans, laborers, and landless peasants—by far the largest class of people in Europe—found the value of their labor constantly shrinking. Throughout Europe, social unrest increased as formerly productive and respected citizens

were reduced to poverty and begging. Overseas expansion seemed an inviting solution to the problem of an impoverished population.

Sitting at the center of the new economy, Philip's Spain had the most to lose from rapid inflation and popular unrest. It also had the most to lose from New World expansion by other European nations; after all, the pope had ordered that it all belonged to them. Philip finally chose to confront building tensions by taking a desperate gamble: he would destroy England. This ploy, he thought, would effectively remove the Protestant threat, rid him of Elizabeth's ongoing harassment, and demonstrate to the rest of Europe that Spain intended to exercise absolute authority over the Atlantic world. In the spring of 1585, when tensions were at their peak, Philip began massing what was to be the largest amphibious force Europe had ever witnessed.

In 1588 Philip launched 132 warships carrying more than three thousand cannons and an invasion force of thirty thousand men. Arriving off the shores of England in July, the so-called "Invincible Spanish Armada" ran up against small, maneuverable British defense ships commanded by Elizabeth's skilled pirate captains. Drake and his fleet harassed the Spanish ships, preventing them from launching a successful attack. Then a storm blowing down from the North Sea scattered the Spanish fleet. Though Spanish power remained great for some time to come, the Armada disaster effectively ended Spain's official monopoly over New World colonization. It also ended Spain's control over Holland, putting another trade-hungry Protestant colonizing power into play.

inflation Rising prices that occur when the supply of currency or credit grows faster than the available supply of goods and services.

☐ **Spanish Armada** Fleet of warships sent by Spain in 1588 to invade England.

Bering 1728

Bering 1741

RUSSIAN AMERICA

160°W

140°W

120°W

PACIFIC OCEAN

Columbia R.

Missouri R.

Arctic Circle

Hudson Bay

HUDSON'S BAY COMPANY

Great Lakes

NEW FRANCE

Québec
Montréal · Port Royal

Joliet and Marquette 1673

Boston

Ft. Detroit

New Haven
New York
Philadelphia
Baltimore
Jamestown
Roanoke I.

THIRTEEN COLONIES

Cahokia

Ohio R.

Wilmington

Quivira

LOUISIANA

Ft. Prudhomme

Arkansas R.

Colorado R.

Ácoma
Taos
Santa Fé
Albuquerque

La Salle 1682

Mabilia

Charles Town

Apalachee

ATLANTIC OCEAN

El Paso del Norte

Natchez

St. Augustine

San Antonio

New Orleans

Rio Grande

NEW SPAIN

Oñate 1598–1605

Mexico City

Bahamas

Tropic of Cancer

Gulf of Mexico

Havana · Cuba

SANTO DOMINGO

BRITISH HONDURAS

Jamaica

SAINT DOMINGUE

Caribbean Sea

60°N
40°W
40°N
60°W
20°N
80°W
100°W

N

ean territorial claims

British
French
Russian
Spanish

♦ Selected Indian settlement
• European settlement
☨ Mission
✖ Fort

0   300   600 Km.
0   300   600 Mi.

MAP 2.1 European and Indian Settlements in the Americas
Although Europeans were at first unsure about the implications of stumbling over a portion of the world that was new to them, they quickly came to understand the economic, political, and military potential involved in American colonization. As the colored arrows show, exploration continued into the seventeenth century as Europeans scrambled to claim individual pieces of New World real estate. © Cengage Learning.

EUROPEAN EMPIRES IN AMERICA

☆ *What similarities and differences characterized Spanish, French, and Dutch patterns of empire building in North America? What role did colonists' experiences play?*

☆ *How did natural environments help shape the colonial enterprises?*

In the seventeenth and eighteenth centuries, Spain, France, England, and a number of other European nations vied for control of the Americas and for domination of the transatlantic trade (see Map 2.1). For reasons explained in Chapter 3, England was somewhat delayed in its colonizing efforts, and by the time it became deeply involved in New World ventures, Spain, France, and Holland had already made major progress toward establishing empires in America. These European settlements not only affected England's colonization process profoundly, but through their interactions among themselves and with the Native Americans, they also created unique societies in North America whose presence influenced the entire course of the continent's history.

The Troubled Spanish Colonial Empire

Although the destruction of the Armada in 1588 struck a terrible blow at Spain's military power and its New World monopoly, the Spanish Empire continued to grow. By the end of the seventeenth century, it stretched from New Mexico southward through Central America and much of South America into the Caribbean islands and northward again into Florida. Governing such a vast empire was difficult, and periodic efforts to reform the system usually failed. Two agencies in Spain, the House of Trade and the Council of the Indies, set Spanish colonial policy. In the colonies, Crown-appointed viceroys wielded military and political power in each of the four divisions of the empire. The Spanish colonies set up local governments as well; each town had a **cabildo secular**, a municipal council, as well as judges and other minor officials. The colonial administrators were appointed rather than elected, and most were envoys from Spain rather than native-born individuals.

Over the centuries, as the layers of bureaucracy developed, corruption and inefficiency developed as well. One major source of corruption and unrest stemmed from a persistent New World problem: the shortage of labor. The Spanish had adapted traditional institutions to address the demand for workers in mines and on plantations. In Spain, work was directed by **feudal** landlords, *encomenderos*, whose military service to the king entitled them to harness the labor of Spanish peasants. In New Spain, Indians took the place of peasants in what was called the *encomienda* system. Under a law passed in 1512, any time Spaniards made first contact with an Indian group, the conquistadores were required to explain to them (in Spanish, of course) that they were subject to the Spanish king and to the Catholic Church, offering to absorb them peacefully. Having satisfied this **requerimiento**, the *encomenderos* gained the right to exploit the Indians' labor for nine months each year. For his part, the *encomendero* paid a tax to the Crown for each Indian he received and agreed to teach his workers the Catholic faith, Spanish language, and a "civilized" vocation.

Despite some commitment to uplifting local Indians, the system in reality was brutally exploitative. As Bartolomé de Las Casas reported both to the Council of the Indies and to the king himself, landlords frequently overworked their Indian **serfs** and failed in their "civilizing" responsibilities. As the result of Las Casas's appeal, the *Leyes Nuevas,* issued in 1542, turned Indian relations in New Spain over to the church, and priests were assigned to enforce the laws. As Las Casas discovered, however, colonists often ignored even these slim protections.

The Dutch Enterprise

Interestingly, it was a former Spanish colony, the Netherlands, that presented one of the most serious threats to Spain's New World monopoly. Holland's first serious claim to American territory came in 1609, when Dutch sea captain **Henry Hudson** sailed up a large river that he hoped would be the rumored **Northwest Passage**. After realizing that he had not found a route to the Far East, he returned to Holland, reporting that the territory surrounding this river was "pleasant with Grasse & Flowers and Goodly Trees" and that the Indians were friendly. Surely, he added, profits could be made there. At first, Hudson's employers did not share his enthusiasm; however, a fashion trend that seized Europe late in the sixteenth century impelled a change of mind. The immense popularity of the broad-brimmed beaver felt hat created a nearly insatiable demand for fur, and the experiences of early explorers and fishermen along America's North Atlantic shore indicated that a near endless supply was ripe for the trapping. Seeking to tap into this "brown gold," the Dutch built **Fort Orange** on the Hudson River and an export station on Manhattan Island in 1614. Real Dutch efforts at New World colonization, however, did not begin until investors formed the **Dutch West India Company** in 1621.

In 1626, the company instructed official Peter Minuit to negotiate a lease for the entire island of Manhattan from the Manhates Indians, but the focus remained upriver; the company did nothing to attract settlers. By 1629, only three hundred colonists had

□ **cabildo secular** Secular municipal council that provided local government in Spain's New World empire.

feudal Relating to a system in which landowners held broad powers over peasants or tenant farmers, providing protection in exchange for loyalty and labor.

□ *requerimiento* Spanish colonial law requiring conquistadores to inform Indians that they were subject to Spanish authority and offer to absorb them peacefully.

serfs Peasants who were bound to a particular estate but, unlike slaves, were not the personal property of the estate owner and received traditional feudal protections.

□ **Henry Hudson** Dutch ship captain and explorer who sailed up the Hudson River in 1609, giving the Netherlands a claim to the area now occupied by New York.

Northwest Passage The much-hoped-for water route from Europe to Asia through North America; the object of much European exploration throughout the colonial era.

□ **Fort Orange** Dutch trading post established near Present-day Albany, New York, in 1614.

□ **Dutch West India Company** Dutch investment company formed in 1621 to develop colonies for the Netherlands in North America.

Its location at the mouth of the Hudson River made the Dutch settlement of New Amsterdam a particularly important colonial trading center. Furs flowed down the river from Fort Orange (near modern Albany, New York), while guns, tools, and other trade goods traveled the other way. This painting of the Capitol Building (*Stadthuys*) on Manhattan Island in 1679, captures the city's solid stability after Peter Stuyvesant and the Dutch burghers merged their power to bring order and prosperity.

spread themselves in a thin ribbon from Manhattan Island upriver to Fort Orange. The situation began to change, however, when the Dutch West India Company drew up a comprehensive business plan to maximize profits and minimize dependence on local Indians for food and other support. To encourage the agricultural development necessary to support the fur industry, the company offered huge estates called **patroonships** to any company stockholder willing to bring fifty colonists to New Netherland at his own expense. In exchange, the patroons would enjoy near-feudal powers over their tenants. But few prosperous Dutchmen were interested in becoming New World barons. The colony's development came to rely instead on many poorer migrants who were drawn by unofficial promises of land ownership and economic betterment.

Settlers from just about anywhere were welcome in New Netherland—the colony attracted an extremely diverse population, including German and French Protestants, free and enslaved Africans, Catholics, Jews, and Muslims. In 1638 the Dutch even encouraged Swedish fur traders to create their own colony, New Sweden, within New Netherland's boundaries. Local government in such a disparate community was a persistent problem. Although the Dutch West India Company was officially in charge, day-to-day affairs were actually run by an elite group of **burghers**, men in New Amsterdam whose economic and political successes gave them significant influence. To reassert its power, the company reorganized its New World operations in

1645, appointing Peter Stuyvesant to manage all of its affairs in the Western Hemisphere. Stuyvesant immediately came into conflict with the local burghers in New Amsterdam, who in 1647 forced him to create a compromise government that gave the burghers an official voice through a council of nine appointed representatives. Six years later, Stuyvesant and the council created a municipal government modeled on those back in Holland. Despite this nod to democratic government, Stuyvesant ran company affairs with an iron hand, significantly tightening operations throughout the colony. In 1655 he even invaded and rooted out the Swedes, eliminating that source of dissension and competition.

The French Presence in America

Although France made a number of efforts to compete with Spain's New World projects during the sixteenth century, Spanish power was sufficient to prevent any

□ **patroonships** Huge grants of land given to any Dutch West India Company stockholder who, at his own expense, brought fifty colonists to New Netherland; the colonists became the tenants of the estate owner, or patroon.

□ **New Netherland** The colony founded by the Dutch West India Company in present-day New York; its capital was New Amsterdam on Manhattan Island.

burghers In New Amsterdam, men who were not Dutch West India Company officials, but who governed civic affairs through their political influence.

It Matters Today

The Felt Hat Fad

Changes in fashion come and go, and we seldom give much thought to them as being historically significant. But the sudden popularity of felt hats in the late sixteenth century had a profound impact on not just America's history, but on the history of the entire world. The flood of new wealth flowing into Europe from America permitted people of means—not just the nobility, but the landed gentry and even urban craftsmen and small business owners—to keep up with the latest fashions. Being in style became increasingly important to status-conscious merchants, manufacturers, and other beneficiaries of the New World boom. Demand for the beaver fur to make the felt became so steep that virtually the entire population of Old World beavers was wiped out, and entire industries arose in France, the Netherlands, Great Britain, and Russia to import this "brown gold" from the Americas. Fur drew Europeans up virtually every waterway in North America, leading to the founding of many of the most prominent cities in America today. It is safe to say that without this seemingly silly fashion trend, little in the United States would be as we know it today.

- Another important trade item during this era was deerskins. Research the demand for deerskins and then discuss what this tells us about socioeconomic changes during this era.
- Identify a current fashion trend and discuss its impact on global society. What differences do you think this trend will make on the future?

major successes. For example, when a force of French Protestants established a colony in Florida in 1564, Spanish authorities sent an army to root them out. This led to increased Spanish vigilance, prompting Pedro Menéndez de Aviles to build the city of **Saint Augustine** the following year.

Unable to penetrate Spain's defenses in the south, the French concentrated their efforts farther north. In 1599, French Protestants facing an increasingly discriminatory environment at home began seeking investment opportunities in the New World. Pierre Chauvin and **Pierre Dugua de Mons** established a year-round trading post at Tadoussac, northeast of the eventual site of Quebec City. De Mons went back to France but in 1604 returned with **Samuel de Champlain** to establish a string of settlements in what would be called **New France**. In 1608 de Mons and Champlain founded the city of Quebec and formed an enduring alliance with the Huron Indians. Two years later, King Henri IV was assassinated, setting off a wave of religious violence in France and destabilizing the French settlement in America. Over the next decade, French colonial authorities took little interest in overseas enterprises.

Finally in 1627, French minister Cardinal Richelieu chartered the **Company of New France**, awarding a group of the king's favorites licenses to establish plantations in Canada, but the venture failed to attract much interest. Frustrated by the lack of profits, Richelieu reorganized the company in 1633, dispatching Champlain with three ships of supplies, workmen, and soldiers who, it was hoped, would breathe new life into the colony. In its new form, the company ignored the government's demands that it establish agricultural settlements and focused instead on the fur trade. Setting up posts in Quebec, Montreal, and a few more remote locations, the company became the primary outfitter of and buyer from the **coureurs de bois** and amassed

▫ **Saint Augustine** First colonial city in the present-day United States; located in Florida and founded for Spain in 1565.

▫ **Pierre Dugua de Mons** French Protestant investor and adventurer who helped to found the French fur trade in Canada.

▫ **Samuel de Champlain** French explorer who traced the St. Lawrence River inland to the Great Lakes, founded the city of Quebec, and formed the French alliance with the Huron Indians.

▫ **New France** The colony established by France in what is now Canada and the Great Lakes region of the United States.

▫ **Company of New France** Company established by Cardinal Richelieu to bring order to the running of France's North American enterprises.

▫ **coureurs de bois** Literally, "runners of the woods"; independent French fur traders who lived among the Indians and sold furs to the French.

huge profits by reselling the furs in Europe. After Richelieu's death in 1642, queen mother and French regent Anne of Austria acted on complaints filed by both fur trade investors and Jesuit missionaries that the Company of New France was not governing effectively. She chose to empower a new company, the **Community of Habitants of New France**, with a monopoly on the fur trade and the privilege of granting land claims. Then, in 1647, Anne approved the formation of a council that consisted of the governor, the local director of the Jesuits, the colony's military commandant, and three elected officials. Meanwhile, the Company of New France continued technically to own the land and retained the power to appoint the governor and court officials in the colony.

Local authorities managed most of the colony's affairs until 1663, when the Crown began to intervene seriously in Canada. Having taken the functions of state into his own hands, young Louis XIV gave his finance minister, Jean-Baptiste Colbert, considerable authority over all monetary matters, including colonial enterprises. Seeking to make New France more efficient and to increase its contribution to the empire at large, Colbert founded the **Company of the West**, modeled on the highly successful Dutch West India Company. He also revoked the land titles held by the Company of New France, putting them directly into the king's hands, and overturned the political power of the Community of Habitants, making New France a royal colony.

In 1673 a French expedition led by Louis Joliet and Jacques Marquette set out on a systematic exploration of New France's many waterways. They discovered what appeared to be a major river, but it fell to **Robert Cavelier, Sieur de La Salle**, to prove the strategic and economic value of that discovery. In 1683 he and a party of French *coureurs de bois* and Indians retraced the earlier expedition and then followed the Mississippi River all the way to the Gulf of Mexico. La Salle immediately claimed the new territory for Louis XIV of France, naming it **Louisiana** in his honor. In 1698 the king sent settlers to the lower Mississippi Valley under the leadership of Pierre Le Moyne d'Iberville, who in 1699 raised Louisiana's first French fort, near present-day Biloxi, Mississippi. In 1718 French authorities built the city of New Orleans to serve as capital of the new territory.

The acquisition of Louisiana was a major accomplishment for La Salle and for France. The newly discovered river way gave the French a rich, untapped source of furs as well as an alternative shipping route, allowing them to avoid the cold, stormy North Atlantic. Also, if an agricultural venture could be started in the new territory, it might serve as an inexpensive source of supplies to support both the fur trade in Canada and France's sugar plantations in the Caribbean.

Royal Ontario Museum.

Although this scene in Quebec was not painted until 1820, back streets in the old part of the city still looked very much as they had during the heyday of the French *coureurs de bois*. So did the people. Shops, like the one on the left, sold provisions and tools—often on credit—to the outward-bound runners of the woods, binding them to bring their next load of furs back to satisfy their debt. Thus, while the French Crown did little to encourage it, the fur business formed the core of Canada's woodland and urban economies.

◻ **Community of Habitants of New France** Company chartered by Anne of Austria to make operations in New France more efficient and profitable; it gave significant political power to local officials in Canada.

◻ **Company of the West** Company chartered after New France became a royal colony, designed to maximize profits to the Crown.

◻ **Robert Cavelier, Sieur de La Salle** French explorer who followed the Mississippi River from present-day Illinois to the Gulf of Mexico in 1683, giving France a claim to the entire river way and adjoining territory.

◻ **Louisiana** French colony south of New France; it included the entire area drained by the Mississippi River and all its tributary rivers.

In the Wider World

Russia's American Frontier

As Western European nations were expanding throughout the Atlantic world, another empire was closing in on the Americas from the opposite direction. Responding to the global demand for furs, Russia engaged in massive eastward expansion to trap valuable fur-bearing animals in Siberia. Although the historical record is murky, it appears that Russian explorer Semyon Ivanovich Dezhnyov may have accidentally stumbled upon Alaska in 1648, but it was not until 1733 that Peter the Great sent a formal expedition under Vitus Bering to explore the region. Though the expedition ended in disaster, the existence of Alaska and its wealth in furs were verified. Over the next sixty years, Russian fur hunters penetrated farther and farther into North America, not only in Alaska but down the Pacific Coast all the way to California. Though its boundaries were fuzzy and certainly challenged by other nations, Russia incorporated the entirety of their new discoveries by imperial decree in 1799, creating the province of Russian America (Русская Америка).

INDIANS AND THE EUROPEAN CHALLENGE

☆ How did changes in the natural environment affect Indian societies during the early colonial period?

☆ How did the arrival of Europeans influence continuing adaptations by Native American groups?

Native Americans did not sit idly by while the European powers carved out empires in North America. Some joined the newcomers, serving as advisers and companions. Others sought to use the Europeans as allies to accomplish their own economic, diplomatic, or military goals (see Map 2.2). Still others, overwhelmed by the onset of European diseases and shifting population pressures, withdrew into the interior. The changes in native America created both obstacles and opportunities, giving shape to the patterns of expansion and conflict that characterized the colonial world.

□ **Don Juan de Oñate** Spaniard who conquered New Mexico and claimed it for Spain in the 1590s.

□ **Ácoma Pueblo** Indian community that resisted Spanish authority in 1598 and was subdued by the Spanish.

□ **Hopi Indians** Indians who were related to the Comanches and Shoshones and took up residence among the Pueblo Indians as agricultural town-dwellers; their name means "peaceful ones."

□ **Santa Fe** Spanish colonial town established in 1609; eventually the capital of the province of New Mexico.

The Indian Frontier in New Spain

Indian assistance had been critical in Spain's successful campaign against the Aztecs. Groups who had been forced to pay tribute to the Aztec Empire gladly allied themselves with the Spanish in what the natives perceived as an opportunity to win their independence. Their hopes were soon dashed when the Spanish simply replaced the Aztecs as the new lords of a tributary empire.

Once Spain's New World empire was firmly rooted, Spanish expansion met little native resistance until 1598, when a particularly brutal conquistador named Don Juan de Oñate led a large expedition to the Rio Grande region of New Mexico. When some Pueblos resisted Oñate's efforts to impose Spanish culture and religion, the conquistador chose to make an example of Ácoma Pueblo. After his troops subdued the pueblo, Oñate ordered eight hundred Indians executed and made slaves of the nearly seven hundred survivors, mostly women and children. In addition, each male survivor over the age of 25 had one foot chopped off to prevent his escape from slavery. Two Hopi Indians who were visiting Ácoma at the time had their right hands cut off and then were sent home as examples of the price of resistance.

This blatant cruelty disgusted even the most cynical authorities in New Spain, and both the church and state stepped in. Oñate was removed, and the surviving Indians were placed under joint military and religious protection. Some members of Oñate's company remained, however, founding the town of Santa Fe in 1609. Others scattered to set up ranches throughout the region.

Thanks in part to Las Casas's efforts, the church played a key role in developing the colonies, especially

Primary economic activity
- Agriculture
- Hunting
- Hunting-gathering
- Fishing
- *FOX* Tribal location
- Original range of bison

MAP 2.2 Indian Economies in North America
Indian economic activities helped to shape patterns of European settlement and investment in the New World. Regions that were primarily agricultural, like the Atlantic shoreline, lent themselves to European farming activities. Farther north and west, however, where hunting played a more prominent role in native life, the fur trade was a more attractive investment for European settlers. © Cengage Learning.

in the stark regions along Mexico's northern frontier where there were no gold mines or profitable plantations. The Franciscan order led church efforts in New Mexico and put a peculiar stamp on the pattern of Indian relations. A highly ascetic and disciplined order, the Franciscans were particularly offended by the Pueblo religion and lifestyle. Indian ceremonies that involved various types of traditional religious objects smacked of idolatry to the Franciscans, and the priests embarked on a wholesale effort to destroy every vestige of the Indians' religion. The priests also interfered in the most intimate social aspects of Pueblo life, imposing foreign ideas about sexual relations and family structure and punishing most of the Pueblos' traditional practices as sinful.

After nearly a century of enduring these assaults on their most fundamental values, the Pueblos struck

ascetic Practicing severe abstinence or self-denial, generally in pursuit of spiritual awareness.

Before the arrival of European explorers like Hernando de Soto in the early 1540s, Indians in the American Southeast had lived in huge cities. This painting by archaeological reconstruction artist Tom Hall captures the bustling marketplace at Moundville, a large pre-Columbian city in present-day Alabama. Moundville was abandoned following the introduction of European diseases. Scholars are unsure about what became of Moundville's survivors, but it is likely that they formed smaller villages that were easier to support in the new environment.

back. In 1680 a traditional leader named Popé led an uprising that united virtually all of the Indians in New Mexico against Spanish rule. The Pueblo Revolt left four hundred Spaniards dead as the rebels captured

◻ **Pueblo Revolt** Indian rebellion against Spanish authority in 1680 led by Popé; succeeded in driving the Spanish out of New Mexico for nearly a decade.

◻ **Creek Confederacy** Alliance of Indians living in the Southeast; formed after the lethal spread of European diseases to permit economic and military cooperation among survivors.

Santa Fe and drove the invaders from their land. It was not until 1689 that troops moved back into the region and over the next several years waged a brutal war to recapture the territory. The fighting continued off and on until the end of the century, but Spanish settlers began returning to New Mexico after the recapture of Santa Fe in 1693.

The Indian World in the Southeast

Members of Spanish exploring expeditions under such would-be conquistadores as Ponce de León and Hernando de Soto were the first Europeans to contact the mound builder societies and other Indian groups in the Southeast. Although their residential and ceremonial centers impressed the Spaniards, these Mississippian agricultural groups had no gold and could not easily be enslaved. The conquistadores moved on without attempting to force Spanish rule or the Catholic religion on them.

Given sufficient incentive, however, the Spanish were quick to strike at Indian independence and culture. In Florida, for example, the need to protect Spanish ships from French settlers led Spain to establish garrisons such as Saint Augustine. With this and other similar military posts in place, Jesuit and Franciscan missionaries ranged outward to bring Catholicism to Indians in the region. By 1600 they had established missions from the Gulf Coast of Florida all the way to Georgia.

Although the Spanish presence in the region was small, its impact was enormous. The Spanish introduced European diseases into the densely populated towns in the Mississippi River region. Epidemics wiped out entire Native American civilizations and forced survivors to abandon their towns and entirely modify their ways of life. Certain groups, among them the Cherokees and Creeks, formed village-based economies that combined agriculture, hunting, and gathering. As had happened earlier in the Northeast among the Powhatans and others, this change in economy led to increased intergroup warfare. And like the Powhatans, many southeastern groups created formal confederacies as a way of coping. One example is the Creek Confederacy, a union of many groups that had survived the Spanish epidemics. Internally, members created an economic and social system in which each population contributed to the welfare of all and differences were settled through athletic competition—a ballgame, the ancestor of lacrosse—rather than warfare. And when new Europeans arrived in the seventeenth and eighteenth centuries, the Creeks and other confederacies found it beneficial to welcome them as trading partners and allies, balancing the competing demands of the Spanish and French, and later the English. To some degree, they took advantage of the European rivalries to advance their own interests against those of neighboring confederacies.

The Indian World in the Northeast

By the time Europeans had begun serious exploration and settlement of the Northeast, the economic and cultural changes among northeastern Woodlands Indians had resulted in the creation of two massive—and opposing—alliance systems. On one side were the Hurons, Algonquins, Abenakis, Mi'kmaqs, Ottawas, and several smaller tribes. On the other was the Iroquois League.

The costs and benefits of sustained European contact first fell to the Hurons and their allies. The Abenakis, Mi'kmaqs, and others who lived along the northern shore of the Atlantic were the first groups drawn into trade with the French, and it was among them that the *coureurs de bois* settled and intermarried. These family ties became firm economic bonds when formal French exploration brought these groups into more direct contact with the European trading world. Seeking advantage against the Iroquois, the Hurons and their neighbors created a great wheel of alliance with the fur trade at its hub.

The strong partnership between these Indians and the French posed a serious threat to the Iroquois. Much of the territory being harvested for furs by the Hurons had once belonged to the Iroquois, and they wanted it back. The presence of the French and the fur trade made this objective all the more desirable. If the Iroquois could push the Hurons and their allies out and take control of the St. Lawrence River, the French would then have to trade exclusively with them. But the French presence also complicated the situation in that the Hurons had a ready source for guns, iron arrowheads, and other tools that gave them a military edge.

The arrival of the Dutch in Albany, however, offered the Iroquois an attractive diplomatic alternative. In 1623 the Dutch West India Company invited representatives from the Iroquois League to a meeting at Fort Orange, offering them friendship and trade. The Iroquois responded enthusiastically, but in a way that the Dutch had not anticipated. They began a bloody war with the Mohicans, who had been the Dutch traders' main source for furs in the Hudson Valley. By 1627 the Iroquois had driven out the Mohicans and had taken control over the flow of furs.

Trade was so vigorous that the Iroquois soon wiped out fur supplies in their own territory and began a serious push to acquire new sources. Beginning in the late 1630s, the Iroquois League entered into a long-term aggressive war against the Hurons and their allies in New France; against the Munsees, Delawares, and other groups in the Susquehanna and Delaware River valleys to the south; and even against the Iroquois-speaking Eries to the west.

The New Indian World of the Plains

Though largely unexplored and untouched by Europeans, the vast area of the Great Plains also underwent profound transformation during the period of initial contacts between Native Americans and Europeans. Climate change, the pressure of shifting populations, and the introduction of novel European goods through lines of kinship and trade created an altogether new culture and economy among the Indians in this region.

Before about 1400, Indians living on the plains rarely strayed far from the waterways that form the Missouri River drainage, where they lived in villages sustained by agriculture, hunting, and gathering. The climate cooldown that affected their neighbors to the east (as discussed in Chapter 1) had a similar effect on the Plains Indians: growing seasons became shorter, and the need to hunt became greater. But at the same time, this shift in climate produced an increase in one food source: buffalo.

A survivor of the Great Ice Ages, the American bison is particularly well adapted to cold climates. Although buffalo had long been a presence on the plains, the cold weather during the Little Ice Age spurred a massive increase in their numbers. Between 1300 and 1800, herds numbering in the millions emerged in the new environment created by the climate change.

Some groups—such as the Caddoan-speaking Wichitas, Pawnees, and Arikaras—virtually abandoned their agricultural villages and became hunters. Others, such as the Hidatsas, split in two: a splinter group calling themselves Crows went off permanently to the grasslands to hunt, while the remainder stayed in their villages growing corn and tobacco. These and

□ **Iroquois League** Probably founded as a response to the Little Ice Age under the influence of Heinwatha (Hiawatha) and Dekanawida, it united the Mohawk, Oneida, Onondaga, Cayuga, and Seneca nations into what is properly called the League of the *Haudenosaunee*.

□ **Mohicans** Algonkian-speaking Indians who lived along the Hudson River, were dispossessed in a war with the Iroquois League, and eventually were all but exterminated.

buffalo The American bison, a large member of the ox family, native to North America and the staple of the Plains Indian economy between the fifteenth and mid-nineteenth centuries.

Caddoan A family of languages spoken by several groups of Plains Indians.

Alfred Jacob Miller based this 1837 painting of eighteenth-century mounted buffalo hunters on interviews with Shoshone Indians he met on a trip through the American West. It illustrates clearly the enormous impact the arrival of horses had on Plains Indian life. Note how few mounted men it took to drive vast numbers of animals over a cliff to their deaths. At the bottom of the cliff, women would butcher the dead animals and the meat, bones, and hides would provide food, clothing, tools, tents, and trade goods sufficient to support an entire band of Indians for some time. The arrival of the horse on the Great Plains in the late 1600s marked the beginning of 150 years of unprecedented wealth and power for the Indians in the region.

others who chose to continue their agricultural ways, the Mandans for example, established a thriving trade with the hunters, exchanging vegetables and tobacco for fresh meat and other buffalo products.

The increase in buffalo not only provided a welcome resource for the Indians already on the Great Plains but also drew new populations to the area. The Blackfeet and other Indians swept down from the subarctic Northeast to hunt on the plains. Other Algonkian-speaking Indians, including the Gros Ventres, Cheyennes, and Arapahos, soon followed, to be joined by other northeastern groups fleeing the

violence and disease that were becoming endemic in the Eastern Woodlands. The Lakotas, for example, once the westernmost family of Siouan agriculturalists, were pushed onto the plains by continuing pressure from the east, but they maintained close relations with their Dakota neighbors in Minnesota, who continued to farm and harvest wild rice and other crops. This continued tie, like that between the Crows and Hidatsas, increased both the hunters' and the farmers' chances for survival in an ever more hostile world: intergroup trade became the key to the welfare of all.

The buffalo also began to play an important role on the southern plains. There, groups such as the Apaches, Comanches, and Kiowas specialized in hunting the ever-increasing herds and then exchanging part of their kill for village-based products from their neighbors and kin, the Navajos, Hopis, and Pueblos. And it was in these intergroup trades that the Plains Indians acquired a new advantage in their efforts to expand their hunting economy: the horse.

◻ **Lakotas/Dakotas** Subgroups of the Sioux Nation of Indians; Lakotas make up the western branch, living mostly on the Great Plains; Dakotas, the eastern branch, live mostly in the prairie and lakes region of the Upper Midwest.

Cowboy and Indian Movies Got It All Wrong

European explorers, Euro-American settlers, and modern makers of Western movies completely misunderstood life among the Plains Indians. To such observers and commentators, the Indians of the Plains seemed unsophisticated hunters and warriors caught in a timeless primitive world. Dragging their tepees from place to place as they nomadically followed herds of buffalo, they seemed no more sophisticated than their big-game hunting ancestors during the Stone Age—and this stereotype persists.

Historians and their colleagues in such fields as archaeology, ethnology, and biology know better. Cross-disciplinary research has revealed, as noted in Chapter 1, that trade among Indian groups in North America before European contact was common, but after Europeans began settling the continent it became even more common, even in areas where Europeans seldom set foot. One unintentional outcome of the Pueblo Revolt was the liberation of thousands of Spanish horses, an animal that had gone extinct in North America at about the same time that the ancestors of the Indians were just entering the continent. The settled agricultural Pueblos had little use for these animals, but their long-standing trading partners, the Kiowas and Comanches, quickly adopted them. Horses could carry much larger loads than dogs and could survive on a diet of grass rather than competing with people for food. In less than a generation, horses became a mainstay of the buffalo-hunting cultures on the southern plains. Following routes outlined on this map, northern plains dwellers such as the Shoshones quickly began acquiring horses from their southwestern kin.

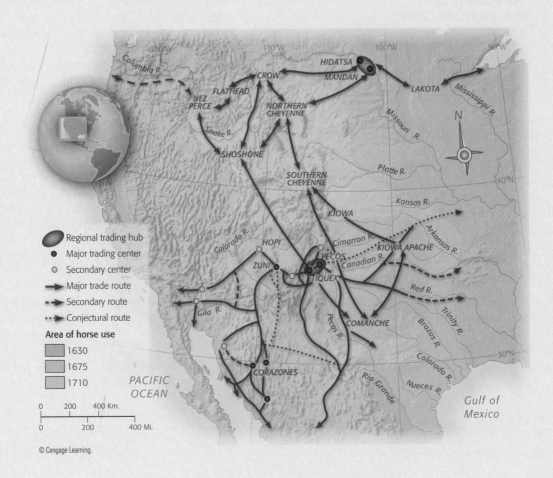

© Cengage Learning.

Horses were passed from one group to another in the complex trading system that came into existence in the Plains region. Both archaeological records and historical documents demonstrate that the steady demand for horses created a new dynamic on the Great Plains and set a new economy into motion.

After the Spanish reconquest of New Mexico, Indians could obtain horses only through warfare and trade, and both increased significantly. Surprise raids to steal horses from neighboring Indian groups and European settlements brought both honor and wealth to those who were successful. But raiding brought reprisals; trade was a safer option. Facing labor shortages, European settlers in New Mexico and elsewhere accepted Indian slaves—especially children—in exchange for horses. Soon, these young captives became another important commodity in the already complex trading and raiding system that prevailed among the southwestern Indians and Spanish New Mexicans.

Along with the horses came other trade items: horse-related technologies like saddles, bridles, and fiber ropes; iron and steel tools and spear and arrow heads—and guns. And, of course, any time there was contact between people, diseases came as well. Long before any European ever laid eyes on the Missouri River, smallpox epidemics had destroyed many thousands of Indian lives. Dramatically, the combination of these forces, along with population pressures from Indians fleeing European encroachment and disease, could cause entire societies that were once sedentary agriculturalists to become horse-borne migratory buffalo hunters in less than a generation.

Thus while long-standing stereotypes portray the Plains Culture that Europeans encountered as backward, primitive, and stagnant, diligent scholarship has revealed that it was actually extremely modern, extraordinarily complex, and dynamic—in some ways more so than the Euro-American pioneering culture that would eventually displace it.

CONQUEST AND ACCOMMODATION IN A SHARED NEW WORLD

☆ *How did settlers and American Indians adapt to changing conditions in the different regions of colonial occupation?*

Old World cultures, Native American historical dynamics, and New World environmental conditions combined to create vibrant new societies in European pioneer settlements. Despite the regulatory efforts of Spanish bureaucrats, French royal officials, and Dutch company executives, life in the colonies developed in its own peculiar ways. Entire regions in what would become the United States assumed cultural contours that would shape all future developments in each.

New Spain's Northern Frontiers

After suppressing the Pueblo Revolt during the 1690s, Spaniards began drifting back into New Mexico. Unlike areas to the south, New Mexico offered no rich deposits of gold or silver, and the climate was unsuitable for large-scale agriculture. With neither mines

nor plantations to support the *encomienda* system, the basic underpinnings of the traditional ruling order never emerged. The church, which was channeling money to missions, and the Spanish government, which allocated both military and civic support funds, were the only major employers in the region. Those not in the church's or the state's employ had to scramble for a living.

Under Pueblo control following the revolt, the small flocks of sheep abandoned by the fleeing Spanish had grown dramatically, and sheep ranching had become a reliable way to make a living. Thus, rather than concentrating near the municipal center in Santa Fe, the population in New Mexico spread out across the land, forming two sorts of communities. South of Santa Fe, people settled on scattered ranches. Elsewhere, they gathered in small villages along streams and pooled their labor to make a living from irrigated subsistence farming.

Like colonists elsewhere in Spain's New World empire, the New Mexico colonists were almost entirely male. Isolated on sheep ranches or in small villages, these men sought Indian companionship and married into local populations. These marriages gave birth not only to a new hybrid population but also to lines of kinship, trade, and authority that were in sharp contrast to the imperial ideal. For example, when Navajo or Apache raiding parties struck, ranchers and villagers turned to their Indian relatives for protection rather than to Spanish officials in Santa Fe.

subsistence farming Farming that produces enough food for survival but no surplus that can be sold.

In this frontier world, unlike the rest of Hispanic America, a man's social status came to depend less on his Spanish connections than on his ability to work effectively in the complicated world of kinship that prevailed in the Indian community. The people who eventually emerged as the elite class in New Mexico were those who best perfected these skills. Under their influence, Santa Fe was transformed from a traditional mission and imperial town into a cosmopolitan frontier trading center. During the next two centuries, this multiethnic elite absorbed first French and then Anglo-American newcomers while maintaining its own social, political, and economic style.

The Dutch Settlements

As noted above, the easygoing community in New Amsterdam appealed to many groups in Europe who were experiencing hardship in their own countries but who, for one reason or another, were unwelcome in the colonies of their homelands. French

The Granger Collection, NYC.

Commenting on conveying indigenous ideas using European languages, Ácoma Pueblo poet Simon Ortiz observed, "a vital sense of cultural continuity [is] maintained because of Indigenous cultural consciousness." The mirror image of this process may be seen in this icon of Jesus wrought using traditional American feather-working techniques. Through such ingenious workmanship, natives indigenized foreign ideas, converting them from colonial to native expressions.

Protestants, for example, were experiencing terrible persecution in France but were forbidden to go to Canada or Louisiana. Roman Catholics, Quakers, Jews, Muslims, and a wide variety of others also chose to migrate to New Netherland. Most of the colonists settled on small farms, called *bouweries* in Dutch, and engaged in the same agricultural pursuits they had practiced in Europe. Thus New Netherland was dotted with little settlements, each having its own language, culture, and internal economy.

Farming was the dominant activity among the emigrants, but some followed the example of the French *coureurs de bois* and went alone or in small groups into the woods to live and trade with the Indians. Called *bosch loopers*, these independent traders traveled through the forests, trading cheap brandy and rum for Indian furs, which they then sold for enormous profits. Although both tribal leaders and legitimate traders complained about such illegal activities, company officials could not control them.

In fact, the Dutch West India Company was unable to control much of anything in New Netherland. The incredible diversity of the settlers no doubt contributed to this administrative impotence. For example, Dutch law and company policy dictated that the Dutch Reform Church was to be the colony's official and only religion. But instead of drawing everyone into one congregation, the policy had the opposite effect. As late as 1642 not a single church of any denomination had been planted. Poor leadership and unimaginative policies also contributed to the general air of disorder. Following Peter Minuit's dismissal by the company in 1631, a long line of incompetent governors ruled the colony. In the absence of any legislative assembly or other local body to help keep matters on track, for years one bad decision followed another. It took a major reorganization by the West India Company and its appointment of Peter Stuyvesant in 1645 to turn the colony around.

Life in French Louisiana

France's colony in Louisiana had many of the same qualities and faced many of the same problems as Holland's and Spain's North American possessions. Like most European settlements, Louisiana suffered from a critical shortage of labor, leading first to dependence on the Indians and eventually to the wholesale

◻ *bosch loopers* Dutch term meaning "woods runners"; independent Dutch fur traders.

◻ **Dutch Reform Church** Calvinistic Protestant denomination; the established church in the Dutch Republic and the official church in New Netherland.

In the late 1690s, officials in Louisiana noted that the absence of women was one serious deterrent to attracting useful colonists and proposed that the government pay the passage of young women of good character to the colony. The first party of these "casket girls"—so-called because of the small chests in which they packed their belongings—arrived in Mobile in 1704. Parties continued to arrive through the 1720s, though their presence made little practical difference in terms of attracting male colonists.

adoption of African slavery. And like all Europeans who settled in North America, Louisianans found themselves embroiled in a complicated Native American world that usually defied European understanding.

Despite the territory's strategic location, fertile soils, and fur-bearing animals, few Frenchmen showed any interest in settling there. In the first years of the colony's existence, the population consisted primarily of three groups: military men, who were generally members of the lower nobility; *coureurs de bois* from Canada looking for new and better sources of furs; and French craftsmen seeking economic independence in the New World. The men in each group had little in common with those in the other groups, and more important, none had knowledge of or interest in food production. In the absence of an agricultural establishment, the small number of settlers in Louisiana had to depend on imported food. At first, ships from France carried provisions to the colonies, but war in Europe frequently interrupted this source. In desperation, the colonists turned to the Indians.

The Natchez, Chickasaws, and Choctaws were all close by and well provisioned. The Chickasaws refused to deal with the French, and the Natchez, divided into quarreling factions, were sometimes helpful and sometimes hostile. But the Choctaws, locked into a war with the Chickasaws and a tense relationship with the Natchez, found the prospect of an alliance with the French quite attractive. In the realignment process, the Choctaws helped shape France's Indian policies and expansion plans. For example, they were able to convince the French to expand onto Natchez land rather than into Choctaw territory. When the Natchez resisted French incursion, the Choctaws helped their European allies destroy the tribe. The Choctaws also assisted the French in a thirty-year-long conflict with the Chickasaws, though with less success.

Despite the Choctaw alliance, which guaranteed ample food supplies and facilitated territorial acquisitions, Louisiana remained unappealing to Frenchmen. Increasingly, settlers in Louisiana followed their Spanish neighbors' example by importing African slaves to do necessary work. By 1732, slaves made up two-thirds of the population.

▢ **Natchez** An urban, mound-building Indian people who lived on the lower Mississippi River until they were destroyed in a war with the French in the 1720s; survivors joined the Creek Confederacy.

▢ **Chickasaws** Another lower Mississippi urban, mound-building Indian people, who became a society of hunters after the change in climate and introduction of disease after 1400; they were successful in resisting French aggression throughout the colonial era.

▢ **Choctaws** Like the Chickasaws, a mound-building people who became a society of hunters after 1400; they were steadfast allies of the French in wars against the Natchez and Chickasaws.

Individual Voices

BARTOLOMÉ DE LAS CASAS
Argues for the American Indians

One of the serious problems in assessing relations between Native Americans and Europeans during the period of early contact is a general lack of evidence about what participants thought about their situations and each other. Fortunately, the Spanish Crown and the Roman Catholic Church kept detailed records. The records of the debate between Juan Ginés de Sepúlveda and Bartolomé de Las Casas before the Council of Valladolid give us insight into how at least some people were thinking. We know, for example, Sepúlveda's view that Indians lacked souls and therefore could never become truly civilized Christians. We also know from Las Casas of Indians' many remarkable accomplishments, both in creating advanced civilizations of their own and in adapting to Spanish civilization. And in the following excerpt, we learn his views about the relationship between the Indians and God. Even so, despite his sympathy for the Indians, Las Casas's voice does not give us a clear insight into how the Indians themselves perceived things.

Bartholeme de Las Casas (1474–1566) (oil on panel) (see also 129762), Spanish School, (16th century)/Archivo de Indias, Seville, Spain/Mithra-Index/The Bridgeman Art Library.

❶ What, exactly, is Las Casas asserting in this sentence? How does this proposition set up the rest of his argument?

❷ What does the reference to writings by Saint Thomas tell us about Las Casas's view of human nature? How does it refute Sepúlveda's claims concerning Indians?

❸ Judging from this brief excerpt from Las Casas's argument, why do you suppose he won the debate? Why would the Catholic Church have chosen to endorse and publicize his views and not Sepúlveda's?

Who, therefore, except one who is irreverent toward God and contemptuous of nature, has dared to write that countless numbers of natives across the ocean are barbarous, savage, uncivilized, and slow witted when, if they are evaluated by an accurate judgment, they completely outnumber all other men? **❶** This is consistent with what Saint Thomas writes: "The good which is proportionate to the common state of nature is to be found in most men and is lacking only in a few. . . . Thus it is clear that the majority of men have sufficient knowledge to guide their lives, and the few who do not have this knowledge are said to be half-witted or fools." Therefore, since barbarians of that kind, as Saint Thomas says, lack that good of the intellect which is knowledge of the truth, a good proportionate to the common condition of rational nature, it is evident that in each part of the world, or anywhere among the nations, barbarians of this sort or freaks of rational nature can only be quite rare. For since God's love of mankind is so great and it is his will to save all men, it is in accord with his wisdom that in the whole universe, which is perfect in all its parts, his supreme wisdom should shine more and more in the most perfect thing: rational nature. **❷**

Again, if we believe that such a huge part of mankind is barbaric, it would follow that God's design has for the most part been ineffective, with so many thousands of men deprived of the natural light that is common to all peoples. And so there would be a great reduction in the perfection of the entire universe—something that is unacceptable and unthinkable for any Christian. **❸**

Source: Bartolomé de Las Casas, *In Defense of the Indians: The Defense of the Most Reverend Lord, Don Fray Bartolome de las Casas, of the Order of Preachers, Late Bishop of Chiapa, Against the Persecutors and Slanderers of the Peoples of the New World Discovered Across the Seas,* translated, edited, and annotated by Stafford Poole (DeKalb, Northern Illinois University Press, © 1974).

Study Tools

SUMMARY

Spain's opening ventures in the Americas had been wildly successful, making the Iberian kingdom the envy of the world. Hoping to cash in on the bounty, other European nations challenged Spain's monopoly on American colonization, creating an outward explosion. Although slow to consolidate an imperial presence in North America, England was the first to confront the Spanish in force, wounding them severely. France and the Netherlands took advantage of the situation to begin building their own American empires.

For Native Americans, the entry of Europeans into their realms combined with other forces to create an air of crisis. Presented with a series of new challenges, Indians sought new ways to solve their problems and created altogether new societies. This often involved difficult choices: perhaps allying with the newcomers, resisting them, or fleeing. As different groups exercised different options, the outcome was a historically dynamic world of interaction involving all of the societies that were coming together in North America.

This dynamic interaction yielded interesting fruit. In New Spain, New France, Louisiana, New Netherland, and throughout the Great Plains, truly cosmopolitan societies emerged. Bearing cultural traits and material goods from throughout the world, these new transatlantic societies set the tone for future development in North America. As we see in Chapter 3, societies on the Atlantic coast, too, were evolving as English colonists interacted with the land and its many occupants. The outcome of such interchange, over the centuries, was the emergence of a multicultural, multiethnic, and extraordinarily rich culture—an essential element in Making America.

CHRONOLOGY
New World Colonies and Native Americans

1512	Creation of the *encomienda* system
1519–1521	Hernán Cortés invades Mexico
1551	Council of Valladolid rules that American Indians are human beings with souls
1558	Elizabeth I becomes queen of England
1565	Spanish found St. Augustine in present-day Florida
1588	English defeat Spanish Armada
1598	Don Juan de Oñate destroys Ácoma Pueblo
1608	French-Huron alliance
1609	Spanish found Santa Fe in present-day New Mexico
1627	Creation of Company of New France
1680	Pueblo Revolt
1683	La Salle expedition down the Mississippi River to the Gulf of Mexico
ca. 1700	Beginning of French-Choctaw alliance

FOCUS QUESTIONS

If you have mastered this chapter, you should be able to answer these questions and to explain the terms that follow the questions.

1. Why did European rulers promote exploration and colonization in North America?

2. How did religious and political rivalries influence each European power's approach to New World colonization?

3. What similarities and differences characterized Spanish, French, and Dutch patterns of empire building in North America? What role did colonists' experiences play?

4. How did natural environments help shape the colonial enterprises?

5. How did changes in the natural environment affect Indian societies during the early colonial period?

6. How did the arrival of Europeans influence continuing adaptations by Native American groups?

7. How did settlers and American Indians adapt to changing conditions in the different regions of colonial occupation?

Study Tools

KEY TERMS

SUGGESTED RESOURCES

Ned Blackhawk. "Violence over the Land: Indians and Empires in the Early American West," http://archive.org/details/LibraryChannel_NedBlackhawk_Lecture_Video_20080128. A 2008 lecture by one of the leading experts on European-indigenous contact summarizing insights from his 2006 book by the same name; a rare opportunity to hear from this renowned Yale University professor.

Legacy Preservation Library. "Great Epochs in American History: Vol. I—Voyages of Discovery and Early Explorations," http://www.usgennet.org/usa/topic/preservation/epochs/vol1/toc.htm. A site maintained by Lynn Waterman, Ginger Cisewski, and Bill Oliver. This portion of the site contains a very nice collection of primary documents from the early colonial era.

Gilder Lehrman Institute. "History by Era: The Americas to 1620," http://www.gilderlehrman.org/history-by-era/americas-1620. An interpretive website on the contact era in the Americas with contributions by Christopher L. Miller, Elliott West, Peter C. Mancall, and Felipe Fernández-Armesto.

Gilder Lehrman Institute. "History by Era: Colonization and Settlement, 1585–1763," http://www.gilderlehrman.org/history-by-era/colonization-and-settlement-1585-1763. Like the previous resource, an interpretive site with many resources. Contributors include John Demos, James Horn, Ira Berlin, Jon Butler, and Francis Bremer.

Public Broadcasting Service. Station KMBH, "Who Was in America in 1628?" http://www.pbs.org/wnet/colonialhouse/history/1628.html. An interactive web resource exploring North America region by region, explaining who was present and the interactions taking place in and around the year 1628. Part of a much larger site that covers the colonial era in its entirety.

3

Founding the English Mainland Colonies, 1585-1732

INDIVIDUAL CHOICES

Nathaniel Bacon

Arriving in Virginia from England in 1674, Nathaniel Bacon was wealthy enough to buy a tobacco plantation near Jamestown and a large tract of land on the frontier. Governor William Berkeley, impressed with the young man, appointed him to his elite advisory council. But within two years, Bacon had become the governor's worst nightmare: the leader of a rebellion by frontier farmers and servants.

What drove Bacon to rebel? And what caused so many frontiersmen to join him? Hard times had come to the backcountry: a drought coupled with falling tobacco prices threatened to destroy these farmers' dreams of prosperity. It had become harder to pay the taxes imposed by the Virginia government, and few of the wealthy planters who monopolized the coastal land seemed willing to provide relief for their struggling fellow colonists. Above all, Bacon and his followers resented that the government refused to use some of the money it collected to keep the backcountry safe from Indian attack. Like most colonists who would move west, these Virginians had little sympathy for the native population they were uprooting.

Nathaniel Bacon

Self Portrait Aged 42 (oil on panel), Bacon, Sir Nathaniel (1585–1627)/Private Collection/The Bridgeman Art Library.

Things came to a head when Bacon demanded that the governor raise a militia to rid the backcountry of Indians. When the governor refused, Bacon took matters into his own hands. He raised a vigilante army that attacked peaceful as well as hostile Indian villages.

Enraged, Governor Berkeley branded Nathaniel Bacon a traitor. But to his neighbors, "General" Bacon was a hero. Over five hundred men and women flocked to his defense and together they seized control of the colony's capital. Soon the rebel army controlled over two-thirds of Virginia. But on October 26, 1676, their leader died suddenly of dysentery. Without the charismatic Bacon, the revolution faltered and by the spring of 1677, it had been crushed.

Before his death, Bacon wrote "The Manifesto of the People," excerpted at the end of this chapter. In it, he declared that he and his followers were fighting for a just cause. The royal governors and the wealthy coastal planters who dominated Virginia's political life over the next century disagreed. To these elite colonists, Bacon and his rebellion symbolized a dangerous breakdown of law and order. To Native Americans, Bacon represented the dangers of land-hungry Europeans. But to backcountry families, he remained a folk hero.

Bacon's Rebellion reflects many of the contradictory themes and patterns of the seventeenth-century English-American world. Colonists struggled to adapt creatively to new circumstances, yet they also worked to preserve old traditions and values. Their strong connections to their homelands came out in such small things as naming their towns or farms after places and people they had left behind. Most colonists dreamed of farming their own land, yet to do this, they often callously uprooted Native American communities. Many colonists came to America seeking religious freedom, but in several colonies this freedom was denied to members of other faiths. Most colonists dreamed of new economic opportunities, yet men of wealth, power, and prestige soon dominated colonial society. In every colony, conflict and violence went hand in hand with cooperation and community building, because differences of religion, race, and social class divided neighbor from neighbor. Finally, despite 3,000 miles of ocean separating their New World from the Old World, colonists were still affected by the political upheavals of their home countries and the great imperial struggles waged between Spain, France, Holland, and England.

The early colonial settlements suffered many hardships. Ships carrying colonists sank in ocean storms or fell victim to pirates or enemy vessels. Diseases unknown in England decimated some of the new settlements, and poor planning and simple ignorance of survival techniques destroyed others. Conflicts with local Indian populations produced violence, bloodshed, and atrocities on both sides, and struggles between backcountry settlers like Bacon's rebels and the more established coastal residents erupted in New England, Pennsylvania, the Carolinas, and Virginia.

Still, by the end of the seventeenth century, twelve distinct colonies hugged the Atlantic coastline of English America. The thirteenth, Georgia, was founded in 1732. Although each colony had its own unique history, the New World's climate and geography produced four distinct regions: New England, the Middle Colonies, the Upper South and the Lower South. The colonies within each region shared a common economy and labor system, or a similar religious heritage, or a special character that defined the population, such as ethnic diversity. Yet certain institutions emerged in every colony. Thus, whether its founders had been religious refugees or wealthy businessmen, each colony developed a representative assembly, established courts, built houses of worship—and constructed jails. Carolinians may have thought they shared little in common with the people of Connecticut, but both sets of colonists were subject to English law, English trade policies, internal English conflicts, and conflicts with rival nations. Separate but linked, they were part of a larger transatlantic world that joined Europe, the Americas, and Africa. Between 1607 and 1700 each of the colonies transformed itself from a struggling settlement to a complex society.

It Matters Today

Exploring New Worlds, Then and Now

When Sir Walter Raleigh declared his intention to create a colony in North America, many people no doubt thought the idea was foolish. The mysterious disappearance of his Roanoke Island colonists seemed to confirm that Raleigh was a dreamer. Yet today there is talk of colonizing the moon—and perhaps even Mars. This is not just the work of science fiction novels or movies; in 2006, President George W. Bush announced plans to plant a colony on the moon, and in 2012, presidential hopeful Newt Gingrich pledged he would do so if elected to office. Even the U.S. space agency, NASA, has a proposal for a project called "Moonbase." The quest to explore and settle new worlds seems to be alive and well in the twenty-first century.

- Research physical conditions on the moon, and list some of the challenges these would pose for colonists.
- Produce a set of criteria for participation in such a colony.
- Given differences in technology and economic and political sophistication between Raleigh's time and today, which venture seems more difficult, Roanoke or the moon colony?

ENGLAND AND COLONIZATION

☆ *What circumstances or conditions in England affected people's willingness to join England's colonizing efforts?*

Unlike France or Spain, the English government was not willing to finance the creation of an American empire. No conquering army and no church-supported missionaries would be provided to aid colonists hoping to settle along the North American coastline. Instead, the Crown relied on private citizens to take on the risks of colonization. Sometimes the king helped by providing huge grants of land to the risk-takers, but the royal treasury was not tapped to create the thirteen colonies that eventually emerged on the mainland.

England's First Attempts at Colonization

When the poet and courtier Sir Walter Raleigh took up the challenge of colonization, he risked his personal fortune. In 1587, Raleigh financed the settlement of a hundred colonists at Roanoke, the island he had chosen off the coast of what became North Carolina. Unfortunately, by 1588 England was locked in naval warfare with Spain, and Raleigh was unable to send supplies to his colony for over three years. When a supply ship finally reached Roanoke, the men on board could find no trace of the colonists. Instead, they found abandoned ruins and a single word carved into the bark of a nearby tree: "Croatan." Whether the Roanoke colonists had fled from an attack by the Croatan Indians, been murdered by them, or rescued by them in the face of starvation, epidemic, or some other natural disaster, no one knows. But news of the mysterious disappearance of the colony spread rapidly. So too did news that Sir Walter Raleigh's wealth had disappeared in the process. It would be almost sixteen years before anyone else dared to establish an English colony in North America.

Turmoil and Tensions in England

No one will ever know what crisis the Roanoke settlers faced, but the crises plaguing those still living in England in the seventeenth century were all too clear. Economic upheaval, bitter religious disagreements, and a political challenge to the Crown that ended in civil war all contributed to decades of unrest, violence, and misery. These crises played an important role in reviving the dream of colonization.

The strains of economic change were apparent everywhere in England. The rise of the woolens industry and the transformation of farmland into sheep pastures left thousands of tenant farm families homeless. "Sheep eat men" became the bitter cry of farmers who, overnight, had become vagabonds, roaming from countryside to cities in search of work. Many turned to crime or prostitution to survive. The nation's more fortunate citizens began to discuss the merits of America as a "dumping ground" for the poor and desperate among them; the poor and desperate began to consider a dangerous ocean voyage and the unknown terrors of the New World a better choice than life on the streets of London or Bristol.

Religious tensions troubled the nation as well. Although the official Church of England that Henry VIII had created in 1531 was Protestant, there were those who felt it had kept too many Catholic rituals and customs. They sought to "purify" the church. To the monarchs of the Stuart dynasty, this Puritan criticism smacked of treason as well as heresy, for the king was not only head of the nation but head of the Anglican Church. The mistrust between Puritan reformers and their kings grew during the reigns of James I and his son Charles I, for both men were rumored to be secretly practicing Catholicism.

The political situation was equally tense. A power struggle between the Crown and Parliament, which was the legislative branch of the English government, erupted into open warfare in 1642. This civil war brought together many of the threads of religious and political discontent and conflict, pitting Puritans, merchants, and members of the rising middle class against the Stuart king. A Puritan army, led by Oliver Cromwell, overthrew the monarchy and, in 1649, Cromwell took the radical step of executing Charles I. This execution established the supremacy of Parliament. Cromwell headed the new Commonwealth government until his death in 1658, but he proved no more popular than the former king. In 1660, the Stuart family was invited to take the throne once again. For the next twenty-five years, during a period called the Restoration, Charles II ruled England. But when the crown passed to his brother, James II, who openly practiced Catholicism, a second revolution began, this time with far less bloodshed, because James wisely fled to the safety of France. His Protestant daughter Mary and her Dutch husband, William, then came to the English throne. This Glorious Revolution of 1688 ended almost a century of political, ideological, and economic instability. But by that time, thousands of English men and women had journeyed across the Atlantic Ocean and twelve colonies covered the mainland shores.

SETTLING THE UPPER SOUTH

☆ What were the goals of the Virginia Company and of the Calvert family in creating their Chesapeake Bay area colonies? Did the colonies achieve these goals?

☆ What events illustrate the racial, class, and religious tensions in the Chesapeake?

Fears of financial ruin had prevented any individual Englishman from following in Sir Walter Raleigh's footsteps. But by the beginning of the seventeenth century, English entrepreneurs had developed a new method of financing high-risk ventures, the joint-stock company. In 1603, King James I granted

a charter to two such companies eager to establish colonies on mainland North America. One company quickly failed. The remaining Virginia Company managed to create the first successful English colony in North America.

The Jamestown Colony

The 101 men and four boys sent by the Virginia Company in 1607 found themselves crammed aboard three small ships. Tempers grew short as the months at sea grew long, and trouble aboard one ship landed an adventurer named John Smith in the ship's brig for his role in attempting to organize a mutiny. The colonists had more to worry about than Mr. Smith's temper, however. The Spanish had proven eager to repel any European competitors from the vast territory stretching from Florida to Maine that the pope had granted them in the sixteenth century. And although the Indians had been friendly on the Caribbean Islands where the English ships had stopped for provisions, the colonists were far from certain of the reception they would receive when they reached the mainland.

The three ships entered Chesapeake Bay five months after they had set sail (see Map 3.1). The colonists settled on a small peninsula that jutted out from a river they named the James, in honor of their king,

□ **Church of England** The Protestant church established in the sixteenth century by King Henry VIII as England's official church; also known as the Anglican Church.

□ **Puritans** Members of the Church of England who wanted to reform its worship service and religious doctrines to make it a more thoroughly Protestant church.

□ **Parliament** The lawmaking branch of the English government, composed of the House of Lords, representing England's nobility, and the House of Commons, an elected body of untitled English citizens.

□ **Commonwealth** The republic established after the victory of Oliver Cromwell in the English civil war; the Commonwealth lasted from 1649 until the monarchy was restored in 1660.

□ **Restoration** The era following the return of monarchy to England, beginning in 1660 with King Charles II and ending in 1688 with the exile of King James II.

□ **Glorious Revolution** A term used to describe the removal of James II from the English throne and the crowning of the Protestant monarchs, William and Mary.

entrepreneur A person who organizes and manages a business enterprise that involves risk and requires initiative.

joint-stock company A business financed through the sale of shares of stock to investors; the investors share in both the profits and losses from a risky venture.

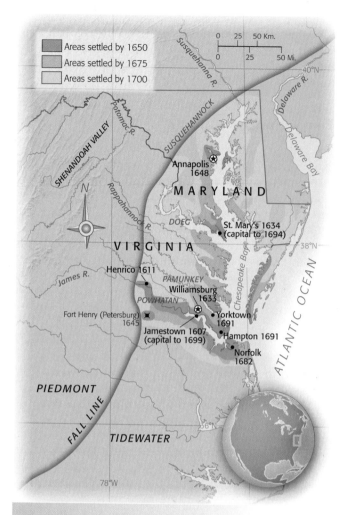

MAP 3.1 Chesapeake Expansion
In Maryland and Virginia, tobacco became the staple crop, making planters who owned land in the tidewater areas quite wealthy. Barrels of dried tobacco were shipped out of the broad Chesapeake Bay, across the Atlantic to England. Increasingly, as the eighteenth century began, ships sailing into the bay carried African slaves who did the backbreaking labor required to produce this profitable "brown gold." © Cengage Learning.

calling their little foothold Jamestown. As they explored their surroundings and met the local Indians, the Englishmen concluded that prospects looked good for forging a peaceful and profitable relationship.

Yet even the least insightful among them should have recognized the wide chasm that separated Englishmen from Indians. To the local tribes, the land on which the colonists had set up their tents and begun to build their fortifications was not Virginia but Tsenacommacah, and it belonged to the confederation of

◻ **Jamestown** First permanent English settlement in mainland America, established in 1607 by the Virginia Company and named in honor of King James I.

some thirty Algonkian-speaking tribes dominated by the Powhatan chieftain Wahunsunacock, as described in Chapter 1. If the English found the Indians exotic—in their body and face paints, their relative nakedness, their religious ceremonies, and their weaponry—the Pamunkeys, Arrohatecks, and Mattoponis found the cumbersome dress and the noisy but less than effective weaponry of the new arrivals equally odd. Each viewed their own culture as superior and, for a brief period, seemed willing to tolerate the misguided beliefs and behaviors of the other.

If the English men and boys had known what lay in store for them in the next decade, they might have sailed for home at once. For the settlers soon faced a seemingly endless series of survival challenges. The site of their encampment proved unhealthy, and one by one, colonists fell ill, suffering from typhus, malaria, or dysentery. Few of them had the skills needed to survive in what was proving to be a hostile and alien environment. Many lacked the experience or the motivation needed to clear fields, plant crops, or build fortifications. These adventurers, as one Englishman bluntly put it, "never knew what a day's labour meant."

The disease, starvation, and exposure to the elements that threatened to destroy the colony were temporarily relieved when the former troublemaker,

Advertisements like this one were designed to promote settlement of England's first permanent mainland colony. Recruiters hoped that the promise of economic opportunity would offset the fears of settling in a dangerous, strange, and distant land.

Who's Telling the Story? And Whose Voice Is Silent?

What if five hundred years from now a historian wanted to learn how people in the early twenty-first century viewed the world around them and what they thought and felt about it? Who would they find telling the story—and whose voice could not be heard? Happily for this future historian, he or she would have no trouble finding documents and artifacts from people of all ages, races, religions, ethnicities, genders, and social classes. There would be letters, e-mails, government documents, television shows, photographs, household furnishings, clothing, court records, tax returns—not to mention Facebook pages.

But today's historians of seventeenth-century North America are not as lucky. Many if not most Indians, enslaved Africans, women, and indentured servants of that era could not write or did not have the leisure time to write down their thoughts. They did not have their portraits drawn or leave any likenesses of themselves. Their homes, their furnishings, their clothes, and other material sources or artifacts rarely survived over the decades and the centuries. Their stories, therefore, often come to us indirectly, from the records of more privileged people such as the ministers, government officials, masters, husbands, judges, and other members of the colonial elite.

The challenge facing modern historians is to uncover more sources that will give ordinary people their voice. We use archaeology and anthropology to help us understand how non-elite men and women lived and worked. We use computer technology to analyze data such as birth, death, and marriage records that reveal the life cycle of ordinary colonists. The result is a collective picture of their lives, yet individual voices remain rare. And, thus the story remains incomplete.

Photo by Ira Block/National Geographic/Getty Images.

Archeological digs like this one at Jamestown can reveal valuable information about the lives of ordinary people. Here, the team has uncovered semicircles that remain from the wall of James Fort's, where early Virginia colonists found safety from the dangers of the New World. Digs like these sometimes provide remains of household equipment, weaponry, and other examples of material culture that speak for the women and men whose own voices have been lost.

John Smith, took command. Smith was hardly a well-liked man: he was overconfident and self-centered, full of exaggerated tales of his heroic deeds as a mercenary in exotic lands. But Smith did have some survival knowledge, and he knew how to discipline men. He established a "no work, no food" policy, and he negotiated with the Powhatans for corn and other supplies. When Smith left in 1609, the discipline and order he had established quickly collapsed. The original colonists and those who joined them the following spring remembered that winter as "the starving time." The desperate colonists burned their housing to keep warm and ate dogs, cats, mice, snakes, even shoe leather in their struggle to survive. Only sixty settlers were alive at winter's end.

The Powhatans had little sympathy for the colonists. Even before Smith had departed, cooperation between the two groups had begun to disintegrate. Despite all their problems, the English exhibited a sense of superiority and entitlement that alienated Wahunsunacock and his confederacy. By 1609 tension and resentment had turned to bloodshed, and raids and counterattacks defined Anglo-Indian relationships for over a decade. Wahunsunacock made several efforts to establish peace, but English encroachments on Indian lands made any lasting truce impossible. Like Wahunsunacock, his successor, Opechancanough, the chief of the Pamunkeys, recognized that dealing with the English colonists would require warfare, not words.

If the settlers were learning hard lessons in survival, the Virginia Company was learning hard lessons, too. The colony was hanging on by a thread, but the stockholders saw no profits, only their yearly expenses of passage for new colonists and supplies for old ones. Prospects for improvement seemed bleak: the investors could see nothing of economic value in the region they called the Chesapeake.

The investors, however, turned out to be wrong. Tobacco, a weed native to the Americas, proved to be the colony's salvation. Pipe smoking had been a steady habit in England since the mid-sixteenth century, and Englishmen were a reliable market for this "brown gold." The local strain of tobacco in Virginia was too harsh for English tastes, but one of the colonists, an enterprising young planter named John Rolfe, managed to transplant a milder strain of West Indian tobacco to the colony. Rolfe made a second contribution to the colony soon afterward, easing the strained Anglo-Indian relations by marrying an Indian princess, Pocahontas, who John Smith insisted had once saved his life.

By 1612, the Virginia Colony's settlers were engaged in a mad race to plant and harvest as many acres of tobacco as possible. Yet the Virginia Company was unable to take full advantage of this unexpected windfall, for it had changed its policies in an effort to ease its financial burdens. In the beginning the company owned all the land but also bore all the costs of colonization. By 1618, however, the company's new policy allowed individual colonists to own land if they paid for their voyage to the colony. This **head right system** granted each male colonist a deed for 50 acres of land for himself and for every man, woman, or child whose voyage he financed. In this way the Virginia Company shifted the cost of populating and developing the colony to others. But the head rights also ended the company's monopoly on the suddenly valuable farmland.

Other important concessions to the colonists soon followed. The military-style discipline instituted by John Smith and continued by later leaders was abandoned. At the same time, a measure of self-government was allowed. In 1618 the company created an elected, representative lawmaking body called the **House of Burgesses**, which gave the landholders—tobacco planters—of Virginia some control over local political matters. In effect, a business enterprise had finally become a colonial society.

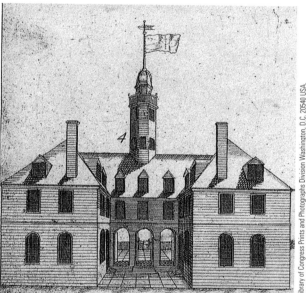

The Virginia House of Burgesses was the first representative assembly to be established in the British colonies. The legislators held their first session in a small Jamestown church, but by 1669, the tobacco planters who served in this assembly had moved into elegant quarters in the colonial capital of Williamsburg. The imposing building sent a clear message to all Virginians that government was the proper domain of gentlemen of wealth and social standing.

□ **head right system** The grant of 50 acres of land for each settler brought over to Virginia by a colonist.

□ **House of Burgesses** The elected lawmaking body of Virginia, established by the Virginia Company in 1618; the assembly first met in 1619.

Religious Conflict in Europe and the Colonies

Although a wide ocean separated the English colonists from Europe, events abroad resonated in their lives. In 1618, a long and devastating war began between Catholics and Protestants that eventually involved conflict both within and among most of the major European powers. The loss of life and resources was so great in this Thirty Years' War that both Protestant and Catholic nations agreed that religious tolerance was preferable to more decades of bloodshed. The peace settlement included a call for "Christian and universal peace, and a perpetual, true and sincere amity" among the combatants. A similar religious warfare, smaller in scale but equally fierce, erupted in Maryland in 1649, and in seventeenth-century Massachusetts, Quakers and other non-Puritans were harassed, jailed, driven out of the colony, and on occasion executed. Although Pennsylvania and Rhode Island did embrace religious toleration, "true and sincere amity" often proved no easier to establish in the New World than in the Old.

The Virginia Company did retain one of the colony's earliest traditions: a bad relationship with the Powhatan Indians. By 1622, with the population growing and tobacco bringing a measure of prosperity, Virginia planters pressed farther inland, seizing Indian land along local rivers. The new Powhatan chief, Opechancanough, decided to strike back. On what the Christian settlers called Good Friday, he mounted a deadly attack on Jamestown, killing a quarter of the colonists in a single day. The company responded as quickly as it could, sending weapons to the Virginians. For two years, war raged between the Indians and the English. Although the bloodshed had become less frequent by 1625, a final peace was not reached for a decade. By that time, disease and violence had taken its toll on the Powhatans. Once over forty thousand strong, they had dwindled to fewer than five hundred people.

The Good Friday Massacre, as the English called it, brought important changes for the colony. King James I had already begun an investigation of the Virginia Company's management record—and the colony's growing profit potential. When he learned of the renewed conflict between Indians and colonists, the king took away the company's charter and declared Virginia to be a royal possession.

If the king's advisers had tallied the cost in human life for planting this first English colony in the same manner that the company tallied expenses in pence and pounds, they would have found the outcome sobering. By 1624, only 1,275 of the 8,500 settlers who had arrived since 1607 remained alive. Fortunately, no other English colony would pay such a price for its creation.

Maryland: A Catholic Refuge

Soon plans for a second southern colony were brewing in England. The man behind this project was not a merchant or entrepreneur, and profit was not his motive. George Calvert, a wealthy Catholic whom King Charles I had just made Lord Baltimore, envisioned a religious refuge in America for fellow Catholics suffering growing harassment and discrimination at home. Calvert acquired a charter from the king for a generous tract of land east and north of Chesapeake Bay. Here, he planned to establish a highly traditional society, dominated by powerful noblemen and populated by obedient tenant farmers. Thus, in the 1630s, George Calvert was a reactionary thinker with a radical vision.

George Calvert, Lord Baltimore, hoped to create a refuge for English Catholics in America. But Maryland soon filled with Protestants, hoping for a new start in a new world. Conflict between colonists of the two faiths followed. Photo by Hulton Archive/ Getty Images.

Calvert died before a single colonist could be recruited for his Maryland. His son, Cecilius Calvert, took on the task of establishing the colony. To Calvert's surprise, few English Catholics showed any enthusiasm for the project. When the first boatload of colonists sailed up the Chesapeake Bay in 1634, most of the two hundred volunteers were young Protestants seeking a better life. Calvert soon adopted the head right system developed by the Virginia Company to attract additional settlers. The lure of land ownership, he realized, was the key to populating Maryland.

Marylanders immediately turned to planting the profitable staple crop, tobacco, and joined the scramble for good riverfront land. Like the Virginians, these colonists used trickery, threats, and violence to pry acres of potential farmland from resisting Indians. By midcentury, the two Chesapeake colonies could claim a modest prosperity, even though their populations grew slowly. But they could not claim a peaceful existence. The political crises that shook England during the mid-seventeenth century sent shock waves across the Atlantic Ocean to American shores. These crises intertwined with local tensions among colonists or between colonists and Indians to produce rebellions, raids, and civil wars.

Troubles on the Chesapeake

In Maryland, tensions ran high between the Catholic minority, who had political influence beyond their numbers because of Lord Baltimore's support, and the Protestant majority in the colony. But with Oliver Cromwell's rise to power in England, Calvert realized that his power to protect Maryland's Catholics was in jeopardy. Hoping to avoid persecution of the Catholic colonists, Calvert offered religious toleration to all Marylanders. In 1649 he issued the innovative Toleration Act, protecting all Christians from being "troubled [or] molested . . . in respect of his or her religion." Cromwell, however, promptly repealed the act. In 1654 Parliament took Maryland away from the Calvert family and established a Protestant assembly in the colony. As Calvert had feared, a wave of anti-Catholic persecution followed.

Within a year, a bloody civil war was raging in Maryland. Protestant forces won the fiercely fought Battle of the Severn, but their victory proved futile when Oliver Cromwell died and the monarchy was restored. Charles II returned Maryland to the Calvert family, who had always been loyal supporters of the Stuart dynasty. Despite this reversal of fortune, Protestants in Maryland continued their struggle, organizing unsuccessful rebellions in 1659, 1676, and 1681. Then, in 1689, the Glorious Revolution prompted Maryland's Protestants to rally once again. Led by an unlikely looking hero, the stooped and nearly crippled minister John Coode, these colonists formed an army they called the Protestant Association. By 1691, Coode had persuaded the Crown to make Maryland a royal colony. The story did not end there, however. In 1715 the fourth Lord Baltimore gave up the Catholic faith and joined the Church of England. Maryland was once again returned to the Calverts.

Virginia was less affected by religious controversy than its neighbor. There, colonists were primarily Anglicans, although small communities of Quakers, Puritans, and even members of the radical Dutch Labadist sect were scattered throughout. Religious differences, however, did not spark hostilities. Instead, the fault lines in Virginia society developed between the wealthy planters of the tidewater region and the ambitious newcomers seeking to make their fortunes in the backcountry. It was this tension that led to Bacon's Rebellion. Many of the problems behind this failed rebellion would resurface one hundred years later during the events leading up to the Revolutionary War.

Colonial Chesapeake Life

Every aspect of life in the Chesapeake colonies, observers noted, seemed to be shaped by tobacco. Its cultivation set rhythms of work and play. Planting, tending, harvesting, and drying tobacco leaves took almost ten months of the year, beginning in late winter and ending just before Christmas. In the short period between the holiday and the start of a new planting cycle, Chesapeake planters, their families, and their servants worked frantically to catch up on other, neglected farm chores. They did repairs, sewed and mended, built new cabins and sheds, cut timber and firewood. They also compressed what meager social life they had into these winter weeks, engaging—whenever possible—in hasty courtships followed by marriage.

Because tobacco quickly exhausted the soil in which it grew, planters moved frequently to new acres on their estates or to newly acquired lands farther west. Since they rarely stayed in one place very long, planters placed little value on permanent homes or social institutions such as schools. Throughout the century, Chesapeake colonists sacrificed many of the familiar forms of community life to the demands of their profitable crop.

Planters needed a labor force large enough and cheap enough to ensure their profits. As long as poverty

staple crop A basic or necessary agricultural item, produced for sale or export.

◻ **John Coode** Leader of a rebel army, the Protestant Association, that won control of Maryland in 1691.

tidewater Low coastal land drained by tidal streams in Maryland and Virginia.

and social unrest plagued England, they found the workers they needed in their homeland. Over 175,000 young, single, and impoverished immigrants flooded the Chesapeake during the seventeenth century, their passages paid by the ship captain or the planter. In exchange for their transatlantic voyage, these indentured servants worked for several years in the tobacco fields without pay. Planters preferred a male workforce, because they shared the general European assumption that farming was a masculine activity. As a result, men outnumbered women in most areas of Virginia and Maryland by 3 to 1. In some areas, the ratio was a remarkable 6 to 1 until the end of the century.

For indentured servants, and often for their masters as well, life was short and brutal. They spent long, backbreaking days in the fields. Their food rations were meager, their clothing and bedding inadequate, and their shoulders frequently scarred by the master's whip. Servants wrote letters home describing their miserable existence. "People cry out day, and night," wrote one young man, who told his father that most servants would give up "any limb to be in England again."

Most servants also expressed doubts that they would survive to win their freedom. In many cases, they were correct. Disease and malnutrition took the lives of perhaps a quarter of these bound laborers. Free colonists fared little better than servants. Typhus, dysentery, and malaria killed thousands. Over one-quarter of the infants born in the Chesapeake did not live to see their first birthdays; another quarter of the population died before reaching the age of 20. One result of this demographic disaster was short-lived marriages, followed by the prompt remarriage of the surviving partner. Complex families emerged, and, after several marriages and remarriages, children could be found in many households who were not related by blood to either of the adult parents in the family.

The last decades of the century saw a change in the labor force. The steady supply of English workers dried up as economic conditions in England improved. At the same time, the cost of purchasing an African slave declined. During the next century, the shift from English servants to African slaves would be completed.

NEW ENGLAND: COLONIES OF DISSENTERS

☆ What type of society did the Puritans create in Massachusetts?

☆ What troubles confronted New England colonists, and how did they respond?

While Captain John Smith was barking orders at the settlers in Jamestown, some religious dissenters in a small English village were preparing to escape King James's wrath. These residents of Scrooby Village were people of modest means, without powerful political allies or a popular cause. But they had gone one step further than the majority of Puritans, who continued to be members of the Anglican Church despite their criticisms of it. The Scrooby villagers had left the church altogether, forming a separate sect of their own. James I despised these separatists and declared his intention to drive them out of England—or worse.

In 1611 the Scrooby separatists fled to the Netherland city of Leyden. They saw themselves as Pilgrims on a spiritual journey to religious freedom. The Dutch welcomed them warmly, but several Pilgrims feared that the comfortable life they had found in Holland was diminishing their devotion to God. By 1620, William Bradford was leading a small group of these transplanted English men and women on a second pilgrimage—to America.

The Plymouth Colony

These Pilgrims set sail on an old, creaky ship called the *Mayflower*. On board, too, were a band of "strangers," outsiders to the religious sect who simply wanted passage to America. Crammed together in close and uncomfortable quarters, Pilgrims and strangers weathered a nightmare voyage of violent storms and choppy waters. After nine weeks at sea, the captain anchored the *Mayflower* at Cape Cod, almost 1,000 miles north of the original Virginia destination (see Map 3.2 on page **64**). The exhausted passengers did not complain; they fell to the ground to give thanks. Once the thrill of standing on dry land had passed, however, many of them sank into depression. Early winter New England was dreary, alien, and disturbingly empty. William Bradford's own wife, Dorothy, may have committed suicide in the face of this bleak landscape.

Talk of setting sail for Virginia spread through the ranks of the ship's crew and the passengers. Mutiny was in the air. To calm the situation, Bradford negotiated

□ **indentured servants** People working out their compulsory service for a fixed period of time, usually from four to seven years; the terms were most often agreed to in exchange for passage to the colonies; a labor contract called an *indenture* spelled out the agreement.

demographic disaster The outcome of a high death rate and an unbalanced ratio of men to women in the Chesapeake colonies.

separatists English Protestants who chose to leave the Church of England because they believed it was corrupt.

□ **Pilgrims** A small group of separatists who left England in search of religious freedom and sailed to America on the *Mayflower* in 1620.

□ **William Bradford** The separatist who led the Pilgrims to America; he became the first governor of Plymouth Plantations.

an unusual contract with every man aboard the ship—Pilgrim, crew, servant, and stranger. This document, known as the Mayflower Compact, granted political rights to any man willing to remain and to abide by whatever laws the new colony enacted. Here was an unheard-of opportunity for poor men to participate in governing themselves. All agreed, and the new colony of Plymouth Plantations began to prepare for the long winter ahead.

Here, as in Virginia, the first winter brought sickness, hunger, and death. Half of the colonists did not survive. When a Patuxet Indian, Squanto, came upon the remaining men and women in the spring of 1621, he found them huddled in flimsy shelters, trapped between a menacing forest and a dangerous ocean. Squanto sympathized with their confusion and their longings for home, because he had crossed the Atlantic in 1605 aboard an English trading ship and spent several years in an alien environment. He also understood

The Bible was the most cherished book, and often the only book, in a colonist's home. To safeguard this treasure, many Pilgrims stored their Bibles in hand-carved boxes like this one belonging to William Bradford. This box, once decorated with the lion and unicorn symbol of England, was politicized during the American Revolution, when the British lion was scraped off.

□ **Mayflower Compact** An agreement drafted in 1620 when the Pilgrims reached America that granted political rights to all male colonists who would abide by the colony's laws.

□ **Squanto** A Patuxet Indian who taught the Pilgrims survival techniques in America and acted as translator for the colonists.

□ **John Winthrop** One of the founders of Massachusetts Bay Colony and the colony's first governor.

□ **Great Migration** The movement of Puritans from England to America in the 1630s, caused by political and religious unrest in England.

what it meant to be a survivor, for the Pilgrims had settled where his own village had once stood. His entire family and tribe had been wiped out by diseases carried by English traders and fishermen.

Squanto helped the colonists, teaching them how to plant corn, squash, and pumpkins. Perhaps his greatest service, however, was in helping William Bradford negotiate a peace treaty with Massasoit, leader of the local Wampanoag Indians. The combined efforts of Squanto and Massasoit saved the Plymouth Colony, and in the fall of 1621, English settlers and Indian guests sat down together in a traditional harvest celebration of thanksgiving.

Plymouth grew slowly, its colonists earning their livings by farming, fishing, and lumbering. A few Pilgrims grew wealthy by developing a fur trade with the Indians. Unlike the Jamestown settlers, the Plymouth community purchased land rather than seizing it, and they were strong allies when warfare broke out between Massasoit's people and their enemies. In fact, the colonists proved to be such ferocious fighters that they were known as Wotoroguenarge, or "Cutthroats."

Massachusetts Bay and Its Settlers

A second colony soon appeared beside Plymouth Plantations. In 1629 a group of prosperous Puritans, led by the 41-year-old lawyer and landowner John Winthrop, secured a charter for their Massachusetts Bay Company from King Charles I. Government harassment, coupled with a deepening economic depression in England, spurred these Puritans to set sail for what would be called New England. As religious tensions and economic distress increased in England, Massachusetts attracted thousands more settlers. This Great Migration continued until Oliver Cromwell's Puritan army took control of England.

While profit motivated the Virginia colonists and a desire to worship in peace prompted the Pilgrims to sail to America, the Puritans of Massachusetts were people on a mission. They hoped to create a model Christian community, a "city upon a hill" that would persuade all English men and women that the reforms they proposed to the Anglican Church were correct. John Winthrop set out their mission in a speech to the passengers aboard the *Arabella*. "The eyes of all peoples are upon us," Winthrop warned and, more importantly, God, too, was watching them. If they abandoned or forgot their mission, the consequences would surely include divine punishment.

This sense of mission influenced the physical as well as spiritual shape of the colony. Massachusetts colonists created tight-knit farming villages and small seaport towns in which citizens could monitor one another's behavior as well as come together in prayer. This settlement pattern fit well with the realities of New England's climate and terrain, since the short growing season and the rocky soil made large, isolated plantations based on staple crops impossible. The colonists, homesick for English villages in regions such as East Anglia, did their best to reproduce familiar architecture and placement of public buildings. The result was often a hub-and-spoke design, with houses tightly clustered around a village green or common pasture, a church beside this green, and most of the fields and farms within walking distance of the village center. This design set natural limits on the size of any village because beyond a certain point—usually measured in a winter's walk to church—a farm family was considered outside the community circle. As a town's population grew and the available farmland was farther from the village green, settlers on the outer rim of the town usually chose to create a new community, a process the Puritans called "hiving off."

Unlike the Chesapeake colonists, many New England settlers came as members of a family. Thus the gender ratio in the northern colonies was never dramatically skewed. And unlike their Chesapeake counterparts, New Englanders never endured a demographic disaster. The cool temperatures and clean drinking water made the region a healthy place for Europeans, healthier than England itself. Infant mortality was low, and most children lived to marry and produce families of their own. A couple could expect to live a long life together and raise a family of five to seven children. One outcome of this longevity was a rare phenomenon in the seventeenth-century English world: grandparents.

Both Puritans and neighboring Pilgrims spoke of the family as "a little commonwealth," the building block on which the larger society was constructed. And, like the larger society, the family was a **hierarchy**. Children were to obey parents; wives were to obey husbands. A husband, however, was expected to care for and be respectful toward his wife. Marriage involved many practical duties as well. Wives were expected to strive to be "notable housewives"—industrious, economical managers of resources and skilled at several crafts. They were to spin yarn, sew, cook, bake, pickle, butcher farm animals, cure meat, churn butter, and set cheeses. Husbands were expected to labor in the fields or in the shop to provide income for their families.

Although obligated to be tender and loving, the husband controlled the resources of the family. This was true in all English colonies, although in the Chesapeake, a husband's early death often left the wife in charge of the family farm or shop and its profits until sons came of age. Under English law, a married woman, as a femme couverte, lost many of her legal rights. Married women could gain basic legal rights only through special contracts made with their husbands. Puritan communities, however, frowned on any such arrangements. A husband also represented

the family's interests in the realm of politics. No matter how wise or wealthy a woman might become, she did not have a political voice.

Government in Puritan Massachusetts

To create the "city upon a hill" the directors of the Massachusetts Bay Company needed, and expected, the full cooperation of all colonists. However, John Winthrop made it clear that this "wilderness Zion" was not intended to be an **egalitarian** society. Like most of his audience, Winthrop believed that it was natural and correct for some people to be rich and some to be poor. Other colonies denied a political voice to women, children, servants, young men, and adult men without property, but Massachusetts further limited political participation. No man in Massachusetts had

---

hierarchy A system in which people or things are ranked above one another.
egalitarian Believing in human equality.

a full political voice unless he was an acknowledged church member, not just a churchgoer. Church membership, or **sainthood**, was granted only after a person testified to an experience of "saving grace," a moment of intense awareness of God's power and a reassuring conviction of personal salvation. Thus Massachusetts made religious qualifications as important as one's sex or economic status in the colony's political life.

Massachusetts differed from the Chesapeake colonies in other significant ways. The colony's government enforced biblical law as well as English civil and criminal law. This meant that the government regulated a colonist's religious beliefs and practices and personal behavior. For example, every colonist was required to attend church and to observe the Sabbath as Puritan custom dictated. The church played a role in supervising business dealings, parent-child relationships, and marital life.

In the early decades of the colony, the Puritan sense of mission left little room for religious toleration. Colonial leaders saw no reason to welcome anyone who disagreed with their religious views. English America was large, they argued, and people of other faiths could settle elsewhere. Winthrop's government was particularly aggressive against members of a new sect called the **Quakers**, who came to Massachusetts on a mission of their own—to convert Puritans to their faith. Quakers entering the colony were beaten, imprisoned, or branded with hot irons, and then thrown out. If they returned, they were hanged. Puritan leaders showed just as little tolerance toward members of their own communities who criticized or challenged the rules of the Bay Colony or the beliefs of its church. They drove out men and women they perceived to be **heretics**, or religious traitors.

Almost anyone could be labeled a heretic—even a popular Puritan minister like **Roger Williams**. Williams attracted a devoted following with his electrifying sermons and his impressive knowledge of scripture. But he soon attracted the attention of local

authorities as well, for his sermons were highly critical of the colonial government. From his pulpit, Williams condemned political leaders for seizing Indian land, calling their tactics of intimidation and violence a "National Sinne." He also denounced laws requiring church attendance.

In 1635 John Winthrop's government banished Roger Williams from the colony. With snow thick on the ground, Williams left Salem and sought refuge with the Narragansett Indians. When spring came, many of his Salem congregation joined him in exile. Together, in 1635, they created a community called Providence that welcomed dissenters of all kinds, including Quakers, Jews, and Baptists. Providence also attracted other Massachusetts colonists tired of the tight controls imposed on their lives by Winthrop and his colleagues. In 1644 the English government granted Williams a charter for his colony, which he eventually called Rhode Island. Within their borders, Rhode Islanders firmly established what was then a radical idea: separation of church and state.

Soon after the Massachusetts authorities rid the colony of Roger Williams, a new challenge arose. In 1634 a merchant named William Hutchinson arrived in Massachusetts with his family. His wife, **Anne Hutchinson**, had received an exceptionally fine education from her father and was eloquent, witty, and well versed in scripture. In addition, she was clearly knowledgeable about the religious debates of the day. Like Williams, Hutchinson put little stock in the power of a minister or in any rules of behavior to assist an individual in the search for salvation.

Hutchinson's opinions, aired in popular meetings at her home, disturbed the Puritan authorities. That she was a woman made her outspoken defiance even more shocking. Men like John Winthrop believed that women ought to be silent in the church and had no business criticizing male authorities. However, male merchants and craftsmen who lacked political rights because they were not members of the saintly elect welcomed her attacks on the authorities. Hutchinson also attracted Puritan saints who resented the tight grip of the colonial government on their lives.

In the end, none of Hutchinson's supporters could protect her against the determined opposition of the Puritan leadership. In 1637 she was arrested and brought to trial. John Winthrop and his colleagues declared her a heretic, "unfit to our society," and banished her from Massachusetts.

Many Puritans who left Massachusetts did so by choice, not because they were banished. For example, in 1636 the Reverend Thomas Hooker and his entire Newton congregation resettled in the Connecticut River valley. Other Puritan congregations followed. In 1644 the Connecticut Valley towns of Hartford, Wethersfield, and Windsor united with the Saybrook settlement at the mouth of the Connecticut River to

sainthood Full membership in a Puritan church.

□ **Quakers** Members of the Society of Friends, a radical Protestant sect that believed in the equality of men and women, pacifism, and the presence of a divine "inner light" in every individual.

heretic A person who does not behave in accordance with an established attitude, doctrine, or principle, usually in religious matters.

□ **Roger Williams** Puritan minister banished from Massachusetts for criticizing its religious rules and government policies; in 1635, he founded Providence, a community based on religious freedom and the separation of church and state.

□ **Anne Hutchinson** A religious leader banished from Massachusetts in 1636 because of her criticism of the colonial government and what were judged to be her heretical beliefs.

This painting captures the hostility colonial Puritans felt for anyone labeled a heretic by their leadership. The close connection between church and state in Massachusetts is evident in the fact that Williams's unorthodox preaching was judged not only a sin against the church but also sedition, that is, a crime against the government. Williams was banished from the colony but built a refuge for other critics of the Puritans in what became Rhode Island.

create the colony of Connecticut. In 1660 the independent New Haven community joined them. Other Bay colonists, searching for new or better lands, made their way north to what later became Maine and New Hampshire. New Hampshire settlers won a charter for their own colony in 1679, but Maine remained part of Massachusetts until it became a state in 1820.

Indian Suppression

Although the Puritan colonists hoped to create a godly community, they were often motivated by greed and jealousy. Between 1636 and the 1670s, New Englanders came into conflict with one another over desirable land. They also waged particularly violent warfare against the Indians of the region.

When the Connecticut Valley towns sprang up, for example, Winthrop tried to assert Bay Colony authority over them. His motives were personal: he and his friends had expected to develop the valley area lands themselves someday. The Connecticut settlers ignored Winthrop's claims and blocked his attempts to prevent their independence from Massachusetts. But they could not ignore the Indians of the area, who understood clearly the threat that all English settlers posed to their territories and their way of life. Sassacus, leader of the Pequots, hoped that an armed struggle would break out between Winthrop and the new Connecticut towns, destroying them both. Instead, however, the two English rivals joined forces to eliminate the Pequots.

By 1636, the Pequot War had begun, with the Indians under attack from both Massachusetts and Connecticut armies, helped by their Indian allies, the Narragansetts and the Mohicans. Atrocities followed. Captain John Mason attacked the defenseless Pequot town of Mystic Village, where only civilians were present. Captain John Underhill of the Massachusetts army recorded the slaughter with obvious satisfaction: "Many [Pequots] were burnt in the fort, both men, women, and children." When the survivors tried to surrender to the Narragansetts, Puritan soldiers killed them. The brutal war did not end until all the Pequot men had been killed and the women and children sold into slavery. If the Narragansett Indians believed their alliance with Winthrop would protect them, they were mistaken. Within five years the Puritans had assassinated the Narragansett chief, an act of insurance against problems with these former Indian allies.

By 1675, Pilgrims, too, were at war with local Indians. Their demands for more land led the Wampanoag chief Metacomet, known to the English as King Philip, to resist. Metacomet's early, devastating raids on white settlements terrified the colonists, but soon the casualties, and atrocities, grew on both sides in what the English called King Philip's War. With the help of Iroquois troops sent by the governor of New York, the colonists finally defeated the Wampanoags. The victors murdered Metacomet and impaled his head on a stick.

Indian objections to colonial expansion in New England had been silenced. Indeed, few native peoples remained to offer resistance of any sort. Several

□ **Pequot War** Conflict in 1636 in which the colonists of Massachusetts Bay and Connecticut and their Indian allies destroyed the Pequot Indians inhabiting eastern Connecticut.

□ **Metacomet** A Wampanoag chief, known to the English as King Philip, who led the Indian resistance to colonial expansion in New England in 1675.

No portrait of Metacomet, or King Philip, was painted during his lifetime. In this nineteenth-century painting, Metacomet wears traditional New England Indian clothing, yet he is armed with a European musket, providing a stark reminder that even the bitterest enemies borrowed from one another's culture.

tribes had been wiped out entirely in the war, or their few survivors sold into slavery in the Caribbean. Those who escaped enslavement or death scattered to the north and the west. The victory had cost the English dearly also. More than two thousand New England colonists lost their lives as the war spread from Plymouth to nearby settlements. And the war left a legacy of hate that prompted Indian tribes west of Massachusetts to block Puritan expansion whenever possible. The costs of New England's Indian policy prompted colonial leaders in other regions to try less aggressive tactics in dealing with local Indians. For the Wampanoags, the Narragansetts, and the Pequots, however, this decision came too late.

□ **Half-Way Covenant** An agreement (1662) that gave partial membership in Puritan churches to the children of church members even if they had not had a "saving grace" experience.

Dominion of New England A megacolony created in 1686 by James II that brought Massachusetts, Plymouth Plantations, Connecticut, Rhode Island, New Jersey, and New York under the control of one royal governor; William and Mary dissolved the Dominion when they came to the throne in 1689.

patronage Jobs or favors distributed by political leadership, usually as rewards for loyalty or service.

Change and Reaction in England and New England

The rise of England's Puritan Commonwealth during the 1640s was celebrated in New England, but many Puritans returned to England to enjoy Cromwell's success. A lot of the newcomers to the colony during the rest of the century were not Puritans at all, but men and women eager to improve their fortunes. Among those Puritans who remained, religious zeal seemed to fade. Few native-born colonists petitioned for full membership, or sainthood, in their local churches as their parents had done, perhaps because of their growing involvement with commerce or because their mission seemed to have been fulfilled by Cromwell and his followers. By 1662, anxious members of the older generation of saints approved a compromise to ensure that their sons would enjoy political rights despite their failure to recount a conversion experience. The resulting Half-Way Covenant kept political power in the hands of Puritans—for the moment.

Pressures from England could not be dealt with so easily, however. After the Restoration in 1660, Charles II cast a doubtful eye on a colony that sometimes ignored English civil law if it conflicted with biblical demands. In 1683 Charles insisted that the Bay Colony revise its charter to weaken the influence of biblical teachings and eliminate the stringent voting requirements. The Massachusetts government said no. With that, Charles revoked the charter. Massachusetts remained in political limbo until 1685, when James II came to the throne. Then conditions grew far worse.

In an effort to centralize administration of his growing American empire, King James decided on a massive reorganization of the mainland colonial world. He combined several of the northern colonies into one large unit under direct royal control. This megacolony, the Dominion of New England, included Massachusetts, Rhode Island, Connecticut, Plymouth Plantations, New Jersey, and New York, both newly acquired from the Dutch. James expected the Dominion to increase the patronage, or political favors, he could provide to his loyal supporters—favors such as generous land grants or colonial administrative appointments. He also expected to increase revenues by imposing duties and taxes on colonial goods in the vast region he now controlled.

What King James did not expect was how strongly colonists resented his Dominion and the man he chose to govern it: the arrogant and greedy Sir Edmund Andros. Andros immediately offended New England Puritans by establishing the Church of England as the official religion of the new colony. Andros also alienated many non-Puritans in Massachusetts by abolishing the representative assembly there. Non-Puritan men had been struggling to be included in the assembly, not to have the assembly destroyed. Andros's high-handed tactics united Massachusetts colonists who had been at odds with each other. When the Dominion governor imposed new taxes, saints and nonsaints alike refused to pay them.

Upon receiving news of the Glorious Revolution, Boston citizens imprisoned Edmund Andros and shipped him back to England to stand trial as a traitor to the nation's new Protestant government. Massachusetts Puritans hoped to be rewarded for their patriotism, but although William and Mary abolished the Dominion, they chose not to restore the Bay Colony charter. In 1691 Massachusetts became a royal colony, its governor appointed by the Crown. **Suffrage**, or voting rights, was granted to all free males who met an English **property requirement**. Church membership would never again be a criterion for citizenship in the colony.

For many colonists, the takeover of Massachusetts by the king was a tragedy. But in 1692, a tragedy of a very different sort struck the colony. In that year, a group of young women and girls in Salem Village began to act strangely. They fell into violent fits, contorting their bodies and crying out in pain. Local authorities might have pronounced them possessed by the devil or a demon, but instead they declared them to be victims of bewitchment. This meant that someone in the colony was practicing witchcraft—but who, and how many? Under questioning, the young women pointed their fingers at several local women, including a West Indian slave named Tituba, as their tormentors. The conviction that the devil had come to Massachusetts spread quickly, and the number of people accused of witchcraft mushroomed. Within months, more than a hundred women, men, and children were crowded into local jails, awaiting trial. Accusations, trials, and even executions—nineteen in all—continued until the new royal governor, Sir William Phips, arrived in the colony and forbade any further arrests. Phips dismissed the court that had passed judgment based on "spectral evidence"—that is, testimony by the alleged victims that they had seen the spirits of those tormenting them. In January 1693, Phips assembled a new court that acquitted the remaining prisoners.

What had prompted this terrible episode in colonial history? In the seventeenth century, it was widely believed in both Europe and America that the devil and his disciples could work great harm in a community. Isolated instances of witchcraft or possession had cropped up in the Chesapeake as well. But the spectacle of the Salem witch trials seemed to have been prompted by more than the affliction of young women or confessions of witchcraft. The transition to

Martha Corey and her husband Giles were among the many Massachusetts Puritans accused of witchcraft in 1692. Although she was admired in her community before the witch hunts began, she was nevertheless found guilty and hanged by the colonial government.

a royal colony had prompted anxieties, and the growing commercial orientation of many colonists seemed a dangerous challenge to the religious mission traditional Puritan colonists still supported. A flood of immigrants from the frontier, driven into the coastal towns by Indian raids, raised the specter for some colonists that the Devil was operating through the Indian population as well. John Winthrop's warning, over a half century before, that God would punish the colonists if they abandoned their faith may not have been totally forgotten. Belief in witchcraft did not end in 1792, but after the Salem tragedy, no colony ever mounted a witch hunt again.

THE PLURALISM OF THE MIDDLE COLONIES

☆ *How did New Netherland develop under English control, and what cultural and economic tensions came to a head during Leisler's Rebellion?*

☆ *What made William Penn's vision for Pennsylvania so distinctive?*

Between the Chesapeake and New England lay the vast stretch of forest and farmland called

suffrage The right to vote.

property requirement The limitation of voting rights to citizens who own certain kinds or amounts of property.

New Netherland, a Dutch colony that was home to settlers from Holland, Sweden, Germany, and France. In the 1660s, Charles II seized the area and drove the Dutch from the Atlantic coast of North America. The English divided the conquered territory into three colonies: New York, New Jersey, and Pennsylvania. Although the region changed hands, it did not change its character: the Middle Colonies remained a multicultural, commercially oriented, and competitive society no matter whose flag flew over them.

From New Netherland to New York

By 1652, England and Holland had become bitter rivals, fighting three naval wars to decide who would control the transatlantic trade in raw materials and manufactured goods. After each war, the Dutch lost ground, and their decline made it likely that their New Netherland settlement would be abandoned.

King Charles II of England wanted New Netherland very much, and James, Duke of York (later King James II), was eager to satisfy his brother's desires. In 1664 Charles agreed to give James control of the region lying between the Connecticut and Delaware Rivers—if James could wrest it from the Dutch (see Map 3.2).

When the duke's four armed ships arrived in New Amsterdam harbor and aimed their cannons at the town, Governor Peter Stuyvesant tried to rally the local residents to resist. They refused. Life under the English, they reasoned, would probably be no worse than life under the Dutch. Perhaps it might be better. The humiliated governor surrendered the colony, and in 1664 New Netherland became New York without a shot being fired.

In many ways, James proved to be a very liberal ruler, allowing the Dutch and other European colonists to keep their lands, practice their religions, and conduct their business in their native languages. But the duke's generosity and tolerance did not extend to taxation matters. James taxed New Yorkers heavily and allowed no representative assembly that might interfere with his use of the treasury. All political offices in the new colony, high or low, went to the duke's friends, creating a patronage system that impressed even King Charles.

James's colony did not develop as he had hoped, however. Settlement did not expand to the north and east as he wished. He could not enlist the aid of influential New Yorkers in his expansion plans, even though he finally offered them the incentive of a representative assembly in 1682. By 1685, James—now king of England—had lost interest in the colony, abandoning his schemes for its growth and abolishing the representative assembly as well.

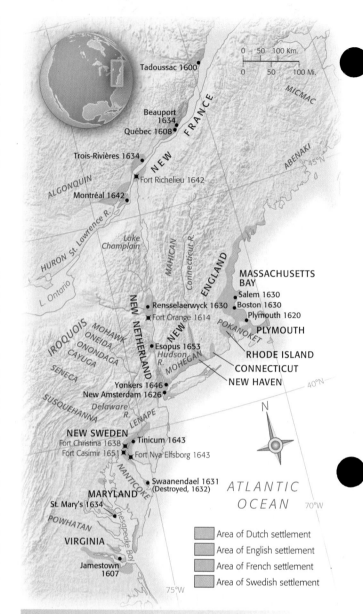

MAP 3.2 European Civilization in the Middle and North Atlantic
In the seventeenth century, several nations competed to establish a colonial foothold along the Atlantic coast of North America. Swedish and Dutch settlements separated the English colonial world of New England from its counterpart in the Chesapeake. While these European colonies hugged the coastline, Native Americans continued to dominate the lands to the west. © Cengage Learning.

Leisler's Rebellion

Although James viewed New York as a failure, the colony actually grew rapidly during his rule. The population doubled between 1665 and 1685, reaching fifteen thousand the year the duke ascended to the English throne. These new settlers added to the cultural diversity that had always characterized the region, for

A prosperous merchant, Jacob Leisler, and his followers seized control of New York in the name of William and Mary when they replaced James II on the English throne. But when the new monarchs sent over a royal governor, Leisler refused to turn power over to him. In the end, Leisler was arrested, tried and convicted of treason against the Crown. His followers continued, however, to be a force in New York politics for many years.

the colony became a religious refuge to French Protestants, English Quakers, and Scottish Presbyterians. New York's diverse community, however, did not always live in harmony. English, Dutch, and German merchants competed fiercely for control of New York City's trade and for dominance in the city's cultural life. An equally intense rivalry existed between Manhattan's merchants and Albany's fur traders. Only one thing united these competitors: a burning resentment of James's political control and the men he chose to enforce his will. Their anger increased when James created the Dominion of New England.

In 1689 news of the Glorious Revolution prompted a revolt in New York City similar to the one that shook Boston. Jacob Leisler, a German merchant, emerged as its leader. Although Leisler lacked the charisma and commanding presence that had allowed Nathaniel Bacon to rise to power in 1676, he was able to take control of the entire colony. When England's new rulers, William and Mary, sent their governor to New York, Leisler refused to surrender the reins of government. This time, the abrasive, headstrong merchant found few supporters, and eventually he was forced to step down. To Leisler's surprise, he was then arrested and charged with treason. Both he and his son-in-law were tried, found guilty, and executed. As befit traitors in the seventeenth century, the two rebels were hanged, disemboweled while still alive, and then beheaded. Afterward, their mutilated bodies were quartered.

In death, Leisler became a hero and a martyr. Popular anger was so great that to quiet the discontent, the new governor had to permit the formation of a representative assembly. Several of the men elected to this new legislature were ardent Leislerians, and for many years New York politics remained a battleground between them and supporters of the royal governor and the king.

William Penn's Holy Experiment

More than most dissenting sects, Quakers had paid a high price for their strongly held convictions. They had been jailed in England and Scotland and harassed by their neighbors throughout the empire. Quaker leaders thus had strong motives to create a refuge for members of their beleaguered sect. In the 1670s, a group of wealthy Quakers purchased New Jersey from its original proprietors and offered religious freedom and generous political rights, even to the Puritans residing there. The best known of these proprietors was William Penn, who had given up a life of privilege, luxury, and self-indulgence in Restoration society and embraced the morally demanding life of the Quakers.

Both Penn and his father were loyal supporters of King Charles. The King rewarded this devotion in 1681, when he granted the younger Penn a charter to a huge area west of the Delaware River. This gave Penn the opportunity to create a refuge for Quakers based on their religious principles.

Presbyterians Members of a Protestant sect that eventually became the established church of Scotland but that in the seventeenth century was sometimes persecuted by Scotland's rulers.

☐ **Jacob Leisler** German merchant who led a revolt in New York in 1689 against royal officials representing the Dominion of New England; he was executed as a traitor when he refused to surrender control of the colony to a governor appointed by William and Mary.

proprietor In colonial America, a proprietor was a wealthy Englishman who received a large grant of land in America from the king or queen in order to create a new colony.

☐ **William Penn** English Quaker who founded the colony of Pennsylvania in 1681.

This sketch of a Quaker meeting highlights one of the most radical of Quaker practices: allowing women to speak in church. Most Protestant denominations, because of their reading of Saint Paul, enforced the rule of silence on women. But Quakers struck a blow at seventeenth-century gender notions by granting women an active ministerial role, a voice in church policy, and decision-making responsibilities on issues relating to the church and the family.

The Bridgeman Art Library/Getty Images.

Penn called his new colony Pennsylvania, meaning "Penn's Woods," in memory of his father. (The southernmost section of Penn's grant, added later by Charles II, developed independently of Penn's control and in 1776 became the state of Delaware.) Like most colonial proprietors, Penn expected to profit from his charter, and he set a *quitrent*, or small fee, on all land purchased within his colony. But Quaker values and principles were the basis for his "holy experiment." At the heart of the Quaker faith was the conviction that the divine spirit, or "inner light," resided in every human being. Quakers thus were expected to respect all individuals. By their plain dress and their refusal to remove their hats in the presence of their social "betters," Quakers demonstrated their belief that all men and women were equal. At the strikingly simple Quaker meeting, or worship service, any member who felt moved to speak was welcome to participate, no matter how poor or uneducated and no matter what sex or age. Although they actively sought converts, Quakers were always tolerant of other religions.

Pennsylvania's political structure reflected this egalitarianism. All free male residents had the right to vote during Penn's lifetime, and the legislature they elected had full governing powers. The political quarrels that developed in Pennsylvania's assembly actually shocked Penn, but his only action was to urge political leaders not to be "so noisy, and open, in your dissatisfactions."

Penn's land policy also reflected Quaker principles. Unlike many proprietors, he wanted no politically powerful landlords or economically dependent tenant farmers. Instead, he actively promoted a society of independent, landowning farm families. Penn also insisted that all land be purchased fairly from the Indians, and he pursued a policy of peaceful coexistence between the two cultures. William Penn took an active role in making Pennsylvania a multicultural society, recruiting non-English settlers through pamphlets that stressed the religious and political freedoms and economic opportunities his colony offered. More than eight thousand immigrants poured into the colony in the first four years. Many did come from England, but Irish, Scottish, Welsh, French, Scandinavian, and German settlers came as well. To their English neighbors who did not speak German, newcomers from Germany such as the Mennonites and Amish were known as the "Pennsylvania Dutch" (*Deutsch*, meaning "German," would have been correct).

When William Penn died in 1717, he left behind a successful, dynamic colony. Philadelphia was already emerging as a great shipping and commercial center, rivaling the older seaports of Boston and New York City. But the commercial orientation here, as in Puritan Massachusetts, attracted colonists who were more secular in their interests and objectives than the colony's Quaker founder. Many newcomers saw Penn's Indian policy as a check on their ambitions and preferred to seize land from the Indians rather than purchase it. The demand for military protection by these land-hungry farmers in the western part of the colony, similar to the demands made decades before by Nathaniel Bacon and his followers, became a major political issue and a matter of conscience for Quakers, whose religious principles included **pacifism**. Eventually many Quakers chose to resign from the colonial government rather than struggle to uphold a holy experiment their neighbors did not support.

COLONIES OF THE LOWER SOUTH

☆ *What type of society did the founders of Carolina hope to create? How did the colony differ from their expectations?*

☆ *Why did philanthropists create Georgia? Why did the king support this project?*

No new colonies were created on the mainland during the Puritan revolution or the Commonwealth. But with the restoration of the monarchy, colonization began once again. In 1663 King Charles II granted eight of his favorite supporters several million acres lying south of Virginia and stretching from the Atlantic to the Pacific Ocean. The gesture was both grand and calculated. France, Spain, Holland, and the Indian tribes who inhabited this area all laid claim to it, and Charles thought it would be wise to secure England's control of the region by colonizing it. The eight new colonial proprietors named their colony Carolina to honor the king's late father, who had lost his head to the Puritan Commonwealth (and whose name in Latin was Carolus; see Map 3.3).

The Carolina Colony

The proprietors' plan for Carolina, called the Fundamental Constitution, was similar to Lord Baltimore's medieval dream. It was an elaborate blueprint for a society of great landowners, **yeomen** (small, independent farmers), and serfs (agricultural laborers) bound to work for their landlords. Like the Calverts, however, the Carolina proprietors discovered that few English people were willing to travel three thousand miles across the ocean to become serfs. Bowing to reality, the proprietors offered the incentive of the head right system.

Many of the early colonists in Carolina were planters relocating from the Caribbean island of Barbados, where sugar growing supported a plantation economy (as further discussed in Chapter 4). They settled the southeastern portion of the colony, drawn there by the fine natural harbor of the port city, Charles Town (later Charleston), and its fertile surroundings. Despite the dangers from the Spanish to the south in Florida and the Yamasee Indians to the southwest, Charles Town grew rapidly, becoming the most important city in the southern colonies.

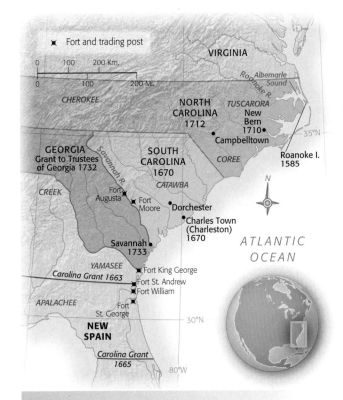

MAP 3.3 The Settlements of the Lower South
This map shows the towns and fortifications of North Carolina, South Carolina, and Georgia, as well as the overlapping claims by the Spanish and the English to the territory south and west of Fort King George. The many Georgia forts reflect that colony's role as a buffer state between rice-rich South Carolina and the Spanish troops stationed in Florida. © Cengage Learning.

The early Carolinians experimented with several moneymaking activities, like trading with some Indians for captive victims of tribal warfare, whom the colonists sold as slaves in the Caribbean, and selling naval stores from their pine forests. Their first real success turned out to be cattle raising, a skill they learned from African slaves brought into the colony by the settlers from Barbados. But by the 1680s rice cultivation became the road to riches. In 1719, Carolina's elite rice planters took control of the southern section of the colony from the original proprietors and named it South Carolina. These planters quickly became the richest English colonists on the mainland.

The northern region of Carolina did not fare as well. Bordered by the Great Dismal Swamp to the north and by smaller swamps to the south, and with a chain of barrier islands blocking access to much of

---

pacifism Opposition to war or violence of any kind.

yeoman Independent landowner entitled to suffrage.

The Lynch family, wealthy rice planters of South Carolina, built this elegant home on the banks of the North Santee River in the 1730s. The Hopsewee Plantation is a striking example of the luxury enjoyed by the small number of elite white planters whose fortunes depended on the labor of enslaved African field workers.

Richard Ellis / Alamy Limited.

the coastline for oceangoing vessels, this isolated area attracted few colonists. Even so, some poor farm families and freed white indentured servants had drifted in from Virginia, searching for unclaimed land and a fresh start. They had modest success in growing tobacco and producing naval stores.

In 1729 the North Carolina colonists followed the lead of their elite neighbors around Charleston and rid themselves of proprietary rule. They then officially separated from the rice-rich southern section of the colony. Thus both South Carolina and North Carolina had become royal colonies.

Georgia, the Last Colony

In 1732 James Oglethorpe, a wealthy English social reformer, and several of his friends requested a charter for a colony on the Florida border. Their goal was to provide a new, moral life for English men and women imprisoned for minor debts. King George II had other motives for granting the charter, however. He was anxious to create a protective buffer between the valuable rice-producing colony of South Carolina

▫ **James Oglethorpe** English philanthropist who established the colony of Georgia in 1732 as a refuge for debtors.

and the Spanish in Florida. He added a clause in the Georgia charter requiring military service from every male settler. Thus, with one stroke of the pen, George II ensured that the poor men of Georgia would protect the rich men of South Carolina (see Map 3.4).

The Georgia trustees believed that poverty was the result of a weak character or, worse, of an addiction to vice and thus did not think debtors could govern themselves. They forbade a representative assembly and denied the settlers a voice in selecting political leaders and military officers. They set other rules, designed to reform the character of their colonists, including a ban on alcohol. To ensure that the settlers worked hard, they kept individual land grants small and banned the use of slave labor.

Oglethorpe envisioned Georgia as a refuge for the "deserving poor." Although he interviewed many imprisoned debtors, few met his standards. Instead, the colony filled slowly with middle-class English immigrants and South Carolinians looking for new land. These colonists resented the trustees' paternalistic attitudes, and they soon challenged all the restrictive rules and regulations in the charter. They won the right to accumulate and sell land. They introduced slave labor in defiance of the trustees. By 1752, Oglethorpe and his fellow trustees had lost enthusiasm for their reform project and, with relief, returned Georgia to the king.

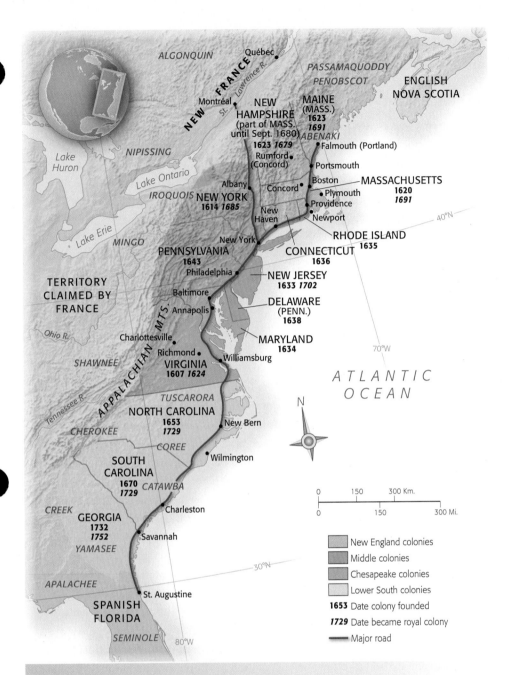

MAP 3.4 The Colonies and Their Major Cities
The creation of the English mainland colonies spanned almost 125 years, from the first settlement at Jamestown, Virginia, in 1607 to the founding of the last colony of Georgia in 1732. This map indicates the year each colony was founded and the date on which eight of these colonies came directly under royal control. The map also locates the major colonial cities in each region. © Cengage Learning.

Individual Voices

NATHANIEL BACON

Manifesto Concerning the Troubles in Virginia, 1676

Sometimes historical figures leave behind a clear statement of the motives and goals for their actions. Nathaniel Bacon is a good example. He was not setting down this information for future generations, of course; he was issuing a ringing statement of the grievances suffered by his followers, and his audience was the governor and his allies, English authorities, and his loyal followers. "The Declaration of the People" was designed to persuade readers of the justice of the rebellion and to ensure that Bacon would be hailed as a defender of the people's rights and liberties rather than condemned as a traitor.

Self Portrait Aged 42 (oil on panel), Bacon, Sir Nathaniel (1585–1627)/Private Collection/The Bridgeman Art Library.

❶ Here Bacon declares that a just God would condone his attacks on the Indian population since they had slaughtered innocent colonists. Yet Bacon attacked peaceful Indians as well. How do Bacon's attacks on these peaceful Indian communities suggest a larger issue of racism in the colonies?

❷ In this section Bacon reminds his readers that the haughty tidewater planters came to Virginia as poor men, not as gentlemen, and are thus no better than his followers.

If virtue be a sin, if piety be guilt, all the principles of morality, goodness and justice be perverted, we must confess that those who are now called rebels may be in danger of those high imputations. Those loud and several bulls would affright innocents and render the defense of our brethren and the inquiry into our sad and heavy oppressions, treason. ❶ But if there be, as sure there is, a just God to appeal to; if religion and justice be a sanctuary here; if to plead the cause of the oppressed; if sincerely to aim at his Majesty's honour and do public good without any reservation or by interest; if to stand in the gap after so much blood of our dear brethren bought and sold; if after the loss of a great part of his Majesty's colony deserted and dispeopled, freely with our lives and estates to endeavour to save the remainders be treason; God Almighty judge and let guilty die. But since we cannot in our hearts find one single spot of rebellion or treason, or that we have in any manner aimed at the subverting of the settled government or attempting of the person of any either magistrate or private man, notwithstanding the several reproaches and threats of some who for sinister ends were disaffected to us and censured our innocent and honest designs, and since all people in all places where we have yet been can attest our civil, quiet, peaceable behaviour far different from that of rebellion and tumultuous persons, let truth be bold and all the world know the real foundations of pretended guilt.... [L]et us trace these men in authority and favour to whose hands the dispensation of the country's wealth has been committed. ❷ Let us observe the sudden rise of their estates composed with the quality in which they first entered this country, or the reputation, they have held here amongst wise and discerning men. And let us see whether their extractions and education have not been vile, and by what pretence of learning and virtue they could so soon [come]

3 Bacon argues that the governor and his friends have done nothing to earn the public's trust or admiration and have failed to provide basic protection for the colony's citizens. One hundred years later, American revolutionaries will make the same claim against the king and Parliament. Do you think Bacon's claims are accurate? Why or why not?

into employments of so great trust and consequence. **3** Let us consider their sudden advancement and let us also consider whether any public work for our safety and defence or for the advancement and propagation of trade, liberal arts, or sciences is here extant in any way adequate to our vast charge. Now let us compare these things together and see what sponges have sucked up the public treasure, and whether it has not been privately contrived away by unworthy favourites and juggling parasites whose tottering fortunes have been repaired and supported at the public charge. Now if it be so, judge what greater guilt can be than to offer to pry into these and to unriddle the mysterious wiles of a powerful cabal; let all people judge what can be of more dangerous import than to suspect the so long safe proceedings of some of our grandees, and whether people may with safety open their eyes in so nice a concern.

SUMMARY

In 1607, the English created their first permanent colony at Jamestown. By 1732, thirteen English colonies hugged the coast of the Atlantic Ocean. Some, like Maryland, Pennsylvania, and Massachusetts, were founded as religious refuges; others were founded for profit. Four distinct regions soon emerged, based primarily on how the settlers made their livings.

Virginia and Maryland made up the Upper South region. Here tobacco shaped every aspect of life. Thousands of poor young Englishmen were brought over to work in the tobacco fields. They came as indentured servants, working without pay in exchange for passage to America. Few women were recruited, and the combination of an unbalanced sex ratio and frequent deaths caused by an unhealthy climate, grueling labor, and poor diet produced what historians call a "demographic disaster" in the seventeenth-century Chesapeake.

The colonies of the Lower South, the Carolinas and Georgia, were established many decades after the Chesapeake by two groups of wealthy Englishmen. Carolina's proprietors tried to create a feudal society, and Georgia's founders wanted to build a haven for debtors. In the end, however, neither goal was achieved. The settlers of what became South Carolina focused on rice production, using African slave labor, and these planters became the richest group in the colonies. North Carolinians were poorer, growing tobacco and farming.

Plymouth Plantations, Massachusetts, Rhode Island, Connecticut, and later New Hampshire made up the New England colonies, with their small farms and shipping and lumbering industries. Here, the earliest settlers were dissenters who sought religious freedom. In 1620, separatists known as the Pilgrims founded the first New England colony, Plymouth Plantations. Their leaders drafted a radical document known as the Mayflower Compact, which assured broad political rights to all the men on board their ship, including the crew and servants. In 1630, Massachusetts Bay was founded by Puritans who intended it to be a model Protestant community. They demanded conformity to their religious views and drove out those who challenged them, especially Quakers. When Puritans like Roger Williams and Anne Hutchinson challenged the colony's leadership and its religious practices, they too were exiled. Williams went on to found Rhode Island on the principle of separation of church and state. Other colonists left Massachusetts voluntarily and founded Connecticut. In 1691, Massachusetts was taken over by the King, and the Puritans' religious experiment ended. The anxiety produced by this political change coupled with economic tensions and Indian attacks on the frontier all contributed to the Salem witch hunts of 1691.

The Middle Colonies region was originally settled by the Dutch and the Swedes, but the English seized the area in 1664. New Sweden and New Netherland became New Jersey and New York. In 1681 William Penn created the colony of Pennsylvania, west of New Jersey, as a home for Quakers. Unlike the Puritans, however, he welcomed people of all faiths into his "holy experiment." The Middle Colonies were noted for their diverse populations and policies of religious toleration.

CHRONOLOGY
Settling the Mainland Colonies

1585	English colonize Roanoke Island
1607	Virginia Company founds Jamestown
1619	Virginia House of Burgesses meets
1620	Pilgrims found Plymouth Plantations
1625	Charles I becomes king of England
1630	Puritans found Massachusetts Bay Colony
1634	Lord Baltimore establishes Maryland
1635	Roger Williams founds Providence
1636	Anne Hutchinson banished from Massachusetts
	Pequot War in New England
	Connecticut settled
1642–1648	English civil war
1649	Charles I executed; Cromwell and Puritans come to power in England

1655	Civil war in Maryland
1660	Restoration of English monarchy
1663	Carolina chartered
1664	New Netherland becomes New York
1675	King Philip's War in New England
1676	Bacon's Rebellion in Virginia
1681	Pennsylvania chartered
1685	James II becomes king of England
1686	Dominion of New England established
1688	Glorious Revolution in England
1689	Leisler's Rebellion in New York
1691	Massachusetts becomes royal colony
1692	Salem witch trials
1732	Georgia chartered

Religious, economic, and political conflicts were common back in England, and it was often no more peaceful in the colonies. In Maryland, Protestants and Catholics warred with each other, and in Virginia, poor backcountry farmers, led by Nathaniel Bacon, rose up against the wealthier coastal planters in 1676. The desire for land also led to bloodshed. Land-hungry colonists in Virginia and New England made war against the Indians. Finally, English policies prompted rebellions, as colonists in Boston and New York rose up to overthrow the hated Dominion of New England in 1689.

As you will see in Chapter 4, most colonists continued to think of England as "home" even as they developed their own societies and their own institutions. Some developments, like widespread African slavery, would seem to widen the differences among the colonial regions; some, like the rise of local representative government, would seem to bring them together. Slowly, however, colonists in all regions developed interests and goals that conflicted with the policies of England's government. One thing was certain: great changes would take place in the eighteenth century.

FOCUS QUESTIONS

If you have mastered this chapter, you should be able to answer these questions and to explain the terms that follow the questions.

1. *What circumstances or conditions in England affected people's willingness to join England's colonizing efforts?*

2. *What were the goals of the Virginia Company and of the Calvert family in creating their Chesapeake Bay area colonies? Did the colonies achieve these goals?*

3. *What events illustrate the racial, class, and religious tensions in the Chesapeake?*

4. *What type of society did the Puritans create in Massachusetts?*

5. *What troubles confronted New England colonists, and how did they respond?*

6. *How did New Netherland develop under English control, and what cultural and economic tensions came to a head in Leisler's Rebellion?*

7. *What made William Penn's vision for Pennsylvania so distinctive?*

8. *What type of society did the founders of Carolina hope to create? How did the colony differ from their expectations?*

9. *Why did philanthropists create Georgia? Why did the king support this project?*

KEY TERMS

Church of England *p. 51*	John Coode *p. 56*	Roger Williams *p. 60*
Puritans *p. 51*	indentured servants *p. 57*	Anne Hutchinson *p. 60*
Parliament *p. 51*	Pilgrims *p. 57*	Pequot War *p. 61*
Commonwealth *p. 51*	William Bradford *p. 57*	Metacomet *p. 61*
Restoration *p. 51*	Mayflower Compact *p. 58*	Half-Way Covenant *p. 62*
Glorious Revolution *p. 51*	Squanto *p. 58*	Jacob Leisler *p. 65*
Jamestown *p. 52*	John Winthrop *p. 58*	William Penn *p. 65*
head right system *p. 54*	Great Migration *p. 58*	James Oglethorpe *p. 68*
House of Burgesses *p. 54*	Quakers *p. 60*	

SUGGESTED RESOURCES

Ric Burns. "The Country and the City," Episode 1 of *New York* (Steeplechase Films documentary, 1999). The story of New York's colonial years with commentary by leading historians. Deerfield History Museum, "Raid on Deerfield: The Many Stories of 1704," www.1704.deerfield.history.museum.

William M. Kelso. *Jamestown, The Buried Truth* (University of Virginia Press, 2008). Uses archaeology to reconstruct life for the earliest English colonists on the mainland. Kelso explains how artifacts—for example, tools or remaining foundations of buildings—are valuable historical sources, especially when documents are missing.

Don Jordan and Michael Walsh. *White Cargo: The Forgotten History of Britain's White Slaves in America* (New York University Press, 2008). A vivid account of the lives of the indentured servants who toiled in the tobacco fields of the Chesapeake in the seventeenth century.

Mary Beth Norton. *In the Devil's Snare: The Salem Witchcraft Crisis of 1692* (Vintage, 2003). An exciting account of the how Indian raids and the colonial refugees these raids produced added to the conviction in 1692 that the devil had come to Massachusetts.

4

The English Colonies in the Eighteenth Century, 1689–1763

INDIVIDUAL CHOICES

Eliza Lucas

Eliza Lucas of South Carolina was only sixteen when her father surprised his neighbors by leaving her in charge of his plantations when he was called away to war. But George Lucas's confidence in his daughter's abilities was not misplaced. Under her management, the family plantations prospered. She even introduced a new crop, **indigo**, from which a valuable blue dye was made. While most other wealthy young women focused on marriage and children, Eliza busied herself with planting, paying bills, directing overseers, and selling crops. But she also made time for traditional female tasks like attending teas, visiting the sick, and learning how to dance and play the piano. To do all this, she set herself a grueling daily schedule, beginning each day at 5:00 A.M., as described in the Individual Voices feature at the end of this chapter.

National Museum of American History, Smithsonian Institution.

Eliza Lucas Pinckney's Gown

Eliza's father had encouraged many nontraditional skills in his daughter. For example, he opened his legal library to her and educated her fully on her legal rights as a single woman, or *femme sole*. Eliza stubbornly protected the independence her father had nurtured. When she finally married it was to an old and respected friend, Charles Pinckney, a widower twice her age who was a leading lawyer and political figure in the colony. As a wife, Eliza turned her full attention to domestic concerns and to the education of her five children. She rejected the traditional notion that children were burdened by original sin and raised her family according to Rousseau's theories of the power of nurture and encouragement. The French philosopher's advice served her well: Eliza and Charles's two surviving sons grew up to be political leaders during the revolutionary struggle and her only daughter followed in Eliza's footsteps, eventually running her own plantation.

The American social and economic landscape was changing dramatically in the eighteenth century. Farms and plantations spread westward, while coastal cities grew larger. Population boomed, as immigrants from Ireland, Scotland, and Germany poured into the colonies, along with thousands of imported African slaves. These immigrants added diversity of language, religion, and customs to colonial communities. Trade among the colonies grew, and ships traveled the coastline almost as frequently as they sailed the Atlantic to Europe or the Caribbean islands.

Although regional differences were growing more pronounced, the colonists continued to share many experiences. They were all part of a common imperial structure as well as a sprawling transatlantic community in which goods, people, and ideas steadily flowed between England, Europe, the Americas, and Africa.

Although Anglo-Americans eagerly awaited news from an England they still called "home," few members of the English elite followed American developments closely—or at all. Members of the English Parliament viewed the colonists as little more than a collective source of endless problems. They expected insubordinate colonial legislatures, defiant merchants who violated trade regulations, and a dangerously unstable political atmosphere in a society that gave common men an *unprecedented* voice in government. Yet it was the colonists who often suffered from decisions made by Parliament and the king. England's fierce rivalries with European nations produced a long series of imperial wars that disrupted communities from the Maine border to Georgia. In the end, England would triumph over every rival for a North American empire. The outcome of this victory would prove surprising to everyone.

THE ENGLISH TRANSATLANTIC COMMUNITIES OF TRADE

☆ What were the main regional differences in colonial commerce and what kind of economic choices did each region offer colonists?

Although the English spoke of "the colonial trade," British North America did not have a single, unified economy. Instead, four distinctive regional economies had developed on the mainland, concentrated along the Atlantic coastline and bordered on the west by the primarily *subsistence society* that was commonly known as the backcountry. To the south, the sugar islands of the Caribbean made up a fifth unique regional economy. Each of these economies was shaped by environmental conditions, natural resources, English commercial policy, the available labor force, and the available technological know-how.

Regions of Commerce

The sugar-producing islands of the West Indies were the brightest jewels in the English imperial crown. Spain had first laid claim to most of these islands,

indigo Shrublike plant with clusters of red or purple flowers, grown on plantations in the South; it was a primary source of blue dye in the eighteenth century.

femme sole From the French for "woman alone"; a legal term for an unmarried, widowed, or divorced woman with the legal right to own or sell property, sue or be sued, or earn wages.

unprecedented Unheard of or novel.

subsistence society A society that produces the food and supplies necessary for its survival but that does not produce a surplus for market.

but England had slowly gobbled up many of them, and thus, by the eighteenth century, the English flag flew over St. Kitts, Barbados, Nevis, Montserrat, and Jamaica. Here, English plantation owners built fabulous fortunes on the sugar that African slaves produced. While the **absentee planters** lived in luxury in England, black slaves lived—and died in staggering numbers—on the islands, working the cane fields and tending the fires that burned day and night under the sugar vats of the boiling houses where the raw sugar, or molasses, was produced.

Few mainland colonists enjoyed the wealth of this "Sugar Interest." Still, planters of South Carolina and Georgia, like Eliza Lucas Pinckney, amassed considerable fortunes by growing rice in the lowlands along the Atlantic coast. Here, as in the Caribbean, slaves formed the planters' labor force. Slavery had been introduced to the region early in the eighteenth century by Barbadian planters who brought their slaves with them when they migrated to the mainland. These slaves taught the English colonists how to cultivate the rice crop that would make their masters wealthy. By the 1730s, this American rice was feeding the people of the Mediterranean, Portugal, and Spain. By midcentury, planters were making additional profits from indigo crops. Unlike the island moguls, the plantation masters here never became permanently absent landowners.

Tobacco, or "brown gold," continued to dominate the economy of the Chesapeake, although the high taxes placed on this crop prompted many eighteenth-century planters to begin producing wheat and other grains for export. Tobacco production shifted west to the area along the Potomac, the James River valley, and the **piedmont** foothills. The second major shift came in the labor force used in tobacco cultivation. By the eighteenth century, African slaves had replaced indentured servants in the fields. Planters who could afford to purchase a number of slaves enjoyed a competitive advantage over their neighbors in both the old and the new tobacco areas, for slave labor allowed them to plant and harvest bigger crops. This large-scale production kept tobacco the number one export of the mainland colonies.

Together, these two southern regions provided the bulk of the mainland's agricultural exports to Great Britain. In contrast, the New England regional economy depended far less on Britain as a market.

Except in the Connecticut River valley, where tobacco was grown, the region's rocky soil made large-scale farming unfeasible for New Englanders. Instead, shipbuilding and the ambitious **carrying trade** dominated New England's economy. Colonists made great profits from this transatlantic trade that carried colonial exports across the Atlantic and to the Caribbean and distributed foreign goods and English manufactured products to the colonies (see Map 4.1). Some merchant-shippers—the slave traders of Newport, Rhode Island, for example—specialized in a certain commodity, but most were willing to carry any cargo that promised a profit. An economy based on the carrying trade made New Englanders rivals of English merchants rather than useful sources of profit for the Mother Country.

Sandwiched between the South and New England, the colonies of New York, New Jersey, Pennsylvania, and the area that later became Delaware developed their own regional economy, creating profits from both staple-crop farming and trade. The forests of the Pocono Mountains and upper New York were a source of wood and wood products for the shipbuilding industry, and locally harvested flaxseed was exported to Ireland for its linen industry. The central crop, however, was wheat, the price of which rose steadily during the eighteenth century. The carrying trade, both along the coast and across the ocean, was equally important in this region's mixed economy. Ships carrying cargoes of grain and flour across the Atlantic and into the Caribbean crossed paths with other colonial ships bringing manufactured goods and luxury items from Europe to the region's two major port cities, New York and Philadelphia.

Not everyone in the colonies participated fully in the market-oriented activities, of course. In the older coastal settlements of each region, harbors and river ways provided the necessary transportation routes for the shipment of crops, goods, and supplies. But most colonies had an inland backcountry that was sparsely populated and farmed by European immigrants, ex-servants, or the families of younger sons from older communities. There, on what white settlers thought of as the frontier and Indians called the invasion line, colonists struggled to produce enough for survival. They lacked both the labor force to clear and work sufficient acreage for a marketable crop and the transport to get a crop to market. And they had few financial or political resources that might help overcome these obstacles. This belt of subsistence extended like a border from Maine to western Pennsylvania, to inland Carolina, along every region of the mainland colonies. But even these backcountry farms had a link to the world of international trade, for settlers brought with them the farm tools and basic household supplies that had been manufactured in England or imported through colonial ports.

---

absentee planter An estate owner who collects profits from farming or rent but does not live on the land or help cultivate it.

piedmont Land lying at the foot of a mountain range.

☐ **carrying trade** The business of transporting goods across the Atlantic or to and from the Caribbean.

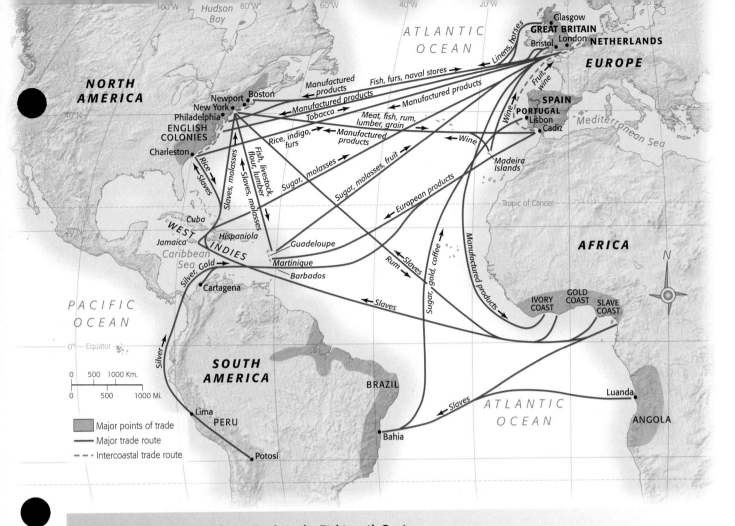

MAP 4.1 Colonial Transatlantic Trade in the Eighteenth Century
This map shows the major trade routes between the British mainland colonies, West Africa, the Caribbean, and Europe, and the most important export and import cargoes carried along these routes. The central role northern seaport cities played in carrying colonial agricultural products across the Atlantic and bringing British manufactured goods into the colonies is clear. Note also the role the northern colonies played in the slave trade. © Cengage Learning.

The Cords of Commercial Empire

England's trade policies were based on the dominant economic theory of the day: mercantilism. Under mercantilism, a government regulated trade to ensure as much self-sufficiency *within* its borders as possible, encouraging the domestic production of essential food and manufactured goods so that they need not be purchased from rival nations. At the same time, the government supported the production of goods other nations might wish to purchase. The result of a successful mercantile policy was that gold and silver—the wealth of the day—would flow into, rather than out of, the country. The colonies played a critical role in the success of British mercantilism, for they produced the wheat and rice that Europe needed and much of the tobacco Europeans wanted. By the eighteenth century, the colonists were also a profitable market for goods manufactured in England or imported for sale by English merchants. Since the end

of the seventeenth century, laws called Navigation Acts had regulated colonial trade. Colonists were required to ship their products in English or colonial-made boats. They were forbidden to manufacture items that might compete with English production such as hats or iron tools. And, they were discouraged from trading directly with enemy or rival nations by the imposition of import taxes. Although these regulations were rarely strictly enforced, they did shape colonial trade patterns.

Thus, although salt, wine, and spices reached colonists' tables from southern Europe, and sugar, rum, and cotton came to their households from French and Spanish West Indian islands, the deepest channels in the transatlantic trade were those that connected England and the colonies. The British purchased over half of all the crops, furs, and mined resources that colonists produced for market and supplied 90 percent of all colonial imports.

The English mainland colonies were also bound to one another, despite a deserved reputation for dispute,

It Matters Today

Women's Opportunities, Then and Now

In her character and her life choices, Eliza Lucas Pinckney seems remarkably modern. Yet she lived in an era when women were assumed to be best suited for the domestic duties known as "housewifery." Of course, Pinckney had advantages many other eighteenth-century women did not enjoy: wealth, social standing, and a father and a husband who had confidence in her abilities. Without these advantages, Pinckney might never have been able to venture outside the domestic realm. Today, Pinckney would find herself among many women who are able to have successful careers in business, medicine, the law, scientific research—and in an area completely closed to Pinckney, politics. The contrast between a life that was extraordinary in the eighteenth century but ordinary in the twenty-first century prompts us to examine what changes have occurred in women's lives between the colonial era and today.

- Choose a profession such as law, medicine, or the military. Research the entrance of women into that profession. What arguments have been offered for and against allowing women into this profession? What factors do you feel have been most significant in opening up opportunities for women in this field? What obstacles still remain?

---

disagreement, and endless rivalries. New Englanders might exchange insults with Pennsylvanians, but in the shops and on the wharfs, Pennsylvania flour, Massachusetts mackerel, Carolina rice, and scores of domestic products and produce changed hands in a lively and cheerful commerce. Domestic trade was greater in volume, although lower in value, than all foreign trade in this eighteenth-century colonial world.

COMMUNITY AND WORK IN COLONIAL SOCIETY

☆ How did the Yankee society of early eighteenth-century New England differ from Puritan society?

☆ Why did colonists in the Chesapeake and Lower South shift to slave labor? What problems faced Africans in slavery?

☆ What distinguished life in the Middle Colonies?

☆ What motivated colonists to migrate to the backcountry?

Despite the belief of many observers that there was an "American character," visitors could not fail to note cultural and social differences as they traveled from New England to the Lower South. Moving from the carefully laid-out towns of New England, through the crowded seaport cities of the Middle Colonies, and into the isolated rural worlds of the plantation South, they could see that the Yankee culture of Connecticut differed strikingly from the lifestyle and social attitudes of South Carolina's elegant planter elite.

The Emergence of the "Yankee"

Once Massachusetts became a royal colony, the Puritan culture of the village gave way to a more secular "Yankee" culture. In this atmosphere, a wealthy man could rise politically without any need to demonstrate his piety. Economic competition and the pursuit of profit eclipsed older notions that the well-being of the community came before the gains of the individual. This shift to a "Yankee" mentality was reflected in the law: Puritan laws regulating prices and interest rates, for example, were repealed or simply ignored. Still, some sense of obligation to the community remained in New Englanders' willingness to create and maintain public institutions such as schools and colleges. In 1701, for example, Yale College opened its doors in New Haven, Connecticut, giving the sons of elite New Englanders an alternative to Massachusetts's Harvard College, founded in 1636. And New Englanders supported newspapers and printing presses that kept their communities informed about local, regional, and international events.

Even in more traditional New England villages, changes were evident. By the eighteenth century, fathers no longer had enough farmland to provide adequately for all their sons. Thus many younger sons left home to seek their fortunes. Some chose to push the frontier of settlement westward as they searched for fertile land. Others went north, to less developed areas such as Maine, causing the number of backcountry New England towns to grow steadily until the end of the colonial period. Still other young men abandoned farming entirely and relocated to

As this 1754 engraving shows, Charles Town, South Carolina was a thriving port city, exporting rice to England and importing luxury goods from Europe. Here, in elegant townhouses, the colony's wealthy families escaped the heat and humidity of their rice plantations and enjoyed a social schedule of theatre, balls, and dinner parties.

the commercial cities of the region. Urban life often disappointed them, for inequality of wealth and opportunity went hand in hand with the overall prosperity. In Boston a growing number of poor widows and landless young men scrambled for employment and often wound up dependent on public charity. As news spread about the scarcity of farmland in the countryside and the poverty and competition for work in the cities, European immigrants to America tended to bypass New England and settle in the Middle Colonies or along the southern frontier.

Planter Society and Slavery

Southern society was changing as dramatically as New England's. By the end of the seventeenth century, the English economy was improving, and young men who might once have signed on as indentured servants in Virginia or Maryland now chose to remain at home. Those who did immigrate preferred to indenture themselves to farmers and merchants of the Middle Colonies, where work conditions were bearable and economic opportunities were brighter. While the supply of indentured servants was declining, however, a different labor supply was growing: enslaved Africans. By the first decades of the eighteenth century, the trade in enslaved Africans and the exploitation of slave labor was one of the defining characteristics of the Atlantic world.

Slavery was well established in the Caribbean in the seventeenth century, both as a legal and an economic system, when it began to develop on the North American mainland. Although a small number of Africans had been brought to Virginia as early as 1619, the legal distinctions between black and white workers here on the mainland remained vague until the 1660s. As the number of African workers slowly increased, white colonists began to adopt the different and harsher treatment that defined slavery in islands like Barbados. By midcentury, it became the custom in the Chesapeake to hold black servants for life terms, although their children were still considered free. By the 1660s, colonists had turned these customs of **discrimination** into law. In 1662 Virginia had taken a major step toward making slavery an inherited condition by declaring that "all children born in this country shall be held bond or free according to the condition of the mother."

Southern planters had long been aware of the advantages of slave labor over indentured servitude. First, slaves, bound for life, would never compete with their former master the way freed white servants did. Second, most white colonists did not believe that the English customs regulating a master's treatment of servants had to be applied to African workers. For example, Christian holidays need not be honored for African laborers, and the workday itself could be lengthened without any outcry from white neighbors. Yet until the late 1600s, Chesapeake planters found investment in African laborers both too costly and too risky. The Dutch controlled the slave trade and this kept purchase prices high and supply low, and the disease environment of the Chesapeake cut human life short. By the 1670s, however, mortality rates fell in the

discrimination Treatment that denies opportunity or rights because of class, gender, or racial or ethnic category; sometimes called *prejudice.*

Chesapeake, and the English broke the Dutch monopoly on the slave trade. Soon fierce competition among English slavers drove prices down and at the same time ensured a steady supply of slaves. Under these conditions, the demand for slaves in the Chesapeake grew rapidly. Although only 5 percent of the roughly 9.5 million Africans brought to the Americas came to the North American mainland colonies, their numbers in Virginia and Maryland rose dramatically in the eighteenth century. By 1700, 13 percent of the Chesapeake population was African or of African descent. In Virginia, where only 950 Africans had lived in 1660, the black population grew to 120,000 by 1756. At the end of the colonial period, blacks made up 40 percent of Virginia's population.

Chesapeake colonists who could not afford to purchase African slaves now moved west, and new immigrants to the colonies avoided the coastal and piedmont plantation society altogether. Colonial merchants and skilled craftspeople also avoided the Chesapeake, for the planters purchased their goods directly from England or used slave labor to manufacture barrels, bricks, and other products. As a result, few towns or cities developed in this region. The Chesapeake region remained a rural society, dominated by a planter class whose prosperity rested on the labor of enslaved African Americans.

If tobacco provided a comfortable life for an eighteenth-century Virginia planter, rice provided a luxurious one for the planters of the Lower South. During the summer months, wealthy South Carolina planters found relief from the heat, humidity, and unhealthy environment of their lowland plantations by moving to their elegant Charles Town homes. Beautiful townhouses, theaters, and parks made this summer retreat the single truly cosmopolitan city of the South and perhaps the most sophisticated of all mainland cities.

The luxurious life these Lower South planters enjoyed depended on the forced labor of slaves. By 1708, one-half of the colonial population in Carolina was black, and by 1720, Africans and African Americans outnumbered their white masters. Georgia, too, depended on slavery for its prosperity.

Slave Experience and Slave Culture

Slaves began their bondage when African slavers, often armed with European weapons, captured men, women, and children and delivered them in chains to European ships anchored along the coast of West Africa (see Map 1.5, page **20**). While many of those enslaved were considered war captives, others had simply been kidnapped. The slave trader John Barbot recounted the kidnapping of "little Blacks" who had been sent by their parents to "scare away the devouring small birds" in the family cornfield. Even before these captives reached the European slave ships, they were introduced to the horrors of slavery. Their captors treated them "severely and barbarously," beating and wounding them. The many who died on the long march from the interior to the coast were left unburied, their bodies to be "devoured by...beasts of prey." As the surviving captives were branded and then rowed to the waiting ships, some committed suicide, leaping overboard into the ocean waters. Slave traders tried to prevent these suicides—every death meant a smaller profit—but were not surprised by them. The slaves, they commented, dreaded life in America more than their captors dreaded hell.

This depiction of the African slave trade focuses on the despair and grief produced by the traffic in human beings during the colonial and early national period. Those taken aboard the slave ship would endure the horrors of the "middle passage," the long voyage across the Atlantic Ocean to the Americas.

The slaves' transatlantic voyage, or **middle passage**, was a nightmare of death, disease, suicide, and sometimes mutiny. The casualties included the white officers and crews of the slave ships, who died of diseases in such great numbers that the waters near Benin in West Africa were known as the "white man's grave." But the loss of black lives was far greater. Slave ships were breeding grounds for scurvy, yellow fever, malaria, dysentery, smallpox, measles, and typhus—each bringing painful death. When smallpox struck his slave ship, one European recorded that "we hauled up eight or ten slaves dead of a morning. The flesh and skin peeled off their wrists when taken hold of." Perhaps 18 percent of all the Africans who began the middle passage died on the ocean.

Until the 1720s, most Chesapeake slaves worked alone on a tobacco farm with the owner and his family or in small groups of two or three in a system known as "gang labor." This isolation made both the creation of a family and the emergence of a slave community almost impossible. Even on larger plantations, community formation was discouraged by the division of women and men into separate gangs. The steady influx of newly imported slaves, or "outlanders," during the first decades of the eighteenth century also made it difficult for African Americans to work together to create a culture of their own. The new arrivals had to be taught to speak English and to adapt to the demands of slavery. Slowly, however, these involuntary immigrants from different African societies, speaking different languages, practicing different religions, and surviving under the oppressive conditions of slavery, did create a sense of community, weaving together African and European traditions. The result was an African American culture that gave meaning to and a sense of identity within the slave's oppressive world.

In the Lower South, where Eliza Lucas Pinckney ran her plantations, slaves were concentrated on large plantations where they had limited or no contact with white society. This isolation from the dominant society allowed them an earlier opportunity to develop a creole, or native, culture. Because slaves in South Carolina, unlike those in the Chesapeake colonies, were imported directly from Africa, they were able to preserve more of their African heritage. For example, they gave their children African names and developed languages that mixed a basic English vocabulary with words from a variety of African tongues. One of these languages, Gullah, remained the local dialect on the Sea Islands off the coast of South Carolina and Georgia until the end of the nineteenth century.

In contrast to gang labor, here a "task labor" system prevailed. Slaves were assigned certain chores to be completed within a certain time period, and this gave rice plantation slaves some control over their pace of work and some opportunities to manage their free time.

TO BE SOLD on board the Ship Bance-Island, on tuesday the 6th of May next, at Ashley-Ferry; a choice cargo of about 250 fine healthy NEGROES, just arrived from the Windward & Rice Coast.—The utmost care has already been taken, and shall be continued, to keep them free from the least danger of being infected with the SMALL-POX, no boat having been on board, and all other communication with people from Charles-Town prevented.

Austin, Laurens, & Appleby.

N. B. Full one Half of the above Negroes have had the SMALL-POX in their own Country.

The Granger Collection, NYC.

Advertisements like this one were common in the eighteenth-century colonies, both north and south. Rewards were usually offered to encourage colonists to turn in the enslaved men and women seeking their freedom.

For many slaves, the bonds of community became a form of resistance to enslavement. But African Americans also developed other ways to show their hatred of slavery. The diary of Virginia planter William Byrd is filled with accounts of daily resistance: slaves who challenged orders, field hands who broke tools and staged work slowdowns, men who pretended sickness and women who claimed pregnancies, household servants who stole supplies and damaged property, and slaves who ran away to the woods for a day or two or to the slave quarters of a neighboring plantation. African Americans with families, and those who understood the odds against escape, preferred to take disruptive actions like these rather than risk almost certain death in open rebellion.

The Urban Culture of the Middle Colonies

The small family farms of Pennsylvania, with their profitable wheat crops, earned the colony its reputation as the "best poor man's country." Tenant farmers, hired laborers, and even African slaves were not unknown in eastern Pennsylvania, but the colony boasted more comfortable middle-class farm families than neighboring New York or New Jersey. In New York great estates along the Hudson River controlled much of the colony's good land, and in New Jersey wealthy owners

▢ **middle passage** The transatlantic voyage of indentured servants or African slaves to the Americas.

Private Collection / Peter Newark American Pictures / The Bridgeman Art Library.

Crowded at the tip of Manhattan, the city of New York boasted one of the busiest harbors in the mainland colonies. Residents complained of the the same problems in the eighteenth century that they do today: high rents, cramped quarters, noisy streets and a fast pace of life. Wits remarked that New York had far more taverns and brothels than churches.

dominated the choicest acreage, which often resulted in tensions between the landlords and their tenants in both colonies.

But what made the Middle Colonies distinctive was the dynamic urban life of the two major cities, New York and Philadelphia. Although only 3 percent of the colonial population lived there, the eighteenth-century cities were magnets for young men and women, widows, free African Americans and slaves, and some of the immigrant population pouring into the colonies from Europe. By 1770, Philadelphia's forty thousand residents made it the second-largest

apprentice A person bound by legal agreement to work for a craftsman for a specific length of time in exchange for instruction in a trade, craft, or business.

milliner A maker or designer of hats.

city in the British Empire. In the same year, twenty-five thousand people crowded onto the tip of New York's Manhattan Island.

New York residents shared their cramped living spaces with chickens and livestock and their streets with roving packs of dogs and pigs. On the narrow cobblestone or gravel streets, pedestrians jostled one another and struggled to avoid being run down by carts, carriages, men on horseback, or cattle being driven to slaughter. Although colonial cities were usually thought to be cleaner than European cities, with better sewage and drainage systems, garbage and excrement left to rot on the streets provided a feast for flies and scavenging animals.

City residents faced more serious problems than runaway carts and snarling dogs. Sailors on the ships docked at Philadelphia or New York often carried venereal diseases. These and other communicable diseases spread rapidly in overcrowded areas. Fires also raced through these cities of wooden houses, wharfs, and shops. And urban dwellers were no strangers to crime—especially robbery and assault—in a community where taverns, brothels, and gambling houses were common.

Despite the dangers, colonial cities attracted many a farmer's daughter or son because they offered a wide range of occupations and experiences. These newcomers were sometimes overwhelmed by city life. One farm boy wrote to his father: "I must confess, the jolts of Waggons, the Ratlings of Coaches, the crying of meat for the Market, the [hollering] of negroes and the ten thousand junggles and Noises, that continually Surround us in every Part almost of the Town, confuse my Thinking."

Young men who could endure the noise and confusion sought work as **apprentices** in artisan trades ranging from the luxury crafts of silversmithing or cabinet making to the profitable trades of shipbuilding or butchering, to the more modest occupations of ropemaking or baking. The poorest might find work on the docks or as servants, or they might go to sea. Young women had more limited choices because few trades were open to them. Some might become dressmakers or **milliners**, but domestic service and prostitution were more likely choices. In Middle Colony cities, as in Boston, widowed farm wives came seeking jobs as nurses, laundresses, teachers, or seamstresses. A widow or an unmarried woman who had a little money could open a shop or set up a tavern or a boarding house.

Although most northern farmers did not employ slave labor, New York and Philadelphia merchants and shippers found enslaved laborers valuable on their docks and wharfs and in domestic service in their homes. New York City had the highest concentration of African Americans, both free and enslaved, in the northern colonies. Perhaps only 5 percent of

Few women worked in the skilled trades or crafts, although widows and daughters might manage a shop after a husband or father died. The mantua maker shown here was considered an artisan and could command a good price for her skills in making fancy gowns and other elaborately sewn clothing.

all mainland colony African Americans were free. Although many remained in the South despite social and legal harassment, others made their way to the cities of New England and the Middle Colonies, eking out a livelihood as laborers, servants, or sailors.

Life in the Backcountry

Thomas Malthus, a well-known English analyst of demographics, believed the eighteenth-century population explosion in the English mainland colonies was "without parallel in history." The colonial white population climbed from 225,000 in 1688 to over 2 million in 1775, and the number of African Americans reached 500,000 in the same year. Natural increase accounted for much of this growth, and over half of the colonists were under age 16 in 1775. But hundreds of thousands of white immigrants arrived during the eighteenth century, risking all on the transatlantic voyage to start life over in America.

The majority of these immigrants ended up in the colonial backcountry.

Migration westward gradually shifted the population center of mainland society. Newcomers from Europe and Britain, as well as descendants of the original New England settlers and the younger sons of the tidewater Chesapeake, all saw their best opportunities in the sparsely settled regions of the interior. Many of these settlers were squatters who cleared a few acres and laid claim by their presence to a promising piece of land.

This westward flow of settlers was part of the American landscape throughout the century, but it became a flood after 1760. A seemingly endless train of carts, sledges, and wagons moved along Indian paths to the west, and the rivers were crowded with rafts and canoes carrying families, farm tools, and livestock. Many of these new immigrants traveled south from Pennsylvania along a wagon road that ran eight hundred miles from Philadelphia all the way to Augusta, Georgia. Others chose to remain in the Middle Colonies. New York's population rose 39 percent between 1760 and 1776, and in 1769, on the day the land office opened at Fort Pitt (Pittsburgh), over twenty-seven hundred applicants showed up to register for land.

By 1760, perhaps seven hundred thousand new arrivals had made their homes in the mainland colonies. In the early part of the century, the largest immigrant group was the Scots-Irish. Later, German settlers dominated. Some one hundred thousand German Protestants, fleeing persecution by Catholic rulers, made the long and grim journey down the Rhine to Rotterdam, then to English port cities, and finally across the Atlantic Ocean to the colonies. But an occasional traveler on the wagon roads might be Italian, Swiss, Irish, Welsh, or a European Jew. Most striking, the number of British immigrants swelled after 1760.

What prompted this transatlantic population shift was not always desperation or oppression. Many arrived with enough resources to finance their new life in the colonies. While unemployment, poverty, the oppression of landlords, and crop failures pushed men and women out of Europe or Britain, it is also true that the availability of cheap land, a greater likelihood of religious freedom, and the chance to pursue a craft pulled others toward the colonies.

demographics The physical characteristics of a population such as age, sex, marital status, family size, education, geographic location, and occupation; usually in the form of statistics.

Scots-Irish Protestant Scottish settlers in British-occupied northern Ireland, many of whom migrated to the colonies in the eighteenth century.

This is a 1709 example of fraktur, a folk art form practiced by Pennsylvania's German population. The artist uses pen and ink and watercolor and traditional forms such as flowers to decorate a document.

CONFLICTS AMONG THE COLONISTS

☆ *What events illustrated the tensions between races in colonial society?*

☆ *What conflicts arose between elites and poorer colonists?*

The strains of economic inequality in every region of mainland British America frequently erupted into violent confrontations. At the same time, tensions between Indians and colonists continued, and tensions between black and white colonists increased as both slave and free black populations grew during the eighteenth century. In almost every decade, blood was shed as colonist battled colonist over economic opportunity, personal freedom, western lands, or political representation.

Slave Revolts, North and South

Southern planters took elaborate precautions to prevent slave rebellions, assembling armed patrols that policed the roads and woods near their plantations. These patrols were usually efficient, and the

◻ **Stono Rebellion** Slave revolt in South Carolina in 1739; it prompted the colony to pass harsher laws governing the movement of slaves and the capture of runaways.

punishment they inflicted was deadly. Even if rebels escaped immediate capture, few safe havens were available to them. Despite the terrible odds, slaves continued to seek their liberty, often timing their revolts to coincide with epidemics or imperial wars that distracted the white community.

The most famous southern slave revolt of the eighteenth century, the **Stono Rebellion**, took place in the midst of a yellow-fever epidemic in Charles Town and just as news of a war between England and Spain reached South Carolina. Early on a Sunday morning in September 1739, about twenty slaves gathered at the Stono River, south of Charles Town. Their leader, Jemmy, had been born in Africa, possibly in the Congo but more likely Angola, for twenty or more of those who eventually joined the revolt were Angolan. The rebels seized guns and gunpowder, killed several planter families and storekeepers, and then marched south, beating drums to invite slaves on nearby plantations to join them in their flight to Spanish Florida. Other slaves answered the call, and the Stono rebels' ranks grew to almost one hundred. Charles Town planters quickly gathered to put an end to the uprising. By late Sunday afternoon white militias had overtaken and surrounded the escaping slaves. The Stono rebels stood and fought, but the militiamen killed almost thirty of them. Those who were captured were executed. Those who escaped into the countryside were hunted down.

The Stono Rebellion terrified white South Carolinians. The government increased both the size and frequency of the slave patrols. It also raised the rewards offered for the capture of runaways to make sure that fleeing slaves taken alive and unharmed, or brought in dead and scalped, were worth hunting down.

Slave revolts were not confined to the plantation colonies. Even before the Stono Rebellion, white New Yorkers' fears of an uprising had become reality. At midnight on April 6, 1712, two dozen blacks armed with guns, hatchets, and swords set fire to a downtown building. The rebels attacked startled whites who rushed to keep the flames from spreading, leaving nine people shot, stabbed, or beaten to death. Six more were wounded. Militia units were called out to quell the riot and to cut off any hope of escape for the rebels. Realizing the hopelessness of their situation, six committed suicide. Those who were taken alive suffered horrible punishment. According to the colonial governor, Robert Hunter, "some were burnt, others were hanged, one broke on the wheel, and one hung alive in chains in the town." Twenty-nine years later, in 1741, the mere rumor of a conspiracy by African Americans to commit arson was enough to move white residents to violent reprisals. Despite the lack of any evidence to support the charge, 101 of the city's black residents were arrested—17 were hanged and 13 burned alive.

Clashes Between the Rich and the Poor

Class tensions often erupted into violence as the gap between rich and poor grew in every colony. In New York and New Jersey during the 1750s and 1760s, tenant farmers frequently mounted "land riots" against their powerful landlords, expressing their resentment and frustration at their inability to acquire land of their own.

In the backcountry, settlers were likely to face two enemies: Indians and the established political powers of their own colonies. Often the clashes with the colonial government were about Indian policy, just as Bacon's Rebellion had been. Eighteenth-century colonial legislatures and governors preferred diplomacy to military action, but western settlers wanted a more aggressive program to push Indians out of the way. Even when frontier hostilities led to bloodshed, the colonists of the coastal communities were reluctant to spend tax money to provide protection along the settlement line.

The revolt by Pennsylvania's **Paxton Boys** was the most dramatic eighteenth-century episode. Pennsylvania's Quaker-dominated government had consistently encouraged settlers to find peaceful ways to coexist with local tribes, but the eighteenth-century Scots-Irish settlers did not share the Quaker commitment to pacifism. Philadelphians often spoke of these settlers as savages, but the frontiersmen saw

themselves as sacrificing their own safety to expand the colonial frontier. To them, every Indian was a potential enemy, even those who pledged friendship. In 1763, when the government failed to provide protection against Indian raids on their isolated homesteads, settlers of Paxton, Pennsylvania, vented their anger on a village of peaceful Conestoga Indians. Although the murder of these Indians solved nothing and could not be justified, hundreds of western colonists supported this vigilante group known as the Paxton Boys. The group marched on Philadelphia to press their demands for an aggressive Indian policy. Philadelphia residents feared their city would be attacked and looted, but the popular printer and political leader Benjamin Franklin met the Paxton Boys on the outskirts of the city and negotiated a truce. The outcome was a dramatic shift in Pennsylvania Indian policy: an official bounty was set for Indian scalps.

Vigilante action was not always connected to Indian conflicts, however. In South Carolina, trouble arose because coastal planters refused to provide basic government services to the backcountry. Settlers in western South Carolina paid their taxes, but because their counties had no courts, they had to travel long distances to register land transactions or file lawsuits. The government provided no sheriffs either, and outlaws preyed on these communities. Since the coastal planters refused to admit any backcountry representatives to the colonial legislature, settlers could do little but complain, petition, and demand relief. In the 1760s, the farmers took matters into their own hands, choosing to "regulate" backcountry affairs themselves. These **Regulators** pursued and punished backcountry outlaws, dispensing justice without the aid of courts or judges.

In North Carolina, a similar power struggle led to a brief civil war. Here, a Regulator movement was organized against corrupt local officials in the backcountry appointed because of their political connections to the colony's slaveholding elite. These officials awarded contracts to friends for building roads and bridges; charged exorbitant fees to register deeds, surveys, or even the sale of cattle; and set high annual taxes on their backcountry neighbors. The North Carolina Regulators wanted these men removed, and when their demands were ignored, they mounted a

□ **Paxton Boys** Settlers in Paxton, Pennsylvania, who massacred Conestoga Indians in 1763 and then marched on Philadelphia to demand that the colonial government provide better defense against the Indians.

□ **Regulators** Frontier settlers in the Carolinas who protested the lack or abuse of government services in their area; the North Carolina Regulators were suppressed by government troops in 1771.

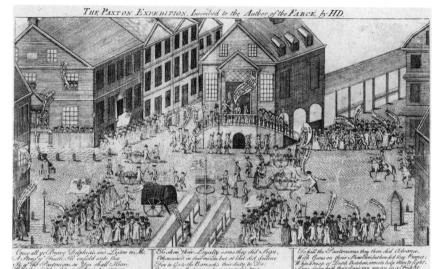

THE PAXTON EXPEDITION, *Inscribed to the Author of the FARCE, by HD.*

Violence between settlers and Indians was common in the eighteenth century, as immigrants moved west in search of land. When the Pennsylvania government refused to send a protective military force to the frontier, the Paxton Boys took matters into their own hands. In 1763, they attacked a peaceful settlement of Conestoga Indians, and the following year, they marched on Philadelphia, demanding assistance from the legislature. Only the intervention of Benjamin Franklin, who promised their complaints would be taken seriously, prevented violence between frontiersmen and city dwellers.

Photo by Fotosearch/Getty Images.

taxpayers' rebellion. When tax collection dried up, the governor raised a militia of twelve hundred men who in 1771 met and easily defeated two thousand poorly armed Regulators near the Alamance River. The brief east-west war ended in North Carolina, but the bitterness remained. During the Revolutionary War, when most of North Carolina's coastal elite cast their lot for independence, many farmers of the backcountry—disgusted with colonial government—sided with England.

REASON AND RELIGION IN COLONIAL SOCIETY

☆ *What political and personal expectations arose from Enlightenment philosophy?*

☆ *What was the impact of the Great Awakening on colonial attitudes toward authority?*

Trade routes tied the eighteenth-century colonial world to parent societies across the Atlantic. The

◻ **Enlightenment** An eighteenth-century intellectual movement that stressed the pursuit of knowledge through reason and challenged the value of religious belief, emotion, and tradition.

philosophe Any of the popular French intellectuals or social philosophers of the Enlightenment, such as Voltaire and Rousseau.

◻ **deism** The belief that God created the universe in such a way that it could operate without any further divine intervention such as miracles.

bonds of language and custom tied the immigrant communities in America to their homelands too. In addition to these economic and cultural ties, the flow of ideas and religious beliefs helped sustain a transatlantic community.

The Impact of the Enlightenment

At the end of the seventeenth century, a new intellectual movement arose in Europe: the Enlightenment. Enlightenment thinkers argued that reason, or rational thinking, rather than divine revelation, tradition, intuition, or established authority, was the true path to reliable knowledge and to human progress. A group of brilliant French thinkers called *philosophes*, including Voltaire, Rousseau, and Montesquieu, were among the central figures of the Enlightenment, along with English intellectuals such as John Locke and Isaac Newton and Scotland's David Hume. These philosophers, political theorists, and scientists disagreed about many issues, but all embraced the belief that nature could provide for all human wants and that human nature was not fatally flawed by original sin. Human beings, they insisted, were rational and capable of making progress toward a perfect society if they studied nature, unlocked its secrets, and carefully nurtured the best human qualities in themselves and their children. It was this idea of nurturing children that guided Eliza Pinckney when she became a mother.

Only the colonial elite had access to the books and essays that Europe's Enlightenment philosophers produced. These colonists were particularly drawn to two aspects of Enlightenment thought: its new religious philosophy of deism and the political theory of the

An Age of Science

The eighteenth century was, in many ways, the golden age of European science. In Berlin, Germany, in St. Petersburg, Russia, and in Turin, Italy, new scientific academies joined the older Paris Academy and the Royal Society of London as centers of scientific research. Scientific journals began to appear in England and across Europe, and popular science magazines brought new discoveries and theories to an eager reading public. One scientific tract, by Leonhard Euler, went through thirty-eight printings in nine languages. Similar explosions of scientific and mathematical knowledge occurred in the Islamic society of the seventh through the sixteenth centuries and in the scientific and technological breakthroughs of the twentieth century. Such expansion of knowledge dramatically changed how people lived and how they thought about their world.

"social contract." Deists believed that the universe operated according to logical, natural laws, without divine intervention. They denied the existence of any miracles after the Creation and rejected the value of prayer in this rational universe. Deism appealed to colonists such as the Philadelphia scientist, writer, and political leader Benjamin Franklin and Virginia planter Thomas Jefferson, men who were intensely interested in science and the scientific method.

Universal Images Group/Getty Images.

This is the frontispiece, or cover page, of John Locke's *Two Treatises*, first published in 1689. Locke was one of England's leading philosophers and his theory of government as a social contract between those who governed and the people they governed was widely accepted by the colonial elite.

The most widely accepted Enlightenment ideas in the colonies were those of the English political theorist John Locke, who published his *Essay Concerning Human Understanding* in 1690 and *Two Treatises of Government* in 1689. In his political essays Locke argued that human beings have certain natural rights, which include the right to own themselves and their own labor and the right to own that part of nature on which they have labored productively—that is, their property. However, in exchange for the government's protection of their natural rights to life, liberty, and property, people make a social contract to give up absolute freedom and to live under a rule of law. According to Locke, the government created by this social contract receives its political power from the consent of those it governs, and it can claim no other right to rule. In Locke's scheme, the people express their will, or their demands and interests, through a representative assembly, and the government is obligated to protect and respect the natural rights of its citizens and serve their interests. If the government fails to do this, Locke said, the people have a right, even a duty, to rebel. Locke's theory was especially convincing because it meshed with political developments in England from the civil war to the Glorious Revolution that were familiar to the colonists.

Religion and Religious Institutions

The growing religious diversity of colonial society led many to see religious tolerance as a practical matter. The commitment to religious tolerance did not come at an even pace, of course, nor did it extend to everyone.

□ **social contract** A theoretical agreement between the governed and the government that defines and limits the rights and obligations of each.

After 1729, no colony allowed Catholics to vote or hold elective office, and even Maryland did not permit Catholics to celebrate Mass openly until Baltimore's Catholics broke the law and founded a church in 1763. Connecticut granted freedom of worship to "sober dissenters" such as Anglicans, Quakers, and Baptists as early as 1708, but in 1750 its legislature declared it a felony to deny the Trinity. When colonists spoke of religious tolerance, they did not mean the separation of church and state. On the contrary, the tradition of an established church supported by taxes went unchallenged in the southern colonies, where Anglicanism was established, and in Massachusetts and Connecticut, where Congregationalism was established.

Although the diversity in churches was growing, the number of colonists who did not regularly attend any church at all was growing too. Some colonists were preoccupied with secular concerns, while others disliked that ministers' sermons were more intellectual than emotionally stirring. Occasionally, religious revivals appeared, urging colonists to return to their religion. The most widespread of these revivals, known as the Great Awakening, began in the 1720s.

The Great Awakening

The Great Awakening was led by a group of charismatic preachers who denounced the obsession with profit and wealth they saw around them, condemned the sinfulness and depravity of all people, warned of the terrible punishments of eternal hell fire, and praised the saving grace of God. In a society divided by regional disputes, racial conflicts, and economic competition, these preachers held out a promise of social harmony based on the surrender of individual pride and a renewed love and fear of God. In voices filled with "Thunder and Lightning," they called for a revival of basic Protestant belief.

This revival was based as much on a new approach to preaching as on the message itself. This new-style preaching first appeared in New Jersey and Pennsylvania, when two itinerant preachers—Theodore Frelinghuysen and William Tennent Jr.—accused local churches of lacking devotion to God and of "cold" preaching. Tennent established what he called a "log college" to train fiery preachers who could spread a Christian revival throughout the colonies. Soon afterward, Jonathan Edwards introduced the revival to Massachusetts. The Great Awakening soon spread rapidly throughout the colonies, carried from town to town by wandering ministers called "awakeners," who stirred entire communities to renewed religious devotion.

The Great Awakening's success was ensured in 1740 when the English minister George Whitefield toured the colonies from Charles Town to Maine. Everywhere this young preacher went, crowds gathered to hear him. His impact was electric. "Hearing him preach gave me a heart wound," wrote one colonist, and even America's most committed deist, Benjamin Franklin, confessed that Whitefield's sermons moved him. Whitefield himself recorded his effect on a crowd: "A wonderful power was in the room and with one accord they began to cry out and weep most bitterly for the space of half an hour."

The Great Awakening did not go unchallenged. Many ministers were angered by the criticisms of their preaching. They launched a counterattack against the revivalists and their "beastly brayings." Members of the colonial elite, disturbed by the Awakening's loud condemnation of worldly amusements such as dancing, gambling, drinking, the theater, and elegant clothing, used their political power against the revivalists. In Connecticut, for example, the assembly passed a law banning itinerant ministers from preaching outside their own parishes.

Bitter fights within congregations and denominations also developed. "Old Light" Congregationalists upheld the established service but "New Lights" chose revivalism, and "Old Side" Presbyterians similarly battled "New Sides." Congregations split, and the minority groups hurriedly formed new churches. Many awakened believers left their own denominations entirely, joining the Baptists or the Methodists. Antirevivalists also left their strife-ridden churches and became Anglicans. These religious conflicts frequently became intertwined with secular disputes. Colonists who had long-standing disagreements over Indian policy or economic issues lined up on opposite sides of the Awakening. Class tensions also influenced religious loyalties, as poor colonists pronounced judgment on activities of their rich neighbors that they considered to be sins.

Trinity In Christian doctrine, the belief that God has three divine aspects—Father, Son, and Holy Spirit.

☐ **established church** The official church of a nation or colony, usually supported by taxes collected from all citizens, no matter what their religious beliefs or place of worship.

Congregationalism A form of Protestant church government in which the local congregation is independent and self-governing; in the colonies, the Puritans were Congregationalists.

☐ **Great Awakening** A series of religious revivals based on fiery preaching and emotionalism that swept across the colonies during the second quarter of the eighteenth century.

charismatic Having a spiritual power or personal quality that stirs enthusiasm and devotion in large numbers of people.

itinerant Traveling from place to place.

☐ **George Whitefield** English evangelical preacher of the Great Awakening whose charismatic style attracted huge crowds during his preaching tours of the colonies.

denomination A group of religious congregations that accept the same doctrines and are united under a single name.

Evangelist George Whitefield drew huge crowds each time he preached, and the men and women in his audiences often fainted or cried out in ecstasy. As the leading figure of the Great Awakening, Whitefield was loved by thousands but criticized by ministers who opposed the religious enthusiasm he represented.

Thus, the Great Awakening increased rather than eliminated strife and tension among colonists. Yet it had positive effects as well. For example, the Awakening spurred the growth of higher education. The revivalists founded new colleges, including Rutgers, Brown, Princeton, and Dartmouth, to prepare their clergy, just as the Old Lights relied on Harvard and Yale to train theirs. One possible effect of the Great Awakening was that it reinforced a belief that protest and resistance were acceptable, not just in religious matters but in the realm of politics as well.

GOVERNMENT AND POLITICS IN THE MAINLAND COLONIES

☆ *What factors affected the struggle for power between the colonial assemblies and the colonial governors?*

The English mainland colonies were part of a large and complex empire, and the English government had created many agencies to set and enforce imperial policy. Parliament passed laws like the Navigation Acts, which regulated trade. The royal navy and army determined colonial defense, and English diplomats decided which foreign nations were friends and which

were foes. But from the beginning, kings and proprietors like the Calverts had also found it convenient to create local colonial governments to handle day-to-day affairs. By 1700 every mainland colony boasted a representative assembly.

Although the British government thought of these assemblies as conveniences, colonists insisted on their right to make local political decisions. From the British point of view, this was **insubordination**, and it led to a long and steady struggle for power between royally appointed colonial governors and colonial assemblies. Over the first half of the century, the colonists did wrest important powers from the governors. But the British government remained adamant that ultimate power, or **sovereignty**, rested with the king and Parliament.

Imperial Institutions and Policies

Although the regulation and governing of the colonies was split among several bureaucracies, these agencies shared one thing in common: lax

insubordination Resistance to authority; disobedience.
sovereignty The ultimate power in a nation or a state.

enforcement. Parliament set the tone for this indifference with a policy known unofficially as **salutary neglect**. As long as specific, or **enumerated**, colonial raw materials continued to flow into British hands and the colonists continued to rely on British manufactured goods, a healthy neglect satisfied the king, Parliament, and most government officials. Looking the other way when rules were broken was, after all, cheaper than hiring scores of customs inspectors and courtroom officials to see that every rule was always obeyed.

Salutary neglect, however, did not mean that the colonists were free to do exactly as they pleased. Even in purely domestic matters, the colonial assemblies could not operate as freely as many of them desired, and this was at the center of the most intense political conflicts before the 1760s.

Local Colonial Government

The eighteenth-century mainland colonies remained a mixture of royal, proprietary, and corporate colonies, although most were held directly by the king. Whatever the form of ownership, however, the local colonial governments were strikingly similar in structure and operation. Each colony had a governor appointed by the king or the proprietor or, in Connecticut and Rhode Island (the only two **corporate colonies**), elected to executive office. Each had a council, usually appointed by the governor, though sometimes elected by the assembly, which served as an advisory body to the governor. And each had an elected representative assembly with lawmaking and taxing powers.

The governor, who represented royal authority and imperial interests in the local setting, was the linchpin of most colonial governments. In theory, his powers were impressive. He alone could call the assembly into session, and he had the power to dismiss it. He also could veto any act passed by the assembly. He had the sole power to appoint and dismiss judges, justices of the peace, and all government officials. He could grant pardons and reprieves. The governor made all land grants, oversaw all aspects of colonial trade, and conducted all diplomatic negotiations with the Indians. Because he was commander in chief of the military and naval forces of the colony, he decided what action, if any, to take in conflicts between colonists and Indians. Armed with such extensive powers, the man who sat in the governor's seat ought to have been respected—or at least obeyed.

A closer look, however, reveals that the governor was not so powerful after all. First, he was bound by a set of detailed and specific instructions written by England's Board of Trade. These instructions often bore little relation to the realities the governor encountered in his colony. Instead, by limiting his ability to improvise and compromise, they proved more burdensome than helpful to many a frustrated governor.

Second, the governor's own skills and experience were often limited. Few men in the prime of their careers sought posts in the provinces, three thousand miles from England. Thus governorships went to **bureaucrats** nearing the end of sometimes unimpressive careers or to younger men who were new to the rough-and-tumble games of politics. Many colonial governors were honorable and competent, but enough of them were fools, scoundrels, or eccentrics to give the office a poor reputation.

Finally, most governors served brief terms, sometimes too brief for them to learn which local issues were critical or to discern friend from foe in the colonial government. For many, the goal was simply to survive the ordeal. They were willing to surrender much of their authority to the local assemblies in exchange for a calm, uneventful, and, they hoped, profitable term in office.

Even the most ignorant or incompetent governor might have managed to dominate colonial politics had he been able to apply the grease that oiled eighteenth-century political wheels: patronage. The kings of England had learned that political loyalty could be bought on the floor of Parliament with royal favors. By midcentury, over half of the members of Parliament held Crown offices or had received government contracts. Unfortunately for the colonial governor, he had few favors to hand out. The king could also bribe voters or intimidate them to ensure the election of his supporters to Parliament, but the governor lacked this option as well. The number of eligible voters in most colonies was far too great for a governor's resources.

However, the most significant restraint on the governor's authority was not his rigid instructions, his inexperience, or his lack of patronage, but that the colonial assembly paid his salary. England expected the colonists to foot the bill for local government, including compensation for the governor. Governors who challenged the assembly too strongly or too often usually found a sudden, unaccountable budget crisis delaying or diminishing their allowances, while

□ **salutary neglect** The British policy of relaxed enforcement of most colonial trade regulations as long as the mainland colonies remained loyal to the government and profitable within the British economy.

enumerated Added to the list of regulated goods or crops.

corporate colony A self-governing colony, not directly under the control of proprietors or the Crown.

bureaucrat A government official, usually appointed, who is deeply devoted to the details of administrative procedures.

those who bent to assembly wishes could expect bonuses in the form of cash or grants of land. William Burnett, the governor of Massachusetts in the 1720s, discovered how stubborn an assembly could be when he pressed them for a permanent, and regularly paid, salary. Although he used every power at his disposal—for example, refusing to allow any business to be conducted until the salary was set, threatening to dissolve the legislature, and moving the assembly from the comforts of Boston to the small towns of Salem and Cambridge—he lost this battle of wills. The assembly stood firm and retaliated by sending two local leaders to London to argue for Burnett's removal. Only Burnett's death from a stroke ended the deadlock.

While the governors learned that their great powers were not so great after all, the assemblies in every colony were making an opposite discovery: they learned they could broaden their powers far beyond the king's intent. They fought for and won more freedom from the governor's supervision and influence, gaining the right to elect their own speaker of the assembly, make their own procedural rules, and settle contested elections. They also increased their power over raising and spending revenues or, in eighteenth-century parlance, their **power of the purse**.

In their pursuit of power, these local political leaders had several advantages besides the governor's weaknesses. They came from a small social and economic elite who were regularly elected to office for both practical and social reasons. First, they could satisfy the high property qualifications set for most officeholders. Second, they could afford to accept an office that cost more to win and to hold than its modest salary could cover. And a colonial habit of **deference** toward the more educated and wealthy men in a community also ensured that they would win seats in the assembly. Although as many as 50 to 80 percent of adult free white males in a colony could vote, few were considered suitable to hold office. Generations of fathers and sons from elite families thus dominated political offices. These men knew one another well, and although they fought among themselves for positions and power, they could effectively unite against outsiders such as an arrogant governor or rebellious backcountry settlers. Finally, through long careers in the legislature they honed the political, administrative, and even **oratorical** skills that would enable them to contend successfully with the royal appointees.

Conflicting Views of the Assemblies

The king and Parliament left many local issues in the hands of the colonial assemblies, giving them the power to raise taxes, pay government salaries, direct the care of the poor, and maintain bridges and roads. To the colonists, this came to mean that the assemblies were a legitimate tier of the British governing system. But most British leaders disagreed. They saw the colonial governments as temporary conveniences, empowered to pass minor laws perhaps, but not sharing in the sovereignty of the king and Parliament. As the governor of Pennsylvania put it in 1726, the assembly's actions and decisions should in "no ways interfere . . . with the Legal Prerogative of the Crown or the true Legislative Power of the Mother State." A vocal if small minority in English politics supported the colonists' view. For example, Thomas Pownall, who served as governor of Massachusetts in the 1750s and later as governor of South Carolina, believed that political powers must be shared between England's legislature, Parliament, and the colonial assemblies. This notion of a dominion government shocked eighteenth-century members of Parliament, yet by the next century it would become the blueprint of the British empire.

NORTH AMERICA AND THE STRUGGLE FOR EMPIRE

☆ What were the diplomatic and military goals of Europeans and American Indians in North America, and what role did American colonists play in the fighting?

☆ How did the English victory in 1763 affect people in North America?

Until the last decades of the 1600s, most of the violence and warfare in colonial America arose from struggles either between Indians and colonists over land or among colonists over political power and the use of revenues and resources. These struggles continued to be important during the 1700s, but by 1690 the most persistent dangers to colonial peace and safety came from the fierce rivalries between the French, Spanish, and English (see Map 4.2). Between 1688 and 1763, these European powers waged five bloody and costly wars. Most of these conflicts were motivated by politics within Europe, although colonial ambitions spurred the last and most decisive of them. No matter where these worldwide wars began, or what their immediate cause, colonists were usually drawn into them.

□ **power of the purse** The power enjoyed by the branch of government that controls taxation and the use of tax monies.

□ **deference** Yielding respectfully to the judgment or wishes of a social or intellectual superior.

oratorical Related to the art of persuasive and eloquent public speaking.

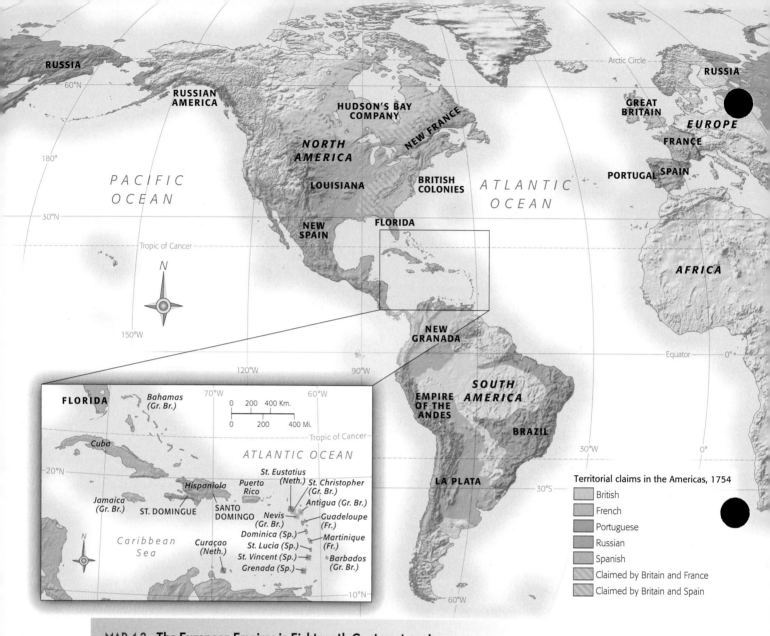

MAP 4.2 The European Empires in Eighteenth-Century America
Three rival powers—Britain, France, and Spain—colonized the Americas. It is clear from the map why British colonists felt vulnerable to attack by England's archenemies, France and Spain, until English victory in the Great War for Empire in 1763. © Cengage Learning.

When imperial wars included fighting in America, English colonists relied on Indian allies and faced Indian enemies as well as European ones. For example, until the mid-seventeenth century, the Huron-dominated confederacy to the north supported the French (see Map 4.3), while the Hurons' rivals, the Iroquois League, gave their support to the English and their colonists. The southern English colonists turned to the Creek Confederacy when wars with Spain erupted. Yet the colonists' own land hunger always worked to undermine—if not unravel—these Indian alliances. Thus the southern tribes' support was

unreliable, and the Iroquois, wary of English westward expansion, often chose to pursue an independent strategy of neutrality.

The wars that raged from 1688 until 1763 were part of a grand effort by rival European nations to control the balance of power at home and abroad. The colonists often felt like pawns in the hands of the more powerful players, and resentment sometimes overshadowed their patriotic pride when England was victorious. Whatever their views on imperial diplomacy, few colonists escaped the impact of this nearly century-long power struggle, for periods of peace

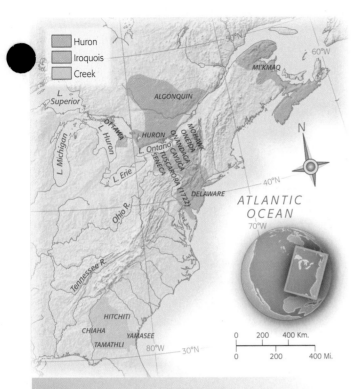

Huron
Iroquois
Creek

MAP 4.3 The Indian Confederacies
This map shows the three major Indian military and political coalitions—the Huron, Iroquois, and Creek Confederacies. Unlike the squabbling English mainland colonies, these Indian tribes understood the value both of military unity in the face of threats to their land and their safety and of diplomatic unity in negotiating with their European allies. © Cengage Learning.

were short and the long shadow of war hung over the colonies until Britain's major triumph in 1763.

An Age of Imperial Warfare

To begin what seemed like an endless series of wars, colonists were enlisted to fight in 1689 against the French in what Europeans called the War of the League of Augsburg but colonists called simply King William's War. In this war, New England and northern New York bore the brunt of what quickly became vicious fighting in the colonies. As reports of atrocities mounted, the governments of Massachusetts, Plymouth, Connecticut, and New York made a rare attempt at cooperation. Their goal was to capture Canada, but when few of the participating colonies made good on their promises of men or money, assaults on Montreal and Quebec both failed. When the war finally ended in 1697 with the Treaty of Ryswick, 659 New Englanders had died in battle, in raids, or in captivity. The death toll for their Iroquois allies was between six hundred and thirteen hundred. The lessons of the war were apparent. First, colonists paid a high price for their lack of cooperation. Second,

no New Englander could ever feel secure until the French had been driven out of Canada. Third, the colonists needed the aid of the English army and navy to effectively drive the French away.

The colonists had little time to enjoy peace. Five years later, in 1702, the conflict colonists called Queen Anne's War began, once again pitting France, with its now dependent ally Spain, against England, Holland, and Austria. In this eleven-year struggle, colonists faced enemies on both their southern and northern borders. Once again, those enemies included Indians. Between 1711 and 1713, southern colonists were caught up in fierce warfare with the Tuscaroras, who were angered by North Carolina land seizures. The casualties were staggering, and both sides outdid one another in cruelty: stakes were run through women's bodies, children were murdered, and colonists roasted Indian captives alive. When the war ended, the Tuscaroras had been decimated. Many of their survivors were sold into slavery, while others took refuge in the land of the Iroquois.

The war in the north was just as deadly. Indian and French raids, such as the one on Deerfield, Massachusetts, cost the lives of many New Englanders. Indeed, the high death toll of King William's War and Queen Anne's War was staggering: nearly one of every four soldiers in uniform had died. The financial cost was equally devastating. Four-fifths of Massachusetts revenues in 1704–1705 went for military expenses. Homeowners in Boston saw their taxes rise 42 percent between 1700 and 1713. Beggars filled the city's streets and widows occupied its homes. In Connecticut and Massachusetts, colonists spoke bitterly of their home country's failure to protect them. Yet England's victory in 1713 brought tangible gains to New Englanders. The English flag now flew over Nova Scotia, Newfoundland, and Hudson Bay, which meant that Maine settlers no longer had to fear enemy raids. New England fleets could fish the cod-rich waters of Newfoundland more safely. And colonial fur traders could profit from Hudson Bay's resources.

For a generation, Europeans kept the peace. In America, however, violence continued along the line of settlement, with New Englanders battling Indian allies of the French and southern colonists making war on their own former allies, the Yamasees. The short but ferociously fought Yamasee War of 1715 left four hundred of South Carolina's five thousand colonists dead in the first twelve months of fighting, a higher death rate than white Massachusetts had sustained in King Philip's War.

Events at the end of the 1730s fractured the calm in Europe. By 1740, France, Spain, and Prussia were at war with England and its ally Austria. This war, known in the colonies as King George's War, again meant enemy attacks on both the northern and southern colonies. New Englanders, swept up in the Great

George Washington was a young man when the British general Edward Braddock was sent to the colonies to drive the French out of the Ohio Valley. Washington volunteered to join this disastrous campaign. When Braddock's troops were caught by surprise and routed by an Indian and French force near the Monongahela River, Washington was one of the officers who carried the mortally wounded Braddock off the field of battle. Washington escaped unharmed.

Awakening, viewed the war as a Protestant crusade designed to rid the continent of Catholicism. Yet when the war ended in 1748, Catholic France still retained its Canadian territories.

The Great War for Empire

Despite three major wars and countless border conflicts, the map of North America had changed very little. Colonial efforts to capture Canada or to rid the southwest of Indian enemies had not succeeded. Yet veterans of the wars and their civilian colonial supporters spoke with pride of the colonial armies as excellent military forces. Without assistance from British regulars or the British navy, militiamen and volunteer armies had defended their communities, defeated Indian enemies, and captured important French forts.

Many colonists remained angry and bewildered, however, by the home country's military neglect. From their perspective, they were being dragged into

□ **French and Indian War** Begun in 1754 and ending with a British victory in 1763, this conflict was known in Europe as the Seven Years War. It was one of a long series of wars between France and England for political dominance in Europe and territorial dominance in North America.

European wars that did not concern them. Then, in 1756, the tables seemed to turn: this time, Europe was dragged into a colonial war. Westward expansion deeper into North America triggered a great war for empire, referred to in Europe as the Seven Years War and in the colonies as the French and Indian War.

The tensions began in the 1740s, as the neutral zone between the French colonial empire and the British mainland settlements began to shrink. As thousands of new immigrants poured into the English colonies, the colonists pressed farther westward, toward the Ohio Valley. Virginia land speculators began to woo the Indians of the region with trading agreements. The English colonial interest in the Ohio Valley alarmed the French, who had plans to unite their mainland empire, connecting Canada and Louisiana with a chain of forts, trading posts, and missions across the valley.

Virginia's governor, Robert Dinwiddie, troubled by the French military buildup in the Ohio Valley, warned the British that a potential crisis was developing thousands of miles from London. In 1754 Britain responded; the government agreed to send an expedition to assess French strength and warn the French to abandon a new fort on French Creek. Dinwiddie chose an inexperienced Virginia planter and colonial militia officer, Major George Washington, to lead the

What's in a Name?

Between 1680 and 1763, the British Empire was involved in six wars. Five of them were known by a different name in Europe than in the English colonies. Is this difference significant to understanding the imperial relationship of the home country and its colonies? Does it hold clues to a difference in perspective between them? Both answers are yes. The British government's terms reflect its concerns with shifts in the balance of power between England and its rivals, with the impact of changing alliances in Europe, and with challenges to its control of trade routes and colonial possessions. The North American names for these wars confirm the subordinate status of the colonies within the British Empire, their belief that the king or queen, rather than Parliament or the people of England, was responsible for the war, and their attention to the composition of enemy alliances on their own side of the Atlantic.

Imperial and Colonial Wars

NAME	DATE	PARTICIPANTS	TREATY
In colonies: King William's War *In Europe:* War of the League of Augsburg	1688–1697	*In Europe:* France vs. England, Holland, Sweden, and Spain *In North America:* Colonists and Iroquois allies vs. French and Indian allies *Area:* New England and northern New York	Treaty of Ryswick (1697) *Results:* Port Royal in Acadia (Nova Scotia) is returned to France France is still a presence in North America
In colonies: Queen Anne's War *In Europe:* War of the Spanish Succession	1702–1713	*In Europe:* England, Holland, and Austria vs. France and Spain *In North America:* English colonists vs. French in North and Spanish in South and their Indian allies	Treaty of Utrecht (1713) *Results:* France renounces plans to unite with Spain under one crown England gains Caribbean islands, St. Kitts, Gibraltar, and Minorca; also Nova Scotia, Newfoundland, and Hudson Bay War takes a financial toll on the colonies
War of Jenkins's Ear	1739–1740	*In Europe:* England vs. Spain *In North America:* Colonists clash with Spanish in interior south	None—conflict expands into King George's War
In colonies: King George's War *In Europe:* War of the Austrian Succession	1740–1748	*In Europe:* Austria and England vs. Prussia, France, and Spain *In North America:* Colonists in New England vs. French and Indian allies	Treaty of Aix-la-Chapelle (1748) *Results:* England returns Louisbourg to French in exchange for Madras (in India)
In colonies: French and Indian War *In Europe:* Seven Years War	1756–1763	*In Europe:* England and Prussia vs. France and Austria *In North America:* English colonists vs. French and their Indian allies *Area:* Global war; in colonies, all regions	Treaty of Paris (1763) *Results:* French Empire shrinks; France loses Canada and trading posts in Africa and exits India Britain takes Florida from Spain and Canada from France France gives up Louisiana to Spain as compensation for Florida British government deeply in debt Borders of Britain's North American colonies secured

expedition. When Washington conveyed the warning, the French commander responded with insulting sarcasm. Tensions escalated rapidly. Dinwiddie later sent Major Washington to challenge the French at Fort Duquesne, near present-day Pittsburgh, but the French forced him to surrender.

Fearing another war, colonial political leaders knew it was time to act decisively—and to attempt cooperation. In June 1754, seven colonies sent representatives to Albany, New York, to organize a united defense. Unfortunately, however, when the Albany Plan of Union was presented to the individual colonial assemblies, not one was willing to approve it. Instead, American colonists looked to Britain to act. This time, Britain did. Parliament sent Major General Edward Braddock, a battle-hardened veteran, to drive the French out of Fort Duquesne. A French ambush routed Braddock's force and killed the general. Braddock's humiliating failure was only the first of many for the English in America.

English and French forces engaged each other in battle four times before war was officially declared in 1756. Soon, every major European power was involved, and the fighting spread rapidly across Europe, the Philippines, Africa, India, the Caribbean, and North America. In America, France's Indian allies joined the war more readily than England's. Iroquois tribes opted for neutrality, waiting until 1759 to throw in their lot with the English. In the south, the Cherokees played the French and English against each other. Given these circumstances, a British defeat seemed likely.

In 1756 the worried British government turned the direction of the war over to the ardent imperialist William Pitt. More than willing to take drastic steps, Pitt committed the British treasury to the largest war expenditures the nation had ever known and then put together the largest military force that North America had ever seen, combining twenty-five thousand colonial troops with twenty-four thousand British regulars. The fortunes of war soon reversed. By the end of 1759, the upper Ohio Valley had been taken from the French. And in August of that year, a force led by British General James Wolfe captured the French fortress city of Quebec. Both Wolfe and the French commander, Louis-Joseph, Marquis de Montcalm, died in the battle on Quebec's Plains of Abraham. In 1760 the city of Montreal also fell to the British. With that, the French Canadian governor surrendered the whole of New France to his enemies, and the war in North America was over. The fighting in this most global of eighteenth-century wars continued elsewhere until 1763. Spain entered the struggle as a French ally in 1761, but English victories in India, the Caribbean, and the Pacific squelched any hopes the French had. The Treaty of Paris established the supremacy of the British Empire.

The Outcomes of the Great War for Empire

The war had redrawn the map of the world. The French Empire had shriveled, with nothing remaining of New France but two tiny islands between Nova Scotia and Newfoundland. Ten thousand Acadians—French colonists of Nova Scotia—were refugees of the war. Deported from their homes by the English because their loyalty was suspect, these Acadians either relocated to France, settled in New England, or made the exhausting trek to French-speaking Louisiana. The only other remnants of the French Empire in the Western Hemisphere were the sugar islands of Guadeloupe, Martinique, and St. Domingue, left to France because England's so-called Sugar Interest wanted no further competition in the British market. Across the ocean, France lost trading posts in Africa, and on the other side of the world, the French presence in India vanished.

The 1763 peace treaty dismantled the French Empire but did not destroy France itself. Although the nation's treasury was empty, its borders were intact and its alliance with Spain held firm. Britain was victorious but did not escape unharmed. The British government was deeply in debt and faced new problems associated with managing and protecting its greatly enlarged empire.

In the mainland colonies, people lit bonfires and staged parades to celebrate Britain's victory and the safety of their own borders. But the tension of being both members of a colonial society and citizens of a great empire could not be easily dismissed. The war left scars, including memories of the British military's arrogance toward provincial soldiers and lingering resentment over the quartering, or housing, of British soldiers at colonial expense. The colonists were aware that the British had grounds for resentment also, particularly the profitable trade some Americans had carried on with the enemy even in the midst of the war. Suspicion and resentment, a growing sense of difference, a tug of loyalties between the local community and the larger empire—these were the unexpected outcomes of a glorious victory.

◻ **Treaty of Paris** The treaty ending the French and Indian War in 1763; it gave all of French Canada and Spanish Florida to Britain.

Individual Voices

ELIZA LUCAS
Challenges Traditional Plantation Life

As one of the few women to manage a large plantation at the time, Eliza Lucas was unique in her desire to experiment with new crops and stretch old gender roles. Because she was both wealthy and educated, Lucas left behind letters and a diary that allow the modern reader to hear her voice more clearly than the voices of most eighteenth-century colonial women. In her letters, Lucas provides insight into the experiences of a woman succeeding in a male-dominated society. In this letter to her young niece, Lucas describes the demanding schedule she maintained to balance her roles as a society woman and a plantation master.

National Museum of American History, Smithsonian Institution.

1 In this section Eliza Lucas shows us some of the ways in which she juggles her feminine and masculine roles. Do you think the men of the period spent the same amount of time devoted to learning?

2 Eliza Lucas hoped that the two African American slave girls she was educating would educate other slaves on the plantation. What arguments could be raised against this program to educate slaves? What benefits might come from the education of slaves?

3 Lucas is clearly proud of her latest moneymaking project, yet she doesn't want to go into too much detail about her plans to her friend. What reason does she give for this hesitancy?

Dr. Miss B.

. . . Why, my dear Miss B, will you so often repeat your desire to know how I triffle away my time in our retirement in my fathers absence. Could it afford you advantage or pleasure I should not have hesitated, but as you can expect neither from it I would have been excused; however, to show you my readiness in obeying your commands, here it is.

1 In general then I rise at five o'Clock in the morning, read till Seven, then take a walk in the garden or field, see that the Servants are at their respective business, then to breakfast. The first hour after breakfast is spent at my musick, the next is constantly employed in recolecting something I have learned least for want of practise it should be quite lost, such as French and short hand. **2** After that I devote the rest of the time till I dress for dinner to our little Polly and two black girls who I teach to read, and if I have my papa's approbation (my Mamas I have got) I intend [them] for school mistres's for the rest of the negro children—another scheme you see. But to proceed, the first hour after dinner as the first after breakfast at musick, the rest of the afternoon in Needle work till candle light, and from that time to bed time read or write. 'Tis the fashion here to carry our work abroad so that having company, without they are great strangers, is no interruption to that affair; but I have particular matters for particular days, which is an interruption of mine. Monday my musick Master is here. Tuesdays my friend Mrs. Chardon (about 3 mile distant) and I are constantly engaged to each other, she at our house one Tuesday—I at hers the next and this is one of the happiest days I spend at Woppoe. Thursday the whole day except what necessary affairs of the family take up is spent in writing, either on the business of the plantations, or letters to my friends. Every other Fryday, if no company, we go a vizeting so that I go abroad once a week and no oftener.

O! I had like to forgot the last thing I have done a great while. I have planted a large figg orchard with design to dry and export them. **3** I have reconed [reckoned] my experience and the propfets [profits] to arise from these figgs, but was I to tell you how great an Estate I am to make this way, and how 'tis to be laid out you would think me far gone in romance. Your good Uncle I know has long thought I have a fertile brain at schemeing. I only confirm him in his opinion; but I own I love the vegitable world extremly. I think it an innocent and useful amusement. Pray tell him, if he laughs much at my project, I never intend to have my hand in a silver mine and he will understand as well as you what I mean . . .

Study Tools

SUMMARY

Important changes emerged in the British mainland colonies during the eighteenth century. In New England, increased commercial activity produced a shift from a "Puritan" culture to a more secular "Yankee" culture. In the South, the planter elite shifted from a labor force of indentured servants to one of African slaves. By midcentury, these enslaved workers had begun to develop their own community life and their own African American culture. The Middle Colonies developed a lively urban culture that contrasted with the backcountry culture of newly arrived immigrants.

Intellectual life in the eighteenth century also changed. The colonial elite embraced the Enlightenment notion that progress would come through the application of reason rather than faith. They developed a skepticism about religious dogmas and accepted John Locke's theory of natural rights. At the same time, the Great Awakening unleashed a second, and opposing, intellectual current aimed at renewing the quest for religious salvation among ordinary colonists. The message of the "awakeners" had radical implications, for they challenged all authority except the individual spirit.

A similar challenge to authority emerged in politics and imperial relations. Despite England's policy of salutary neglect in governing the colonies, colonial assemblies resented royal officials and asserted their own claims to power as the legitimate representatives of the local interests.

England, France, and Spain fought five major wars between 1688 and 1763. Colonists were expected to defend their own borders in most of the wars. In the French and Indian War, however, the British played an active role in driving the French out of mainland America. Their victory in 1763 altered the colonial map of North America and changed power relations throughout the European world.

Dramatic events like the British victory often have unexpected consequences. As you will see in the next chapter, that victory carried with it a long trail of problems for the British government. Perhaps most surprising, tensions between the English colonists and the home country intensified as colonial celebration and appreciation quickly turned into resentment, protest, and resistance.

CHRONOLOGY
From Settlements to Societies

1690–1691	John Locke's essays *Concerning Human Understanding* and *Two Treatises of Government*
1702	Queen Anne's War begins
1704	Pro-French Indians attack Deerfield, Massachusetts Tuscarora War begins in North Carolina
1712	New York City slave revolt
1715	Colonists defeat Creek and Yamasee Indians of Georgia
1734	Great Awakening spreads to New England
1739	Stono Rebellion in South Carolina
1740	King George's War begins George Whitefield begins his preaching tour
1756	Great War for Empire begins
1763	Treaty of Paris
1771	North Carolina Regulator movement defeated

Study Tools

FOCUS QUESTIONS

If you have mastered this chapter, you should be able to answer these questions and to explain the terms that follow the questions.

1. What were the main regional differences in colonial commerce, and what kind of economic choices did each region offer colonists?

2. How did the Yankee society of early eighteenth-century New England differ from Puritan society?

3. Why did colonists in the Chesapeake and Lower South shift to slave labor? What problems faced Africans in slavery?

4. What distinguished life in the Middle Colonies?

5. What motivated colonists to migrate to the backcountry?

6. What events illustrated the tensions between races in colonial society?

7. What conflicts arose between elites and poorer colonists?

8. What political and personal expectations arose from Enlightenment philosophy?

9. What was the impact of the Great Awakening on colonial attitudes toward authority?

10. What factors affected the struggle for power between the colonial assemblies and the colonial governors?

11. What were the diplomatic and military goals of Europeans and American Indians in North America, and what role did American colonists play in the fighting?

12. How did the English victory in 1763 affect people in North America?

KEY TERMS

carrying trade   *p. 76*

middle passage   *p. 81*

Stono Rebellion   *p. 84*

Paxton Boys   *p. 85*

Regulators   *p. 85*

Enlightenment   *p. 86*

deism   *p. 86*

social contract   *p. 87*

established church   *p. 88*

Great Awakening   *p. 88*

George Whitefield   *p. 88*

salutary neglect   *p. 90*

power of the purse   *p. 91*

deference   *p. 91*

French and Indian War   *p. 94*

Treaty of Paris   *p. 95*

SUGGESTED RESOURCES

Ira Berlin. *Generations of Captivity: A History of African-American Slavery* (Harvard University Press, 2004). [LP1]A leading scholar on slavery looks at the changing and varied nature of the institution from the seventeenth century to Emancipation.

Patricia Bonomi. *Under the Cope of Heaven: Religion, Society and Politics in Colonial America* (Oxford University Press, 2003). Bonomi examines the role of religion in shaping the character of American colonists in the eighteenth century.

***The Last of the Mohicans* (1992).** Film of the classic novel by James Fenimore Cooper; a romanticized but powerful look at the impact of imperial wars on the lives of Indians and white colonists.

"Voyages: The Transatlantic Slave Trade Database," http://www.slavevoyages.org. A rich source of information on the ships, the cargo, and the countries of origin and destination in the African slave trade.

5

Deciding Where Loyalties Lie, 1763–1776

INDIVIDUAL CHOICES

James Otis Jr.

James Otis Jr. was the oldest of thirteen children, born on February 5, 1725, to the lawyer James Sr. and his wife Mary Allyne Otis. He grew up in West Barnstable, Massachusetts, and, like the sons of many prosperous families, attended Harvard College. He went on to become a Boston lawyer. In 1756, he willingly accepted a royal appointment as advocate general of the region's vice admiralty, or maritime, court. Until 1761, he rigorously prosecuted New England merchants who were caught smuggling goods into the region to avoid British trade regulations and import taxes. Yet something happened that turned James Otis Jr. into a fiery critic of the British.

What caused him to become a political radical and a thorn in the royal governor's side? In part, it was the government's decision to introduce general search warrants, or writs of assistance, that gave customs officials broad leeway to enter businesses and homes just on the suspicion of contraband. In part, it was his anger that the Massachusetts governor did not choose his father to be the colony's new chief justice of the superior court.

Otis resigned as advocate general and agreed to serve as the attorney for some merchants fighting against the writs of assistance. Although he lost the case, his argument (summarized at the end of this chapter in the Individual Voices feature) that the writs violated the colonists' natural rights

The Granger Collec

and were thus null and void made him an instant celebrity. Massachusetts lawyer and revolutionary John Adams would later claim that "then and there, the child Independence was born."

For almost a decade, Otis remained a defender of colonial rights. He served in the Massachusetts assembly and in 1764 published *The Rights of the British Colonies Asserted and Proved,* in which Otis confronted the dilemma facing the colonists: to reject any law made by Parliament was to reject the authority of Parliament entirely. Even Otis was not ready to take that radical step.

In 1769, a political enemy—angered at Otis's newspaper attacks on royal officeholders—confronted Otis in a local coffee shop. Words quickly turned to blows, and James Otis received a severe head injury. Perhaps he was already showing signs of failing mental health, but the blow left him struggling with bouts of insanity. On May 23, 1783—the very year the colonies officially won their independence—James Otis Jr. was killed by a bolt of lightning. John Adams summed up his friend's impact on the political life of his country: "Otis was a flame of fire!"

Many colonists believed that Britain's victory over France in 1763 would usher in a new era of economic growth, westward expansion, and improved cooperation between the home country and its colonies. But these hopes for harmony and goodwill were quickly dashed. Less than two years after the Treaty of Paris ended the war, colonists were protesting British policy and resisting new trade regulations.

In the next thirteen strife-filled years, the colonists and the British government discovered that fundamental political differences existed between them. They found that they did not agree over the proper division of power between Parliament and the local elected assemblies. And they found themselves in conflict over major imperial policies. English officials, for example, thought it made good sense to curtail westward settlement to prevent costly Indian wars. But American colonists believed loyal citizens deserved the economic opportunity that westward settlement would provide. The British insisted that the Americans ought to help pay the costs of maintaining the empire, but the colonists believed that this was the duty of those who remained in the home country.

By the 1770s, Americans who had once toasted the king and his government now drank instead to liberty and resistance to tyrants. By 1775, a new choice faced the colonists: loyalty or rebellion. And colonists such as James Otis Jr. seemed caught in the midst of a struggle they had never anticipated and could not avoid.

The colonists who chose to protest taxation by the British government in 1765 and 1767, or to oppose the creation of juryless courts, or to complain of the presence of troops in their towns in peacetime did not know they were laying the groundwork for a revolution. Indeed, most of them would have been shocked at the suggestion that they were no longer loyal British patriots. Yet events between 1763 and 1776 forced these colonists to choose between two versions of patriotism—loyalty to the king or loyalty to colonial independence—and between two visions of the future—as members of a great and powerful empire or as citizens of a struggling new nation. These events also forced Indians and African American slaves to choose an alliance with the king or with the rebels.

VICTORY'S NEW PROBLEMS

☆ Why did Prime Minister Grenville expect the colonists to accept part of the burden of financing the British Empire in 1764?

☆ How did colonists understand their obligations to the empire?

☆ Why were the colonists alarmed by Grenville's 1765 stamp tax?

☆ How did the colonists protest Parliament's taxation policies?

In the midst of the French and Indian War, King George II died in his bed. Loyal subjects mourned the old king and in 1760 welcomed his grandson George III. At age 22, the new monarch was already

□ **George III** King of England (r. 1760–1820); his government's policies produced colonial discontent that led to the American Revolution in 1776.

In the Wider World

showing the symptoms of an illness that produced delusions and severe depression. Although he was inexperienced in matters of state, George III meant to rule—even if he had to deal with politicians, whom he distrusted, and engage in politics, which he disliked. He chose George Grenville, a no-nonsense, practical man, to assist him. Grenville's two most pressing postwar tasks were negotiating England's victory treaty with France and designing Britain's peacetime policies.

At the peace table with France, England had the opportunity to decide what the spoils of war would be: a French Caribbean sugar island or the mainland territory of Canada. English sugar planters opposed adding a new competitor to their profitable market, and so the government opted for the vast region north and west of the thirteen colonies. American colonists could not help but be pleased. With one sweep of the pen, their worst enemies had been eliminated from their borders. The treaty also held out the promise of profitable fishing off the Newfoundland coast and new farmlands in the fertile Ohio Valley. By the end of 1763, George III and his subjects could look with pride on an empire that had grown in physical size, on a nation that dominated the markets of Europe, and on a navy that ruled the seas.

delusion A false belief strongly held in spite of evidence to the contrary.

□ **George Grenville** British prime minister who sought to tighten controls over the colonies and to impose taxes to raise revenues.

□ **Covenant Chain** An alliance of Indian tribes established to resist colonial settlement in the Ohio Valley and Great Lakes region and to oppose British trading policies.

□ **Pontiac** Ottawa chief who led the unsuccessful resistance against British policy in 1763.

Unfortunately, victory also brought new problems. First, to win the war, Secretary of State William Pitt had spent vast sums of money, leaving the new king with an enormous war debt. English taxpayers, who had groaned under the wartime burden, now demanded tax relief, not tax increases. Second, the new Canadian territory posed serious governance problems because the Indians were unwilling to pledge their allegiance to the English king and the French Canadians were unwilling to abandon their traditions, their laws, or the Catholic Church.

Dealing with Indian and French Canadian Resistance

Both the Canadian tribes and Spain's former Indian allies along the southeastern borders of the English colonies felt threatened by Britain's victory. For decades, Indian diplomats had protected their lands by playing European rivals against one another, but with the elimination of France and the weakening of Spain in mainland America, this strategy was now impossible. Warfare rather than diplomacy had become their only option. When settlers from the southern colonies poured into Creek and Cherokee lands, the Cherokees mounted a full-scale, but ultimately futile, resistance along the Virginia and Carolina western settlement line. Defeated, the Cherokee leaders were forced to sign treaties opening up their lands to both English settlement and military bases.

In the Ohio Valley, Indian tribes were determined to resist not only the settlers' invasion of their homelands but also the increase in the price British traders set on tools, clothing, and liquor. Together, Senecas, Ojibwas, Potawatomis, Hurons, Ottawas, Delawares, Shawnees, and Mingoes formed an alliance known as the Covenant Chain. Led by the Ottawa chief Pontiac, the Indians mounted their attack on British forts and colonial settlements in the spring of 1763 (see Map 5.1). By fall, however, their

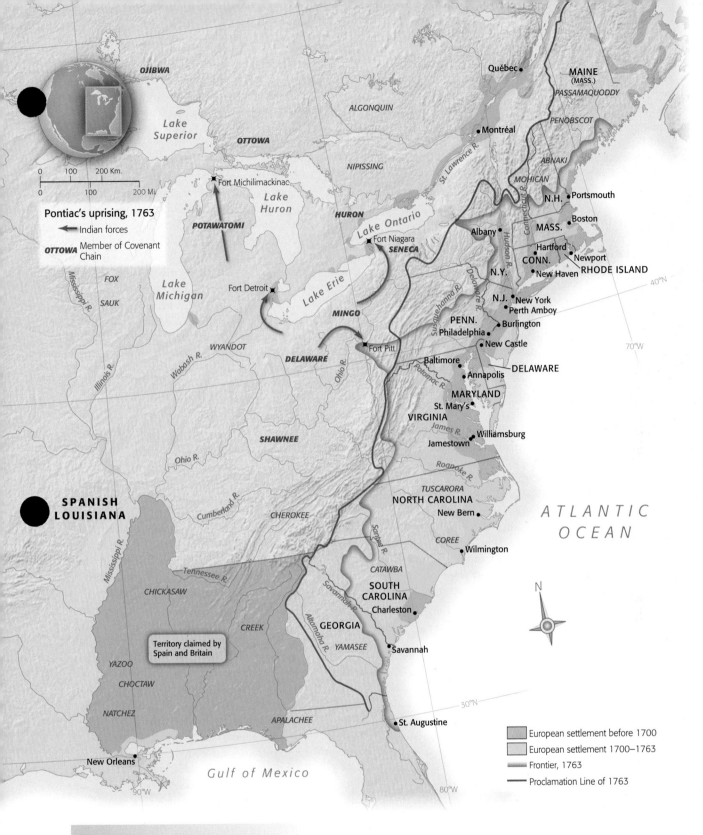

OJIBWA

Lake Superior

OTTOWA

Lake Huron

POTAWATOMI

★ Fort Michilimackinac

Lake Michigan

Fort Detroit ★

Lake Erie

FOX

SAUK

Mississippi R.

Illinois R.

Wabash R.

WYANDOT

DELAWARE

Ohio R.

MINGO

Fort Pitt ★

★ Fort Niagara

SENECA

Lake Ontario

St. Lawrence R.

ALGONQUIN

NIPISSING

HURON

OTTOWA

Québec ●

Montréal ●

MAINE (MASS.)

PASSAMAQUODDY

PENOBSCOT

ABNAKI

MOHICAN

N.H. ● Portsmouth

● Boston

MASS.

Albany ● Hartford

CONN. ● Newport

N.Y. ● New Haven RHODE ISLAND

N.J. ● New York

● Perth Amboy

PENN. ● Burlington

Philadelphia ●

● New Castle

DELAWARE

Baltimore ●

● Annapolis DELAWARE

MARYLAND

St. Mary's ●

VIRGINIA

James R. ● Williamsburg

Jamestown ●

Roanoke R.

40°N

70°W

Hudson R.

Connecticut R.

Delaware R.

Susquehanna R.

Potomac R.

SPANISH LOUISIANA

Cumberland R.

CHEROKEE

Tennessee R.

CHICKASAW

YAZOO

CHOCTAW

NATCHEZ

CREEK

Altamaha R.

Savannah R.

APALACHEE

New Orleans ●

SHAWNEE

Ohio R.

Santee R.

TUSCARORA

NORTH CAROLINA

New Bern ●

COREE

● Wilmington

CATAWBA

SOUTH CAROLINA

Charleston ●

YAMASEE

GEORGIA

● Savannah

● St. Augustine

30°N

80°W

90°W

Gulf of Mexico

ATLANTIC OCEAN

N

Pontiac's uprising, 1763

→ Indian forces

OTTOWA Member of Covenant Chain

0   100   200 Km.

0   100   200 Mi.

Territory claimed by Spain and Britain

■ European settlement before 1700
□ European settlement 1700–1763
━ Frontier, 1763
━ Proclamation Line of 1763

MAP 5.1 The Proclamation Line of 1763

Victory over the French in 1763 meant that the Ohio Valley region was now British territory. But the Indians living in this region united under a Covenant Chain to fiercely resist white settlement there. Pontiac's Rebellion, centered around Lake Erie, led the British government to declare a moratorium on settlement west of the Proclamation Line. This restriction outraged Colonists. © Cengage Learning.

resistance had evaporated, and the Covenant Chain tribes were forced to acknowledge British control of the Ohio Valley.

The British realized that their victories did not mean a permanent peace in the West. As long as the "middle ground" between Indian and colonial populations continued to shrink, Indians would rise up against what Creeks bluntly called "people greedily grasping after the lands of red people." Settlers would then demand expensive military protection as they pushed westward. If the army did not respond, settlers were ready to take vigilante action on their own. Violence would lead to violence—unless Grenville could keep Indians and settlers at arm's length. Grenville's solution was a proclamation, issued in 1763, temporarily banning all colonial settlement west of the Appalachian Mountains.

Grenville's **Proclamation Line of 1763** (see Map 5.1) outraged colonists hoping to move west and wealthy land speculators hoping to reap a profit from their western investments. Many colonists simply ignored the Proclamation Line. Over the next decade, areas such as Kentucky began to fill with eager homesteaders, creating a wedge that divided northern from southern Indian tribes and increasing Indian anxiety about their own futures.

Because of their long tradition of anti-Catholic sentiment, American colonists also objected to Grenville's strategy of winning over Britain's new French-speaking Catholic Canadian subjects rather than strong-arming them. To balance their loss of fishing and fur-trading industries, Grenville promised the Canadians the right to preserve their religious and cultural way of life, a concession that scandalized American colonists.

Demanding More from the Colonists

Colonists were not the only ones growing discontent. In London, the king and many members of Parliament were impatient with colonial behavior and attitudes. "Hadn't the colonists benefited more than anyone from the French defeat?" asked George Grenville. And hadn't they contributed less than anyone to securing that victory? Such questions revealed the subtle but important rewriting of the motives and goals of the French and Indian War. Although Britain had waged the war to win dominance in European affairs, not to benefit the colonies, Grenville now declared that the war had been fought to protect the colonists.

This new interpretation fit well with the government's increasing sense that something had gone wrong in the economic relationship between England and its mainland colonies. Colonial cities such as Boston, Philadelphia, and New York had grown considerably, yet their growth did not make England as rich as **mercantile theory** said it should. One reason was that in every colony locally produced goods competed with English-made goods. A more important reason, however, was widespread illegal trade with Britain's rivals. In fact, to English amazement, colonists had continued to trade with the French Caribbean islands throughout the French and Indian War. In peacetime, colonists avoided paying the required **import duties** on foreign goods by bribing customs officials or landing cargoes where no customs officers were stationed.

Grenville discovered that by the 1760s, the Crown had collected less than £2,000 in revenue from colonial trade with other nations, yet the cost of collecting these duties was over £7,000 a year. Such discoveries fueled British suspicions that the colonies were underregulated and undergoverned, not to mention ungrateful and uncooperative. When the strong doubts about colonial loyalty met the reality of British government debts and soaring expenses, something drastic could be expected to follow. And it did. In 1764 Parliament approved Grenville's dramatic reforms of colonial trade policy. Colonists greeted these new policies with resentment and alarm.

Separately, each of Grenville's measures addressed a loophole in the proper relationship between home country and colonies. For example, a **Currency Act** outlawed the use of paper money as legal tender in the colonies. Grenville reasoned that this would drive colonial manufacturers, who were paid with paper money, out of business and ensure that colonists bought their manufactured goods from England.

Grenville's main focus was the widespread practice of colonial smuggling. Lawbreakers were so common, and customs officers so easily bribed, that smuggling had become an acceptable, even respectable form of commerce. To halt this illegal traffic, Grenville created the American Revenue Act. This 1764 act increased the powers of the customs officers, allowing them to use blanket warrants, called writs of assistance, to search ships and warehouses for smuggled goods. It was these writs that James Otis Jr. so eloquently opposed. Grenville also changed the regulations regarding key foreign imports, including sugar, wine, and coffee. This startling shift in policy, known popularly

◻ **Proclamation Line of 1763** Boundary that Britain established in the Appalachian Mountains, west of which white settlement was banned; it was intended to reduce conflict between Indians and colonists.

mercantile theory The economic notion that a nation should amass wealth by exporting more than it imports; colonies were seen as a source of raw materials and a market for manufactured goods.

import duties Taxes on imported goods.

◻ **Currency Act** British law of 1764 banning the printing of paper money in the American colonies.

as the Sugar Act, revealed Grenville's practical bent. He knew that any attempt to stop the flow of French sugar into the colonies was a waste of time and resources. So he decided to make a profit for the Crown from this trade. He would lower the tax on imported sugar—but he would make sure it was collected. He would also change the way in which alleged smugglers were brought to justice. Until 1764, a colonist accused of smuggling was tried before a jury of his neighbors in a civil court. He expected, and usually got, a favorable verdict from his peers. Grenville now declared that anyone caught smuggling would be tried in a juryless vice-admiralty court, where a conviction was far more likely. Once smuggling became too costly and too risky, Grenville reasoned, American shippers would declare their cargoes of French sugar and pay the Crown for the privilege of importing them.

The Colonial Response

Grenville's reforms were spectacularly ill timed as far as Americans were concerned. The colonial economy was suffering from a postwar depression, brought on in part by the loss of the British army as a steady market for American supplies and of British soldiers as steady customers who paid in hard currency rather than paper money. In 1764 unemployment was high among urban artisans, dockworkers, and sailors, and colonial merchants were caught in a credit squeeze— unable to pay their debts to British merchants because their colonial customers had no cash to pay for their purchases. These colonists opposed a Currency Act that shut off a source of money and a Sugar Act that established a new get-tough policy on foreign trade. In the eyes of many anxious colonists, the English government was turning into a greater menace than the French army had ever been.

Protests and proposals for action soon filled the pages of colonial newspapers. To many colonists, Grenville's reforms had raised profound issues about the rights of citizens and the relationship between Parliament and the colonial governments— issues that needed to be resolved. The degree to which Parliament had, or ought to have, power over colonial economic and political life required serious, public pondering. Years later, with the benefit of hindsight, John Adams stressed the importance of the Sugar Act in starting America down the road to independence. "I know not why we should blush to confess," wrote Adams, "that molasses [liquid sugar] was an essential ingredient in American independence." But in 1764 colonists were far from agreement over the issue of parliamentary and local political powers. They were not even certain how to respond to the Sugar Act.

The Stamp Act

Did Grenville stop to consider the possibility of grave problems arising from his postwar policies? Probably not. He was hardly a stranger to protest and anger, for he had often heard British citizens grumble about taxes and assert their rights against the government. As he saw it, his duty was to fill the treasury, reduce the nation's staggering debt, arm its troops, and keep the royal navy afloat. The duty of loyal British citizens, he believed, was to obey the laws of their sovereign government. Grenville had no doubt that the measures he and Parliament were taking to regulate the colonies and their revenue-producing trade were constitutional. Some colonists, however, had doubts. To settle the issue, Grenville proposed another piece of legislation designed not only to raise revenue but to assert the principle of parliamentary sovereignty. The new law was called the Stamp Act.

The Stamp Act of 1765 was to be the first direct tax ever laid on the colonies by Parliament. There was nothing startling or novel about this revenue-collecting method. A stamp tax raised money by requiring the use of government "stamped paper" on certain goods or as part of the cost for certain services. It was simple and efficient, and several colonial legislatures used this method themselves. What was startling, however, was that this tax had nothing to do with foreign trade. Until 1765, Parliament had passed many acts regulating colonial trade, and if these regulations generated revenue for the Crown, the colonists did not complain. They accepted this as a form of external taxation. But colonists were convinced that only their local assemblies had the power to impose direct taxes like the stamp tax. Grenville's Stamp Act was a sharp break with the traditional understanding

□ **Sugar Act** British law of 1764 that taxed sugar and other colonial imports to pay for some of Britain's expenses in protecting the colonies.

civil court Any court that hears cases regarding the rights of private citizens.

vice-admiralty court Nonjury British court in which a judge heard cases involving shipping.

depression A period of drastic economic decline, marked by decreased business activity, falling prices, and high unemployment.

□ **Stamp Act** British law of 1765 that directly taxed a variety of items, including newspapers, playing cards, and legal documents.

direct tax A tax imposed to raise revenue rather than to regulate trade.

external taxation Revenue raised in the course of regulating trade with other nations.

of the relationship between Britain and the colonies, and it challenged the distribution of political power between colonial assemblies and Parliament.

Most members of Parliament, however, saw the Stamp Act as an efficient and modest redistribution of the burden of the empire—and a constitutional one. Colonists were certainly not being asked to shoulder the entire burden, since the estimated £160,000 in revenue from the stamped paper would cover only one-fifth of the cost of maintaining a British army in North America.

The new law, passed in February 1765, was set to go into effect in November. The nine-month delay gave Grenville time to print the stamped paper and ship it across the Atlantic and to appoint agents to receive and distribute the stamps in each colony. News of the tax, however, crossed the ocean rapidly and was greeted with outrage. Virtually every free man and woman was affected by a tax that required stamps on all legal documents, newspapers and pamphlets, playing cards and dice. Grenville was reaching into the pockets of the rich, who would need stamped paper to draw up wills and property deeds and to bring suit in court. And he was emptying the pockets of the poor, who would feel the pinch when dealing a hand of cards in a tavern or buying a printed broadside filled with advertising. Colonial merchants and ship captains would have to use stamped clearances for all shipments or risk the seizure of their cargoes by the royal navy. Lawyers feared the loss of clients if they had to add the cost of the stamps to their fees. Thus, with the stamp tax Grenville united northern merchants, southern planters, rural women, and urban workingmen, and he riled the most articulate and argumentative of all Americans: lawyers and newspaper publishers.

The Popular Response

Many colonists proved ready to resist the new legislation. Massachusetts, whose smugglers were already choking on the new customs regulations, and whose assembly had a long history of struggle with local Crown officers, led the way. During the summer of 1765, a group of Bostonians formed a secret resistance organization called the Sons of Liberty. The Sons were led by the irrepressible Samuel Adams, a Harvard-educated member of a prominent Massachusetts family who preferred the company of local working men and women to the comfortable parlors of his relatives. Adams was a quick-witted, dynamic champion of working-class causes. He had a genius for writing propaganda and for mobilizing popular sentiment on political and community issues.

Many members of the Sons of Liberty were artisans and shopkeepers, but the group's main support came from men of the city's laboring classes who had been hard hit by the postwar depression and would suffer from the stamp tax. These colonists had little influence in the legislature or with Crown officials, but they compensated by staging public demonstrations and protests. By January 1765, New York City also had a Sons of Liberty organization, and by August, the Sons could be found in other cities and towns across the colonies.

Boston led the way in the demonstrations and protests that soon erupted. On August 14, shoemaker Ebenezer McIntosh led a crowd to protest the appointment of the colony's stamp agent, the wealthy merchant Andrew Oliver. The crowd, which included a number of the city's gentlemen disguised as workingmen, paraded through the city streets carrying an effigy of Oliver. They then destroyed Oliver's dockside warehouse and went on to break all the windows in his home. The message was clear—and Oliver understood it well. The following day Andrew Oliver resigned as stamp agent. Boston Sons of Liberty celebrated by declaring the tree on which they hanged Oliver's effigy the "liberty tree."

But Oliver's resignation did not end the protest. Customs officers and other Crown officials living in Boston were threatened with words and worse. The chief target of abuse, however, was the wealthy merchant and political officeholder Thomas Hutchinson. Hutchinson was resented by many of the ambitious younger political leaders because he monopolized appointive offices in the colony's government and hated by the workingmen because of his disdain for ordinary people. Late one August evening, a large crowd surrounded Hutchinson's elegant brick mansion. Hutchinson and his family, warned of trouble, had wisely fled, escaping just before rocks began to shatter the parlor windows. By dawn, the house was in ruins, and Hutchinson's furniture, clothing, and personal library had been trashed. The attack on Hutchinson revealed that sometimes protests were not simply over British policies but over local issues and against local elites as well. It was not surprising, therefore, that

broadside An advertisement, public notice, or other publication printed on one side of a large sheet of paper.

▢ **Sons of Liberty** A secret organization first formed in Boston to oppose the Stamp Act.

▢ **Samuel Adams** Massachusetts revolutionary leader and propagandist who organized opposition to British policies after 1764.

Ebenezer McIntosh Boston shoemaker whose workingman's organization, the South End "gang," became the core of the city's Sons of Liberty in 1765.

▢ **Thomas Hutchinson** Boston merchant and judge who served as lieutenant governor and later governor of Massachusetts; Stamp Act protesters destroyed his home in 1765.

The Sons of Liberty were able to silence many who criticized them. In 1765, the Boston Sons demanded the resignation of local stamp agent Andrew Oliver (*left*). In 1774, New York's pro-British editor, James Rivington, used the illustration on the right while reporting that a New Brunswick mob had hanged him in effigy. The New York Sons promptly attacked his office, destroyed his press, and forced his paper to close.

prosperous merchants and shippers soon saw a potential danger in the mobilization of lower-class crowds like the Sons of Liberty. For elites like Hutchinson, crowd protest was a double-edged sword, a useful weapon that could be deadly in the wrong hands.

The campaign against the stamp agents spread like a brushfire across the colonies. Agents in Connecticut, Rhode Island, Maryland, and New York were mercilessly harassed. Most stamp agents resigned. When the stamps reached colonial ports in November, only the young and conservative colony of Georgia could produce anyone willing to distribute them. Colonial governors retaliated by refusing to allow any colonial ships to leave port, hoping to persuade local merchants to help end the resistance. Their strategy backfired. Violence increased as hundreds of unemployed sailors took to the streets, terrorizing customs officers and any colonists suspected of supporting the king's taxation policy.

Political Debate

While the Sons of Liberty and their supporters demonstrated in the streets, colonial political leaders were proceeding with caution. Virginia lawyer and planter Patrick Henry briefly stirred passions in the House of Burgesses when he suggested that the Stamp Act was evidence of the king's tyranny. Not everyone agreed with him that the measure was so serious. Many did agree with James Otis, however, that the heart of the matter was not stamped paper but parliamentary sovereignty versus the rights of colonial citizens. "No taxation without representation"—the principle that citizens cannot be taxed by a government unless they are represented in it—was a fundamental assumption of free white Englishmen on both sides of the

Atlantic. The crucial question was this: Did the House of Commons represent the colonists even though no colonist sat in the House and none voted for its members? If the answer was no, then the Stamp Act violated the colonists' most basic "rights of Englishmen."

Stating the issue in this way led to other concerns. Could colonial political leaders oppose a single law such as the Stamp Act without completely denying the authority of the government responsible for its passage? This was the question that troubled James Otis Jr. He, for one, was not prepared to become a rebel. Instead he proposed that Parliament give seats in the government to colonial representatives.

Like Otis, most political leaders shrank from denying Parliament's authority. But his suggestion that Parliament admit colonial representatives satisfied no one. A small contingent of colonial members of Parliament would have little power and was likely to find its views ignored. The only solution seemed to be to protest against the Stamp Act, demand its repeal, and warn Parliament that Americans would resist further efforts to infringe on their rights and liberties.

Many members of the colonial legislatures felt more was needed than strong words and implicit threats. Their own authority was at stake, for if Parliament asserted its right to govern the colonies directly, their powers would be diminished. These men had much to lose—status, prestige, and the many benefits that

□ **Patrick Henry** Member of the Virginia House of Burgesses and American revolutionary leader noted for his oratorical skills.

came from deciding how tax monies would be allocated. Thus, when Massachusetts suggested an intercolonial meeting of delegates be held to discuss the Stamp Act crisis, the idea was greeted with enthusiasm.

Grenville's policies appeared to be bringing about what had once seemed impossible: united political action by the colonies. Yet in the fall of 1765 delegates from nine colonies met in New York "to consider a general and unified, dutiful, loyal and humble Representation [petition]" to the king and Parliament. The petitions this historic Stamp Act Congress ultimately produced were far bolder than the delegates first intended. While conceding parliamentary authority over the colonies, they denied Parliament's right to impose any direct taxes on them. "No taxes," the Congress said, "ever have been, or can be Constitutionally imposed" on the colonies "but by their respective Legislatures." Clearly Americans expected this tradition to be honored.

Repeal of the Stamp Act

Neither the protest in the streets nor the arguments of the Stamp Act Congress moved the king or Parliament to repeal the stamp tax. But the most powerful weapon in the colonial arsenal was a refusal to purchase English goods, for English manufacturers relied heavily on their colonial markets. On the night before the stamp tax officially went into effect, two hundred New York merchants announced that they would not import any new British goods. Local artisans and laborers rallied to support this boycott. The movement for a boycott, which colonists called nonimportation and nonconsumption, spread quickly. By the end of November, several colonial assemblies had publicly endorsed the boycott agreements signed by local merchants. Popular support widened as well.

English exporters complained bitterly of the damage done to their businesses and pressured Parliament to take colonial protest seriously. Meanwhile, colonists were simply ignoring the hated law anyway, continuing to sue their neighbors, sell their land, publish their newspapers, and buy their playing cards as if the stamped paper and the Stamp Act did not exist.

◻ **Stamp Act Congress** A meeting convened in October 1765 to call for the repeal of the Stamp Act. Delegates from nine colonies attended this first example of colonial cooperation.

◻ **boycott** An organized political protest, used by the colonists to protest British taxation, in which people refuse to buy goods from a nation or group of people whose actions they oppose; also called *nonimportation.*

◻ **Declaratory Act** A statement of Parliament's authority over the American colonies "in all cases whatsoever," passed on the same day as the repeal of the Stamp Act.

For unrelated reasons, by winter's end, Grenville had been replaced by Lord Rockingham, and for the new prime minister the critical issue was how to repeal the Stamp Act without appearing to cave in to colonial pressure. In 1766, the government came up with a satisfactory solution. Great Britain repealed the Stamp Act but at the same time passed a Declaratory Act, which asserted that the colonies were "subordinate unto, and dependent upon the imperial Crown and parliament of Great Britain." Thus, this act reaffirmed as absolute Parliament's right to pass legislation for and raise taxes from the North American colonies.

Colonists celebrated the repeal with public outpourings of loyalty to England that were as impressive as their public protests had been. There were cannon salutes, bonfires, parades, speeches, grand gestures of loyalty, and public toasts to the king and Rockingham. In one spectacular but poorly executed gesture, the Liberty Boys of Plymouth, Massachusetts, tried to move Plymouth Rock to the center of town. When the famous rock on which the Pilgrims were said to have landed split in two, half of it was carried to Liberty Pole Square, where it remained until 1834. As for the Declaratory Act, colonists who commented on it at all dismissed it as a face-saving device. To a degree, they were correct. But the Declaratory Act expressed the views of powerful men in Parliament, and within a year they put it to the test.

ASSERTING AMERICAN RIGHTS

☆ *Why did Charles Townshend expect his revenue-raising measures to be successful?*

☆ *What forms of resistance did the colonists use against Townshend's measures and what were the results?*

By the summer of 1766, William Pitt, who had resigned from George III's government, had returned to power. But Pitt was old and preoccupied with his failing health. A young playboy named Charles Townshend, serving as Chancellor of the Exchequer, rushed in to fill the leadership void. This brash young politician wasted little time foisting a new package of taxes on the colonies.

The Townshend Acts and Colonial Protest

During the Stamp Act crisis, Benjamin Franklin had assured Parliament that American colonists accepted indirect taxation through trade regulations, even if they violently protested a direct tax such as the Stamp Act. In 1767 Townshend decided to test this distinction by proposing new regulations on a variety of imported necessities and luxuries. But unlike any import taxes the colonies had ever seen, the Townshend Acts taxed products made within the British Empire.

The Townshend Acts taxed glass, paper, paint, and lead products, all made in England. The acts also placed a three-penny tax on tea, considered a necessity by virtually all colonists. Townshend wanted to be certa in these taxes were collected, so he ordered new customs boards in the colonies and created new vice-admiralty courts in the major port cities of Boston, Charleston, and Philadelphia to try cases of smuggling or tax evasion. In case Americans tried to harass customs officials, Townshend ordered British troops transferred from the western regions to the major colonial port cities. To help finance this military occupation of key cities, Townshend invoked the 1766 Quartering Act, a hated law requiring colonists to provide room and board to troops stationed in their midst, including "candles, firing, bedding, cooking utensils, salt and vinegar," and a ration of beer, cider, or rum. Clearly taking every precaution to avoid the embarrassment Grenville had suffered in the Stamp Act disaster, Townshend relied on the presence of uniformed soldiers—known as "redcoats" because of their scarlet jackets—to keep the peace.

When news of the new regulations reached the colonies, however, the response was immediate, determined, and well-organized resistance. Newspaper accounts indicate that the colonists were united in their opposition to the Townshend Acts and the repressive enforcement policies. In Boston, Samuel Adams voiced his outrage: "Is it possible to form an idea of Slavery, more compleat, more miserable, more disgraceful?" Others worried more about the economic burden of new taxes and quartering troops than about political rights. Boston lawyer Josiah Quincy Jr. asked readers of the *Boston Gazette*: "Is not the bread taken out of the children's mouths and given unto the Dogs?"

John Dickinson, a well-respected Pennsylvania landowner and lawyer, laid out the basic American position on imperial relations in his pamphlet *Letters from a Farmer in Pennsylvania* (1767). Direct taxation without representation violated the colonists' rights as English citizens, Dickinson declared. But by imposing any tax that did not regulate foreign trade, Parliament also violated those rights.

Dickinson also considered, and rejected, the British claim that Americans were represented in the House of Commons. According to the British argument, colonists enjoyed "virtual representation" because the House of Commons represented the interests of all citizens in the empire who were not members of the nobility, whether those citizens participated directly in elections to the House or not. Like most Americans, Dickinson discounted virtual representation. What Englishmen were entitled to, he wrote, was *actual* representation by men they had elected to government to protect their interests. For qualified voters in the colonies who enjoyed actual representation in their local assemblies, virtual

The Granger Collection, NYC.

Samuel Adams, whose family owned a Boston brewery, was the undisputed leader of the popular protest movement in Massachusetts during the 1760s and 1770s. Adams was one of the organizers of the Sons of Liberty, a group responsible for many of the demonstrations against British policies as well as some of the violence against British officials. After the Revolution, he served as governor of Massachusetts.

representation was nothing more than a weak excuse for exclusion and exploitation. As one American quipped: "Our privileges are all virtual, our sufferings are real."

Popular resistance began when Samuel Adams set in motion a massive boycott of British goods to begin on January 1, 1768. Simple economics contributed forcefully to support for the boycott. Boston artisans remained enthusiastic about any action that stopped the flow of inexpensive English-made goods to America, because it would make it easier to sell their own goods. Small-scale merchants who had little access to British goods were also eager to see nonimportation enforced. The large-scale merchants who had led the 1765 boycott were not enthusiastic, however. By 1767, their warehouses were no longer overflowing with English stock unsold during the postwar depression, and the boycott might cut off their livelihoods. Many of these elite merchants delayed signing the agreements. Others did not sign at all.

Those who opposed resistance to the Townshend Acts most strongly were colonists holding Crown-appointed

◻ **Townshend Acts** Revenue-raising measure imposing duties, for the first time, on colonial imports from within the British Empire.

TOWARD A MORE PERFECT UNION

Direct Representation vs. Virtual Representation

In 1689, the English Bill of Rights forbade any taxes imposed without the consent of Parliament. The goal of this Bill of Rights was to limit the power of the monarch. As one of the political writers who supported the Glorious Revolution put it, "what an English King has no right to demand, an English subject has a right to refuse." But in the seventeenth and eighteenth centuries, did Parliament represent all English citizens, even those who lived across the ocean in the colonies? Most English political leaders said yes. Taxation was initiated in the House of Commons and, by virtue of the fact that the House represented all commoners, the colonists too were represented. American political leaders in the 1760s and 1770s rejected this notion of virtual representation. They demanded actual representation, the right to elect the people who served in office and taxed them. Thus "No taxation without representation" became a rallying cry of the American Revolution.

Yet the framers of the U.S. Constitution incorporated the notion of indirect election in 1787 in two ways. The Constitution explicitly stated that the Senate was to be chosen by state legislatures, and this did not change until 1913, when the Seventeenth Amendment was ratified. And, implicitly, during the nineteenth century wives were said to be represented by virtue of the fact that their husbands could vote. This did not change until 1920 with the ratification of the Nineteenth Amendment.

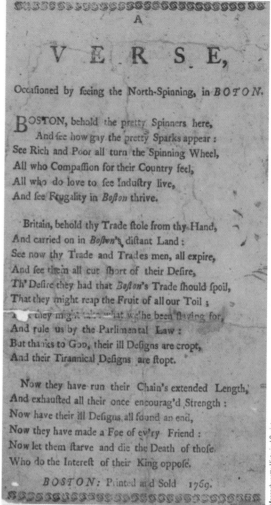

"A Verse Occasioned by Seeing the North-Spinning in Boston, 1769." When political leaders called for a boycott of English goods, including cloth, to force the repeal of the Townsend Acts, women became crucial to its success. They organized spinning bees, replacing British cloth with their own "liberty cloth." Both the women spinners and admirers like the author of this verse realized this was a form of female political protest.

government offices. These fortunate few—including judges and customs men—had sworn to uphold the policies of the British government. They were inclined to see British policymakers as well intentioned, and they saw acceptance of British policy as a patriotic duty. Jonathan Sewall, the king's attorney general in Massachusetts, was perhaps typical of these royal officeholders.

Sewall's family went back many generations, and he had deep roots in his colonial community. His closest friend was John Adams, cousin of Samuel Adams, and the wealthy Boston merchant and smuggler John Hancock would soon become his brother-in-law. Yet Sewall became a staunch public defender of Crown policy. In his newspaper articles, he urged his neighbors to ignore the call to resistance, and he questioned the motives of the leading activists, suggesting that greed, thwarted ambition, and envy rather than high-minded principles motivated the rabble-rousers. But despite their prestige and their positions of authority, Crown officers like Sewall were unable to prevent the boycott or slow the spread of resistance.

The 1768 boycott brought politics into the lives of women just as the Stamp Act mobilized working-class men. Women's boycott of English cloth was critically important and many women rose to the challenge, resurrecting the tedious skill of spinning yarn for cloth. Taking a bold political stance, women, including wealthy mothers and daughters, formed groups called the Daughters of Liberty and staged large public spinning bees to show support for the boycott. Wearing clothing made of "homespun" became a mark of honor and a political statement. As one male observer noted, "The ladies...may vie with the men in contributing to the preservation and prosperity of their country and equally share in the honor of it." Through the boycott, politics had entered the domestic circle.

The British Humiliated

Although the Townshend Acts met with defiance in almost every colony, Massachusetts provided the greatest embarrassment for Parliament and the king. The assembly defied the colonial governor, Francis Bernard, by issuing a Circular Letter to other colonies, calling for united protest against the Townshend Acts. The helpless governor could do nothing to save face except dismiss the assembly, leaving the colony without any representative government.

Bernard's ability to ensure law and order then eroded rapidly. Throughout 1768, enforcers of the boycott roamed the streets of Boston, intimidating pro-British merchants and harassing anyone wearing British-made clothing. Boston mobs of men and women openly threatened customs officials, and the Sons of Liberty protected the colony's thriving business in smuggling foreign goods and the items listed in the hated Townshend Acts. The flamboyant John Hancock, one of the town's most notorious smugglers, grew more popular with his neighbors each time he unloaded his illegal cargoes of French and Spanish wines or West Indian sugar. When customs officers seized Hancock's vessel, aptly named the *Liberty*, in June 1768, protesters beat up senior customs men, and mobs visited the homes of other royal officials. The now-desperate Governor Bernard sent an urgent plea for help to the British government.

In October 1768, four thousand troops arrived in Boston—one soldier for every four citizens. John Adams marveled at what he considered British thickheadedness. The presence of so many young soldiers, far from home and surrounded by a hostile community, was certain to worsen the situation. Military occupation of Boston, Adams warned, made more violence inevitable.

Adams was right. With time on their hands, the soldiers passed the hours courting any local women who would speak to them and pestering those who would not. They angered local dockworkers by moonlighting in the shipyards when off duty and taking jobs away from colonists by accepting lower pay. For their part, civilians taunted the sentries, insulted the soldiers, and refused the military any sign of hospitality. News of street-corner fights and tavern brawls inflamed feelings on both sides. Samuel Adams and his friends did their best to fan the flames of hatred, publishing daily accounts of both real and imaginary confrontations in which soldiers threatened the honor or endangered the safety of innocent townspeople.

The military occupation dragged on through 1769 and early 1770. On March 5, the major confrontation most people expected occurred. An angry crowd began throwing snowballs—undoubtedly laced with bricks and rocks—at British sentries guarding the customs house. The redcoats, under strict orders not to fire on civilians, issued a frantic call for help in withdrawing

Paul Revere's engraving of the Boston Massacre appeared in newspapers the day after the confrontation between redcoats and Boston citizens. Even though Captain Preston and most of his soldiers were found innocent of wrongdoing, Revere's striking image of innocent civilians and murderous soldiers remained fixed in the popular mind. It reinforced suspicion that the British were plotting to deprive Americans of their rights and liberties.

to safety. When Captain Thomas Preston and his men arrived to rescue the sentries, the growing crowd immediately enveloped them. How, and under whose orders, Preston's soldiers began to fire is unknown, but they killed five men and wounded eight other colonists. Four of the five victims were white laborers. The fifth, Crispus Attucks, was a free black sailor.

Massachusetts protest leaders immediately labeled the confrontation the Boston Massacre. Their account appeared in colonial newspapers everywhere and included a dramatic anti-British illustration engraved by silversmith Paul Revere. A jury of colonists later cleared Preston and all but two of his men of the charges against them. But nothing that was said at their trial—no sworn testimony, no lawyer's arguments—could erase the image of British brutality against British subjects.

Even before the bloodshed of March 5, Edmund Burke, a member of Parliament known for his sympathy to the colonial cause, had warned the House of Commons that the relationship between Britain and the colonies was both desperate and tragic. "The

◻ **Boston Massacre** A clash between Boston citizens and British soldiers on March 5, 1770, that resulted in the deaths of five civilians and the trials of nine British soldiers.

Americans," Burke said, "have made a discovery, or think they have made one, that we mean to oppress them; we have made a discovery, or think we have made one, that they intend to rise in rebellion. We do not know how to advance; they do not know how to retreat." Parliament was ready to act to ease the crisis and make a truce possible. A new minister, Frederick, Lord North, was given the reins of government, and on the very day Captain Preston's men fired on the crowd at Boston, Lord North repealed the Townshend Acts and allowed the hated Quartering Act to expire. Yet Lord North wanted to give no ground on the question of parliamentary control of the colonies. For this reason, he kept the tax on tea—to preserve a principle rather than fill the king's treasury.

Success Weakens Colonial Unity

Repeal of the Townshend Acts allowed the colonists to return to the ordinary routine of their lives. But it was not true that all tensions had vanished. Troubling ones remained—and they were largely among the colonists themselves. Struggling artisans and laborers now found themselves at odds with their former allies, the merchants. In fact, many elite colonists gladly abandoned the radical activism they had shown in the 1760s in favor of social conservatism. Their fear of British tyranny dimmed, but their fear of the lower classes' clamor for political power grew. "Many of the poorer People," observed one supporter of expanded political participation, "deeply felt the Aristocratic Power, or rather the intolerable Tyranny of the great and opulent." The new political language in which common men justified their demands made their social superiors uneasy. Their own impassioned appeals for rights and liberties were returning to haunt some of the colonial elite.

THE CRISIS RENEWED

☆ *What British policies led Americans to imagine a plot against their rights and liberties?*

☆ *How did the king hope to crush resistance in Massachusetts and how did the Continental Congress respond?*

Lord North's government took care not to disturb the calm created by the repeal of the Townshend Acts. Between 1770 and 1773, North proposed no new taxes on the colonists and made no major changes in colonial policy. American political leaders took equal care not to make any open challenges to British authority. Both

◻ **committees of correspondence** Committees appointed by the legislatures of all the mainland colonies except Pennsylvania and North Carolina to speed intercolonial communication of political news.

sides recognized that their political truce had its limits. It did not extend to smugglers and customs men, who continued to lock horns; it did not end the bitterness of southern colonists who wished to settle beyond the Proclamation Line; it did not erase the distrust colonial political leaders and the British government felt for each other.

Disturbing the Peace of the Early 1770s

The British effort to crack down on American smuggling continued to disturb New England merchants whose fortunes were built on trade with the Caribbean. They resented the sight of customs officers at the docks and of customs ships patrolling the coastline. Rhode Island merchants took revenge against the determined—and highly effective—customs operation in their colony. One June day in 1772, the customs patrol boat *Gaspée* ran aground as it chased an American vessel off Rhode Island. That evening a band of colonists boarded the *Gaspée,* taunted the stranded customs men, and then set fire to their boat. Rhode Islanders called the burning of the *Gaspée* an act of political resistance. The English called it an act of vandalism and appointed a royal commission to investigate. To their amazement, no witnesses came forward, and no evidence could be gathered to support any arrests.

Many American political leaders were convinced that the British government had intended to bring its suspects to England for trial and thus deprive them of a jury of their peers. They read this as further evidence of the plot to destroy American liberty, and they decided to keep in close contact to monitor British moves. Following the Virginia assembly's lead, five colonies organized a communications network called the committees of correspondence, instructing each committee to circulate detailed accounts of any questionable royal activities in its colony. These committees of correspondence were also a good mechanism for coordinating protest or resistance should the need arise. Thus the colonists put in place their first permanent machinery of protest.

The Tea Act and the Tea Party

During the early 1770s, colonial activists worked to keep the political consciousness of the 1760s alive. Without major British provocation, however, a revival of mass action was unlikely.

In 1773 Parliament provided that provocation. This time the government was not setting new colonial policy but trying to save a major commercial enterprise, the East India Tea Company. Mismanagement, coupled with the American boycott and the tendency of colonists to buy smuggled Dutch tea, had left the company in serious financial trouble, its warehouses bursting with unsold tea.

The company directors had a plan: if Parliament allowed them to ship their tea directly to the colonial market, eliminating the English merchants who served as middlemen, they could lower their prices and compete effectively against the smuggled Dutch tea. Even with the three-penny tax on tea that remained from the Townshend era, smart consumers would see this as a bargain. Lord North liked the plan and saw in it the opportunity for vindication: Americans who purchased the cheaper English tea would be confirming Parliament's right to tax the colonies. With little debate, Parliament made the company's arrangement legal through passage of the Tea Act. No one expected the colonists to object.

Once again, British politicians had seriously misjudged the impact of their decisions. Colonists read the Tea Act as an insult, a challenge, another chilling sign of a conspiracy against their liberty. They distrusted the arrangement, believing that the East India Tea Company would raise its prices dramatically once all foreign teas were driven off the market. And they were concerned that if other British companies marketing products in the colonies followed the East India Tea Company's example, prices for scores of products would soar. These objections, however, paled beside the colonists' immediate grasp of Lord North's strategy: purchasing cheaper English tea would confirm Parliament's right to tax the colonies. The tea that Americans drank might be cheap, but the price of conceding the legitimacy of the tea tax was too high.

Colonists mobilized their resistance in 1773 with the skill acquired from a decade of experience. In several cities, crowds met the ships carrying the East India tea and prevented the unloading of their cargoes. They used the threat of violence to persuade ship captains to return to England with the tea still on board. As long as both the captains and the local royal officials gave in to these pressures, no serious confrontation occurred. But in Massachusetts, the most famous victim of mob violence, now Governor Thomas Hutchinson, was not willing to give in. A stalemate resulted: colonists refused to allow crews to unload the tea, but Hutchinson refused to allow the tea ships to depart without unloading. Boston activists broke the stalemate on December 16, 1773, when some sixty men, thinly disguised as Mohawk Indians, boarded the tea ships. Working calmly and methodically, they dumped 342 chests of tea, worth almost £10,000, into the waters of Boston harbor.

Americans throwing the Cargoes of the Tea Ships into the River, at Boston

As this illustration shows, during the famous "Boston Tea Party" of December 1773 city men boarded British ships to toss thousands of pounds' worth of tea into the harbor. Although the radicals donned Indian disguises, most of them were no doubt easily recognized by their supporters.

The Intolerable Acts (Coercive Acts)

The Boston Tea Party delighted colonists everywhere. The Crown, however, failed to see the humor in this deliberate destruction of valuable private property. The tea chests had barely settled into the harbor mud before Parliament retaliated. The king and his minister meant to make an example of everyone in Boston, the source of so much trouble and embarrassment over the past decade. Americans on the scene in England warned friends and family back home of the growing rage against the colonies. Arthur Lee, serving in London as Massachusetts's colonial agent, drew a gloomy picture in a letter to his brother. "The storm, you see, runs high," he wrote, "and it will require great prudence, wisdom and resolution, to save our liberties from shipwreck."

The four acts known as the Coercive Acts that Parliament passed in 1774 to discipline Massachusetts were as harsh and uncompromising as Arthur Lee predicted. The colonists called them the Intolerable Acts. The Port Act closed the port of Boston to all

□ **Intolerable Acts** Three acts Parliament passed in 1774 to punish Massachusetts for the Boston Tea Party; also called the Coercive Acts; colonists also considered the Quebec Act and the Quartering Act to be part of Britain's new and more coercive policy.

trade until the citizens compensated the East India Tea Company fully for its losses. This was a devastating blow to the colony's economy. The Massachusetts Government Act transferred much of the power of the colony's assembly to the royal governor, including the right to appoint judges, sheriffs, and members of the colonial legislature's upper house. The colony's town meetings, which had served as forums for anti-British sentiment and protests, also came under the governor's direct control. A third measure, the Justice Act, allowed royal officials charged with capital crimes to stand trial in London rather than before local juries. And a new Quartering Act gave military commanders the authority to house troops in private homes. To see that these laws were enforced, the king named General Thomas Gage, commander of the British troops in North America, as the acting governor of Massachusetts.

At the same time that Parliament passed these punitive measures, the British government issued a comprehensive plan for the government of Canada. The timing of the Quebec Act may have been a coincidence, but its provisions infuriated Americans. The Quebec Act granted the French in Canada the right to worship as Catholics, retain their language, and keep many of their legal practices—all marks of a tolerance that the Crown had refused to show its English colonists. The Quebec Act also expanded the borders of Canada into the Ohio Valley at the expense of the English-speaking colonies' claim to western land. This dealt a harsh blow to Virginia planters who hoped to profit from land speculation in the region. The king expected the severe punishment of Massachusetts to isolate that colony from its neighbors. But the Americans resisted this divide-and-conquer strategy. In every colony, newspaper essays and editorials urged readers to see Boston's plight as their own. "This horrid attack upon the town of Boston," said the *South Carolina Gazette,* "we consider not as an attempt upon that town singly, but upon the whole Continent." George Washington, by now an influential Virginia planter and militia officer, declared that "the cause of Boston now is and ever will be the cause of America." Indeed, the Intolerable Acts produced a wave of sympathy for the beleaguered Bostonians, and relief efforts sprang up across the colonies.

In pamphlets and political essays, colonists placed the Intolerable Acts into the larger context of systematic oppression by the home country. Political writers referred to the British government as the "enemy,"

conspiring to deprive Americans of their liberty, and urged colonists to defend themselves against the "power and cunning of our adversaries."

This unity of sentiment, however, was more fragile than it appeared. In the cities, bitter divisions quickly developed, and artisans struggled with merchants to control the mass meetings that would make strategy choices. Samuel Adams and the radical artisans and workers of Boston suggested what might be at stake in this struggle between elites and ordinary citizens when they formed a "solemn league and covenant" to lead a third intercolonial boycott of British goods. As most Bostonians knew, the words *solemn league* referred to a pact between the Scottish Presbyterians and English Puritans who had overthrown the royal government in the 1640s and beheaded a king. Adams and his allies had made their choice: armed rebellion. Yet even in crisis-torn Boston, not everyone wanted matters to go that far. And in the southern colonies, planters worried that slave revolts and class antagonisms between the elite and the poorer farmers might be the ultimate outcome of escalating protest.

Creating a National Forum: The First Continental Congress

On September 5, 1774, delegates from every colony but Georgia gathered in Philadelphia for a continental congress. Few of the delegates or the people they represented thought of themselves as revolutionaries. "We want no revolution," a North Carolina delegate bluntly stated. Yet in the eyes of their British rulers, he and other colonists were treading dangerously close to treason. After all, neither the king nor Parliament had authorized the congress, which was intent on resisting acts of Parliament and defying the king. English men and women had been hanged as traitors for far less serious betrayals of the English government.

Some of the most articulate political leaders in the colonies attended this First Continental Congress. Conservative delegates such as Joseph Galloway of Pennsylvania hoped to slow the pace of colonial resistance by substituting petitions to Parliament for the total boycott proposed by Samuel Adams. Their radical opponents—including Samuel Adams and his cousin John, Patrick Henry, and delegates from the artisan community of Philadelphia—demanded the boycott and more. Most of the delegates were desperately searching for a third choice: a way to express their grievances and demand that injustices be corrected without further eroding their relationship with England.

The mounting crisis in Massachusetts diminished the chances of a moderate solution. Rumors spread that the royal navy was planning to bombard Boston and that General Gage was preparing to invade the

□ **First Continental Congress** A gathering of delegates from twelve colonies in 1774 that demanded the repeal of the Intolerable Acts, established a new boycott of British goods, and issued a Declaration of Rights and Grievances.

countryside. Thousands of Massachusetts militiamen had begun mustering in Cambridge. The growing conflict drove many delegates into the radical camp. In this atmosphere of dread and anxiety, the Continental Congress approved the Continental Association, a boycott of all English goods to begin on December 1, 1774. The Congress also passed strong resolutions demanding the repeal of the Intolerable Acts.

This First Continental Congress had chosen radical tactics, but many delegates were torn between loyalty to Great Britain and loyalty to colony. Thomas Jefferson, a young Virginia planter and intellectual, tried to find a way out of this dilemma by separating loyalty to the king from resistance to Parliament. He argued that the colonists owed allegiance to the nation's king, not to Parliament, and that each colony did indeed have the right to legislate for itself. Not everyone agreed.

If no compromise could be reached, the delegates—and Americans everywhere—would have to choose where their strongest loyalties lay. Joseph Galloway believed that he had worked out the necessary compromise. In his Plan of Union, Galloway called for a Grand Council, elected by each colonial legislature, that would share with Parliament the right to originate laws for the colonies.

Congress rejected Galloway's compromise by the narrowest of margins. Then it was John Adams's turn to propose a solution. Under his skillful urging and direction, the Congress adopted the Declaration of Rights and Grievances, which politely but firmly established the colonial standard for acceptable legislation by Parliament. Colonists, said the declaration, would consent to acts meant to regulate "our external commerce." But they absolutely denied the legitimacy, or lawfulness, of an "idea of taxation, internal or external, for raising revenue on the subjects of America, without their consent."

The delegates knew that the force behind the declaration came from the unspoken but nevertheless real threat that rebellion would occur if the colonists' demands were not met. To make this threat clearer, Congress endorsed a set of resolutions rushed to Philadelphia from Suffolk County, Massachusetts. These Suffolk Resolves called on the residents of that county to arm themselves and prepare to resist British military action. Congressional support for these resolves sent an unmistakable message that American leaders were willing to choose rebellion if politics failed.

The delegates adjourned and headed home, bringing news of the Congress's decisions with them to their families and their communities. There was nothing to do now but wait for the Crown's response. When it came, it was electric. "Blows must decide," declared King George III, "whether they are to be subject to this country or independent."

George III, or George William Frederick, was only 22 when he became the king of Great Britain and Ireland in 1760. During his reign, Britain won a major war against France in 1763, but lost most of its mainland colonies in 1783, when American independence was recognized. Thomas Paine called him the "royal brute"; American revolutionaries called him a tyrant; but supporters viewed him as a statesman. In this portrait George III shows no signs of the illness that would lead to blindness and senility, as well as bouts of insanity, later in his life.

THE DECISION FOR INDEPENDENCE

☆ *What compromises were still available in 1775–1776 and how might the Revolutionary War have been avoided?*

☆ *What motivated some colonists to become loyalists and others to become patriots?*

Americans were anxious while they waited for the king and Parliament to respond to the Declaration of Rights and Grievances, but they were not idle. In most colonies, a transfer of political power was occurring as the majority of Americans recognized the authority of anti-British, patriot governments.

Taking Charge and Enforcing Policies

Imperial control broke down as communities in each colony refused to obey royal laws or acknowledge the authority of royal officers. For example, when General Thomas Gage, the acting governor of Massachusetts, refused to convene the Massachusetts assembly, its members met anyway, taking up preparations for military resistance to Gage and his army. While the redcoats occupied Boston, the rebellious assembly openly ordered the colonists to stockpile military supplies near the town of Concord (see Map 5.2).

The transition from royal to patriot political control was peaceful in communities where anti-British sentiment was strong. Where it was weak, or where the community was divided, radicals used persuasion, pressure, and open intimidation to advance the patriot cause. In most colonial cities and towns, patriot committees arose to enforce compliance with the boycott of British goods. These committees publicly exposed those who did not obey the Continental Association, publishing violators' names in local newspapers and calling on the community to shun them. These tactics were effective.

Colonists suspected of sympathizing with the British were brought before committees and made to swear oaths of support for the patriot cause. When public shaming or political pressure did not work, most committees were ready to use threats of physical violence and to make good on them. In Connecticut a group of patriots hauled a 70-year-old Anglican man from his bed, dragged him naked into the winter night, and beat him brutally because his loyalty to the Church of England made him suspect. In New England, many pro-British citizens, or loyalists, came to fear for their lives. In the wake of the Intolerable Acts, hundreds of them fled to the city of Boston, hoping General Gage could protect them from their neighbors.

The Shot Heard 'Round the World

King George continued to believe that resistance in most colonies would fade if the Massachusetts radicals were crushed. In January 1775, he ordered General Gage to arrest the most notorious leaders of rebellion in that colony, Samuel Adams and John Hancock. Gage made plans to send redcoats to Concord with orders to seize the rapidly growing stockpile of weapons and arrest the two radical leaders along the way.

The patriots, of course, had their spies in Boston. Reports of the arrest orders and of suspicious troop preparations reached the militias gathered outside the occupied city. The only question was when and where Gage would attack. The Americans devised a warning system: as soon as Gage's troops began to move out of Boston, spies would signal the route with lanterns hung in the bell tower of the North Church. On April 18, 1775, riders waiting outside Boston saw two

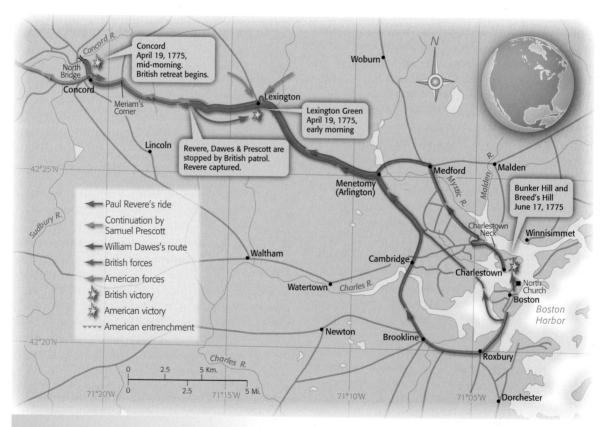

MAP 5.2 Battles in Eastern Massachusetts, 1775
This map shows the British march to Concord and the routes taken by the three Americans who alerted the countryside of the enemy's approach. Also shown is the battle fought on June 17, discussed in the next chapter. © Cengage Learning.

The Right to Dissent

As the colonists moved toward declaring independence, men and women who remained loyal to the king were pressured to keep silent. Many, like Jonathan Sewall, who had publicly opposed independence, had to flee their home and country and find refuge in England or Canada. Others were forced to sign loyalty oaths to the new independent governments. Throughout American history, men and women have opposed political and social choices made by the nation, including the entrance of the United States into World War I, woman suffrage, Prohibition, and the wars in Vietnam and Iraq. The right to dissent, guaranteed by the Constitution, has been a critical part of the American political tradition since the nation began. Examining how dissent has been voiced and how it has been received is part of the story of all major controversial events.

- Consider your position on dissent in times of national crisis. Do you believe the government has the right to suppress dissent during war or major disasters? Why or why not?
- Discuss the impact modern technology has had on the ability of citizens to voice opposition and organize resistance to government policies.

lanterns flash from the bell tower. Within moments, silversmith Paul Revere and his fellow messengers rode off to give news of the British army's approach.

Around sunrise on April 19, an advance guard of a few hundred redcoats reached the town of Lexington, where they expected to apprehend Adams and Hancock. In the pale light, they saw about seventy colonial militiamen waiting on the village green. As the badly outnumbered colonists began to disperse, eager and nervous redcoats broke ranks and rushed forward, sending up a triumphant cheer. No order came to fire, but in the confusion shots rang out. Eight Americans were killed, most of them shot in the back as they ran for safety. Nine more were wounded. Later Americans who told the story of the skirmish at Lexington would insist that the first musket fired there sounded a "shot heard 'round the world."

The British troops marched from Lexington to Concord. Surprised to find the town nearly deserted, they began a methodical search for weapons. All they uncovered were five hundred musket balls, which they dumped into a nearby pond. They then burned the town's liberty tree. Ignoring this act of provocation, the Concord Minutemen, in hiding nearby, waited patiently. When the moment seemed right, they swooped down on the unsuspecting British troops guarding the town's North Bridge.

The sudden attack by the Americans shocked the redcoats, who fled in a panic back toward Boston. The Minutemen followed, gathering more men along the path of pursuit. Together, these American farmers, artisans, servants, and shopkeepers terrorized the young British soldiers, firing on them from behind barns, stone walls, and trees; 73 redcoats were killed, 174 were wounded, and 26 were missing. The day after the Battles of Lexington and Concord, thousands of New England militiamen poured in from the surrounding countryside, dug trenches, and laid siege to Boston. As far as they and thousands of other Americans were concerned—including the loyalist refugees crowded into the city—war had begun.

The Second Continental Congress

When the Continental Congress reconvened in May 1775, it began at once to ready the colonies for war. This Second Continental Congress authorized the printing of American paper money for the purchase of supplies and appointed a committee to oversee foreign relations. It approved the creation of a Continental Army and chose George Washington, the Virginia veteran of the French and Indian War, to serve as its commander.

The Congress was clearly ready to defend Americans' rights and protect their liberties. But some delegates still hoped to find a peaceful solution to the crisis, despite the bloodshed at Lexington and Concord. This sentiment led the Congress to draft the Olive Branch Petition, which offered the king a

Minutemen Nickname first given to the Concord militia because of their speed in assembling and later applied generally to colonial militia during the Revolution.

☐ **Battles of Lexington and Concord** Confrontations in April 1775 between British soldiers and patriot Minutemen; the first recognized battles of the Revolution.

Olive Branch Petition Resolution, adopted by the Second Continental Congress in 1775, after the Battles of Lexington and Concord, that offered to end armed resistance if the king would withdraw his troops and repeal the Intolerable Acts.

The State House in 1778, from a Drawing at that date by CW Peale corrected by WI Breton.

The Pennsylvania State House in Philadelphia is best known to modern-day Americans as Independence Hall. It was here that the Declaration of Independence was debated and approved, and it was here that delegates gathered to draft a new Constitution for the United States in the hot and humid summer of 1787. Although the State House boasted large windows in the East Room where the delegates met, the shutters were tightly closed—to preserve the secrecy of the debates and to prevent the huge bottlenecked flies swarming throughout the city from entering the room.

choice: the colonists would end their armed resistance if the king would withdraw the British military and revoke the Intolerable Acts. Many delegates must have doubted the king's willingness to make such concessions, for the very next day the Congress issued a public statement in defense of the war preparations. This "Declaration of the Causes and Necessity of Taking Up Arms" boldly accused the British government of tyranny. It stopped short, however, of declaring colonial independence.

Across the Atlantic, British leaders struggled to find some negotiating points despite the king's refusal to bend. Almost two months before the battles at Lexington and Concord, Lord North had drafted a set of Conciliatory Propositions for Parliament and the American Continental Congress to consider. North's proposals gave no ground on Parliament's right to

American Prohibitory Act British law of 1775 that authorized the royal navy to seize all American ships engaged in trade; it amounted to a declaration of war.

◻ **Common Sense** Revolutionary pamphlet written by Thomas Paine in 1776; it attacked George III, argued against monarchy, and advanced the patriot cause.

tax the colonies, but they did offer to suspend taxation if Americans would raise funds for their own military defense. Members of Parliament who were sympathetic toward the Americans also pressed for compromise. They insisted that it made better sense to keep the colonies as a market for English goods than to lose them in a battle over raising revenue.

Cooler heads, however, did not prevail. Americans rejected Lord North's proposals in July 1775. The king, loath to compromise, rejected the Olive Branch Petition. George III then persuaded Parliament to pass an **American Prohibitory Act** instructing the royal navy to seize American ships engaged in any form of trade, "as if the same were the ships . . . of open enemies." For all intents and purposes, King George III declared war on his colonies before the colonies declared war on their king.

The Impact of *Common Sense*

War was a fact, yet few American voices were calling for a complete political and emotional break with Britain. Even the most ardent patriots continued to justify their actions as upholding the British constitution. They were rebelling, they said, to preserve the rights guaranteed English citizens, not to establish an independent nation. Their drastic actions were necessary because a corrupt Parliament and corrupt ministers were trampling on those rights.

If any American political leaders believed the king was as corrupt as his advisers and his Parliament, they did not make this view public. Then, in January 1776, Thomas Paine, an Englishman who had come to America a few years earlier, published a pamphlet he called *Common Sense*. Paine's pamphlet broke the silence about King George III.

Tom Paine was a corset maker by trade but a political radical by temperament. He directed *Common Sense* at ordinary citizens, not their political leaders. Like the preachers of the Great Awakening, Paine rejected the formal language of the elite, adopting instead a plain, urgent, and emotional vocabulary and writing style designed to reach a mass audience.

Common Sense was unique in its content as well as its style. Paine made no excuses for his revolutionary zeal. He expressed no admiration for the British constitution

The English political radical, Thomas Paine, arrived in the colonies in 1774. Two years later Paine wrote and published *Common Sense*, a widely read pamphlet appealing to Americans to declare their independence and establish a republic. Paine argued that men had the right and the ability to govern themselves, without king or nobility to guide or oppress them. When Paine dismissed George III as nothing more than a 'royal brute' he helped colonists cut the last ties to the Great Britain.

or reverence for the British political system. Instead, he attacked the **sanctity** of the monarchy head-on. He challenged the idea of a hereditary ruler, questioned the value of monarchy as an institution, and criticized the personal character of the men who ruled as kings. Paine put it bluntly and sarcastically: "Of more worth is one honest man to society, and in the sight of God, than all the crowned ruffians that ever lived." He dismissed George III as nothing more than a "Royal Brute," and he urged Americans to establish their own **republic**.

Common Sense sold 120,000 copies in its first three months in print. The impact of Paine's words resounded in the taverns and coffeehouses, where ordinary farmers, artisans, shopkeepers, and laborers took up his call for independence and the creation of a republic. Political leaders acknowledged Paine's importance, although some begrudged the popular admiration lavished on this poorly educated artisan whose flamboyant writing style they found unsuitable.

Declaring Independence

The Second Continental Congress, lagging far behind popular sentiment, inched its way toward a formal declaration of independence. John Adams fumed at its snail's pace. But finally, on June 7, 1776, Adams's close ally, Virginia lawyer Richard Henry Lee, rose on the floor of the Congress and offered this straightforward motion: "That these United Colonies are, and of right ought to be, free and independent States, that they are absolved from all allegiance to the British Crown, and that all political connection between them and the State of Great Britain is, and ought to be, totally dissolved."

Lee's resolution was no more than a statement of reality, yet the Congress chose to postpone its final vote until July. The delay would give members time to win over the few fainthearted delegates from the Middle Colonies. It also would allow the committee appointed to draft a formal declaration of independence time to complete its work.

To draft the declaration, Congress chose John Adams, Connecticut's Roger Sherman, Benjamin Franklin, and New York landowner Robert Livingston. But these men delegated the task of writing the document to the fifth and youngest member of the committee, Thomas Jefferson. The 33-year-old Virginian was not a social radical like Samuel Adams and Tom Paine. He was not an experienced politician like John Adams and Benjamin Franklin. And he lacked the reputation of fellow Virginians George Washington and Richard Henry Lee. But the committee members recognized that Jefferson could draw on a deep and broad knowledge of political theory and philosophy. He had read the works of Enlightenment philosophers, classical theorists, and seventeenth-century English revolutionaries. And though shy and somewhat halting in his speech, Thomas Jefferson was a master of written prose.

Jefferson began the **Declaration of Independence** with a defense of revolution based on "self-evident" truths about humanity's "inalienable rights"—rights that included life, liberty, and the pursuit of property. (In a later draft, the rights became "unalienable" and "property" became "happiness.") Jefferson argued that these rights were natural rather than historical. In other words, they came from the "Creator" rather than developing out of human law, government, or tradition. Thus they were broader and more sacred than the specific "rights of Englishmen." With this philosophical groundwork in place, Jefferson moved on to list the grievances that demanded America end its relationship with Britain. He focused on the king's abuse of

sanctity Saintliness or holiness; the quality of being sacred or beyond criticism.

☐ **republic** A nation in which supreme power resides in the citizens, who elect representatives to govern them.

☐ **Declaration of Independence** A formal statement, adopted by the Second Continental Congress in 1776, that listed justifications for rebellion and declared the American mainland colonies to be independent of Britain.

In 1776, patriots everywhere celebrated independence by destroying local symbols of royal authority. New Yorkers, however, combined the practical with the symbolic, tearing down an imposing statue of King George III that had stood near the tip of Manhattan since 1770 and recycling its lead to make ammunition for the Revolutionary army.

power rather than on the oppressive legislation passed by Parliament. All government rested on the consent of the governed, Jefferson asserted, and the people had the right to overthrow any government that tyrannized rather than protected them, that threatened rather than respected their unalienable rights.

The genius of Jefferson's Declaration was not that it contained novel ideas but that it contained ideas that were commonly accepted by most colonists. Jefferson gave voice to these beliefs, clearly and firmly. He also gave voice to the sense of abuse and injustice that had been growing in colonial society for several decades.

Declaring Loyalties

Delegates to the Second Continental Congress approved the Declaration of Independence on July 2, 1776, and made their approval public on July 4. (The text of the Declaration is reprinted in the Documents section at the end of this book.) As John Adams was fond of saying, "The die had been cast," and Americans had to weigh loyalty to king against loyalty to a new nation. In the face of such a critical choice, many wavered. Throughout the war that followed the Declaration, a surprising number of colonists clung to neutrality, hoping that the breach could be resolved without their having to participate or choose sides.

Those who did commit themselves based their decisions on deeply held beliefs and personal considerations as well as fears. For some of the perhaps one hundred and fifty thousand active loyalists, their commitment was a matter of personal character. Reluctance to break a solemn oath of allegiance to

the king or fear of the chaos and violence that were a real part of revolution could motivate a colonist to remain loyal rather than rebel. Many loyalists believed that tradition and common sense argued for acknowledging parliamentary supremacy and the king's right to rule. These colonists had an abiding respect for the structure of the British government. In addition, in their judgment, the advantages of remaining within the protective circle of Europe's most powerful nation seemed too obvious to debate, and the likelihood of swift and bloody defeat at the hands of the British army and navy too obvious to risk. Many of the men who articulated the loyalist position were members of the colonial elite. They frankly admitted their fears that a revolution would unleash the "madness of the multitude." The tyranny of the mob, they argued, was far more damaging than the tyranny of which the king stood accused.

For many colonists who chose loyalism, however, the deciding issues were economic. Holders of royal offices and merchants who depended on trade with British manufacturers found loyalty the compelling option. The loyalist ranks were also filled with colonists from the "multitude." Many small farmers in the Carolinas and tenant farmers in New York gave their support to the Crown when their political and economic foes—the great planters or the wealthy manor lords—became patriots. The choice of which side to back often hinged, therefore, on local struggles and economic conflicts rather than on beliefs about government and imperial issues.

For African Americans, the rallying call of liberty was familiar long before the Revolution began. Decades of slave resistance and rebellion demonstrated that black colonists needed little reminder of the value of freedom. Instead, many slaves viewed the Revolution as they viewed epidemics and imperial warfare: as a potential opportunity to gain their own liberty. In the same way, many free blacks saw the Revolution as a possible opportunity to win civil rights they had been denied before 1776.

African Americans had pointed out the inconsistencies of the radical position even before the Declaration of Independence. In 1773, a group of enslaved blacks in Boston petitioned the governor and the assembly for their freedom, "in behalf of all those, who...are held in a state of SLAVERY, within the bowels of a FREE country." Some white colonists appreciated these sentiments. In 1774, while John Adams debated the threat of political slavery for colonial Englishmen in the First Continental Congress, his wife Abigail observed: "It always appeared a most iniquitous [sinful] scheme to me—to fight ourselves for what we are daily robbing and plundering from those who have as good a right to freedom as we have."

It's Complicated!

Wander through your school library or your local bookstore. You might see a dozen books on the American Revolution by a dozen different historians. In fact, you might see many more. Ever wonder why?

It's not that historians can't agree on most of the "facts," that is, on *what* happened. The problem—or the challenge—is that we also want to explain *why* it happened. And with an event as dramatic as a revolution—and even with the most ordinary events like why a basketball team won a championship, or why the whole class failed a biology exam—we know that the answer won't be simple. In fact, if historians had a motto it would surely be "It's Complicated."

With most events, we start by asking, "What were the immediate causes?" In the case of the Revolution, we could look at the growing tension between England and the colonies after the French and Indian War. We could cite the end of salutary neglect, the Stamp Act, the Townshend Acts, the boycotts, the congresses, the political essays, the violence in Boston, the Coercive Acts, and the "shot heard 'round the world." This succession of events and actions might be thought of as the tinder for the blaze of revolution.

But we also realize that there were long-term causes that shaped the American and the British response to events in the 1760s and 1770s. Some were structural: the emergence of the colonial assemblies, their rising power, and the vested interest political leaders had in retaining that power. Some were economic: the growth of the notion that British regulation no longer protected but instead hindered economic growth and prosperity in the colonies. Some were ideological: the very different definitions of representation held by colonists and Parliament that led to misunderstandings and mistrust; or the conflicting interpretations of the new legislation, which colonists labeled as a sign of tyranny and political decadence, while the British government saw it as a necessary policy change.

Every historian tries to weigh these and other causes carefully. But we often disagree about how much weight to give each of them in explaining why the American Revolution occurred. If you were asked to explain the Revolution, what would you point to as its major cause? Was a clash of economic interests the driving force behind revolution? Were ideas and ideals the most powerful factor in the move for independence? Did self-interest motivate leaders more than principles? Did the personalities and character of leading figures shape events?

Not sure? Now you understand why your library shelf is filled with books about the American Revolution: because it's complicated.

In 1819, the noted artist John Trumbull recreated the moment when the committee assigned to draft a Declaration of Independence presented their handiwork to the full Continental Congress in 1776.

De Agostini/Getty Images

Peter Salem (1750–1816) was an African American soldier who fought in the battle of Concord on April 19, 1775, and later in the Battle of Bunker Hill. He reenlisted in 1776 and fought once again in the battles of Saratoga and Stony Point. After the war, he returned to his home state of Massachusetts where he died in a poorhouse at the age of 66.

Tom Paine agreed. Writing as "Humanus" in a Philadelphia newspaper, Paine urged white patriots to abolish slavery and give freed blacks western land grants.

Other patriots worried that slaves would seek their freedom by supporting the British in the war. Indeed, in 1775 the royal governor of Virginia, Lord Dunmore, expressed his intention to "arm all my own Negroes and receive all others that will come to me whom I shall declare free." Rumors of this plan horrified neighboring Maryland planters, who demanded that their governor issue arms and ammunition to protect against a slave **insurrection**. Throughout the South, white communities braced themselves for a black struggle for freedom that would emerge in the midst of the colonial struggle for independence.

When Dunmore did offer freedom to "all indentured Servants, negroes or others…able and willing to bear Arms who escaped their masters," he was more interested in disrupting the slave-based plantation economy of his American enemies than in African American rights. Yet slaves responded, crossing into British lines in great enough numbers to create an "Ethiopian Regiment" of soldiers. These black loyalists wore a banner across their uniforms that read "Liberty to Slaves." In the southern campaigns of the long war that followed, thousands of black men, women, and children made their way to the British lines. Once in uniform, black soldiers were usually assigned to work in road construction and other manual labor rather than participate in combat. Perhaps as many as fifty thousand slaves gained

insurrection An uprising against a legitimate authority or government.

their freedom during the war as a result of either British policy or the disruptions that made escape possible.

Indians' responses to news of the war were far from uniform. At first, many considered the Revolution a family quarrel that should be avoided. The revolutionaries would have been satisfied to see Indians adopt this policy of neutrality. They knew they were unlikely to win Indian support given the legacy of border warfare and the actions of land-hungry settlers. As early as 1775, the Second Continental Congress issued a proclamation warning Indians to remain neutral. But the British, recognizing their advantage, made strong efforts to win Indian support. Indian leaders proceeded cautiously, however. When a British negotiator boasted to Flying Crow that British victory was inevitable, the Seneca chief was unimpressed. "If you are so strong, Brother, and they but as a weak Boy, why ask our assistance?…You say they are all mad, foolish, wicked, and deceitful—I say you are so and they are wise for you want us to destroy ourselves in your War and they advise us to live in Peace."

The British continued to press for Indian participation in the war, and many Indian tribes and confederations eventually decided that the Crown would better serve their interests and respect their rights than would the colonists. First, the British were much more likely than the colonists to be able to provide a steady supply of the manufactured goods and weapons the Indians relied on in the eighteenth century. Second, colonial territorial ambitions threatened the Indians along the southern and northwestern frontiers. Third, an alliance with the British offered some possibility of recouping land and trading benefits lost in the past. No uniformity emerged, however. Intertribal rivalries and Indians' concerns about the safety of their own villages often determined alignments. Even among the Iroquois, pro-British Senecas burned the crops and houses of Oneidas who had joined forces with the patriots. In the southern backcountry, fierce fighting between Indians and revolutionaries seemed a continuation of the century's many border wars. But there, too, alignments could shift. Although the Cherokees began the war as British allies, a split developed, producing an internal civil war.

Fewer than half of the colonists threw in their lot immediately with the revolutionaries. Among those who did were people whose economic interests made independence seem worth the risk, including artisans and urban laborers as well as merchants who traded outside the British Empire, most large and some small farmers, and many members of the southern planter elite. For these Americans, it was not simply a matter of escaping unfair taxation. A release from Britain's mercantile policies, which restricted colonial trade with other nations, held out the promise of expanded trade and an end to the risks of smuggling. Sometimes the pressure for independence came from below rather than from a colony's political leadership, most notably in Virginia where many elite planters were pressed by more radical ordinary farmers to support independence or lose their positions of authority. Colonists affected by the Great Awakening's message of egalitarianism often chose the patriot side. Americans with a conscious, articulated radical vision of society—the Tom Paines and Samuel Adamses—supported the Revolution and its promise of a republic. Many who became revolutionaries shared the hope for a better life under a government that encouraged its citizens to be virtuous and to live in simplicity.

As Americans—of English, European, Indian, and African heritage—armed themselves or fled from the violence and bloodshed they saw coming, they realized that the conflict wore two faces: this was a war for independence, but it was also a civil war. In the South, it pitted slave against master, Cherokee against Cherokee, and frontier farmer against coastal planter. In New England, it set neighbor against neighbor, forcing scores of loyalist families to flee. In some instances, children were set against parents, and wives refused to support the cause their husbands had chosen. Whatever the outcome of the struggle ahead, Americans knew that it would come at great cost.

Individual Voices

JAMES OTIS JR.
Argues Against the Writs of Assistance

In 1761, the British government decided to reissue writs of assistance that would allow customs officials to search any premises for contraband without stating the exact nature of the materials they were seeking. James Otis Jr. served as the lawyer for the Massachusetts merchants opposing this policy. Some colonists believed this was the first salvo in the war for independence. In his courtroom presentation, Otis condemned the writs, as he explains in the following excerpt.

The Granger Collection, NYC.

❶ The fear of tyranny became a common theme in the protest against British policies in the years before the American Revolution. Would you say the policies of the king and Parliament rose to the level of tyranny?

❷ Jews and Christians believed that the Archangel Gabriel would blow a trumpet to signal Judgment Day.

❸ This phrase is an old English proverb, but the famous English jurist Sir Edward Coke frequently cited this notion and established the legal principle that no one may enter a person's home without permission.

It appears to me the worst instrument of arbitrary power, the most destructive of English liberty and the fundamental principles of law, that ever was found in an English law-book.... Every one with this writ may be a tyrant. ❶ ... Every man may reign secure in his petty tyranny, and spread terror and desolation around him, until the trump of the Archangel shall excite different emotions in his soul. ❷ ... a person with this writ, in the daytime, may enter all houses, shops, etc., at will, and command all to assist him ... even their menial servants, are allowed to lord it over us.... Now, one of the most essential branches of English liberty is the freedom of one's house. A man's house is his castle; ❸ and whilst he is quiet, he is as well guarded as a prince in his castle. This writ, if it should be declared legal, would totally annihilate this privilege. Custom-house officers may enter our houses when they please; we are commanded to permit their entry. Their menial servants may enter, may break locks, bars, and everything in their way; and whether they break through malice or revenge, no man, no court can inquire. Bare suspicion without oath is sufficient. ❹

❹ If you were the lawyer defending the use of these writs, what arguments would you make to justify their use in colonial Massachusetts?

Study Tools

SUMMARY

The British victory in the Great War for Empire produced many new problems. The British had to govern the French population in Canada and maintain security against Indians on a greatly expanded colonial frontier. They had to pay an enormous war debt but continue to finance strong and well-equipped armed forces to keep the empire they had won. To deal with these new circumstances, the English government chose to impose revenue-raising measures on the colonies.

The Sugar Act of 1764 tightened customs collections, the Stamp Act of 1765 placed a direct tax on legal documents, and the Townshend Acts of 1767 set import taxes on English products such as paint and tea. Colonists protested each of these sharp shifts in policy, for they saw Parliament's revenue-raising actions as an abuse of power. Political debate in the colonies began to focus on the possibility that the British government meant to curtail American liberties.

Crowds directed by the Sons of Liberty attacked royal officials, and in Boston five civilians died in a clash with British troops known as the Boston Massacre. But colony-wide boycotts of British goods proved to be the most effective form of protest. They led to the repeal of all three taxes.

Political activists prepared for a quick and united response to any new crises by creating organizations such as the committees of correspondence. In 1773 the British expected little American opposition to the Tea Act, but they were wrong. In Boston a group of activists dumped thousands of pounds' worth of tea into the harbor, enraging British officials, who as a punishment closed the port of Boston to all trade. This and other Intolerable Acts infuriated colonists, and they took united action in support of Massachusetts. A new colonial forum, the First Continental Congress, met in 1774 to debate the colonies' relationship to England and to issue a united protest, sending the king a Declaration of Rights and Grievances. But George III rejected the colonists' appeal for compromise, instead declaring that "blows must decide."

After British troops fought militiamen at Lexington and Concord, the Second Continental Congress prepared for war. Tom Paine's pamphlet *Common Sense* pushed many reluctant colonists into the revolutionary camp. In July 1776, Congress issued the Declaration of Independence, drafted by Thomas Jefferson, which defended the colonists' right to resist a tyrannical king.

In 1776 Americans faced the difficult task of choosing sides: loyalty to the Crown or revolution. African Americans and Indians had to decide whether to support one side or the other or try to remain neutral in the midst of revolution. For thousands, the outcome of this crisis of loyalty was exile from home and family. For others, it meant death or injury on the battlefield, widowhood, or life as an orphan. In 1776, however, its outcome was unclear.

CHRONOLOGY
Loyalty or Rebellion?

1763	Treaty of Paris ends French and Indian War
	Pontiac's Rebellion
	Proclamation Line
1764	Sugar Act
1765	Stamp Act
	Sons of Liberty organized
	Stamp Act Congress
	Nonimportation of British goods
1766	Stamp Act repealed
	Declaratory Act
1767	Townshend Acts
1768	Renewed boycott of British goods
1770	Boston Massacre
	Townshend Acts repealed
1773	Tea Act and Tea Party
1774	Intolerable Acts
	First Continental Congress
	Continental Association
	Declaration of Rights and Grievances
1775	Battles of Lexington and Concord
	Second Continental Congress
	Olive Branch Petition
1776	Tom Paine's *Common Sense*
	Declaration of Independence

Study Tools

FOCUS QUESTIONS

If you have mastered this chapter, you should be able to answer these questions and to explain the terms that follow the questions.

1. Why did Prime Minister Grenville expect the colonists to accept part of the burden of financing the British Empire in 1764?

2. How did colonists understand their obligations to the empire?

3. Why were the colonists alarmed by Grenville's 1765 stamp tax?

4. How did the colonists protest Parliament's taxation policies?

5. Why did Charles Townshend expect his revenue-raising measures to be successful?

6. What forms of resistance did the colonists use against Townshend's measures and what were the results?

7. What British policies led Americans to imagine a plot against their rights and liberties?

8. How did the king hope to crush resistance in Massachusetts and how did the Continental Congress respond?

9. What compromises were still available in 1775-1776 and how might the Revolutionary War have been avoided?

10. What motivated some colonists to become loyalists and others to become patriots?

KEY TERMS

George III *p. 101*
George Grenville *p. 102*
Covenant Chain *p. 102*
Pontiac *p. 102*
Proclamation Line of 1763 *p. 104*
Currency Act *p. 104*
Sugar Act *p. 105*
Stamp Act *p. 105*

Sons of Liberty *p. 106*
Samuel Adams *p. 106*
Thomas Hutchinson *p. 106*
Patrick Henry *p. 107*
Stamp Act Congress *p. 108*
boycott *p. 108*
Declaratory Act *p. 108*
Townshend Acts *p. 109*
Boston Massacre *p. 111*

committees of correspondence *p. 112*
Intolerable Acts *p. 113*
First Continental Congress *p. 114*
Battles of Lexington and Concord *p. 117*
Common Sense *p. 118*
republic *p. 119*
Declaration of Independence *p. 119*

SUGGESTED RESOURCES

"The American Revolution." Issue 21 of the online journal *History Now*. This issue offers highly readable essays by distinguished scholars on topics such as "The Indians' War of Independence," "Unruly Americans in the Revolution," and "Women and Wagoners: Camp Followers in the American War for Independence."

"Liberty! The American Revolution." (PBS DVD, 2004). Originally aired on PBS, in this three-part series actors tell the story of the Revolution in the words of its actual participants. Historians appear as commentators.

Gordon S. Wood. *The American Revolution: A History* (2003). A very readable narrative account of the events leading up to the revolution.

6

Re-Creating America: Independence and a New Nation, 1775–1783

INDIVIDUAL CHOICES

Esther de Berdt Reed

Esther de Berdt was born in London, but came to Philadelphia in 1770 as the bride of a young lawyer, Joseph Reed. She began her life as a colonial wife and mother in the midst of the crisis that would lead to the American Revolution. By 1778, her husband was the governor of the state of Pennsylvania and, though Esther had no formal political voice, she was determined to make her own contribution to the Revolution.

Working with Ben Franklin's daughter, Sarah Bache, Esther de Berdt Reed organized the first major fund drive in American history. Together these two "daughters of liberty" mobilized some of the most prominent Philadelphia women to go door to door, collecting money for Washington's army. Over fifteen hundred people contributed $300,000 in paper money and almost $7,500 in gold and silver. Reed shared her fund-raising plan with patriot women in Maryland, New Jersey, and Virginia, and they, too, collected money for the troops.

Realizing that the fund-raising campaign was a radical act for "proper women," Reed issued a bold statement entitled "Sentiments of an American Woman" that defended women's active participation in the patriot cause. Later, in this chapter's Individual

Courtesy of Andrew B. Reed.

Voices feature, you will be able to read part of her argument for women's entrance into the public sphere.

Reed did not live to see the full success of her plan. She died in September 1780 at the age of 34. She had shocked some Philadelphians by her actions, but many agreed with a French government representative who declared Esther de Berdt Reed "the most zealous and active" patriot the Revolution had inspired.

No matter what eighteenth-century Americans felt about the war, no matter which side they supported or what role they played, they shared the experience of extraordinary events and the need to make extraordinary choices when the war disrupted their lives. In this most personal and immediate sense, the war was as revolutionary for them as it was for the farm boys who would become, for a brief but critical moment, soldiers in the name of liberty.

Great Britain expected an easy victory over the colonial rebels and, on paper at least, the odds against an American victory were staggering. Great Britain could commit vast human and material resources to crush the rebellion. The well-trained and harshly disciplined British ground troops were assisted and supplied by the most powerful navy in the world, and they carried the flag of Europe's richest imperial power. Many Indian tribes, including most of the Iroquois, allied with the British, and the Crown could expect thousands of white and black loyalists to fight beside them as well.

The American resources were far less impressive. The Continental Congress had a nearly empty treasury, and the country had none of the foundries or factories needed to produce arms, ammunition, or other military supplies. Through most of the war, therefore, American officers and enlisted men could expect to be underpaid or not paid at all. They were likely to go into battle poorly equipped, often half-starved, and frequently dressed in rags. Unlike the British redcoats, these Americans had little military skill or formal military training.

Britain's advantage was not absolute, however. The British had to transport arms, provisions, and men across thousands of miles of ocean. They risked delays, disasters, and destruction of supplies on the open seas. The Americans, on the other hand, were fighting on familiar ground, and geography gave them an additional advantage: their vast, rural society could not be easily conquered even if major colonial cities were taken or an entire region was occupied. Long-standing European rivalries gave the Americans potentially valuable allies, since Holland, France, and Spain all stood to gain from England's distress. In 1778, when France and Spain decided to formally recognize American independence, the war suddenly expanded into a global struggle that stretched British resources thin.

THE FIRST TWO YEARS OF WAR

☆ What were the British and American strategies in the early years of the war?

☆ What decisions and constraints kept the British from achieving the quick victory many expected?

In 1775 General Thomas Gage, the military governor of Massachusetts and commander of the British army of occupation there, surely wished he were anywhere but Boston. The town was unsophisticated by British standards, many of its inhabitants were unfriendly, and its taverns and lodging houses bulged at the seams with complaining loyalist refugees from the countryside. Gage's army was restless, and his officers were bored. The American encampments outside the city were growing daily, filling with thousands of local farmers and artisans. These colonial militiamen were clearly the military enemy, yet in 1775 they were still citizens of the British Empire, not foreign invaders or foes. Gage, like his American opponents, was caught up in the dilemma of an undeclared war.

The Battle for Boston

The Americans knew that artillery could do serious damage to Gage's army in Boston, but they had no cannons. To obtain them, New Haven druggist Benedict Arnold joined Vermont farmer Ethan Allen, and in

Thomas Gage British general who was military governor of Massachusetts and commander of the army occupying Boston in 1775.

□ **militiamen** Soldiers who were not members of a regular army but ordinary citizens called out in an emergency.

□ **Benedict Arnold** Pharmacist turned military leader whose bravery and daring made him an American hero and a favorite of George Washington until he committed treason in 1780.

American artist John Trumbull painted "The Battle of Bunker Hill" in 1786, over a decade after the bloody encounter between redcoats and American militiamen. He had not witnessed the battle and thus the painting was based on secondhand accounts and Trumbull's desire to express the patriotism of his fellow Americans.

May of 1775 their troops captured Fort Ticonderoga in New York and began transporting the fort's cannon across hundreds of miles of mountains and forests to Boston. By the time the artillery reached the city, however, a bloody battle between Gage and the American militia had already taken place.

In early June, Gage had issued a proclamation declaring all armed colonists traitors but offering amnesty to any rebel who surrendered to British authorities. When the militiamen ignored the general's offer, Gage decided a show of force was necessary. On June 17, 1775, Gage's fellow officer William Howe led a force of twenty-four hundred soldiers against rebel-held Breed's Hill (see Map 5.2, page 116). Despite the day's oppressive heat and humidity, General Howe ordered his men to advance in full dress uniform, weighed down with wool jackets and heavy knapsacks.

amnesty A general pardon granted by a government, especially for political offenses.

□ **William Howe** British general in command at the Battle of Bunker Hill; three years later he became commander in chief of British forces in America.

Battle of Bunker Hill British assault on American troops on Breed's Hill near Boston in June 1775; the British won the battle but suffered heavy losses.

Howe also insisted on making a proper frontal attack on the Americans. From the top of the hill, Captain William Prescott's militiamen immediately opened fire on the unprotected redcoats. The result was a near massacre. The tables turned, however, when the Americans ran out of ammunition. Most of Prescott's men fled in confusion, and the British soldiers bayoneted the few who remained to defend their position.

Even battle-worn veterans were shocked at the carnage. The British suffered more casualties that June afternoon than they would in any other battle of the war. The Americans, who retreated to the safety of Cambridge, learned a costly lesson: an effective supply line of arms and ammunition was vital for victory. Little was gained by either side. That the battle was misnamed the Battle of Bunker Hill captured perfectly the confusion and the absurdity of the encounter.

Congress Creates an Army

In Philadelphia, the Continental Congress was busy taking its first steps toward recruiting and supplying an army. The "regular" army that took shape was actually a collection of small state armies whose recruits preserved their local or regional identities. This army was expected to follow the war wherever it led, while state militias were expected to join in any battles that took place within their own borders.

Congress chose French and Indian War veteran George Washington to command the Continental forces. Washington wrote gloomily of the task before him. Nothing he saw when he reached Massachusetts on July 3, 1775, made him more optimistic. A carnival atmosphere seemed to prevail inside the militiamen's unsanitary camps. Farm boys turned soldiers fired their muskets at random, often using their weapons to start fires or to shoot at geese flying overhead. In the confusion, they sometimes accidentally wounded or killed themselves and others. "Seldom a day passes but some persons are shot by their friends," Washington noted in amazement. He was disturbed but not surprised by what he saw. He knew that the men in these camps were country boys, away from home for the first time in their lives. The chaos they created resulted from a combination of fear, excitement, boredom, inexperience, and plain homesickness. Despite his sympathy for these young men, Washington acted quickly to reorganize the militia units, replace incompetent officers, and tighten discipline within the camps.

The British meanwhile laid plans to evacuate Boston, spurred in part by the knowledge that Arnold's wagon train of cannon was nearing Massachusetts. In March 1776 a fleet carried Thomas Gage, his officers, the British army, and almost a thousand loyalist refugees north to the safety of Halifax, Nova Scotia. The king now turned the war over to two brothers, General William Howe and Admiral Richard Howe. Their assignment was clear: bring the rebellion to a speedy end.

The British Strategy in 1776

General Howe's strategy was to locate areas with high concentrations of loyalists and use these Americans to secure the allegiance of their undecided and rebellious neighbors. Howe targeted two reputed centers of loyalist strength. The first—New York, New Jersey, Pennsylvania—had a legacy of social and economic conflicts that led many of the region's elite families to see independence as a threat to their prosperity. But loyalism was not confined to the conservative and wealthy. Among the poor settlers of the Carolina backcountry, decades of bitter struggle with coastal planters had led to the Regulator movement and to intense loyalist sentiment among the embattled frontier men and women.

General Howe's strategy had its flaws, however. First, although many people in these two regions were loyal, their numbers were never as great as the British assumed. Second, everywhere they went, British and hired Hessian troops left behind a trail of destruction and abuse that alienated potentially loyal men and women. Howe was not likely to win over families who saw wives and daughters raped and "cattle killed and lying about the fields and pastures...household furniture hacked and broken into pieces...wells filled up and...tools destroyed."

In 1776 Howe launched his first major military assaults in the South and the mid-Atlantic region. In North Carolina, loyalists did turn out to fight for the Crown, but the British General Henry Clinton failed to provide them the military support they needed. Poorly armed and badly outnumbered, Carolina loyalists were decisively defeated by the rebel militia on February 27 in the Battle of Moore's Creek. The British then abandoned their loyalist allies in favor of taking revenge on South Carolina. An impressive fleet of fifty ships and three thousand men sailed into Charleston harbor. But the Americans had unexpected good luck. Working frantically to defend the harbor, they constructed a flimsy fort out of local palmetto wood. To the surprise of both sides, the cannon balls fired by British ships sank harmlessly into the absorbent, pulpy palmetto stockade. The fort—and the city of Charleston—remained standing.

Embarrassed and frustrated, the British abruptly ended the southern campaign, and General Clinton sailed north. The North and South Carolina loyalists, however, could not escape British failures. They had been denounced, mobbed, imprisoned, and sometimes tortured since 1775. Their situation grew even worse after the British withdrew.

Escape from New York

While Clinton was failing in the Carolinas, the Howe brothers were preparing a massive invasion of the mid-Atlantic region. In July 1776, the Howes sailed into New York harbor with the largest expeditionary force of the eighteenth century. With thirty thousand men, one-third of them Hessian mercenaries, this British army was larger than the peacetime population of New York City.

The Howes did not plan to demolish New York, however. Unlike most British officers, the brothers were genuinely fond of Americans, and they preferred to be agents of compromise and negotiation rather than of destruction. They hoped that a spectacular show of force and a thorough humiliation of rebel

George Washington Commander in chief of the Continental Army; he led Americans to victory in the Revolution and later became the first president of the United States.

☐ **Richard Howe** British admiral who commanded British naval forces in America; he was General William Howe's brother.

Hessian troops German soldiers from the state of Hesse who were hired by Britain to fight in the American Revolution.

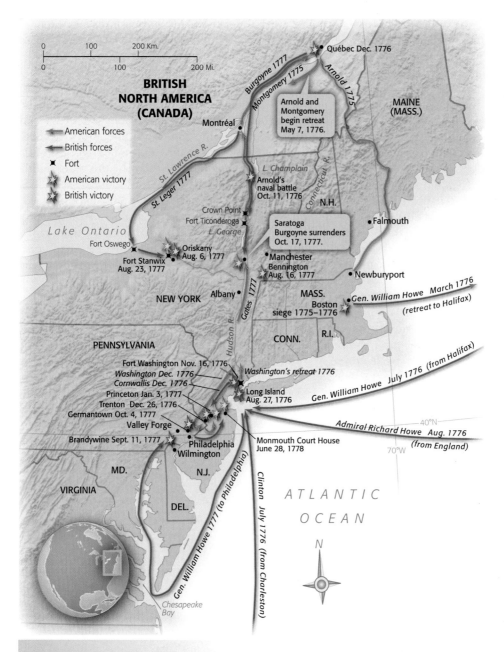

MAP 6.1 The War in the North
This map details the movements of both British and American troops during the Northern Campaign, and it indicates the victories and defeats for both armies. The American attempt to capture Canada and General George Washington's effort to save New York from British occupation were failures, but Washington did manage to stage successful raids in New Jersey before retreating to safety in the winter of 1777. Discussion of Burgoyne's failed New York campaign begins on the next page.
© Cengage Learning.

commander George Washington would be enough to bring the Americans to their senses.

General Washington rushed his army south from Massachusetts to defend the city, but he had few illusions that his twenty-three thousand men, many of them sick and most of them inexperienced at war, could repel the invading British forces. For a month, the Howes made no move on the city. Finally, on the morning of August 22, 1776, the British began their advance, landing unopposed and moving toward the Brooklyn neck of Long Island (see Map 6.1). Just as Washington had feared, five days later when fighting began almost all of his raw and inexperienced troops surrendered or ran. Washington, at the scene himself, might have been captured had the Howes pressed their advantage. But they withdrew, content that they had made the American commander look foolish.

Washington took advantage of the Howes' delay to bring his troops to the safety of Manhattan Island. But on September 15, a British attack again sent his army into flight. Angry and frustrated, Washington threw his hat to the ground and shouted, "Are these the men with whom I am to defend America!"

Washington's army fled north with the British in hot pursuit. In a skirmish at Harlem Heights, the American commander was relieved to see his men stand their ground and win their first combat victory. He was even more relieved by the strange failure of the British to press their advantage. When the redcoats finally engaged the Continentals again at White Plains, the Americans managed to retreat safely. Soon afterward, Washington took his army across the Hudson River to New Jersey and marched them farther west, across the Delaware River into Pennsylvania.

Winter Quarters and Winter Victories

Before the cold set in, General Howe established winter quarters for his troops in the New York area and in Rhode Island. He expected Washington to make camp somewhere as well. But Washington, safe for the moment in Pennsylvania, was too restless to settle in just yet. Enlistment terms in his army would soon be up, and without some encouraging military success he feared few of his soldiers would reenlist. Thus Washington looked eagerly for a good target to attack—and found one: a garrison near Trenton, manned by two or three thousand Hessian troops.

On Christmas night, amid a howling blizzard, General Washington led twenty-four hundred of his men back across the river. Marching 9 miles, the Americans arrived to find the Hessians asleep. The surprised enemy surrendered immediately. Without losing a single man, Washington had captured nine hundred prisoners and many badly needed military supplies. Taking full advantage of the moment, Washington made a rousing appeal to his men to reenlist. About half of the soldiers agreed to remain.

The Battle of Trenton was a sweet victory, but Washington enjoyed his next success even more. In early January he attacked the British garrison at Princeton. On the way, his advance guard ran into two British regiments. As both sides lined up for battle, Washington rode back and forth in front of his men, shouting encouragement and urging them to stand firm. His reckless behavior put him squarely in the line of fire, but it was effective. When the British turned in retreat, Washington rashly rode after them, clearly delighted to be in pursuit for once in the war.

The Trenton and Princeton victories raised the morale of the Continental Army as it settled at last into its winter quarters near Morristown, New Jersey. They also stirred popular support for the raids that many called Washington's "nine-day wonder."

Of course, General Howe was still poised to march on Philadelphia when warm weather returned. And Congress still had few resources to spare for Washington's army. When Washington pleaded for supplies, Congress urged him to commandeer what he needed from civilians nearby. The general wisely refused. English high-handedness and cruelty had turned many people of the area into staunch supporters of the Revolution, and Washington had no intention of alienating them.

Burgoyne's New York Campaign

In July 1777 General William Howe sailed up the Chesapeake Bay toward Philadelphia with fifteen thousand men. The Continental Congress had already fled the city, knowing that Washington could not prevent the enemy occupation, and the British had little difficulty capturing Philadelphia. The problems they did face in 1777 came from the poor judgment of a flamboyant young British general named John Burgoyne.

Burgoyne had won approval for an elaborate plan to separate New England from the rest of the American colonies. He would move his army south from Montreal, while a second army of redcoats and Iroquois, commanded by Colonel Barry St. Leger, would veer east across the Mohawk Valley from Fort Oswego. At the same time, William Howe would send a third force north from New York City. The three armies would rendezvous at Albany, effectively isolating New England and, it was assumed, giving the British a perfect opportunity to crush the rebellion.

On paper, this daring plan seemed to have every chance of success. In reality, however, it had serious flaws. First, neither Burgoyne nor the British officials in England had any knowledge of the American terrain that had to be covered. Second, they badly misjudged the Indian support St. Leger would receive. Third, General Howe, no longer in New York City, knew absolutely nothing of his own critical role in the plan. Blissfully unaware of these problems, Burgoyne and his army began their march southward from Montreal in June 1777 (see Map 6.1). The troops floated down Lake Champlain in canoes and flat-bottom boats and easily retook Fort Ticonderoga. But from this point on, things began to go badly for Burgoyne.

In true eighteenth-century British style, Burgoyne chose to travel well rather than lightly. The thirty

□ **Battle of Trenton** Battle on December 26, 1776, when Washington led his troops by night across the Delaware River and captured a Hessian garrison wintering in New Jersey.

□ **John Burgoyne** British general forced to surrender his entire army at Saratoga, New York, in October 1777.

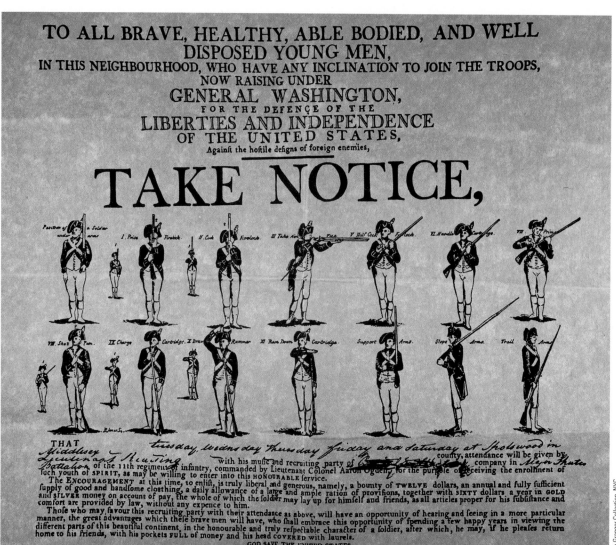

This recruiting poster for the Continental Army invites young men to join in the defense of American liberty and independence. The bounty of $12, along with "good and handsome clothing," a daily allowance of provisions, and $60 a year paid in gold, tempted many poor farm and city boys.

wagons moving slowly behind the general contained over fifty pieces of artillery for the campaign. They also contained Burgoyne's mistress, her personal wardrobe and his, and a generous supply of champagne. When this caravan encountered New York's swamps and gullies, movement slowed to a snail's pace. Ethan Allen and his Green Mountain Boys added to Burgoyne's problems by harassing his troops as they entered Vermont. A bloody, head-on battle near Bennington further slowed Burgoyne's progress. Then, when the general's army finally reached Albany in mid-September, neither St. Leger nor Howe were in sight.

The degree of Iroquois support St. Leger had counted on failed to materialize, and he met fierce resistance in the Mohawk Valley. When news reached him that Benedict Arnold and an army of a thousand

Americans were approaching, St. Leger simply turned around and took his exhausted men to the safety of Fort Niagara. Howe, of course, had no idea that he was expected in Albany. This left John Burgoyne stranded in the heart of New York with dangerously low supplies and a hungry and tired army. On September 19, Burgoyne attacked the American lines, hoping to clear a path of retreat toward Canada. The American general, Horatio "Granny" Gates, was neither bold nor particularly clever, but it took little daring or genius to defeat Burgoyne's weary soldiers. On October 17, 1777, General John Burgoyne surrendered.

On both sides of the Atlantic, news that a major British army had been defeated was a powerful boost to American confidence and an equally powerful blow to British self-esteem. The rebel victory also reversed the fortunes of American diplomatic efforts. Until the Battle of Saratoga, American appeals to Spain, France, and Holland for supplies, loans, and military support had met with only moderate success. Now, hopes ran high that Britain's rivals would recognize independence and join the war effort.

Winter Quarters in 1777

John Adams, who never wore a uniform, had once toasted a "short and Violent war." After Burgoyne's defeat, many Americans believed that Adams's wish was coming true. General Washington, however, did not share their optimism. French help might be coming, he pointed out, but who knew when? In the meantime, he reminded Congress, his army still needed funds and supplies. Congress ignored all his urgent requests. The result was the long and dreadful winter at Valley Forge, twenty miles from Philadelphia, where General Howe and his army were comfortably housed for the winter. Throughout December 1777, Washington's men labored to build the huts and cabins they needed not only for themselves but also for the hundreds of women and children who flocked to the safety of the camp. The presence of enlisted men's families, fleeing starvation or physical abuse by enemy soldiers, transformed the army camp into a crowded temporary city. Washington could not turn these families away, so he quickly set the women to work cooking, laundering, and nursing sick soldiers.

Rations were a problem from the start. Most soldiers and civilians at Valley Forge lived primarily on a diet of fire cakes, made of flour and water baked on the fire. Blankets were scarce, coats were rare, and firewood was precious. An army doctor summed up conditions when he wrote: "Poor food—hard lodgings—cold weather—fatigue—nasty clothes—nasty cookery—vomit half my time—smoked out of my senses—the devil's in it—I can't endure it." The doctor, however, did endure it. So did the soldiers he tended to daily, men such as the barefoot, half-naked, dirty young man who cried out in despair, "I am sick, my feet lame, my legs are sore, my body covered with this tormenting itch." While civilians in comfortable homes mastered the steps of the latest dance craze, the soldiers at Valley Forge traded the remains of their uniforms and sometimes their muskets for the momentary warmth and sense of well-being provided by liquor.

The enlisted men who survived the winter at Valley Forge were strangers to luxury even in peacetime. Most were from the humblest social classes: farm laborers, servants, apprentices, even former slaves. But if poverty had driven them into the army, a commitment to see the war through kept them there. The contrast between their own patriotism and the apparent indifference of much of the civilian population made many of these soldiers bitter. Private Joseph Plumb Martin expressed the feelings of most when he said "a kind and holy Providence" had done more to help the army at Valley Forge than "the country in whose service we were wearing away our lives."

These suffering soldiers did get one thing they desperately needed—professional military training. In the spring of 1778, an unlikely Prussian volunteer arrived at Valley Forge. Baron Friedrich von Steuben was almost 50 years old, dignified, elegantly dressed, with a dazzling gold and diamond medal always displayed on his chest. Like most foreign volunteers, many of whom plagued Washington more than they helped him, the baron claimed to be an aristocrat, to have vast military experience, and to have held high rank in a European army. In truth, he had purchased his title only a short time before fleeing his homeland in bankruptcy, and he had only been a captain in the Prussian army. He had not, however, exaggerated his talent as a military drillmaster. All spring, the baron could be seen drilling Washington's troops, alternately shouting in rage and applauding with delight. Washington considered von Steuben a most unexpected and invaluable surprise.

In the spring of 1778, Washington received the heartening news that France had formally recognized the independence of the United States. He immediately declared a day of thanks and issued brandy to each enlisted man at Valley Forge. American diplomacy had triumphed.

DIPLOMACY ABROAD AND PROFITEERING AT HOME

☆ What strategy did Benjamin Franklin pursue to win recognition from the French?

☆ How did the French alliance affect the war effort and wartime spending?

Like most wars, the American Revolution was not confined to the battlefields. Diplomacy was essential, and American diplomats hoped to secure supplies, safe harbors for American ships, and if at all possible, formal recognition of independence and open military

□ **Battle of Saratoga** American victory in October 1777 that helped convince France to openly aid the American rebellion and turned the tide in the war.

□ **Valley Forge** Winter encampment of Washington's army in Pennsylvania in 1777–1778, where the soldiers suffered greatly from cold and hunger.

□ **Baron Friedrich von Steuben** Prussian military officer who served as Washington's drillmaster at Valley Forge, helping to turn American soldiers into a disciplined army.

Friedrich Wilhelm Augustus von Steuben, or Baron von Steuben, came to America in 1777 and served as an effective drillmaster to General George Washington's troops at Valley Forge. Because he spoke little or no English, he swore and yelled at the troops in German and French. When this proved ineffective, he instructed his French-speaking aide to deliver the curses for him in English!

assistance. General Burgoyne's defeat made the widening of the war into an international struggle a real possibility.

The Long Road to Formal Recognition

In 1776 England had many enemies and rivals in Europe who were only too happy to see George III expend his resources and military personnel to quell a colonial rebellion. Although these nations expected the American Revolution to fail, they were eager to keep the conflict going as long as possible. Before Saratoga, they preferred to keep their support for the Revolution unofficial. After Saratoga, the Americans had reason to hope for more.

In December 1776, Congress had sent the printer-politician-scientist **Benjamin Franklin** to France to pursue formal recognition of American independence. The charming and witty Franklin was the toast of Paris, adored by aristocrats and common people alike, but even he could not persuade the king to support the Revolution openly. Burgoyne's surrender changed everything. The British government had begun scrambling to end a war that had turned embarrassing, and the French government began scrambling to reassess its diplomatic position. If the American Congress

□ **Benjamin Franklin** American writer, inventor, scientist, and diplomat instrumental in bringing about a French alliance with the United States in 1778; he later helped negotiate the treaty ending the war.

agreed to a compromise ending the rebellion, France could gain nothing more. But if the French helped keep the war alive, perhaps they could recoup some of the territory and prestige lost to England in the Seven Years War. This meant, of course, recognizing the United States and entering a war with Britain. French foreign minister Charles Gravier, comte de Vergennes, knew a choice had to be made—but he was not yet certain what to do.

Meanwhile, the English government was indeed preparing a new peace offer for Congress. The king was willing to make large concessions: he would agree never to tax the colonies again and to repeal any objectionable legislation such as the Intolerable Acts that had been passed since 1763. The Americans, however, were unimpressed by this offer. For Congress, a return to colonial status was now unthinkable.

Benjamin Franklin knew that Congress would reject the king's offer. But he was too shrewd to relieve the comte de Vergennes's fear that a compromise was in the works. Franklin warned that France must act quickly and decisively or accept the consequences. His gamble worked, and in 1778 France and the United States signed a treaty linking French and American fates tightly together. Under its provisions neither country could make a separate peace with Great Britain. By 1779, Spain had also formally acknowledged the United States, and in 1780 the Netherlands did so too. George III had little choice but to declare war against these European nations.

The Revolution had thus grown into an international struggle that taxed British resources further

A Deeper Understanding of History

What's That Mean?

The impact of a political cartoon or a political poster usually depends on its use of familiar, easily recognizable symbols. Unless the viewer is familiar with those symbols, the cartoon often makes little sense and has little power to persuade. Imagine, for example, that you did not know that the figure of Uncle Sam personified America. So if you saw a cartoon featuring a tall slim man, dressed in red, white, and blue, who is pointing his finger at the viewer and declaring "Uncle Sam needs you!" what might you think? "Whose uncle is this? I don't have an uncle named Sam. What does this man need me for?"

American political cartoons have had a number of stock, repeating symbols: for example, Uncle Sam, a screaming eagle, a donkey and an elephant, a woman dressed in a long flowing white robe, holding a lamp or a sword or perhaps a scale, a pair of shackles, or a snake cut into several pieces. You will probably recognize these as a form of shorthand for the U.S. government, for the two major political parties, for Liberty, for slavery, and for the need for unity. Some symbols are more universal, of course, and are not tied to American history; for example, the dove means peace and the hawk means war in the symbolism of many countries.

There is an economy in every good political cartoon; that is, nothing in it is extraneous, everything in it symbolizes or evokes something. Each element in the drawing is part of a story or a message the cartoonist wants to convey. If there is a caption to the cartoon, it too is there as a clue to the cartoonist's message.

Consider the cartoon below, drawn in 1778 when Britain sent a peace commission to America. There are six characters: five white men and an American Indian. The men are wealthy, for they are dressed in wigs and brocaded coats. Their posture—heads bowed and hands clasped as if in prayer—suggests that the words above their heads are pleas made to the Indian sitting elevated above them. The Indian, on the other hand, is almost nude, her only clothing a cloth draped over her lower torso and thighs, much like the women in Roman and Greek statues. Over her head a halo shines and in her right hand she holds a spear.

To interpret the cartoon, a viewer must understand who, or what, these figures and their attire represent. An eighteenth-century viewer would have no trouble deciphering the message. The clothing of the commissioners represents the decadence and love of luxury that American patriots believed led to the corruption into which the British government had sunk. The Indian, on the other hand, needs no silk or satins to convey her natural majesty.

The halo surrounding her head symbolizes purity and nobility, but the spear in her hand symbolizes a readiness to defend the realm she rules. She is a common symbol of America, vigilant in the protection of her people's liberty. Her authority and power rest upon the natural bounty of America—wheat, rice, tobacco, and other crops desired by the English and Europeans. Her head is turned away from the commissioners. She will not give in to their pleas or promises.

Once the symbols are deciphered, the message is clear: America will not surrender, it will not compromise with a corrupt Great Britain.

As you read through this textbook, look for other cartoons. Decipher their messages by decoding their symbols. Only then will the picture be worth a thousand words.

In this political cartoon, the members of a British peace commission, sent to America in 1778, make their offers of compromise to America in hopes of ending the revolution. While these men are dressed in wigs and brocade coats—representing luxury and decadence, America appears in the natural simplicity of an Indian woman. Notice however that this defender of liberty carries a weapon and sits confidently upon the agricultural bounty of a new nation.

and made it impossible for Britain to concentrate all its military might and naval power in America. Diverting ships to the Caribbean and to the European coast undermined Britain's blockade of American ports and its ability to transport troops. Above all, if the Americans could count on the cooperation of the French fleet, a British army could be trapped on American soil, cut off by French ships from supplies, reinforcements, and any chance of escape.

War and the American Public

News of the alliance with France unleashed an orgy of spending in America, especially among those who had profited from the sale of supplies to the army. The treaty with France meant that European goods could flow across the ocean once again, and Americans with money welcomed the chance to purchase them. Many of the goods imported into America over the next few years were actually British-made. A black market in English goods grew rapidly, for American consumers apparently saw no contradiction between patriotism and the purchase of enemy products. Optimism, cheap money, and plentiful foreign goods thus combined to create a wartime spending bonanza.

The government and the military also succumbed to this spirit of self-indulgence. Corruption and graft grew common as both high- and low-ranking officials sold government supplies for their own profit or charged the army excessive rates for goods and services. Cheating the government and the army was a game civilians could play, too. Wagoners carting pickled meat to military encampments drained the brine from the barrels to lighten their load so they could carry more. The results were spoiled meat, soldiers suffering from food poisoning—and a greater profit for the cartmen. Soldiers became accustomed to defective weapons, defective shoes, and defective ammunition, but many of them joined the profit game by selling off their army-issued supplies to any available buyers. Recruiters pocketed the bounties given to them to attract enlistees. Officers accepted bribes from enlisted men seeking discharges.

---

black market The illegal business of buying and selling goods that are banned or restricted.

cheap money Paper money that is readily available but has declined in value.

graft Misuse of one's position for profit or advantage.

□ **Sir Henry Clinton** General who replaced William Howe as commander of the British forces in America in 1778 after the British surrender at Saratoga.

General Charles Lee Revolutionary general who tried to undermine Washington's authority on several occasions; he was eventually dismissed from the military.

Congress seemed to be the only group unable to join in this spending spree. Bluntly put, by 1778, the government was broke. When Congress tried to deal with its financial crisis by printing more paper money, the result was rampant inflation. The value of the "continental," as the congressional paper money was called, dropped steadily with each passing day. The government's inability to pay soldiers became widely known—and enlistments plummeted. Both the state militias and the Continental Army resorted to impressment, or forced military service, to fill their ranks. Men forced to serve, however, were men more likely to mutiny or to desert. Officers did not know whether to sympathize with their unpaid and involuntary soldiers or to enforce stricter discipline upon them. Congress acknowledged the justice of the soldiers' complaints by giving them pay raises in the form of certificates they could redeem—after the war.

FROM STALEMATE TO VICTORY

☆ *What factors produced a stalemate in the war?*

☆ *What characterized warfare in the South and what led to General Cornwallis's surrender at Yorktown?*

☆ *What were the most important results of the peace treaty negotiations?*

The French presence in the war did not immediately affect its course. The war in the North fell into a stalemate because English generals had grown overly cautious and Washington could not mount a major campaign without the support of the French fleet. In late 1778, the active war shifted to the South once again, as the British mounted a second major campaign in the Carolinas.

The War Stalls in the North

Sir Henry Clinton, now the commander of the British army in North America, knew that the French fleet could easily blockade the Delaware River, cutting off supplies to occupied Philadelphia. So, as spring arrived in 1778, the British forces made their way east through New Jersey, en route to New York. Clinton's slow-moving caravan, with its long train of bulky supply wagons, made an irresistible target—and Washington decided to strike.

Washington entrusted a former British career officer, General Charles Lee, with the initial attack. Lee marched his men to Monmouth, New Jersey, and as the British approached, the Americans opened fire. Yet as soon as the British army began to return fire, Lee ordered his men to retreat. When Washington arrived on the scene, the pursuing British troops were closing in. Washington rallied the retreating

In the Wider World

Americans, calling on them to re-form their lines and stand their ground. Trained by von Steuben, the men moved forward with precision and speed to drive the redcoats back. The Battle of Monmouth was not a decisive victory, but Washington had saved it from becoming a defeat. He saw to it that Lee, who had long been a critic and rival, was discharged from the army.

If Monmouth was a disappointment, the first American and French joint effort was a disaster. In August a combined land and naval force targeted the British base at Newport, Rhode Island. But at the last minute, French admiral D'Estaing decided the casualty rate would be too high. He abruptly gathered up his own men and sailed to safety on the open seas, leaving Washington's American troops to retreat as best they could.

Throughout the fall and winter of 1778, Washington waited glumly for effective French naval support for a major campaign. The news coming from the western front did little to improve his bleak mood. In Kentucky and western Virginia, deadly Indian attacks had decimated many American settlements. The driving force behind these attacks was a British official named Harry Hamilton, nicknamed "Hair Buyer" because of the bounties he paid for American scalps. In October Hamilton led Indian troops from the Great Lakes tribes into the Illinois-Indiana region and captured the fort at Vincennes. The American counterattack was organized by a stocky young frontiersman, George Rogers Clark, whose own enthusiasm for scalping earned him the nickname "Long-Knife." To Washington's relief, Clark and his volunteer forces managed to drive the British from Vincennes.

Border conflict with Britain's Indian allies remained a major problem, and when loyalist troops joined these Indians, the danger increased. So did the atrocities. When patriot General John Sullivan's regular army was badly defeated by local loyalists and followers of Mohawk chief Thayendanegea, Sullivan took revenge by burning forty Indian villages. It was

The Bridgeman Art Library/Getty Images.

Mohawk chief Thayendanegea (Joseph Brant) believed that Iroquois lands would be lost if the Americans were victorious. He urged an Iroquois alliance with the British, fought for the British, and directed a series of deadly raids against settlements in New York. After the war—as Brant had feared—his people were forced to relocate to Canada.

Battle of Monmouth New Jersey battle in June 1778 in which Charles Lee wasted a decisive American advantage.

◻ **George Rogers Clark** Virginian who led his troops to successes against the British and Indians in the Ohio Territory in 1778.

◻ **Thayendanegea** Mohawk chief known to the Americans as Joseph Brant; his combined forces of loyalists and Indians defeated John Sullivan's expedition to upstate New York in 1779.

an act of violence and cruelty that deeply shocked and shamed General Washington.

Spring and summer of 1779 passed and still Washington waited for the French navy's cooperation. Fall brought the general the worst possible news: Admiral D'Estaing and his fleet had sailed for the West Indies under orders to protect valuable French possessions in the Caribbean and, if possible, to seize English possessions there. News of D'Estaing's departure spurred a new wave of discipline problems among Washington's idle troops. Mutinies and desertions increased. From his winter headquarters in Morristown

Heights, New Jersey, Washington wrote to von Steuben: "The prospect, my dear Baron, is gloomy, and the storm thickens." The real storm, however, was raging not in New Jersey but in the Carolinas.

The Second Carolinas Campaign

Since the fall of 1778, the British had been siphoning off New York–based troops for a new invasion of the South. The campaign began in earnest with the capture of Savannah, Georgia (see Map 6.2). Then, in the winter of 1779, General Henry Clinton sailed

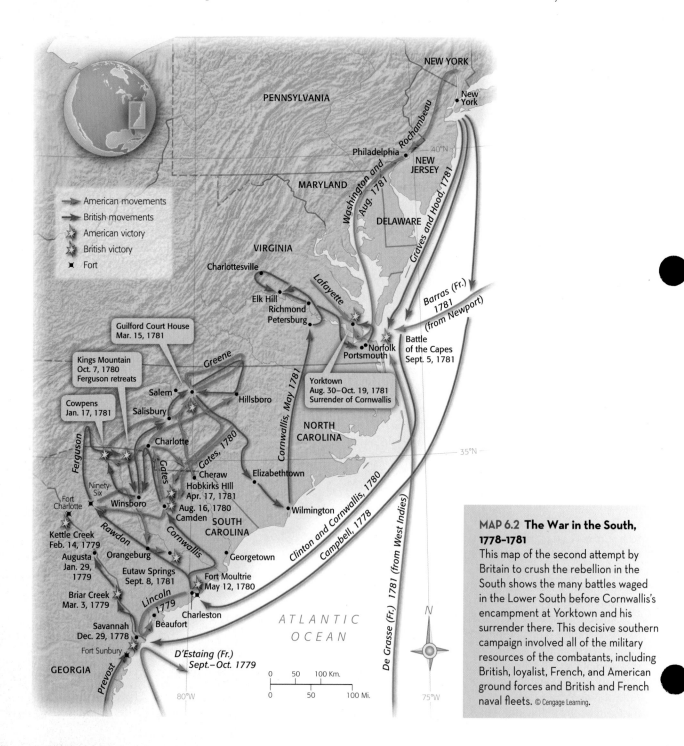

MAP 6.2 The War in the South, 1778–1781
This map of the second attempt by Britain to crush the rebellion in the South shows the many battles waged in the Lower South before Cornwallis's encampment at Yorktown and his surrender there. This decisive southern campaign involved all of the military resources of the combatants, including British, loyalist, French, and American ground forces and British and French naval fleets. © Cengage Learning.

for Charleston, South Carolina, eager to avenge his embarrassing retreat in the 1776 campaign. Five thousand Continental soldiers hurried to join the South Carolina militia in defense of the city. From the Citadel, a fortification spanning the northern neck of the city's peninsula, these American forces bombarded the British with all they could find, firing projectiles made of glass, broken shovels, hatchets, and pickaxes. From aboard their ships, the British answered with a steady stream of mortar shells. On May 12, 1780, after months of deadly bombardment and high casualties on both sides, the Citadel fell. The American commander, General Benjamin Lincoln, surrendered his entire army to the British, and a satisfied General Clinton returned to New York.

Clinton left the southern campaign in the hands of Charles Cornwallis, an ambitious and able general who set out with more than eight thousand British regulars, joined by loyalist troops as eager to defeat their enemies as Clinton had been. Since the British had abandoned the South in 1776, small, roving bands of loyalist guerrillas had kept resistance to the Revolution alive in a bloody civil war of ambush, arson, and brutality between the Carolinas' tidewater patriots and backcountry loyalists. By the summer of 1780, the fortunes in this war-within-a-war had reversed: the revolutionaries were now the resistance, using guerrilla tactics against the loyalists who were in control.

The revolutionary resistance produced legendary guerrilla leaders. Francis Marion, known as the "Swamp Fox," organized raiding bands of white and black recruits who steadily harassed Cornwallis's army and effectively cut British lines of communication between Charleston and the interior. Other guerrilla leaders, including Thomas Sumter, focused their energies on the loyalists. When these patriots and loyalists met head-on in battle, they honored few of the rules of war. In October 1780, for example, in the Battle of King's Mountain, revolutionaries surrounded loyalist troops and picked them off one by one. As this bitter civil war continued, marauding bands, often made up of outlaws posing as soldiers, terrorized civilians and plundered their farms.

The regular American army, under the command of the Saratoga hero "Granny" Gates, had little success against Cornwallis. In August 1780, Gates suffered a crushing defeat at Camden, South Carolina. That fall, Washington wisely replaced Gates with a younger, more energetic officer from Rhode Island, Nathanael Greene. When he arrived in South Carolina, Greene found that the fourteen hundred Continental soldiers who remained were tired, hungry, and clothed in rags. Their officers had been unable to prevent them from plundering local communities. To ease the strains caused by civil war and atrocities, Gates offered pardons to loyalists and proposed alliances with local

Indian tribes. In the end, he managed to win all but the Creeks away from the British.

Greene's military strategy was attrition: wear the British out by making them chase his small army across the South. He sent Virginian Daniel Morgan and six hundred riflemen to western South Carolina to tempt troops under the command of Banastre Tarleton into pursuit. Tarleton finally caught up with Morgan on an open meadow called the Cowpens in January 1781. When the outnumbered Americans stood their ground, ready to fight, the tired and frustrated British soldiers panicked and fled. Annoyed by this turn of events, Cornwallis decided to take the offensive. Now it was Greene's turn to lead the British on a long, exhausting chase. In March 1781, the two armies finally met at Guilford Courthouse, North Carolina. Although the Americans lost the battle and withdrew, British losses were so great that a disgusted Cornwallis ordered his army northward to Virginia.

Treason and Triumph

In the fall of 1780, one of Washington's favorite officers, Benedict Arnold, defected to the British. Although the Americans foiled Arnold's plot to turn over the fort at West Point, New York, to the British, his treason saddened Washington and damaged American morale. News the following spring raised Washington's spirits, however: French help was at last on its way. When Washington met with the French general Rochambeau in May of 1781, Rochambeau insisted on a move against Cornwallis in Virginia and had already ordered Admiral de Grasse and his fleet to the Chesapeake. Having little choice, Washington agreed.

On July 6, 1781, Washington's Continental forces and a French army began a long march from north of Manhattan to Virginia. The French soldiers, elegant in their sparkling uniforms, were openly amazed and impressed by their bedraggled allies. "It is incredible," wrote one French officer, "that soldiers composed

□ **Charles Cornwallis** British general who was second in command to Henry Clinton; his surrender at Yorktown in 1781 brought the Revolution to a close.

□ **Francis Marion** South Carolina leader of guerrilla forces during the war; known as the "Swamp Fox," he harassed British forces during the second southern campaign.

Battle of King's Mountain Battle fought in October 1780 on the border between the Carolinas in which revolutionary troops defeated loyalists.

□ **Nathanael Greene** American general who took command of the Carolinas campaign in 1780.

West Point Site of a fort overlooking the Hudson River, north of New York City.

When fighting in the Revolutionary war moved to the south, Loyalists as well as English soldiers served under the command of a bold Irish officer named Banastre Tarleton. Tarleton's men engaged in some of the most bitterly fought battles in what was not only a war for independence but a civil war in the Carolinas. Accused of allowing his men to massacre surrendering patriot troops, the young Lt. Colonel came to be known among the patriot forces as "No Quarter" Tarleton. Victorious American troops, however, often gave no quarter to surrendering loyalists as well.

Photo by MPI/Getty Images.

of whites and blacks, almost naked, unpaid, and rather poorly fed, can march so well and stand fire so steadfastly."

Within a few months, General Cornwallis too would be forced to admire the American army's stamina. Unaware that an enemy army and navy were headed his way, Cornwallis decided to move his own forces to the peninsula port of Yorktown. It was a choice he would heartily regret.

By September 1781, Washington's army had reached Virginia, and Admiral de Grasse's fleet was in place in Chesapeake Bay. General Clinton, still in New York, had been devastatingly slow to realize what the enemy intended. With most of the British fleet in the Caribbean, the desperate Clinton had only a single naval squadron to dispatch to Cornwallis's rescue.

Admiral de Grasse had no trouble fending off Clinton's rescue squadron. Then he turned his naval guns on the redcoats at Yorktown. From his siege positions on land, Washington also directed a steady barrage of artillery fire against the British, producing a deafening roar both day and night. On October 19, 1781, Lord Cornwallis admitted the hopelessness of his situation and surrendered. It is said that, at the surrender ceremony, a British army band played a tune called "The World Turned Upside Down."

□ **Yorktown** Site of the last major battle of the Revolution; American and French troops trapped Cornwallis's army on a peninsula on the York River near the Chesapeake Bay and forced him to surrender.

Despite the American victory at Yorktown, fighting continued in some areas. Loyalists and patriots kept on fighting in the South for another year, and bloody warfare against the Indians continued along the frontier. The British still occupied Charleston, Savannah, and New York. But the British had given up all hope of military victory against their former colonies. On March 4, 1782, Parliament voted to cease "the further prosecution of offensive war on the Continent of North America, for the purpose of reducing the Colonies to obedience by force." The war for independence had been won.

Winning Diplomatic Independence

What Washington and his French and Spanish allies had won, the American diplomats Benjamin Franklin, John Adams, and John Jay had to preserve. At first glance, these men made an odd trio. Franklin was witty and sophisticated; Adams, competitive, self-absorbed, and socially inept; Jay, aristocratic and reserved. Yet they proved to be a highly effective combination. Franklin brought a crafty skill and a love of strategy to the team as well as a useful knowledge of French politics. Adams provided the backbone, for in the face of any odds he was a stubborn and determined watchdog of American interests. Jay was calm, deliberate, and a match for Adams in patriotism and integrity.

Franklin, Adams, and Jay understood what was at stake at the peace table. They knew that their chief ally, France, had its own agenda and that England still wavered on the degree of independence America had actually won at Yorktown. Thus, the American diplomats

John Trumbull celebrates the surrender of Cornwallis at Yorktown in this painting. However, neither Cornwallis nor Washington actually participated in the surrender ceremonies. The British commander claimed illness and sent his general of the guards as his deputy. Washington, always sensitive to status and protocol, promptly appointed an officer of equal rank, General Benjamin Lincoln, to serve as his deputy.

issued a direct challenge to Britain: you must formally recognize American independence as a precondition to any negotiations at all. The British commissioner reluctantly agreed. Negotiations continued for more than a year, with all sides debating, arguing, and compromising until the terms of a treaty were finally set.

In the **Treaty of Paris of 1783**, the Americans emerged with two clear victories. First, the boundaries of the new nation were extensive (see Map 6.3). Second, the treaty granted the United States unlimited access to the fisheries off Newfoundland, a particular concern of New Englander John Adams. It was difficult to measure the degree of success on other issues, however, since the terms for carrying out the agreements were so vague. For example, although Britain ceded the Northwest to the United States, the treaty offered no provisions for Indian approval of the transfer of this land, and no timetable for British evacuation of its western forts. In some instances, the treaty's vague language worked to American advantage. For example, it included only a general promise that the American government would help British merchants collect the extensive prewar debts owed by Southern planters and an equally general pledge that the government would urge states to return confiscated property to loyalists.

The peacemakers were aware of the treaty's shortcomings and its lack of clarity on key issues. But this was the price for avoiding stalemate and dangerous confrontation on controversial issues. Franklin, Adams, and Jay knew the consequences might be serious, but for the moment they preferred to celebrate rather than to worry.

REPUBLICAN EXPECTATIONS IN A NEW NATION

☆ *How did the Revolution affect Americans' expectations regarding individual rights, social equality, and the role of women in American society?*

☆ *What opportunities were open to African Americans during and after the Revolution?*

☆ *What was the fate of the loyalists?*

As an old man, John Adams insisted that the Revolution was more than battlefield victories and defeats. The Revolution took place, he said, "in the hearts and the minds of the people." What he meant was that changes in American social values and political ideas were as critical as artillery, swords, and battlefield

◻ **Treaty of Paris of 1783** Treaty that ended the Revolutionary War in 1783 and secured American independence.

MAP 6.3 North America in 1783
This map shows the North and Central American territory held by the British, Spanish, French, and Russians in the year the United States became a nation. From the Great Lakes, to the Mississippi River, to the coastline of the Gulf of Mexico, the young republic was surrounded by the claims of nations more powerful than itself. It would be many decades before the United States could declare it stretched "from sea to shining sea." © Cengage Learning.

Territorial claims
- United States
- British
- Spanish
- French
- Russian
- Disputed by Russia, Britain, and Spain

strategies in creating the new nation. "The people" were, of course, far more diverse than Adams was ever willing to admit. And they often differed in their "hearts and minds." Race, region, social class, gender, religion, even the national origin of immigrants all played a part in creating diverse interests and diverse interpretations of the Revolution. Adams was correct, however, that significant changes took place in American thought and behavior during the war and the years immediately after.

The Protection of Fundamental Rights

The Declaration of Independence expressed the commonly held American view that government must protect the fundamental rights of life, liberty, property, and as Jefferson put it, "the pursuit of happiness." The belief that Britain was destroying these rights was a major justification for the Revolution. Thus, Americans were certain to demand the protection of these fundamental rights from their new governments.

The protection of many individual rights—freedom of speech, assembly, and the press, and the right to a trial by jury—were written into the new constitutions of several states. But some rights were more difficult to define than others. While many Americans supported "freedom of conscience," not all of them supported separation of church and state. Virginia approved George Mason's Declaration of Rights, which guaranteed its citizens "the free exercise of religion," yet that state continued to use tax monies to support the Anglican Church. It was not until 1786 that the Statute of Religious Freedom ended tax-supported churches in Virginia and guaranteed complete freedom of conscience, even for atheists. Other southern states followed Virginia's lead.

The battle was more heated in New England, where some wished to continue government support of the Congregational Church, while others simply wished to keep the principle of an established church alive. The compromise was to require every town to make one church its established church but to let the communities decide which denomination that would be. New England did not separate church and state entirely until the nineteenth century.

Protection of Property Rights

In the decade before the Revolution, much of the protest against British policy had focused on the right to private property and the government's duty to protect that right. For free, white, property-holding men—and for their sons and those white male servants, tenant farmers, or apprentices who hoped to join their ranks someday—life, liberty, and happiness were tightly connected to the right of landownership.

The property rights of some infringed on the freedoms of others, however. White American claims to western land denied the rights of Indians to that same land. A master enjoyed a claim to the time and labor of his servants or apprentices. In the white community, a man's property rights usually included the restriction of his wife's right to own or sell land, slaves, and even her own personal possessions. And the institution of slavery transformed human beings into the private property of others.

Even for white men, the right to property was sometimes an unattainable ideal. When the Revolution began, one-fifth of free American people lived in poverty or depended on the community's charity. For some, taking advantage of opportunities to acquire property was difficult even when they arose. Washington's Continental soldiers, for example, were promised western lands as delayed payment for their military service. But when they left the army in 1783, most were penniless, jobless, and sometimes homeless. They had

TOWARD A MORE PERFECT UNION

Separating Church and State

The founders of our nation knew their history. They had witnessed or read about the destructive religious wars that had plagued Europe for centuries, as Catholics battled Protestants, Puritans rebelled against Anglicans, and monarchs executed, banished, or harassed men and women they labeled as heretics to the established church. Even within their own new country, religious battles had led to bloodshed—in the conflict between Catholics and Protestants in Maryland and the hanging of Quakers in Massachusetts. Although many states were reluctant to give up the tradition of an official, or established religion, supported by taxes on all their citizens, the framers of the Constitution carefully avoided linking any religion or denomination to their national government. There would be no established church in the United States—and, with the Bill of Rights, "freedom of religion" became a founding principle of the nation. Individuals might practice any faith they wished, but they could not impose their beliefs on others.

little choice but to sell their land warrant certificates, trading their future as property owners tomorrow for bread and shelter today.

Although economic inequality actually grew in the decades after the Revolution, a republican commitment to social equality led to reforms that reshaped political realities in some states. Pennsylvania and Georgia eliminated all property qualifications for voting among free white males. Other states lowered their property requirements for voters but refused to go as far as universal white manhood suffrage. They feared that the outcome of such a sweeping reform was unpredictable. Even women might demand a political voice.

Women in the New Republic

The war did not erase differences of class, race, region, or age among women, but many wartime experiences were universally shared. Rich or poor, white or black, most women would remember the war years as a time of constant danger, anxiety, harassment, and unfamiliar and difficult responsibilities. As their men went off to war, these women took on the task of managing shops and farms in addition to caring for large families and coping with shortages of food and supplies. Some, like the woman who pleaded with her soldier husband to "pray come home," may have

feared they would fail in these new circumstances. Yet many spoke with satisfaction about their new roles. They expressed their sense of accomplishment in letters to husbands that no longer spoke of "your farm" and "your crop" but of "our farm" and even "my crop."

Some women found they enjoyed the sudden independence from men and from the domestic hierarchy that men ruled in peacetime. Even women in difficult circumstances experienced this new sense of freedom. Grace Galloway, wife of loyalist exile Joseph Galloway of Pennsylvania, remained in America during the war in an effort to preserve her husband's property. Shunned by her patriot neighbors, reduced from wealth to painful poverty, Grace Galloway nevertheless confided to her diary that "Ye liberty of doing as I please Makes even Poverty more agreable than any time I ever spent since I married." If Galloway experienced new self-confidence and liberty during wartime, not all women were so fortunate. For the victims of rape and physical attack by soldiers, the war meant more traditional experiences of vulnerability.

For women, just as for men, the war meant adapting traditional behavior and skills to new circumstances. Women who joined husbands or fathers in army camps took up the familiar domestic chores of cooking, cleaning, laundering, and providing nursing

A Society of Patriotic Ladies at Edenton. This anti-American cartoon published in London illustrates the negative response to American women's involvement in the protest against British policies. By signing a petition to boycott English goods, these women abandon their femininity and their domestic duties as mothers and become crudely and unattractively masculine.

care on a larger scale than in their own household. Throughout the war, loyalist and patriot women used traditional assumptions about women's nonpolitical nature to their advantage: they slipped unnoticed through enemy lines as spies and couriers; they turned their homes into havens for soldiers; and in their cellars they stored weapons along with food preserved for the winter.

Many such conscious acts of patriotism did not fit within traditional wifely duties. When women burned their crops or destroyed their homes to prevent the enemy from using them, they were acting as "daughters of liberty." And in the battle zones, women crossed gender boundaries dramatically. Although few disguised themselves as men to enlist as soldiers, many became accidental combatants. "Molly Pitchers" like Mary Ludwig who carried water to cool down the cannons in a fort under siege would take the place of fallen soldiers, loading and firing the weapons. After the war, female veterans like Margaret Corbin, who was wounded while firing cannon against the British army, applied to the government for pensions, citing as evidence the wounds they had received in battle.

In the postwar years, members of America's political and social elite engaged in a public discussion of women's role in their new republican society. The Enlightenment had dispelled earlier notions that women were incapable of rational thought, and women's many contributions to the war effort proved their capacity for patriotic commitment and political loyalty. Thus, opinion makers urged a new role for women within the family: the moral upbringing of their children. The republic, they said, must rely on wives and mothers to inculcate patriotism and republican principles in both their sons and their daughters.

This new ideal, "republican womanhood," had practical roots as well as intellectual ones. Even before the revolution, the growth of a prosperous urban class able to purchase many household necessities freed these urban wives and mothers from domestic production. Because they no longer needed to make cloth or candles or butter, they had time to devote to raising children. Republican womanhood probably had little immediate impact in the lives of ordinary free women who remained unable to purchase essential goods or to pay others to do household chores, or in the lives of African American or Indian women.

□ **Mary Ludwig** Wife of a soldier, William Hayes, at Fort Monmouth; one of many women known popularly as "Molly Pitchers" because they carried water to cool down the cannon their husbands fired in battle.

□ **republican womanhood** A role for mothers that became popularized following the Revolution; it stressed women's importance in instructing children in republican virtues such as patriotism and honor.

Although women's active role in the education of the next generation was often applauded as a public, political contribution, it did not lead to formal political participation for female Americans. The Constitution left suffrage qualifications to the state governments, and only one state, New Jersey, failed to stipulate "male" as a condition for suffrage in its first constitution, but this oversight was soon revised.

Communities were also given a critical role in educating future citizens. Arguing that a citizen could not be both "ignorant and free," several states allotted tax money for public elementary schools. Some went even further. By 1789, for example, Massachusetts required every town to provide free education to its children. After the Revolution, *children* meant girls as well as boys.

This new emphasis on female education was a radical departure for women. Before the Revolution, the education of daughters was haphazard at best. Colleges and the preparatory schools that trained young men for college were closed to female students. A woman got what formal knowledge she could by reading her father's or her brother's books. Most women had to be content to learn domestic skills. After the Revolution, however, educational reformers reasoned that mothers must be well versed in history and even political theory if they were to teach their children the essential principles of citizenship. By the 1780s, private academies had opened in every state to educate the daughters of wealthy American families. These privileged young women enjoyed the rare opportunity to study mathematics, history, geography, and political theory. Although their curriculum was often as rigorous as that in a boys' preparatory school, the addition of courses in fancy needlework reminded the girls that their futures lay in marriage and motherhood, not government or the professions.

The War's Impact on Slaves and Slavery

Liberty and freedom were major themes of the Revolution. Yet the denial of liberty was a central reality in the lives of most African Americans. To win their freedom, thousands of slaves had opposed the patriot cause and risked their lives to escape to the British army. In contrast, only about five thousand African American men joined the Continental Army once Congress opened enlistment to them in 1776. Black soldiers were generally treated better by the British, but in both armies they received lower pay than white soldiers and were often assigned to the most dangerous or menial duties. Slaves found other routes to freedom besides military service during the war. Some escaped from farms and plantations to the cities, where they passed as free people. Others fled to the frontier, where they joined sympathetic Indian tribes. Women and children, in particular, took advantage of wartime disruptions to flee their masters' control.

It Matters Today

Tracking Changes in Gender Roles

Eighteenth-century women like Mary Ludwig Hayes and Esther de Berdt Reed tested the limits of traditional gender roles, demonstrating bravery on the battlefield and political organizing skills during the American Revolution. But it would be over 140 years before their descendants could vote in a national election and decades more before they could serve in the military. The impact of this social change can be seen today in the accomplishments of women such as Lt. General Claudia J. Kennedy, the U.S. Army's first female three-star general; Sandra Day O'Connor, the first woman to become a Supreme Court justice; Madeleine Albright, the first woman secretary of state; and Shirley Chisholm, the first woman to run for the presidency of the United States. Tracking major changes in gender roles and examining why those changes occurred is a critical part of the historian's task.

- Do you think a woman president is likely to be elected in your lifetime? Explain the factors on which you base your opinion.

With American victory in 1781, thousands of former slaves boarded British transport ships, headed to what they hoped would be a better life in Canada, England, British Florida, or the Caribbean. But their dreams often went unrealized. Three thousand former slaves settled initially in Nova Scotia, but the racism of their white loyalist neighbors led more than a thousand of these veterans to emigrate a second time. Led by an African-born former slave named Thomas Peters, they sailed to Sierra Leone, in West Africa, where they established a free black colony.

During the war, loyalists had taunted patriots, asking, "How is it that we hear the loudest yelps for liberty among the drivers of negroes?" The question made the contradiction between revolutionary ideals and American reality painfully clear, especially to patriots in the northern states where slavery was not widespread or integral to the economy. In the 1760s and 1770s, influential political leaders such as James Otis, Thomas Paine, and Benjamin Rush campaigned to end slavery. In Boston, Phillis Wheatley, a young African-born slave whose master recognized

Scenes from a Seminary for Young Ladies, c. 1810–1820. One of the reforms that followed the Revolution was the movement to educate the young women of the new nation. Young ladies academies were established in all thirteen of the new states and for the first time girls studied geography and philosophy, history and political theory. The academies did not ignore domestic skills, however, and fine needlework, dancing, and singing were part of the curriculum. The purpose of the academies was not to produce merchants or political leaders but devoted mothers who would instill patriotism in their sons and daughters. Scenes from a Seminary for Young Ladies (Detail of girls & globe) St. Louis Art Museum, Purchase Funds Given by Decorative Arts Society /Bridgeman Art Library.

Phillis Wheatley was brought from Africa as a child. The Boston couple who purchased her encouraged her literary talent. Wheatley's patriotic poetry won approval from George Washington and praise from many revolutionary leaders. She died free but in poverty in the 1780s. Library of Congress.

and encouraged her literary talents, called on the revolutionaries to acknowledge the universality of the wish for freedom. "In every human breast," Wheatley wrote, "God had implanted a Principle, which we call

▫ **manumission** Freedom from slavery or bondage.

love of freedom; it is impatient of Oppression, and pants for Deliverance...."

Free black Americans joined with white reformers to mount antislavery campaigns in Pennsylvania, Massachusetts, Rhode Island, and Connecticut. In Boston and Philadelphia, slaves petitioned on their own behalf to be "liberated from a state of Bondage, and made Freemen of this Community." In the North, it proved easier to acknowledge the truth in the slave's cry: "We have no property!...we have no children!...we have no city!...we have no country!"

In 1780, Pennsylvania became the first state to pass an emancipation statute, making **manumission** a public policy rather than a private matter of conscience. Pennsylvania lawmakers, however, compromised on a gradual rather than an immediate end to slavery. Only slaves born after the law was enacted were eligible, and they could not expect to receive their freedom until they had served a twenty-eight-year term of indenture. By 1804, all northern states except Delaware had committed themselves to a slow end to slavery.

Slavery was far more deeply embedded in the South, where it was a labor system and a system that regulated race relations. In the Lower South, slaveowners ignored the debate over slavery and took immediate steps to replace missing slaves and to restore tight control over work and life on their plantations. Manumissions did occur in the Upper South. Free black communities grew in both Maryland and Virginia after the Revolutionary War, and planters openly debated the morality of slavery in a republic and the practical benefits of slave labor. They did not all reach the same

Pass for black loyalist, 1783. The British army promised freedom and land to African Americans who chose loyalism over rebellion. In 1783, thousands of black men, women, and children boarded ships with white loyalists, headed to Nova Scotia and a new life. Unfortunately, racism made them unwelcome in this Canadian refuge, and within a decade, many black loyalists relocated to Sierra Leone.

> 196   Qand M G / vol. 948
>
> NEW-YORK, 21st April 1783.
>
> THIS is to certify to whomsoever it may concern, that the Bearer hereof
>
> Cato Ramsay
>
> a Negro, resorted to the British Lines, in consequence of the Proclamations of Sir William Howe, and Sir Henry Clinton, late Commanders in Chief in America; and that the said Negro has hereby his Excellency Sir Guy Carleton's Permission to go to Nova-Scotia, or wherever else he may think proper. —
>
> By Order of Brigadier General Birch,

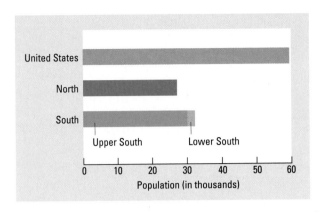

FIGURE 6.1 Free Black Population, 1790
This graph shows the number of free African Americans in the United States in 1790, as well as their regional distribution. These almost sixty thousand free people were less than 10 percent of the African American population of the nation. Although 40 percent of northern blacks were members of this free community, only about 5.5 percent of the Upper South African Americans and less than 2 percent of those in the Lower South lived outside the bounds of slavery. ©Copyright Cengage Learning

conclusions. George Washington freed all his slaves on the death of his wife, but Patrick Henry, who had often stirred passions with his spirited defense of American liberty, justified his decision to continue slavery with blunt honesty. Freeing his slaves, he said, would be inconvenient (see Figure 6.1).

The Fate of the Loyalists

After 1775, America's loyalists flocked to the safety of British-occupied cities, crowding first into Boston and later into New York City and Philadelphia. When the British left an area, the loyalists evacuated with them. More than a thousand Massachusetts loyalists boarded British ships when Boston was abandoned in 1776, and fifteen thousand more sailed out of New York harbor when the war ended in 1781. Altogether, as many as a hundred thousand men, women, and children left their American homes to take up new lives in England, Canada, and the West Indies.

Wealth often determined a loyalist's destination. Rich and influential men such as Jonathan Sewall of Massachusetts took refuge in England during the war. But life in England was so expensive that it quickly ate up their resources and drove them into debt. Accustomed to comfort, many of these exiles passed their days in seedy boarding houses in the small cities outside London. They lost more than servants and fine clothes, however. In a society dominated by aristocrats and royalty, loyalist men who had enjoyed status and prestige in America suddenly found themselves socially insignificant, with no work and little money. Loyalists in England grew more desperately homesick each day.

When the war ended, most of the loyalists in England departed for Nova Scotia, New Brunswick, or the Caribbean. Many of these exiles were specifically forbidden to return to the United States by the new state governments. Others refused to go back to America because they equated the new republican society with mob rule. Those who were willing to adjust to the new American nation returned slowly.

Less prosperous loyalists, especially those who served in the loyalist battalions during the war, went to Canada after 1781. Many of these exiles suffered depression and despair as they faced separation from family and friends and the bleak climate of Canada. One woman who had bravely endured the war and its deprivations broke down and cried when she landed at Nova Scotia. Like the revolutionaries, these men and women had chosen their political loyalty based on a mixture of principle and self-interest. Unlike the revolutionaries, they had chosen the losing side. They lived with the consequences for the rest of their lives.

Canada became the refuge of another group of loyalists: members of the Indian tribes that had supported the Crown. The British ceded much of the Iroquois land to the United States in the Treaty of Paris, and American hostility toward "enemy savages" made peaceful postwar coexistence unlikely. Thus, in the 1780s, Mohawks, Onondagas, Tuscaroras, Senecas, Oneidas, and Cayugas along with Delawares, Tutelos, and Nanticokes created new, often multiethnic settlements on the banks of the Grand River in Ontario. These communities marked an end to the dislocation and suffering many of these refugees had experienced during the Revolution, when steady warfare depleted Indian resources and made thousands dependent on the British for food, clothing, and military supplies.

ESTHER DE BERDT REED

Glories in the Usefulness of Women

Esther de Berdt Reed knew that many Philadelphians might consider her fund-raising drive for the Continental soldiers a scandalous undertaking. Proper women were not supposed to go door to door, talking to strangers and asking them to contribute to a political cause. To defend this fund drive, Reed issued a broadside entitled "Sentiments of an American Woman," in which she reminded her readers that throughout history women had risen up to support a just cause. She cited Deborah and Esther from the Old Testament, Queen Elizabeth I, and Joan of Arc as examples of patriotic women of the past. Could American women do less for the great cause of independence? We too, she declared, were "born for liberty." The following excerpt is from her defense of women's activism in the cause of liberty.

Courtesy of Andrew B. Reed.

❶ Reed uses the word "constitution" here to refer to women's mental and physical capacities. In the eighteenth century, many Americans still believed that women were intellectually inferior to men and physically incapable of contributing on the battlefield. How have our opinions and customs changed?

❷ Reed knows that some critics will blame her radical behavior on the fact that she is educated and knows about brave women in history. Do you think that education radicalizes people?

On the commencement of actual war, the Women of America manifested a firm resolution to contribute as much as could depend on them, to the deliverance of their country. Animated by the purest patriotism . . . they aspire to render themselves . . . really useful. . . . Our ambition is kindled by the same of those heroines of antiquity, who have rendered their sex illustrious, and have proved to the universe, that, if the weakness of our Constitution, if opinion and manners did not forbid us to march to glory by the same paths as the Men, **❶** we should at least equal and sometimes surpass them in our love for the public good. . . . Who knows if persons disposed to censure, and sometimes too severely with regard to us, may not disapprove our appearing acquainted even with the actions of which our sex boasts? **❷** We are at least certain, that he cannot be a good citizen who will not applaud our efforts for the relief of the armies which defend our lives, our possessions, our liberty. **❸**

❸ Reed defends women's entrance into the public sphere by insisting that the country is in a crisis and needs help from every citizen. Is she suggesting that women should only be politically active in times of war or catastrophe?

Study Tools

SUMMARY

In 1776, few patriots or loyalists believed that America could win its independence from Britain. The British outnumbered and outgunned the Americans, and their troops were better trained and better equipped. The Americans' major advantage was logistical: they were fighting a war on familiar terrain.

The early British strategy was to invade New York and the southern colonies, where they expected to rally strong loyalist support. This strategy failed, not only because they were waging war on unfamiliar ground but also because they had overestimated loyalist strength and alienated would-be sympathizers. Washington's hit-and-run tactics made it impossible for the British to deliver a crushing blow.

The turning point in the war came in 1777 when British general John Burgoyne's plan to isolate New England from the other rebel colonies failed. Burgoyne was forced to surrender at Saratoga, New York. The surprising American victory led to an alliance between France and the United States and the expansion of the war into an international conflict. The British invaded the South again in 1778, but despite early victories, their campaign ended in disaster when French and American forces defeated General Cornwallis at Yorktown, Virginia, in October 1781. Fighting continued for a time, but in March 1782, the British Parliament ended the conflict.

The Treaty of Paris was negotiated in 1783, and to the surprise of many European diplomats, the Americans gained important concessions.

Victory led to significant transformations in American society. Individual rights were strengthened for free white men. A republican spirit changed the outlook, if not the condition, of many Americans, as customs of deference gave way to more egalitarian behavior. The wartime experiences of women led American intellectuals to reconsider women's "nature" and their abilities. Although no state granted full citizenship, white women's capacity for rational thought was acknowledged, and their new role as the educators of their children led to expanded formal education for women. Black Americans also made some gains. Fifty thousand slaves won their freedom during the war by fleeing to the British or by serving in the Continental Army. Northern states moved to outlaw slavery, but southern slaveholders decided to preserve the institution despite intense debate. For most loyalists, black or white, the end of the war meant permanent exile from their homeland.

Independence had been won. But could it be preserved? In Chapter 7, you will read about the struggles of both the federal and the state governments to protect the young nation and preserve the liberties its citizens had fought to ensure.

CHRONOLOGY
Rebellion and Independence

1775	Battle for Boston
	George Washington assumes command of the Continental Army
1776	Declaration of Independence
	British campaigns in South and mid-Atlantic regions
1777	Burgoyne's New York campaign
	Battle of Saratoga
	Winter at Valley Forge

1778	American-French alliance
	British begin second southern campaign
1780	Fall of Charleston
	Treason of Benedict Arnold
	Pennsylvania enacts manumission statute
1781	Cornwallis surrenders at Yorktown
	Loyalists evacuate United States
1782	British Parliament votes to end war
1783	Treaty of Paris signed

Study Tools

FOCUS QUESTIONS

If you have mastered this chapter, you should be able to answer these questions and to explain the terms that follow the questions.

1. What were the British and American strategies in the early years of the war?

2. What decisions and constraints kept the British from achieving the quick victory many expected?

3. What strategy did Benjamin Franklin pursue to win recognition from the French?

4. How did the French alliance affect the war effort and wartime spending?

5. What factors produced a stalemate in the war?

6. What characterized warfare in the South and what led to General Cornwallis's surrender at Yorktown?

7. What were the most important results of the peace treaty negotiations?

8. How did the Revolution affect Americans' expectations regarding individual rights, social equality, and the role of women in American society?

9. What opportunities were open to African Americans during and after the Revolution?

10. What was the fate of the loyalists?

KEY TERMS

militiamen   *p. 127*

Benedict Arnold   *p. 127*

William Howe   *p. 128*

Richard Howe   *p. 129*

Battle of Trenton   *p. 131*

John Burgoyne   *p. 131*

Battle of Saratoga   *p. 133*

Valley Forge   *p. 133*

Baron Friedrich von Steuben   *p. 133*

Benjamin Franklin   *p. 134*

Sir Henry Clinton   *p. 136*

George Rogers Clark   *p. 137*

Thayendanegea   *p. 137*

Charles Cornwallis   *p. 139*

Francis Marion   *p. 139*

Nathanael Greene   *p. 139*

Yorktown   *p. 140*

Treaty of Paris of 1783   *p. 141*

Mary Ludwig   *p. 144*

republican womanhood   *p. 144*

manumission   *p. 146*

SUGGESTED RESOURCES

Carol Berkin. *Revolutionary Mothers: Women in the Struggle for America's Independence* (2006). A lively examination of women's many contributions to the American Revolution, including stories of female spies, saboteurs, and soldiers.

David McCullough. *1776* (2007). A highly readable account of Washington's victories and defeats during the first year of the war for independence.

Music of the American Revolution: The Birth of Liberty (New World Records audio, 1996). Twenty popular tunes sung by soldiers and civilians during the war.

Ray Raphael. *A People's History of the American Revolution: How Common People Shaped the Fight for Independence* (2002). Using diaries and letters of soldiers, women, farmers, enslaved African Americans, and others, Raphael shows us the revolution through the eyes of ordinary Americans.

Novia Scotia Museum. "Remembering Black Loyalists," http://museum.gov.ns.ca/black loyalists. Covers the history of African American exiles who settled in Canada after the war.

7

Competing Visions of the Virtuous Republic, 1770–1796

INDIVIDUAL CHOICES

Gouverneur Morris

Gouverneur Morris was one of the most brilliant men of his revolutionary generation. As the heir to a vast fortune, Morris was free to study political philosophy, languages, and the law and to travel widely. When the Constitutional Convention met in Philadelphia, this veteran of the war was eager to serve as a delegate from the state of Pennsylvania. When he rose to speak, which he did more often than most, his fellow delegates forgot about his damaged right arm and his peg leg—souvenirs of childhood accidents. Instead they listened with respect, or annoyance, to his insightful, bold, but often sarcastic comments on the issues facing the convention (see the Individual Voices feature at the end of this chapter). He viewed himself, he declared, as a representative of the "whole human race," not simply the people of Pennsylvania, and for their sake, he advocated the principle that the consent of the governed was fundamental in government. Whether they agreed or disagreed with his views, everyone acknowledged that Morris was a master orator and a gifted writer. It was no surprise, then, that the

Portrait of Gouverneur Morris (1752–1816) (oil on canvas), Sharples, James (c.1751–1811)/ Bristol City Museum and Art Gallery, UK/The Bridgeman Art Library.

delegates turned to him to bring clarity and organization to their work and to polish the language of their proposed Constitution. It was Morris who penned the preamble and who created the orderly list of articles in the document.

Unlike most delegates, Morris did not actively campaign for ratification of the Constitution nor run for office once the new government was approved. Instead, he left for Europe, spending a decade there before returning to his family's estate in New York. In Paris he watched the French Revolution's promise of liberty fall victim to the bloody Reign of Terror—a tragedy he was proud to say his own young nation had avoided. He knew, he wrote to a friend, that his nation's republican government had its flaws; but he "took it knowing all its bad qualities" because he loved its virtues.

Between 1776 and 1783, Americans fought to create an independent nation. But what kind of nation would that be? Most free white Americans embraced the idea of a republic. Yet a republic could take many forms, and Americans who enjoyed a political voice disagreed on what form was best.

During the years following the Revolution, Americans grappled with critical questions. How should power be divided between state and national governments? How should laws be made, and by whom? Who should administer those laws? What programs and policies should the national government pursue? How could the government be designed to protect the unalienable individual rights of free white Americans? These questions had to be answered, and soon.

The Articles of Confederation were the nation's first effort at republican government. But many political leaders believed this government was too limited in its powers to solve America's economic and social problems. In 1787 delegates to a Constitutional Convention produced a new plan of government, the Constitution. The result of many difficult compromises, the Constitution created a stronger national government, but Antifederalists, who opposed its adoption, argued that it threatened the basic ideals of the Revolution, especially the commitment to local representative government. Federalists argued that America's survival required the new Constitution. Leading patriots of the 1760s and 1770s could be found on both sides of this debate, but the Federalists carried the day.

The adoption of the Constitution did not magically solve all of America's problems. Tensions remained between competing visions for the new nation. Nevertheless, when President George Washington said his farewells to public life in 1796, most Americans were confident that their young United States would survive.

AMERICA'S FIRST CONSTITUTIONS

☆ *What types of legislatures did the states create?*

☆ *What were the major elements of the Articles of Confederation?*

☆ *What problems arose in ratifying the Articles?*

The writers of state constitutions were the first to deal with troubling but fundamental issues—in particular, the definition of citizenship and the extent of political participation. Could landless men, servants, free blacks, or apprentices enjoy a political voice? Should women with property be allowed to vote? These were exactly the kinds of questions John Adams feared might arise in any discussion of voting rights, or suffrage. They raised the specter of democracy, which he and most other revolutionary leaders considered a dangerous system. Once the question was posed, he predicted, "There will be no end of it . . . women will demand a vote, lads from twelve to twenty-one will think their rights are not enough attended to, and every man who has not a **farthing** will demand an equal voice with any other in all acts of state."

English political tradition supported Adams's view that political rights were not universal. Under English law "rights" were, in fact, particular *privileges* that a group enjoyed because of special social circumstances—including age, sex, wealth, race, or

farthing A British coin worth one-fourth of a penny and thus a term used to indicate something of very little value.

religious affiliation. In their first constitutions, several states extended voting rights to all free white men, a democratic reform but one that still set special conditions of race and sex.

The state constitutions reflected the variety of opinion on this matter of democracy within a republic. At one end of the spectrum was Pennsylvania, whose constitution abolished all property qualifications and granted the vote to all white males. At the other end were states such as Maryland, whose constitution continued to link the ownership of property to voting. To hold office, a Marylander had to meet even higher standards of wealth than the voters.

While constitution writers in every state believed that in a republic the legislature was the primary branch of government, they remained divided over other issues. Should there be a separate executive branch? Should the legislature have one house or two? What qualifications should be set for officeholders? Again, Pennsylvania produced the most democratic answer to this question, concentrating all power to make and to administer laws in a one-house, or **unicameral**, elected assembly, and eliminating the executive office. In contrast, Maryland and other states divided powers between a governor, or executive branch, and a **bicameral** legislature, although the legislature enjoyed the broader powers. Members of the upper house in Maryland's legislature had to meet higher property qualifications than those in the lower house, or assembly. Thus political leaders in this state ensured their elite citizens a secure voice in lawmaking.

Pennsylvania and Maryland represented the two ends of the democratic spectrum. The remaining states fell between these poles. The constitutions of New Hampshire, North Carolina, and Georgia followed the more democratic tendencies of Pennsylvania. New York, South Carolina, and Virginia chose Maryland's more conservative and traditional approach. New Jersey and Delaware took the middle ground, with at least one surprising result. New Jersey's first constitution, written in 1776, gave the vote to "all free inhabitants" who met certain property qualifications. This requirement denied the ballot to propertyless men but, because it did not stipulate "male" inhabitants, it granted voting rights to property-holding women. A writer in the *New York Spectator* in 1797 snidely remarked that New Jersey women "intermeddl[ing] in political affairs" made that state's politics as strange as those of the "emperor of Java [who] never employs any but women in his embassies." Nevertheless, for thirty-one years, at least a few New Jersey women regularly exercised their right to vote.

A state's particular history often determined the type of constitution it produced. For example, New Hampshire, South Carolina, Virginia, and North

The men who drafted the New Jersey constitution took care to include a property qualification for voting but forgot to specify the sex of an eligible voter. Thus women who owned property had the right to vote from 1776 to 1807, when state lawmakers corrected the "error," arguing that "the weaker sex" was too easily manipulated by political candidates to be allowed to vote.

Carolina, where the colonial governments had been dominated by coastal elites and lowland gentry, ensured representation to small farming districts in interior and frontier regions. The memory of high-handed colonial governors and elitist upper houses in the legislature led Massachusetts lawmakers to severely limit the powers of their first state government. The constitutions in all of these states reflected the strong political voice that ordinary citizens had acquired during the Revolution.

Beginning in the 1780s, however, many states revised their constitutions, increasing the power of the government. At the same time, they added safeguards they hoped would prevent abuse. The 1780 Massachusetts' constitution was the model for many of these revisions, building in a system of checks and balances among the legislative, judicial, and executive branches to ensure that no branch could grow too powerful or overstep its assigned duties. Most of these revised constitutions also restored wealth as a qualification to govern, although they did not allow the wealthy to tamper with the basic individual rights of citizens. In seven states, these individual rights were

unicameral A legislature with a single house.
bicameral A legislature with two houses.

safeguarded by a **bill of rights** guaranteeing freedom of speech, religion, and the press as well as the right to assemble and to petition the government.

The Articles of Confederation

But what of the national government? Soon after the Declaration of Independence was approved, the Continental Congress set about drafting a national Constitution. The frame of government they produced, called the **Articles of Confederation**, was primarily a response to the injustices that had led them to revolution. For example, because they wanted to avoid the tyranny experienced under King George III and the royal governors, the Articles eliminated the executive branch entirely. Because the colonial councils, or upper houses of the legislature, had been the domain of the richest and often the most conservative men in a colony, the Congress gave the Confederation a unicameral or one-house legislature. Because Britain's trade regulations had stifled American trade and kept colonies from expanding their markets, they gave the Confederation no power to regulate the new nation's commerce. In addition, the men who wrote the Articles refused to give the central government the power to tax. Most members of the Continental Congress shared the popular belief that only men the voters knew, who lived among them and shared their economic interests, had the right to impose taxes on citizens; that is, that the power of the purse belonged to local governments.

This highly restricted national government suited most voters, who expected their state governments to remain sovereign, independent entities. In 1776, it was reasonable to come together in a "league of friendship" to wage the war and make the peace, but most patriots would approve John Adams's characterization of the national government: "a Confederacy of States, each of which must have a separate government."

The debate over other clauses in the Articles revealed how eager the delegates were to protect and enhance the power of state governments. The majority of Continental Congress agreed that the state legislatures, not the voters themselves, should choose the members of the Confederation Congress. But they did not agree on how many members each state should have. Should the states have equal representation or **proportional representation** based on population? **John Dickinson**, who had written the first draft of the Articles, argued for a one-state, one-vote rule, but Benjamin Franklin insisted that large states such as his own Pennsylvania deserved more influence in the new government. Dickinson's argument carried the day, and the Articles established that each state was entitled to a single vote when the Confederation roll was called. The same jealous protection of state power also shaped the Confederation's amendment process. Any amendment required the unanimous consent of the states.

Arguments over financial issues were as fierce as those over representation and sovereignty. Because the Confederation would not have the power to tax, it was agreed that it should be supported by contributions from the states. But how was each state's share of the Confederation's operating budget to be determined? Dickinson reasoned that a state's contribution should be based on its population, including inhabitants of every age, sex, and legal condition (free or unfree). Southern political leaders protested this proposal. Because their states had large, dependent slave populations, the burden of tax assessment would fall heavily on slave masters and other free white men. In the end, state assessments were based on the value of land, buildings, and improvements rather than on population. The Continental Congress thus shrewdly avoided any final decision on the larger question of whether slaves were property or people.

When Congress finally submitted the Articles to the states for their approval in November of 1777, the fate of the western territories proved to be the major stumbling block to **ratification**. In his draft of the Articles, Dickinson had designated the Northwest Territory as a national domain. But states with colonial charters granting them land from the Atlantic to the Pacific Oceans each claimed the exclusive right to the lands beyond the Appalachian mountains (see Map 7.1). Delegates from Maryland, a state with no claim to western territory, dug in their heels, insisting that citizens of every state ought to have the right to pioneer the northwestern territories. Maryland's ultimatum—no national domain, no ratification—produced a long stalemate, but it finally ended when the states with western land claims ceded their claims to Congress. In 1781 Maryland became the thirteenth and final state to ratify the Articles of Confederation. Establishing this first national government had taken an agonizing five and a half years.

bill of rights A formal statement of essential rights and liberties under law.

□ **Articles of Confederation** The first constitution of the United States; it created a central government with limited powers, and it was replaced by the Constitution in 1788.

□ **proportional representation** Representation in the legislature based on the population of each state.

□ **John Dickinson** Philadelphia lawyer and revolutionary pamphleteer who drafted the Articles of Confederation.

ratification The act of approving or confirming a proposal.

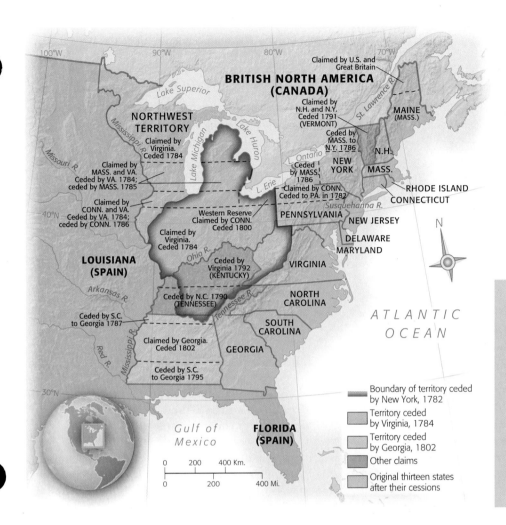

MAP 7.1 Western Land Claims After American Independence
This map shows the claims, based on colonial charters, made by several of the thirteen original states to land west of the Appalachian Mountains and in the New England region. Until this land was ceded to the federal government, new states could not be created here. © Cengage Learning.

Map labels:
- 100°W, 90°W, 80°W, 70°W
- BRITISH NORTH AMERICA (CANADA)
- Claimed by U.S. and Great Britain
- Lake Superior
- NORTHWEST TERRITORY
- Claimed by N.H. and N.Y. Ceded 1791 (VERMONT)
- St. Lawrence R.
- MAINE (MASS.)
- Claimed by Virginia. Ceded 1784
- Missouri R.
- Mississippi R.
- Lake Michigan
- Lake Huron
- Ceded by MASS. to N.Y. 1786
- N.H.
- Claimed by MASS. and VA. Ceded by VA. 1784; ceded by MASS. 1785
- Ontario
- Ceded by MASS. 1786
- NEW YORK
- MASS.
- 40°N
- L. Erie
- Claimed by CONN. Ceded to PA. in 1782
- RHODE ISLAND
- CONNECTICUT
- Claimed by CONN. and VA. Ceded by VA. 1784; ceded by CONN. 1786
- Western Reserve Claimed by CONN. Ceded 1800
- Susquehanna R.
- PENNSYLVANIA
- NEW JERSEY
- Claimed by Virginia. Ceded 1784
- DELAWARE
- MARYLAND
- LOUISIANA (SPAIN)
- Ohio R.
- Ceded by Virginia 1792 (KENTUCKY)
- VIRGINIA
- N
- Arkansas R.
- Ceded by N.C. 1790 (TENNESSEE)
- Tennessee R.
- NORTH CAROLINA
- ATLANTIC OCEAN
- Ceded by S.C. to Georgia 1787
- SOUTH CAROLINA
- Claimed by Georgia. Ceded 1802
- GEORGIA
- Red R.
- Mississippi R.
- 30°N
- Ceded by S.C. to Georgia 1795
- Gulf of Mexico
- FLORIDA (SPAIN)

Legend:
- Boundary of territory ceded by New York, 1782
- Territory ceded by Virginia, 1784
- Territory ceded by Georgia, 1802
- Other claims
- Original thirteen states after their cessions

Scale: 0 200 400 Km. / 0 200 400 Mi.

CHALLENGES TO THE CONFEDERATION

☆ *What problems faced the Confederation?*

☆ *What gains did nationalists expect from a stronger central government?*

☆ *How did the Confederation establish relations with other nations?*

The members of the first Confederation Congress had barely taken their seats in 1781 when Cornwallis surrendered at Yorktown and peace negotiations began in Paris. These political leaders realized that the new nation faced a number of daunting problems. The long home-front war had left physical, psychological, and economic scars. In New Jersey and Pennsylvania, communities were still recovering from the rape and looting by British occupying armies. In the South, where civil war had raged, a steady stream of refugees filled the cities. In New England postwar economic depression and food shortages became

worse when an insect attack destroyed the local wheat crops.

The postwar depression seemed to touch everyone's life. Four years after the American victory, Thomas Jefferson might boast that Americans "adore [their] country, its climate, its equality, liberty, laws, people and manners." But America's unemployed sailors, debt-ridden farmers, and destitute widows and orphans would have found it difficult to share his enthusiasm.

Depression and Financial Crisis

Financial problems plagued wealthy Americans as well as poor farmers and unpaid Revolutionary War veterans. Many merchants had overextended their credit importing foreign goods after the war. Wealthy land **speculators** had borrowed too heavily in order

speculator A person who buys and sells land or some other commodity in the hope of making a profit.

It Matters Today

Having a Vision for the Future

In 1791, Alexander Hamilton outlined his vision for the economic future of the United States. When Hamilton predicted that manufacturing would, and should, overtake agriculture as the basis for the American economy, he knew he would be setting himself against some of the most important people in the nation. Hamilton's *Report on Manufactures* was not adopted by Congress, but the ideas it set forth would eventually become central to the economy of the United States. Hamilton's belief that a strong central government with broad economic powers could encourage the fledgling manufacturing industries of the new country set the stage for this country to become the economic superpower it is today.

- Newly elected presidents often outline their vision for the nation's future in their inaugural addresses. Select one such inaugural address and analyze the vision it offers.
- If you had the chance to put forward your vision of the future, what priorities would you insist upon?

to grab confiscated loyalist lands or portions of the Northwest Territory. Southern planters were hard hit when the demand for staple crops such as rice dropped dramatically after the war. By 1786 the New England fisheries were operating at only about 80 percent of their prewar level. Not surprisingly, the English did nothing to ease the plight of their former colonists. In fact, Britain banned the sale of American farm products in the West Indies and limited American shipping there. These restrictions hit New England shipbuilding so hard that whole communities were impoverished.

The Confederation government was itself helpless to solve its own most pressing problem—debt. To finance the war, the Continental Congress had printed more than $240 million in paper money backed by "good faith" rather than by the hard currency of gold and silver. As doubts grew that the government could ever **redeem** these continentals for hard currency, their value fell rapidly. The scornful phrase "not worth a continental" indicated popular attitudes about a government that owed money both to its own citizens and to allies abroad.

redeem To pay a specified sum in return for something; in this case, to exchange hard currency, silver or gold, for paper money issued by the government.

◻ **Robert Morris** Pennsylvania merchant and financial expert who advised the Continental Congress during the Revolution and served as a fundraiser for the Confederation government.

◻ **tariff** A tax on imported or exported goods.

◻ **Northwest Ordinances** Three laws (1784, 1785, 1787) that dealt with the sale of public lands in the Northwest Territory and established a plan for the admission of new states to the Union.

In 1781 the government turned to Philadelphia shipper and merchant **Robert Morris** for advice on how to raise funds. Morris, known as a financial wizard, came up with a solution: ask the states to approve federal **tariffs**, or import taxes, on certain foreign goods. The tariffs would provide desperately needed income for the Confederation and relieve the states of having to contribute funding that many could scarcely afford. But even this modest plan failed. Both Virginia and Rhode Island said no, and, to add insult to injury, some states promptly passed their own tariffs on imported goods. The failure of the tariff strategy prompted one critic of the Confederation government to comment: "Thirteen wheels require a steady and powerful regulation to keep them in good order." Until Congress could act without the unanimous consent of all states, nothing could prevent the machine from becoming useless.

The Northwest Ordinances

The Confederation turned to the sale of western lands to solve its financial problems. Here at least Congress had the authority to act, for it could set policy for the settlement and governance of all national territories. In 1784, 1785, and 1787, a national land policy took shape in three **Northwest Ordinances**.

The 1784 ordinance established that five new states would be carved out of the region, each to stand on an equal footing with the older, original states. In the earliest stages of settlement, each territory would have an appointed governor. As soon as the number of eligible voters in the territory increased sufficiently, however, they could elect a representative assembly, and the territory could begin to govern itself. Once a state constitution was drafted and approved by the

MAP 7.2 **Competing Claims in the West, 1783–1796**
This map shows American westward settlement before 1800. Congress approved the eventual creation of five new states in the Northwest Territory, ensuring that the citizens of these states would enjoy the same political rights as those in the original thirteen states. But settlement in this region, as in the area west of Georgia, was challenged by territorial claims of Native American tribes. As the map indicates, the issue was settled in the 1790s by military action and treaty negotiations. French and Spanish claims west of the Mississippi and in Florida would prompt diplomatic efforts at treaty negotiations.
© Cengage Learning.

territory's voters, the new state could send elected representatives to the Confederation Congress. Ohio, Indiana, Illinois, Michigan, and Wisconsin would each follow this path to full statehood (see Map 7.2).

The ordinance of 1785 spelled out the terms for sale of the land. Mapmakers divided the region into five districts and subdivided each district into townships. Each township, covering 36 square miles, was broken down in a gridlike pattern of thirty-six 640-acre plots. Congress intended to auction off these plots to individual settlers rather than to land speculators, but when the original selling price of $1 per acre in hard currency proved too high for the average farm family, Congress lowered the price and lifted the ban on sales to speculators.

The ordinance of 1787 established that sixty thousand adult white males were needed for a territory to apply for admission as a state. Thomas Jefferson, who drafted this ordinance, took care to protect the liberties of the settlers with a bill of rights and to ban slavery north of the Ohio River. Yet these provisions trampled on the rights of American Indians whose claims to the land were ignored.

Diplomatic Problems

The Confederation's diplomatic record was as discouraging as its financial plight. Problems with the British and the Indians arose as settlers began to pour into the Northwest Territory. According to the Treaty of Paris, the British were to evacuate their western forts, but they refused to do so until the Americans honored their treaty promises to repay war debts and return confiscated property to loyalists. Instead, the British encouraged Indian resistance by selling arms and supplies to the Shawnees, Miamis, and Delawares who denied the legitimacy of the two treaties that turned over the northwest territories to the Americans.

In the Wider World

Rebellion

The last decades of the eighteenth century witnessed a number of revolutions, rebellions, and independence movements. In 1789, the year after the U.S. Constitution was ratified, French radicals stormed the Paris prison, the Bastille, setting in motion that country's revolution. In that same year, in the Portuguese colony of Brazil, colonists like Joaquim José da Silva Xavier were inspired by the American Revolution to give their lives in an attempt to win their independence. Two years later, men like Dutty Boukman led slaves on the French sugar island of Haiti in launching a revolt that became a decade of civil war and ended in the first independent nation in Latin America (see Chapter 8 feature, In the Wider World, page 190). And in 1798, in Ireland, a coalition of Protestants and Catholics led by men such as Henry Joy McCracken and Henry Munro would mount an unsuccessful revolt to win their independence from England.

American claims to western lands rested on the 1784 Treaty of Fort Stanwix and the 1785 Hopewell Treaties. But these treaties had not been approved by all the tribes of either area. The Shawnees and their allies challenged both treaties, arguing that other tribes had no right to speak for them. Throughout the 1780s, the Confederation and the Indians resorted to warfare rather than negotiation (see Map 7.2).

The Confederation preferred diplomacy to armed conflict when dealing with European powers. The new nation desperately needed trade concessions from Britain, for commercial ties with France and Holland had not developed as rapidly as some patriots had predicted. American merchants thus remained economically dependent on England as a source of manufactured goods, and on British possessions in the Caribbean for trade. Congress sent John Adams to Great Britain, but the American bargaining position was weak. Britain had no desire to help America end its economic woes.

The Confederation had problems with allies as well as with enemies. Spain, for example, was alarmed to find thousands of Americans ready to join the almost fifty thousand Americans who had already moved into what would become Kentucky and Tennessee. The Spanish government, which controlled access to the Mississippi River and the port of New Orleans, responded to this threat by banning all American traffic on the river. The Confederation appointed John Jay, fresh from his success as a Paris peace commissioner, to negotiate with Spain on this and other issues, but Jay could make no headway.

The Confederation had no better luck in dealing with the Barbary pirates. For many years, the rulers of Algiers, Tunisia, Tripoli, and Morocco had taken advantage of their location along the Barbary Coast of North Africa to attack European vessels engaged in Mediterranean trade. Most European nations kept this piracy under control by paying blackmail or by providing armed naval escorts for their merchant ships. The Barbary pirates found a new target in the American merchant marine, for American ships no longer sailed under the protection of the British royal navy. In 1785 a New England ship was captured, its cargo seized, and the crew stripped and sold into slavery. The Confederation Congress was outraged, but with no navy and no authority to create one, it could do nothing to ensure American safety in the Mediterranean.

A Farmers' Revolt

The postwar economic depression weighed heavily on backcountry farmers, and these Americans began to protest burdens they had long resented—high rents and land prices, heavy taxes, debts, oppressive legal fees, and the failure of their governments to provide protection from Indian attacks and frontier bandits. They used the language of republicanism to defend their position and to justify the occasional violence that erupted in their areas. "We fought for land & liberty,"

◻ **Treaty of Fort Stanwix** A 1784 treaty by which the Iroquois opened all of their lands to white settlement.

◻ **Hopewell Treaties** Treaties signed by 1785 in which the Choctaws, Chickasaws, and Cherokees granted American settlement rights in the Southwest.

◻ **John Jay** New York lawyer and diplomat who negotiated with Great Britain and Spain on behalf of the Confederation; he later became the first chief justice of the Supreme Court and negotiated Jay's Treaty with England.

◻ **Barbary pirates** Pirates along the Barbary Coast of North Africa who attacked European and American vessels engaged in Mediterranean trade.

wrote one **squatter** in response to a land speculator's claim to his farm. "Who can have a better right to the land than we who have fought for it, subdued it & made it valuable?" Members of the political and economic elite, who remembered the violence of the Regulator movement and the Paxton Boys revolt, grew uneasy. When farmers in western Massachusetts began an organized protest in 1786, this uneasiness reached crisis proportions.

Western Massachusetts farmers were among those hardest hit by the postwar depression. Many were deeply in debt to creditors who held mortgages on their farms. In the 1780s, these farmers looked to the state government for temporary relief, hoping that it would pass **stay laws** that would temporarily suspend creditors' rights to foreclose on lands and farm equipment. The Massachusetts assembly responded sympathetically but met stubborn resistance from the merchants and creditors who were themselves deeply in debt to foreign manufacturers. The upper house of the state legislature, with its more elite members, sided with the creditors and blocked the passage of stay laws. The Massachusetts government then shocked the farmers by raising taxes.

In 1786 hundreds of farmers revolted. They believed they were protecting their rights and their communities as true republicans must do. To their creditors, though, the farmers appeared to be dangerous lawbreakers threatening the state with "anarchy, confusion, and total ruin." The farmers, led by men such as Revolutionary War veteran **Daniel Shays**, closed several courts and freed a number of their fellow farmers from debtors' prison.

Their actions struck a chord among desperate farmers in other New England states, and fear of a widespread uprising spurred the Massachusetts government to action. It sent a military force of six hundred to Springfield, where more than a thousand farmers, most armed with pitchforks rather than guns, had gathered to close the local courthouse. The troops let loose a cannon barrage that killed four protesters and set the remaining men to flight. Although Daniel Shays managed to escape, by February 4, 1787, the farmers' revolt was over.

Shays's Rebellion brought to a head long-standing antagonisms between farmers and the coastal merchant elite, and the farmers who joined Shays were acting as they had been encouraged to act in the prerevolutionary years. When the government did not respond to their needs, they organized, and they protested—and when government still did not respond, they took up arms against what they considered to be injustice. Across the country, many Americans sympathized with these farmers. But just as many did not. Abigail Adams, adopting language earlier used against her husband by his loyalist opponents, condemned the leaders of the farmers' revolt as "ignorant, restless, desperadoes, without conscience or principles."

The revolt stirred fears of slave rebellions and pitched battles between debtors and creditors, haves and have-nots. Above all, it raised doubts among influential political figures about the ability of either state governments or the Confederation to preserve the basic rule of law. To George Washington, Shays's Rebellion was also a tragedy for the reputation of the United States. When the farmers' protest began, Washington wrote to authorities in Massachusetts urging them to act fairly but to end the unrest decisively for, Washington said, "To be more exposed to the eyes of the world, and more contemptible than we already are, is hardly possible."

A Call for Change

By 1786, many political leaders believed the survival of the nation was in question. They regretted having created a national government so restricted that it could not deal with the problems it faced both at home and abroad. Washington predicted "the worst consequences from a half-starved, limping government, always moving upon crutches and tottering at every step." For him, for Alexander Hamilton, and for others like them who thought of themselves as **nationalists**, the solution was clear. "I do not conceive we can long exist as a nation," Washington remarked, "without having lodged somewhere a power which will pervade the whole Union" in the way the state governments held power in their states. Here was a different form of republican government to consider.

Support for a stronger national government grew in the key states of Virginia, Massachusetts, and New York. Leaders in these states wanted to give the central government taxing powers, devise an easier amendment process, and provide some legal means to enforce national government policies that a state might oppose. They wanted a government that could establish stable diplomatic and trade relations. They also wanted a national government able to preserve their property and their peace of mind. At Alexander Hamilton's urging, in 1786 a group of influential Virginians called for a meeting on problems of interstate trade. With the approval of the Confederation

squatter A person who settles on unoccupied land to which he or she has no legal claim.

stay laws Laws suspending the right of creditors to foreclose on, or seize, debtors' property; they were designed to protect indebted farmers from losing their land.

◻ **Daniel Shays** Revolutionary War veteran considered the leader of the farmers' uprising in western Massachusetts called Shays's Rebellion.

◻ **nationalists** Americans who preferred a strong central government rather than the limited government prescribed in the Articles of Confederation.

Alexander Hamilton was a true American success story: an illegitimate son of a Scottish merchant, he immigrated from the West Indies to the mainland during his teenage years. Hamilton served as Washington's aide-de-camp, became a leader of the New York bar, and married into New York's social elite. As the author of many of the *Federalist Papers* essays and the first secretary of the treasury, Hamilton helped shape the future of the new nation. In 1804, a political enemy, Aaron Burr, killed Hamilton in a duel.

Alexander Hamilton, c.1804 (oil on canvas), Trumbull, John (1756–1843)/© Collection of the New-York Historical Society, USA/The Bridgeman Art Library.

him sat men from eleven of the thirteen states (New Hampshire's delegates did not arrive until late July), closeted behind curtained windows and locked doors despite the heat and humidity of a Philadelphia summer. These secrecy precautions stemmed in large part from the delegates' ultimate purpose. Rhode Island, refusing to participate in the deliberations, accused the nationalists of plans to drastically revise the national government. The accusation was correct. The convention did expect to make significant changes in the structure of the government. This objective and the need to freely make the many compromises it would require were ample reasons to keep the deliberations secret.

Most of the fifty-five men gathered in that room were lawyers, merchants, or planters—and many of them had served as officers in the Continental Army. When Thomas Jefferson later referred to the convention members as "demigods," he was probably thinking of the likes of 81-year-old Benjamin Franklin, whose sparkling wit and crafty political style set him apart from his colleagues despite his advanced age; or of the articulate, brilliant Alexander Hamilton of New York, whose reputation as a financial mastermind equaled that of Confederation adviser Robert Morris; or of James Madison, the prim Virginia planter who turned out to be the chief architect of a new constitution; or of Pennsylvania's Gouverneur Morris. Even delegates of lesser intellect enjoyed the advantages of education and long political experience.

Several notable men were absent. Thomas Jefferson was abroad serving as ambassador to France. John Adams was representing the United States in the same capacity in London. The charismatic Patrick Henry, and the two great propagandists of the Revolution, Samuel Adams and Thomas Paine, were absent by choice. When asked about the intentions of the convention, Henry replied, "I smell a rat."

Revise or Replace?

Most of the delegates were nationalists, but they did not necessarily agree on how best to proceed. Should they revise the Articles or abandon them? Virginia planter and former governor Edmund Randolph provided the convention with the answer. The Virginia proposal he presented effectively amended the Articles of Confederation out of existence.

Although Randolph introduced this Virginia Plan on the convention floor, James Madison was its guiding spirit. The 36-year-old Madison was small, frail, charmless, and a hypochondriac. But he was highly respected as a scholar of philosophy and history and as an astute political theorist, and his long service in the Virginia legislature and the Confederation Congress gave him a practical understanding of politics and government. At the convention, Madison first

Congress, delegates met at Annapolis, Maryland. But beyond trade issues, the meeting organizers had a second agenda: to test the waters on revising the nation's Constitution. Although only a third of the states participated in the Annapolis conference, nationalists were convinced that their position had substantial support. They asked Congress to call a delegates' convention in Philadelphia so that political leaders could continue to discuss interstate commerce problems—and other aspects of government reform. Some members of Congress were reluctant, but news of Shays's Rebellion tipped the balance in favor of the convention.

CREATING A NEW CONSTITUTION

☆ *What major compromises did the framers make in writing the new constitution?*

☆ *What safeguards did James Madison see in his "checks and balances" system?*

Late in May 1787, George Washington called the delegates convention to order in Philadelphia. Before

considered one question: What was the best form of government for a strong republic? He concluded, as John Adams had done early in the 1780s, that the fear of tyranny should not rule out a powerful national government. The abuse of power could be curtailed by building internal checks and balances into the republican structure.

Madison's Virginia Plan called for a government with three distinct branches—legislative, executive, and judicial—to replace the Confederation's Congress, which was performing all three functions. By dividing power in this way, Madison believed the plan could prevent an individual or group of men from wielding too much authority, especially for self-interested reasons. Madison's plan also gave Congress the power to **veto** laws passed by the state legislatures and the right to intervene directly if a state acted to interrupt "the harmony of the United States."

The delegates endorsed Madison's notion of a strong government able "to control the governed" but also "obliged to control itself." But they were in sharp disagreement over many specific issues in the Virginia Plan. The greatest controversy swirled around representation in the legislative branch—Congress—a controversy familiar to those who had helped draft the Articles of Confederation. Madison proposed a two-house or bicameral legislature. Membership in both houses would be based on proportional representation. Large states supported the plan, for representation based on population worked to their advantage. Small states objected heatedly, arguing that proportional representation would leave them helpless against a national government dominated by the large ones. Small-state delegates threw their support behind a second proposal, the **New Jersey Plan**, which also called for three branches of government and gave Congress the power to tax and to control national commerce. This plan, however, preserved an equal voice and vote for every state within a unicameral legislature.

Debate over the two plans dragged on through the steamy days of a June heat wave. Tempers flared, and threats to walk out of the convention came from both sides. Ultimately, a compromise, hammered out by a special committee, was presented by Roger Sherman of Connecticut. This **Great Compromise** proposed a two-house legislature to satisfy both sides, with proportional representation in the lower house (the House of Representatives) and equal representation in the upper house (the Senate).

The Great Compromise resolved the first major controversy at the convention but opened the door to the next one: how the representatives in each house were to be elected. A compromise also settled this issue. State legislatures would select senators, and the eligible voters of each state would directly elect their members of the House. This formula allowed the delegates to acknowledge the sovereignty of the state governments but also to accommodate the republican commitment to popular elections in a representative government. For the strong nationalists, however, both of these compromises were a serious blow. They had hoped to keep the states out of the national government entirely. Nevertheless, nationalists such as Madison and Hamilton accepted the will of the convention.

The delegates faced one last stumbling block over representation in the House: Which Americans were to be counted to determine a state's population? This issue remained as divisive as it had been when the Articles of Confederation were drafted, but this time the positions of the southern and northern states were reversed. Southern delegates argued that slaves, who composed as much as one-third and sometimes more of each plantation state's residents, should be included in the population count. Northern delegates protested that slaves should be considered property. They were motivated by self-interest rather than a desire for consistency, for if slaves were considered property, not people, their region would dominate the lower house.

The compromise that settled this question defied reason but made brilliant political sense. The **Three-Fifths Compromise** established that three-fifths of the slave population would be included in a state's critical headcount. A clause was then added guaranteeing that the slave trade could continue for a twenty-year period. Some southern leaders, especially in South Carolina, wanted this extension badly because they had lost many slaves during the Revolution. But not all slaveowners concurred. Virginia's George Mason, a slaveowner himself, spoke passionately of the harm slavery did to his region. It not only prevented white

□ **James Madison** Virginia planter and political theorist known as the "father of the Constitution"; he would become the fourth president of the United States.

Virginia Plan Fourteen proposals by the Virginia delegation to the Constitutional Convention for a more powerful central government giving states proportional representation in a bicameral legislature.

veto The power or right of one branch of government to reject the decisions of another branch.

New Jersey Plan A proposal submitted by the New Jersey delegation to the Constitutional Convention for a government in which the states would have equal representation in a unicameral legislature.

□ **Great Compromise** A proposal calling for a bicameral legislature with equal representation for the states in one house and proportional representation in the other.

□ **Three-Fifths Compromise** An agreement to count three-fifths of a state's slave population for purposes of determining a state's representation in the House of Representatives.

The Maze of History

Historians know that properly understanding the past requires them to appreciate the uncertainty men and women faced as they tried to resolve problems that were big or small. Reading history, as it was lived and created by past generations, is like finding a way through a maze. People who made history faced multiple paths, and historians investigate why they followed the ones they did. The road to the future is filled with a confusing number of choices—and the only road map to the right choice is what people have learned from the past and what seems possible in the present.

Consider, for example, one of the thorniest problems facing the Philadelphia convention: how to elect the president. The delegates debated and discussed this issue repeatedly, but no agreement could be reached. In the last days of the convention, the weary framers sent the question to an aptly named Committee on Postponed Matters. The result was the Electoral College.

To understand why this solution was adopted, a historian would have to answer three key questions:

1. How did these eighteenth-century men define the problem?
2. What were the real and ideological constraints they faced in 1787?
3. What alternative solutions were posed—and why were they rejected?

The first of these questions can be partially answered by examining the records of the convention, especially those kept by James Madison. But it can also be answered by studying the framers' understanding of why republics had failed in the past and what lessons the Revolution had taught them about power. You would find, for example, that they were deeply concerned about a president becoming a tyrant. They believed power corrupted, as they had seen repeatedly with colonial governors, Parliament, and the king himself. But they were also concerned about the potential corruption of a group of men who might be given the task of selecting the president. For instance, if the Senate chose the president, would they pick a man who they could control and force to do their bidding? The framers knew that an oligarchy, or small group of ruling men, was another form of tyranny. And they were just as fearful that agents of foreign countries, far more powerful than their own fledgling nation, would manage to put a man they controlled in office. Remember, they did not know how well checks and balances would work.

The second key question requires, among other things, a knowledge of transportation, communication, and educational limits in the eighteenth century. The framers lived in an era before railroads, airplanes, or cars; before universal public education, cheap books, or electronic communications. Information and people simply did not travel fast enough to make campaigning for office among the voters practical.

Finally, although popular election and selection by the Senate or by state legislatures were proposed as alternative mechanisms, they were rejected because the problems they raised seemed greater than those that might arise from an electoral college. For instance, having the state legislatures choose the president would give the states additional power in the national government, something the nationalists did not want. And popular election of the president would, they reasoned, lead to dozens if not hundreds of candidates put forward by local groups.

In the end, the delegates settled on a solution they knew was imperfect: the electoral college. If we understand their trip through the maze of history, we realize that criticizing their choices from a modern perspective is a form of "Monday morning quarterbacking."

In 1867, Thomas Pritchard Rossiter painted his *Signing of the Constitution of the United States* honoring a group of statesmen that included James Madison, Alexander Hamilton, and George Washington, who presided over the Constitutional Convention.

MPI/Stringer/Hulton Archive/Getty Images.

immigration to the South, Mason said, but infected the moral character of the slave master. "Every master of slaves," Mason argued, "is born a petty tyrant."

Drafting an Acceptable Document

The Three-Fifths Compromise ended weeks of debate over representation. No other issue arose to provoke such controversy, and the delegates proceeded calmly to implement the principle of checks and balances. For example, the president, or executive, was named commander in chief of the armed forces and given primary responsibility for foreign affairs. To balance these **executive powers**, only Congress was given the right to declare war and to raise an army. Congress received the critical "power of the purse," but this power to tax and spend was checked in part by the president's power to veto congressional legislation. As yet another balance, Congress could override a presidential veto by the vote of a two-thirds majority. Following the same logic of distributing power, the delegates gave the president authority to name federal court judges, but the Senate had to approve all such appointments. The concern for checks and balances arose in part from the delegates' belief that all men would succumb to the lure of power, even themselves. To prevent the rise of tyranny in any branch of the government, its power must be held in check.

Occasionally, as in the system for electing the president, the convention chose awkward or cumbersome procedures. For example, many delegates opposed direct popular election of the president. A few agreed with George Mason, who said this "would be as unnatural…as it would [be] to refer a trial of colours to a blind man." Others simply doubted that the citizens of one state would be familiar enough with a candidate from a distant state to make a valid judgment. In an age of slow communication, few men besides George Washington had a truly national reputation. Popular voting might lead to dozens of candidates who were favorites in local politics. When it was proposed that state legislatures select the president, delegates objected that this solution put too much power in the legislators' hands. As a somewhat clumsy compromise, the delegates created the **Electoral College**, a group of special electors to be chosen by the states to vote for presidential candidates. Each state would be entitled to a number of electors equal to the number of its senators and representatives sitting in Congress, but no one serving in Congress at the time of a presidential election would be eligible to be an elector. If two presidential candidates received the same number of Electoral College votes, or if no candidate received a majority of the Electoral College votes, then the House of Representatives would choose the new president. This complex procedure honored the **discretion** of the state governments in appointing the electors but limited the power of individuals already holding office.

The long summer of conflict and compromise ended with a new plan for a national government. Would the delegates be willing to put their names to the document they had created in secrecy and by overreaching their authority? Benjamin Franklin fervently hoped so. Though sick and bedridden, Franklin was carried by friends to the convention floor, where he pleaded for unanimous support for the new government. When a weary George Washington at last declared the meetings adjourned on September 17, 1787, only a handful of delegates left without signing what the convention hoped would be the new American Constitution.

RESOLVING THE CONFLICT OF VISION

☆ What were the Antifederalists' arguments against the Constitution? What were the Federalists' arguments in its favor?

☆ What was the outcome of the ratification process?

The framers of the Constitution called for special state **ratifying conventions**, with delegates chosen by voters, to discuss and then vote on the proposed change of government. The conventions would bypass the state legislatures, which stood to lose power under the new government and were thus likely to oppose it. The framers added to their advantage by declaring that the approval of only nine states was necessary to establish the Constitution. Reluctantly, the Confederation Congress agreed to all these terms and procedures. By the end of September 1787, Congress had passed the proposed Constitution on to the states, triggering the next round of debates over America's political future.

The Ratification Controversy

As Alexander Hamilton boasted, "The new Constitution has in favor of its success…[the] very great weight

---

executive powers Powers given to the president by the Constitution.

□ **Electoral College** A body of electors chosen by the states to elect the president and vice president; the number of each state's electors equals the number of its senators and representatives in Congress.

discretion The power or right to act according to one's own judgment.

□ **ratifying conventions** A meeting of delegates in each state to determine whether that state would ratify the Constitution.

of influence of the persons who framed it." Hamilton was correct. Men of wealth, political experience, and frequently great persuasive powers put their skills to the task of achieving ratification. But many revolutionary heroes and political leaders opposed the Constitution with equal intensity—most notably Patrick Henry, Samuel Adams, George Mason, and George Clinton, the popular governor of New York. Boston's most effective revolutionary propagandist, Mercy Otis Warren, immediately took up her pen to attack the Constitution as an assault on republican values. Thus the leadership on both sides of the issue was drawn from the political elite of the revolutionary generation.

The pro-Constitution forces won an early and important victory by clouding the language of the debate. They abandoned the label "nationalists," which drew attention to their belief in a strong central government, and chose to call themselves Federalists, a name originally associated with a system of strong state governments and limited national government. This shrewd tactic cheated opponents of the Constitution out of their rightful name. The pro-Constitution forces then dubbed their opponents Antifederalists, which implied that their adversaries were negative thinkers and pessimists who lacked a program of their own.

Although the philosophical debate over the best form of government for a republic was an important one, voters considered other, practical factors in choosing a Federalist or Antifederalist position. Voters in states with a stable or recovering economy were likely to oppose the Constitution because the Confederation system gave their states greater independent powers. Those in small, geographically or economically disadvantaged states were likely to favor a strong central government that could protect them from their competitive neighbors. Thus the small states of Delaware and Connecticut ratified the Constitution quickly, but in New York and Virginia ratification was hotly contested.

To some degree, Federalist and Antifederalist camps matched the divisions between the relatively urban, market-oriented communities of the Atlantic coast and the frontier or rural communities of the inland areas (see Map 7.3). For example, the backcountry of North and South Carolina and the less economically developed areas of Virginia saw little benefit in a stronger central government, especially

one that might tax them. But coastal centers of trade and overseas commerce such as Boston, New York City, and Charleston wanted an aggressive and effective national policy regarding foreign and interstate trade. In these urban centers, artisans, shopkeepers, and even laborers joined wealthy merchants and shippers to support the Constitution as they had once joined them to make the Revolution. No generalization can explain every political choice, of course. No economic or social group was unified under the Federalist or the Antifederalist banner. On the whole, however, it can be said that the Federalists were better organized, had more resources at their disposal, and campaigned more effectively than the Antifederalists.

Public debates sharply defined the political differences between the Federalists and Antifederalists. Antifederalists rejected the claim that the nation was in a "critical period," facing economic and political collapse. As one New Yorker put it: "I deny that we are in immediate danger of anarchy and commotions." Nevertheless, the Federalists were successful in portraying the moment as a crisis or turning point for the young republic—and in insisting that their plan for recovery was better than no plan at all.

The Antifederalists struck hard against the dangerous elitism they believed they saw in the Constitution. They portrayed the Federalists as a privileged, sophisticated minority, ready and able to tyrannize the people if their powerful national government were ratified. Be careful, one Massachusetts man warned, because "these lawyers, and men of learning, and moneyed men, that talk so finely and gloss over matters so smoothly, to make us poor illiterate people swallow down the pill, expect to get into Congress themselves." And New York Antifederalist Melancton Smith predicted that the proposed new government would lead inevitably to rule by a wealthy, unrepresentative minority. The Virginia revolutionary leader Richard Henry Lee was flabbergasted that his generation would even consider ratifying the Constitution. "Tis really astonishing," he wrote to a New York opponent in the summer of 1788, "that the same people, who have just emerged from a long and cruel war in defense of liberty, should agree to fix an elective despotism upon themselves and posterity."

The Antifederalists' most convincing evidence of elitism and its potential for tyranny was that the proposed Constitution lacked a bill of rights. It contained no written guarantees of the people's right to assemble or to worship as they saw fit, and it gave no assurances of a trial by jury in civil cases or the right to bear arms. The framers believed these rights were secure because most state constitutions contained strong guarantees of them. But Antifederalists put the question to both voters and delegates: What did this glaring omission tell Americans about the framers'

□ **Federalists** Supporters of the Constitution; they desired a strong central government.

□ **Antifederalists** Opponents of the Constitution; they believed a strong central government was a threat to American liberties and rights.

despotism Rule by a tyrant.

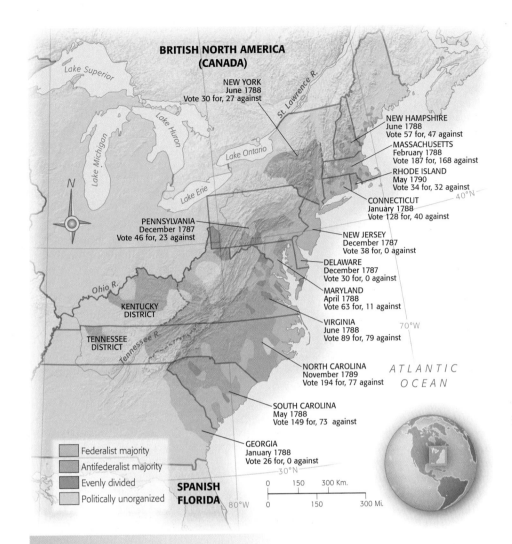

BRITISH NORTH AMERICA
(CANADA)

NEW YORK
June 1788
Vote 30 for, 27 against

NEW HAMPSHIRE
June 1788
Vote 57 for, 47 against

MASSACHUSETTS
February 1788
Vote 187 for, 168 against

RHODE ISLAND
May 1790
Vote 34 for, 32 against

CONNECTICUT
January 1788
Vote 128 for, 40 against

PENNSYLVANIA
December 1787
Vote 46 for, 23 against

NEW JERSEY
December 1787
Vote 38 for, 0 against

DELAWARE
December 1787
Vote 30 for, 0 against

MARYLAND
April 1788
Vote 63 for, 11 against

VIRGINIA
June 1788
Vote 89 for, 79 against

KENTUCKY
DISTRICT

TENNESSEE
DISTRICT

NORTH CAROLINA
November 1789
Vote 194 for, 77 against

ATLANTIC
OCEAN

SOUTH CAROLINA
May 1788
Vote 149 for, 73 against

GEORGIA
January 1788
Vote 26 for, 0 against

Federalist majority
Antifederalist majority
Evenly divided
Politically unorganized

SPANISH
FLORIDA

0   150   300 Km.
0   150   300 Mi.

MAP 7.3 The Federalist and Antifederalist Struggle over the Constitution
The battle over ratification of the Constitution was fierce throughout 1787 and 1788. This map shows the areas of strong antifederalism, the areas of Federalist strength, and the scattered pockets where opinion was evenly divided. The date of each state's ratification and its convention vote are also shown. © Cengage Learning.

respect for republican ideals? The only conclusion, Antifederalists argued, was that the Constitution was a threat to republican principles of representative government, a vehicle for elite rule, and a document unconcerned with the protection of the people's individual liberties. Federalists countered by insisting that the Constitution fulfilled and could preserve the republican ideals of the Revolution far better than the Articles had done. Their cause was put forward most convincingly by Alexander Hamilton, James Madison, and John Jay, who entered the newspaper wars over ratification in the key state of New York. Together, they produced a series of essays known today as the *Federalist Papers*. Although these eighty-five essays were all signed "Publius," Hamilton wrote fifty-one of them, Madison twenty-nine, and Jay five.

Their common theme was the link between American prosperity, American liberties, and a strong central government.

The Federalist Victory

Practical politics rather than political theory seemed to influence the outcome of many of the ratifying conventions. The small states of New Jersey and Georgia joined Delaware and Connecticut and quickly approved the Constitution. In Pennsylvania, Antifederalists in the rural western regions lost control of the

☐ *Federalist Papers* Essays written by Alexander Hamilton, John Jay, and James Madison in support of the Constitution.

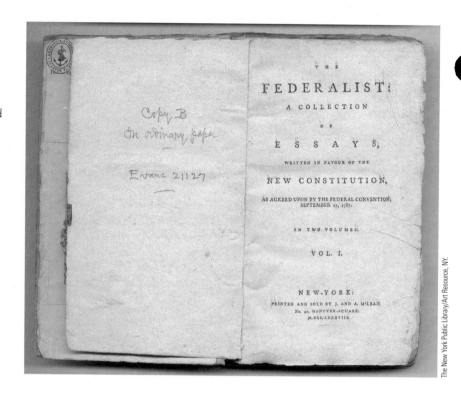

The battle over ratification of the new U.S. constitution, drafted in Philadelphia in 1787, was intense. To help the constitution's supporters, called Federalists, John Jay, Alexander Hamilton, and James Madison wrote a series of essays defending the need for the new government and explaining its advantages. The essays, known collectively as *The Federalist Papers*, were printed under the pseudonym Publius, in honor of the Roman Consul Publius Valerius Publicola.

convention to the Federalists and thus that state also endorsed the Constitution. In the remaining states, including Massachusetts, Virginia, and New York, the two sides were more evenly matched.

Antifederalists were in the majority in the Massachusetts convention, where most of the delegates were small farmers from the western counties and more than twenty of them had participated in Shays's Rebellion. The Federalists' strategy was to make political deals with key delegates, winning over Antifederalists such as Samuel Adams and John Hancock, for example, with promises to demand the addition of a bill of rights to the Constitution. At the final count, a nineteen-vote margin gave the Federalists a narrow victory in Massachusetts. In New Hampshire too, a close vote gave a victory to the Federalists.

Rhode Island, true to its history of opposition to strong central authority, rejected the Constitution decisively. But Maryland and South Carolina ratified it. In Virginia, James Madison and George Washington directed the Federalist effort against intense opposition. In the end, the presence of Washington proved irresistible because Virginians knew that this war hero and admired colleague was certain to be the first president of the United States if the

This political cartoon captures the celebration that followed the ratification of the nation's new government. Gathered around the flag, the celebrants salute the shrine of liberty resting solidly upon the rock of a written constitution and written laws, guaranteeing the success of a nation made up of citizens from many different backgrounds.

Constitution went into effect. When the vote was taken on June 25, 1788, Virginia became the tenth state to ratify the new government.

New York's battle was equally intense. Acknowledging its absence as a major political error, Federalist leaders Jay and Hamilton made a public pledge to support inclusion of a Bill of Rights. By then, however, ten states had already ratified the Constitution, so the new government was a *fait accompli*. Realizing this, on July 26, 1788, a majority of New York delegates voted yes on ratification.

President George Washington

The election of senators and Congress members was almost complete by February 4, 1789, when presidential electors met in each state to choose the nation's first president. Although George Washington did not seek the position, he knew the nation expected him to serve. Hailed as the hero of the Revolution, looking and acting the part of the dignified, virtuous patriot, Washington became president by a unanimous vote of the Electoral College. For regional balance, New Englander John Adams was chosen vice president.

In April 1789, as Washington made his way from Virginia to his inauguration in New York City, the temporary national capital, Americans thronged to greet him with parades, sharply dressed military escorts, and choruses of church bells and cannon fire. Thousands of supporters gathered to see him take the oath of office. Yet amid the celebration, Washington and his closest advisers knew the future was uncharted and uncertain. "We are in a wilderness," Madison observed, "without a single footstep to guide us."

Washington agreed and proceeded with caution and deliberation. He labored carefully over each of his selections to the almost one thousand federal offices waiting to be filled. He took particular care in choosing the men to head four executive departments created with approval from Congress. Naming his **protégé** Alexander Hamilton to the Treasury Department was probably Washington's easiest decision. He asked the Massachusetts military strategist Henry Knox to lead the War Department and fellow Virginian Edmund Randolph to serve as attorney general. Washington chose another Virginian, Thomas Jefferson, to be secretary of state. Over time, the president established a pattern of regularly meeting with this **cabinet** of advisers to discuss policy matters. Together, they made major decisions and, as Washington expected, expressed serious disagreements that exposed him to differing viewpoints on policy.

The unknown artist of *The Federal Procession in New York, 1788*, captured the jubilant mood of Americans as they celebrated their new Constitution with parades, bonfires, and banquets. As the "Ship of State" float indicates, New Yorkers were particularly eager to acknowledge the role of their own Alexander Hamilton in launching the new government.

COMPETING VISIONS REEMERGE

☆ *How did Alexander Hamilton's expectations for the new nation differ from those of Thomas Jefferson? What were the consequences of this conflict of vision?*

☆ *How did the French Revolution affect Washington's diplomatic policy?*

A remarkable but, as it turned out, short-lived spirit of unity marked the early days of Washington's administration. Federalists had won the overwhelming majority of seats in the new Congress, and this success enabled them to work quickly and efficiently on matters they felt had priority. But the unity was fragile. By 1792, as the government debated foreign policy and domestic affairs, two distinct groups, voicing serious differences of opinion, began to form. Alexander Hamilton's vision for America guided one group, Thomas Jefferson's vision the other.

Unity's Achievements

In addition to creating the four executive departments that became the cabinet, the First Congress

---

fait accompli An accomplished deed or fact that cannot be reversed or undone.

protégé An individual whose welfare or career is promoted by an influential person.

▫ **cabinet** A body of officials appointed by the president to run the executive departments of the government and to act as the president's advisers.

The Amendment Process

The men who wrote the Constitution did not spend much time debating the future; they saw their task as securing their nation's survival in the present. Yet they assumed that the nation's size, population, and economy would change over time and that the needs of generations to come might differ from the needs of their own generation. This is one of the reasons they included an amendment process in the Constitution. The process did not allow for hasty decisions; it was slow and deliberate and designed to promote consensus. But amendments such as those that ended slavery and gave women the vote did ensure that the Constitution could keep abreast of an ever-changing world.

passed the Judiciary Act of 1789. This act established a Supreme Court, thirteen district courts, and three circuit courts. It also empowered the Supreme Court to review the decisions of state courts and to nullify any state laws that violated either the Constitution or any treaty made by the federal government. President Washington chose John Jay to serve as first chief justice of the Supreme Court.

James Madison wanted the nationalists to keep their promise, and so he prodded Congress to draft the Bill of Rights. On December 15, 1791, ten amendments guaranteeing numerous rights were added to the Constitution. Soon after, both Rhode Island and North Carolina ratified the Constitution and joined the union. Eight of these original constitutional amendments spelled out the government's commitment to protect individual civil liberties. They

□ **Judiciary Act of 1789** Law establishing the Supreme Court and the lower federal courts; it gave the Supreme Court the right to review state laws and state court decisions to determine their constitutionality.

□ **Bill of Rights** The first ten amendments to the U.S. Constitution, added in 1791 to protect certain basic rights of American citizens.

civil liberties Fundamental individual rights such as freedom of speech and religion, protected by law against interference from the government.

free trade Trade between nations without any protective tariffs.

□ **Federalists** Political group formed during Washington's first administration (after and distinct from those who supported the Constitution); led by Alexander Hamilton, they favored an active role for government in encouraging commercial and manufacturing growth.

guaranteed that the new national government could not limit free speech, interfere with religious worship, deny U.S. citizens the right to keep or bear arms, force the quartering of troops in private homes, or allow homes to be searched without proper search warrants. The amendments prohibited the government from requiring persons accused of crimes to testify against themselves, nor could it deny citizens the right to a trial by jury. The government also could not deprive a citizen of life, liberty, or property without "due process of law," or impose excessive bail, or administer "cruel and unusual punishments." The Ninth Amendment made clear that the inclusion of these protections and rights did not mean that others were excluded. The Tenth Amendment stated that any powers not given to the federal government or denied to the states belonged solely to the states or the people.

Condensed into these ten amendments was a rich history of struggle for individual rights in the face of abusive power. It was a history that recalled the illegal search and seizure of cargoes in Boston Harbor, the British government's insistence on quartering troops in New York homes, and the religious persecution of men and women who dissented from established churches both in England and in the colonies.

Hamilton and Jefferson's Differences

Alexander Hamilton was consumed by a bold dream: to transform agricultural America into a manufacturing society that rivaled Great Britain. His blueprint for achieving this goal called for protective tariffs to assist developing American industry rather than simply raise revenue. It also called for subsidies, or government financial support, for new enterprises and for incentives to support new industries. And it relied on strong economic and diplomatic ties with the mercantile interests of England. Hamilton's vision had great appeal in the Northeast but few advocates in the southern states. Indeed, his ambitious development program seemed to confirm Patrick Henry's worst fear that the new government would produce "a system which I have ever dreaded—subserviency of Southern to Northern Interests."

Virginia planters Thomas Jefferson and James Madison offered a different vision of the new nation: a prosperous, agrarian society. Instead of government tariffs designed to encourage American manufacturing, they advocated a national policy of free trade to keep consumer prices low. They did not rule out commerce and industry in the United States but believed it should remain only as "a handmaiden to agriculture." In the same fashion, Hamilton was content to see agriculture thrive as long as it did not stand in the way of commercial or industrial growth. Hamilton and men of similar vision spoke of themselves as true Federalists. Those who agreed with Jefferson and Madison identified themselves as Republicans.

The emergence of two political camps was certain to trouble even the men who played a role in creating them. The revolutionary generation believed that factions, or special-interest parties, were responsible for the corruption of English politics. John Adams seemed to speak for all these political leaders when he declared: "A division of the republic into two great parties . . . is to be dreaded as the greatest political evil." Yet as President Washington was quick to see, sectionalism fueled the growth of just such a division.

Hamilton's Economic Plan

As secretary of the treasury, Alexander Hamilton was expected to seek solutions to the nation's fiscal problems, particularly the foreign and domestic debts hanging over America's head. His proposals were the source of much of the conflict that divided Congress in the early 1790s.

In January 1790 Hamilton submitted a *Report on Public Credit* to the Congress. In it, he argued that the public debt fell into three categories, each requiring attention: (1) foreign debt, owed primarily to France; (2) state debts, incurred by the individual states to finance their war efforts; and (3) a national debt in the form of government securities (the notorious paper continentals) that had been issued to help finance the war. To establish credit, and thus to be able to borrow money and attract investors in American enterprises, Hamilton declared that the nation had to make good on all it owed.

Hamilton proposed that the federal government assume responsibility for the repayment of all three categories of debt. He insisted that continentals be redeemed for the amount shown on the certificate, regardless of what their current value might be. And he proposed that *current* holders of continentals should receive that payment. These recommendations, and the political agenda for economic growth they revealed, raised furious debate within Congress.

Before Hamilton's *Report on Public Credit,* James Madison had been the voice of unity in Congress. Now Madison leapt to his feet to protest the treasury secretary's plan. The government's debt, both financial and moral, Madison argued, was not to the current creditors holding the continentals but to the *original* holders, many of whom were ordinary citizens and Continental soldiers who had sold these certificates to speculators at a tremendous loss during the postwar depression. The state treasuries of New York, Pennsylvania, and Maryland were three of the largest speculators, having bought up great quantities of these bonds when they were disgracefully cheap. If Hamilton's plan were adopted, Madison protested, these speculators, rather than the nation's true patriots, would reap enormous unfair profits.

Although enslaved men and women performed the work done on Madison's plantation, the Virginia planter believed that wealth acquired by this productive labor was moral, whereas wealth gained by the manipulation of money was corrupt. Hamilton simply sidestepped the moral issue by explaining the difficulty of identifying and locating the original holders of the continentals. Whatever the ethical merits of Madison's argument, Hamilton said, his solution was impractical. Congress supported Hamilton, but the vote reflected the growing rift between regions.

Far from silenced, Madison next led the opposition to Hamilton's proposal that the federal government assume, or take over, the states' debts. Here, Hamilton's motives were quite transparent: as a fierce nationalist, he wished to concentrate both political and economic power in the federal government at the expense of the states. He knew that creditors, who included America's wealthiest citizens, would take a particular interest in the welfare and success of any government that owed them money. Hamilton also knew that a sizable debt provided a compelling reason for raising revenue. By assuming the state debts, the federal government could undercut state governments' need for new taxes—and justify its own.

Congress saw the obvious inequities of the plan. States such as Maryland and Virginia had paid all their war debts during the 1780s. If the national government assumed state debts and raised taxes to repay them, responsible citizens of Maryland and Virginia would be taxed for the failure of Massachusetts or New York to honor their obligations. Although the Senate approved the assumption of state debts, members of the House strongly objected and deferred a decision. Hamilton, realizing he faced defeat, sought a behind-the-scenes compromise with Madison and his ally Jefferson, using the location of the national capital as a bargaining chip.

In 1789 the new government had made New York its temporary home until Congress could settle on a permanent site. Hamilton was willing to put the

---

□ **Republicans** Political group opposing Federalists; led by Thomas Jefferson and James Madison, they favored limited government involvement in encouraging manufacturing and the continued dominance of agriculture in the national economy.

factions A political group with shared opinions or interests.

□ **sectionalism** Competition between regional interests, for example, Southern versus Northern interests.

fiscal Relating to finances.

□ *Report on Public Credit* Hamilton's proposal, ultimately adopted, that the federal government pay debts incurred to finance the Revolution, including debts to foreign countries, continentals at face value, and debts owed by the states.

inequities Unfair circumstances or proceedings.

capital right in Jefferson's backyard in exchange for the Virginian's support on assumption of state debts. Madison and Jefferson agreed to the deal. Like many good Republicans, they believed it was important to monitor the deliberations of a powerful government. In an age of slow land travel and communication, it was difficult to keep watch from a distance. New Englanders knew that "watching" from nearby meant the chance to influence the government. Nevertheless, by trading away the capital location, Hamilton ensured the success of his debt assumption plan.

As the year 1791 began, Hamilton outlined another controversial proposal—a plan for chartering a national bank, modeled on the Bank of England, to serve as fiscal agent for the federal government. The bank would not be an exclusively public institution but instead would be funded by both the government and private sources in a partnership that fit nicely with Hamilton's plan to tie national prosperity to the interests of private wealth.

Once again, James Madison led the opposition. He argued that the government had neither the express right nor the implied power to create a national institution such as the bank. The majority of Congress did not agree, and the bill passed. But Madison's argument caused President Washington to hesitate over signing the bill. Turning to his advisers as usual, Washington asked both Secretary of State Jefferson and Treasury Secretary Hamilton to set down their views on the matter.

Like Madison, Jefferson was at that time a strict constructionist in his interpretation of the Constitution. On February 15, 1791, he wrote of the dangers of interpreting the government's powers broadly. "To take a single step beyond the boundaries...specifically

drawn around the powers of Congress," he warned, "is to take possession of a boundless field of power." A broad constructionist, Hamilton saw no such danger in the bank. He based his argument on Article 1, Section 8, of the Constitution, which granted Congress the right to "make all Laws which shall be necessary and proper" to exercise its legitimate powers. Because it seemed obvious that "a bank has a natural relation to the power of collecting taxes," Hamilton believed there could be no reasonable constitutional argument against it. Hamilton's argument persuaded the president, and the Bank of the United States was chartered on February 25, 1791, with stock offered for sale by July 4, 1791.

To complete his vision, in 1792 Hamilton issued his *Report on Manufactures*, a package of aggressive policies aimed at industrializing the nation. It included protective tariffs and government incentives and subsidies. But this time his program was too extreme to win support in Congress. Still, the Bank of the United States, which provided much-needed working capital for new commercial and manufacturing enterprises, and the establishment of sound national credit, which attracted foreign capital to the new nation, had gone far toward moving the economy in the direction of Hamilton's vision.

Foreign Affairs and Deepening Divisions

In 1789, just as George Washington became the first president of the United States, the French Revolution began. In the next years it would stir new controversy within American politics.

On July 14, 1789, as crowds took to the streets in the name of broad social reform, Parisian radicals stormed the Bastille prison, a symbol of royal oppression, tearing down its walls and liberating its political prisoners. The crowds filling the Paris streets owed some of their political rhetoric and ideals to the American Revolution, a debt the marquis de Lafayette, who had volunteered in the American Revolution, acknowledged when he sent his old friend President Washington the key to the Bastille. Like most Americans in these early days of the French Revolution, Washington was pleased to be identified with this new struggle for the "rights of man." Briefly, enthusiasm for the French Revolution united Hamilton's Federalists and Jefferson's Republicans.

By 1793, however, American public opinion began to divide sharply on the French Revolution. Popular support faded when the revolution's most radical party, the Jacobins, executed King Louis XVI and his wife. Many shocked Americans denounced the revolution completely when the Jacobins, in their Reign of Terror against any who opposed their policies, began marching moderate French reformers as well

---

implied power Power that is not specifically granted to the government by the Constitution but can be viewed as necessary to carry out the governing duties that the Constitution does list.

strict constructionist A person who believes the government has only the powers specifically named in the Constitution.

broad constructionist A person who believes the government can exercise implied powers in keeping with the spirit of the Constitution.

☐ **Bank of the United States** National bank, proposed by Hamilton and funded by the government and private investors, to ensure the country's financial stability.

capital Money needed to start or sustain a commercial enterprise.

☐ **French Revolution** Political rebellion against the French monarchy and aristocratic privileges; it began in 1789 and ended in 1799.

☐ **Reign of Terror** The period from 1793 to 1794 in the French Revolution when thousands of people were executed as enemies of the state.

MASSACRE of the Unfortunate FRENCH KING, with a View of LA GUILLOTINE, or the Modern French BEHEADING MACHINE.
1 The Monarch   3 General Santerre
2 His Confessor   4 The Mayer of Paris
Published by Alex.r Hogg March 1 1793

In 1793, French revolutionaries executed both the King and the Queen of France. More executions would follow in what came to be known as the years of "The Terror." Here King Louis XIV is about to be beheaded on the guillotine while soldiers and citizens look on.

as members of the nobility to the guillotine to be beheaded.

Soon, the Jacobin government vowed to bring "liberty, equality, and brotherhood" to the peoples of Europe, by force if necessary. This campaign to spread the revolution led France into war with England, Spain, Austria, and Prussia. At the very least, France expected the Americans to honor the terms of the treaty of 1778, which bound the United States to protect French possessions in the West Indies from enemy attack. The enemy most likely to strike was England, which suddenly made a second war between England and the United States a possibility.

American opinion on a second war with England was contradictory and complex. Some felt the United States should honor its treaty obligations. But others who continued to support the French Revolution, including Thomas Jefferson, did not want the United States to become embroiled in a European war. On the other hand, many who condemned the French Revolution were eager to use any excuse to attack the British, who still were occupying forts in the Northwest and restricting American trade in the Caribbean. Political leaders such as Hamilton who were working toward better relations with England denounced the French assault on other nations and opposed any American involvement.

The French, meanwhile, plotted to mobilize American support. In 1793 the new French republic sent a diplomatic minister to the United States. When Citizen Edmond Genêt arrived in Charleston, he wasted no time on formal matters such as presenting his diplomatic credentials to either the president or the secretary of state. Instead, he immediately launched a campaign to recruit Americans to the war effort. By all accounts, Genêt was charming, affable, and in the words of one observer, so humorous that he could "laugh us into the war." President Washington, however, was infuriated by Genêt's total disregard for formal procedures. Genêt's bold attempts to provoke incidents between the United States and Spain stunned Hamilton. Even Thomas Jefferson grew uncomfortable when the Frenchman used the port of Philadelphia to transform a captured British ship into a French privateer!

On April 22, 1793, Washington decided to act. Publicly, the president issued a proclamation that declared American neutrality without actually using the term, making clear that the United States would give no military support to the French. Privately, Washington asked the French government to recall Genêt.

The Genêt affair had domestic as well as diplomatic repercussions. For the first time, George Washington came under public attack. A Republican newspaper whose editor was employed by Jefferson in the State Department, questioned the president's integrity in refusing to honor the Franco-American treaty. Washington was furious with this assault on his character. Federalist newspapers struck back, insisting that Jefferson and his followers had actively encouraged

Prussia A northern European state that became the basis for the German Empire in the late nineteenth century.

☐ **Edmond Genêt** Diplomat sent by the French government to bring the United States into France's war with Britain and Spain.

diplomatic credentials Papers certifying that a government has empowered someone to represent it to another government; protocol calls for credentials to be formally presented upon arrival.

neutrality The policy of treating both sides in a conflict the same way and thus favoring neither.

In 1794, the new federal government passed an excise tax on whiskey, made from grain. Farmers in western Pennsylvania rose up in protest against what they considered an unfair assault on their livelihood. Using tactics straight out of the pre-Revolutionary War era, including tarring and feathering the "revenooer" assigned to collect the taxes, the "Whiskey Rebels" challenged the federal government's authority. President Washington assembled an army of almost thirteen thousand men to put down the Whiskey Rebellion. Critics declared the president's response excessive. Do you agree?

the outrageous behavior of Genêt. By the end of 1793, Jefferson had resigned from Washington's government, more convinced than ever that Hamilton and his supporters posed a serious threat to the survival of the American republic.

More Domestic Disturbances

Hamilton's Federalists agreed that the republic was in danger—from Jefferson's Republicans. By Washington's second term (he was reelected in 1792), both political groups were trying to rouse popular sentiment for their programs and policies. Just as in the prerevolutionary years, these appeals to popular opinion broadened participation in the national debate, and organizations rose up to make demands on the government. The most troubling of these to President Washington were the Democratic-Republican societies.

Between 1793 and 1794, thirty-five Democratic-Republican societies were created. Made up primarily of craftsmen and men of the "lower orders," these

pro-French political groups also had their share of professional men, merchants, and planters. No matter what the background of the membership, these societies shared a common agenda: to serve as a platform for expressing the public's will. They insisted that political officeholders were "the agents of the people," not their leaders, and thus should act as the people wished.

In 1794, protest turned violent. That July, a crowd in western Pennsylvania, angry about a new federal excise tax on the whiskey they produced, ransacked and burned the home of the federal excise inspector and then threatened to march on Pittsburgh if the tax were not repealed.

President Washington, haunted by the memory of Shays's Rebellion and worried that the radical spirit of the French Revolution was spreading throughout America, determined to crush this Whiskey Rebellion firmly. Calling up thirteen thousand militiamen, the president marched into the countryside to do battle with a few hundred citizens armed with rifles and pitchforks. In the face of such an overwhelming military force, the whiskey rebels abruptly dispersed.

Washington publicly laid the blame for the western insurrection on the Democratic-Republican societies, and Federalists in Congress rushed to propose a resolution condemning those groups. By 1796, the Democratic-Republican organizations had vanished from the American political scene. The president's public condemnation and Congress's censure undoubtedly damaged them. But improvements on the western borders also diminished the farmers' interest

□ **Democratic-Republican societies** Political organizations formed in 1793 and 1794 to demand greater responsiveness by the state and federal governments to the needs of the citizens.

excise A tax on goods or services produced and sold within the country.

□ **Whiskey Rebellion** A protest by grain farmers against the 1794 federal tax on whiskey; militia forces led by President Washington put down this Pennsylvania uprising.

The Treaty of Greenville, 1795. This painting, done in 1805, commemorates the treaty between a coalition of American Indian tribes, known as the Western Confederacy, and the United States. The treaty (discussed on the next page) followed the victory of General "Mad" Anthony Wayne at the Battle of Fallen Timbers in 1794. By this treaty, the new nation acquired most of what would become Ohio.

in protest organizations. In October 1795, Carolina planter Thomas Pinckney won the concession from Spain that Jay had earlier been unable to obtain: free navigation of the Mississippi River. Pinckney's **Treaty of San Lorenzo** not only gave western farmers an outlet to ocean trade through the port of New Orleans but also ensured that Indian attacks would not be launched from Spanish-held territories.

Jay's Treaty and the West

During Washington's second administration, the diplomatic crisis continued to worsen. England resented America's claim to neutrality, believing it helped France. The British, therefore, ignored American claims that "free ships made free goods" and began to seize American vessels trading with the French Caribbean islands. These seizures prompted new calls for war with Great Britain.

Anti-British emotion ran even higher when the governor of Canada actively encouraged Indian resistance to American settlement in the Northwest. Efforts to crush the Miamis of Ohio had recently ended in two embarrassing American defeats, and in February 1794, as General Anthony Wayne headed west for a third attempt against the Miamis, the Canadian governor's fiery remarks were particularly disturbing.

Anti-British sentiment showed itself in the House of Representatives, where Republicans considered restricting trade with England. Outside the government, war hysteria led mobs to attack English seamen

and tar and feather Americans expressing pro-British views. What would Washington do?

Early in 1794, the president sent Chief Justice John Jay to England as his special **envoy**. Jay's mission was to produce a compromise that would prevent war. Jay, however, was pessimistic. Britain wanted to avoid war with the United States, but what would British diplomats concede to his weak nation?

Jay's negotiations did resolve some old nagging issues. In the treaty that emerged, Britain agreed to evacuate the western forts, although it did not promise to end support for Indian resistance to American western settlement. Britain also granted some small trade favors to America in the West Indies. For its part, the United States agreed to see that all prewar debts owed to British merchants were at last paid. Jay, a fierce opponent of slavery, did not press for any provision to pay slaveholders for slaves lost during the Revolution. In the end, Jay knew he had given up more than he gained: he had abandoned America's demand for freedom of the seas and acknowledged the British navy's right to remove French property from any neutral ship.

□ **Treaty of San Lorenzo** A 1795 treaty negotiated by Thomas Pinckney in which Spain granted the United States the right to navigate the Mississippi River and use the port of New Orleans.

envoy A government representative charged with a special diplomatic mission.

Competing Visions Reemerge **173**

Although Federalists in Congress credited Jay's Treaty with preserving the peace, Republicans condemned it as an embarrassment and a betrayal of France. Once again, the president came under attack, and Kentucky settlers threatened rebellion, warning Washington that if he signed Jay's Treaty, "western America is gone forever—lost to the Union." The treaty finally squeaked through the Senate in the spring of 1795 with only two southern senators supporting ratification. Despite the criticism heaped upon him, Jay knew he had accomplished his mission, for American neutrality in the European war continued.

Although Jay's Treaty damaged the prestige and authority of Washington's administration, the president did far better in military and diplomatic affairs in the West. In August 1794, Anthony Wayne's army defeated the northwestern Indians at the Battle of Fallen Timbers. Wayne then lived up to his reputation as "Mad Anthony" by rampaging through enemy villages, destroying all he could. These terror tactics helped produce the Treaty of Greenville in August 1795. By this treaty, the Indians ceded most of the land that later became the state of Ohio. These victories, combined with the auspicious terms of Pinckney's Treaty of San Lorenzo, won praise for the troubled president.

Washington's Farewell

As his second term drew to a close, George Washington made a precedent-setting decision: he would not seek a third term as president. Instead, in 1796 he would return to his beloved Virginia home, Mount Vernon, and resume the life of a gentleman planter.

When Washington retired, he left behind a nation very different from the one whose independence he had helped win and whose survival he had helped secure. The postwar economic depression was over, and the war raging in Europe had produced a steadily rising demand for American foodstuffs. More fundamentally, in the fifteen years since the Revolution, the U.S. economy had moved decisively in the direction that Alexander Hamilton had envisioned. The values and expectations of a market economy—with its stress on maximizing profit and the pursuit of individual economic interests—had captured the imagination and shaped the actions of many white Americans. Hamilton's policies as secretary of the treasury had both reflected and advanced a growing interest in the expansion of trade, the growth of markets, and the development of American manufacturing and industry. In its political life, the republic had been reorganized and the relationships between the states and the central government redefined. The new Constitution granted greater diplomatic and commercial powers to the federal government but protected individual citizens through the Bill of Rights. America's political leaders, though convinced that factions were dangerous to the survival of the republic, had nevertheless created and begun to work within an evolving party system.

In his Farewell Address to the public, Washington expressed his thoughts on many of these changes. Although Jefferson had viewed the president as a partisan Federalist, Washington spoke with feeling against parties in a republic, urging the nation to return to nonpartisan cooperation. Washington also warned America and its new leaders not to "entangle our peace and prosperity in the toils of European ambition." An honorable country must "observe good faith and justice toward all nations," said the aging Virginian, but Americans must not let any alliance develop that draws the nation into a foreign war. The final ingredient in Washington's formula for America's success and its "permanent felicity" was the continuing virtue of its people.

□ **Jay's Treaty** Controversial 1794 treaty between the United States and Great Britain negotiated by John Jay to ensure American neutrality in the war between France and England.

□ **Battle of Fallen Timbers** A 1794 battle in which Kentucky riflemen defeated Indians of several tribes, helping to end Indian resistance in the Northwest.

□ **Treaty of Greenville** A 1795 treaty in which the United States agreed to pay northwestern Indians about $10,000 for the land that later became the state of Ohio.

market economy An economy in which production of goods is geared to sale or profit.

partisan Taking a strong position on an issue out of loyalty to a political group or leader.

Individual Voices

GOUVERNEUR MORRIS
Speaks as More Than a Nationalist

At the Constitutional Convention, Pennsylvania delegate Gouverneur Morris called on his fellow political leaders to set aside local and provincial interests and, as Alexander Hamilton put it, "think continentally." But Morris urged more than a concern for national interest; he believed that the principles embodied in the Constitution these men were writing would inspire people throughout the world. Morris's impassioned speech would be lost to us if delegate James Madison had not been secretly taking notes on the convention's debates. Historians of the era are fortunate that Madison disobeyed the convention rules and thus preserved Morris's vision of America as an inspiration to everyone.

Portrait of Gouverneur Morris (1752–1816) (oil on canvas), Sharples, James (c.1751–1811)/Bristol City Museum and Art Gallery, UK/The Bridgeman Art Library.

❶ Most Americans identified themselves by their town, state, or region rather than as citizens of the United States. What events or cultural changes might have helped forge a strong national identity in the decades that followed the Constitutional Convention?

❷ Does Morris's tone, as described by Madison, strike you as optimistic or pessimistic? Does he seem to doubt the integrity of his fellow delegates?

❸ What does Morris's admission that the sentiments of the people cannot be known suggest about the limits of communication in the 18th century? What tools do we have today that would allow us to gauge popular opinion?

❹ What recent civil commotion do you think would spring to the delegates' minds when Morris painted this dire scenario?

He came here as a Representative of America; he flattered himself he came here in some degree as a Representative of the whole human race; for the whole human race will be affected by the proceedings of this Convention. He wished gentlemen to extend their views beyond the present moment of time; beyond the narrow limits of place from which they derive their political origin. **❶** If he were to believe some things which he had heard, he should suppose that we were assembled to truck and bargain for our particular States. He can-not descend to think that any gentlemen are really actuated by these views. We must look forward to the effects of what we do. These alone ought to guide us. **❷** Much has been said of the sentiments of the people. They were unknown. They could not be known. All that we can infer is that if the plan we recommend be reasonable & right; all who have reasonable minds and sound intentions will embrace it, notwithstanding what had been said by some gentlemen. **❸** . . . This Country must be united. If persuasion does not unite it, the sword will. He begged that this consideration might have its due weight. The scenes of horror attending civil commotion can not be described, and the conclusion of them will be worse than the term of their continuance. The stronger party will then make traytors of the weaker; and the Gallows & Halter will finish the work of the sword. **❹** . . . State attachments, and State importance have been the bane of this Country. We can not annihilate; but we may perhaps take out the teeth of the serpents. He wished our ideas to be enlarged to the true interest of man, instead of being circumscribed within the narrow compass of a particular Spot. And after all how little can be the motive yielded by selfishness for such a policy. Who can say whether he himself, much less whether his children, will the next year be an inhabitant of this or that State.

Source: James Madison, Notes on Debates in the Federal Convention of 1787.

Study Tools

SUMMARY

After independence was declared, Americans faced the challenge of creating a new nation out of thirteen distinct states. The new nation faced enormous debt and was still surrounded by real and potential enemies, and its ability to survive seemed doubtful to many.

As colonies became states, they drafted their own constitutions. Some put in place democratic forms of government, while others built in more restrictive features such as high property qualifications for officeholding. The first national government, created by the Articles of Confederation, reflected the states' desire to preserve their individual sovereignty. It also embodied the revolutionary generation's opposition to a strong centralized government. The Confederation government thus lacked basic powers: it could not raise taxes or regulate commerce. However, it negotiated the peace treaty of 1783, and it established, through three Northwest Ordinances, the process by which territories became states. But with limited powers, the Confederation could not resolve the nation's financial problems, deal effectively with foreign nations, or ensure social order within its borders. By the time Massachusetts farmers rose up in revolt in 1786, many of the nation's elite political figures were calling for a stronger national government.

In the summer of 1787, these nationalists met in Philadelphia to consider a new Constitution. The Constitution they produced, after long months of debate, steered a middle ground between a central government that was too powerful and one that was too limited. It established executive, legislative, and judicial branches that could "check and balance" one another and thus, it was hoped, safeguard the nation from tyranny. The new government could both raise taxes and regulate commerce. After intense battles between pro-Constitution forces, known as Federalists, and their Antifederalist opponents, the new Constitution was ratified by the states in 1788.

Soon after George Washington took office as the first president, serious differences in political opinion again emerged. Alexander Hamilton's vision of a vigorous commercial and industrial nation conflicted with Thomas Jefferson's desire for an agrarian republic. The two resulting factions disagreed over economic and foreign policy. The French Revolution intensified the divisions: while Hamilton argued against American support for the French in their war with England, Jefferson pressed the administration to support their fellow revolutionaries. Washington managed to steer a neutral course in this European conflict.

By the end of Washington's second term, the United States had expanded its borders, negotiated with Spain for access to the Mississippi River, and under Hamilton's guidance, established a national bank at the center of an economic system that promoted market-oriented growth. The departing Washington urged Americans to continue to cooperate and cautioned them not to allow competing visions of America's future to harm the new nation.

CHRONOLOGY
From Revolution to Nationhood

1770s	State constitutions developed
1776	Oversight in New Jersey constitution gives property-holding women the right to vote
1781	States ratify Articles of Confederation / Cornwallis surrenders at Yorktown
1784–1787	Northwest Ordinances
1786	Annapolis Convention / Shays's Rebellion
1787	Constitutional Convention
1787–1788	States ratify U.S. Constitution
1789	First congressional elections / George Washington inaugurated as first president / Judiciary Act of 1789
1791	First Bank of the United States chartered / Bill of Rights added to Constitution / Alexander Hamilton's *Report on Manufactures*
1792	Washington reelected
1793	Genêt affair / Jefferson resigns as secretary of state
1794	Whiskey Rebellion in Pennsylvania / Battle of Fallen Timbers
1795	Congress approves Jay's Treaty / Treaty of San Lorenzo
1796	Washington's Farewell Address

FOCUS QUESTIONS

If you have mastered this chapter, you should be able to answer these questions and to explain the terms that follow the questions.

1. What types of legislatures did the states create?

2. What were the major elements of the Articles of Confederation?

3. What problems arose in ratifying the Articles?

4. What problems faced the Confederation?

5. What gains did nationalists expect from a stronger central government?

6. How did the Confederation establish relations with other nations?

7. What major compromises did the framers make in writing the new Constitution?

8. What safeguards did James Madison see in his "checks and balances" system?

9. What were the Antifederalists' arguments against the Constitution? What were the Federalists' arguments in its favor?

10. What was the outcome of the ratification process?

11. How did Alexander Hamilton's expectations for the new nation differ from those of Thomas Jefferson? What were the consequences of this conflict of vision?

12. How did the French Revolution affect Washington's diplomatic policy?

KEY TERMS

Articles of Confederation *p. 154*

proportional representation *p. 154*

John Dickinson *p. 154*

Robert Morris *p. 156*

tariff *p. 156*

Northwest Ordinances *p. 156*

Treaty of Fort Stanwix *p. 158*

Hopewell Treaties *p. 158*

John Jay *p. 158*

Barbary pirates *p. 158*

Daniel Shays *p. 159*

nationalists *p. 159*

James Madison *p. 160*

Great Compromise *p. 161*

Three-Fifths Compromise *p. 161*

Electoral College *p. 163*

ratifying conventions *p. 163*

Federalists *p. 164*

Antifederalists *p. 164*

Federalist Papers *p. 165*

cabinet *p. 167*

Judiciary Act of 1789 *p. 168*

Bill of Rights *p. 168*

Federalists *p. 168*

Republicans *p. 169*

sectionalism *p. 169*

Report on Public Credit *p. 169*

Bank of the United States *p. 170*

French Revolution *p. 170*

Reign of Terror *p. 170*

Edmond Genêt *p. 171*

Democratic-Republican societies *p. 172*

Whiskey Rebellion *p. 172*

Treaty of San Lorenzo *p. 173*

Jay's Treaty *p. 174*

Battle of Fallen Timbers *p. 174*

Treaty of Greenville *p. 174*

SUGGESTED RESOURCES

Yale Law School. Lillian Goldman Law Library, "*The Avalon Project*," http://avalon.law.yale.edu. This rich eighteenth-century collection of founding documents includes Madison's notes on the Constitutional Convention as well as those of Alexander Hamilton and Charles Pinckney.

"Founding Fathers." (History Channel DVD, 2012), An in-depth look at the men who wrote the constitution and the men who opposed it, with commentary by noted historians.

Linda Monk. *The Words We Live By: Your Annotated Guide to the Constitution* (Hyperion, 2004). Monk's commentary on the American Constitution makes this vital document accessible to every reader.

The Avalon Project. avalon.law.yale.edu/. This rich eighteenth century collection of founding documents includes Madison's notes on the constitutional convention as well as those of Alexander Hamilton and Charles Pinckney.

The Early Republic, 1796–1804

INDIVIDUAL CHOICES

Charles Cotesworth Pinckney

Charles Cotesworth Pinckney was born in South Carolina in 1746 to one of the leading families in colonial America; he was the son of Eliza Lucas Pinckney, the featured individual in Chapter 4, and planter/diplomat Charles Pinckney. He accompanied his father on a diplomatic mission to England in 1753 and stayed to graduate from Oxford University and then study law at the prestigious Middle Temple in London. He returned to the United States in 1770 and immediately became embroiled in politics. When the Revolution broke out, he volunteered for the Continental Army, eventually earning the rank of brigadier general. And like many of his fellow former officers, he became a delegate to the Constitutional Convention in 1787. Thus he was quite accustomed to the intrigues that haunted politics and international affairs during the raucous era of the late eighteenth century. But nothing in his background had prepared him for the shock he would receive as an American minister to France in 1797 and the momentous choice this would force him to make.

The presidential election in 1796 was hotly contested between Federalist John Adams and Republican Thomas Jefferson. Archrivals France and Great Britain each supported one of the candidates: Great Britain favored Adams, while France favored Jefferson. Adams emerged as the victor, but that did not end the controversy. On May 16, 1797, Adams called a special joint session of Congress and informed the legislature that "the French government

National Portrait Gallery, Smithsonian Institution/Art Resource, NY.

had expressed serious discontents at some proceedings of the government of these states" to which he had responded by sending a special envoy to smooth over differences. But he went on to say that the French government refused to receive the envoy "until after the redress of grievances demanded of the American government." He then announced his intention to "institute a fresh attempt at negotiation." Three delegates were to convene immediately in Paris with Pinckney in charge.

The French foreign minister received the delegation gladly, but The Directory refused them an audience. As days of diplomatic stalemate spun out, a man who would later be referred to as "Mr. X." approached the delegation explaining that he and other businessmen were in a position to get them a hearing if they paid a sizable bribe (see the Individual Voices feature at the end of this chapter). Confronted with this serious affront to American dignity and the diplomatic sovereignty of the United States, Pinckney immediately consulted with his colleagues and then, having reached his decision, broke off negotiations, launching what would be called the "Quasi-War" between the United States and France.

When George Washington retired as president, the stability that his leadership lent to a new and uncertain government retired with him. And Washington's replacement, John Adams, seemed incapable of calming national anxieties. Under his watch, the United States became involved in an undeclared war with France and saw its international reputation consistently decline. And domestic unrest prevailed as well. Led by Alexander Hamilton, Federalists had tried to undermine the electoral process in 1796 and then used the war crisis to attack their political enemies. Far from succeeding in the destruction of their critics, these Federalist efforts actually helped to crystallize opposition, giving Hamilton's key rival, Thomas Jefferson, a forum from which to assault the party in power. In 1800 the Federalists were soundly defeated and turned out of office.

Assuming the presidency in 1801, Jefferson ushered in a new era in American politics, launching the country on a freewheeling adventure of continental expansion and global trade. At the same time, Jefferson waged an aggressive foreign policy designed to restore American international trading and win new territory along the nation's borders. His successes could be measured by a mounting federal treasury surplus, increased national income, and expanding borders.

Under Jefferson's leadership most Americans saw significant improvement in their everyday lives, and the nation became increasingly optimistic. But the Jeffersonian promise was not made to everyone. For women, Native Americans, and African Americans, life improved for some, but underlying prejudices and rigid codes of public behavior prevented full realization of new opportunities. Contradictions shot through the whole of Jeffersonian America, counterbalancing the enthusiastic optimism and giving a peculiar shape to national life.

CONFLICT IN THE ADAMS ADMINISTRATION

☆ How did Federalists manipulate the crisis with France in 1798 for their own political advantage?

☆ What steps did Republicans take to counter Federalist manipulations?

Retiring president George Washington spoke for many in 1796 when he warned in his Farewell Address of "the baneful effects of the spirit of party." Followers of both Hamilton and Jefferson were thoroughgoing republicans, but their conceptions of republicanism were different. Hamiltonians tended to be "classical republicans," and espoused the belief that governments are fragile and must be led by an aristocracy that could protect the people from themselves.

□ **The Directory** (*Directoire exécutif*) The committee of government ministers that exercised executive authority in France between 1795 and 1799.

□ **Quasi-War** Diplomatic crisis triggered by the XYZ affair; fighting occurred between the United States and France between the early summer of 1798 and the official end of the conflict in September 1800, but neither side issued a formal declaration of war.

Jeffersonians, on the other hand, tended to be "liberal republicans," asserting that government existed solely to guarantee free and equal participation for citizens. For Federalists, aristocratically led republicanism in England provided the appropriate model; for Republicans, the populism in revolutionary France came closer to the ideal. These views were fundamentally incompatible and led each side to the conviction that the other sought to destroy "real" republicanism. These differences led to serious political conflict during the years following Washington's retirement.

The Split Election of 1796

As the broadly accepted leader of the opposition to Hamilton's policies, Thomas Jefferson was the Republicans' logical choice to represent them in the presidential election in 1796. Most people at the time were not surprised that Republicans chose **Aaron Burr**, a brilliant young New York attorney and member of the Senate, to balance the ticket.

Although he styled himself a spokesman for the common man, Burr definitely was not one—his grandfather was the famous evangelical minister Jonathan Edwards (see page 88), and his family continued to have enormous influence. During the Revolutionary War, Burr accepted a commission in the Continental Army, where he found common cause with the radical democrats who had formed the Sons of Liberty. By 1784, he had used his political connections and backing from the Sons of Liberty to win a place in the New York state assembly. In 1791 the New York Sons of Liberty, now calling themselves the Society of St. Tammany, maneuvered Burr's election to the U.S. Senate.

Approaching the election of Washington's successor, most Federalists assumed that Vice President Adams would be their candidate, but Hamilton and some other hardcore party members favored Thomas Pinckney of South Carolina. The younger brother of Charles Cotesworth Pinckney, Thomas had emerged as a major political force when he successfully negotiated the Treaty of San Lorenzo. This coup won Pinckney the unreserved admiration of both southerners and westerners; Hamilton supported him, though, because he was unwaveringly loyal while Adams was more independent.

☐ **Aaron Burr** New York lawyer and vice-presidential candidate in 1796; he became Thomas Jefferson's vice president in 1801 after the House of Representatives broke a deadlock in the Electoral College.

statesman A political leader who acts out of concern for the public good and not out of self-interest.

factionalism In politics, the emergence of various self-interested parties (factions) that compete to impose their own views onto either a larger political party or the nation at large.

Most Federalists, however, aligned behind the old warhorse from Massachusetts. A descendant of New England Puritans, Adams was a man of strong principles, fighting for what he believed was right despite anyone's contrary opinion. Though formally a Federalist, he remained Thomas Jefferson's close friend: both he and his wife, Abigail, maintained a spirited correspondence with the Virginian. Like Washington, Adams was seen by many old revolutionaries as above politics, as a statesman whose conscience and integrity would help the new nation avoid the pitfalls of factionalism.

Hamilton sought to use a loophole in the Constitution to rig the election for Pinckney. According to the Constitution, each member of the Electoral College could cast votes for any two candidates; the highest vote getter became president, and the runner-up became vice president. Hamilton urged Pinckney supporters to cast only one vote—for Pinckney—so that Adams could not get enough votes to win the presidency. But Hamilton miscalculated: he did not expect Adams's supporters to learn of the plot, and when they did, they withheld votes from Pinckney.

Because of the squabbling within the Federalist faction, Jefferson received the votes of disgruntled Federalist electors as well as electors within Republican ranks. He thus ended up with more votes than Pinckney—and only three fewer than Adams. So the nation emerged from the first truly contested presidential election with a split administration: the president and vice president belonged to different factions and held opposing political philosophies. Adams compounded partisan divides by retaining Hamilton loyalists Oliver Wolcott, James McHenry, and Timothy Pickering from Washington's cabinet. This disunity enticed interested parties both at home and abroad to try to undermine Adams's authority and influence.

XYZ: The Power of Patriotism

One group seeking to take advantage of the divisions in the United States was the revolutionary government in France. The pro-British impact of Jay's Treaty and the antirevolutionary rhetoric adopted by Federalists led the French to question American friendship. During the election of 1796, France sought to influence American voting by actively favoring Republican candidates, threatening to terminate diplomatic relations if the vocally pro-British Federalists won. True to its word, the French Directory broke off relations with the United States as soon as Adams was elected.

Although angry at the French, Adams still vowed to pursue a diplomatic solution by sending Charles Cotesworth Pinckney, John Marshall, and Elbridge Gerry to Paris, where they were to arrange a peaceful settlement of the two nations' differences. At the same time, Adams told Congress that the United States would not be "humiliated under a colonial spirit of

One of the fathers of the American Revolution, John Adams seemed the perfect choice to step into the presidency when George Washington chose to step down at the end of his second term. Though many were comforted by Adams's conservative statesmanship, the rigid New Englander was poorly qualified to deal with the partisan politics that came to haunt his administration.

Library of Congress.

fear and a sense of inferiority," and he pressed the legislature to build up America's military defenses.

The French Directory ordered foreign minister **Charles Maurice de Talleyrand-Périgord** to keep the American delegation waiting, even as the French provocatively began to seize American ships. After the attempted intervention by interested business people (see the Individual Choices and Individual Voices features in this chapter), Pinckney cleverly postponed further talks in an effort to stop French predations on American shipping so he and his party could safely leave France. Later, when sharing the diplomatic dispatches with Congress, Adams ordered that the names of the businessmen be replaced with the initials "X," "Y," and "Z."

Americans' response to the **XYZ affair** was overwhelming. France's diplomatic slight seemed a slap in the face to a new nation seeking international respect. In Philadelphia, people paraded in the streets to protest French arrogance. The crowds chanted Pinckney's reported response: "No; no, not a sixpence!" This wave of patriotism gave the president a virtually unified Congress and country. In the heat of the moment, Adams pressed for increased military forces, and in short order Congress created the

Department of the Navy and appropriated money to start building a fleet of warships. Then, on July 7, 1798, Congress rescinded all treaties with France and authorized privateering against French ships. Congress also created a standing army of twenty thousand troops and ordered that the militia be expanded to thirty thousand men. Washington added his prestige to the effort by coming out of retirement to lead the new army, with Hamilton as his second-in-command. Although running sea battles between French and American ships resulted in the sinking or capture of many vessels on both sides, Congress shied away from actually declaring war, which led to the conflict being labeled the Quasi-War.

The Home Front in the Quasi-War

Federalists immediately seized upon the war as a means to crush their political enemies. In Congress, they began referring to Jefferson and his supporters as the "French Party." Arguing that the presence of this "French Party" constituted a danger to national security, congressional Federalists proposed a series of new laws to destroy all opposition to their conception of true republicanism.

One source of opposition was **naturalized** American citizens. The revolutionary promises of "life, liberty, and the pursuit of happiness" had attracted many immigrants to the United States. They were drawn to Jefferson's political rhetoric—especially his stress on equal opportunity and his attacks on aristocracy. In 1798 Federalists in Congress passed three acts designed to counter political activities by immigrants. The Naturalization Act extended the residency requirement for citizenship from five to fourteen years. The Alien Act authorized the president to deport any foreigner he judged "dangerous to the peace and safety of the United States." The Alien Enemies Act permitted the president to imprison or banish any foreigner he considered dangerous. The Naturalization Act was designed to prevent recent immigrants from supporting the Republican cause by barring them from the political process. The other two acts served as a constant reminder that the president or his

☐ **Charles Maurice de Talleyrand-Périgord** French foreign minister appointed by the revolutionary government in 1797; he later aided Napoleon Bonaparte's overthrow of that government and served as his foreign minister.

☐ **XYZ affair** A diplomatic incident in which American envoys to France were told that the United States would have to loan France money and bribe government officials as a precondition for negotiation.

naturalized Granted full citizenship (after having been born in a foreign country).

The majority of Americans were scandalized by the XYZ affair and convinced that French radicalism and corruption threatened their security. In this cartoon from 1798, the French Directory is depicted as a five-headed monster threatening the American delegation with a dagger. In the background French dignitaries share a feast at the base of the guillotine. Such images ginned up American resentment as the Quasi-War unfolded.

agents could arbitrarily imprison or deport any resident alien who stepped out of line.

The other source of support for Jefferson was the Republican press. Both political factions were notorious for maintaining partisan newspapers that spewed biased stories and scurrilous editorials. Congressional Federalists passed the Sedition Act, which, in addition to outlawing conspiracies to block the enforcement of federal laws, prohibited the publication or utterance of any criticism of the government or its officials. In the words of one Federalist newspaper, "It is patriotism to write in favour of our government, it is **sedition** to write against it." Federalists brandished the law against all kinds of criticism directed toward either the government or the president, including perfectly innocent political editorials. Not surprisingly, most of the defendants in the fifteen cases brought by federal authorities under the Sedition Act were prominent Republican newspaper editors.

Republicans complained that the **Alien and Sedition Acts** violated the Bill of Rights, but Congress and the federal judiciary, controlled as they were by Federalists, paid no attention. Dissidents had little choice but to take their political case to the state governments, which they did in the fall of 1798. One statement, drafted by Madison, came before the Virginia legislature, and another, by Jefferson, was considered in Kentucky.

Madison and Jefferson based their **Virginia and Kentucky Resolutions** on the Tenth Amendment, contending that powers not specifically granted to the federal government under the Constitution or reserved to the people in the Bill of Rights fell to the states. By passing laws such as the Alien and Sedition Acts that were not explicitly permitted in the text of the Constitution, Congress had violated the states' rights. The two authors differed, however, in how the states should respond. For his part, Madison asserted that when the majority of states agreed that a federal law had violated their Tenth Amendment rights, they could collectively overrule federal authority. But Jefferson argued for the principle of **interposition**, recognizing each state's "natural right" to interpose its authority between the federal government and its own citizens.

The Virginia and Kentucky Resolutions passed in their respective state legislatures, but no other states followed suit. Even within Kentucky and Virginia, great disagreement arose over how far state authority should extend. Nevertheless, this response to the Federalists' use of federal power brought the disputed relationship between federal law and **states' rights** into national prominence.

Another bone of contention was the methods used to finance the Quasi-War and the impact these methods had on various groups of Americans. Consistent with Hamilton's views on finance, tariffs and excises were to be the primary source of revenue, and they had the greatest impact on people who needed manufactured or imported items but had little hard cash. In addition, Federalists imposed a tax on land, hitting cash-poor farmers especially hard. In 1799 farmers in Northampton County, Pennsylvania, refused to pay the

sedition Conduct or language inciting rebellion against the authority of a state.

◻ Alien and Sedition Acts Collectively, the four acts—Alien Act, Alien Enemies Act, Naturalization Act, and Sedition Act—passed by Congress in 1798 designed to prevent immigrants from participating in politics and to silence the anti-Federalist press.

◻ Virginia and Kentucky Resolutions Statements that the Virginia and Kentucky legislatures issued in 1798 in response to the Alien and Sedition Acts; they asserted the right of states to overrule the federal government.

interposition To Jefferson, the principle of interposition meant that states had the right to use their sovereign power as a barrier between the federal government and the states' citizens when the natural rights of those citizens were at risk.

◻ states' rights The political position in favor of limiting federal power to allow the greatest possible self-government by the individual states.

tax and began harassing tax collectors. Several tax resisters were arrested, but local Federalist John Fries raised an armed force to break them out of jail. Later, federal troops sent by Adams to suppress what was characterized as Fries's Rebellion arrested Fries and two of his associates. Charged with treason, the three were tried in federal court, found guilty, and condemned to death.

Settlement with France

The Federalists' seeming overreaction to French provocation and domestic protest alienated increasing numbers of Americans. In the heat of the moment, Pennsylvania Republican George Logan undertook a personal crusade to end the conflict, voyaging to France to negotiate peace. When Logan sent news that Foreign Minister Talleyrand was asking that a new American delegation be sent, Adams seized the opportunity to end the Quasi-War. Telling the Federalist-dominated Congress that he would give them the details later, Adams instructed the American minister to the Netherlands, William Vans Murray, to go immediately to Paris. As rumors of negotiations began to circulate, Hamilton and his supporters became furious, all but accusing Adams of treason. This gave the president the ammunition he needed: he fired Hamilton loyalists Pickering, Wolcott, and McHenry and then embarrassed the Federalist judiciary by granting a presidential pardon to John Fries and his fellow Pennsylvania rebels.

Adams's diplomatic appeal to France was well timed. When Murray and his delegation arrived in Paris in November 1799, they found that whatever ill feeling might have existed toward the United States had been swept away. On November 9, 1799, Napoleon Bonaparte had overthrown The Directory. Napoleon was more interested in establishing an empire in Europe than in continuing an indecisive conflict with the United States. After some negotiation, Murray and Napoleon drew up and signed the Convention of Mortefontaine, ending the Quasi-War on September 30, 1800.

THE "REVOLUTION OF 1800"

☆ How did Federalists respond to losing the election of 1800? What does this response reveal about their political attitudes?

☆ What did Thomas Jefferson mean by the statement "Every difference of opinion is not a difference of principles"?

☆ How did Jefferson's vision for America differ from that of Hamilton, Adams, and other Federalists?

According to the partisan press, the political situation in 1800 was as simple as the contrast between the personalities of the major presidential candidates.

The Republican press characterized Adams as an aristocrat and claimed that his efforts to expand the powers of the federal government were really attempts to rob citizens of freedom. In contrast, it characterized Jefferson as a man of the people, sensitive to the appeals of southern and western agricultural groups who felt perpetually ignored or abused by northeastern elites. According to Federalist newspapers, however, Vice President Jefferson was a dangerous radical and an atheist. By their reckoning, Adams was a man whose policies and steady-handed administration would bring stability and prosperity, qualities that appealed to elite propertied interests. The rhetoric became so hateful that even Adams and Jefferson got caught up in it—the old friends stopped speaking to each other; nearly twenty years passed before they renewed their friendship.

The Lesser of Republican Evils

As the election of 1800 approached, the split between Adams and Hamilton widened. Both agreed on the necessity of dumping Jefferson as vice president, putting forward Charles Cotesworth Pinckney to replace him. But Adams's behavior in the wake of Logan's mission to France had angered Federalists; they now wanted Adams to be gone as well. Having gotten Pinckney into the Electoral College balloting, Hamilton again tried to steal the 1800 election. As before, he advised delegates to withhold votes, but this time he engaged in direct lobbying, even writing a pamphlet in which he questioned Adams's suitability for the presidency.

Hamilton's methods backfired again: Federalists cast one more vote for Adams than for Pinckney. But more important, Hamilton's scheming and his faction's consistent pro-manufacturing stance had so alienated southern Federalists that many chose to support Jefferson. With Jefferson pulling in the southern vote and his running mate—Burr again—pulling in the craftsmen and small-farm vote in New York and Pennsylvania, the Republicans outscored the Federalists by 16 votes in the Electoral College. But that still did not settle the election. Burr and Jefferson won the same number of electoral votes, throwing the contest into the still Federalist-dominated House of Representatives (see Map 8.1).

□ **Fries's Rebellion** A tax revolt by Pennsylvania citizens in 1799 that was suppressed by federal forces; leader John Fries was condemned to death for treason but received a presidential pardon from John Adams.

□ **Napoleon Bonaparte** General who took control of the French government in November 1799, at the end of France's revolutionary period; he eventually proclaimed himself emperor of France and conquered much of the continent of Europe.

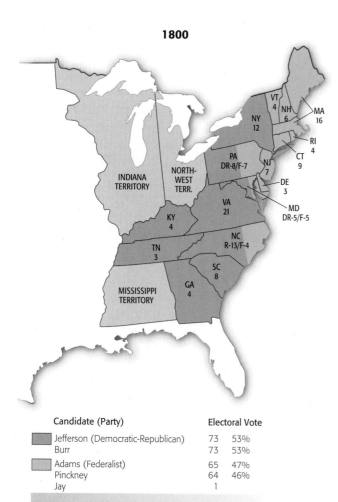

1800

Candidate (Party)	Electoral Vote	
Jefferson (Democratic-Republican)	73	53%
Burr	73	53%
Adams (Federalist)	65	47%
Pinckney	64	46%
Jay	1	

MAP 8.1 Election of 1800

The political partnership between Thomas Jefferson and Aaron Burr allowed the Republicans to unseat Federalist John Adams in the election of 1800. As this map shows, only New England voted as a bloc for the Federalist, while Burr's political home, New York, went entirely to Jefferson. © Cengage Learning.

☐ **Twelfth Amendment** Constitutional amendment, ratified in 1804, that provides for separate balloting in the Electoral College for president and vice president.

lame duck An officeholder who has failed to win reelection or is ineligible for reelection, but whose term in office has not yet ended.

☐ **Judiciary Act of 1801** Law that the Federalist Congress passed to increase the number of federal courts and judicial positions; President Adams rushed to fill these positions with Federalists before his term ended.

☐ **John Marshall** Virginia lawyer and politician whom President Adams made chief justice of the Supreme Court; his legal decisions helped shape the role of the Supreme Court in American government.

conciliatory Striving to overcome distrust or to regain goodwill.

Federalists in the House now faced the task of choosing between two men whom most of them viewed as being dangerous radicals. Indecision was plain: in ballot after ballot over six grueling days early in 1801, neither Jefferson nor Burr could win the necessary majority. Eventually, two things combined to break the deadlock. First, Hamilton convinced several Federalists that even though Jefferson's rhetoric was dangerous, the Virginian was a gentleman of property and integrity—a suitable guardian under classical republican theory—whereas Burr was "the most dangerous man of the community." Second, intent on preventing a "legislative usurpation" of the popular will, Virginia and Pennsylvania mobilized their militias. As Delaware senator James Bayard described the situation, "we must risk the Constitution and a Civil War or take Mr. Jefferson." Finally, on the thirty-sixth ballot, on February 17, 1801, Jefferson emerged as the winner.

Federalists and Republicans agreed about very little, but the threat of civil war frightened both factions equally. Not long after Jefferson's election, both parties aligned briefly to pass the Twelfth Amendment to the Constitution, which requires separate balloting in the Electoral College for president and vice president, thereby preventing deadlocks like the one that nearly wrecked the nation in 1800.

Federalist Defenses and a Loyal Opposition

The Federalists had outmaneuvered themselves in the election of 1800, but they were not about to leave office without erecting some defenses for the political and economic machinery they had constructed. The Federalist-controlled judiciary, which had proved its clout during the controversy over the Alien and Sedition Acts, appeared to offer the strongest bulwark to prevent Republicans from tampering with the Constitution. Thus, during their last days in office, the Federalist lame ducks in Congress passed the Judiciary Act of 1801, which greatly expanded the federal court system. President Adams then rushed to fill all these positions with loyal Federalists, signing appointments right up to midnight on his last day in office. The appointments came in such large numbers and so late in the day that John Marshall, Adams's secretary of state, was unable to deliver all the appointment letters before his own term ran out. But Marshall did deliver one letter promptly: the one making him chief justice of the Supreme Court.

Considering the ill will evident in the Alien and Sedition Acts and the presidential electioneering, Jefferson's inaugural address was oddly conciliatory. "We are all Republicans; we are all Federalists," Jefferson said, seeming to abandon partisan politics and align himself with those who had recently

This monumental statue of Chief Justice John Marshall, which sits on the ground floor of the Supreme Court Building, captures the jurist's imposing presence—he dominated the Supreme Court and American constitutional law for over thirty years after his appointment in 1801, setting many precedents that remain in force today.

Photograph by Steve Petteway, Collection of the Supreme Court of the United States.

labeled him a "contemptible hypocrite." In his mind, all Americans shared the same republican goals, but even Jefferson considered the election of 1800 a revolution—"as real a revolution in the principles of our government as that of 1776 was in its form."

Jefferson was right in many respects about the revolutionary nature of the election of 1800. Although his inaugural address preached kinship between Federalists and Republicans, the new president repeatedly criticized his opponents for their lack of faith in the American people. "If there be any among us who would wish to dissolve this Union or to change its republican form," he said, "let them stand undisturbed as monuments of the safety with which error of opinion may be tolerated, where reason is left free to combat it."

As a result of Jefferson's reassuring address, the nation began to share the president's view that "Every difference of opinion is not a difference of principles." Even extreme Federalists such as Fisher Ames came to understand that a "party is an association of honest men for honest purposes." Ames went on to describe how a loyal **opposition party** should behave. "We are not to revile or abuse magistrates, or lie even for good cause," he said. "We must act as good citizens, using only truth, and argument, and zeal to

impress them." With parties such as these, a system of loyal opposition could become a permanent part of a republican government without risk to security or freedom. And in keeping with the two-party spirit and Jefferson's philosophical commitment to free speech, Congress eliminated the Alien and Sedition Acts.

Jefferson's Vision for America

Jefferson had a strong, positive vision for the nation, and the party made every effort to put his policies into effect. The greatest dangers to a republic, he believed, were (1) high population density and the social evils it generated, and (2) the concentration of money and power in the hands of a few. Accordingly, Jefferson wanted to steer America away from the large-scale, publicly supported industry so dear to Hamilton and toward an economy founded on yeoman farmers— men who owned their own land, produced their own food, and were beholden to no one. Such men, Jefferson believed, could make political decisions based solely on pure reason and good sense.

But Jefferson was not naive. He knew Americans would continue to demand the comforts and luxuries found in industrial societies. His solution was simple. In America's vast lands, he said, a nation of farmers could produce so much food that "its surplus [could] go to nourish the now perishing births of Europe, who in return would manufacture and send us in exchange our clothes and other comforts." Overpopulation and **urbanization**—the twin causes of corruption in Europe—would not occur in America, for here, Jefferson said, "the immense extent of uncultivated and fertile lands enables every one who will labor, to marry young, and to raise a family of any size."

Making such a system work, however, would require a radical change in economic policy. The government would have to let businesses make their own decisions and succeed or fail in a marketplace free of government interference. In an economy with absolutely free trade and an open marketplace, the iron law of **supply and demand** would determine the cost of goods and services. This view of the economy was a direct assault on mercantilist notions of governments controlling prices and restricting trade to benefit the nation-state.

opposition party A political party opposed to the party or government in power.

urbanization The growth of cities in a nation or region and the shifting of the population from rural to urban areas.

☐ **supply and demand** The two factors that determine price in an economy based on private property: (1) how much of a commodity is available (supply), and (2) how many people want it (demand).

It Matters Today

The Peaceful Transit of Power

Beginning with debates over the ratification of the Constitution and continuing with ever-increasing stridency through the Quasi-War, questions about the legitimacy of opposition politics ran rampant. Many among the nation's founders wondered if *loyal* opposition was even possible. In 1798, one Federalist in Congress accused the Republican opposition of outright treason, charging that they "believe it to be their duty to do all in their power to overturn the whole system, to effect which, they may think a French army and a French invasion necessary." Republican John Nicholas countered that the Federalists were far more dangerous than the French, seeking to "subvert all the liberties of our country," and many suspected that they were not above using a British army to attain that end. Such charges and countercharges became increasingly strident as the presidential election approached in 1800, and many feared that a truly contested election would result in civil war. Despite these realistic fears, the election came and went, the Federalists were swept from power, and both parties settled into a comfortable, though seldom affable, pattern of permanent opposition. With a few minor exceptions, the two-party system has dominated the political process ever since, and while claims of treason or of subverting liberties continue to muddle our political rhetoric, the precedent of a peaceful transit of power set in the election of 1800 remains fundamental to our success as a nation.

- Consider the impact of a two-party political system on national life. Has the impact been generally positive? Why or why not?
- Though the two-party system has dominated politics in the United States, there have been some significant exceptions. Examine a period during which there was either only one political party or more than two parties and analyze what caused this exception and how it played out.

REPUBLICANISM IN ACTION

☆ *What legal maneuvers did Republicans initiate to deal with defenses Federalists put in place in 1801? What were the political and constitutional consequences?*

☆ *What policies did Jefferson pursue to carry out his vision for the country? What obstacles did he encounter?*

When Jefferson assumed office, he ushered a new spirit into national politics and the presidency. A combination of circumstances moved him to lead a much simpler life than had his predecessors. For one thing, he was the first president to be inaugurated in the new national capital, the still largely uncompleted Washington City, which afforded quite different and much more limited amenities. Washington lacked the taverns and entertaining social circles that both previous capitals, New York and Philadelphia, had offered. Personal preferences also moved him in a simpler direction. He refused, for example, to ride in a carriage,

choosing to go by horseback through Washington's muddy and rutted streets. He sometimes entertained with startling informality, wearing frayed slippers and work clothes, and seated his guests at a round table so that no one might be seen as more important than the others.

But this show of simplicity and his conciliatory inaugural address were misleading. Jefferson was a hard-working partisan politician whose main objective was to bring the nation around to his vision of republican virtue with all possible speed. He quickly launched a program to revamp the American economy and give the United States a place in the international community. Along the way, he captured many Americans' affection and their political loyalty but also alienated those who did not share his vision.

Assault on Federalist Defenses

Aware of the partisan purpose behind the Judiciary Act of 1801 and Adams's midnight appointments, Republicans chose to wage an equally aggressive partisan war to reverse Federalist control of the justice system. In January 1802, Republicans in Congress proposed the repeal of the 1801 Judiciary Act, arguing that the expanded court system was unnecessary.

amenities Conveniences, comforts, and services.

Suffering a lifelong sensitivity to cold as well as a dislike for formality, Thomas Jefferson usually chose to dress practically, in fairly plain clothes that kept him warm. This 1822 portrait by Thomas Sully captures the former president in his customary greatcoat, unadorned suit, and well-worn boots.

Federalists countered that repealing the act would violate the separation of powers. Congress proceeded anyway, replacing the Judiciary Act of 1801 with the Judiciary Act of 1802, and awaited the response of the Federalist courts.

Eventually in the case of *Stuart v. Laird* (1803) the Supreme Court approved Congress's action, but six days earlier another decision loomed even larger. Upon taking office, Jefferson's secretary of state, James Madison, held back the appointment letters that John Marshall had been unable to deliver before the expiration of his term. One jilted appointee was William Marbury, who was to have been a **justice of the peace** for the newly created federal District of Columbia. Marbury, with the support of his party, filed suit in the Supreme Court. According to Marbury, the Judiciary Act of 1789 gave the federal courts the power to order the executive branch to deliver his appointment.

Marbury v. Madison was Chief Justice Marshall's first major case, and in it he proved his political as well as his judicial ingenuity. Marshall was keenly aware that in a direct confrontation between the executive and judicial branches, the judiciary was sure to lose. Rather than risking a serious blow to the dignity of the Supreme Court, Marshall ruled in 1803 that the Constitution contained no provision for the Supreme Court to issue such orders as the Judiciary Act of 1789 required and that therefore that portion of the law was unconstitutional.

This decision put Jefferson and Madison in a difficult political position. On one hand, the authors of the Virginia and Kentucky Resolutions were on record for arguing that the states and not the courts should determine the constitutionality of federal laws. But political realities forced them to accept Marshall's decisions in these cases if they wanted to block Adams's handpicked men from assuming lifetime appointments in powerful judicial positions. Although these **precedents** for **judicial review** did not immediately invalidate the principles set forth in Jefferson's and Madison's earlier **manifestos**, they established the standard that federal courts, rather than states, could decide the constitutionality of acts of Congress.

Marshall's decision in *Marbury v. Madison* gave the Republicans the power to withhold undelivered letters of appointment from the Adams administration, but it gave them no power to control the behavior of judges whose appointments were already official. Thus, in the aftermath of the *Marbury* decision, Republican radicals in Congress decided to take aim at particularly partisan Federalist judges.

John Pickering of New Hampshire was an easy first target. Mentally ill, he was known to rave incoherently both on and off the bench. No one, not even staunch Federalists, doubted that the man was incompetent, but it was far from certain that he had committed the "high crimes and misdemeanors" for which he was **impeached** in 1803. Whether he had or not, the Senate found him guilty and removed him from office.

justice of the peace The lowest level of judge in some state court systems, usually responsible for hearing small claims and minor criminal cases; because the District of Columbia is a federal territory rather than a state, the justices of the peace for that district are federal appointees.

◻ *Marbury v. Madison* Supreme Court decision (1803) declaring part of the Judiciary Act of 1789 unconstitutional, thereby establishing an important precedent in favor of judicial review.

precedent An event or decision that may be used as an example in similar cases later on.

judicial review The power of the Supreme Court to review the constitutionality of laws passed by Congress and by the states.

manifesto A written statement publicly declaring the views of its author.

impeach To formally charge a public official with criminal conduct in office; once the House of Representatives has impeached a federal official, the official is then tried in the Senate on the stated charges.

Judicial Review over the Acts of Congress

Article III of the Constitution makes two related statements: "The judicial power of the United States shall be vested in one Supreme Court . . ." and "The judicial power shall extend to all cases, in law and equity, arising under this Constitution, the laws of the United States, and treaties made . . .". What was not clear from these assertions was whether the Supreme Court had the power to overrule acts of Congress viewed as unconstitutional or if the separation of powers prohibited that. In their Virginia and Kentucky Resolutions, Madison and Jefferson had each argued that the Tenth Amendment gave this power to the states.

Two cases that went before the Supreme Court in 1803 asserted an answer to this question. In *Marbury v. Madison*, the court decided that a portion of the Judiciary Act of 1789 was unconstitutional and struck it down. Less than a week later, in *Stuart v. Laird*, the court upheld Congress's action in repealing the Judiciary Act of 1801. Political realities at the time forced Jefferson and Madison to accept these decisions, opening the door to what is now universally recognized as the Supreme Court's power of judicial review over acts of Congress.

Emboldened by that easy victory, radical Republicans took on Supreme Court Justice Samuel Chase. Chase was notorious for making partisan decisions—such as condemning John Fries to death—and for using the federal bench as an anti-Republican soapbox. Unlike Pickering, Chase defended himself very competently, making the political motivations behind the impeachment effort obvious to all observers. In the end, both Federalists and many Republicans voted to dismiss the charges, reconfirming Chase to the Court.

Implementing a New Economy

Still, Republicans were determined on one partisan agenda item: tearing down Hamilton's economic structure and replacing it with a new one more consistent

▢ **Albert Gallatin** Treasury secretary in Jefferson's administration; he favored limited government and reduced the federal debt by cutting spending.

internal taxes Taxes collected directly from citizens, like Alexander Hamilton's various excise taxes, as opposed to tariffs or other taxes collected in connection with foreign trade.

with Jefferson's vision. One key economic difference between Federalists and Republicans was their position on government debt: Jeffersonians believed in a balanced budget, while Hamiltonians understood the practical ends to which debt might be useful. Treasury Secretary **Albert Gallatin**, in true Republican fashion, immediately set out to retire the nation's debt, seeking to make the United States entirely debt free by 1817. With Jefferson's approval, Gallatin implemented a radical course of budget cutting. But even this measure had other, more direct partisan goals.

First, through staff reductions, Gallatin was able to mask the firing of loyal Federalists still employed in civil service in a seemingly nonpartisan appeal to fiscal responsibility, and in drastically reducing the size of the military, he removed many Federalist officers. He accomplished another ideological goal by reducing the overall federal presence, putting more responsibilities onto the states, where Jefferson's philosophy said they belonged. In addition, Gallatin's plan called for a significant change in how the government raised money. In 1802 the Republican Congress repealed all **internal taxes**, leaving customs duties and the sale of western lands as the sole sources of federal revenue. With this one sweeping gesture, Gallatin struck a major blow for Jefferson's economic vision by tying the nation's financial future to westward expansion and foreign trade. But this vision would soon face serious challenges.

Threats to Jefferson's Vision

One threat to Jefferson's commitment to foreign trade came from pirates who patrolled the northern coast of Africa from Tangier to Tripoli, controlling access to the Mediterranean Sea. Ever since gaining independence, the United States had in effect been bribing the Barbary pirates not to attack American ships. By 1800, fully a fifth of the federal budget was earmarked for this purpose, a cost Gallatin wished to see eliminated as he tried to balance the nation's books. To Jefferson, principle was as important as financial considerations. Deciding on war, Jefferson asserted presidential privilege as commander in chief to dispatch navy ships to the Mediterranean in 1801.

What followed was a fiasco from anyone's point of view. After some indecisive engagements between the American fleet and the pirates, Jefferson's navy suffered a major defeat with the capture of a prize warship, the *Philadelphia,* and its entire crew. A bold but unsuccessful attempt to invade Tripoli by land across the Libyan Desert led only to a threat to kill the crew of the *Philadelphia* and other hostages. The war dragged along until 1805, when the United States finally negotiated peace terms, agreeing to pay $60,000 for the release of the hostages and accepting the pirates' promise to stop raiding American shipping.

In the meantime, France and Spain posed a serious threat to Jefferson's dream of rapid westward expansion. As settlers continued to pour into the region between the Appalachian Mountains and the Mississippi River, the commercial importance of that inland waterway increased. Whoever controlled the mouth of the Mississippi—the place where it flows past New Orleans and into the Gulf of Mexico and the open seas—would have the power to make or break the interior economy.

In accordance with the Treaty of San Lorenzo, Spain had granted American farmers the right to ship cargoes down the Mississippi without paying tolls and had given American merchants permission to **transship** goods from New Orleans to Atlantic ports without paying export duties. In 1800, however, Napoleon had traded some of France's holdings in southern Europe to Spain in exchange for Spain's land in North America. The United States had no agreement with France concerning navigation on the Mississippi, so the deal between Spain and France threatened to scuttle American commerce on the river. Anxiety over this issue turned to outright panic when, preparatory to the transfer of the land to France, Spanish officials suspended free trade in New Orleans.

Jefferson responded on two fronts. Backing away from his usual anti-British position, he announced, "The day France takes possession of New Orleans we must marry ourselves to the British fleet and nation," and he dispatched James Monroe to talk with the British about a military alliance. He also had Monroe instruct the American minister to France, Robert Livingston, that he could spend as much as $2 million to try to purchase New Orleans and as much adjacent real estate as possible.

Napoleon may have been considering the creation of a Caribbean empire when he acquired Louisiana from Spain, but a series of setbacks prevented his following through, including a slave revolt on the island of **Saint-Domingue** led by **François Dominique Toussaint Louverture**. Stymied in the Caribbean, Napoleon turned his full attention back to extending his holdings in Europe and was seeking funds to finance a continental war. Thus, by the time Monroe and Livingston entered into negotiations with the French in 1803, Napoleon had instructed Foreign Minister Talleyrand to offer the whole of Louisiana to the Americans for $15 million.

Pushing Westward

Although Livingston and Monroe had been authorized to spend only $2 million for the purchase of Louisiana,

Although Jefferson largely failed in efforts to stop Barbary pirate looting against American shipping in the Mediterranean, the struggle provided a wonderful training ground for future military leaders. Young naval commander Stephen Decatur was one such figure. Decatur led his men in boarding a pirate ship and engaged in hand-to-hand fighting against the crew, eventually winning the fight despite having been shot through the arm.

they jumped at Talleyrand's offer. The president was overjoyed. The deal contained three important benefits for Jefferson and the Republican vision for the nation. It removed one European power—France—from the continent and saved Jefferson from having to ally the United States with Britain. It secured the Mississippi River for shipments of American agricultural products to industrial Europe. And it doubled the size of the United States, opening uncharted new expanses for settlement by yeoman farmers.

The **Louisiana Purchase** was immensely popular among most Americans, but it raised significant

transship To ship cargo to a port and then transfer it to other ships for transport to a final destination; cargoes shipped by barge down the Mississippi River to New Orleans were then loaded onto ocean-going vessels bound for American ports along the Atlantic coast.

☐ **Saint-Domingue** Caribbean island originally named Hispaniola by Christopher Columbus and also known as Santo Domingo; today shared by the nations of Haiti and the Dominican Republic.

☐ **François Dominique Toussaint Louverture** Black revolutionary who liberated the island of Saint-Domingue, only to see it reinvaded by the French in 1802.

☐ **Louisiana Purchase** The U.S. purchase of Louisiana from France for $15 million in 1803; the Louisiana Territory extended from the Mississippi River to the Rocky Mountains.

In the Wider World

The Republic of Haiti

The Louisiana Purchase came about largely owing to dramatic events elsewhere in the Americas. Between 1791 and 1804, slaves on the Caribbean island of Saint-Domingue waged a successful rebellion against their Spanish and French masters. It began on August 22, 1791, as a general slave revolt. Through the rest of that year, pitched fighting between the slave rebels and their masters left thousands dead on both sides. In the course of the fighting, one self-educated former slave, François Dominique Toussaint Louverture, emerged as a dominant figure, liberating the island from colonial control in 1801.

The sugar-rich island may have figured in Napoleon's plans for exploiting the North American interior, and in the following year, he sent an expeditionary force against the former slaves. The French were able to defeat and capture Toussaint, but no more. The rebels' military skills and yellow fever destroyed the French force. And on January 1, 1804, Toussaint's successor, Jean-Jacques Dessalines, announced the birth of the Republic of Haiti, the first postcolonial black-led nation in the world.

---

ideological and constitutional questions. Some Federalists *and* Republicans questioned whether the United States could acquire this territory and its many residents without becoming an empire—something entirely at war with the rhetoric of our Revolution against the British. To this Jefferson responded by spinning the term "empire" into the phrase "empire of liberty," emphasizing that the new territory would aid Americans in securing and extending the benefits of our revolutionary tradition. Members of both parties also pointed out that the framers of the Constitution had made no provision for the acquisition of new territories by the United States, saying that the nation was prohibited from extending westward beyond its then-current boundaries without specific constitutional authorization. Again Jefferson parried with rhetoric, saying: "Strict observance to the written laws is doubtless one of the high duties of a good citizen, but it is not the highest. The laws of necessity, of self-preservation, of saving our country when in danger, are of a higher obligation." In the end, Jefferson got his way: Congress voted overwhelmingly for ratification of the treaty in November 1803.

□ **Meriwether Lewis** Jefferson aide who was sent to explore the Louisiana Territory in 1803; he later served as its governor.

□ **William Clark** Soldier and explorer who joined Meriwether Lewis as co-leader on an expedition to explore the Louisiana Territory; he was responsible for mapmaking.

□ **Sacajawea** Shoshone woman who served as guide and interpreter on the Lewis and Clark expedition.

Even before the Louisiana Purchase, "laws of necessity" had led Jefferson to exert presidential power in an unusual way. When rumors of the land transfer between France and Spain began circulating, Jefferson started preparations for a series of covert spy missions. In a series of confidential letters, Jefferson instructed his private secretary, Meriwether Lewis, to form a party that would pretend to be on a scientific expedition into Louisiana.

Lewis, his co-commander William Clark, and the rest of the "Corps of Discovery" set out by boat in the spring of 1804. Pushing its way up the Missouri River, the party arrived among the Mandan Indians (see page 11) in present-day North Dakota in the late fall. They chose to winter among the Mandans, a decision that may have ensured the expedition's success. The Mandans were a settled agricultural group who had been farming along the upper Missouri for thousands of years. Their villages, which offered food and shelter for the wandering hunting tribes, became hubs in the evolving Plains trading and raiding system after the arrival of horses (see Deeper Understanding of History, Chapter 2). By wintering with the Mandans, the expedition came into contact with many of the Indian and European groups that participated in the complex economy of the West. Lewis and Clark acted on Jefferson's secret instructions by learning all they could from the Mandans and their visitors about the fur trade, the nature of military alliances, and the tribes that lived farther west.

One particularly important contact Lewis and Clark made during the Mandan winter was with a French trapper named Charbonneau and his Shoshone wife, Sacajawea. Between the two of them, Sacajawea and Charbonneau spoke several of the languages understood by the Indians in the Far West and possessed knowledge about the geography and the various peoples in the area. With their help, Lewis and Clark were able to make contact with the Shoshones, who aided them in crossing the Rocky Mountains. From there, the expedition passed from Indian group to Indian group along a chain of friendship. Following this chain of Indian hospitality, the expedition finally reached the Pacific Ocean in November 1805.

Challenge and Uncertainty in Jefferson's America

☆ *How did American life change during Jefferson's presidency?*

☆ *How did Native Americans and African Americans figure into Jefferson's vision of America? How did each group respond to its circumstances?*

Jefferson's policies not only put the nation on a new road politically and economically but also brought a new spirit into the land. The Virginian's commitment to opportunity and progress, to openness and frugality, offered a stark contrast in approach and style to the policies of his predecessors. The congressional

elections of 1802 and the presidential election in 1804 proved Jefferson's popularity and the Republican Party's strong appeal. Nevertheless, some disturbing social and intellectual undercurrents began to surface during his second term. National expansion strained conventional social institutions as white farmers, entrepreneurs, and adventurers seized the opportunities that Republican economic and expansion policies offered. Adding to the strain was the fact that the Jeffersonian spirit was more of a promise than a commitment: Jefferson's vision for the republic excluded many.

The Heritage of Partisan Politics

The popularity of Jefferson's party was abundantly clear in 1804. Jefferson had won an extremely narrow victory in 1800, and his Republican Party had won significant but hardly overwhelming majorities in Congress. The congressional elections of 1802, however, had virtually eclipsed Federalist power, and Federalists faced the presidential election of 1804 with dread. Former president John Adams commented, "The power of the Administration rests upon the support of a much stronger majority of the people throughout the Union than the former administrations ever possessed since the first establishment of the Constitution."

Despite an abiding faith in the emerging two-party system, staunch Federalist congressman Fisher

One of the key objectives for the Lewis and Clark Expedition was to map portions of the newly acquired Louisiana Territory. Here we see a copy of William Clark's map of their journey rendered by map publisher Samuel Lewis. For help drawing accurate maps--not to mention finding their way--the expeditioncarried sophisticated navigation hardware like the chronometer and box compass shown here. The original chronometer (now lost) was the single-most-expensive item carried by the explorers on their way west.

A Deeper Understanding of History

Jefferson's Covert Spy Missions

The entire nation celebrated the Lewis and Clark Expedition immediately after the party successfully returned from its transcontinental trek. But what few knew at the time, and few still know today, is that this was only one of four similar ventures personally sponsored by Thomas Jefferson in his role as president of the United States. What historians discovered many decades later, buried in volumes of Jefferson's correspondence and other documents, was that all four expeditions had top secret missions hidden from the public and from many in government itself.

Writing to fellow Virginian George Rogers Clark in 1780, Jefferson voiced the anticipation that should the Americans be victorious in the Revolution, the United States would acquire the vast lands extending at least to the Rocky Mountains, calling it the "Empire of Liberty." Over the next twenty years, he continued to dream of his anticipated empire. But no sooner had he been elected president than he learned this territory was being transferred from relatively weak Spain to incredibly powerful France, potentially threatening his desires. What he needed was more information and a diplomatic edge, and he needed them quickly—without tipping off potential rival nations to his intentions.

There had been little systematic exploration of the continent's interior and even less diplomatic outreach between the United States and the various interior Indians. For an empire of liberty to arise, these deficits would have to be overcome. Jefferson immediately made a choice: he commenced secret correspondence with supporters in Congress asking for appropriations to support four covert missions, as shown on the accompanying map. The first was the Lewis and Clark expedition. The second was assigned to Scottish-born naturalist and Natchez planter William Dunbar. The third was put under the command of Thomas Freeman, an astronomer and surveyor. The fourth was to be led by Captain Zebulon Pike.

The government issued papers to all four expeditions claiming that they were purely scientific in nature, designed for no other purpose than to collect biological and other intelligence. But historians later learned from their actual instructions that their primary mission was clearly military and diplomatic. Among other things, they were to note the numbers of French, Spanish, and other agents in the areas each explored, along with the numbers and condition of the Indians, and to chart major waterways

Ames withdrew from public life, followed by John Jay and other prominent leaders. Charles Cotesworth Pinckney, however, stepped forward to head the Federalists' 1804 presidential ticket. For the vice presidency, the Federalists chose Rufus King, a defender of the notion of loyal opposition and the two-party system. But Federalists had trouble identifying issues on which to build a viable platform. Pinckney accused Jefferson of violating his own political principles by exerting the federal authority to purchase Louisiana. Beyond that, there was little to complain about: the economy had continued to grow at the same rate during Jefferson's tenure in office as it had under the Federalists. Such economic growth permitted Jefferson to maintain a favorable **balance of payments** throughout his first administration, a feat the Federalists had never achieved. And with Gallatin's help, Jefferson had proved his fiscal responsibility by building up a multimillion-dollar Treasury surplus.

The enormous scope of Jefferson's successes and the limited scope of his opponent's platform helped swing the election of 1804 firmly over to the Republicans. Jefferson won 162 electoral votes to Pinckney's 14, carrying every state except Connecticut and Delaware.

Westward Expansion and Social Stress

As new territories opened in the West, young people streamed into the region at a rate that had an unsettling effect on communities in the East. Economic opportunities available in the West fed a new air of independence even among young people who did not migrate, leading them to question traditional authority. Business interests in the East were also upset as they witnessed westward expansion drawing off

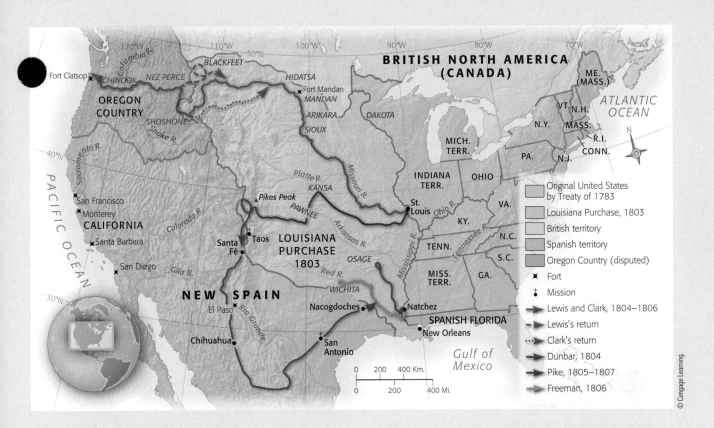

and other important strategic sites. They were also to open the way for direct dealings between the Indians and the United States, seeking to undermine the Indians' relations with other nations. Thus when Lewis and Clark returned from their venture in 1806 and the nation celebrated their great scientific achievement, they were celebrating only one small part of a much larger project. The science was merely a cover for more practical, if unspoken, aims of the American president. It is often the case that nations, like individual people, use deception to get their way, and it is frequently up to historians to figure out what real objectives lay behind what was revealed to the public.

population, which in time would drive up the price of labor and reduce profits.

Conditions in the newly opened West were incredibly unstable as rapid growth put enormous stress on conventional institutions. The population of Ohio, for example, grew from 45,000 in 1800 to 231,000 in 1810, and similar rates of growth occurred in the new states of Tennessee and Kentucky and in territories from Louisiana north to Michigan and west to Missouri. Authorities in the West found these increases challenging as they tried to deal with the practical matters of maintaining governments, economies, and peaceful relations among the new settlers and between the settlers and neighboring Indians.

Most of the people who moved west looked forward to achieving the agrarian self-sufficiency that Jefferson advocated, but life in the West was far more complicated. Inexpensive, reliable transportation was impossible in the vast, rugged interior, and Jefferson's notion of breadbasket America trading with industrial Europe was doomed without it. No navigable streams ran eastward from America's interior across the Appalachians to the Atlantic, and the ridges of those mountains made road building extremely difficult.

Only one realistic route existed for transporting produce from the interior to shipping centers in the East. The Ohio-Mississippi-Missouri drainage system provided a reliable watercourse, and huge cargoes

balance of payments The difference between a nation's total payments to foreign countries and its total receipts from abroad.

flowed along its stream. Shipping goods on the Mississippi, however, was dangerous and expensive. Because of the river's strong current, loads could be shipped only one way—downstream. Rafts were built for the purpose and then were broken up and sold for lumber in New Orleans. Shippers had to return home by foot. On both legs of the journey, travelers risked attack by river pirates, Indians, and sickness. Moreover, it was virtually impossible for shippers to take manufactured goods back with them because of the condition of the roads and the distances involved.

As a result of geographical isolation and the rapid pace of settlement, the economy in the West became highly localized. Settlers arriving with neither food nor seed bought surplus crops produced by established farmers. The little capital that was generated in this way supported the development of local industries in hundreds of farming villages. Enterprising craftsmen ranging from coopers to wheelwrights produced hand-manufactured items on demand. As long as people kept moving into an area, local economies boomed. But when new arrivals slowed and then stopped, the market for surplus crops and local manufactures collapsed, and the economy went bust. Swinging from boom to bust and back again became a way of life in newly settled areas.

Along with economic instability, social instability was also common. The odd mixture of ethnic, religious, and national groups found in western villages did little to bring cohesiveness to community life.

The Religious Response to Social Change

The changes taking place in the young republic stirred conflicting religious currents. One was liberalism in religious thought. The other was a new evangelicalism.

Born of the Enlightenment (see page 86–87) in France, Scotland, and England, liberal religious thought

cooper A person who makes or repairs wooden barrels.

wheelwright A person who makes or repairs wheels for carts, wagons, or other vehicles.

The Mississippi River drainage system was the only reliable transportation route for Americans moving into the West during the early 1800s. Farmers moved produce to market on keelboats like the one depicted here. On the open deck, cargo and livestock endured weather and exposure to mosquitoes and other river menaces. In the central cabin, however, people could eat, drink, and sleep in comfort during the trip downriver. One problem with this mode of transport was that the current on the giant river made upstream travel impossible during much of the year, so boats like this one were often sold for lumber after they reached New Orleans.

The New York Public Library/Art Resource, New York.

emphasized the connection between **rationalism** and faith. To rationalists like both Jefferson and Adams, the possibility that a being as perfect as God might behave irrationally was unthinkable. In fact, for such men, the more plain, reasonable, and verifiable religious claims were, the more likely it was that they emanated from God. Less perfect than God, it was man who had cluttered the plain revealed truth with irrational claims and unsolvable mysteries. For his part, Jefferson was so convinced of this logic that he edited his own version of the Bible, keeping only the moral principles and the solid historical facts and discarding anything supernatural.

This liberal creed led many, including Jefferson, to abandon organized religion altogether. Not all liberals were so quick to bolt organized worship, however. John Adams, for example, continued to adhere to New England Congregationalism, but he and others used their influence to promote a young and more liberal clergy who sought to insert a heavy dose of rationalism into the old Puritan structure. Rejecting such traditional mysteries as the **Trinity** and the literal divinity of Christ, **Unitarianism** expanded inside Congregational churches during the years just before and following the American Revolution. Liberal influence within Congregationalism became so prominent in New England that Unitarians were able to engineer the election of their own **Henry Ware** as the senior professor of theology at Harvard College, formerly the educational heart of orthodox American Protestantism.

While deism and Unitarianism were gaining strong footholds in eastern cities, disorder, insecurity, and missionizing activities were helping to foster a very different kind of religious response in the West. Although Methodists, Baptists, Presbyterians, and evangelical Congregationalists disagreed on many specifics, they all emphasized the spirited preaching that could bring about the emotional moment of conversion—the moment of realization that without the saving grace of God, every soul is lost. Each of these denominations concentrated on training a new, young ministry and sending it to preach in every corner of the nation. In this way, another religious awakening swept across America, beginning in Cane Ridge, Kentucky, in 1801 and spreading throughout the South and West.

The new evangelicalism stressed the individual nature of salvation but at the same time emphasized the importance of Christian community. Looking back to the first generation of Puritans in America, evangelicals breathed new life into the old Puritan notion of God's plan for the universe and the leading role that Americans were to play in its unfolding. As early nineteenth-century Presbyterian divine Lyman Beecher put it, "It was the opinion of [Jonathan] Edwards that the millennium would commence in America . . . all providential signs of the times lend corroboration to it."

In addition to numerous official evangelical councils and conventions, hundreds of informal associations came together to carry out what they characterized as God's plan for America. These organizations helped counterbalance the forces of extreme individualism and social disorder by providing ideological underpinnings for the expansive behavior of westerners and a sense of mission to ease the insecurities produced by venturing into the unknown. They also provided an institutional framework that brought some stability to communities in which traditional controls were lacking. These attractive features helped evangelicalism to sweep across the West. During the early nineteenth century, it became the dominant religious persuasion in that region.

Exceptions in Jefferson's Vision

Jefferson's policies enabled many Americans to benefit from the nation's development, but they certainly did not help everyone. Neither Native Americans nor African Americans had much of a role in Jefferson's republic, and each group was subject to different forms of unequal treatment. And women were to occupy a special, but far from equal place in the envisioned society.

A slaveholder himself, Jefferson expressed strong views about African Americans. In his *Notes on the State of Virginia* (1781), Jefferson asserted that blacks were "inferior to whites in the endowments both of body and mind." He was convinced, and

evangelicalism A Protestant religious persuasion that emphasizes the literal truth of the Gospels and salvation through faith alone; in the early nineteenth century, it became infused with increasing amounts of romantic emotionalism and an emphasis on converting others.

rationalism The theory that the exercise of reason, rather than the acceptance of authority or spiritual revelation, is the only valid basis for belief and the best source of spiritual truth.

Trinity The Christian belief that God consists of three divine persons: Father, Son, and Holy Spirit.

□ **Unitarianism** A religion that denies the Trinity, teaching that God exists only in one person; it also stresses individual freedom of belief and the free use of reason in religion.

□ **Henry Ware** Liberal Congregationalist who was elected senior theologian at Harvard College in 1805, making Unitarianism the dominant religious view at the previously orthodox stronghold.

Evangelical denominations gained ever wider followings during the early nineteenth century as the uncertainties accompanying rapid expansion and social change took their toll. Both black and white communities engaged in enthusiastic worship. This painting, attributed to Russian travel writer and artist Pavel Svinin, captures an African American Methodist service that Svinin attended in 1811.

stated publicly on many occasions, that the white and black races could not live together without inevitably polluting both. This was the key reason for what little opposition he voiced to slavery and for his continued involvement in various projects to remove African Americans by colonizing them in Africa. And yet despite this attitude, many of his contemporaries believed that he kept a slave mistress, Sally Hemings, by whom he fathered several children, a contention that modern DNA evidence has demonstrated as likely. Even so, almost no documentary evidence about the relationship exists despite the fact that hundreds of the nation's most prolific writers (and gossips) passed through Jefferson's home regularly. Circumstantial evidence, however, suggests that their relationship was an exclusive one and lasted for a long time. And traditions passed down through generations of Sally Hemings's descendants claim that theirs was a sentimental, even romantic bond.

Given his belief in racial inequality, it seems contradictory that Jefferson could have had a long-term affectionate relationship with an African American woman. If so, it reflects equally deep-seated contradictions that shot through American society at the time. Truly a man of his century and his social class, Jefferson was convinced that women, like slaves, existed to serve and entertain men. For example, when asked if a woman could hold public office, Jefferson

replied, "The appointment of a woman to office is an innovation for which the public is not prepared, nor am I." Thus his entanglement with Hemings, who probably was the half-sister of Jefferson's deceased wife, seemed no more unequal or unnatural than his marriage. But while the relationship may have seemed perfectly natural behind closed doors, the race code to which Jefferson gave voice defined it as entirely unacceptable in public. This rigid separation between public and private behavior led Jefferson to keep the relationship secret, and his friends and family—even most of his political enemies—joined him in a conspiracy of silence.

Throughout the Jeffersonian era, the great majority of African Americans lived in the South, and most of them were slaves. But during the late eighteenth century, conditions for slaves underwent some serious modifications and the number of free blacks increased steadily. In northern states like New York and Pennsylvania slavery was in the process of gradual legislative abolition, and even the plantation states showed increasing flexibility in dealing with slavery, as some elite southerners began to recognize the unprofitability, though generally not the immorality, of the institution. After Virginia authorized owners to free their slaves in 1782, Delaware and Maryland soon did likewise. But an event that took place in 1800 revealed that slavery would continue to be a source of enormous anxiety.

In the more relaxed racial atmosphere that was coming into existence in late-eighteenth-century Virginia, skilled slave workers like a blacksmith named Gabriel, owned by a Henrico County planter named Thomas Prosser, exercised significant freedom, hiring himself out for wages and learning to read and write. Gabriel came into contact with a wide variety of people and learned about the promises of greater freedom mouthed by Jeffersonian reformers and of the successful slave revolution in Saint-Domingue. Frustrated by the impotence of Republican rhetoric and emboldened by Toussaint Louverture's successes, Gabriel enlisted at least two white partners and a number of fellow slaves to wage an armed revolt. On August 30, they armed themselves in preparation to invade nearby Richmond, but torrential rainfall bogged down the effort. Eventually Gabriel, along with his two brothers and twenty-four other slaves, were captured and hanged. It appears that Virginia governor James Monroe was aware that there were white participants, but did not pursue the evidence in fear that the information would hurt Jefferson's election efforts.

Gabriel's Rebellion had a chilling effect on race relations throughout the country. In Virginia and throughout the slave South, new restrictions were placed on the freedoms accorded to both enslaved and free African Americans. Even in northern states blacks were not permitted to testify in court, vote, attend schools, or exercise other fundamental freedoms accorded to whites. Even churches were often closed to blacks who wished to worship.

Some African Americans began to respond to systematic exclusion and to express their cultural and social identity by forming their own institutions. In Philadelphia, tension between white and free black Methodists led former slave Richard Allen to form the Bethel Church for Negro Methodists in 1793. Two years later, Allen became the first black deacon ordained in America. Ongoing tension with the white Methodist hierarchy, however, eventually led Allen to secede from the church and form his own African Methodist Episcopal Church (Bethel) in 1816. Similar controversies in New York led black divine James Varick to found an African Methodist Episcopal Church (Zion) in that city in 1821.

African American leadership was not confined to the religious realm. James Forten, for example, a free-born African American, followed up on his experience as a sailor in the Revolutionary navy with a career as a sail maker in Philadelphia. Despite both overt and subtle racial discrimination, he acquired his own company in 1798, eventually becoming a major employer of both African American and white workers. In cooperation with other African American entrepreneurs, such as Boston's Paul Cuffe, Forten invested expertise, capital, and personal influence in an effort to create jobs for black city-dwellers and opportunities for budding black businessmen. Despite these efforts, the overall racial atmosphere in Jefferson's America significantly limited the number of African American leaders who attained positions of wealth or influence.

Jefferson thought differently of Native Americans than he did of African Americans. He considered Indians to be "savages" but was convinced that "They are formed in mind as well as in body on the same module with the 'Homo Sapiens Europaeus.'" Jefferson attributed the differences between Indians and Europeans to what he saw as the Indians' cultural retardation. He was confident that if whites lifted Indians out of their "uncivilized state" and put them on an equal footing with Europeans, Indian populations would grow, their physical condition would improve, and they would be able to participate in the yeoman republic on an equal footing with whites.

Jefferson's Indian policy reflected this attitude. Jefferson created a series of government-owned trading posts at which Indians were offered goods at cheap prices. He believed that Indians who were exposed to white manufactures would come to agree that white culture was superior and would make the rational decision to adopt that culture wholesale. At the same time, both the government and right-minded philanthropists should engage in instructing Native Americans in European methods of farming, ensuring that these former "savages" would emerge as good, Republican-voting frontier farmers. Until this process of acculturation was complete, however, Jefferson believed the Indians, like women and children, should be protected from those who might take advantage of them or lead them astray. Also like women and children, the Indians were not to be trusted to exercise the rights and responsibilities

□ **Gabriel's Rebellion** Attempted slave revolt led by a slave blacksmith in 1800; although a failure, the affair led to greater restrictions on African Americans both slave and free in the South.

□ **African Methodist Episcopal Church** African American branch of Methodism established in Philadelphia in 1816 and in New York in 1821.

□ **James Forten** African American entrepreneur with a successful sail-making business in Philadelphia who provided leadership for black business enterprises and advocated both racial integration and equal rights during the Jeffersonian era.

acculturation Changes in the culture of a group or an individual as a result of contact with a different culture.

Unlike many of his contemporaries, Thomas Jefferson was convinced that the American Indians could eventually become full participants in the American republic. Members of the "Five Civilized Tribes" (Cherokee, Choctaw, Chickasaw, Creek, and Seminole) often owned large plantations and practiced lifestyles not unlike those of their white neighbors. Unfortunately, Jefferson's hopes fell before the racism and greed of white settlers. Even sophisticated leaders like Cherokee chief Tooan Tuh (Spring Frog), pictured here, were driven from their land; he eventually took up residence in Indian Territory to escape persecution in his native Tennessee.

of citizenship. Thus Indian rights were left to the whims of the Senate, which drafted and ratified Indian treaties, and of the army, which enforced those treaties.

The chief problem for Jeffersonian Indian policy was not the Indians' supposed cultural retardation but their rapid modernization. Among groups such as the Cherokees and Creeks, members of a rising new elite led their people toward greater prosperity and diplomatic independence. Alexander McGillivray of the Creeks, for example, deftly manipulated American, French, and Spanish interests to Creek advantage while building a strong economic base founded on both communally and privately owned plantations. In similar fashion, the rising Cherokee elite in 1794 established a centralized government that began pushing the Cherokees into a new era of wealth and power.

Although Jefferson might have greeted such acculturation with enthusiasm, the Indians' white neighbors generally did not. Envisioning all-out war between the states and the Indians—war that his reduced government and shrunken military were helpless to prevent—Jefferson advanced an alternative. Having acquired Louisiana, Jefferson suggested the creation of large reserves to which Indians currently residing within states could relocate, taking themselves out of state jurisdictions and removing themselves from the corrupting influence of the "baser elements" of white society. Although he did not advocate the use of force to move Indians west of the Mississippi, he made every effort to convince them to migrate. This idea of segregating Native Americans from other Americans formed the basis for Indian policy for the rest of the century.

CHARLES COTESWORTH PINCKNEY
and the XYZ Dispatches

Following the presidential election in 1796, the French Directory broke off diplomatic relations with the United States to protest the election of the seemingly pro-British John Adams. In a fiery speech to a joint session of Congress, Adams announced that he was sending a delegation headed by Charles Cotesworth Pinckney to negotiate with the French but also asking for military preparations should the delegation fail in its mission. In November 1797 Pinckney posted dispatches announcing the delegation's failure and relating the odd circumstances surrounding the affair. The following is an excerpt from these dispatches.

National Portrait Gallery, Smithsonian Institution/Art Resource, NY.

❶ This is a reference to Adams's speech to the joint session of Congress on May 16, 1797.

❷ Given the way this passage is phrased, who is Pinckney saying was actually responsible for the demands of a bribe and forced loan?

❸ Why did Pinckney choose to make this answer rather than just a flat statement that the demanded payments would not be made? Why might he have wanted to stall under these particular circumstances?

M. X. replied, that the Directory, and particularly two of the members of it, were exceedingly irritated at some passages of the President's speech, ❶ and desired that they should be softened, and that this step would be necessary previous to our reception: that besides this, a sum of money was required for the pocket of the Directory and ministers, which would be at the disposal of M. Talleyrand: and that a loan would also be insisted on. M. X. said, if we acceded to these measures, M. Talleyrand had no doubt that all our differences with France might be accommodated. ❷

On enquiry, M. X. could not point out the particular passages of the speech that had given offense, nor the quantum of the loan, but mentioned that the douceur [bribe] for the pocket was twelve hundred thousand livres, about fifty thousand pounds sterling.

We committed immediately to writing the answer we proposed, in the following words: "Our powers respecting a treaty are ample: but the proposition of a loan in the form of Dutch inscriptions, or in any other form, is not within the limits of our instructions: upon this point therefore the government must be consulted: one of the American ministers will, for the purpose, forthwith embark for America: provided the Directoire will suspend all further captures on American vessels, and will suspend proceedings on those already captured." ❸

Study Tools

SUMMARY

Americans faced a difficult choice in 1796: to continue in a Federalist direction with John Adams or to move into new and uncharted regions of republicanism with Thomas Jefferson. Factionalism and voter indecision led to Adams's election as president and Jefferson's as vice president. The split outcome frightened Federalists, and they used every excuse to make war on their political opponents. Diplomatically, they let relations with France sour to the point that the two nations were at war in all but name. At home, they used repressive measures such as the Alien and Sedition Acts to try to silence opponents, and they imposed tariffs and taxes that were hateful to many. Reminded of what they had rebelled against in the Revolution, in 1800 the American people decided to give Jefferson and the Republican faction a chance.

Although Jefferson called the election "the revolution of 1800," even hard-line Federalists such as Hamilton were sure that the general direction in government would not change. Just to be safe, however, Federalists stacked the court system so that Republicans would face insurmountable constraints if they tried to change government too much.

Jefferson's inaugural address in 1801 seemed to announce an end to partisan warfare, but both Madison and hard-line Republicans in Congress attempted to restrict Federalist power in the court system. The Republican program, however, was not entirely negative. Jefferson looked toward a future in which most Americans could own enough land to produce life's necessities for themselves and were beholden to no one and thus free to vote as their consciences and rationality dictated. To attain this end, Jefferson ordered massive reductions in the size of government, the elimination of internal federal taxes, and rapid westward expansion, including the purchase of the vast territory called Louisiana. For some the outcome was a spirit of excitement and optimism, but not everyone was so hopeful. Many were unsure and fearful of the new order's novelty and of the stresses that rapid expansion engendered.

Jefferson clearly wanted most Americans to share in the bounty of an expanded nation, but not all were free to share equally. For American Indians, the very success of Jefferson's expansion policy meant a contraction in their freedom of action. African Americans also found that the equality Jefferson promised to others was not intended for them, though many grasped for it anyway. As to women, they were encouraged to play an active role in the new nation but were expected to do so only through their roles as wives and mothers.

CHRONOLOGY
Partisan Tension and Jeffersonian Optimism

1796	George Washington's Farewell Address
	First contested presidential election: John Adams elected president, Thomas Jefferson vice president
1797	XYZ affair
1798	Quasi-War with France begins
	Alien and Sedition Acts
	Kentucky and Virginia Resolutions
1799	Napoleon seizes control in France
1800	Convention of Mortefontaine ends Quasi-War
1801	Jefferson elected president in House of Representatives; Burr vice president
	Judiciary Act of 1801
	John Marshall becomes chief justice
	War begins between American navy ships and Barbary pirates
1802	Congress repeals all internal taxes
	Congress repeals Judiciary Act of 1801
	French invade Saint-Domingue
1803	*Marbury v. Madison* and *Stuart v. Laird*
	Louisiana Purchase
1804	Twelfth Amendment ratified
	Jefferson reelected
1804–1806	Lewis and Clark expedition
1816	African Methodist Episcopal Church formed in Philadelphia

Study Tools

FOCUS QUESTIONS

If you have mastered this chapter, you should be able to answer these questions and to explain the terms that follow the questions.

1. How did Federalists manipulate the crisis with France in 1798 for their own political advantage?

2. What steps did Republicans take to counter Federalist manipulations?

3. How did Federalists respond to losing the election of 1800? What does this response reveal about their political attitudes?

4. What did Thomas Jefferson mean by the statement "Every difference of opinion is not a difference of principles"?

5. How did Jefferson's vision for America differ from that of Hamilton, Adams, and other Federalists?

6. What legal maneuvers did Republicans initiate to deal with defenses Federalists put in place in 1801? What were the political and constitutional consequences?

7. What policies did Jefferson pursue to carry out his vision for the country? What obstacles did he encounter?

8. How did American life change during Jefferson's presidency?

9. How did Native Americans and African Americans figure into Jefferson's vision of America? How did each group respond to its circumstances?

KEY TERMS

The Directory   *p. 179*

Quasi-War   *p. 179*

Aaron Burr   *p. 180*

Charles Maurice de Talleyrand-Périgord   *p. 181*

XYZ affair   *p. 181*

Alien and Sedition Acts   *p. 182*

Virginia and Kentucky Resolutions   *p. 182*

states' rights   *p. 182*

Fries's Rebellion   *p. 183*

Napoleon Bonaparte   *p. 183*

Twelfth Amendment   *p. 184*

Judiciary Act of 1801   *p. 184*

John Marshall   *p. 184*

supply and demand   *p. 185*

Marbury v. Madison   *p. 187*

Albert Gallatin   *p. 188*

Saint-Domingue   *p. 189*

François Dominique Toussaint Louverture   *p. 189*

Louisiana Purchase   *p. 189*

Meriwether Lewis   *p. 190*

William Clark   *p. 190*

Sacajawea   *p. 190*

Unitarianism   *p. 195*

Henry Ware   *p. 195*

Gabriel's Rebellion   *p. 197*

African Methodist Episcopal Church   *p. 197*

James Forten   *p. 197*

SUGGESTED RESOURCES

Gilder Lehrman Institute. "The New Nation, 1783–1815," http://www.gilderlehrman.org/history-by-era/new-nation-1783-1815. An interpretive website with many resources on the early national era.

U.S. Department of State, Office of the Historian. "Milestones, 1784–1800," http://history.state.gov/milestones/ 1784-1800; also "Milestones 1801–1829," http://history.state.gov/milestones/1801-1829. These websites present summaries of key issues in diplomatic history from the era of the early Republic; they include maps, images, and many other useful resources.

U.S. National Archives. "Teaching with Documents: The Lewis and Clark Expedition," http://www.archives.gov/education/lessons/lewis-clark. A brief overview of the circumstances surrounding the "Corps of Discovery," with a varied collection of primary documents illustrating different aspects of the expedition.

Yale Law School, Lillian Goldman Law Library. "The Avalon Project: The Barbary Treaties," http://avalon.law.yale.edu/subject_menus/barmenu.asp. A comprehensive collection of primary documents relating to the Barbary pirate wars with full texts of treaties as well as supporting diplomatic and legal documents.

9

Increasing Conflict and War, 1805–1815

INDIVIDUAL CHOICES

Tecumseh

Tecumseh stood in stark contrast to dominant white perceptions about Indian life. Whites thought of Indians as living in isolated and constantly warring tribes, yet Tecumseh's father was a Shawnee from Ohio and his mother was a Creek from Alabama. In the sophisticated Indian world of the American interior, such things were common.

A combination of his family connections and a distinguished military career led to Tecumseh's emergence as war chief in the late 1780s. But defeat at the Battle of Fallen Timbers in 1794 temporarily broke Indian defenses. Taking advantage of Indian vulnerability, American agents used a combination of bribery, coercion, and violence to convince **accommodationist** leaders to cede more land (see the Individual Voices feature at the end of this chapter). Seeking to stop these new invasions, Tecumseh approached war chiefs from a variety of tribes suggesting a vast alliance system in which the warriors would stop the accommodationists from selling land and form a military force to turn back the Americans.

Bent on continuing expansion, white leaders like Indiana territorial governor William Henry Harrison found Tecumseh's actions frightening. Finally in November 1811

North Wind Picture Archives. Translated and modernized by Berkin from the original transcript.

Harrison resorted to direct action, leading an army to invade Tecumseh's headquarters at Prophetstown on Tippecanoe Creek. Tecumseh was absent, seeking new allies, and Harrison's forces were able to overcome a spirited defense and burn the town, destroying its winter food supply. By the time Tecumseh reached Tippecanoe in January, few of his followers remained. Thinking first of the survivors' welfare, Tecumseh traveled to Canada seeking emergency supplies.

While he was in Canada, war broke out between the United States and Great Britain. He decided that the only hope for the Shawnees' future lay in a British victory, and he committed what was left of his alliance to the British. His army enjoyed great success against the Americans, but at the Battle of the Thames, on October 5, 1813, Tecumseh's forces were overrun, and Tecumseh was shot. After the battle, triumphant American troops mutilated his body and left it lying on the field.

Tecumseh's situation in Indiana reflected many of the more troubling problems that beset the nation during the opening decades of the nineteenth century. Sitting at the juncture of three worlds—the dynamic republican world of Jeffersonian America, the European imperial world in Canada, and his own Native American world—Tecumseh perceived that unless something happened soon, all three worlds were heading for crisis.

Jefferson had set an ambitious agenda for the country that was extremely popular with many Americans, but it created serious stresses within the nation and across the world. Along the Atlantic frontier, imperial powers such as Great Britain and France challenged Jefferson's commitment to open trade and freedom of the seas. A war of words, blustering threats, and some open confrontations pushed the United States increasingly toward crisis and triggered economic disaster. Along the western frontier, a variety of Indian groups opposed Jefferson's vision of rapid westward expansion. Here too, verbal and some armed conflicts engendered an air of crisis. And to many, including Indiana's Harrison, these seemed not to be isolated phenomena. Convinced that a conspiracy was afoot between Indian dissidents like Tecumseh and imperial agents from Great Britain, an increasing number of Jeffersonians demanded aggressive action.

No one could stem the tide of crisis. Harrison finally took matters over the edge: his attack on Prophetstown precipitated a general call for a war that set the nation on a new course altogether.

TROUBLING CURRENTS IN JEFFERSON'S AMERICA

☆ How did varying regional interests complicate Jefferson's political situation during his second term as president?

☆ How did European politics affect the American economy between 1804 and 1808?

Jefferson's successes, culminating in his victory in the 1804 election, seemed to prove that Republicans had absolute control over the nation's political reins. But factions challenging Jefferson's control were forming. A small but vocal coalition of disgruntled Federalists threatened to **secede** from the Union. Even within his own party, Jefferson's supremacy eroded and dissidents emerged. Diplomatic problems joined domestic ones to trouble Jefferson's second administration.

accommodationist Willing to give up something in an attempt to avoid conflict or get something desirable, or both; accommodationist Indians were willing to cede—give up ownership of—Indian lands, expecting peace and items of value in return.

◻ **secede** To withdraw formally from membership in a political union; threats of secession were used frequently during the early nineteenth century to bring attention to political issues.

Fletcher v. Peck

Although Article 6, Clause 2, of the Constitution, the so-called "Supremacy Clause," specifies that "The Constitution and the laws of the United States which shall be made in pursuance thereof . . . shall be the supreme law of the land," it nevertheless was not clearly stated anywhere how the constitutionality of state laws was to be determined. This would be tested in the case of *Fletcher v. Peck* (1810), which grew out of the "Yazoo affair" in which the Georgia state legislature had contracted to sell vast tracts of land to private investors. The public was outraged at what was a clear case of bribery and voted the governor and the legislature out of office. The newly elected government then overturned the deal. When the case came before the Supreme Court, the majority decided that Article 1, Section 10, of the Constitution, which specifies that "No state shall . . . pass any . . . law impairing the obligation of contracts," prevented Georgia from canceling the sale. In the process, the Court extended the power it had asserted in *Marbury v. Madison* and *Stuart v. Laird* over acts of Congress to the acts of states as well.

Emerging Factions in American Politics

The Federalists' failure in the election of 1804 nearly spelled the troubled party's demise. With the West and the South firmly in Jefferson's camp, disgruntled New England Federalists found their once-dominant voice being drowned out by those who shared Jefferson's rather than Hamilton's view of America's future (see pages 168–169). Proclaiming that "the people of the East cannot reconcile their habits, views, and interests with those of the South and West," Federalist leader Timothy Pickering advocated changes in the Constitution that he thought might restore balance. Among other things, northeasterners demanded much stricter standards for admitting new states in the West and the elimination of the Three-Fifths Compromise. Pickering brought together a tight political coalition called the Essex Junto to press for these changes.

Regional fissures began to appear inside Jefferson's party as well. Throughout Jefferson's first administration, some within his party, especially those from the South, criticized the president for turning his back on republican principles by expanding federal power and interfering with states' rights. One of Jefferson's most vocal critics was his cousin John Randolph.

On the eve of the 1804 election, the two Virginia Republicans clashed over the Yazoo affair, a complicated legal tangle arising from land fraud in Georgia. Traditional Republicans thought the matter should have been worked out at the state level. Jefferson, however, chose to involve the federal courts in the affair. He irritated Randolph again in 1806 by approaching Congress for a $2 million appropriation to be used to win French influence in convincing Spain to sell Florida to the United States. Randolph split with Jefferson to form a third party, the Tertium Quid, which fractured the Republicans' united political front.

A second fissure in the party opened over controversial vice president Aaron Burr's political scheming. Jefferson virtually ignored Burr for four years and then dropped him as vice-presidential nominee in 1804. With Burr in political limbo, Pickering saw an opportunity: he offered to help Burr become governor of New York if Burr would commit the state to the Essex Junto. Mainstream New York Federalists were furious, especially Alexander Hamilton, who actively opposed the move. Burr lost the election in a landslide. Never willing to accept defeat gracefully, he challenged Hamilton to a duel. Hamilton was personally opposed to dueling, but in the honor-driven culture that permeated early nineteenth-century politics, he could not refuse. Burr was an excellent shot and his well-aimed bullet killed Hamilton.

Though his political career was now in shambles, Burr was not finished meddling in the nation's future. Calling in outstanding political favors, he arranged for James Wilkinson to become governor of the Louisiana Territory. To this day, no one is entirely certain what Wilkinson and Burr had in mind, but in 1805, Burr ventured west, sailing down the Mississippi to recruit associates. Amid rumors of intrigue, federal authorities received a letter from Wilkinson late in 1806 implicating Burr in a "deep, dark, wicked, and widespread conspiracy" against the United States. Learning that Wilkinson had turned him in, Burr tried to

□ **Essex Junto** A group of political conspirators who sought power outside of the regular political process—composed of radical Federalists in Essex County, Massachusetts, who at first advocated constitutional changes that would favor New England politically and later called for New England and New York to secede from the United States.

□ **John Randolph** Virginia Republican politician who believed in limited government and objected to several of Jefferson's policies.

□ **Yazoo affair** Corrupt deal in which the Georgia legislature sold a huge tract of public land to speculators for a low price but later overturned the sale; the basis for the Supreme Court case of *Fletcher v. Peck*.

□ **Tertium Quid** Republican faction formed by John Randolph to protest Jefferson's plan for acquiring Florida from Spain; the name is Latin and means a "third thing," indicating Randolph's rejection of both the Federalist and Republican parties.

reach Spanish Florida but was captured early in 1807 and put on trial for treason.

Burr's trial provided an open arena for Jefferson and his critics to air their views on such touchy subjects as presidential power, westward expansion, and national loyalty. Jefferson used the powers of his office to pardon conspirators who would testify against Burr and he leaked information that made his former vice president look guilty. Chief Justice John Marshall presided over the case. He advised the jury that treason consisted of, and *only* of, "levying war against the United States or adhering to their enemies." Burr had done neither, and so the jury was forced to acquit, to the glee of Jefferson's critics.

The Problem of American Neutrality

Internal tensions in American politics were matched by growing stress in the nation's diplomatic and economic relations. Jefferson's economic successes had been the product of continuing warfare in Europe. With their fleets engaged in naval battles, their people locked in combat, and their lands crisscrossed by opposing armies, Europeans needed American ships and the fruits of American labor, especially food. American neutrality ensured continued prosperity as long as the contending parties in Europe agreed to recognize that neutrality.

Americans immediately grasped at this opportunity. An upsurge in European campaigning in 1803 helped raise the total value of American exports by over 65 percent. A significant proportion of the increase came from the shipment of foreign goods to foreign markets by way of neutral American ports: sugar from the Caribbean, for example, frequently passed through the United States on its way to Europe. Such shipments rose in value from $14 million in 1803 to $60 million in 1807, prompting a rapid growth in earnings for American shipping. In 1790, net income from shipping amounted to a mere $5.9 million; by 1807 the volume had surged to $42.1 million.

Prospects seemed bright for America's economic and diplomatic future and for Jefferson's dream of agricultural America feeding overcrowded, war-torn Europe. But politicians in both England and France constantly threatened to disrupt American trade and created an atmosphere of hostility. One source of tension was impressment. For decades, British sailors had protested the exceedingly cruel conditions and low pay in His Majesty's navy by jumping ship in American ports and enlisting as merchant sailors on American vessels. Strapped for mariners by renewed warfare, England pursued a vigorous policy of reclaiming

The impressment of sailors into the British navy from American ships was one of the more prominent causes of the War of 1812. This 1790 engraving shows an American sailor being seized at gunpoint while those who might try to assist him are elbowed aside.

Picture Research Consultants & Archives.

British sailors after 1803, even if they were on neutral American ships and, more provocatively, even if they had become citizens of the United States. It is estimated that the British abducted as many as eight thousand sailors from American ships between 1803 and 1812. The loss of so many seamen hurt American shippers economically, but it wounded American pride even more. Like the XYZ affair, impressment seemed to be a direct denial of the United States' status as a legitimate nation.

Economic Warfare

Pressure on American neutrality increased after 1805, when a military deadlock emerged in the European war: Britain was supreme at sea, while France was in control on the ground. The war then changed from one of military campaigning to one of diplomatic and economic maneuvering. Seeking to close off foreign supplies to England, in November 1806 Napoleon issued the Berlin Decree, barring ships that had

□ **impressment** Procedure permitted under British maritime law that authorized commanders of warships to force English civilian sailors into military service.

□ **Berlin Decree** Napoleon's order declaring the British Isles under blockade and authorizing the confiscation of British goods from any ship found carrying them.

anchored at British harbors from entering ports controlled by France. The British Parliament responded by issuing a series of directives that permitted neutral ships to sail to European ports only if they first called at a British port to pay a transit tax. It was thus impossible for a neutral ship to follow the laws of either nation without violating the laws of the other. All this European blustering, however, had little immediate effect on the American economy. From the issuance of the Berlin Decree to the end of 1807, American exports and shipping rose more than they had risen during any similar period.

But such good fortune was not to last. Seeking to break France's dependence on America as a source for food and other supplies, Napoleon sought an alliance with Russia, and in the spring of 1807 his diplomatic mission succeeded. Having acquired an alternative source for grain and other foodstuffs, Napoleon immediately began enforcing the Berlin Decree, hoping to starve England into submission. The British countered by stepping up enforcement of their European blockade and aggressively pursuing impressment to strengthen the Royal Navy.

The escalation in both France's and Britain's economic war efforts quickly led to confrontation with Americans and a diplomatic crisis. A pivotal event occurred in June 1807. The British frigate *Leopard*, patrolling the American shoreline, confronted the American warship *Chesapeake*. The *Leopard* ordered the American ship to halt and hand over any British sailors on board. When the *Chesapeake*'s captain refused, the *Leopard* fired several broadsides, crippling the American vessel, killing three sailors, and injuring eighteen. The British then boarded the *Chesapeake* and dragged off four men, three of whom were naturalized citizens of the United States. Americans were outraged.

Americans were not the only ones galvanized by British aggression. Shortly after the *Chesapeake* affair, word arrived in the United States that Napoleon had responded to Britain's belligerence by declaring a virtual economic war against neutrals. In the Milan Decree, he vowed to seize any neutral ship that so

much as carried licenses to trade with England. What was worse, the Milan Decree stated that ships that had been boarded by British authorities—even against their crew's will—were subject to immediate French capture.

Believing that Europeans were far more dependent on American goods and ships than Americans were on European money and manufactures, Jefferson chose to violate one of his cardinal principles: the U.S. government would interfere in the economy to force Europeans to recognize American neutral rights. In December 1807, the president announced the Embargo Act, which would, in effect, close down all American foreign trade as of January 1 unless the Europeans agreed to recognize America's neutral rights.

CRISES IN THE NATION

☆ How did Jefferson's economic and Indian policies influence national developments after 1808?

☆ How did problems in Europe, coupled with the actions of frontier politicians such as William Henry Harrison, lead the nation into war in 1812?

Jefferson's reaction to European aggression immediately began strangling American trade and with it America's domestic economy. In addition, European countries still had legitimate claims on much of North America, and the Indians who continued to occupy most of the continent could pose a serious threat to the United States if properly motivated. While impressment, blockade, and embargo paralyzed America's Atlantic frontier, a combination of European and Indian hostility along the western frontier added to the air of national emergency. The resulting series of domestic crises played havoc with Jefferson's vision of a peaceful, prosperous nation.

Economic Depression

Although Jefferson felt justified in suspending free trade to protect neutral rights, the result was the worst economic depression since the founding of the British colonies in North America. Critics such as John Randolph pronounced Jefferson's solution worse than the problem—like trying "to cure corns by cutting off the toes." And while Jefferson's "damn-bargo," as critics called it, was only halfheartedly enforced, the economy slumped disastrously. Taken together, all American exports fell from $109 million to $22 million, and net earnings from shipping fell by almost 50 percent. During 1808, earnings from legitimate business enterprise in America declined to less than a quarter of their value in 1807.

New Englanders, whose economy was almost entirely focused on shipping and international trade,

frigate A very fast warship, rigged with square sails and carrying from thirty to fifty cannons on two gun decks.

broadside The simultaneous discharge of all the guns on one side of a warship.

□ **Milan Decree** Napoleon's order authorizing the capture of any neutral vessels sailing from British ports or submitting to British searches.

□ **Embargo Act** Embargo (a government-ordered trade ban) announced by Jefferson in 1807 to pressure Britain and France to accept neutral trading rights; it went into effect in 1808 and closed down all U.S. foreign trade.

screamed loudest about the impact of the embargo. Indeed, the depression shattered economic and social life in many eastern towns. It has been estimated that thirty thousand sailors were thrown out of work and that as many as a hundred thousand people employed in support industries were laid off. In light of Jefferson's policies and the collapsing economy, the extremism expressed by the Essex Junto three years earlier began to sound reasonable.

Southerners and westerners, however, were just as seriously affected by the embargo. The economy of the South had depended on the export of staple crops like tobacco since colonial times and was rapidly turning to cotton. There, embargo meant near-death to all legitimate trade. In response to the loss of foreign markets, tobacco prices fell from $6.75 per hundredweight to $3.25, and cotton from 21 to 13 cents per pound. In the West, wholesale prices for agricultural products spiraled downward also. Overall, the prices of farm products were 16 percent lower between 1807 and 1811 than they had been between 1791 and 1801. At the same time, the price of virtually every consumer item went up. For example, the price of building materials—hardware, glass, and milled lumber—rose 11 percent during the same period, and the price of textiles climbed 20 percent. In fact, the only consumer item that did not go up in price was the one item farmers did not need to buy: food. Faced with dropping incomes and soaring costs, farmers probably felt the trade restrictions more profoundly than others.

Rather than blaming their problems on the Republican administration, however, disaffected farmers directed their anger at the British. Frontiersmen believed, rightly or wrongly, that eliminating British interference with American trade would restore the boom economy that had drawn so many of them to the edge of American settlement. Thus westerners banded together to raise their voices in favor of war against Britain.

Political Upheaval

Despite the escalating crisis in the country, Jefferson remained popular and powerful, but like Washington, he chose to step down from the presidency after serving two terms, making it clear to party officials that he favored James Madison to replace him. Although Madison and Jefferson had much in common and were longtime friends, they seemed very different from each other. Few could say they knew Madison well, but those who did found him captivating: a man of few words but of piercing intellect and unflinching conviction. Those less well acquainted with him thought the quiet Virginian indecisive: where Jefferson tended to act on impulse, Madison approached matters of state as he approached matters of political philosophy—with caution, patience, and reason.

Dissatisfied with Jefferson's policies, both southern and northeastern party members contested Madison's succession. The Tertium Quid challenged Jefferson's authority in the party caucus and tried to secure the nomination for the stately and conservative James Monroe. Jefferson managed to hold the party's southern wing in line, but northeasterners, stinging under the pressure of the embargo, bucked the decision of the party caucus and nominated their own presidential candidate: New Yorker George Clinton. Although Clinton polled only six electoral votes, his nomination was a sign of growing divisions over the problems that the United States faced in 1808. Despite all the political contention, Madison easily defeated his Federalist opponent, Charles Cotesworth Pinckney. But Federalist criticism of Jefferson's policies, especially of the embargo, was finding a growing audience as the depression deepened, and in the congressional elections the Republicans lost twenty-four seats to Federalists.

During Madison's first two years in office, lack of any progress toward resolving the nation's woes seemed to confirm critics' perception of his indecisiveness. Nevertheless, Republicans actually made gains in the congressional elections in 1810: they regained fourteen of the seats they had lost in the House in 1808 and picked up two additional Senate seats. But this was no vote of confidence in Madison. Though the new congressmen were Republicans, sixty-three of them did not support Madison or his commitment to a conciliatory policy toward the British. These congressmen, mostly very young and extremely patriotic, represented frontier constituents who were being ravaged by the agricultural depression. Among them were Henry Clay and John Calhoun, who would become political lions in the years ahead. In the months to come, their increasingly strident demands for aggressive action against England, and especially against Canada, earned them the nickname War Hawks.

The Rise of the Shawnee Prophet

A key reason for War Hawk militancy was the unsettled conditions along the western frontier. Relations with Indians in the West had been peaceful since the Battle of Fallen Timbers in 1794. The Shawnees and other

party caucus A meeting of members of a political party to decide on questions of policy, leadership, or candidates running for office.

□ **James Monroe** Republican politician from Virginia who served in diplomatic posts under George Washington, John Adams, and Thomas Jefferson; he later became the fifth president of the United States.

□ **War Hawks** Members of Congress elected in 1810 from the West and South who campaigned for war with Britain in the hopes of stimulating the economy and annexing new territory.

groups had been thrown off their traditional home-lands in Ohio by the Treaty of Greenville and forced to move to new lands in Indiana. There, food shortages, disease, and continuing encroachment by settlers caused many young Indians to lose faith in their traditional beliefs and in themselves as human beings.

In the midst of the crisis, one disheartened, diseased alcoholic rose above his afflictions to lead the Indians into a brief new era of hope. Like others of his generation, Lalawethika felt increasingly hopeless, turned to alcohol, and finally in 1805 became critically ill. He claimed that he remembered dying and meeting the Master of Life and then awoke cured of his illness. Launching a religious and cultural revival designed to teach the ways revealed to him by the Master of Life, he adopted the name Tenskwatawa ("the open door"). Whites called him The Prophet.

Blaming the decline of his people on their adoption of white ways, the Prophet taught them to go back to their traditional lifestyle—to discard whites' clothing, religion, and especially alcohol—and live as their ancestors had lived. He also urged his followers to unify against the temptations and threats of white exploiters and to hold on to what remained of their lands. If they followed his teachings, the Prophet insisted, the whites would vanish from their world. In 1807 the Prophet established a religious settlement, Prophetstown, on the banks of Tippecanoe Creek in Indiana Territory.

Although the Prophet preached a message of ethnic pride, nonviolence, and passive resistance, as white settlers continued to pressure his people, he began to advocate more forceful solutions. In a speech to an intertribal council in April 1807, he suggested for the first time that warriors unite to resist white expansion. He made it clear that the Master of Life would defend his followers if war were pressed on them.

Prophecy and Politics in the West

While Tenskwatawa continued to stress spiritual means for stopping white aggression, his brother Tecumseh pushed for a more political course of action. Seven years older than the Prophet, Tecumseh was known as a brave fighter and a persuasive political orator. Tecumseh traveled throughout the western frontier, working out political and military alliances designed to put a stop to white expansion once and for all (see Map 9.1). Although he did not want to start an aggressive war against white settlers, Tecumseh exhorted Indians to defend every inch of land that remained to them. Rumors soon were flying up and down the frontier filled with speculations about Tecumseh's ultimate objectives, including the suggestion that he was a British agent and part of a plot against the Americans.

Like many along the frontier, Indiana governor William Henry Harrison had good reason to advance the impression of a conspiracy between Tecumseh and the British. Harrison and men like him believed the United States had the right to control all of North America and, accordingly, to brush aside anything standing in the way. Britain and the Indians were thus linked in their minds. Both were seen as obstacles to national destiny, and many War Hawks prayed for the outbreak of war between the United States and the British with the Indians in between. Such a war would provide an excuse to attack the Indians and dispossess them of their land. In addition, a war would justify invading and seizing Canada, fulfilling what many considered a logical but frustrated objective of the American Revolution. Taking Canada from the British would open rich timber, fur, and agricultural lands for American settlement. It would also secure American control of the Great Lakes and St. Lawrence River—potentially a very valuable shipping route for agricultural produce.

Choosing War

With the nation reeling from the economic squeeze of the embargo, Congress replaced it with the Non-Intercourse Act early in 1809. The new law forbade trade only with England and France and gave the president the power to reopen trade if either of the combatants lifted its restrictions against American shipping. Even though this act was much less restrictive than the embargo, American merchants were relieved when it expired in the spring of 1810. At that point, Congress passed an even more permissive boycott, Macon's Bill No. 2. According to this new law, merchants could trade with the combatants if they wanted to take the risk, but if either France or England lifted its blockade, the United States would stop trading with the other.

Hoping to cut England off from needed outside supplies, Napoleon responded to Macon's Bill in August by promising to suspend French restrictions on American shipping while secretly ordering the continued seizure of American ships. Despite Napoleon's devious intentions, Madison sought to use the French peace overture as a lever: he instructed the American mission in London to tell the British that he would

□ **The Prophet (Tenskwatawa)** Shawnee religious visionary who called for a return to Indian traditions and founded the community of Prophetstown on Tippecanoe Creek in Indiana.

□ **Non-Intercourse Act** An 1809 law reopening trade with all nations except France and Britain and authorizing the president to reopen trade with them if they lifted restrictions on American shipping.

□ **Macon's Bill No. 2** An 1810 law that offered exclusive trading rights to France or Britain, whichever recognized American neutral rights first.

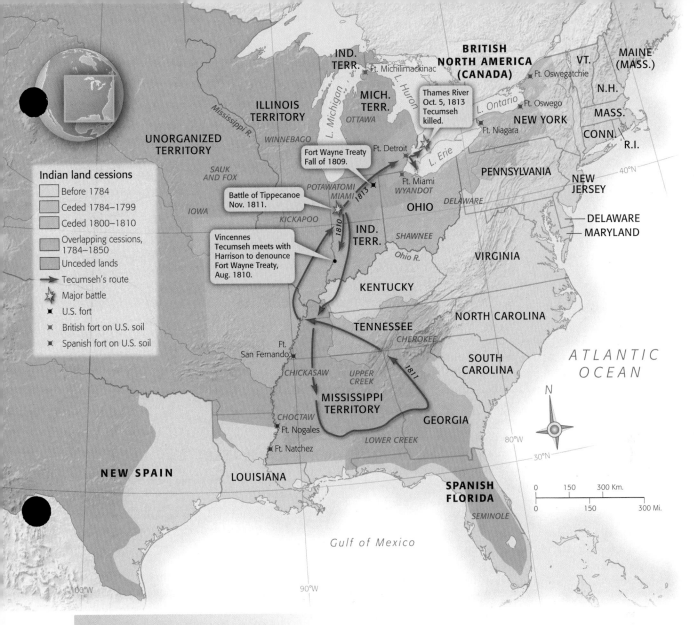

Indian land cessions

- Before 1784
- Ceded 1784–1799
- Ceded 1800–1810
- Overlapping cessions, 1784–1850
- Unceded lands
- → Tecumseh's route
- ★ Major battle
- ⚔ U.S. fort
- ⚔ British fort on U.S. soil
- ⚔ Spanish fort on U.S. soil

Thames River
Oct. 5, 1813
Tecumseh
killed.

Fort Wayne Treaty
Fall of 1809.

Battle of Tippecanoe
Nov. 1811.

Vincennes
Tecumseh meets with
Harrison to denounce
Fort Wayne Treaty,
Aug. 1810.

MAP 9.1 Tecumseh's Potential Alliance

Between 1806 and the outbreak of the War of 1812, Tecumseh traveled up and down the Trans-Appalachian West recruiting allies for a unified Indian confederacy to oppose any further American westward expansion. Had Tecumseh succeeded, the history of the United States would undoubtedly have been very different.
© Cengage Learning.

close down trade with them unless they joined France in dropping trade restrictions. Sure that Napoleon was lying, the British refused, backing the president into a diplomatic corner. In February 1811, the provisions of Macon's Bill forced Madison to close down trading with Britain for its failure to remove economic sanctions, stepping up tensions all around.

Later in the year, events in the West finally triggered a crisis. The origin of the problem was an agreement, the Fort Wayne Treaty, signed in the fall of 1809 between the United States and representatives of the Miami, Potawatomi, and Delaware Indians. In return for an outright bribe of $5,200 and individual

annuities ranging from $250 to $500, accommodationists among these three tribes sold over 3 million acres of Indian land in Indiana and Illinois—land already occupied by many other Indian groups.

In August 1810, Tecumseh met with Governor Harrison in Vincennes, Indiana, to denounce the Fort Wayne Treaty. Harrison insisted that the agreement was legitimate. Speaking for those whose lands had been sold out from under them, Tecumseh said,

annuity An allowance or income paid annually.

Although they had enormous respect for each other, Indiana territorial governor William Henry Harrison and Tecumseh were both ferocious when it came to defending their political and diplomatic positions. This painting of their confrontation at the 1810 peace conference held at Vincennes makes this point clearly. The two never actually came to blows at this meeting or at another held one year later, but they never were able to find common ground.

"They want to save that piece of land, we do not wish you to take it.... I want the present boundary line to continue. Should you cross it, I assure you it will be productive of bad consequences." But Harrison refused to budge.

The Vincennes meeting convinced the Indians that they must prepare for a white attack. Tecumseh traveled up and down the American frontier, enlisting additional allies in his growing Indian confederacy. Meanwhile, Harrison grew more and more eager to attack the Indians before they could unite fully. He got his chance when a second peace conference in the summer of 1811 also failed. Citing the failed peace effort and sporadic skirmishes between frontier settlers and renegade bands of Indians, none of which were connected to Tecumseh, Harrison ordered an attack on their village near the Wabash River. On November 7, in the Battle of Tippecanoe, an army of enraged frontiersmen burned Prophetstown. Then, having succeeded in setting the Indian frontier ablaze, Harrison called for a declaration of war against the Indians and the British.

Headlining Harrison's call for war, a Kentucky newspaper proclaimed, "The war on the Wabash is purely BRITISH, the SCALPING KNIFE and TOMAHAWK of British savages, is now, again devastating our frontiers." Coming as it did while Congress was already embroiled in debate over economic sanctions and British impressment, the outbreak of violence on the frontier was finally enough to push legislators into action. Chairman of the House Foreign Relations Committee John C. Calhoun put the situation bluntly: "The mad ambition, the lust of power, and the commercial avarice of Great Britain have left to neutral nations an alternative only between the base surrender of their rights, and a manly vindication of them." He then introduced a war bill in Congress, which passed 79 to 49 in the House and 19 to 13 in the Senate.

THE NATION AT WAR

☆ What geographic and economic factors impeded American war efforts?

☆ What part did events in Europe and Britain play in ending the war and what were the results from Americans' point of view?

With its woefully neglected army and navy, the United States was taking a terrible risk in engaging Britain, a nation that was fast becoming the most awesome military power in the world. Not surprisingly, defeat and humiliation were the main fruits of American efforts as the two nations faced off.

The Fighting Begins

Despite years of agitation, the war's actual arrival in 1812 caught the United States terribly unprepared. Republican cost cutting had virtually disbanded the military during Jefferson's first term in office. Renewed fighting with pirates in the Mediterranean and building tensions in the Atlantic had forced Republicans to increase military spending, but the navy still had fewer than twenty vessels, and the army could field fewer than seven thousand men. And for all its war fever, Congress balked at appropriating new funds even after war had been declared. Thus the first ventures in the war went forward with only grudging financial support.

In line with what the War Hawks wanted, the first military campaign was a three-pronged drive toward Canada and against the Indians (see Map 9.2). One force, commanded by Harrison, successfully raided

▫ **Battle of Tippecanoe** Battle near Prophetstown in 1811, where American forces led by William Henry Harrison defeated the followers of the Shawnee Prophet and destroyed the town.

It Matters Today

The Battle of Tippecanoe

Many Americans today think that Indians never really mattered in the nation's history. This modern dismissal of Indian significance is entirely incorrect. For years before the Battle of Tippecanoe, William Henry Harrison warned officials in Washington that if Tecumseh was successful he almost certainly would stop American westward expansion. This was not baseless exaggeration. As Harrison himself said of Tecumseh, "He is one of those uncommon geniuses, which spring up occasionally to produce revolutions and overturn the established order of things." We will never know how close Tecumseh came to overturning the established order. We do know that he experienced considerable success in raising a unified defense, and there is no question that such a unified force would have compelled politicians like Jefferson to reconsider their policies. Undoubtedly, America today would be a profoundly different place had Harrison not destroyed Prophetstown and undermined the growing Indian confederacy.

- How might the Jefferson administration have dealt differently with the demands made by Tecumseh and his allies? In what ways would the United States be different today had this alternative course been followed?

- Since the early nineteenth century, the United States has encountered resistance to national expansion on a number of fronts. Choose another situation from later in the nation's history in which such resistance was dealt with. What similarities or differences, or both, do you see between this event and the handling of Tecumseh's resistance movement?

While the army experienced a string of embarrassing losses during the opening days of the War of 1812, the navy outperformed all expectations. This contemporary engraving celebrates the victory of the U.S.S. *Constitution* over the British H.M.S. *Guerrière*. In a protracted battle, the Americans splintered the British ship, damaging it so badly that any salvage was impossible; what remained of the *Guerrière* was burned by the victorious Americans.

U.S. territory after an inconclusive battle against the British.

American sailors fared much better during the war's opening days. Leading the war effort at sea were three frigates: the *Constitution* (popularly known as Old Ironsides), the *President,* and the *United States.* In mid-August, the *Constitution* outmaneuvered and eventually captured what the British described as "one of our stoutest frigates," the H.M.S. *Guerrière.* The *United States,* under the command of Stephen Decatur, both endured and delivered horrific broadsides while subduing the British *Macedonian.* The carnage Decatur described when he boarded the crippled vessel was typical of naval warfare at the time: "fragments of the dead scattered in every direction, the decks slippery with blood." American privateers also enjoyed success, capturing 450 British merchant ships valued in the millions during the first six months of the war.

American naval victories were all that kept the nation's morale alive in 1812. Former

undefended Indian villages but was unable to make any gains against British troops. Farther east, a force led by Major General Stephen Van Rensselaer was defeated by a small British and Indian army. Meanwhile, the third force, commanded by Henry Dearborn, lunged at Montreal but nervously withdrew back into

▫ **Old Ironsides** Nickname of the U.S.S. *Constitution*, the forty-four-gun American frigate whose victory over the British H.M.S. *Guerrière* bolstered sagging national morale during the War of 1812.

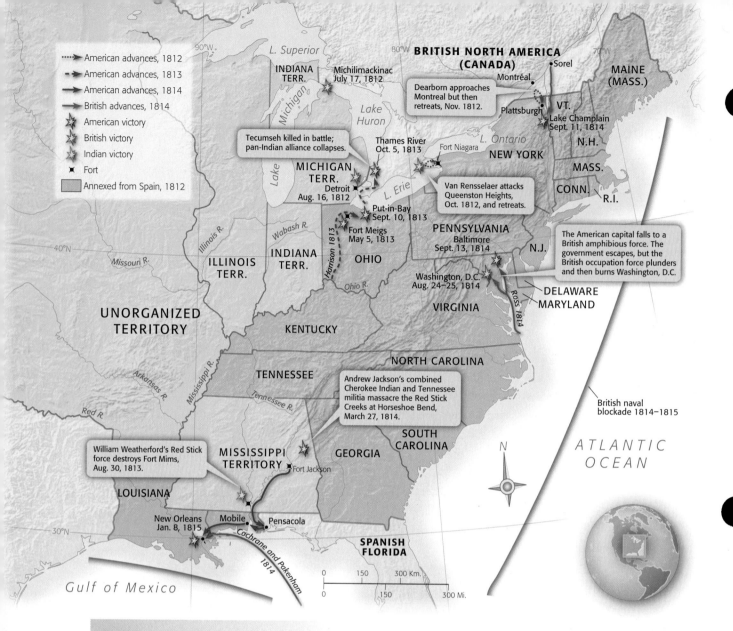

Legend:
- American advances, 1812
- American advances, 1813
- American advances, 1814
- British advances, 1814
- American victory
- British victory
- Indian victory
- Fort
- Annexed from Spain, 1812

Michilimackinac July 17, 1812

Dearborn approaches Montreal but then retreats, Nov. 1812.

Tecumseh killed in battle; pan-Indian alliance collapses.

Thames River Oct. 5, 1813

Fort Niagara

Lake Champlain Sept. 11, 1814

Detroit Aug. 16, 1812

Put-in-Bay Sept. 10, 1813

Fort Meigs May 5, 1813

Van Rensselaer attacks Queenston Heights, Oct. 1812, and retreats.

Baltimore Sept. 13, 1814

The American capital falls to a British amphibious force. The government escapes, but the British occupation force plunders and then burns Washington, D.C.

Washington, D.C. Aug. 24–25, 1814

British naval blockade 1814–1815

Andrew Jackson's combined Cherokee Indian and Tennessee militia massacre the Red Stick Creeks at Horseshoe Bend, March 27, 1814.

William Weatherford's Red Stick force destroys Fort Mims, Aug. 30, 1813.

Fort Jackson

New Orleans Jan. 8, 1815

Mobile

Pensacola

Cochrane and Pakenham 1814

MAP 9.2 The War of 1812

The heaviest action during the first two years of the War of 1812 lay along the U.S./Canadian border. Then, in 1814 the British sought to knock the United States out of the war by staging three offensives: one along the northern frontier at Plattsburgh, New York; one into the Chesapeake; and a third directed at the Mississippi River at New Orleans. All three offensives failed. © Cengage Learning.

Treasury secretary Albert Gallatin summarized the nation's humiliating military efforts: "The series of misfortunes exceeds all anticipations made even by those who had least confidence in our inexperienced officers and undisciplined men." The land war had been, as another politician recalled, a "miscarriage, without even the heroism of disaster." Vowing to reverse the situation, Congress increased the size of the army to fifty-seven thousand men and offered a $16 bonus to encourage enlistments.

Thus in 1812 Madison stood for reelection at a time when the nation's military fate appeared uncertain and his own leadership equally so. Although the majority of his party's congressional caucus supported him for reelection, nearly a third of the Republican congressmen—mostly those from New York and New England—rallied around New Yorker DeWitt Clinton. Like his uncle George Clinton, DeWitt Clinton was a Republican who favored Federalist economic policies and agreed with New England Federalists that the war was unnecessary. Most Federalists supported Clinton, and the party did not field a candidate of its own.

The campaign's outcome mirrored the congressional vote on the war bill earlier in the year. New York and New England rallied behind Clinton. The South and West continued to support Madison, the Republicans, and war. Madison won, but his share of electoral votes had fallen from 72 percent in 1808 to

58.9 percent. At the same time, Republican Party strength in the House dropped by over 13 percent, and in the Senate by about 8 percent.

The War Continues

When military campaigning resumed in the spring of 1813, it appeared that the U.S. Army would fare as badly as it had the previous fall. Fighting resumed when British colonel Henry Proctor and Tecumseh, with a joint force of nine hundred British soldiers and twelve hundred Indians, laid siege to Harrison's command camped at Fort Meigs on the Maumee Rapids in Ohio. An army of twelve hundred Kentucky militiamen finally arrived and drove the enemy off but were so disorganized that they lost nearly half their number in pursuing the British and Indian force. Harrison was shocked, proclaiming the Kentuckians' "excessive ardour scarcely less fatal than cowardice." Having escaped virtually unscathed, Proctor and Tecumseh continued to harass American forces throughout the summer. Then, with winter approaching, the British and Indians withdrew to Canada. Harrison, who had been busy raising additional troops, decided to pursue.

No doubt Harrison's new effort would have proved as fruitless as his earlier ones, but an unexpected event turned the odds in his favor. One key problem plaguing Harrison and other commanders in the field was that the British controlled the Great Lakes and so could depend on an uninterrupted supply line. In contrast, American forces and their supplies moved along undeveloped roads and were easy targets for Indian and British attackers. Oliver Hazard Perry, a young naval tactician, had been given command of a small fleet assigned to clear the lakes of British ships. He got his chance at Put-in-Bay on Lake Erie in September 1813. After three hours of close combat, Perry's command subdued and captured six British ships. Perry immediately sent a note to Harrison stating, "We have met the enemy and they are ours."

Buoyed by this news, Harrison's army closed in on Proctor and Tecumseh at the Thames River, about 50 miles northeast of Detroit, on October 5. The British force faced a piercing cavalry charge and, lacking naval support, abandoned their Indian allies and fled. The Indians held out longer, but when word spread that Tecumseh had been killed, they melted into the woods, leaving the body of their fallen leader to be torn apart by the victorious Americans.

Another war front had also opened farther south during 1813. Although the Creek Confederacy as a whole wished to remain neutral, one faction calling themselves the Red Sticks had allied with Tecumseh in 1812. In the summer of 1813, Red Stick leader William Weatherford led a force against Fort Mims on the Alabama frontier, killing all but about thirty of the more than three hundred occupants. The Fort

Mims massacre enraged whites in the Southeast. In Tennessee, twenty-five hundred militiamen rallied around Andrew Jackson, a young brawler and Indian fighter. Already called "Old Hickory" because of his toughness, Jackson made a bold promise: "The blood of our women & children shall not call for vengeance in vain." In the course of that summer and fall, Jackson's frontier ruffians fought multiple engagements against the Red Stick Creeks, driving them into hiding.

While these battles raged on land, the British shut down American forces at sea. Embarrassed by the success of Old Ironsides and the other American frigates, the British admiralty ordered that "the naval force of the enemy should be quickly and completely disposed of" and sent sufficient ships to do the job. The American naval fleet and merchant marine found themselves bottled up in port by the world's strongest navy.

The Politics of War

The war had wound down for the winter by the time Congress reconvened in December 1813, but the outlook was not good. President Madison tried to be optimistic. Recalling the victories during the year, he said, "The war, with its vicissitudes, is illustrating the capacity and destiny of the United States to be a great, a flourishing, and a powerful nation." Madison's optimism seemed justified later in December when the British offered to open direct peace negotiations with the Americans. The president quickly formed a peace commission, but until its work was done, Madison and Congress still had to worry about the practical issues of troops and money, both of which were in critically short supply.

Despite increases in army pay and bonuses for new recruits, enlistments were falling off in 1813. Congressional Republicans responded by adding further enticements, including grants of 160 acres of land in the western territories. Congress also authorized the president to extend the term of enlistment for men already in service. By 1814, the army had increased to more than sixty-two thousand men but Congress had not figured out how to pay them.

Traditional enemies of internal taxes, the Republicans faced a dilemma: in the federal budget for 1814

□ **Oliver Hazard Perry** American naval officer who led the fleet that defeated the British in the Battle of Put-in-Bay during the War of 1812.

□ **Andrew Jackson** General who defeated the Creeks at Horseshoe Bend in 1814 and the British at New Orleans in 1815; he later became the seventh president of the United States.

merchant marine A nation's commercial ships.

vicissitudes Sudden or unexpected changes in circumstances.

the government's income would be approximately $16 million, but its expenses would amount to over $45 million. Congress had already passed a set of new taxes and could not imagine explaining another increase to their constituents. So congressional Republicans decided to borrow instead, authorizing a $35 million deficit.

Adding to the money problem, the United States, to this point in the war, had permitted neutral nations to trade freely in American ports, carrying American exports to England and Canada and English goods into the U.S. ports. As a result American food was rolling directly into British military commissaries, strengthening the enemy's ability and will to fight.

In a secret message to Congress, the president proposed an absolute embargo on all American ships and goods—neither were to leave port. Federalists, especially those from New England, screamed in protest. They called the proposal "an engine of tyranny." But congressional Republicans passed the embargo a mere eight days after Madison submitted it. What emerged, the Embargo of 1813, was the most far-reaching trade restriction bill ever passed by Congress. It confined all trading ships to port, and even fishing vessels could put to sea only if their masters posted sizable bonds. Government officials charged with enforcing the new law had unprecedented discretionary powers. The impact was devastating: the embargo virtually shut down the New England and New York economies, and it severely crippled the economy of nearly every other state.

New British Offensives

While Congress debated matters of finance and trade restrictions, events in Europe were changing the entire character of the war. On March 31, 1814, the British and their allies took Paris, forcing Napoleon to abdicate his throne. Napoleon's defeat left the United States as Great Britain's sole military target.

In frustration at failing to capture members of the U.S. government, the British pillaged Washington in August 1814 and then burned the public buildings. This painting captures the disordered scene as city dwellers try to quench the flames while the capitol building blazes in the background.

Republican Joseph Nicholson expressed a common lament when he observed, "We should have to fight hereafter not for 'free Trade and sailors rights,' not for the Conquest of the Canadas, but for our national Existence." As Nicholson feared, a flood of combat-hardened British veterans began arriving in North America, and the survival of the United States as an independent nation was indeed at issue. By the late summer of 1814, British troop strength in Canada had risen to thirty thousand men. From this position of power, the British prepared a chain of three offensives to bring the war to a quick end.

In the first of these, twenty British warships and several troop transports sailed up Chesapeake Bay toward Washington, D.C. The British arrived outside Washington at midday on August 24. The troops defending the city could not withstand the force of hardened British veterans, but they slowed the invasion long enough for the government to escape. Angered at being foiled, the British sacked the city, torching most of the buildings. They then moved on toward the key port city of Baltimore.

At Baltimore, the British navy had to knock out Fort McHenry and take the harbor before the army could take the city. On September 13, British ships armed with heavy mortars and rockets attacked the fort. Despite the pounding, when the sun rose on September 14, the American flag continued to wave over Fort McHenry. The sight moved a young prisoner of war held on a British ship, Francis Scott Key, to

□ **Embargo of 1813** An absolute embargo on all American trade and British imports.

bond A sum of money paid as bail or security.

discretionary powers Powers to be used at one's own judgment; in government, powers given to an administrative official to be used without outside consultation or oversight.

mortar A portable, muzzle-loading cannon that fires large projectiles; traditionally used against fixed fortifications.

□ **Francis Scott Key** Author of "The Star-Spangled Banner," which chronicles the British bombardment of Fort McHenry in 1814; Key's poem, set to music, became the official U.S. national anthem in 1931.

As part of a three-pronged British offensive designed to bring the war to an end, Governor-General George Prevost led an invasion from Canada into New York. As illustrated here, in the Battle of Plattsburgh, American defenders were able to defeat the British support fleet and turn back the invasion.

record the event in a poem that was later set to music and became the national anthem of the United States. Having failed to reduce the fort, the British were forced to withdraw, leaving Baltimore undisturbed.

While this strike at the nation's midsection was raging, Sir George Prevost, governor-general of Canada, massed ten thousand troops for an invasion in the north. The British force arrived just north of Plattsburgh, New York, on September 6, where it was to join the British naval fleet that controlled Lake Champlain. However, a small American flotilla under the command of Lieutenant Thomas Macdonough outmaneuvered the imposing British armada and forced a surrender on September 11. Prevost had already begun his attack against the defenders at Plattsburgh, but when he learned that the British lake fleet was defeated, he lost his nerve and ordered his men to retreat.

On yet another front, the British pressed an offensive against the Gulf Coast designed to take pressure off Canada and close transportation on the Mississippi River. The defense of the Gulf Coast fell to Andrew Jackson and his Tennesseans. Having spent the winter raising troops and collecting supplies, in March 1814 Jackson and his army of four thousand militiamen and Cherokee volunteers resumed their mission to punish the Red Stick Creeks. Learning that the Red Sticks had established a camp on the peninsula formed by a bend in the Tallapoosa River, Jackson led his men on a forced march to attack. On March 27 in the Battle of Horseshoe Bend, Jackson's force trapped the Creeks and slaughtered nearly eight hundred people, destroying Red Stick opposition and severely crippling Indian resistance in the South.

After the massacre at Horseshoe Bend, Jackson moved his army toward the Gulf of Mexico, where a British offensive was in the making. Arriving in New Orleans on December 1, he found the city ill prepared to defend itself. The local militia, consisting mostly of French and Spanish residents, would not obey American officers. "Those who are not for us are against us, and will be dealt with accordingly," Jackson proclaimed. He turned increasingly to unconventional sources of support. Free blacks in the city formed a regular army corps, and Jackson created a special unit of black refugees from Saint-Domingue. He also accepted a company of river pirates under the command of Jean Lafitte, awarding them a blanket pardon for all past crimes. "Hellish Banditti," Jackson himself called them, but the pirate commander and the general hit it off so well that Lafitte became Jackson's constant companion during the campaign.

Having pulled his ragtag force together, Jackson settled in to wait for the British attack. On the morning of January 8, 1815, it came. The British force emerged from the fog at dawn, directly in front of Jackson's defenses. Waiting patiently behind hastily constructed barricades, Jackson's men began firing cannon, rifles, and muskets as the British moved within range. According to one British veteran, it was

□ **Battle of Horseshoe Bend** Attack in 1814 in which Tennessee militia massacred Creek Indians in Alabama, ending Red Stick resistance to white westward expansion.

□ **Jean Lafitte** Leader of a band of pirates in southeast Louisiana; he offered to fight for the Americans at New Orleans in return for a pardon for his men.

"the most murderous fire I have ever beheld before or since."

When it was all over, more than two thousand British troops had been killed or wounded in the Battle of New Orleans. This was by far the most successful battle fought by American forces during the War of 1812. But ironically, it was fought after the war was over.

The War's Strange Conclusion

While the British were closing in on Washington in the summer of 1814, treaty negotiations designed to end the war were beginning in Ghent, Belgium. Confident that their three-pronged attack against the United States would soon knock the Americans out of the war, the British delegates were in no hurry to end it by diplomacy. They refused to discuss substantive issues, insisting that all of the matters raised by Madison's peace commission were nonnegotiable.

At that point, however, domestic politics in England began to play a deciding role. After nearly a generation of armed conflict, British taxpayers were war weary. As one official put it, "Economy & relief from taxation … are the real objects to which public attention is turned." The failures at Plattsburgh and Baltimore made it appear that the war would drag on at least another year, adding another $44 million to the British tax burden. Moreover, continuation of the American war was interfering with Britain's European diplomacy: "We do not think the Continental Powers will continue in good humour with our Blockade of the whole Coast of America," one British diplomat observed.

In the end, the Treaty of Ghent, completed on December 24, 1814, simply restored diplomatic relations between England and the United States to what they had been prior to the outbreak of war. The treaty said nothing about impressment, blockades, or neutral trading rights. Neither military action nor diplomatic finagling netted Canada for the War Hawks. And the treaty did nothing about the alleged conspiracies between Indians and British agents. Although Americans called the War of 1812 a victory, they actually won none of the prizes that Madison's war statement had declared the nation was fighting for.

□ **Battle of New Orleans** Battle in January 1815 in which American troops commanded by Andrew Jackson destroyed the British force attempting to seize New Orleans.

□ **Treaty of Ghent** Treaty ending the War of 1812, signed in Belgium in 1814; it restored peace but was silent on the issues over which the United States and Britain had gone to war.

mechanize To substitute machinery for human labor.

PEACE AND THE RISE OF NEW EXPECTATIONS

☆ How did events during the War of 1812 help to move the American economy in new directions after peace was restored?

☆ How did changes in the economy affect the institution of slavery and the lives of slaves?

Despite repeated military disasters, loss of life, and diplomatic failure, the war had a number of positive effects on the United States. Just to have survived a war against the British was enough to build national confidence, but to have scored major victories such as those at Plattsburgh, Baltimore, and especially New Orleans was truly worth boasting about. Americans emerged from the conflict with a new sense of national pride and purpose. And many side effects from the fighting itself gave Americans new hopes and stimulated new plans.

New Expectations in the Northeastern Economy

Although trading interests in the Northeast suffered following Jefferson's embargo and were nearly ruined by the war and Madison's embargo, a new avenue of economic expansion opened in New England: cut off from European manufactured goods, Americans started to make more textiles and other items for themselves.

Samuel Slater, an English immigrant who had been trained in manufacturing in Britain, introduced the use of machines for spinning cotton yarn to the United States in 1790, but even with shipping expenses, tariffs, and other added costs, buying and selling machine-made British cloth was still more practical than investing large sums at high risk to build competing factories in the United States. After the embargo went into effect in 1808, however, British fabrics became increasingly unavailable, and prices soared. Slater and his partners moved quickly to expand their spinning operations to fill the void, but it was another entrepreneur, Francis Cabot Lowell, who would truly revolutionize American industry.

On a trip to England in 1810, Lowell engaged in wholesale industrial espionage, making detailed notes and sketches of British textile-manufacturing practices and machinery. Returning to the United States just before war broke out in 1812, Lowell formed the Boston Manufacturing Company. In 1813 the company used the plans Lowell had smuggled back to the United States to build a factory in Waltham, Massachusetts. The new facility included spinning machines, power looms, and all the equipment necessary to mechanize every stage in the production

Luddites

As Americans began to embrace mechanized manufacturing, many in Great Britain were protesting its unsettling impact. During 1811 and 1812, men calling themselves Luddites—a name taken from a fictional leader, "King Ludd"—began attacking and destroying mechanized factories. Although we now use the term Luddite to describe people who oppose modernization, that was not the point among the original Luddites. It took no special training, no craft skill, to run a power loom, and so weavers and other traditional craftsmen found themselves losing status, wages, and control over their own labor. They protested these losses by destroying the machines they blamed for demeaning them. The Luddites were eventually put down by the British military, and in 1812 Parliament passed the Frame Breaking Act, which made destroying factory equipment an offense punishable by death.

of finished cloth, bringing the entire process under one roof.

The spread of textile manufacturing was astonishing. Prior to 1808, only fifteen cotton mills had been built in the entire country. But between the passage of the embargo and the end of 1809, eighty-seven additional mills had sprung up, mostly in New England. And when war came, the pace increased, especially when Lowell's idea of a fully integrated factory proved to be highly efficient and profitable. The number of people employed in manufacturing increased from four thousand in 1809 to perhaps as many as a hundred thousand in 1816. In the years to come, factories in New England and elsewhere supplied more and more of the country's consumer goods.

New Opportunities in the West

Different kinds of development took place in the West following the war. Settlers poured into western regions in astounding numbers. The population of Ohio had already soared from 45,000 in 1800 to 231,000 in 1810, but it more than doubled again by 1820, reaching 581,000. Indiana, Illinois, Missouri, and Michigan experienced similar growth. Most of those who flooded into the newly opened West were small farmers, but subsistence agriculture was not the only economic opportunity that drew expectant Americans into the region.

One of the designs behind the Lewis and Clark expedition had been to gain entry for the United States into the burgeoning economy in North America's interior. That economy was complex, with many commodities being traded, and few entirely understood all of its intricacies. There was one facet, though, that was well known and very desirable to entrepreneurs: the brown gold of beaver, otter, and other animal furs. Even before the War of 1812, John Jacob Astor, a German immigrant, announced that he intended to establish "a range of Posts or Trading houses" along

the route that Lewis and Clark had followed from St. Louis to the Pacific (see page 191).

Another visionary entrepreneur sought a similar fortune in the Southwest. Auguste Chouteau

From the Collections of The St. Louis Mercantile Library Association.

This portrait of fur-trader extraordinaire, Auguste Chouteau, captures this captain of finance and industry at the peak of his career. Totally unlike the stereotype of the wild mountain man, Chouteau and his extended family combined entrepreneurial daring with sound financial planning to build a fortune based on the fur trade.

Following the War of 1812 and the death of Tecumseh, aggressive American expansionists put great pressure on Indians living on the eastern side of the Mississippi River to move farther west. In location after location, American Indian agents and their military escorts set up treaty negotiations designed to acquire ever-increasing amounts of land that would accommodate ambitious would-be farmers. This painting captures one of the largest of these, the Prairie du Chien conference of 1825, at which the Sauk, Fox, Chippewa, and other Indians in Illinois, Wisconsin, and Michigan ceded huge portions of land in hopes of winning peace.

was French by birth, but like many frontiersmen, he changed nationalities as frequently as the borderlands changed owners. Chouteau had helped to found the town of St. Louis and had been instrumental in establishing that city as the capital for a fur-trading empire. He, his brother Pierre, and an extended family of business partners used intermarriage to create a massive kinship network that included important French, Spanish, and Indian connections. The Chouteaus were able to extend their reach deep into the Missouri region and establish trade between St. Louis and the Spanish far western trading capital at Santa Fe. As Americans began to penetrate the area, the Chouteaus took the change in stride, inviting William Clark of the Corps of Discovery and fur entrepreneur Andrew Henry to join forces with them in founding the Missouri Fur Company in 1809.

After the war, the Chouteaus and various American partners pushed continually farther into the West and branched into other businesses. They operated flour mills and distilleries and speculated in real estate. Members of the extended family later helped to found Kansas City, pioneered mining in Colorado, and financed railroad building in the Dakotas.

Such economic expansion into the West posed a terrible threat to Native Americans. When Harrison's soldiers burned Prophetstown and later killed Tecumseh, they wiped out all hopes for a pan-Indian confederacy. In addition, the civil war among the Creeks, followed by Jackson's victories against the Red Stick faction, removed all meaningful resistance to westward expansion in the South. Many Indian groups continued to wield great power, but accommodationist leaders increasingly suggested that cooperation with federal authorities was the best course. Collaboration helped to prevent renewed warfare, but at enormous cost to the Indians. Within a year of the Battle of Horseshoe Bend, Jackson forced the Creeks to sign the Treaty of Fort Jackson, which confiscated over 20 million acres of land from the Creek Confederacy.

A similar but more gradual assault on Indian landholding began in the Northwest in 1815. In a council meeting at Portage des Sioux in Illinois Territory, the United States signed peace accords with the various tribes that had joined the British during the war. Both sides pledged to live in "perpetual peace and friendship," but the northwestern Indians possessed some

2 million acres of prime real estate between the Illinois and Mississippi Rivers—land that the U.S. government had already given away as enlistment bonuses to white war volunteers. Moving the Indians off that land as quickly as possible thus became a matter of national priority.

Over the next several years, federal Indian agents used every tactic they could think of to coerce groups like the Kickapoo Indians into ceding their lands. Finally, in 1819, the Kickapoo Nation signed the Treaty of Edwardsville, turning over most of the land the United States had demanded. Having secured this massive tract, government agents then turned their attention to the vast holdings of more distant tribes—the Sauk, Fox, Chippewa, and Dakota Indians in western Illinois, Wisconsin, and Michigan. As they had done with the Kickapoos, American negotiators used bribery, threat, and manipulation of local tensions to pursue their goal, eventually winning an enormous cession of land in the Prairie du Chien treaties of 1825.

A Revolution in the Southern Economy

Indian dispossession and westward expansion also promised great economic growth for the South. In the years before the War of 1812, the southern economy had been sluggish, and the future of the region's single-crop agricultural system was doubtful. However, the technological and economic changes that came in the war's wake pumped new energy into the South. In only a few decades, an entirely new South emerged.

The mechanization of the British textile industry in the late eighteenth century created an enormous new demand for cotton. Southern planters had been growing the plant and harvesting its fibrous cotton bolls since colonial times, but soil and climatic conditions limited the growing area for the sort of long-staple cotton that could be harvested and sold economically. Large areas of the South and Southwest had proved suitable for growing short-staple cotton, but the time and labor required to pick the sticky seeds from the compact bolls made the crop unprofitable. In 1793 a young Yale College graduate, Eli Whitney, was a guest at a plantation in Georgia where he learned about the difficulty of removing the seeds from short-staple cotton. In a matter of weeks, Whitney helped to perfect a machine that allowed a small and unskilled workforce to quickly comb out the seeds without damaging the fibers.

The outcome of Whitney's inventiveness was the rapid spread of short-staple cotton throughout inland South Carolina and Georgia. Then, just as it seemed that the southern economy was about to bloom, embargo and war closed down exports to England. Although some cotton growers were able to shift sales from England to the rising new factories in New England, a true explosion of growth in cotton cultivation had to await war's end.

With the arrival of peace and the departure of the British naval blockade, cotton growing began to spread at an astounding rate. Southerners rushed into frontier areas, spreading cotton agriculture into Alabama and Mississippi and then into Arkansas and northern Louisiana. In 1821 Spanish authorities gave long-time western land speculator Moses Austin permission to settle three hundred American families within a 200,000-acre tract in Texas between the Brazos and Colorado Rivers. When the elder Austin died, his son, Stephen F. Austin, took over the enterprise and was able to offer families large plots of land for a filing fee of only 12½ cents an acre. "I am convinced," he exclaimed, "that I could take on fifteen hundred families as easily as three hundred if permitted to do so." Throughout the 1820s and 1830s, Austin and other empresarios helped thousands of hopeful cotton capitalists to expand into Mexican territory. As a result of such expansion, the South's annual cotton crop grew by leaps and bounds. By 1840, annual exports reached nearly a million and a half bales, and increasing volumes were consumed within the United States by the mushrooming textile factories in the Northeast.

Reviving and Reinventing Slavery

Before the emergence of cotton, when the South's agricultural system was foundering, many southerners began to question slavery. In 1784 Thomas Jefferson proposed (but saw defeated) a land ordinance that would have prohibited slavery in all of the nation's territories after 1800. Some southern leaders advocated abolishing slavery and transporting freed blacks to Africa. But the booming southern economy after the

---

federal Indian agents Government officials who were responsible for negotiating treaties with Native American groups; at this time they were employed by the War Department.

cotton boll The pod of the cotton plant; it contains the plant's seeds surrounded by the fluffy fiber that is spun into yarn.

long-staple cotton A variety of cotton with long and loosely packed bolls of fiber that is easy to comb out and process.

short-staple cotton A variety of cotton with short and tightly packed bolls of fiber in which the plant's seeds are tangled.

□ **Eli Whitney** American inventor and manufacturer; his perfecting of the cotton gin (short for "cotton engine") revolutionized the cotton industry.

□ **Stephen F. Austin** American colonizer in Texas and later a leading voice in the Texas Revolution.

empresario In the Spanish colonies, a person who organized and led a group of settlers in exchange for land grants and the right to assess fees.

Charting the Growth of Cotton and Slavery

Historians use several ways to visualize historical information and then convey it to their readers. Map 9.3, for example, illustrates, on a county-by-county basis, how the spatial expansion of cotton agriculture and the institution of slavery overlapped between 1820 and 1860. It becomes quite clear that in those areas where cotton production was greatest, the concentration of slaves was also greatest. By 1860 most of South Carolina, lowland Georgia, central Alabama, much of Mississippi, and large portions of Louisiana were heavily dominated by cotton and slavery, while in Missouri, Kentucky, Florida, and Texas both cotton production and the slave population were quite limited. The map thus makes clear the links between this particular industry and its peculiar institution of labor, and it also conveys this information graphically to readers.

But there is much that this map cannot explain. For example, it does not tell us *why* both cotton and slavery increased over the early decades of the nineteenth century, nor does it tell us exactly how much both increased.

To answer these questions, the historian would have to reconfigure the information.

Putting the same information on a graph provides a completely different correlation between the growth of slavery and the growth of cotton production. As the figure included here shows very clearly, in 1790—when the first census of U.S. population was taken and three years before Eli Whitney had perfected the cotton gin—there was virtually no cotton being produced in the country. By 1820, however—the time plotted on the top figure in Map 9.3—we can see that production had grown to about 500,000 bales. At the same time, the number of slaves counted in the census had risen from about 750,000 to double that. Note, too, that by the middle of the 1820s cotton production began a steep increase until, by 1860, production had reached just short of 4 million bales. Slavery, however, maintained a fairly steady, though steep increase over the same period. By the end of the period shown, the raw number of slaves and the raw number of cotton bales was just about equal.

That nearly equal number of slaves and cotton bales might suggest that each slave was producing approximately one five-hundred-pound bale of cotton, but this would be a misleading conclusion. Going back to the bottom figure in Map 9.3, we can see that there were a great many slaves in places where cotton was not being produced: in northern Virginia, for example, which remained heavily slave occupied throughout this period. So, while each of these graphic representations can aid in analyzing this important information, neither is adequate on its own to tell the whole story; it is up to historians to determine what parts of the story they want to tell and then choose the best way of framing that information for both analytical and expressive clarity.

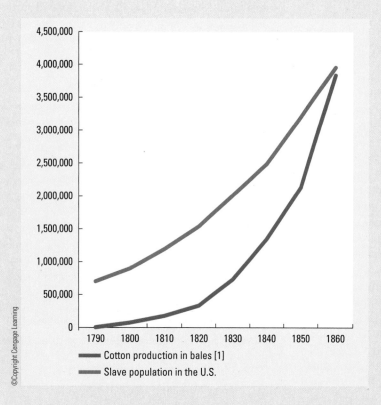

Cotton production in bales [1]

Slave population in the U.S.

©Copyright Cengage Learning

Slavery and Cotton Production in the United States 1790–1860

Data from U.S. Department of Agriculture, *Atlas of American Agriculture*, V, Sec. A, Cotton, Table IV, p. 18. Crop year begins October 1 for 1790–1840 and July 1 for 1845–1860. Production is measured in equivalent 500-pound bales, gross weight.

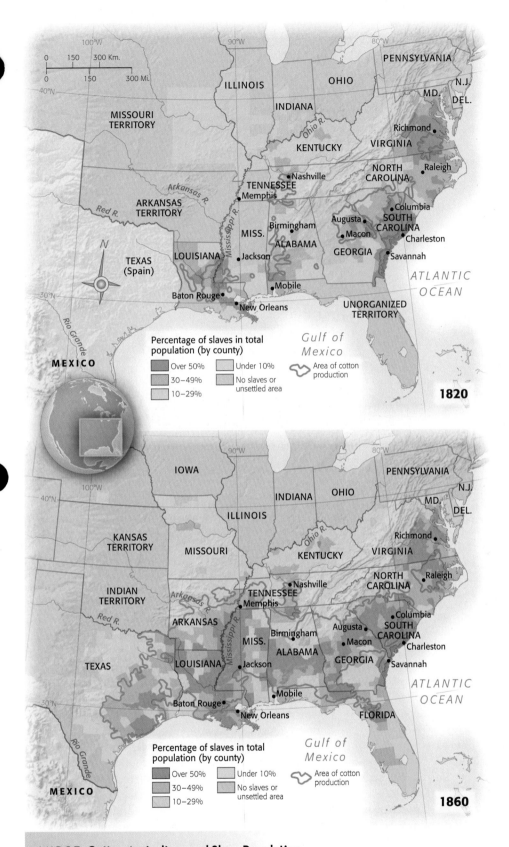

MAP 9.3 Cotton Agriculture and Slave Population

Between 1820 and 1860, the expansion of cotton agriculture and the extension of slavery went hand in hand. As these maps show, cotton production was an isolated activity in 1820, and slavery remained isolated as well. By 1860, both had extended westward. © Cengage Learning.

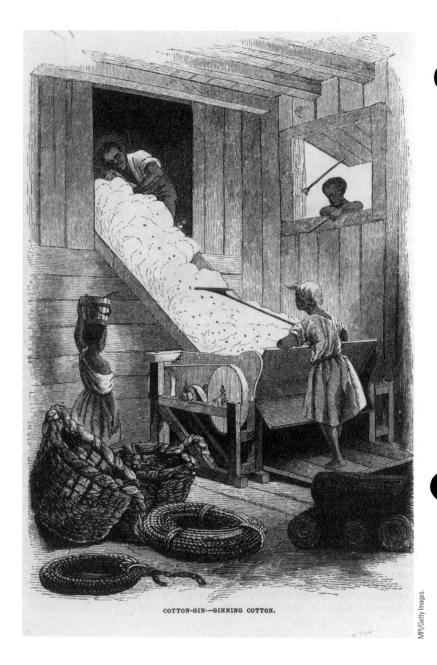

The invention of the cotton gin and the spread of cotton agriculture throughout the American South created an enormous new demand for slave workers and changed the nature of their work. A handful of slaves (only two in this illustration of the process) could comb through large amounts of fiber, but it took armies of field workers to produce the raw cotton that kept the machinery (and the plantation system) working.

COTTON-GIN.—GINNING COTTON.

MPI/Getty Images.

War of 1812 required more labor than ever. As a result, African American slavery expanded as never before. Viewed side by side, a map showing cotton agriculture and one showing slave population appear nearly identical (see Map 9.3).

The virtually universal shift to cotton growing throughout the South brought about not only the expansion and extension of slavery but also substantial modifications to the institution itself. The wide variety of economic pursuits in which slave labor had been employed from the colonial period onward led to varied patterns in slave employment. In many parts of the South, slaves traditionally exercised a great deal of control over their work schedules as they completed assigned tasks (see page 81). But the cotton business called for large gangs of predominantly unskilled workers, and increasingly slaves found themselves regimented like machines in tempo with the demands of cotton production.

At the same time, as northeastern factories were able to provide clothing, shoes, and other manufactured goods at ever more attractive prices and western farmers shipped cheap pork and grain into southern markets, plantation managers found it more practical to purchase such goods rather than to produce them. Thus slaves who formerly had performed various skilled tasks such as milling and weaving found themselves pressed into much less rewarding service as brute labor in the cotton fields. To a large extent, then, specialized manufacturing in the North and large-scale commercial food production in the West permitted an intensified cotton industry in the South and helped foster the increasing dehumanization of the peculiar labor system that drove it.

Individual Voices

TECUMSEH

Describes American Indian Policy Under William Henry Harrison

All too frequently we have to rely on biased non-Indian sources when exploring the troubled relations between Native Americans and the American government. Fortunately, we have transcripts of Shawnee political spokesman Tecumseh's views about what was happening on the Indiana frontier. Displaying very different understandings from those of territorial governor William Henry Harrison, Tecumseh expresses extreme impatience over Harrison's intractable ignorance about Indian life and customs. (*Note:* The original handwritten transcript of this speech contains many abbreviations as well as some unusual spelling and punctuation; the excerpt that follows has been modernized for easier reading.)

North Wind Picture Archives. Translated and modernized by Berkin from the original transcript.

❶ What exactly is Tecumseh accusing Harrison and his agents of doing? What does this suggest about Tecumseh's understanding of the nature of Indian organization and Harrison's misunderstandings about it?

❷ The Wea Indians, a small Miami Indian group, did not sign the Fort Wayne Treaty but later were pressured by Harrison and his accomplice, Winamac, a political headman among the Potawatomi Indians, to give their approval.

❸ How did Tecumseh propose to deal with accommodationists like Winamac? Why do you think he chose this particular approach? What was the implied threat against Harrison and the white settlers?

The reason I tell you this is [that] you want by your distinctions of Indian tribes in allotting to each a particular tract of land to make them to war with each other. You never see an Indian come and endeavor to make the white people do so. You are continually driving the red people when at last you will drive them into the great Lake where they can't either stand or work. **❶**

You ought to know what you are doing with the Indians. Perhaps it is by direction of the President to make those distinctions. It is a very bad thing and we do not like it. Since my residence at Tippecanoe, we have endeavored to level all distinctions to destroy village chiefs by whom all mischief is done; it is they who sell our land to the Americans [so] our object is to let all our affairs be transacted by Warriors.

This land that was sold and the goods that were given for it was only done by a few. The treaty was afterwards brought here and the Weas were induced to give their consent because of their small numbers. The treaty at Fort Wayne was made through the threats [by] Winamac, **❷** but in future we are prepared to punish those chiefs who may come forward to propose to sell their land. If you continue to purchase [land from] them, it will produce war among the different tribes, and at last I do not know what will be the consequences to the white people....

I now wish you to listen to me. If you do not it will appear as if you wished me to kill all the chiefs that sold you the land. I tell you so because I am authorized by all the tribes to do so. I am at the head of them all. I am a Warrior and all the Warriors will meet together in two or three moons from this. Then I will call for those chiefs that sold you the land and shall know what to do with them. If you do not restore the land, you will have a hand in killing them. **❸**

SUMMARY

After Jefferson's triumphal first four years in office, factional disputes at home and diplomatic deadlocks with European powers began to plague the Republicans. Although the Federalists were in full retreat, many within Jefferson's own party rebelled against some of his policies. When Jefferson decided not to run for office in 1808, tapping James Madison as his successor, Republicans in both the Northeast and the South bucked the president, supporting George Clinton and James Monroe, respectively.

To a large extent, the Republicans' problems were the outcome of external stresses. On the Atlantic frontier, the United States tried to remain neutral in the wars that engulfed Europe. On the western frontier, the Prophet and Tecumseh were successfully unifying dispossessed Indians into an alliance devoted to stopping U.S. expansion. Things went from bad to worse when Jefferson's use of economic sanctions gave rise to the worst economic depression since the beginnings of English colonization. The Embargo Act strangled the economy in port cities, and the downward spiral in agricultural prices threatened to bankrupt many in the West and South.

The combination of economic and diplomatic constraints brought aggressive politicians to power in 1808 and 1810. Men such as William Henry Harrison expected that war with England would permit the United States finally to realize independence—forcing freedom of the seas, eliminating Indian resistance, and justifying the conquest of the rest of North America. Despite Madison's continuing peace efforts, southern and western interests finally pushed the nation into war with England in 1812.

Although some glimmering moments of glory heartened the Americans, the war was mostly disastrous. But after generations of fighting one enemy or another, the English people demanded peace. When their final offensive in America failed to bring immediate victory in 1814, the British chose to negotiate. Finally, on Christmas Eve, the two nations signed the Treaty of Ghent, ending the war. From a diplomatic point of view, it was as though the war had never happened.

Nevertheless, in the United States the war created strong feelings of national pride and confidence, and Americans looked forward to even better things to come. In the Northeast, entrepreneurs explored new industries, creating the first stage of an industrial revolution. In the West, the defeat of Indian resistance combined with bright economic opportunities to trigger a wave of westward migration. In the South, the economy was revolutionized by the cotton gin and the growing demand for fiber among English and then American manufacturers. Throughout the country, economic progress promised to improve life for most Americans, but as before, both African Americans and Native Americans bore much of the cost.

CHRONOLOGY
Domestic Expansion and International Crisis

1794	Eli Whitney perfects the cotton gin
1803	Britain steps up impressments
1804	Duel in which Aaron Burr kills Alexander Hamilton
	Jefferson reelected
1807	Burr conspiracy trial
	Prophetstown founded amid Shawnee religious revival
	Chesapeake affair
1808	Embargo of 1808
	Economic depression begins
	James Madison elected president
1809	Non-Intercourse Act
	Fort Wayne Treaty
	Chouteau brothers form Missouri Fur Company
1810	Macon's Bill No. 2
	Vincennes Conference between Harrison and Tecumseh
	War Hawk faction forms
1811	United States suspends trade with Britain
	Battle of Tippecanoe destroys Prophetstown
1812	United States declares war against England, invades Canada
	James Madison reelected
1813	Fort Mims massacre
	Embargo of 1813
	First mechanized textile factory, Waltham, Massachusetts
1814	Battle of Horseshoe Bend
	British burn Washington, D.C.
	Treaty of Ghent
1815	Battle of New Orleans
	Treaty of Fort Jackson
	Portage des Sioux treaties
1819	Treaty of Edwardsville
1825	Prairie du Chien treaties

Study Tools

FOCUS QUESTIONS

If you have mastered this chapter, you should be able to answer these questions and to explain the terms that follow the questions.

1. How did varying regional interests complicate Jefferson's political situation during his second term as president?

2. How did European politics affect the American economy between 1804 and 1808?

3. How did Jefferson's economic and Indian policies influence national developments after 1808?

4. How did problems in Europe, coupled with the actions of frontier politicians such as William Henry Harrison, lead the nation into war in 1812?

5. What geographic and economic factors impeded American war efforts?

6. What part did events in Europe and Britain play in ending the war and what were the results from Americans' point of view?

7. How did events during the War of 1812 help to move the American economy in new directions after peace was restored?

8. How did changes in the economy affect the institution of slavery and the lives of slaves?

KEY TERMS

Secede   *p. 203*

Essex Junto   *p. 204*

John Randolph   *p. 204*

Yazoo affair   *p. 204*

Tertium Quid   *p. 204*

impressment   *p. 205*

Berlin Decree   *p. 205*

Milan Decree   *p. 206*

Embargo Act   *p. 206*

James Monroe   *p. 207*

War Hawks   *p. 207*

The Prophet (Tenskwatawa)   *p. 208*

Non-Intercourse Act   *p. 208*

Macon's Bill No. 2   *p. 208*

Battle of Tippecanoe   *p. 210*

Old Ironsides   *p. 211*

Oliver Hazard Perry   *p. 213*

Andrew Jackson   *p. 213*

Embargo of 1813   *p. 214*

Francis Scott Key   *p. 214*

Battle of Horseshoe Bend   *p. 215*

Jean Lafitte   *p. 215*

Battle of New Orleans   *p. 216*

Treaty of Ghent   *p. 216*

Eli Whitney   *p. 219*

Stephen F. Austin   *p. 219*

SUGGESTED RESOURCES

Jim Barnett and H. Clark Burkett. "The Forks of the Road Slave Market at Natchez," *Mississippi History Now.* http://mshistorynow.mdah.state.ms.us/articles/47/the-forks-of-the-road-slave-market-at-natchez. A detailed summary of the history of one of the most active domestic slave markets in America providing keen insights into the workings and incredible scale of this business.

Th. Jefferson, Monticello. "Embargo of 1807," http://www.monticello.org/site/research-and-collections/embargo-1807. A comprehensive overview, with many excerpts from primary documents, of the various developments during the early nineteenth century that led to Jefferson's decision to close down foreign trade in 1807.

Public Broadcasting Service. "The War of 1812," http://www.pbs.org/wned/war-of-1812/essays. Associated with its 2011 documentary drama about the war, this portion of the PBS site contains a series of experts' essays framing different perspectives on the war.

U.S. National Archives. "Teaching with Documents: Eli Whitney's Patent for the Cotton Gin," http://www.archives.gov/education/lessons/cotton-gin-patent. Teaching site created and maintained by the National Archives showcasing original documents and teaching aids associated with the cotton gin.

Wisconsin Historical Society. "Treaty Councils, from Prairie Du Chien to Madeline Island," http://www.wisconsinhistory.org/turningpoints/tp-013. A very rich site loaded with primary documents concerning various negotiations between the U.S. government and Indian nations in the aftermath of the War of 1812.

Woonsocket Connection. "Samuel Slater: Father of the American Industrial Revolution," http://www.woonsocket.org/slaterhist.htm. A set of interlinked websites exploring Slater's contribution to early textile factory development and many particulars involved in the organization of that industry.

The Rise of a New Nation, 1815–1836

INDIVIDUAL CHOICES

John C. Calhoun

Little in John C. Calhoun's background would have suggested the direction his life would take. A political prodigy from South Carolina, he had been elected to the U.S. House of Representatives at age 29, where he joined forces with other up-and-coming legislators as part of the hyperpatriotic War Hawk faction. After the War of 1812, he continued to act as a dedicated nationalist, working closely with Henry Clay of Kentucky to build the American System— Clay's plan for a national market economy. Calhoun quickly established a reputation as a solid nationalist: his admiring colleague John Quincy Adams described him as "above all sectional and factious prejudices more than any other statesman of this Union with whom I have ever acted."

But in the wake of the economic Panic of 1819, Calhoun began entertaining serious "sectional and factious prejudices." To a large extent this was because of proposals on the part of his northeastern colleagues to use tight credit and higher tariffs as a way of fighting off the effects of the depression. These solutions threatened to strangle the growing cotton industry that was fast becoming the South's economic centerpiece. But population growth in the Northeast and increasing economic specialization in parts of the West gave pro-tariff forces all the votes they needed to promote their political agenda. Calhoun came to believe that the Northeast would emerge as a tyrannical mother country and the rest of the nation would become its oppressed colonies.

In 1828 Calhoun drafted a pamphlet called *The South Carolina*

National Portrait Gallery, Smithsonian Institution/Art Resource, NY.

Exposition and Protest. Drawing on ideas enunciated years before by James Madison and Thomas Jefferson in their Virginia and Kentucky Resolutions (see page 182), Calhoun argued that the federal union was nothing more than a convenient mechanism for carrying out the collective will of the states. As such, its sovereignty was not superior to that of the states. More importantly, if a state determined that a federal law violated the basic rights of its citizens, a popular assembly could declare that law null—having no legal force—within its borders. This doctrine became known as **nullification**.

The crisis itself centered on a hodgepodge of tariff legislation passed by Congress in 1828. By 1832, this so-called **Tariff of Abominations** had so alienated South Carolinians that they chose to act on Calhoun's nullification principle: a popular assembly declared the tariff null. President Andrew Jackson responded by building up federal forces in South Carolina and threatening to use federal troops to establish martial law in the state. South Carolina in turn mobilized its militia to defend its sovereignty. And Calhoun, the once proud nationalist, chose to resign as Jackson's vice president to stand with his state.

Though civil war was avoided in 1832—cooler heads in Congress were able to craft a temporary solution to the tariff conflict—Calhoun's decision to apply his considerable political talent to the cause of **sectionalism** helped bring the nation to the very brink of war. In the years to come, Calhoun would continue to fan the flames of sectionalism. By the time of his death in 1850, Calhoun had become a virtual patron saint for the southern cause, and most people had forgotten that this paragon of sectionalism had at one time been an equally rabid nationalist.

John C. Calhoun was typical of a growing number of Americans in politics. Like his contemporaries Henry Clay and William Henry Harrison, Calhoun made politics a career from very early in life. Of course, Calhoun, Clay, and Harrison were property owners and their families had always exercised political rights, but during the 1820s more and more Americans gained access to the levers of government. In this highly charged atmosphere, matters of state became for the first time in the nation's history a topic for debate among people from all regions and from a broad cross-section of occupations and communities. Like Calhoun, these newly enfranchised voters did not think politics was some gentleman's game but a form of personal combat designed to make their own lives better and to test their wills and their loyalties. Clearly a new day was dawning for American politics and for the whole of American society as well.

AN "ERA OF GOOD FEELINGS"

☆ What were the sources for Americans' optimism as they emerged from the War of 1812 and how did the American government capitalize on this optimism?

☆ How did new developments in the nation influence foreign affairs?

James Madison had been the butt of jokes and the cause of dissension within his own party during the

nullification Refusal by a state to recognize or enforce a federal law within its boundaries.

◻ **Tariff of Abominations** Tariff package designed to win support for anti-Adams forces in Congress; its passage in 1828 discredited Adams but set off sectional tension over tariff issues.

sectionalism In politics, emphasizing the interests of one region of the country over the interests of the country at large.

War of 1812, but he emerged from the war with considerable political clout. After the war Madison immediately seized the political initiative to inaugurate vigorous new diplomatic and domestic programs. His successor, James Monroe, then picked up the beat, pressing on with a new nationalistic Republican agenda. The nationalism that arose after the war seemed to bring political dissension to a close; a Federalist newspaper in Boston proclaimed the dawn of an "Era of Good Feelings."

The "American System" and New Economic Direction

The nation was much more unified politically in 1815 than it had been for years. The war's outcome and the growth that began to take place immediately following the peace settlement had largely silenced Madison's critics within the Republican Party. And during the waning days of the war, extreme Federalists had so embarrassed their party that they were at a severe political disadvantage.

The Essex Junto was primarily responsible for the Federalists' embarrassment. The junto had capitalized on the many military blunders and growing national debt to cast Republicans in a bad light and was drawing increasing support in the Northeast. In mid-December 1814 they staged the Hartford Convention, voting to secede from the Union unless Congress repealed the Embargo of 1813 and passed the slate of constitutional reforms the junto had been pushing since its formation. However, many viewed the Federalists' efforts as either foolish or treasonous, and party popularity underwent a steep decline.

Facing no meaningful opposition, Madison chose in December 1815 to launch an aggressive new domestic policy. He challenged Congress to correct the economic ills that had caused the depression and helped to propel the nation into war. He also encouraged the states to invest in the nation's future by financing transportation systems and other internal improvements. Former critics such as DeWitt Clinton, Henry Clay, and John C. Calhoun quickly rallied behind the president and his nationalistic economic and political agenda.

Clay took the lead. He had come to Congress as one of the War Hawks in 1810 and had quickly become the dominant voice among the younger representatives. Born in Virginia in 1777, Clay had moved to the wilds of Kentucky to practice law and carve out a career in politics. He was fantastically successful, becoming Speaker of the Kentucky state assembly when he was only 30 years old and winning a seat in the House of Representatives four years later. He became Speaker of the House during the prewar crisis. Now aligning himself firmly with the new economic agenda, Clay became its champion, calling it the American System.

What congressional Republicans had in mind was to create a national market economy. In the colonial period and increasingly thereafter, local market economies grew up around the trading and manufacturing centers of the Northeast. Individuals in these areas produced single items for cash sale and used the cash they earned to purchase goods produced by others. Specialization was the natural outcome. Farmers, for example, chose to grow only one or two crops and to sell the whole harvest for cash, which they used to buy various items they had once raised or made for themselves. Clay and others wanted to see such interdependence on a much larger scale. They envisioned a time when whole regions would specialize in producing commodities for which the geography, climate, and the temperament of the people were most suitable. Agricultural regions in the West, for example, would produce food for the industrializing Northeast and the fiber-producing South. The North would depend on the South for efficiently produced cotton, and both South and West would depend on the Northeast for manufactured goods. Advocates of the American System were confident that the balance eventually established among regions would free the nation as a whole from economic dependence on Europe.

Nationalists recognized that one of the first steps in bringing all this about would have to be a national banking authority. Republicans had persistently opposed the Bank of the United States and had killed it in 1811, but the postwar call for a unified national economy prompted Republicans to press again for a national currency and for a national bank to regulate its circulation. In 1816 Calhoun introduced legislation chartering a Second Bank of the United States, which Congress approved overwhelmingly. The Second Bank had many of the same powers and responsibilities as the first. Congress provided $7 million of its $35 million in opening capital and appointed one-fifth

□ **"Era of Good Feelings"** The period from 1816 to 1823, when the decline of the Federalist Party and the end of the War of 1812 gave rise to a time of political cooperation.

□ **Hartford Convention** A meeting held late in 1814 at which Federalist extremists threatened secession from the Union unless their political demands were met.

□ **DeWitt Clinton** Nephew and political heir of New York Republican leader George Clinton; several times governor of New York, the younger Clinton ran the imposing political machine founded by his uncle.

□ **Henry Clay** Former congressional War Hawk who became the leading advocate for nationalistic reforms following the War of 1812. He remained in politics well into the 1850s, holding many government offices.

□ **American System** An economic plan sponsored by nationalists in Congress; it was intended to capitalize on regional differences to spur U.S. economic growth and the domestic production of goods previously bought from foreign manufacturers.

Before the transportation revolution, traveling was highly risky and uncomfortable. This painting shows a rather stylish stagecoach, but its well-dressed passengers are clearly being jostled. Note how the man in the front seat is bracing himself, while the man behind him loses his hat under the wheels.

of its board of directors. The Second Bank opened for business in Philadelphia on January 1, 1817.

Proponents also saw improvements in transportation and communications as essential. Announcing that they would "bind the republic together with a perfect system of roads and canals," Republicans in Congress put forward a series of proposals designed to achieve this result.

Finally, they advocated **protective tariffs** to help the fledgling industries that had hatched during the war. Helped by the embargoes, American cotton-spinning plants had increased rapidly between 1808 and 1815. But with the return of open trade at war's end, British merchants dumped accumulated inventories of cotton and woolen cloth onto the U.S. market. Although some New England voices protested tariffs as unfair government interference, most northeasterners supported protection. Most southerners and westerners, however, remained leery of its impact on consumer prices. Still, shouting with nationalistic fervor about American economic independence, westerners like Clay and southerners like Calhoun were able to raise enough support to pass Madison's proposed **Tariff of 1816**, opening the way for continued tariff legislation in the years to come.

The popularity of these measures was apparent in the outcome of the 1816 elections. The Republican caucus nominated Virginian James Monroe who won by a decisive electoral majority: 184 votes to Federalist Rufus King's 34. Congressional Republicans enjoyed a similar sweep, winning more than three-fourths of the seats in the House of Representatives and the Senate. The triumphant Republicans immediately set about expanding on the new nationalistic agenda.

The Transportation Problem in the West and South

It was clear to many after the War of 1812 that only the large-scale resources available to state and federal governments could make a practical difference in the transportation picture. Immediately after the war, Calhoun introduced legislation in Congress to finance a national transportation program tying the South and West to the rest of the nation. Congress approved, but Madison vetoed the bill, stating that the Constitution did not authorize federal spending on such

protective tariff Tax on imported goods intended to make them more expensive than similar domestic goods, thus protecting the market for goods produced at home.

□ **Tariff of 1816** First protective tariff in U.S. history; its purpose was to protect America's fledgling textile industry.

TOWARD A MORE PERFECT UNION

Establishing Federal Supremacy over Commerce

Three cases decided by the Marshall Court helped to greatly expand the reach of the federal government in matters of commerce. In the first, *Dartmouth College v. Woodward* (1819), the court was asked to decide whether New Hampshire could modify the charter of Dartmouth College, changing it from a private to a public school. College officials argued that the existing charter was a contract, the obligations of which could not be impaired under Article I, Section 10, of the Constitution. The Court agreed. The second, *McCulloch v. Maryland* (1819), stemmed from an attempt on the part of that state to tax federal currency. Here again, the Court asserted that federal authority was superior and overruled Maryland's actions. The third, *Gibbons v. Ogden* (1824), involved two companies offering ferry service between New Jersey and New York. Aaron Ogden's company operated on the basis of a New York charter, which granted him a monopoly. Thomas Gibbons, however, operated on the basis of a federal charter, which he asserted should allow him to ferry goods and passengers between the two states. The Court ruled that federal authority was superior to state authority: New York could not prevent Gibbons from operating his ferry. More significantly, the Court declared that in all matters of interstate commerce, Congress's authority is "complete in itself" and cannot be challenged by states.

□ **Dartmouth College v. Woodward** Supreme Court case (1819) in which the majority ruled that private contracts are sacred and cannot be modified by state legislatures.

□ **McCulloch v. Maryland** Supreme Court case (1819) in which the majority ruled that federal authority is superior to that of individual states and that states cannot control or tax federal operations within their borders.

□ **Gibbons v. Ogden** Supreme Court case (1824) in which the majority ruled that the authority of Congress is absolute in matters of interstate commerce.

□ **Cumberland Road** The initial section of what would be called the "National Road," a highway built with federal funds; this section stretched from Cumberland, Maryland, to Wheeling, Virginia. Later the road would be extended to Vandalia, Illinois, and beyond.

□ **Erie Canal** A 350-mile canal stretching from Buffalo to Albany; it revolutionized shipping in New York State.

projects. But Calhoun finally won Madison's support by convincing the president that a government-funded national road between Cumberland, Maryland, and Wheeling, Virginia, was a military and postal necessity and therefore the initial federal expenditure of $30,000 for the Cumberland Road was constitutional. Construction began in 1815.

Though Calhoun had eased Madison's constitutional concerns regarding federal investment in economic development, it was going to take more than federal authority and money to revolutionize the economy. Private money would be needed as well, and that too required some constitutional clarification. This clarification came through the cases described in the Toward a More Perfect Union feature.

Although people and light cargoes might move efficiently along the proposed national road, water transportation remained the most economical way to ship bulky freight. Unfortunately, with few exceptions, navigable rivers and lakes did not link up conveniently to form usable transportation networks. Before the War of 1812, some Americans had considered canals as a likely solution, but enormous costs and engineering problems had limited canal construction to less than 100 miles. After the war, however, the entry of the state and federal governments into transportation development opened the way to an era of canal building. New York State was most successful at canal development. In 1817 the state started work on a canal that would run more than 350 miles from Lake Erie at Buffalo to the Hudson River at Albany. Three thousand workers dug the huge ditch that would eventually form the Erie Canal. The last leg was completed in 1825, and the first barge made its way from Buffalo to Albany and then on to New York City.

Canals were really little more than extensions of natural river courses, and fighting the currents of great rivers remained a problem. Pushed along by current and manpower, a barge could make the trip south from Pittsburgh to New Orleans in about a month. Returning north, against the current, took more than four months, if a boat could make the trip at all. In 1807, however, Robert Fulton's 160-ton steam-powered ship, the *Clermont*, ran upstream from New York City to Albany in an incredibly quick thirty-two hours. Unfortunately, the design of the *Clermont* made it impractical for most of America's rivers. After the war Henry M. Shreve borrowed the hull design of the shallow-draft, broad-beamed keelboats that had been sailing up and down inland streams for generations. Shreve added two lightweight steam engines, each one driving an independent side wheel. He also added an upper deck for passengers, creating the now-familiar multistoried steamboats of southern lore. Funded by merchants in Wheeling, Virginia— soon to be the western terminus for the Cumberland Road—Shreve successfully piloted one of his newly

With a long and distinguished career as a diplomat behind him, the handsome and elegant James Monroe brought a statesmanlike demeanor to the White House. He managed to soothe long-standing disputes between various political factions, ushering in what would be called the "Era of Good Feelings."

designed boats upriver, from Wheeling to Pittsburgh. Then, in 1816, he made the first successful run south, all the way to New Orleans.

James Monroe and the Nationalist Agenda

While Congress and the courts were firmly in the hands of forward-looking leaders, the presidency passed in 1816 to the seemingly old-fashioned James Monroe. Personally conservative, Monroe nonetheless was a strong nationalist as well as a graceful statesman. He had served primarily as a diplomat during the contentious period that preceded the War of 1812, and as president he turned his diplomatic skills to the task of calming political disputes. He was the first president since Washington to take a national goodwill tour, during which he persistently urged various political factions to merge their interests for the benefit of the nation at large.

Monroe's cabinet was well chosen to carry out the task of smoothing political rivalries while flexing nationalistic muscles. He selected John Quincy Adams, son and heir of Yankee Federalist John Adams, as secretary of state because of his diplomatic skill and to win political support in New England. Monroe tapped John C. Calhoun, still a devoted nationalist at the time, for secretary of war and balanced his appointment with that of southern states' rights

advocate William C. Crawford as secretary of the treasury. With his team assembled, Monroe launched the nation on a course designed to increase its control over the North American continent and improve its position in world affairs.

Madison had already taken steps toward initiating a more aggressive diplomatic policy, setting the tone for the years to come. Taking advantage of U.S. involvement in the War of 1812, Barbary pirates (see page 158) had resumed their raiding activity against American shipping. In June 1815, Madison ordered a military force back to the Mediterranean to put an end to those raids. Naval hero Stephen Decatur, commanding a fleet of ten warships, trained his guns on the port of Algiers itself, threatening to level the city if the pirates did not stop raiding American shipping. The Algerians and the rest of the Barbary pirates signed treaties ending the practice of exacting **tribute**. They also released all American hostages and agreed to pay compensation for past seizures of American ships. Celebrating the victory, Decatur gave voice to a militant new American nationalism, proclaiming, "Our Country! In her intercourse with foreign nations may she always be in the right; but our country, right or wrong."

Meanwhile, Adams began addressing loose ends left dangling by the Treaty of Ghent (1814). One problem had been the **demilitarization** of the Great Lakes boundary between the United States and British Canada. In the 1817 Rush-Bagot Agreement, both nations agreed to cut back their Great Lakes fleets to only a few vessels. A year later, the two nations drew up the Convention of 1818: the British agreed to honor American fishing rights in the Atlantic, to recognize the 49th parallel as the boundary between the Louisiana Territory and Canada, and to occupy the Oregon Territory jointly with the United States.

With these northern border issues settled, Adams set his sights on defining the nation's southern and southwestern frontiers. Pirates and other renegades used Florida as a base for launching raids against American settlements and shipping, and runaway slaves found it a safe haven in their flight from southern plantations. Reflecting on the situation in December 1817, General Andrew Jackson wrote to the president advocating the invasion of Spanish Florida. A short time later, Secretary of War Calhoun ordered Jackson to lead a military expedition into southern Georgia, but Jackson crossed the border and forced the Spanish government to flee. Though Calhoun privately recommended that the general be court martialed, Adams saw

tribute A payment of money or other valuables that one group makes to another as the price of security.

demilitarization The removal of military forces from a region and the restoration of civilian control.

an opportunity to settle the Florida border issue. He announced that Jackson's raid was an act of self-defense that would be repeated unless Spain could police the area adequately. Fully aware that Spain could not guarantee American security, Adams knew that the Spanish would either have to give up Florida or stand by and watch the United States take it by force. Understanding his country's precarious position, Spanish minister Don Luis de Onís chose to cede Florida in the **Adams-Onís Treaty** of 1819. The United States got all of Florida in exchange for releasing Spain from $5 million in damage claims resulting from border raids.

Spain's inability to police its New World territories also led to a more general diplomatic problem. As the result of Spain's weakness, many of its colonies in Latin America had rebelled and established themselves as independent republics. Fearful of the anticolonial example being set in the Western Hemisphere, several European powers were poised to help Spain reclaim its overseas empire. Neither England, which had developed a thriving trade with the new Latin American republics, nor the United States wanted recolonization to occur. In 1823 the British foreign minister proposed that the United States and England form an alliance to end European meddling in Latin America. Adams protested that America would be reduced to a "cock-boat in the wake of the British man-of-war," suggesting instead a **unilateral** statement saying that "the American continents by the free and independent condition which they have assumed, and maintain, are henceforth not to be considered as subject for future colonization by any European power."

Monroe remained uncommitted, but nevertheless conceded the nationalistic necessity for the United States to "take a bolder attitude . . . in favor of liberty." In November 1823 European support to restore Spain's colonies was faltering, so with the immediate threat removed, Monroe announced that the United States would regard any effort by European countries "to extend their system to any portion of this hemisphere as dangerous to our peace and safety."

□ **Adams-Onís Treaty** Treaty between the United States and Spain in 1819 that ceded Florida to the United States, ended any Spanish claims in Oregon, and recognized Spanish rights in the American Southwest.

unilateral Undertaken or issued by only one side and thus not involving an agreement made with others.

□ **Monroe Doctrine** President Monroe's 1823 statement declaring the Americas closed to further European colonization and discouraging European interference in the affairs of the Western Hemisphere.

□ **Napoleonic wars** Wars in Europe waged by or against Napoleon Bonaparte between 1803 and 1815.

installments Partial payments of a debt made at regular intervals until the entire debt is repaid.

He went on to define any attempt at European intervention in the affairs of the Western Hemisphere as a virtual act of war against the United States. The **Monroe Doctrine** was exactly the proud assertion of the principle "in favor of liberty" that Monroe had deemed necessary, and it immediately won the support of the American people.

DYNAMIC GROWTH AND POLITICAL CONSEQUENCES

☆ *How did the global economic situation combine with postwar economic optimism to lead to economic panic in 1819?*

☆ *How did economic growth and panic contribute to sectional conflict and political contention?*

After the **Napoleonic wars** ended in 1815, Europeans continued to need American food and manufactures as they rebuilt a peacetime economy. Encouraged by a ready European market and expanding credit offered by both public and private banks, budding southern planters, northern manufacturers, and western and southwestern farmers embarked on a frenzy of speculation. They rushed to borrow against what they were sure was a golden future to buy equipment, land, and slaves.

Although all shared the same sense of optimism, entrepreneurs in the North, West, and South had different ideas about the best course for the American economy. As the American System drew the regions together into increasing mutual dependency, the tensions among them increased as well. As long as economic conditions remained good, there was little reason for conflict, but when the speculative boom collapsed, sectional tensions increased dramatically.

The Panic of 1819

Early changes in federal land policy had contributed to the rise of speculation. In 1800 and again in 1804, Congress had passed bills lowering the minimum number of acres of federal land an individual could purchase and the minimum price per acre. After 1804 the minimum purchase became 160 acres and the minimum price, $1.64 per acre. The bill also permitted farmers to pay the government in **installments**. For most Americans, the minimum investment of $262.40 was still out of reach, but the installment option encouraged many to take the risk and buy farms they could barely afford.

Land speculators then complicated matters. Taking advantage of the new land prices, they too jumped into the game, buying land on credit. Unlike farmers, however, speculators never intended to put the land into production. They hoped to subdivide it and sell it to people who could not afford to buy 160-acre lots directly from the government. Speculators also offered installment loans, pyramiding the already huge tower of debt.

Banks—both relatively unsupervised state banks and the Second Bank of the United States—then added to the problem. Farmers who bought land on credit seldom had enough cash to purchase farm equipment, seed, materials for housing, and the other supplies necessary to put the land to productive use. So the banks extended liberal credit on top of the credit already extended by the government and by land developers. Farmers thus had acreage and tools, but they also had an enormous debt.

Several developments in the international economy combined to undermine the nation's tower of debt. The economic optimism that fed the speculative frenzy rested on profitable markets. But as the 1810s drew to a close and recovery began in Europe, the profit bandwagon began to slow, and optimism to slip. Not only was Europe able to supply more of its own needs, but Europeans were also importing from other regions of the globe. Led by Great Britain, European nations were establishing colonies in Asia, Africa, and the Pacific. In addition, the recent independence of many of Europe's Latin American colonies deprived the Europeans of the gold and silver that had driven international economics since the discovery of America. Europe became less and less dependent on American goods and, at the same time, less and less able to afford them. Thus the bottom began to fall out of the international market that had fueled speculation within the United States.

Congress noted the beginning of the collapse late in 1817 and tried to head off disaster by tightening credit. The government stopped installment payments on new land purchases and demanded that they be transacted in hard currency. The Second Bank of the United States followed suit in 1818, demanding immediate repayment of loans in either gold or silver. State banks then followed and were joined by land speculators. Instead of curing the problem, however, government austerity drove the economy over the edge. The speculative balloon burst, leaving nothing but a mass of debt behind. This economic catastrophe became known as the **Panic of 1819**.

Six years of economic depression followed. As prices declined, individual farmers and manufacturers, unable to repay loans for land and equipment, faced **repossession** and imprisonment for debt. In Cincinnati and other agricultural cities, bankruptcy sales were a daily occurrence. In New England and the West, factories closed, throwing both employees and owners out of work. In New York and other manufacturing and trading cities, the ranks of the unemployed grew steadily. The number of **paupers** in New York City nearly doubled between 1819 and 1820, and in

THE REMEMBRANCER,
OR
DEBTORS PRISON RECORDER.

" HE WHO'S ENTOMB'D WITHIN A PRISON'S WALLS
ENDURES THE ANGUISH OF A LIVING DEATH "

VOL. I.   NEW-YORK, SATURDAY, APRIL 8, 1820.   No. 1.

THE
DEBTORS PRISON RECORDER
IS ISSUED FROM THE PRESS OF
CHARLES N. BALDWIN,
AND PUBLISHED BY
JOHN B. JANSEN,
No. 15 Chatham-street,
NEW-YORK,
At two dollars per annum, payable quarterly in advance.
Persons at a distance may have the paper regularly forwarded to them by mail, provided they forward the requisite advance, post paid.

TO THE PUBLIC.
THE chief object of this publication will be to spread before an enlightened public the deplorable effects resulting from the barbarous practice of imprisonment for debt—to exhibit the misery of its wretched victims, and the unfeeling conduct of unpitying creditors. By these means, " with truth as its guide, and justice for its object," it will, it is hoped, gradually prepare the minds of the community for the entire abolition of a law which exists a dishonor to the precepts of Christianity, and as a blot on the statute book.
It will be published weekly, in an octavo form, each number to consist of eight pages, comprising a succinct and correct history of the interesting incidents which daily occur in the debtors prison—a correct Journal of prisoners received and discharged from

time to time, with such remarks as may grow out of peculiar persecution or other causes; nor will it neglect to announce the number of those who are supplied with food from that inestimable body, the Humane Society, to whom the profits of this publication will be faithfully applied, as a small testimonial of the gratitude felt by the unfortunate inmates of the prison, for their distinguished beneficence. It will contain interesting extracts from the latest European and American publications. In its columns will be found a variety of communications on various interesting subjects, from gentlemen without the prison walls, who have kindly volunteered their services to furnish us with essays on the ARTS and SCIENCES, criticisms on the DRAMA, POETRY, &c.
This work will be edited, and its matter carefully revised by several prisoners, who, if they cannot themselves enjoy the benefits of their labor, may at least feel a pleasure in the reflection that after ages will bestow a pitying tear on their sufferings, and bless them for the exertions made to rescue their country from the only vestage of feudal tyranny remaining in a land that boasts of freedom.
The small pittance paid for its perusal, will, it is believed, procure for it the patronage of a generous public, who will be amply remunerated in performing a duty subserving the great and benign ends of Charity, while in return they are furnished with a species of reading not to be met with in any other publication.

Vol. 1., No. 1, New York, Saturday, April 8, 1820.

Before the adoption of modern bankruptcy laws, it was common for people to be put in prison when they could not pay their debts. One impact of the Panic of 1819 was a huge upturn in such imprisonments. Newspapers like *The Remembrancer, or Debtors Prison Recorder*, which began publication with this issue on April 8, 1820, called for reform in debtor laws and also reported gruesome stories about the sufferings of previously respectable people who found themselves in debtors' prison through no fault of their own.

Boston thirty-five hundred people were imprisoned for debt. Shaken by the enormity of the problem, John C. Calhoun observed in 1820: "There has been within these two years an immense revolution of fortunes in every part of the Union; enormous numbers of persons utterly ruined; multitudes in deep distress."

▢ Panic of 1819 A financial panic that began when the Second Bank of the United States tightened credit and recalled government loans.

repossession The reclaiming of land or goods by the seller or lender after the purchaser fails to pay installments due.

paupers A term popular in the eighteenth and nineteenth centuries to describe poor people; cities like New York and Boston often registered paupers so as to provide local relief.

Economic Woes and Political Sectionalism

Despite Monroe's efforts to merge southern, northern, and nationalist interests during the Era of Good Feelings, the Panic of 1819 drove a wedge between the nation's geographical sections. The depression touched each of the major regions differently, calling for conflicting solutions. For the next several years, the halls of Congress rang with debates rooted in each section's particular economic needs.

Tariffs were one proven method for handling economic emergencies, and as the Panic of 1819 spread economic devastation throughout the country, legislators from Pennsylvania and the Middle Atlantic states, southern New England, and then Ohio and Kentucky began clamoring for protection. Others disagreed, turning tariffs into the issue that would pit region against region more violently than any other during these years.

Farmers were split on the tariff issue. Irrespective of where they lived, so-called yeoman farmers favored a free market that would keep the price of the manufactures they had to buy as low as possible. In contrast, the increasing number of commercial farmers—those who had chosen to follow Henry Clay's ideas and were specializing to produce cash crops of raw wool, hemp, and wheat—joined mill owners, factory managers, and industrial workers in supporting protection against the foreign dumping of such products. So did those westerners who were producing raw minerals such as iron and tin that were in high demand in the industrializing economy.

Southern commercial farmers, however, did not join with their western counterparts in favoring protection. After supporting the protective Tariff of 1816, Calhoun and other southerners became firm opponents of tariffs. Their dislike of protection reflected a complex economic reality. Britain, not the United States, was the South's primary market for raw cotton and its main supplier of manufactured goods. Protective tariffs raised the price of such goods as well as the possibility that Britain might enact a retaliatory tariff

on cotton imports from the South. If that happened, southerners would pay more for manufactures but receive less profit from cotton.

When, in 1820, northern congressmen proposed a major increase in tariff rates, small farmers in the West and cotton growers in the South combined to defeat the measure. Northerners then began engaging in log rolling with congressmen from the West. The northerners supported one bill that lowered the minimum price of public land to $1.25 per acre and another that allowed farmers who had bought land before 1820 to pay off their debts at the reduced price. The bill also extended the time over which those who were on the installment plan could make payments. Then, in 1822, northerners backed a bill authorizing increased federal spending on the Cumberland Road, an interest vital to westerners. The strategy succeeded: in 1824 western congressmen repaid northern manufacturing interests by voting for a greatly increased tariff.

This victory demonstrated an important new political reality. Of the six western states admitted to the Union after 1800, three—Ohio, Indiana, and Illinois—were predominantly farming states, split between commercial and subsistence farming. The other three—Louisiana, Mississippi, and Alabama—were increasingly dominated by cotton growing. As long as northern commercial interests could pull support from Ohio, Indiana, and Illinois, the balance of power in Congress remained relatively even. But new expansion in either the North or South had the potential to tip the political scale. As all three regions fought to implement specific solutions to the nation's economic woes, the regional balance of power in Congress became a matter of crucial importance.

The Missouri Compromise

The delicate balance in Congress began to wobble immediately in 1819 when the Missouri Territory applied for statehood. New York congressman James Tallmadge Jr. realized that if Missouri was admitted as a free state, its economy would resemble the economies of states in the Old Northwest, and its congressmen would be susceptible to northern log rolling. This realization led Tallmadge to propose that Missouri be closed to slavery. Southerners likewise understood that if Missouri was admitted as a slave state, it would undoubtedly support the southern position on tariffs and other key issues. They unified to oppose the Tallmadge Amendment.

Both sides in the debate were deeply entrenched, but in 1820 Henry Clay suggested a compromise. Late in 1819, Maine applied for admission to the United States. The compromise proposed by Clay was to admit Missouri as a slave state and Maine as a free state. Clay also proposed that after the admission

retaliatory tariff A tariff on imported goods imposed neither to raise revenue nor control commerce but to retaliate against tariffs charged by another nation.

log rolling The trading of favors, such as vote trading, by legislators to obtain passage of bills that would otherwise lack sufficient votes to pass.

□ Tallmadge Amendment An amendment to a statehood bill for Missouri proposed by New York congressman James Tallmadge Jr. that would have banned slavery in the new state; it created a deadlock in Congress that necessitated the Missouri Compromise.

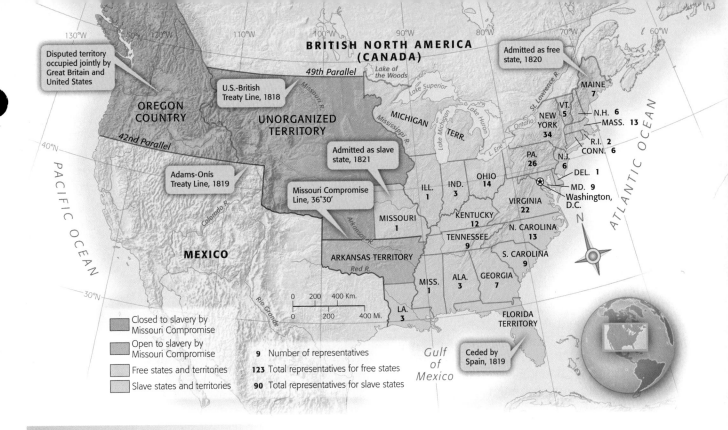

MAP 10.1 Missouri Compromise and Representative Strength
The Missouri Compromise fixed the boundary between free and slave territories at 36°30′ north latitude. This map shows the result both in geographical and political terms. While each section emerged from the compromise with the same number of senators (24), the balance in the House of Representatives and Electoral College tilted toward the North. © Cengage Learning.

of Missouri, slavery be banned forever in the rest of the Louisiana Territory above 36°30′ north latitude, the line that formed Missouri's southern border (see Map 10.1). With this provision, Congress approved the Missouri Compromise.

Though solved in the short term, the Missouri crisis had echoes that would haunt the nation. Although economic strategies had caused the conflict, slavery—its expansion and, for a few, its very existence—had become part of a struggle between sections over national power. From this point on, the issue would smolder beneath all such sectional debates. In addition, through such debates, many African Americans became aware that the nation was divided on the subject of slavery. One, Denmark Vesey, had been able to buy his freedom in 1799 and became a carpenter in Charleston, South Carolina. Over the next two decades, however, white authorities continually harassed Vesey and the African American community: in 1818 and again in 1820 they closed down the African Methodist Episcopal Church that Vesey had helped to build. In part emboldened by northern attacks on slavery, in July 1822 Vesey organized a rebellion designed to seize the city of Charleston, but the plot was reported to authorities, who arrested and charged 131 free and enslaved alleged conspirators. In the end, 72 were found guilty, of whom 35 were executed, including Vesey. As with Gabriel's Rebellion two decades earlier, Vesey's conspiracy terrorized whites and led to even greater restrictions on slaves in the years to come.

New Politics and the End of Good Feelings

Conducted in the midst of the Missouri crisis, the presidential election of 1820 went as smoothly as could be: Monroe was reelected with the greatest majority ever enjoyed by any president except George

☐ **Missouri Compromise** Law proposed by Henry Clay in 1820 admitting Missouri to the Union as a slave state and Maine as a free state and banning slavery in the Louisiana Territory north of the latitude 36°30′.

☐ **Denmark Vesey** Free African American carpenter who plotted a rebellion to seize Charleston; although reported to authorities and broken, the plot terrified whites, who further restricted African Americans.

In the Wider World

Banning Slavery in the British Empire

Though the Missouri crisis revolved around slavery, economic concerns were far more prominent in people's minds than slavery's morality. But at the same time in Great Britain, great public debate raged over the institution and its continued existence in the empire. The British had outlawed the slave trade in 1807, the same year as the United States, but political leaders like William Wilburforce and Thomas Clarkson joined with religious and other reformers to form the Anti-Slavery Society in 1823, pushing for the total abolition of slavery in all British realms. Over the next decade the Houses of both Lords and Commons debated, but with masterful legislative steering by the society, Parliament finally voted a limited end to slavery in 1834. It would take the United States over thirty more years to follow suit.

Washington. Despite economic depression and sectional strife, the people's faith in Jefferson's party held strong, but as the election of 1824 approached, it became clear that the nation's continuing problems had broken Republican unity and destroyed the public's confidence in the party's ability to solve domestic problems. Although Monroe and many others probably favored John Quincy Adams to take over Republican leadership, the southern-dominated party caucus tapped Georgia states' rights advocate William Crawford for the presidency. Certainly Clay and Adams were disappointed: each immediately defied party discipline by deciding to run against Crawford without the approval of the caucus. Encouraged by the apparent death of the caucus system for nominating presidential candidates, the Tennessee state legislature chose to put forward its own candidate, Andrew Jackson.

The election that followed was a painful demonstration of how deeply divided the nation had become. Northern regional political leaders rallied behind Adams, southern sectionalists supported Crawford, and northwestern commercial farmers and other backers of the American System lined up behind Clay. But a good portion of the American people—many of them independent yeoman farmers, traditional craftsmen, and immigrants—defied their political leaders by supporting the hero of New Orleans: Jackson.

Though a political **dark horse**, Jackson won the popular election, but the Electoral College vote was another matter (see Map 10.2). Jackson had 99 electoral votes to Adams's 84, Crawford's 41, and Clay's 37, but although Jackson won a **plurality** of electors, it was not the "majority of the whole number of electors" required by the Constitution. The Constitution specifies that in such cases, a list of the top three vote getters be passed to the House of Representatives for a final decision.

By the time the House had convened to settle the election, Crawford, the third-highest vote getter, had suffered a disabling stroke, so the list of candidates had only two names: John Quincy Adams and Andrew Jackson. Because Clay had finished fourth, he was not in contention in the **runoff election**, but as Speaker of the House he was in a particularly strategic position to influence the outcome. Adams's and Clay's views on tariffs, manufacturing, foreign affairs, and other key issues were quite compatible. Clay therefore endorsed Adams, who won the House election and in 1825 became the nation's sixth president.

Jackson and his supporters were outraged. They considered Clay a betrayer of western and southern interests, calling him the "Judas of the West." Then when Adams named Clay as his secretary of state—the position that had been the springboard to the presidency for every past Republican who held it—Jacksonians exploded. Proclaiming Adams's election a "corrupt bargain," Jackson supporters withdrew from the party of Jefferson, bringing an end to the one-party system that had emerged under the so-called **Virginia Dynasty** and dealing the knockout blow to the Era of Good Feelings.

dark horse A political candidate who has little organized support and is not expected to win.

plurality In an election with three or more candidates, the number of votes received by the leading candidate but which amount to less than half of the total number of votes cast.

runoff election A final election held to determine a winner after an earlier election has eliminated the weakest candidates.

▢ **Virginia Dynasty** Term applied to the U.S. presidents from Virginia in the period between 1801 and 1825: Jefferson, Madison, and Monroe.

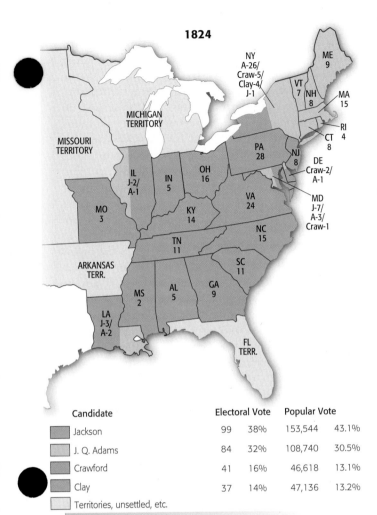

1824

Candidate		Electoral Vote		Popular Vote	
■	Jackson	99	38%	153,544	43.1%
□	J. Q. Adams	84	32%	108,740	30.5%
■	Crawford	41	16%	46,618	13.1%
■	Clay	37	14%	47,136	13.2%
□	Territories, unsettled, etc.				

MAP 10.2 Election of 1824
This map showing the 1824 presidential election illustrates how divided the nation had become politically. William Crawford, the official Republican Party nominee, placed third in the Electoral College. The two most successful candidates, Andrew Jackson and John Quincy Adams, represented no political party. Speaker of the House Henry Clay, who finished fourth, played a key role in the outcome. Under his leadership, the House elected Adams. © Cengage Learning.

THE "NEW MAN" IN POLITICS

☆ What factors helped change Americans' political options during the mid-1820s?

☆ How did the election of Andrew Jackson in 1828 reflect those new options?

Since Washington's day the presidency had been considered an office for gentlemen and statesmen. The first several presidents had tried to maintain an air of polite dignity while in office, and voters were generally pleased with that orderly approach. But with the massive social changes taking place after the War of 1812, the conduct of national politics changed drastically.

New voters from new occupations with radically varying political and economic views began making demands. Many felt isolated from a political system that permitted the presidency to pass from one propertied gentleman to another. Clearly, changing times called for political change, and the American people began to press for it in no uncertain terms.

Adams's Troubled Administration

John Quincy Adams may have been the best-prepared man ever to assume the office of president. As the son of former president John Adams, John Quincy had been born and raised in the midst of America's most powerful political circles. By the time of his controversial election in 1825, Adams had been a foreign diplomat, a U.S. senator, a Harvard professor, and an exceptionally effective secretary of state. Adams conducted himself in office as his father had, holding himself above partisan politics and refusing to use political favors to curry support. As a result, Adams had no effective means of rallying those who might have supported him or of pressuring his opponents. Thus, despite his impressive résumé, Adams's administration was a deeply troubled one.

Adams's policy commitments did nothing to boost his popularity. The new president promised to increase tariffs to protect American manufacturing and to raise funds necessary to pay for "the improvement of agriculture, commerce, and manufactures." He also wanted the Second Bank of the United States to stabilize the economy while providing ample loans to finance new manufacturing ventures. And he advocated federal spending to improve "the elegant arts" and advance "literature and the progress of the sciences, ornamental and profound." High-sounding though Adams's objectives were, Thomas Jefferson spoke for many when he observed that such policies would establish "a single and splendid government of an aristocracy . . . riding and ruling over the plundered ploughman and beggared yeomanry." Jefferson's criticism seemed particularly apt in the economic turmoil that followed the Panic of 1819. Moreover, the increase in federal power implied by Adams's policies frightened southerners, and this fear, combined with their traditional distaste for tariffs, virtually unified opposition to Adams in the South.

Led by John C. Calhoun, Adams's opponents tried to manipulate tariff legislation to undercut the president's support. Calhoun proposed an unprecedented increase in tariff rates, thinking that Northeastern Jacksonians would then voice support for the increase, whereas Jackson supporters in the West and South would oppose them. Calhoun and his colleagues envisioned a win–win situation: first, they envisioned lining up enough votes to block the tariff's passage, but northeastern Jacksonians would win increasing support from manufacturing interests in their region by appearing to support tariffs while southern and western Jackson supporters could take credit for sinking tariff increases, cementing support in their districts; and Adams, who had promised increases as part of his political agenda, would appear ineffectual. But Calhoun and his fellow conspirators had miscalculated: when the tariff package came to the floor in May 1828, key northeastern congressmen engineered its passage. The resulting **Tariff of Abominations** was not what Calhoun had expected, but it served his ends by establishing tariff rates that were unacceptable to almost every segment of the population, and the unpopular president would bear the blame.

Democratic Styles and Political Structure

Adams's demeanor and outlook compounded his problems. He seemed more a man of his father's generation than of his own. The enormous economic and demographic changes that occurred during the first decades of the nineteenth century created a new political climate, one in which Adams's archrival Andrew Jackson felt much more at ease than did the stiff Yankee who occupied the White House.

One of the most profound changes in the American political scene was an explosion in the number of voters. Throughout the early years of the republic's history, voting rights were limited to white men who held real estate. In a nation primarily of farmers, most men owned land, so the fact of limited suffrage raised little controversy. But as economic conditions changed, a smaller proportion of the population owned farms, and while bankers, lawyers, manufacturers, and other such men often were highly educated, economically stable, and politically concerned, their lack of real estate barred them from political participation. Not surprisingly, such elite and middle-class men urged

□ **Martin Van Buren** New York politician known for his skillful handling of party politics; he helped found the Democratic Party and later became the eighth president of the United States.

influence peddling Using one's influence with people in authority to obtain favors or preferential treatment for someone else, usually in return for payment.

Masons An international fraternal organization with many socially and politically prominent members, including a number of U.S. presidents.

□ **Thomas Hart Benton** U.S. senator from Missouri and legislative leader of the Democrats; he was a champion of President Jackson and a supporter of westward expansion.

□ **Democratic Party** Political party that brought Andrew Jackson into office; it recalled Jeffersonian principles of limited government and drew its support from farmers, craftsmen, and small businessmen.

suffrage reform. In 1800 only three of the sixteen states had no property qualifications for voting, and another three permitted taxpayers to vote even if they did not own real property. By 1830, only five of the twenty-four states retained property qualifications, nine required tax payment only, and ten made no property demands at all. The raw number of voters grew enormously and rapidly. In 1824, 356,038 men cast ballots for the presidency. Four years later, more than three times that number voted. In addition, states increasingly dropped property qualifications for office holding as well as voting, opening new opportunities for breaking the gentlemanly monopoly on political power. Of course, all of the states continued to bar women from voting, and most refused the ballot to African Americans, whether free or slave.

Political opportunists were not slow to take advantage of the new situation. Men such as New Yorker **Martin Van Buren** quickly came to the fore, organizing political factions into tightly disciplined local and statewide units. Opposing Governor DeWitt Clinton's faction in New York, Van Buren molded disaffected Republicans into the so-called Bucktail faction. In 1820 the Bucktails used a combination of political patronage—the ability of the party in power to distribute government jobs—**influence peddling**, and fiery speeches to draw newly qualified voters into the political process and swept Clinton out of office.

Many new voters were gratified at finally being allowed to participate in politics but sensed that their participation was not having the impact it should. They resented the "corrupt bargain" that had denied the presidency to the people's choice—Andrew Jackson—in the election of 1824. Voters in upstate New York and elsewhere pointed at organizations such as the **Masons**, claiming that they used secret signs and rituals to ensure the election of their own members, thwarting the popular will.

What was happening in New York was typical of party and antiparty developments throughout the country. As the party of Jefferson dissolved, a tangle of political factions broke out across the nation. This was precisely the sort of petty politics that Adams disdained, but the chaos suited a man like Jackson perfectly, and Van Buren was busy forging with the hero of New Orleans an alliance that would fundamentally alter American politics.

The Rise of "King Andrew"

Within two years of Adams's election, Van Buren had brought together northern outsiders like himself, dissident southern Republicans like John C. Calhoun, and western spokesmen like **Thomas Hart Benton** of Missouri and John H. Eaton of Tennessee into a new political party. Calling themselves Democratic-Republicans—the **Democratic Party** for short—this

As suffrage requirements loosened, politics went from being a sedate parlor game among gentlemen to a rough-and-tumble contest that often spilled out into the streets of the nation's cities and villages. This painting by George Caleb Bingham captures the colorful spirit of the new politics in depicting a county election in early nineteenth-century Missouri.

party railed against the neofederalism of Clay's and Adams's National Republican platform. The Democrats called for a return to Jeffersonian simplicity, states' rights, and republican principles. Behind the scenes, however, they employed the tight organizational discipline and manipulative techniques that Van Buren had used to such good effect against the Clintons in New York. Lining up behind the recently defeated popular hero Andrew Jackson, the new party appealed to both opportunistic political outsiders and democratically inclined new voters. In the congressional elections of 1826, Van Buren's coalition drew the unqualified support of both groups, unseating enough National Republicans to gain a twenty-five-seat majority in the House of Representatives and an eight-seat advantage in the Senate.

In the presidential election that followed, having Andrew Jackson as a candidate was probably as important to the Democrats' success as their ideological appeal and tight political organization. In many ways, Jackson was a perfect reflection of the new voters. Like many of them, he was born in a log cabin under rustic circumstances. His family had faced more than its share of hardships: his father had died two weeks before Andrew's birth, and he had lost his two brothers and his mother during the Revolutionary War. In

the waning days of the Revolution, at the age of 13, Jackson joined a mounted militia company and was captured by the British. His captors beat their young prisoner and then let him go, a humiliation he would never forgive.

At the end of the war, Jackson chose the legal profession as the route to advancement. Driven by an indomitable will and a wealth of native talent, Jackson became the first U.S. congressman from the state of Tennessee and eventually was elected to the Senate. He also was a judge on the Tennessee Supreme Court. Along the way, Jackson's exploits established his solid reputation as a heroic and natural leader: in the popular view, it was Jackson's brashness, not Adams's diplomacy, that had finally won Spanish Florida for the United States.

Jackson's popular image as a rough-hewn man of the people was somehow untarnished by his political alliance with business interests, his activities as a land speculator, and his large and growing personal fortune and stock of slaves. In the eyes of frontiersmen, small farmers, and to some extent urban workingmen, he remained a common man like them. Having started with nothing, Jackson seemed to have drawn from a combination of will, natural ability, and divine favor to become a man of substance without becoming a snob.

A Deeper Understanding of History

The Case of William Morgan: We Just Can't Know

One of the most interesting and important political events that took place during the 1820s is also one of the most puzzling. In the fall of 1826, William Morgan, a New York bricklayer, decided to have a booklet published that revealed some low-level secrets about the inner workings of the Masons. At this time, many leading politicians, judges, and local officials were members of that organization, and some voters wondered if politics was being unfairly influenced under the veil of the organization's secrecy. In any case, Morgan was promptly arrested—charged with owing a debt of $2.69—and jailed. Some unknown person then paid Morgan's debt and he was released. But as he emerged from jail, he was seized, bound and gagged, and dragged into a carriage that whisked him out of town.

Morgan's disappearance caused a popular outcry, and political outsiders demanded a complete investigation. When no clues turned up, many assumed that a Masonic conspiracy was afoot. Within a year, opportunistic young politicians, including New Yorkers Thurlow Weed and William Seward and Pennsylvanian Thaddeus Stevens, had harnessed this political anxiety by forming the Antimasonic Party.

Based exclusively on the alienation felt by small craftsmen, farmers, and other marginalized groups, the Antimasons had no platform beyond their shared antagonism to the conspiracies they were sure were being directed against political transparency. It was a classic illustration of what historian Richard Hofstadter describes as the "paranoid style in American politics." Nonetheless, the party scored major victories in New York state elections in 1828 and after that year was the most powerful force in the state standing in opposition to Martin Van Buren and Andrew Jackson, both of whom were Masons. The organization spread from New York outward. It also expanded its policy positions; it supported the use of public money for building internal improvements like canals and roads, and it supported federal tariff legislation.

In 1831, the party went national, holding the first ever political party convention in Baltimore. They nominated former U.S. Attorney General William Wirt, who oddly enough, had been a Mason, and Amos Ellmaker, a Pennsylvania attorney and railroad pioneer, as their candidates to run against Jackson and Van Buren in 1832. Although they won only seven electoral votes, they were more successful at the state level, electing governors in the states of Pennsylvania and Vermont, but they were not powerful enough to overcome the Democratic machine in New York. Eventually the Antimasonic Party was drawn into the coalition that formed the Whig Party, and it went out of existence as quickly as it had emerged.

Athough historians would love to know what happened to William Morgan when his disappearance launched this incredible political activity, sometimes there are mysteries in history that historians cannot solve. The few legal inquests that were conducted at the time turned up virtually no reliable information about Morgan's disappearance. The official secrecy of the Mason's themselves was maintained loyally by anyone who might have been able to offer evidence. And, according to the Antimasons, the judges, prosecutors, and other officials charged with digging up the facts actually were burying them. No body was ever found nor, despite rumors to the contrary, was Morgan ever seen again. We know that what happened was important but simply do not have enough evidence to know "whodunit." Unless some new, formerly lost documents show up—always a possibility, but in this case highly unlikely—we simply will have to settle for the fact that we just can't know.

Caricature and image making rather than substantive issues dominated the election campaign of 1828. Jackson supporters accused Adams of being cold, aristocratic, and corrupt in bowing to speculators and special interests when defining his tariff and land policies. Adams supporters charged Jackson with being a dueler, an insubordinate military adventurer, and an uncouth backwoodsman. The characterization of Adams as cold was accurate, but charges of corruption were entirely untrue. The charges against Jackson were all too true, but rather than damaging Jackson's image, such talk made him appear romantic and daring. When all was said and done, the Tennessean polled over a hundred thousand more popular votes than did the New Englander and won the vast majority of states, taking every one in the South and West (see Map 10.3).

As if in response to his supporters' desires and his opponents' fears, Jackson swept into the White House on a groundswell of unruly popular enthusiasm. Ten thousand visitors crammed into the capital to witness Jackson's inauguration on March 4, 1829. Showing his usual disdain for tradition, Jackson took the oath of office and then pushed through the crowd and mounted his horse, galloping off toward the White House followed by a throng of excited onlookers. When they arrived, the mob flowed behind him into the presidential mansion, where a spontaneous party broke out. The new president was finally forced to flee the near-riot by climbing out a back window. Clearly a boisterous new spirit was alive in the nation's politics.

Launching Jacksonian Politics

That he was a political outsider was a major factor in Jackson's popularity. Many were convinced that politics consisted primarily of conspiracies among political insiders, and Jackson curried their support by promising retrenchment and reform in the federal system. In the process he initiated a personal style in government unlike that of any of his predecessors in office and alienated many both inside and outside Washington.

Retrenchment was first on the new president's agenda. Jackson challenged the notion that government work required an elite core of professional civil servants. Such duties, Jackson declared, were "so plain and simple that men of intelligence may readily qualify themselves for their performance." And in order to keep such men from becoming entrenched, Jackson promised to institute regular rotation in office for federal bureaucrats: appointments in his administration would last only four years, after which civil servants would have to return to "making a living as other people do."

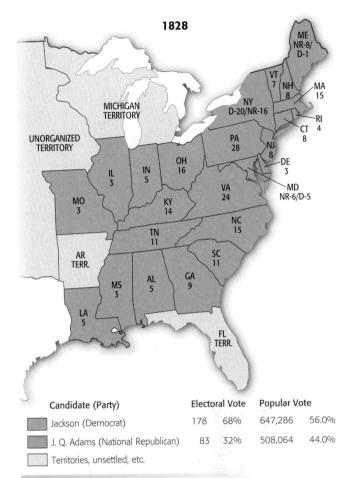

1828

Candidate (Party)	Electoral Vote		Popular Vote	
Jackson (Democrat)	178	68%	647,286	56.0%
J. Q. Adams (National Republican)	83	32%	508,064	44.0%
Territories, unsettled, etc.				

MAP 10.3 Election of 1828
This map shows how the political coalition between Andrew Jackson and Martin Van Buren turned the tables in the election of 1828. Jackson's Democratic Party won every region except Adams's native New England. © Cengage Learning.

□ **Thaddeus Stevens** Opportunistic politician who was one of the founders of the Antimasonic Party; he later became a leader of the "Conscience Whigs" and later still became one of the key organizers of the Republican Party. During and after the Civil War, he was the leader of the Radical Republican faction in Congress.

□ **Antimasonic Party** Political party formed in 1827 to capitalize on popular anxiety about the influence of the Masons; it opposed politics-as-usual without offering any particular substitute.

caricature An exaggerated image of a person, usually enhancing his or her most uncomplimentary features.

special interest A person or organization that seeks to benefit by influencing legislators to support particular policies.

retrenchment In government, the elimination of unnecessary jobs or functions for reform or cost-cutting purposes.

The presidential election of 1828 pitted two totally opposite kinds of men against each other. The staid John Quincy Adams (*left*), who had been involved in national politics for over a quarter of a century, represented old-style gentlemanly politics. The flamboyant military hero Andrew Jackson (*right*), on the other hand, was a political outsider and seemed to have much more in common with the new generation of American voters.

Like many of Jackson's policies, this rotation system was designed to accomplish more than a single goal. Because no new party had come to power since Jefferson's election in 1800, Jackson inherited some ten thousand civil servants who owed their jobs to Republican patronage. Rotation in office gave the president the excuse to fire people whom he associated with the "corrupt bargain" and felt he could not fully trust. It also opened up an unprecedented opportunity for Jackson to reward his loyal supporters by placing them in the newly vacated civil service jobs. The Jacksonian adage became "To the victor belong the **spoils**," and the Democrats made every effort to advance their party's hold on power by distributing government jobs to loyal party members.

Patronage appointments extended to the highest levels in government. Jackson selected cabinet members not for their experience or ability but for their political loyalty and value in satisfying the various factions that formed his coalition. The potential negative impact of these appointments was minimized by Jackson's decision to abandon his predecessors' practice of regularly seeking his cabinet members' advice on major issues: the president called virtually no cabinet meetings and seldom asked for his cabinet's opinion. Instead, he surrounded himself with an informal network of friends and advisers. This so-called **Kitchen Cabinet**, under the deft leadership of Van Buren, worked closely with the president on matters of both national policy and party management.

Jackson's relationship with everyone in government was equally unconventional. He was known to rage, pout, and storm at suspected disloyalty. Earlier presidents had at least pretended to believe in the equal distribution of power among the three branches of government, but Jackson avowed that the president was the only member of the government elected by all the people, making it clear that he would stand in opposition to both private and congressional opponents. Reflecting his generally testy relationship with the legislative branch, he vetoed more bills than all his predecessors combined. Nor did he feel any qualms about standing up to the judiciary. Such arrogant assertions of executive power led Jackson's opponents to call the new president "King Andrew."

spoils Jobs and other rewards for political support.

Kitchen Cabinet President Jackson's informal advisers, who helped him shape both national and Democratic Party policy.

THE REIGN OF "KING ANDREW"

☆ *How did regional conditions influence the national divisions reflected in the Bank War and the nullification crisis?*

☆ *What was President Jackson's role in shaping U.S. Indian policy?*

Jackson had promised the voters "retrenchment and reform." He delivered retrenchment, but reform was more difficult to arrange. Jackson tried to implement reform in four broad areas: (1) the nation's banking and financial system, (2) internal improvements and public land policy, (3) Indian affairs, and (4) the collection of revenue and enforcement of federal law. The steps that Jackson took appealed to some of his supporters but strongly alienated others. Thus, as Jackson tried to follow through on his promise to reform the nation, he nearly tore the nation apart.

Jackson and the Bank

The Second Bank of the United States was an essential part of the American System. In addition to serving as the depository for federal funds, the Second Bank issued national currency, which could be exchanged directly for gold, and it served as a national clearinghouse for notes issued by state and local banks. In that capacity, the Second Bank could regulate currency values and credit rates and help to control the activities of state banks by refusing to honor their notes if the banks lacked sufficient gold to back them. The Second Bank could also police state and local banks by calling in loans and refusing credit—actions that had helped bring on the Panic of 1819 and had made the Second Bank very unpopular.

In 1823 Nicholas Biddle became president of the bank. An able administrator and talented economist, Biddle enforced firm and consistent policies that restored some confidence in the bank and its functions. But many Americans still were not ready to accept the notion of an all-powerful central banking authority. The vast majority did not understand the function of the Second Bank, viewing it as just another instrument for helping the rich get richer. These critics tended instinctively to support the use of specie. Other critics, including many state bankers, opposed the Second Bank because they felt that Biddle's controls were too strict and that they were not receiving their fair share of federal revenues. Speculators and debtors also opposed the bank: when they gambled correctly, they could benefit from the sort of economic instability the bank was designed to prevent.

Hoping that Democratic Party discipline would break down before the upcoming 1832 presidential election, Jackson's opponents in Congress proposed to renew the bank's twenty-year charter four years early.

Congress passed the renewal bill, and as expected, Jackson vetoed it, but an anticipated rift between Jackson and congressional Democrats did not open. The president stole the day by delivering a powerful veto message geared to appeal to the mass of Americans on whose support his party's congressmen depended. In line with his political supporters, Jackson denounced the Second Bank for serving the interests of "the few at the expense of the many" and injuring "humbler members of society—the farmers, the mechanics, and laborers—who have neither the time nor the means of securing like favors to themselves."

Although the charter was not renewed, the Second Bank could operate for four more years on the basis of its unexpired charter. Jackson, however, wanted to "deprive the conspirators of the aid which they expect from its money and power." Withdrawing federal deposits would do just that, although doing so was illegal. Jackson nonetheless ordered Treasury Secretary Louis McLane to make the withdrawals. When he refused, the president fired him and replaced him with William J. Duane, who also refused. Jackson quickly fired him too and appointed Kitchen Cabinet member Roger B. Taney to head the Treasury Department. Taney chose to step around the law rather than breaking it by paying the government's bills from existing accounts in the Second Bank while placing all new deposits in so-called pet banks.

Powerless to stop Taney's diversion of federal funds, Biddle sought to replace dwindling assets by raising interest rates and calling in loans owed by state banks. In this way, the banker believed, he would not only head off the Second Bank's collapse but also trigger a business panic that might force the government to reverse its course. "Nothing but the evidence of suffering . . . will produce any effect," Biddle said as he pushed the nation toward economic instability. Biddle was correct that there would be "evidence of suffering," but the full effect of the Bank War would not be felt until after the reign of "King Andrew" had ended.

☐ **Nicholas Biddle** President of the Second Bank of the United States; he struggled to keep the bank functioning when President Jackson tried to destroy it.

specie Coins minted from precious metals.

☐ **pet banks** State banks into which Andrew Jackson ordered federal deposits to be placed to help deplete the funds of the Second Bank of the United States.

☐ **Bank War** The political conflict that occurred when Andrew Jackson tried to destroy the Second Bank of the United States, which he thought represented special interests at the expense of the common man.

GENERAL JACKSON SLAYING THE MANY HEADED MONSTER.

Jackson slaying the many headed monster', 1828 (colour litho), American School, (19th century)/Private Collection/Peter Newark American Pictures/The Bridgeman Art Library.

Published in 1833, this political cartoon entitled "General Jackson Slaying the Many Headed Monster [The Second Bank of the United States]" pokes fun at Jackson's battle with the bank. Wielding a cane labeled "Veto," Jackson shouts "Biddle thou Monster Avaunt!! avaunt I say! or by the Great Eternal I'll cleave thee to the earth." Though this lampoons Jackson's efforts, most Americans agreed that the bank was a monster and deserved destruction.

Jackson and the West

Although Jackson was a westerner, his views on federal spending for roads, canals, and other internal improvements seemed based more on politics than on ideology or regional interest. For example, when Congress passed a bill calling for federal money to build a road in Kentucky—from Maysville, on the Ohio border, to Lexington—Jackson vetoed it, claiming that it would benefit only one state and was therefore unconstitutional. But three practical political issues influenced his decision. First, party loyalists in places such as Pennsylvania and New York, where Jackson hoped to gain support, opposed federal aid to western states. Second, Lexington was the hub of Henry Clay's political district, and by denying aid that would benefit that city, Jackson was putting his western competitor in political hot water. Finally, Jackson's former congressional district centered on Nashville—already the terminus of a national road and therefore a legitimate recipient of federal funds. Thus Jackson could lavish money on his hometown while seeming to stand by strict constitutional limitations on federal power.

Disposing of the **public domain** was the other persistent problem Jackson faced. By the time he came to power, land policy had become a major factor in sectional politics. Currying support from western voters, Jackson abandoned his predecessors' notion that public land sales should profit the government, taking the position that small farmers should be able to buy federal land for no more than it cost the government to **survey** the plot and process the sale.

Jackson thus directed Congress that "public lands shall cease as soon as practicable to be a source of revenue," and western Jacksonians responded immediately. One of them, Senator Thomas Hart Benton of Missouri, proposed in 1830 that the price of government land be dropped gradually from $1.25 to just 25 cents an acre and that any lands not sold at that price simply be given away. He also suggested that squatters—people who were currently settled illegally on public land—be given the first chance to buy the tract where they were squatting when the government offered it for sale.

Such measures pleased Jackson's western supporters but frightened easterners and southerners. His supporters in the East and South feared that migration would give the West an even bigger say in the nation's economic and political future. In addition, southerners

public domain Land owned and controlled by the federal government.

survey To determine the area and boundaries of land through measurement and mathematical calculation.

244 CHAPTER 10 The Rise of a New Nation, 1815–1836

The Squatters, 1850 (oil on canvas), Bingham, George Caleb (1811–79)/Museum of Fine Arts, Boston, Massachusetts, USA/Bequest of Henry Lee Shattuck in memory of Ralph W. Gray/The Bridgeman Art Library.

Throughout the West, people without money simply camped on publicly owned land. This painting by George Caleb Bingham captures one such family as they pause outside their log cabin. Western politicians like Thomas Hart Benton argued that such "squatters" had a legitimate right to claim the land they settled and fought for legislation protecting squatters' rights.

were concerned that Congress would replace revenues lost from the sale of public land by raising tariffs, threatening the South's economic relationship with Europe. Northerners were afraid that as people moved west, the drain on population would drive up the price of labor, increasing the cost of production and lowering profits. The result was nearly three years of debate in Congress. A frustrated Henry Clay, desperate to save any scrap of his economic plans for the nation, suggested that the distribution of public land be turned over to the states. Congress, relieved to have the matter taken out of its hands, passed Clay's bill in 1833, but Jackson vetoed it.

Jackson and the Indians

At the end of the War of 1812, the powerful Cherokees, Choctaws, Seminoles, Creeks, and Chickasaws—the so-called Five Civilized Tribes—numbered nearly seventy-five thousand people and occupied large holdings within the states of Georgia, North and South Carolina, Alabama, Mississippi, and Tennessee. These Indians had embraced Jefferson's vision of acculturation but were seen as an obstruction to westward migration, especially by grasping planters who coveted Indian land for cotton fields. A similar situation prevailed in the Northwest. Though neither as numerous

nor as Europeanized as the Civilized Tribes, groups such as the Peorias, Kaskaskias, Kickapoos, Sauks, Foxes, and Winnebagos were living settled and stable lives along the northern frontier.

Throughout the 1820s, the federal government tried to convince tribes along the frontier to move farther west. Promised money, new land, and relief from white harassment, many Indian leaders agreed. Others, however, resisted, insisting that they stay where they were. The outcome was terrible factionalism within Indian societies as some lobbied to sell out and move west while others fought to keep their lands. Playing on this factionalism, federal Indian agents were able to extract land cessions that consolidated the eastern tribes onto smaller and smaller holdings. One such transaction, the 1825 Treaty of Indian Springs, involved fraud and manipulation so obnoxious that President Adams overturned the ratified treaty and insisted on a new one.

Adams at least paid lip service to honest dealings with the Indians and the sanctity of treaties. Jackson

□ **Five Civilized Tribes** Term used by whites to describe the Cherokee, Choctaw, Seminole, Creek, and Chickasaw Indians, many of whom were planters and merchants.

scoffed at both. In 1817 he had told President Monroe, "I have long viewed treaties with the Indians an absurdity not to be reconciled to the principles of our government." As president, Jackson advocated removing all the eastern Indians to the west side of the Mississippi, by force if necessary (see Map 10.4). Following Jackson's direction, Congress passed the Indian Removal Act in 1830, appropriating the funds necessary to purchase all of the lands held by Indian tribes east of the Mississippi River and to pay for their resettlement in the West.

It did not take Jackson long to begin implementing his new authority. When white farmers penetrated Sauk Indian territory during the summer of 1831, the Jackson administration authorized federal troops to forcibly move the entire band of more than a thousand Indian men, women, and children across the Mississippi.

At the same time, whites were exerting similar pressure on the southern tribes. The case of the Cherokees provides an excellent illustration of the new, more aggressive attitude toward Indian policy. Having allied with Jackson against the Creeks in 1813, the Cherokees emerged from the War of 1812 with their lands pretty well intact, and a rising generation of accommodationist leaders pushed strongly for the tribe to embrace white culture. In the early 1820s the Cherokees created a formal government with a bicameral legislature, a court system, and a professional, salaried civil service. In 1827 the tribe drafted and ratified a written constitution modeled on the Constitution of the United States. In the following year the tribe began publication of its own newspaper, the *Cherokee Phoenix,* printed in both English and Cherokee, using the alphabet devised earlier in the decade by tribal member George Guess (Sequoyah).

Rather than winning the acceptance of their white neighbors, however, those innovations led to even greater friction. From the frontiersmen's point of view, Indians were supposed to be dying out, disappearing into history, not founding new governments and competing successfully for economic power.

MAP 10.4 Indian Removal

The outcome of Andrew Jackson's Indian policy appears clearly on this map. Between 1830 and 1835, all of the Civilized Tribes except Osceola's faction of Seminoles were forced to relocate west of the Mississippi River. Thousands died in the process. © Cengage Learning.

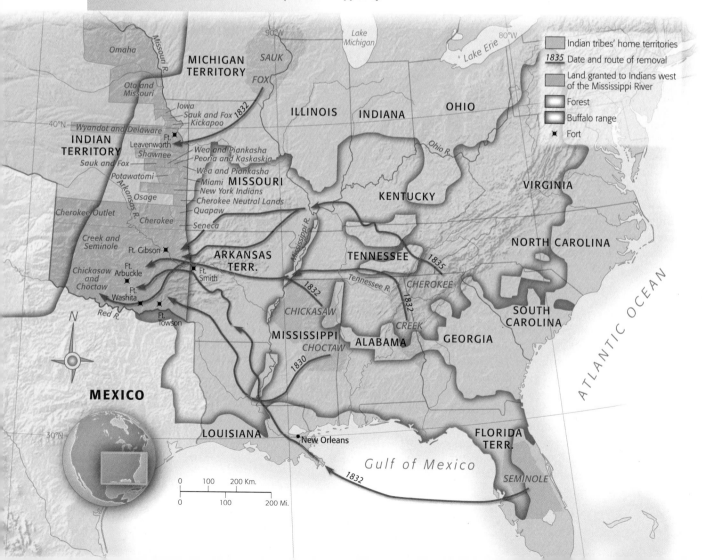

It Matters Today

Establishing Indian Sovereignty

Although the cases of *Cherokee Nation v. Georgia* (1831) and *Worcester v. Georgia* (1832) had very little impact on conditions for Native Americans when they were initially decided, both have had an enormous impact on Indians today. In the first of these cases, the Supreme Court maintained that the Cherokee Nation was a nation, but not a foreign nation and therefore had no right to sue in the federal courts. In the second, the Court made clear that all matters relating to the regulation of Indian nations belonged exclusively to the federal government, acknowledging a sovereign-to-sovereign relationship between Indians and the United States. In the twentieth century, Indian groups began citing these cases regularly when seeking protection from incursions by states on such matters as fishing rights, access to sacred sites, and economic development on reservations. Perhaps most profoundly, these cases shielded Indian communities from state interference with gambling operations on reservations, leading to an economic renaissance among many Native American nations.

- Based on what you have read in this and the previous chapter concerning John Marshall's Supreme Court, why do you think the Court reached the decisions they did in these cases?
- Go online to investigate a twentieth- or twenty-first-century case in which one or both of these cases was cited in support of Native American claims of sovereignty. How was the case or cases used? How was the question of sovereignty decided in this case?

Thus in 1828 the Georgia legislature nullified the Cherokee constitution. In the following year, gold was found on Cherokee land. As more than three thousand greedy prospectors violated tribal territory, the state of Georgia extended its authority over the Cherokees and ordered all communal tribal lands seized.

That was the first in a series of laws that the Georgia legislature passed to make life as difficult as possible for the Cherokees in hopes of driving them out of the state. When Christian missionaries living with the tribe protested the state's actions and encouraged the Cherokees to seek federal assistance, Georgia passed a law that required teachers among the Indians to obtain licenses from the state—a law expressly designed to eliminate the missionaries' influence. When two missionaries, Samuel Austin Worcester and Elizur Butler, refused to comply, a company of Georgia militia invaded the Cherokee reservation, arrested the teachers, and marched them off to jail.

Two notable lawsuits came out of the combined efforts of the missionaries and Cherokees to get justice. In the first case, *Cherokee Nation v. Georgia* (1831), the Cherokees claimed that Georgia's action in extending authority over them and enforcing state law within Cherokee territory was illegal because they were a sovereign nation in a treaty relationship with the United States. The U.S. Supreme Court refused to hear this case. Speaking for the Court, Chief Justice John Marshall stated that the Cherokee Nation was neither a foreign nor a domestic state but was

a "domestic dependent nation" and as such had no standing in federal court.

As American citizens, however, Worcester and Butler did have legitimate standing under federal law, and in 1832 Marshall was able to render a decision in the case of *Worcester v. Georgia*. In this case, the Court ruled that the Cherokee Nation was a distinct political community recognized by federal authority and that Georgia did not have legitimate power to pass laws regulating Indian behavior or to invade Indian land. He thus declared all the laws Georgia had passed to harass the Cherokees null and void and ordered the state to release Worcester and Butler from jail.

Although the Cherokees had grounds for celebration, their joy was short-lived. Jackson refused to use

◻ **Indian Removal Act** Law passed by Congress in 1830 providing for the removal of all Indian tribes east of the Mississippi and the purchase of western lands for their resettlement.

◻ **George Guess (Sequoyah)** Cherokee silversmith and trader who created an alphabet that made it possible to transcribe the Cherokee language according to the sounds of its syllables.

◻ ***Cherokee Nation v. Georgia*** Supreme Court case (1831) concerning Georgia's annulment of all Cherokee laws; the Supreme Court ruled that Indian tribes did not have the right to appeal to the federal court system.

◻ ***Worcester v. Georgia*** Supreme Court case (1832) concerning the arrest of two missionaries who were working with the Cherokees in Georgia; the Court found that Georgia had no right to rule in Cherokee territory.

It is easy to gloss over the brutality that was part of removing the Cherokees and other Indians from the Southeast during the 1830s, but this blockhouse at the former site of Fort Marr in Tennessee provides gruesome testimony to the actualities of the "Trail of Tears." It was one of four corner guard towers that were connected by high walls that contained Indians waiting to be transported to Indian Territory. Confinement often lasted for months, during which time food, fresh water, adequate shelter, and sanitary facilities were either minimal or not supplied at all. Armed sentinels in the blockhouses could shoot through specially drilled gun ports if the Indian detainees protested their inhumane treatment.

Picture Research Consultants & Archives

any federal authority to carry out the Court's order. When the Cherokees and their sympathizers pressed Jackson on the matter, he claimed that he was powerless to help and that the only way the Indians could get protection from the Georgians was to relocate west of the Mississippi.

Under this sort of pressure, tribal unity broke down. The majority of Cherokees stood fast with their stalwart leader John Ross, fighting Georgia through the court system. But another faction emerged advocating relocation. Preying on the division, federal Indian agents named the dissenters as the true representatives of the tribe and convinced them to sign the **Treaty of New Echota** (1835), in which the minority

□ **Treaty of New Echota** Treaty in 1835 by which a minority faction gave all Cherokee lands east of the Mississippi to the U.S. government in return for $5 million and land in Indian Territory.

□ **Trail of Tears** Forced march of the Cherokee people from Georgia to Indian Territory in the winter of 1838, during which thousands of Cherokees died.

faction sold the last 8 million acres of Cherokee land in the East to the U.S. government for $5 million.

A similar combination of pressure, manipulation, and outright fraud led to the dispossession of all the other Civilized Tribes. During the winter of 1831–1832, the Choctaws in Mississippi and Alabama became the first tribe to be forcibly removed from their lands to a designated Indian Territory in what is now Oklahoma. They were joined by the Creeks in 1836 and by the Chickasaws in 1837. John Ross and the other antitreaty Cherokee leaders continued to fight in court and to lobby in Congress, but in 1838 federal troops rounded up the entire Cherokee tribe and force-marched them to Indian Territory. Like all of the Indian groups who were forcibly removed from their native lands, the Cherokees suffered terribly. In the course of the **Trail of Tears** (see Map 10.4), nearly a fourth of the twenty thousand Cherokees who started the march died of disease, exhaustion, or heartbreak.

Only one of the Civilized Tribes resisted militarily: the Seminoles. Like the other tribes, the Seminoles were deeply divided. Some chose peaceful relocation;

others advocated rebellion. After the conciliatory faction signed the Treaty of Payne's Landing in 1832, a group led by Osceola broke with the tribe, declaring war on the protreaty group and on the United States. After years of guerrilla swamp fighting, Osceola was finally captured in 1837, but the antitreaty warriors fought on. The struggle continued until 1842, when the United States withdrew its troops, having lost fifteen hundred men during the ten-year conflict. Eventually, even the majority of Osceola's followers agreed to move west, though a small faction of the Seminoles remained in Florida's swamps, justly proud that they were neither conquered nor dispossessed by the United States.

The Nullification Crisis

Southern concerns about banking and rising tariffs reflected the South's abiding political and economic posture during the Jackson administration. For years, southerners had complained that tariffs discriminated against them. From their point of view, they were paying at least as much in tariffs as the North and West but were not getting nearly the same economic benefits. The banking system, too, seemed to benefit others more than it did them.

This matter had come to a head in 1829 when the impact of the ill-considered Tariff of Abominations began to be felt throughout the nation. The new tariffs roused loud protest from states such as South Carolina, where soil exhaustion and declining agricultural prices were putting strong economic pressure on men who were deeply invested in land and slaves. Calhoun, who took office as Jackson's vice president in 1829, spearheaded the protest. Though it guarded the author's identity, the South Carolina legislature published Calhoun's *South Carolina Exposition and Protest* in 1828, a ringing endorsement of nullification.

Calhoun's position on states' rights contributed to a running feud with Jackson. Just before the election in 1828, Van Buren had leaked information that Calhoun had called for Jackson to be severely disciplined for disobeying orders when he invaded Florida. Then, shortly after Jackson took office, Calhoun and his wife became embroiled in a social scandal that rocked Washington: the "petticoat affair." One of Jackson's closest friends, John Eaton, who Jackson appointed as secretary of war, had recently married the widowed daughter of a Washington boardinghouse keeper. Rumors suggested that Peggy Eaton had engaged in multiple affairs with influential men and that her husband had committed suicide out of despair. Calhoun's wife, Floride, convinced Washington high society, including the wives of other cabinet members, to shun the Eatons. Jackson found this behavior disgraceful and, more provocatively, disloyal and reprimanded Calhoun, who refused to back down.

The tension continued to build until, in 1832, nullification advocates in South Carolina called for a special session of the state legislature, which voted overwhelmingly to nullify the despised tariff. The legislature also elected Robert Y. Hayne, nullification's most prominent spokesman, as governor and named Calhoun as his replacement in the Senate. Calhoun then chose to act on the bad blood between him and the president, finally admitting to writing the *Exposition and Protest* and resigning from the vice presidency to lead the pro-nullification forces from the Senate floor.

Bristling that nullification violated the Constitution and was "destructive of the great object for which it was formed," Jackson immediately reinforced federal forts in South Carolina and sent warships to guarantee the tariff's collection. He also asked Congress to pass a "force bill" giving him the power to invade the rebellious state if doing so proved necessary to carry out federal law. In hopes of placating southerners and winning popular support in the upcoming election, Congress passed a reduced tariff, but it also voted to give Jackson the power he requested.

South Carolina nullifiers immediately called a new convention, which withdrew its nullification of the previous tariff but passed a resolution nullifying the force bill. Because Jackson no longer needed the force bill to collect the new tariff, he chose to ignore this action. Thus there was no real resolution to the problem, and the gash over federal versus states' rights remained unhealed. The wound continued to fester until it was finally cauterized thirty years later by civil war.

□ **Osceola** Seminole leader in Florida who opposed removal of his people to the West and led resistance to U.S. troops; he was captured by treachery while bearing a flag of truce.

Individual Voices

JOHN C. CALHOUN
Justifies the Principle and Practice of Nullification

In February 1833, one year after resigning from the vice presidency and being appointed by the South Carolina legislature to fill a vacancy in its U.S. Senate delegation, John C. Calhoun stood before the Senate to defend South Carolina's actions and the principle of nullification. In a brief statement, Calhoun summarized his views and attempted to justify his home state's act of disobedience in refusing to comply with federal tariff laws.

National Portrait Gallery, Smithsonian Institution/Art Resource, NY

❶ What is the significance of Calhoun's assertion that the federal union is a "union of States" and "not of individuals"?

❷ How does Calhoun's description of the process by which the Constitution was ratified justify his claims concerning the rights of a state-wide convention to declare federal laws null and void?

❸ The expression "meum and tuum" is Latin for "mine and thine." Here Calhoun is saying that a citizen's claim that the government has wrongly taken his or her property— a conflict between "mine and thine"—would be an appropriate matter to take to court. In cases, however, where all citizens believe themselves deprived by the government, it falls to the state and not to the courts to act on their behalf.

❹ On what basis does Calhoun justify the expulsion of federal authorities from a state? What assumptions is he making about federal rights versus states' rights?

The people of Carolina believe that the Union is a union of States, and not of individuals; that it was formed by the States, and that the citizens of the several States were bound to it through the acts of their several States; that each State ratified the Constitution for itself, and that it was only by such ratification of a State that any obligation was imposed upon its citizens. ❶ Thus believing, it is the opinion of the people of Carolina that it belongs to the State which has imposed the obligation to declare, in the last resort, the extent of this obligation, as far as her citizens are concerned; and this upon the plain principles which exist in all analogous cases of compact between sovereign bodies. On this principle the people of the State, acting in their sovereign capacity in convention, precisely as they did in the adoption of their own and the Federal Constitution, have declared, by the ordinance, that the acts of Congress which imposed duties under the authority to lay imposts, were acts not for revenue, as intended by the Constitution, but for protection, and therefore null and void. ❷

. . . It ought to be borne in mind that, according to the opinion which prevails in Carolina, the right to resistance to the unconstitutional acts of Congress belongs to the State, and not to her individual citizens; and that, though the latter may, in a mere question of meum and tuum, ❸ resist, through the courts an unconstitutional encroachment upon their rights, yet the final stand against usurpation rests not with them, but with the State of which they are members; and such act of resistance by a State binds the conscience and allegiance of the citizen. . . .

The Constitution has admitted the jurisdiction of the United States within the limits of the several States only so far as the delegated powers authorize; beyond that they are intruders, and may rightfully be expelled; and that they have been efficiently expelled by the legislation of the State through her civil process, as has been acknowledged on all sides in the debate, is only a confirmation of the truth of the doctrine for which the majority in Carolina have contended. ❹

Study Tools

SUMMARY

With the end of the War of 1812, President Madison and the Republicans promoted a strong agenda for the nation. Joining with former critics such as Henry Clay and John C. Calhoun, Madison pushed for a national market economy by sponsoring federal legislation for a national bank, controlled currency, and tariff protection for American industry. In addition, Madison gave free rein to nationalists such as Stephen Decatur, John Quincy Adams, and Andrew Jackson, who succeeded in enhancing the nation's military reputation and expanding its sphere of influence.

While the nation moved forward in accomplishing its diplomatic goals, the Republicans' economic agenda suffered from a lack of viable transportation and communication systems. Expecting quick and enormous profits, New York built the Erie Canal, the first successful link between the increasingly urban and manufacturing East and the rural, agricultural West. Convinced finally that transportation improvements were necessary for carrying out the work of the government, Madison and his successors joined with state officials to begin the process of building a truly national system of roads and canals.

But what had begun as an age of optimism closed in a tangle of conflict and ill will. A much-hoped-for prosperity dissolved in the face of shrinking markets, resulting in economic panic in 1819 and a collapse in the speculative economy. Economic hard times, in turn, triggered increased competition between the nation's geographical sections, as leaders wrestled for control over federal power in an effort to rid particular areas of economic despair. Supporters of the American System tried to craft a solution, but their compromise did not entirely satisfy anyone. And in the sea of contention that swelled around the Missouri Compromise, the Era of Good Feelings collapsed.

Meanwhile, an army of newly enfranchised voters, common men of moderate means, distressed by what seemed an elite conspiracy to run American affairs, swept the gentlemanly John Quincy Adams out of office and replaced him with the more exciting and presumably more democratic Andrew Jackson. Backed by a political machine composed of northern, western, and southern interests, Jackson had to juggle each region's financial, tariff, and Indian policy demands while trying to hold his political alliance and the nation together. The outcome was a series of regional crises—the Bank War, Indian removal, and nullification—that alienated each region and together constituted a crisis of national proportions.

CHRONOLOGY
New Optimism and a New Democracy

1814	Treaty of Ghent ends War of 1812
1814–1815	Hartford Convention
1815	Government funds Cumberland Road
	Stephen Decatur defeats Barbary pirates
1816	Tariff of 1816
	First successful steamboat run, Pittsburgh to New Orleans
	James Monroe elected president
1817	Second Bank of the United States opens
1818	Andrew Jackson invades Spanish Florida
1819	*McCulloch v. Maryland*
	Adams-Onís Treaty
	Panic of 1819
1820	Monroe reelected
	Missouri Compromise
1823	Monroe Doctrine
1824–1828	Suffrage reform triples voter population
1825	House of Representatives elects John Quincy Adams president
	Completion of Erie Canal
1826	Disappearance of William Morgan and beginning of Antimasons
1827	Ratification of Cherokee constitution
1828	Tariff of Abominations
	Jackson elected president
	Publication of Calhoun's *The South Carolina Exposition and Protest*
	First issue of the *Cherokee Phoenix*
1830	Indian Removal Act
1831	Federal removal of Sauks and Choctaws
1832	*Worcester v. Georgia*
	Bank War
	Nullification crisis
	Seminole War begins
1836–1838	Federal removal of Creeks, Chickasaws, and Cherokees

Study Tools

FOCUS QUESTIONS

If you have mastered this chapter, you should be able to answer these questions and to explain the terms that follow the questions.

1. What were the sources for Americans' optimism as they emerged from the War of 1812 and how did the American government capitalize on this optimism?

2. How did new developments in the nation influence foreign affairs?

3. How did the global economic situation combine with postwar economic optimism to lead to economic panic in 1819?

4. How did economic growth and panic contribute to sectional conflict and political contention?

5. What factors helped change Americans' political options during the mid-1820s?

6. How did the election of Andrew Jackson in 1828 reflect those new options?

7. How did regional conditions influence the national divisions reflected in the Bank War and the nullification crisis?

8. What was President's Jackson role in shaping U.S. Indian policy?

KEY TERMS

Tariff of Abominations   p. 227
"Era of Good Feelings"   p. 228
Hartford Convention   p. 228
DeWitt Clinton   p. 228
Henry Clay   p. 228
American System   p. 228
Tariff of 1816   p. 229
Dartmouth College v. Woodward   p. 230
McCulloch v. Maryland   p. 230
Gibbons v. Ogden   p. 230
Cumberland Road   p. 230
Erie Canal   p. 230

Adams-Onís Treaty   p. 232
Monroe Doctrine   p. 232
Napoleonic wars   p. 232
Panic of 1819   p. 233
Tallmadge Amendment   p. 234
Missouri Compromise   p. 235
Denmark Vesey   p. 235
Virginia Dynasty   p. 236
Martin Van Buren   p. 238
Thomas Hart Benton   p. 238
Democratic Party   p. 238
Thaddeus Stevens   p. 240
Antimasonic Party   p. 240

Kitchen Cabinet   p. 242
Nicholas Biddle   p. 243
pet banks   p. 243
Bank War   p. 243
Five Civilized Tribes   p. 245
Indian Removal Act   p. 246
George Guess (Sequoyah)   p. 246
Cherokee Nation v. Georgia   p. 247
Worcester v. Georgia   p. 247
Treaty of New Echota   p. 248
Trail of Tears   p. 248
Osceola   p. 249

SUGGESTED RESOURCES

Teaching History.Org. "Denmark Vesey," http://teachinghistory.org/history-content/beyond-the-textbook/24126. An excellent treatment of Vesey and his "uprising" discussing the historiography of the event and providing a number of primary sources.

U.S. Library of Congress. "Primary Documents in American History," http://www.loc.gov/rr/program/bib/ourdocs. Nice collections of links to primary documents relating to key events during the era discussed in this chapter.

U.S. Senate. "Famous Senate Speeches: Henry Clay 'In Defense of the American System,'" http://www.senate.gov/artandhistory/history/common/generic/Speeches_ClayAmericanSystem.htm. Contains a nice, concise account of the American System as an introduction to the text of Clay's three-day-long speech in the Senate attacking the Jackson Administration.

Modernization and Expansion, 1828–1848

INDIVIDUAL CHOICES

Jarena Lee

Though few people today have ever heard of Jarena Lee, she was a most remarkable woman for her time and quite well known among her contemporaries. An African American, she was born in Cape May, New Jersey, in 1783. Although slavery was still legal and fairly widely practiced in New Jersey until a gradual emancipation bill was passed in 1804, it is unclear whether Lee was a slave or not. All she says in her memoir, published in 1836, is that "At the age of seven years I was parted from my parents, and went to live as a servant maid." Whatever her condition was, she explains that in 1804 she "left the lady" she had been with and ventured to the Philadelphia area. Throughout her early life she remained mindful that "My parents being wholly ignorant of the knowledge of God, had not therefore instructed me in any degree in this great matter," and she experimented with various religious bodies until she finally encountered Reverend Richard Allen, who had founded the Bethel Church for Negro Methodists in Philadelphia in 1793.

As she listened to a sermon by Allen she experienced an epiphany: "there appeared to my view, in the centre of the heart, *one* sin; and this was *malice* against one particular individual, who had strove deeply to injure me, which I resented. At this discovery I said, Lord I forgive every creature." At that moment, she leapt to her feet and declared "that God, for Christ's sake, had pardoned the sins of my soul." For a period of four years she

Library of Congress.

253

attended church regularly and wrestled with doubts about her deservedness, but after a series of visitations by the Holy Spirit she felt called to preach the gospel. She visited Bishop Allen to seek license, but he refused, telling her "as to women preaching . . . our Discipline knew nothing at all about it—that it did not call for women preachers" (see the Individual Voices feature at the end of this chapter). Dejected, she gave up on the idea and married Reverend Joseph Lee, settling into an unhappy domestic routine.

Eight years after her rejection by Bishop Allen, Lee's husband died. Suddenly her thoughts turned back to her previous call: "I now began to think seriously of breaking up housekeeping, and forsaking all to preach the everlasting Gospel." With no license or any sort of official permission, she immediately embarked on the first of what would be a lifelong series of crusades carrying the Methodist word throughout much of the country. In one year alone she attested to traveling "two thousand three hundred and twenty-five miles, and preached one hundred and seventy-eight sermons." Despite facing serious discrimination on account of both her race and her gender, she persevered, and eventually even Bishop Allen came around, granting her the license she had once been denied on account of being a woman.

Jarena Lee's choices were unusual at a time when both African Americans and women were seen as incapable of independent thought and action. In her travels she witnessed a vastly changing America as she visited slaves and slaveholders; great merchants, manufacturers, and factory workers; poor farmers; and the urban homeless. Her restless, driven movement, although unusual in its extent, was certainly not uncommon; this was a restless age and movement was everywhere. It was exactly the restlessness of the whole of American society that caused Lee and a great many people like her to cut ties with convention and launch themselves into new spaces and new occupations. Modernization and expansion were the key characteristics of the age.

THE NEW COTTON EMPIRE IN THE SOUTH

☆ Why did living conditions for southerners—black and white—change after 1820?

☆ How did elite white southerners respond to the change? How did their response affect slaves, free blacks, and poor whites?

antebellum The decades before the Civil War, the period from 1815 to 1860; Latin for "before the war."

The South exploded outward, seeking new lands on which to grow the glamour crop of the century: cotton. In 1820 cotton was being grown heavily in parts of Virginia, South Carolina, and Georgia. Within a matter of decades, the cotton empire had expanded to include most of the South and Southwest. The new dependence on a single crop changed the outlook and experiences not just of large planters but also of the slaves, free blacks, and poor whites whose labor made cotton king.

A New Birth for the Plantation System

Often characterized as the direct heirs of colonial era patriarchs and the conservators of an older, stately way of life, the cotton barons of the antebellum South generally were not related to the colonial plantation gentry, but had begun their careers as land speculators, financiers, and rough-and-tumble yeoman farmers whose lucky speculations in the burgeoning cotton market netted large landholdings and armies of slaves. And these planters were far from typical among southerners in general. First, the total number of slaveholders constituted less than one-third of all white southerners. Of the minority who actually owned slaves, nearly three-quarters owned only 80 to 160 acres of land and fewer than ten slaves; another 15 percent owned up to 800 acres and between ten and twenty slaves, leaving only about 12 percent who possessed more than 800 acres and twenty or more slaves. Though a minority, large-scale planters controlled the biggest share of productive land and labor. As a result, their economic, political, and social importance was far out of proportion to their numbers.

This is not to say that the image of grand plantations and lavish aristocratic living is entirely false. The owners of cotton plantations made an excellent living from the labor of their slaves. Although they often complained of debt and poor markets, it appears that large-scale planters could expect an annual return on capital equivalent to what the most successful northern industrialists were making. Agricultural profits in non-cotton-producing areas were significantly lower, but even there slavery netted white landowners major profits. The enormous demand for workers in the heart of the Cotton Belt created a profitable interstate trade in slaves, especially after Congress outlawed the international slave trade in 1808. Thus even planters who did not grow cotton came to have a significant investment in its cultivation and in the labor system that was its cornerstone.

The increasing demand for slaves had a terribly unsettling effect on social stability in the plantation world. Whereas generations of slaves had coexisted with generations of slaveowners on the traditional plantations in the colonial South, now the appeal of quick profits led planters in places like Virginia and Maryland to sell off their slaves, often breaking up families and deeply rooted social connections. This fragmentation of slave society helped to further dehumanize an already dehumanizing institution and drove a deeper wedge between the races.

The enormous profits earned from cotton in the 1840s and 1850s permitted some planters to build elegant mansions and to affect the lifestyle that they associated with a noble past. Women decked out in the latest gowns flocked to formal balls and weekend parties. Young men were sent to academies where they could learn the twin aristocratic virtues of militarism and honor. Young women attended private "seminaries" where they were taught, in the words of one southern seminary mistress, "principles calculated to render them useful and rational companions."

Practical concerns, however, always threatened to crack this romantic veneer. Although cotton planting might yield huge profits, successful ventures required major capital investment. If land suitable for cotton could be purchased directly from the federal government, it might be had for as little as 25 cents an acre, but efficient planting called for huge blocks

Despite the popular image that antebellum planters lived lives of idle luxury in great mansions, most actually lived in modest homes and worked alongside their employees and slaves, as this 1838 painting by an anonymous artist shows.

of land, and planters often had to pay a premium to get them. And contrary to popular perception, slave labor was not free: at the height of the slave trade, a healthy male field hand sold for an average of $1,800, the equivalent of almost $45,000 in current money. Often planters purchased slaves and fields on credit and genuinely feared that their carefully constructed empires and lifestyles might collapse in an instant. Aristocratic parents sought to use marriage as a way to enhance family and economic security. "As to my having any sweethearts that is not thought of," one young southern woman complained. "Money is too much preferred, for us poor Girls to be much caressed."

Even those girls whose fortunes earned caresses faced a strange and often difficult life. Planters' wives bore little resemblance to their counterparts in popular fiction. Far from being frail, helpless creatures, southern plantation mistresses carried a heavy burden of responsibility. A planter's wife was responsible for all domestic matters. She supervised large staffs of slaves, looked out for the health of everyone, and managed all plantation operations in the absence of her husband. All those duties were complicated by a sex code that relegated southern women to a peculiar position in the plantation hierarchy—between white men and black slaves. Southern white women were

return on capital The yield on money that has been invested in an enterprise or product.

◻ **Cotton Belt** The region in the southeastern United States in which cotton is grown.

expected to exercise absolute authority over their slaves while remaining absolutely obedient to white men. "He is master of the house," said plantation mistress Mary Boykin Chesnut about her husband. "To hear [him] is to obey." She also remarked, anxiously, "All the comfort of my life depends upon his being in a good humor." It is little wonder that Chesnut concluded her observations about southern womanhood with the statement, "There is no slave . . . like a wife."

And while in some respects planters treated their slaves like machines, slaves were nonetheless human—and sexual—beings. One southerner rationalized the sexual exploitation of slaves, saying, "The intercourse which takes place with enslaved females is less depraving in its effects than when it is carried on with females of their own caste." Of course what he meant was that it was "less depraving" on white men and women, dismissing entirely the impact that such sexual assault had on slaves and their families. But it may have been more depraving in its effects on southern society at large, imposing a veneer of respectability on a culture of rape that may never be entirely erased.

Life Among Common Southern Whites

As noted above, fully two-thirds of free southern families owned no slaves. A small number of these families owned stores, craft shops, and other businesses in southern cities. Some were attorneys, teachers, doctors, and other professionals. The great majority, however, were proud small farmers who owned, leased, or simply squatted on the land they farmed.

Often tarred with the label "poor white trash" by their planter neighbors, these people were often productive stock raisers and farmers. They concentrated on producing what they needed to live, but all aspired to produce surpluses or to grow cotton in an effort to raise cash, though they generally could not do so on a large scale. Whatever cash they raised they usually spent on necessary manufactures, as well as on land and slaves.

These small farmers had a shaky relationship with white planters. On the one hand, many wanted to join the ranks of the great planters, hoping they could transform their small holdings into cotton empires. On the other hand, they resented the aristocracy and envied the planters' exalted status and power. They also feared the expansion of large plantations, which often forced smallholders to abandon their hard-won farms and slaves.

noblesse oblige The belief that members of the elite are duty-bound to treat others charitably, especially those of lower status than themselves.

Although they seldom rebelled openly against their social superiors, common white people often used the power of the ballot box to make their dissatisfactions known. For despite the enormous power of the plantation elite, they were greatly outnumbered by the lesser class of whites, who had the power to wreck the entire social and economic structure if they became sufficiently disgruntled. Thus the *noblesse oblige* practiced by aristocrats toward poorer whites was as much a practical necessity as it was a romantic affectation.

Large-scale planters also used racial tensions as a device for controlling their contentious neighbors. Although they were not above taking slave concubines or trusting African Americans with positions of authority on plantations, the white elite nonetheless emphasized white supremacy when conversing with their poorer neighbors. They acknowledged that poor farmers felt underprivileged but stressed that slavery spared them from the most demeaning work. Planters asserted that should slavery ever end, whether because of poor white political maneuverings or outside pressures, it would be the farmers who would have the most to lose. And for their part, poor southern whites accepted and acted on these prejudices.

Free Blacks in the South

Caught in the middle between southern planters, slaves, and poor white farmers, free African Americans in the South often faced extreme discrimination. Some communities of free blacks could trace their origins back to earliest colonial times, when Africans, like Europeans, served limited terms of indenture. The majority, however, had been freed recently because of diminishing plantation profits during the late 1700s. Most of these people lived not much differently from slaves, working for white employers as day laborers.

Mounting restrictions on free blacks during the first half of the nineteenth century limited their freedom of movement, their economic options, and the protection they could expect to receive by law. In the town of Petersburg, Virginia, for example, when a free black woman named Esther Fells irritated her white neighbor, he took it upon himself to whip her for disturbing his peace. The sheriff did not arrest the assailant but instead took Mrs. Fells into custody, and the court ordered that she be given fifteen more lashes for "being insolent to a white person." Skin color left free African Americans open to abuses and forced them to be extremely careful in their dealings with their white neighbors.

Still, some opportunities were available for a handful of free blacks who had desirable skills. In the Upper South—Delaware, Maryland, and Virginia—master

Conditions for free African Americans in the South were always perilous, but not all suffered the same treatment. The wood engraving on the left illustrates the fate of free blacks who were caught out by white patrols; according to the caption, this man was beaten to death and left lying in the road. Whereas the image on the right shows a prosperous urban barber in Richmond, Virginia.

craftsmen hired young African American boys as apprentices, and those who could stick out their apprenticeship might eventually make an independent living. African American girls, however, had few opportunities as skilled laborers, although some became seamstresses or cooks. Others became washers, and a few grew up to run small groceries, taverns, and restaurants. And a small minority, like Jarena Lee, might make their way as religious exhorters or teachers.

Living Conditions for Southern Slaves

A delicate balance between power and profit shaped planters' policies toward slaves and set the tone for slave life. Maintaining profitability prompted slaveowners to enforce severe discipline and exercise careful supervision over slaves, leading southern states to write increasingly harsh slave codes during the early nineteenth century, which gave slaveowners virtual life-and-death control over their human property. But slaves were expensive: damaging a healthy slave meant taking a significant financial loss. Still, given the need to keep up productivity, slaveowners readily used measured force. But in a power structure so rigid and overwhelming, the temptation to abandon reason and engage in sadism was always present: the historical record is filled with accounts of slaveowners who were willing to take a financial loss by beating slaves until they became useless or even died.

In keeping with demands for profitability, housing for slaves was seldom more than adequate. Most slaves lived in one-room log cabins with dirt floors. Mindful of the need to maintain control and keep slaves productive, slaveowners tried to avoid crowding people into slave quarters. Census figures suggest that the average slave cabin housed five or six people. As one slaveowner explained, "The crowding [of] a number into one house is unhealthy. It breeds contention; is

destructive of delicacy of feeling, and it promotes immorality between the sexes." The cabins had windows, but generally only wooden shutters and no glass, so that occupants had to choose between shutting out the light or letting in flies in summer and cold in winter. The usual source of artificial light was an open fireplace or stove, also used for heat and cooking. Ever-present fires increased the danger of cabins burning down, especially because chimneys were generally made of sticks held together with dried mud. As one slave commented, "Many the time we have to get up at midnight and push the chimney away from the house to keep the house from burning up."

Furnishings in slave houses were usually fairly crude and often crafted by the residents themselves. Bedding normally consisted of straw pallets stacked on the floor or occasionally mounted on rough bedsteads. Other furnishings were equally simple—rough-hewn wooden chairs or benches and plank tables. Clothing was also very basic. One Georgia planter itemized the usual yearly clothing allowance for slaves: "two suits of cotton for spring and summer, and two suits of woolen for winter; four pair of shoes and three hats." Women commonly wore simple dresses or skirts and blouses, while children often went naked in the summer and were fitted with long, loose hanging shirts during the colder months.

It appears that the slave diet, like slave clothing and housing, was barely sufficient. One slave noted that there was "plenty to eat sich as it was," but in summer flies swarmed all over the food. Her master, she said, would laugh about that, saying the added

☐ **slave codes** Laws that established the status of slaves, denying them basic rights and classifying them as the property of slaveowners.

This early photograph, taken on a South Carolina plantation before the Civil War, freezes slave life in time, giving us a view of what slave cabins looked like, how they were arranged, how the largest majority of slaves dressed, and how they spent what little leisure time they had.

nutrition provided by the flies "made us fat." Despite justified complaints, slaves in the American South ate significantly more meat than workers in the urban North. In addition to meat, slaves consumed milk and corn, potatoes, peas and beans, molasses, and fish. The planter usually provided this variety of food, but owners also occasionally permitted slaves to hunt and fish and to collect wild roots, berries, and vegetables.

Although the diet provided to slaves kept them alive, the southern diet in general lacked important nutrients, and diet-related diseases plagued southern communities. Slaves were also subject to occupational ailments like hernia, pneumonia, and lockjaw.

lockjaw A popular name for tetanus, an often fatal disease resulting primarily from deep wounds.

cholera An infectious disease of the small intestines contracted mainly from bacteria in untreated water.

endemic Present in a particular group of people or geographical area.

field hands People who did agricultural work such as planting, weeding, and harvesting.

Because of inadequate sanitation, slaves also suffered from dysentery and cholera. Heart and circulatory diseases were also endemic among slaves. Recent research reveals that most slave children were undernourished because slaveowners would not allocate enough food for people who did not work. Once children were old enough to work, however, they had access to a very high-calorie diet. Such early malnutrition followed by an abrupt switch to a high-calorie and often high-fat diet may well have led to the high incidence of heart attacks, strokes, and similar ailments that the historical record indicates among slaves. And given the balance-sheet mentality among plantation owners, this phenomenon may not have been unwelcome. Old people who could not work hard were a liability; thus having slaves die from circulatory disease in middle age saved planters from unnecessary expenditures later on.

As to the work itself, cotton planting led to increasing concentration in the tasks performed by slaves. A survey of large and medium-size plantations during the height of the cotton boom shows that the majority of slaves (58 percent of the men and 69 percent of the women) were employed primarily as field hands. Of the rest, only 2 percent of slave men and 17 percent

As American industry became increasingly mechanized in the decades after 1820, suitable mill sites—places with solid foundations for factory buildings and reliable water flow for powering machinery—became highly prized. Often long stretches of riverbanks would sprout factory after factory. Lowell, Massachusetts, the site of the first fully mechanized textile plant in America, was one such site.

of slave women, were employed as **house slaves**. The remaining 14 percent of slave women were employed in nonfield occupations such as sewing, weaving, and food processing. Seventeen percent of slave men were employed in nonfield activities such as driving wagons, piloting riverboats, and herding cattle. Another 23 percent were managers and craftsmen.

The percentage of slave craftsmen was much higher in cities, where slave **artisans** were often allowed to hire themselves out on the open job market in return for handing part of their earnings over to their owners. In Charleston, Norfolk, Richmond, and Savannah, slave artisans formed **guilds**. Feeling threatened by their solidarity, white craftsmen appealed to state legislatures and city councils for restrictions on slave employment in skilled crafts. Such appeals, and the need for more and more field hands, led to a decline in the number of slave artisans during the 1840s and 1850s.

Whether on large plantations or small farms, the burden of slavery was a source of constant stress for both slaves and masters in the newly evolving South. The precarious nature of family life, the ever-present threat of violence, and the overwhelming sense of powerlessness weighed heavily on slaves. Among masters, the awareness that they often were outnumbered and thus vulnerable to organized slave rebellion was a source of anxiety. Locked into this fear- and hate-laden atmosphere, everyone in the cotton South was drawn into what would become a long-lasting legacy of racial tension and distrust.

THE MANUFACTURING EMPIRE IN THE NORTHEAST

☆ How did manufacturing and the nature of work change in the United States after 1820?

☆ In what ways did the American system of manufacturing change the traditional pattern of U.S. foreign trade?

☆ How did the developing factory system affect the lives of artisans, factory owners, and middle-class Americans?

Although the South changed radically during the opening years of the nineteenth century, one thing persisted: the economy remained rooted in households. Before the 1820s, households in the North also produced most of the things they used. For example, more than 60 percent of the clothing that Americans wore was spun from raw fibers and sewn by women in their own homes. Some householders even crafted sophisticated items—furniture, clocks, and tools—but skilled artisans usually made such products. These

house slaves People who did domestic work such as cleaning and cooking.

artisan A person who works at a craft, such as a blacksmith, cabinet maker, or stone mason.

guild An association of craftspeople with the same skills who join together to protect their common interests.

A Deeper Understanding of History

Immigration: Visualizing the Numbers

Between 1820 and 1830 slightly more than 151,000 people immigrated into the United States. In the decade that followed, that number increased to nearly 600,000, and then to well over a million-and-a-half between 1840 and 1850. This enormous increase in immigration changed the cultural, economic, and political face of the nation. The massive influx of new people presents a serious problem for historians: how can we visualize the changes that were taking place?

In the map here, four different elements will help you visualize what was happening throughout the nation as the result of immigration:

First, the map is color coded to illustrate those regions of the country that experienced the highest and the lowest concentrations of new immigrants. Second, informational balloons help explain why immigration took place in different regions of the country. Third, at the bottom right a simple bar graph illustrates the radical increase in overall immigration between 1820 and 1850. Fourth, a pie chart shows the approximate numbers of immigrants from different places.

Using these multiple visualizations, the next step is to analyze what this all means. One key question, answerable from the pie chart, is: Where did most immigrants come from? With the exception of Canada and the catchall category of "other," most came from western or central Europe, the vast majority from Ireland. This makes us wonder what was happening in Ireland and elsewhere at this moment in time. That is where the informational balloons come in handy. We learn, for example, that a famine in Ireland was pushing people toward America. We learn, too, about population growth and political upheaval in Germany, land shortages in Quebec, and overpopulation in England.

Looking at the map itself and its color-coded legend addresses some other interesting questions. Where were most immigrants going? One fact that jumps out is that, with the minor exception of Louisiana, they were not going to the South; the biggest pockets of immigration were in the Northeast and West. Why might that be? As one balloon explains, many of the new immigrants from England were skilled manufacturing workers, and during this period, manufacturing was pretty much confined to the Northeast. A great many more newcomers, especially the Irish and French Canadians, were peasants who either needed low-skill jobs in factories or small farms they could settle on. The Western frontier certainly had an abundance of relatively inexpensive land and, as manufacturing became more automated and prevalent, Northeastern jobs opened up for them as well. In the South, though, most land was already controlled by plantation owners and most of the unskilled labor was supplied by slaves. There simply was no incentive for immigrants to go there.

The historical significance of these questions and their answers will become clearer in the chapters to come. For the moment, this serves as an excellent illustration of how historians can use multiple visual tools to frame their analysis of the past.

---

craftsmen, too, usually worked in their homes, assisted by family members and an extended family of artisan employees: apprentices and **journeymen**.

Beginning with the cotton-spinning plants that sprang up during the War of 1812, textile manufacturing led the way in pushing production out of the home: from 1820 onward, manufacturing increasingly moved into factories, and cities began to grow up around them. Such changes severed the intimate ties between manufacturers and workers, and both found themselves surrounded by strangers in the new urban environments. "In most large cities there may be said to be two nations, understanding as little of one another, having as little intercourse, as if they lived in different lands," said one insightful observer. "This estrangement of men from men, of class from class, is one of the saddest features of a great city."

journeyman A person who has finished an apprenticeship to learn a trade or craft and is a qualified worker in the employ of another.

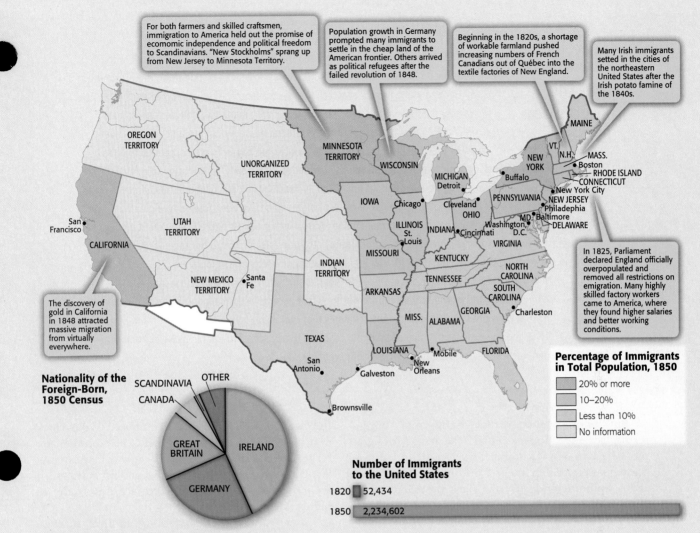

For both farmers and skilled craftsmen, immigration to America held out the promise of ecomomic independence and political freedom to Scandinavians. "New Stockholms" sprang up from New Jersey to Minnesota Territory.

Population growth in Germany prompted many immigrants to settle in the cheap land of the American frontier. Others arrived as political refugees after the failed revolution of 1848.

Beginning in the 1820s, a shortage of workable farmland pushed increasing numbers of French Canadians out of Québec into the textile factories of New England.

Many Irish immigrants setted in the cities of the northeastern United States after the Irish potato famine of the 1840s.

In 1825, Parliament declared England officially overpopulated and removed all restrictions on emigration. Many highly skilled factory workers came to America, where they found higher salaries and better working conditions.

The discovery of gold in California in 1848 attracted massive migration from virtually everywhere.

Nationality of the Foreign-Born, 1850 Census

SCANDINAVIA
CANADA
OTHER
GREAT BRITAIN
IRELAND
GERMANY

Percentage of Immigrants in Total Population, 1850
- 20% or more
- 10–20%
- Less than 10%
- No information

Number of Immigrants to the United States

1820	52,434
1850	2,234,602

Origin and Settlement of Immigrants, 1820–1850. © Cengage Learning.

The "American System of Manufacturing"

The transition from home manufacturing to factory production did not take place overnight, and the two processes often overlapped. Pioneer manufacturers such as Samuel Slater relied on home workers to carry out major steps in the production of textiles. Using what was called the putting-out system, cotton spinners supplied machine-produced yarn to individual households, where families then wove fabric on their own looms during their spare time. Such activities provided much-needed cash to farm families, enabled less productive family members (like the elderly or children) to contribute, and gave entire families worthwhile pastimes during lulls in the farming calendar.

☐ **putting-out system** Manufacturing system through which machine-made components were distributed to individual families who used them to craft finished goods.

Manufacturing and the Revolution in Time

In 1838, Chauncey Jerome introduced the first mass-produced brass clock to the consumer market at a price that virtually any American could afford. The distribution of clocks and the means by which they were manufactured reinforced each other. Factory production required that workers, clerks, managers, shippers, and others essential to industry be coordinated if factories were going to function effectively.

All of these employees, from the highest to the lowest in status, needed to have a reliable way of telling time. Mass-produced clocks provided that reliability, contributing to a revolution in the way Americans began thinking about time itself. Increasingly people looked to mechanical devices to punctuate their lives. Time management, a concept that would have been foreign to a previous generation of Americans, had now become a reality. Today we are almost entirely dependent on day planners or electronic personal information managers to keep track of time, a heritage of the revolution in timekeeping that was born in 1838 with the introduction of cheap brass clocks.

- How were the lives of Americans in the early nineteenth century changed by the increased regimentation and mechanical perceptions of time that accompanied the manufacturing revolution? In what ways does your life reflect these changes that took place so long ago?
- Try to imagine experiencing one day without referring to any sort of mechanical or electronic time management device. Describe what your day would be like.

But innovations in manufacturing soon began to displace such home crafting. The factory designs pioneered by Francis Cabot Lowell and his various partners were widely copied during the 1820s and 1830s. Spinning and weaving on machines located in one building significantly cut both the time and the cost of manufacturing. Quality control became easier because the tools of the trade, owned by the manufacturer rather than by the worker, were standardized and employees were under constant supervision. As a result, the putting-out system for turning yarn into cloth went into serious decline, falling off by as much as 90 percent in some areas of New England. Even home production of clothes for family use declined. Women discovered that spending their time producing cheese or eggs or other marketable items could bring in enough cash to purchase clothing and still have money left over. Throughout the 1830s and 1840s, ready-made clothing became standard wearing apparel.

A major technological revolution helped to push factory production into other areas of manufacturing as well during these years. In traditional manufacturing, individual artisans crafted each item one at a time, from the smallest part to the final product. A clock maker, for example, either cast or carved individually by hand all of the clock's internal parts. As a result, the mechanisms of a clock worked together only in the clock for which they had been made. If that clock ever needed repair, new parts had to be custom-made for it. The lack of interchangeable parts made manufacturing extremely slow and repairs difficult, and it limited employment in the manufacturing trades to highly skilled professionals.

After years of experimentation, in 1821 an engineer named John H. Hall brought together the necessary skill, financing, and tools at the Harper's Ferry federal armory to prove that manufacturing using interchangeable parts was practical. Within twenty years this "American system of manufacturing," as it was called, was being used to produce a wide range of products—farm implements, padlocks, sewing machines, and clocks. Formerly, clocks had been a status symbol setting apart people of means from common folks; however, using standardized parts, pioneer manufacturers like Chauncey Jerome revolutionized clock making to the point where virtually all Americans could afford them. Such manufacturing breakthroughs produced a number of goods so inexpensive and reliable that even Europeans began importing them, reversing the long-standing pattern of manufactures moving exclusively from Europe to America and launching a trend that would grow in the years to come.

New Workplaces and New Workers

With machines now producing standardized parts for complex mechanisms such as clocks, the worker's job was reduced to simply assembling premade

◻ **interchangeable parts** Parts that are identical and can be substituted for one another.

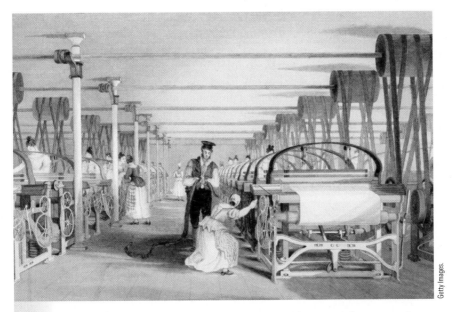

Water-powered textile factories were complex, noisy, and dangerous places to work. As shown here, many machines were powered by a common drive shaft and so remained in motion all the time. Working around the constantly whirring equipment often led to injury or death for what one nineteenth-century magazine described as "the human portion of the machine."

In New York, Philadelphia, and other cities, immigrant slums offered opportunistic manufacturers an alternative source of labor. In the shoe industry, for example, one family would make soles, while a neighboring family made heels, and so forth. This type of operation was not as efficient as large shoe factories, but the money that urban manufacturers saved by not building factories and by paying rock-bottom wages to desperate slum-dwellers made it possible for the companies to compete successfully in the open market.

The combination of machine production and a growing pool of labor proved economically devastating to workers. No longer was the employer a master craftsman or a paternalistic entrepreneur who felt some responsibility to look out for his workers' domestic needs. Factory owners were obligated to investors and bankers and had to squeeze the greatest possible profit out of the manufacturing process. They kept wages low, regardless of the workers' cost of living. As the swelling supply of labor allowed employers to offer lower and lower wages, increasing numbers of working people faced poverty and squalor.

Immigration supplied much of this labor. The flood of immigrants collected in the port and manufacturing cities of the Northeast, where they joined Americans fleeing financial depression in the countryside. Adding to the resulting brew were former master craftsmen, journeymen, and apprentices who no longer had a secure place in the changing economy. Together, though seldom cooperatively, these groups helped to form a new social class in America.

Not only were the new immigrants poor and often unskilled, but also most were culturally different from native-born Americans. Religion was their most notable cultural distinction: the majority were Roman Catholic. This made them suspect in the minds of people steeped in anti-Catholic sentiments handed down from earlier generations of Protestant immigrants. Immigrants' languages, dress, and eating and

components. The centuries-old guild organization for artisans—preserved in the hierarchical system of apprentices, journeymen, and master craftsmen—rapidly fell away as extensive training in the manufacturing arts became irrelevant.

At first, owners found they had to use creative means to attract workers into the new factories. Some entrepreneurs developed company towns. In New England these towns resembled traditional New England villages. Families recruited from the economically depressed countryside were installed in neat row houses, each with its own small vegetable garden. The company employed each family member. Women worked on the production line. Men ran heavy machinery and worked as **millwrights**, carpenters, haulers, or as day laborers dredging out the **millraces**. Children did light work in the factories and tended gardens at home.

Lowell's company developed another system at its factories. Hard-pressed to find enough families to leave traditional employment and come to work in the factories, Lowell recruited unmarried farm girls. The company built dormitories to house these young working women, offering cash wages and reasonable prices for room and board, as well as cultural events and educational opportunities. Because most of the girls saw factory work as a transitional stage between girlhood and marriage, Lowell assured them and their families that the company would strictly control the moral atmosphere so that the girls' reputations would remain spotless.

millwright A person who designs, builds, or repairs mills or mill machinery.
millrace The channel for the fast-moving stream of water that drives a mill wheel.

drinking habits also set them off, making them targets of discrimination.

Such discrimination and a desire to live among people who understood their ways and spoke their language brought new immigrants to neighborhoods where their countrymen had already found places to live. In New York, Philadelphia, and other cities, people with the same culture and religion built churches, stores, pubs or beer halls, and other familiar institutions that helped them cope with the shock of transplantation from Europe and gave them a chance to adapt gradually to life in the United States.

Because the new immigrants were poor, housing in their neighborhoods was often substandard, and living conditions were crowded, uncomfortable, and unsanitary. Lacking the resources to buy farms and the skills to enter professional trades, the fresh immigrants were the perfect workforce for the newly evolving industrial economy. As the flow of immigrants increased, the traditional labor shortage in America was replaced by a labor glut, and the social and economic status of all workers declined accordingly.

Living Conditions in Blue-Collar America

Working conditions for blue-collar workers in factories reflected the labor supply, the amount of capital available to the manufacturing company, and the personal philosophy of the factory owner. Girls at Lowell's factories described an environment of familiar paternalism. Factory managers and boardinghouse keepers supervised every aspect of their lives in much the same manner that authoritarian fathers saw to the details of life on traditional New England farms. As for the work itself, one mill girl commented that it was "not half so hard as . . . attending the dairy, washing, cleaning house, and cooking." What bothered factory workers most was the repetitive nature of the work and the resulting boredom. One Lowell employee described the tedium. "The time is often apt to drag heavily till the dinner hour arrives," she reported. "Perhaps some part of the work becomes deranged and stops; the constant friction causes a belt of leather to burst into a flame; a stranger visits the room, and scans the features and dress of its inmates inquiringly; and there is little else to break the monotony."

labor glut Oversupply of labor in relation to the number of jobs available.

blue-collar workers Workers who wear work clothes, such as coveralls and jeans, on the job; their work is likely to involve manual labor.

tenement An urban apartment house, usually with minimal facilities for sanitation, safety, and comfort.

She went on to note that daydreaming provided relief from the boredom, but daydreaming in front of fast-moving equipment could have disastrous consequences. Inattentive factory workers were likely to lose fingers, hands, or whole arms to whirring, pounding, slashing mechanisms. Not a few lost their lives. Investors vetoed any additional costs that safety devices might have incurred: Samuel Slater, for example, complained bitterly to his investors after a child was chewed up in a factory machine, "You call for yarn but think little about the means by which it is to be made."

Gradually Slater's and Lowell's well-meaning paternalism became rare as factory owners withdrew from overseeing day-to-day operations. The influx of laborers from the depressed countryside and of foreign immigrants wiped out both decent wages and the sorts of incentives the early manufacturing pioneers had employed. Not only did wages fall but laborers were also expected to find their own housing. Soon hulking tenements sprang up, replacing the open fields and clusters of small homes that once had dominated the urban landscape. Large houses formerly occupied by domestic manufacturers and their apprentices were broken up into tiny apartments by profit-hungry speculators who rented them to desperate laborers. In cities like New York, laborers lived fifty to a house in some working-class areas. As the population soared, sewage disposal, drinking water, and trash removal became difficult to provide. Life in such conditions was grossly unpleasant and extremely unhealthy: epidemics of typhus, cholera, and other crowd diseases swept through the slums regularly.

Investigating living and working conditions, a *New York Tribune* reporter found them deplorable. "The floor is made of rough plank laid loosely down, and the ceiling is not quite so high as a tall man," he reported of a tenement dwelling. "The walls are dark and damp and the miserable room is lighted only by a shallow sash partly projecting above the surface of the ground and by the light that struggles from the steep and rotting stairs." In this dark and tiny space, he observed, "often lives the man and his work bench, the wife, and five or six children of all ages; and perhaps a palsied grandfather and grandmother and often both. Here they work, here they cook, they eat, they sleep, they pray."

Life and Culture Among a New Middle Class

Large-scale manufacturing not only changed industrial work but also introduced demands for a new class of skilled managerial and clerical employees. Under the old system of manufacturing, the master craftsman or his wife had managed the company's accounts, hired journeymen and apprentices, purchased raw materials, and seen to the delivery of finished products. The size of the new factories made such direct

Living conditions for working people in America's new industrializing cities were often terrible, as this illustration of a working class tenement apartment makes clear. "The walls are dark and damp and the miserable room is lighted only by a shallow sash," a *New York Tribune* reporter observed. "Here they work, here they cook, they eat, they sleep, they pray."

contact between owners, workers, and products impossible. To fill the void, a new class of professionals came into being. In these days before the invention of the typewriter, firms such as Lowell's Boston Manufacturing Company employed teams of young men as clerks. These clerks kept accounts, wrote orders, and drafted correspondence, all in longhand. As elite owners such as Lowell and his partners became wrapped up in building new factories, pursuing investors, and entering new markets, both clerical and manufacturing employees were increasingly supervised by professional managers.

One distinguishing characteristic of the new white-collar workers was their relative youth. These young people, many of them the sons and daughters of rural farmers, had flocked to newly emerging cities in pursuit of formal education. They stayed to seek employment, leaving behind the economic instability and provincialism of the farm.

While middle-class men found employment as clerks, bookkeepers, and managers, middle-class women parlayed their formal education and their gender's perceived gift for nurturing children into work as teachers. It became acceptable for women to work as teachers for several years before marriage, and many avoided marriage altogether to pursue their hard-won careers.

Middle-class men and women tended to put off marriage as long as possible while they established themselves socially and economically. They also tended to have fewer children than their parents. In the new urban middle-class setting, parents felt compelled to send their children to school so that they could take their place on the career ladder chosen by their parents. Adding nothing to family income, children thus became economic liabilities rather than assets, and middle-class adults used a combination of late marriage and various forms of birth control to keep families small.

A lack of traditional ties affected the lives of both married and unmarried middle-class people. Many unmarried men and women seeking their fortunes in town boarded in private homes or rooming houses. After marriage, they often moved into private town homes, isolating themselves and their children from perceived dangers in the faceless city but also losing the comforting sociability of traditional country life. Accordingly, these young people crafted new urban structures that might provide the missing companionship and guidance. Many found companionship

□ **white-collar workers** Workers able to wear white shirts on the job because they do no grubby manual labor.

provincialism The limited and narrow perspective thought to be characteristic of people in rural areas.

Voluntary associations and fraternal organizations sprang up by the hundreds in the new urban America that was emerging in the 1830s and 1840s. These organizations provided companionship and, more important, a sense of order for the newwly emerging middle class. The Odd Fellows was one prominent example. Often these organizations used complex symbolism to convey core values. On the ceremonial axes shown here, the top image represents the admonition "Whatever the hand goes forth to do the heart should go forth in unison" and the three links in the lower image represent the values of Friendship, Love, and Truth.

Oddfellows Art & Antiques.

in **voluntary associations**. Students in colleges and universities formed a variety of discussion groups, preprofessional clubs, and benevolent societies. After graduation, groups such as the Odd Fellows and the Masons brought people together for companionship. Such organizations helped enforce traditional values through rigid membership standards stressing moral character, upright behavior, and, above all, order.

The *Odd Fellows' Manual* summarized the philosophy of these organizations well. "In the transaction of our business we pursue strict parliamentary rules, that our members may be qualified for any public stations to which they may be called by their fellow-citizens. . . . And when business has been performed, we indulge in social intercourse, and even in cheerful and innocent hilarity and amusement. But all in strict order and decorum, good fellowship and prudence are constantly to be kept in view." Young people also created and joined professional and trade groups. These associations served a social function, but they also became forums for training novices and for setting standards for professional methods and modes of conduct.

Members of the new middle class also used their organizing skills to press for reforms. While the elite class of factory owners and financiers generally formed the leadership for such organizations as the American Tract Society, the American Bible Society, and the American Board of Commissioners for Foreign Missions—each a multimillion-dollar reforming enterprise—young middle-class men and women provided the rank and file of charity workers.

In addition to their youth, another characteristic that prevailed among this newly forming class was deep anxiety. Although their education and skills earned them jobs with greater prestige than those of the average worker, these clerks and supervisors could be laid off or demoted to working-class status at any time. Also, because of the anonymity in the new cities, it was virtually impossible to know if a stranger was truly a member of one's own class or an imposter who might use the trappings of gentility to take advantage of the new urban scene. Such suspicions led to a very strict set of rules for making social connections.

Social Life for a Genteel Class

The changes in lifestyle that affected working-class and middle-class Americans were in large part an outcome of changes in the daily lives of those who owned and operated manufacturing businesses. In earlier years, when journeymen and apprentices had lived with master craftsmen, they were in effect members of a craftsman's extended family. Such working arrangements blurred the distinction between employee and employer. The factory system ended this relationship. The movement of workers out of the owners' homes permitted members of the emerging elite class to develop a **genteel** lifestyle that set them off from the

□ **voluntary association** An organization or club through which individuals engage in voluntary service, usually associated with charity or reform.

genteel The manner and style associated with elite classes, usually characterized by elegance, grace, and politeness.

army of factory workers and lesser number of clerks. Genteel families aimed at the complete separation of their private and public lives. Men in the manufacturing elite class spent their leisure time in new activities. Instead of drinking, eating, and playing with their employees, business owners began to socialize with one another in private clubs and in church and civic organizations. Instead of attending the popular theater, elite patrons began endowing opera companies and other highbrow forms of entertainment.

The lives of the factory owners' wives also changed. The mistress of a traditional manufacturing household had been responsible for important tasks in the operation of the business. Genteel women, in contrast, were expected to leave business dealings to men. Ensconced in private houses set apart from the new centers of production and marketing, genteel women found themselves with time on their hands. To give themselves something to do, they sought areas of activity that would provide focus and a sense of accomplishment without imperiling their elite status by involving them in what was now perceived as the crass, masculine world of commerce. Many found outlets for their creative energies in fancy needlework, reading, and art appreciation societies.

One activity that consumed genteel women was motherhood. Magazines and advice manuals, which began appearing during the 1820s and 1830s, rejected the traditional adage of "spare the rod, spoil the child," replacing it with an insistence on gentle nurturing. One leader in this movement was author and teacher Bronson Alcott. Alcott denied the concept of **infant depravity** that had so affected Puritan parents during the colonial era and led them to break their children's will, often through harsh measures. Instead, he stated emphatically that "the child must be treated as a free, self-guiding, self-controlling being." Alcott was equally emphatic that child rearing was the mother's responsibility. As his wife, Abigail, wrote of family management in Alcott's household, "Mr. A aids me in general principles, though nobody can aid me in the detail."

Books like Alcott's *Conversations with Children on the Gospels* (1836) flooded forth during these years and appealed greatly to isolated and underemployed women. Many adopted the advertised **cult of domesticity** completely. Turning inward, these women centered their lives on their homes and children. In doing so, they believed they were performing an important duty for God and country and fulfilling their most important, perhaps their only, natural calling.

Other genteel women agreed with the general tone of the domestic message but widened the woman's supposedly natural sphere outward, beyond the nursery, to encompass the whole world. Sarah Huntington Smith, for example, a member of Connecticut's elite, spoke for many when she complained in 1833, "To make and

receive visits, exchange friendly salutations, attend to one's wardrobe, cultivate a garden, read good and entertaining books, and even attend religious meetings for one's own enjoyment; all this does not satisfy me." Women like Smith banded together with like-minded women to get out into the world in order to reform it, involving themselves in a variety of reform movements, such as founding Sunday schools or opposing alcohol abuse. These causes let them use their nurturing and purifying talents to improve what appeared to be an increasingly chaotic and immoral society.

A NEW EMPIRE IN THE WEST

☆ Who generally were the first pioneers to move into the West? How did they and those who followed actually move westward and establish communities there?

☆ In what ways did the natural and cultural environment shape various societies that came to dominate in different regions in the West?

While life in the cotton South and manufacturing Northeast underwent radical change, the American West too was experiencing wholesale transformation. Enterprising capitalists often led the way in systematic exploration, looking for furs, gold, and other sources of quick profit. But it did not take long before a wide variety of others followed. Whether they expected a wasteland, a paradise, or something in between, what all of these newcomers to the West did find was a natural and cultural world that was much more complex than anything they had imagined.

Moving Westward

The image of the solitary trapper braving a hostile environment and even more hostile Indians is the stuff of American adventure novels and movies. Although characters like John "Liver Eating" Johnston really did exist, these men were merely advance agents for an **extractive industry** geared to the efficient removal of animal pelts.

What drew men like Johnston Meek into the Far West in the 1830s and 1840s was an innovation in the fur business instigated by long-time entrepreneur

infant depravity The idea that children are naturally sinful because they share in the original sin of the human race but have not learned the discipline to control their evil instincts.

◻ **cult of domesticity** The belief that women's proper role lies in domestic pursuits.

◻ **extractive industry** An industry, such as fur trapping, logging, or mining, that removes natural resources from the environment.

The mountain fur trade is a colorful part of the nation's history and folklore. While millionaire fur entrepreneurs like John Jacob Astor lived in luxury in eastern cities, trappers like Joe Meek (pictured here) occupied the wild and lawless territory of the upper Missouri River. Like many of his contemporaries, Meek survived his wilderness experiences to become an economic and political leader in the Far West when the fur business finally wound down in the 1840s.

William Henry Ashley. Taking advantage of the large numbers of underemployed young men seeking fortune and adventure in the West, Ashley broke the long tradition of depending exclusively on Indian labor for collecting furs. In 1825 he set up the highly successful rendezvous system. Under this arrangement, individual trappers—white adventurers like Johnston Meek, African Americans such as James Beckwourth, and a large number of Indians—combed the upper Missouri, trapping, curing, and packing furs. Once each year Ashley conducted a fur rendezvous in the mountains, where the trappers brought their furs and exchanged them for goods.

Often the first people to join the former fur trappers in settling the West were not rugged yeoman farmers but highly organized and well-financed land

□ **Joseph Smith Jr.** Founder of the Church of Jesus Christ of Latter-Day Saints, also known as the Mormon Church, who transcribed the Book of Mormon and led his congregation westward from New York to Illinois; he was later murdered by an anti-Mormon mob.

speculators and developers. From the earliest days of the republic, federal land policy favored those who could afford large purchases and pay in cash. Liberalization of the land laws during the first half of the nineteenth century put smaller tracts—for less money and on credit terms—within reach of more citizens, but speculators continued to play a role in land distribution by often offering even smaller tracts and more liberal credit. This was particularly true as states granted rights-of-way, first to canal companies and then, increasingly, to railroad developers as a way of financing internal improvements. Land along transportation routes was especially valuable, and developers could often turn an outright grant into enormous profits.

A third group of expectant fortune hunters was lured into the Far West by the same magnet that had drawn the Spanish to the American Southwest: gold. Since colonial times, Americans had persistently hunted precious metals, usually without much success. The promise of gold continued to draw people westward, however, onto Winnebago lands in 1827 and into Cherokee territory in 1829. Also even more mundane metals drew fortune seekers into the West. Industrialization called for iron, tin, and other minerals and the promise of profits from finding reliable deposits of ore made westward migration attractive. So, too, did the vast forests of the upper Midwest, lumber from which would go to build the nation.

Distinct waves of Americans pushed westward into the areas opened by loggers, miners, fur trappers, and land speculators. All of these migrants were responding to promises of abundant land in America's interior. But different groups were reacting to very different conditions in the East, and those differences gave shape to their migrations and to the settlements they eventually created.

"To make money was their chief object," one young pioneer woman in Texas commented; "all things else were subsidiary to it." Many were pushed by economic forces in the East. Throughout New England, for example, people facing persistent agricultural depressions had to choose between moving into cities or migrating westward. Others, however, saw the unsettled West as a refuge for establishing or expanding particular religious or social practices. Many Protestant sects sent battalions of settlers and missionaries to carve out new "Plymouth Colonies" in the West. The most notable of these religious pioneer groups was the Mormons.

This movement was founded in upstate New York in 1830 by Joseph Smith Jr. Announcing that he had experienced a revelation that called for him to establish a community in the wilderness, Smith led his congregation out of New York in 1831 to settle in the northeastern Ohio village of Kirtland. There the Mormons thrived for a while, stressing notions of community, faith, and hard work. But religious persecution eventually convinced Smith to lead

Pioneer Jesuit missionary Pierre Jean de Smet called the annual Rocky Mountain fur rendezvous "one of the most picturesque features of early frontier life in the Far West." This painting by Alfred Jacob Miller gives some sense of the scope of this event as encampments stretch all the way to the horizon. Miller attended the 1837 rendezvous in the entourage of Scottish adventurer William Drummond Stuart, just one of many celebrities who were drawn to the spectacle of this exciting and colorful, as well as extremely profitable, event.

his followers farther west into Missouri and then to the Illinois frontier, where they founded the city of Nauvoo in 1839. Continuing conversions to the new faith brought a flood of Mormons to Smith's Zion in Illinois. In 1844 Nauvoo, with a population of fifteen thousand, dwarfed every other Illinois city.

Despite their growth in numbers and prosperity, Smith's community in Nauvoo continued to be victims of religious and economic persecution. On June 27, 1844, Smith was murdered by a mob in neighboring Carthage, Illinois. The remaining church leaders concluded that the Mormons would never be safe until they moved far from mainstream American civilization. Brigham Young, Smith's successor, decided to search for a safe refuge beyond the Rocky Mountains and set off with sixteen hundred Mormons to the valley of the Great Salt Lake.

Whether they were hopeful cotton planters from the South or Yankee farmers from New England, most people went west not as the stalwart individualists immortalized by Western movies, but as part of a larger community. Beginning with early parties going to Ohio or Texas in the 1820s, most traveled in small to medium-size groups. Even those few who arrived alone seldom stayed that way. "Those of us who have no families of our own, reside with some of the families in the settlement," one young migrant observed. "We remain here notwithstanding the scarcity of provisions, to assist in protecting the settlement."

During the 1830s and 1840s, migrating parties became larger and more organized. It took six months to cross the more than 2,000 miles separating the settled part of the nation from the Oregon Country. Describing an Oregon-bound wagon train in the 1840s, one young woman reported that "Probably there were sixty-five or seventy, or possibly more than that, wagons in our train, and hundreds of loose cattle and horses." "We were not allowed to travel across the plains in any haphazard manner," she continued. "No family or individual was permitted to go off alone from the company." Among such groups on the Oregon Trail, life remained much as it had been at home. "Everybody was supposed to rise at daylight, and while the women were preparing breakfast, the men rounded up the cattle, took

▫ **Brigham Young** Mormon leader who took over in 1844 after Joseph Smith's death and guided the Mormons from Illinois to Utah, where they established a permanent home for the church.

▫ **Great Salt Lake** A shallow, salty lake in the Great Basin near which the Mormons established a permanent settlement in 1847.

▫ **Oregon Country** The region to the north of Spanish California extending from the crest of the Rocky Mountains to the Pacific Coast.

▫ **Oregon Trail** The overland route from St. Louis to the Pacific Northwest followed by thousands of settlers in the 1840s.

This fairly early daguerreotype captures an actual overland wagon party on the move in California. As was often the case, the women, dressed in long dresses and bonnets, stand by in safety while the men pilot the wagons through a narrow mountain pass.

by their own misfortune or mismanagement often settled wherever they could find a spread that seemed unoccupied. Thousands of squatters living on unsold federal lands were a problem for the national government when the time came to sell off the public domain. Always with an eye to winning votes, western politicians frequently advocated "squatter rights." Western congressmen finally maneuvered the passage of a **preemption bill** in 1841, allowing squatters to purchase the lands they occupied. Of course, this right did not guarantee that they would have the money or that they would make profitable use of the land. Thus shoestring farming, perpetual debt, and an uncertain future continued to challenge frontier farmers.

Pioneer Life in the New Cotton Country

Migrants to cotton country in the Mississippi Valley and beyond brought a particular lifestyle with them. Often starting out as landless herders, migrating families carved out claims beyond the **frontier line** and survived on a mixture of raised and gathered food until they could put the land into agricultural production. The Indians who preceded them in the Mississippi Valley unintentionally simplified life for these families, having already cleared large expanses of land for agriculture. Removal of the Indians to the Far West and the continuing devastation of Indian populations by disease meant that southern frontiersmen could plant corn and cotton quickly and reap early profits with minimal labor.

Although some areas were cleared and extremely fertile, others were swampy, rocky, and unproductive. In these less desirable locales, settlers were allowed to survey their own claims. The result was the re-creation of the southern class system in the new lands: those fortunate enough to get profitable plots might become great planters; those not so fortunate had to settle for lesser prosperity and lower status.

During the pioneer phase of southern frontier life, all the members of migrating families devoted most of their time to the various tasks necessary to keep the family alive. Even their social and recreational lives tended to center on practical tasks. House building, planting, and harvesting were often done in cooperation with neighbors. On such occasions participants consumed plenty of food and homemade whiskey, and at day's end, music and dancing often lasted long into the night. Women gathered together separately for large-scale projects such as group quilting. Another community event for southwestern settlers was

down the tents, yoked the oxen to the wagons and made everything ready for an immediate start after the morning meal was finished." Even social customs remained the same. "Life on the plains was a primitive edition of life in town or village," the same pioneer woman remarked.

One other thing most pioneers had in common was that hard cash was always in short supply. Frontier farmers in every region of the West lived on a shoestring, barely making ends meet when conditions were good and falling into debt when weather or other hazards interrupted farming. Still, those who were lucky and exercised careful management were able to carve out excellent livings. Many, however, had to sell out to satisfy creditors or saw their land confiscated for debts. Pulling up stakes again, they often moved to new lands exhausted of furs and opened to settlement by merchant-adventurers and Indian agents.

Many pioneers had no legal claim to their lands. People bankrupted by unscrupulous speculators or

□ **preemption bill** A temporary law that gave squatters the right to buy land they had settled on before it was offered for sale at public auction.

frontier line The outer limit of agricultural settlement bordering on areas still under Indian control or unoccupied.

Although modern movies and traditional folklore portray early Texas as a barely settled cowboy frontier, the region actually was attractive because vast areas in its eastern and central regions could support large-scale cotton, sugar, and other lucrative plantation businesses. This painting from 1845 captures the more genteel side of Texas life during the pioneer era.

the periodic religious revival, which brought people from miles around to revival meetings that might last for days. Here they could make new acquaintances, court sweethearts, and discuss the common failings in their souls and on their farms.

Life Among Westering Yankees

For migrants to areas such as Michigan and Oregon, the overall frontier experience differed in many respects from that in the Mississippi Valley. In the Old Northwest, Indians had also cleared the land for planting; pioneers snatched up the Indians' deserted farms. Here, however, professional surveyors had already carved the land into neat rectangular lots. These surveys generally included provision for a township, where settlers quickly established villages similar to those left behind in New England. Here they re-created the social institutions they already knew and respected—first and foremost, law courts, churches, and schools.

Conditions in the Oregon Country resembled those farther east in most respects, but some significant differences did exist. Most important, the Indians in the Oregon Country had never practiced agriculture—their environment was so rich in fish, meat, and wild vegetables that farming was unnecessary—and they still occupied their traditional homelands and outnumbered whites significantly. Although both of these facts might have had a profound impact on life in Oregon, early pioneers were bothered by neither. Large open prairies flanking the Columbia, Willamette, and other rivers provided abundant fertile farmland. And the Indians helped rather than hindered the pioneers.

Like their southwestern counterparts, pioneers in both the Old and the Pacific Northwest cooperated in house building, annual planting and harvesting, and other big jobs, but a more sober air prevailed at these gatherings among the descendants of New England Puritans. Religious life was also more solemn. Religious revivals swept through Yankee settlements during the 1830s and 1840s, but the revival meetings tended to be held in churches at the center of communities rather than in outlying campgrounds. As a result, they were usually briefer and less emotional than their counterparts on the cotton frontier and strongly reinforced the Yankee notion of village solidarity.

The Hispanic Southwest

In addition to a physical environment very different from that in the Pacific Northwest, the Southwest bore the lasting cultural imprint of Spain's and then Mexico's control of the region.

Using Indian labor, Franciscan missionaries transformed the dry California coastal hill country into a blooming garden and built a long string of missions in which to celebrate their religion. This painting of Mission San Gabriel conveys the beauty and the awesome size of these mission establishments.

Although Spain could assert a claim extending back to the mid-1500s, systematic Spanish exploration into most of the American Southwest did not begin until the eighteenth century. In California, for example, Russian expansion into the Oregon region prompted the Spanish to begin moving northward; garrisons were established at San Diego and Monterey in 1769 and 1770. Junípero Serra, a Franciscan friar, accompanied this expedition and established a mission, San Diego de Alcalá, near the present city of San Diego. Eventually Serra and his successors established twenty-one missions extending from San Diego to the town of Sonoma, north of San Francisco.

The mission system provided a framework for Spanish settlement in California. Established in terrain that resembled the hills of Spain, the missions were soon surrounded by groves, vineyards, and lush farms. California Indians were exploited to provide the labor needed to create this new landscape: the missionaries often forced them into the missions, where they became virtual slaves. The death rate from disease and harsh treatment among the mission Indians was terrible, but their labor turned California's coastal plain into a vast and productive garden.

The Franciscans continued to control the most fertile and valuable lands in California until after Mexico won independence from Spain. Between 1834 and 1840, however, the Mexican government seized the mission lands in California and sold them off to private citizens living in the region. An elite class of Spanish-speaking Californios snatched up the rich lands.

At first, the Californios welcomed outsiders as neighbors and trading partners. Ships from the United States called at California ports regularly, picking up cargoes of beef tallow, cow hides, and other commodities to be shipped around the world, and settlers who promised to open new lands and businesses were given generous grants and assistance. John Sutter, for example, received an outright grant of land extending from the Sierra foothills southwest to the Sacramento Valley, where in 1839 he established a colony called New Helvetia, eventually a thriving cosmopolitan center.

A similar pattern of cosmopolitan cooperation existed in other Spanish North American provinces. In 1821 trader William Becknell began selling and trading goods along the Santa Fe Trail from St. Louis to New Mexico. By 1824, the business had become

◻ **Junípero Serra** Spanish missionary who went to California in 1769; he and his successors established near the California coast a chain of missions that depended on Indian labor.

◻ **Californios** Spanish colonists in California in the eighteenth and nineteenth centuries.

tallow Hard fat obtained from the bodies of cattle and other animals and used to make candles and soap.

◻ **John Sutter** Swiss immigrant who founded a colony in California.

In the Wider World

so profitable that people from all over the frontier moved in to create a permanent Santa Fe trade. As had taken place in St. Louis, an elite class emerged in Santa Fe from the intermingled fortunes and intermarriages among Indian, European, and American populations, and a strong kinship system developed. Thus, based on kinship, the Hispanic leaders of New Mexico consistently worked across cultural lines, whether to fight off Texan aggression or eventually to lobby for annexation to the United States.

Intercultural cooperation also characterized the early history of Texas settlement. Spanish and then Mexican officials aided the empresarios, hoping that the aggressive Americans would form a frontier line between southern Plains Indians and prosperous silver-mining communities south of the Rio Bravo. Tensions rose, however, as population increased. Despite the best efforts of the Mexican government to encourage Hispanics to settle in Texas, fully four-fifths of the thirty-five hundred land titles perfected by the empresarios went to non-Hispanics. Cultural insensitivity and misunderstanding created disharmony between Texians and Tejanos and each tended to cling to their own ways.

Tying the West to the Nation

Rapid expansion created an increased demand for reliable transportation and communications between the new regions in the West and the rest of the nation. An early first step in meeting this demand was building the so-called National Road, which between 1815 and 1820 snaked its way across the Cumberland Gap in the Appalachian Mountains and wound from the Atlantic shore to the Ohio River at Wheeling, Virginia. By 1838 this state-of-the-art highway—with its evenly graded surface, gravel pavement, and stone

bridges—had been pushed all the way to Vandalia, Illinois. Within a few more years, it reached St. Louis, the great jumping-off point for the Far West.

At the same time, a series of other roads was beginning to merge into a transportation network. The so-called Military Road connecting Nashville to New Orleans also earned federal funding, as did the Nashville Road that, in turn, connected Nashville to Knoxville, where a traveler could pick up the Great Valley Road to Lynchburg, Virginia, and from there the Valley Turnpike, which connected with the Cumberland Road. Eventually towns from Portland, Maine, to Saint Augustine, Florida, and from Natchez, Mississippi, to New Haven, Connecticut, were linked by intersecting highways (see Map 11.1). Increasing numbers of people used these new roads to head west looking for new opportunities. Farmers, craftsmen, fur hunters, and others already settled in the West used them too, moving small loads of goods to the nearby towns and small cities that always sprang up along the unfolding transportation routes. And these networks made it possible for Jarena Lee to perform her miraculous feat of traveling thousands of miles a year. But the new roads did little to advance large-scale commerce. Heavy and bulky products were too expensive to move:

annexation The incorporation of a territory into an existing political unit such as a neighboring country.

Rio Bravo The Spanish and then Mexican name for the river that now forms the border between Texas and Mexico; the Rio Grande.

Texians Non-Hispanic settlers in Texas in the nineteenth century.

Tejanos Mexican settlers in Texas in the nineteenth century.

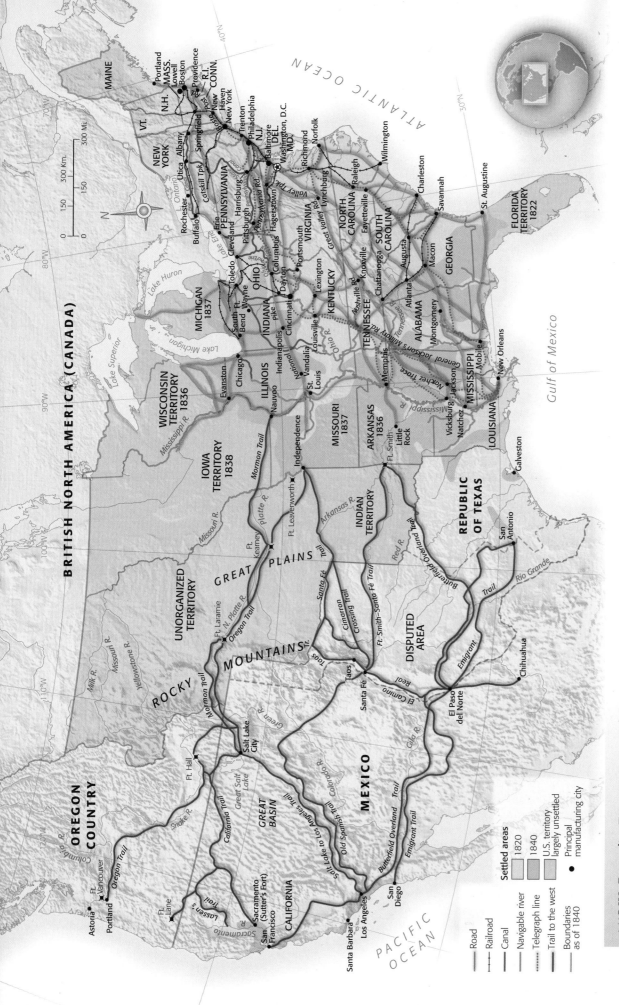

MAP 11.1 Expanding Transportation and Communications to 1850

As settlers followed a web of wagon trails into the Far West, the already settled portion of the nation was experiencing a transportation and communications revolution between 1820 and 1850. Roads, canals, rails, and telegraph lines reached out to bind the nation together. The connections made by the lines of communications shown here ensured economic growth but brought to light the vast differences between regional cultures.

© Cengage Learning.

Surprisingly enough, the first steam locomotive manufactured in the United States did not go into service in the rapidly modernizing Northeast but rather in the equally, though differently, modernizing South. The *Best Friend of Charleston* was commissioned by the Charleston and Hamburg Railroad to haul cotton and other bulky freight as well as passengers in South Carolina.

Picture Research Consultants & Archives.

at a minimum, hauling a ton of freight along the nation's roads cost 15 cents a mile. At that rate, the cost of shipping a ton of oats from Buffalo to New York City amounted to twelve times the value of the cargo.

But the new roads also linked rural America to an ever-expanding network of waterways that made relatively inexpensive long-distance hauling possible. Completed in 1825, the Erie Canal revolutionized shipping: the cost of transporting a ton of oats from Buffalo to Albany fell from $100 to $15, and the transit time dropped from twenty days to just eight. The spectacular success of the Erie Canal prompted businessmen, farmers, and politicians throughout the country to promote canal building. State governments offered exclusive charters to canal-building companies, giving them direct financial grants, guaranteeing their credit, and easing their way in every possible manner. The result was an explosion in canal building that lasted through the 1830s (see Map 11.1).

This new mobility did not come cheaply. Canals cost as much as $20,000 to $30,000 a mile to build, and financing was always a problem. Hoping for large profits, entrepreneurs invested heavily in canal building. Before 1836, careful investors could make a 15 to 20 percent return on capital in canal building, but after that, most canal companies faced bankruptcy, as did the states that had helped finance them.

Steam power took canal building's impact on inland transportation a revolutionary step further. After Henry Shreve's pioneer voyage in 1816 (see page 230), the cost of shipping a ton of goods down American rivers fell annually. By 1840, the price had declined from an average of 1¼ cents a mile to less than half a cent, and the cost of upstream transport from over 10 cents a mile to less than a cent. In addition, steamboats could carry bulky and heavy objects that could not be hauled upstream for any price by any other means. The impact of steam technology on

the economies of the South and West was staggering. The presence of dependable transportation on the Mississippi drew cotton cultivation farther into the nation's interior, western farmers flooded into the Ohio Valley, and fur trappers and traders pressed up the Missouri River.

Steam technology also began to have applications for towns lacking water routes to the interior. As they began losing inland trade revenue to canal towns such as Albany and Philadelphia, entrepreneurs in places like Baltimore looked for other ways to move cargo. Demands from Baltimore merchants spurred Maryland to take the lead in developing a new transportation technology: the steam railroad. In 1828 the state chartered the **Baltimore and Ohio Railroad** (B&O). The B&O soon demonstrated its potential when inventor Peter Cooper's steam locomotive *Tom Thumb* sped 13 miles along B&O track. South Carolina also invested in steam technology and chartered a 136-mile rail line from Charleston to Hamburg. Here, the first full-size American-built locomotive, the *Best Friend of Charleston*, successfully pulled cars until the engine exploded, taking much of the train and many of its passengers with it. The Charleston and Hamburg Railroad, however, had the engine rebuilt and began experimenting with making trains safer. Massachusetts followed this practice as well as it tried to siphon off trade from New York by building a railroad from Boston to Albany.

Although rail transport enjoyed some success during this early period, it could not rival water-based transportation systems. By 1850 individual companies

□ **Baltimore and Ohio Railroad** First steam railroad commissioned in the United States.

had laid approximately 9,000 miles of track, but not in any coherent network. Rails were laid with little or no standardization of track size, and as a result, railcars could not be transferred from one company's line to another's. Other problems plagued the fledgling industry. Boiler explosions, fires, and derailments were common because pressure regulators, spark arresters, and brakes were inadequate. And in state capitals, investors who hoped to profit from canals, roads, and steam shipping lobbied to prevent legislatures from supporting rail expansion.

Distance impaired not only American commerce but also the conduct of the republic itself. Since the nation's founding, American leaders had expressed the fear that the continent's sheer size would make true federal democracy impractical. Voting returns, economic data, and other information crucial to running a republic seemed to take an impossibly long time to circulate, and the problem promised to get worse as the nation grew. During the 1790s, for example, it took a week for news to travel from Virginia to New York City and three weeks for a letter to get from Cincinnati to the Atlantic coast. The transportation revolution, however, made quite a difference in how quickly news got around. After the Erie Canal opened, letters posted in Buffalo could reach New York City within six days and might get to New Orleans within two weeks.

circulation The number of copies of a publication sold or distributed.

◻ **electric telegraph** Device invented by Samuel F. B. Morse in 1836 that transmits coded messages along a wire over long distances; the first electronic communications device.

As the nation expanded, and as economics and social life became more complicated, Americans felt growing pressure to keep up with news from across the nation and its new territories. Transportation improvements helped them do so by moving printed matter faster and more cheaply. At the same time, revolutions in printing technology and paper production significantly lowered the cost of printing and speeded up production. Organizations such as the American Bible Society and the American Tract Society joined newspaper and magazine publishers in producing a flood of printed material. In 1790 the 92 newspapers being published in America had a total **circulation** of around 4 million. By 1835 the number of periodicals had risen to 1,258, and circulation had surpassed 90 million.

The explosion in the volume and velocity of communications was enhanced by an even greater revolution in information technology that was in its starting phases. In the mid-1830s, Samuel F. B. Morse began experimenting with the world's first form of electronic communication: the **electric telegraph**. Morse developed a code consisting of dots (short pulses) and dashes (longer pulses) that represented letters of the alphabet. With this device, a skilled operator could quickly key out long messages and send them at nearly the speed of light. Over the next several years, Morse worked on improvements to extend the distance that the impulses would travel along the wires. Finally, in 1843, Congress agreed to finance an experimental telegraph line from Washington, D.C., to Baltimore. Morse sent his first message on the experimental line on May 24, 1844. His message, "What hath God wrought!" was a fitting opening line for the telecommunications revolution.

Individual Voices

JARENA LEE
My Call to Preach the Gospel

Some four or five years after having a "sanctification" experience with the disembodied voice of the holy spirit, Jarena Lee had another supernatural encounter: "there seemed to sound a voice which I thought I distinctly heard, and most certainly understand, which said to me, 'Go preach the Gospel.'" Two days later, she resolved to go see Reverend Richard Allen of the African Methodist Episcopal Church to tell him "I felt it my duty to preach the gospel." In the excerpt that follows, written many years after the event, she explains what happened and her thoughts about it.

Library of Congress.

---

1 In Lee's way of thinking, what is it that justifies a person to serve as a preacher? What, exactly, is she accusing her critics of doing in advocating "not a whole Saviour"?

2 What is she implying in saying that the original meaning of the term *preach* may have been different from what "it is now *made* to mean"? How does this relate to her earlier warning about being careful in applying "our by-laws of church government and discipline"?

3 How does she here twist the argument that critics leveled against women preaching to her own advantage? What possible defense could a Christian man make against this argument?

I now told him, that the Lord had revealed it to me, that [I] must preach the gospel. He replied, by asking, in what sphere I wished to move in? I said, among the Methodists.... But as to women preaching, he said that our Discipline knew nothing at all about it—that it did not call for women preachers....

O how careful ought we to be, lest through our by-laws of church government and discipline, we bring into disrepute even the word of life. For as unseemly as it may appear now-a-days for a woman to preach, it should be remembered that nothing is impossible with God....

If the man may preach, because the Saviour died for him, why not the woman? seeing he died for her also. Is he not a whole Saviour, instead of a half one? as those who hold it wrong for a woman to preach, would seem to make it appear. **1**

Did not Mary *first* preach the risen Saviour, and is not the doctrine of the resurrection the very climax of Christianity—hangs not all our hope on this, as argued by St. Paul? Then did not Mary, a woman, preach the gospel? for she preached the resurrection of the crucified Son of God.

But some will say that Mary did not expound the Scripture, therefore, she did not preach, in the proper sense of the term. To this I reply, it may be that the term *preach* in those primitive times, did not mean exactly what it is now *made* to mean; perhaps it was a great deal more simple then, than it is now—if it were not, the unlearned fishermen could not have preached the gospel at all, as they had no learning. **2**

To this it may be replied, by those who are determined not to believe that it is right for a woman to preach, that the disciples, though they were fishermen and ignorant of letters too, were inspired so to do.... If then, to preach the gospel, by the gift of heaven, comes by inspiration solely, is God straitened; must he take the man exclusively? May he not, did he not, and can he not inspire a female to preach the simple story of the birth, life, death, and resurrection of our Lord, and accompany it too with power to the sinner's heart. As for me, I am fully persuaded that the Lord called me to labor according to what I have received, in his vineyard. If he has not, how could he consistently bear testimony in favor of my poor labors, in awakening and converting sinners? **3**

Study Tools

SUMMARY

Although seemingly the most old-fashioned region of the country, the South that emerged during the years leading up to 1840 was a profoundly different place from what it had been before the War of 1812. As an industrial revolution overturned the economies in Great Britain and the American Northeast, economic options for southerners also changed radically. Although elite southerners clothed their new society in romanticized garb, they were creating an altogether new kind of economy and society. The efficient production of cotton by the newly reorganized South was an essential aspect of the emerging national market economy.

Change in the North was more obvious, as factories replaced craft shops and cities replaced towns. The new economy and new technology created wonderful new opportunities but also imposed serious constraints. A revamped social structure replaced the traditional order as unskilled and semiskilled workers, a new class of clerks, and the genteel elite carved out new lives. As in the South, the outcome was a remarkable transformation in the lives of everyone in the region.

Meanwhile, the westward movement of Americans steadily gained momentum. Some successful entrepreneurs such as William Henry Ashley made enormous profits from their fur-trading empires. Land speculators and gold seekers, too, helped open areas to settlement. Such pioneers were usually followed by distinct waves of migrants who went west in search of land and opportunity. In Texas, Oregon, California, and elsewhere in the West, communities sprang up like weeds. Here they interacted—and often clashed—with one another, with those who had prior claims to the land, and with the land itself. As a result, a variety of cultures and economies developed in the expansive section of the country.

Tying the regions together, a new network of roads, waterways, and communications systems accelerated the process of change. After 1840, it was possible to ship goods from any one section of the country to any other, and people in all sections were learning more about conditions in far distant parts of the growing nation. Often this new information promised prosperity, but it also made more and more people aware of the enormity of the transformation taking place and the glaring differences between regions. The twin outcomes would be greater integration in the national economy and increasing tension between mutually dependent participants in the new marketplace.

CHRONOLOGY
The Dawn of Modernization

1821	William Becknell opens Santa Fe Trail to American traders
1822	John H. Hall perfects interchangeable parts for gun manufacturing
1828	Baltimore and Ohio Railroad commissioned
1830	Church of Latter-Day Saints (Mormons) founded in New York
1830–1840	Ten-year immigration figure for United States exceeds 500,000
1835	Number of U.S. periodicals exceeds 1,250, with combined circulation of 90 million
1836	Samuel F. B. Morse invents electric telegraph
Bronson Alcott's *Conversations with Children on the Gospels*
1838	National Road completed to Vandalia, Illinois
First mass-produced brass clock
1839	John Sutter founds New Helvetia
Mormons build Nauvoo, Illinois
1841	Congress passes preemption bill
1844	Murder of Joseph Smith

Study Tools

FOCUS QUESTIONS

If you have mastered this chapter, you should be able to answer these questions and to explain the terms that follow the questions.

1. Why did living conditions for southerners—black and white—change after 1820?

2. How did elite white southerners respond to the change? How did their response affect slaves, free blacks, and poor whites?

3. How did manufacturing and the nature of work change in the United States after 1820?

4. In what ways did the American system of manufacturing change the traditional pattern of U.S. foreign trade?

5. How did the developing factory system affect the lives of artisans, factory owners, and middle-class Americans?

6. Who generally were the first pioneers to move into the West? How did they and those who followed actually move westward and establish communities there?

7. In what ways did the natural and cultural environment shape various societies that came to dominate in different regions in the West?

KEY TERMS

Cotton Belt   *p. 255*

slave codes   *p. 257*

putting-out system   *p. 261*

interchangeable parts   *p. 262*

blue-collar workers   *p. 264*

white-collar workers   *p. 265*

voluntary association   *p. 266*

cult of domesticity   *p. 267*

extractive industry   *p. 267*

Joseph Smith Jr.   *p. 268*

Brigham Young   *p. 269*

Great Salt Lake   *p. 269*

Oregon Country   *p. 269*

Oregon Trail   *p. 269*

preemption bill   *p. 270*

Junípero Serra   *p. 272*

Californios   *p. 272*

John Sutter   *p. 272*

Baltimore and Ohio Railroad   *p. 275*

electric telegraph   *p. 276*

SUGGESTED RESOURCES

California Missions Resource Site. http://www.missionscalifornia .com. An extremely rich collection of information concerning virtually every aspect of the mission system in California.

National Park Service. Santa Fe National Historic Trail, http:// www.nps.gov/safe/index.htm. A very rich site, especially the "History & Culture" and "Photos and Multimedia" sections.

National Park Service. "When Rice Was King," http://www.nps .gov/nr/twhp/wwwlps/lessons/3rice/3rice.htm. Explores another major plantation system in the American South: rice cultivation. Very rich with resources.

Oracle Thinkquest. "Oregon Trail," http://library.thinkquest .org/CR0210182. A hands-on site that covers multiple aspects of the wagon train experience; also includes a long list of references for further exploration.

Public Broadcasting System. "Africans in America: Conditions of Antebellum Slavery, 1830–1860," http://www.pbs.org/wgbh/ aia/part4/4p2956.html. An excellent overview of changing conditions for slaves during this era with a number of associated primary sources and historical essays.

Deborah L. Ziel. "Childhood Disease and Malnutrition on the Plantations of the American Antebellum South: A What Came First? Conundrum," http://www.academia.edu/ 1788392/Childhood_Disease_and_Malnutrition_on_the_ Plantations_of_the_American_Antebellum_South_A_What_ Came_First_Conundrum. A scholarly article tracing the connections between childhood diet and other conditions among slaves and the prevalence of disease; technical but fascinating.

Responses to Expansion and Change, 1828–1848

INDIVIDUAL CHOICES

Elizabeth Cady Stanton

Elizabeth Cady Stanton was, from her earliest childhood, a person of privilege. Born into a prominent New York family, she had an extended kin group of distinguished relatives and enjoyed great personal freedom. Like the male members of her family, she took a full academic course at the local academy that included Latin, Greek, mathematics, religion, science, French, and writing. She also read the law and debated with the clerks in her father's practice. She clearly was an unusually accomplished young woman by the time she graduated at the age of 16. It was then, however, that she realized that her freedoms were not as extensive as she

thought: like her older brother and many of her class-mates, she aspired to attend Union College but was refused admission because she was female. Undeterred, she chose to continue her education by attending Emma Willard's Troy Female Seminary, one of America's pioneering women's educational institutions.

In 1840 she married journalist Henry Brewster Stanton and

Bettmann/Corbis.

embarked on a honeymoon trip to London. Two things happened on that trip that forever altered Elizabeth's life. First, while she was there, London was site of the first World Anti-Slavery Convention, which her activist husband attended but from which she was barred on account of her gender. That, however, led to the second significant event: ushered into a curtained-off area reserved for women, she met **Lucretia Mott**, who had also been refused entry. Shortly thereafter, America's most prominent abolitionist, **William Lloyd Garrison**, arrived at the convention and, upon learning that the women had been segregated from the proceedings, he joined Stanton and Mott in the women's area. The three of them became lifetime friends.

After returning from London, Henry Stanton began to study law, joining the Massachusetts bar in 1843, and in 1847 the couple moved to Seneca Falls, New York. There, cut off from the cosmopolitan social world of Boston, Elizabeth, who already had three sons, became a homemaker. She later wrote:

> The general discontent I felt with woman's portion as wife, housekeeper, physician, and spiritual guide, the chaotic conditions into which everything fell without her constant supervision, and the wearied, anxious look of the majority of women, impressed me with a strong feeling that some active measures should be taken to remedy the wrongs of society in general, and of women in particular.

Calling upon her friends Mott and Garrison and the extended circle of reformers who surrounded them, Stanton resolved to hold a women's rights convention in Seneca Falls. In 1848, over three hundred people converged there on July 19 and 20 to discuss conditions for women in the United States. When it was all over, Stanton presented a "Declaration of Sentiments" (see the Individual Voices feature at the end of this chapter) laying out all the disabilities that society imposed on women and calling for immediate redress. All of the proposals she made were approved by the convention, though it was to be more than seventy years before one of the key provisions became reality: women's right to vote.

Elizabeth Cady Stanton reflected many of the forces that were shaping America in the years before midcentury. These were years of both growing anxiety and growing hopefulness. Anxiety was rising over the industrialization and urbanization that was sweeping across the American North and over the expansion of cotton capitalism in the American South. Cady Stanton shared with born-again Christians, transcendentalists, socialists, and other communitarians a belief in human perfectibility that drove them all into a frenzy of work and experimentation. In northern cities, on southern plantations, and at western revival meetings, members of all social classes were crafting cultural expressions designed to give meaning to their lives and lend shape to a society that seemed to be losing all direction. At the same time, ambitious politicians were re-creating the art of politics in line with new economic and cultural imperatives. A new, modern, and much more complicated America clearly was in the making.

And looming over it all was the promise and the challenge of the American West. For many, the West offered a destination for those who sought wealth or free expression. For others, the region provided an arena in which to contest economic and political issues facing the nation at large. Most agreed that the nation's destiny lay in the largely unexplored region, but exactly how this destiny was to unfold remained murky and divided loyalties at every level of society.

◻ **Lucretia Mott** Quaker minister who founded the Philadelphia Female Anti-Slavery Society (1833) and co-organized the Seneca Falls Women's Rights Convention in 1848.

◻ **William Lloyd Garrison** Abolitionist leader who founded and published *The Liberator,* an antislavery newspaper.

☆ *How did developments in American arts and letters reflect the spirit of change during the Jacksonian era?*

☆ *To what extent did international forces influence American cultural expressions?*

As industrialization and urbanization mushroomed in the Northeast, cotton cultivation and its peculiar cultural and labor systems expanded across the South, and hundreds of communities grew up in the West. At the same time, however, increasing economic interdependence between regions and revolutionary transportation and communications systems pulled the geographically expansive nation closer together. These opposing forces helped define not only the social and political tendencies throughout the country but also the trends that would shape a distinctive American culture.

Romanticism and Genteel Culture

Underlying the new mood in American culture was an artistic and philosophical attitude that swept across the Atlantic and found a fertile new home in North America. Romanticism stressed the heart over the mind, the wild over the controlled, the mystical over the rational. The United States, with its millions of acres of wilderness, was the perfect setting for Romanticism to flower.

This new influence had its earliest impact in the religious realm. Reeling under the shock of social change that was affecting every aspect of life, many young people sought a religious anchor to engender some stability. Many, especially in the rising cities in the Northeast, found a voice in New Englander Ralph Waldo Emerson.

Pastor of the prestigious Second Unitarian Church in Boston, Emerson experienced a religious crisis in 1831 when his young wife, Ellen Louisa, died. Looking

▢ **romanticism** Artistic and intellectual movement characterized by interest in nature, emphasis on emotion and imagination over rationality, and rebellion against social conventions.

▢ **Ralph Waldo Emerson** Philosopher, writer, and poet whose essays and poems made him a central figure in the transcendentalist movement and an important figure in the development of literary expression in the United States.

▢ **transcendentalism** A philosophical and literary movement asserting that God exists within human beings and in nature, and that intuition is the highest source of knowledge, opening the way to the *transcendent*—that which lies beyond the range of normal experience.

▢ **Henry David Thoreau** Writer and naturalist and friend of Ralph Waldo Emerson; his best-known work is *Walden* (1854).

for new inspiration, he traveled to Europe where he met the famous Romantic writers William Wordsworth and Thomas Carlyle, who influenced him to seek truth in nature and spirit rather than in rationality and order. Emerson combined this Romantic influence with his already strong Unitarian leaning to create a new philosophical creed called transcendentalism. He returned to the United States to begin a career as an essayist and lecturer, spreading the transcendentalist message.

"Historical Christianity has fallen into the error that corrupts all attempts to communicate religion," Emerson told the students at the Harvard Divinity School in 1838. "Men have come to speak of revelation as somewhat long ago given and done, as if God were dead." But for Emerson, God was "everywhere active, in each ray of the star, in each wavelet of the pool." Only through direct contact with the transcendent power in the universe could men and women know the truth.

Emerson's writings were in tune with the cultural and economic currents of his day. In celebrating the individual, Emerson validated the surging individualism of Jacksonian America. In addition, because each person had to find his or her own path to knowledge, Emerson could extol many of the disturbing aspects of modernizing America as potentially liberating forces. Rather than condemning the money grubbing that many said characterized Jacksonian America, Emerson stated that money represented the "prose of life" and was, "in its effects and laws, as beautiful as roses."

Emerson not only set the tone for American philosophical inquiry but also suggested a bold new direction for American literature. His 1837 address at Harvard University entitled "The American Scholar" was a declaration of literary independence from European models. Young American writers responded enthusiastically. During the twenty years following this speech, Henry David Thoreau, Walt Whitman, Henry Wadsworth Longfellow, and other writers and poets elaborated the nationalistic and transcendentalist gospels, emphasizing the uniqueness of the individual and the role of literature as a vehicle for self-discovery: "I celebrate myself, and sing myself," Whitman wrote. They also carried the Romantic message, celebrating the primitive and the common. Longfellow sang the praise of the village blacksmith, and in "I Hear America Singing," Whitman conveyed the poetry present in the everyday speech of America's common folk.

Perhaps the most radical of the transcendentalists was Emerson's good friend and frequent houseguest Henry David Thoreau. Emerson and his other followers made the case for self-reliance, but Thoreau embodied it, camping on the shore of Walden Pond near Concord, Massachusetts, where he did his best to live independent of the rapidly modernizing market economy. "I went to the woods because I wished to live deliberately," Thoreau wrote, "and not, when I came to die, discover that I had not lived."

Popular Media and the Question of Moral Decency

During the 1830s and 1840s, literacy for both men and women expanded enormously: at the time the Constitution was ratified only about 60 percent of white Americans could read, but by 1850 that number was closer to 80 percent and rising rapidly. Entrepreneurial publishers rushed to capitalize on this growing potential market, and a flood of new books, magazines, newspapers, and publications of all kinds entered the marketplace. As exciting as this may have seemed, many greeted this change with dread. The American Tract Society, one of the foremost Christian publishers in the era, warned that "This misnamed 'literature' had demoralized thousands of the unsuspecting, and is known to have been the occasion of ruin to many of both sexes by its polluting pages." Interestingly, however, the society did not call for government or other legal censorship of this "licentious" material. Instead, it proposed to flood the marketplace with uplifting literature at either extremely inexpensive cost or, often, at no cost at all, and let market forces do their work. Consequentially at a time when advocates for public decency were on the rise and highly influential, Americans avoided the temptation of resorting to any sort of official censorship where popular literature was concerned, a situation that has continued more or less consistently ever since.

- Why might groups like the American Tract Society have been suspicious of mass literacy and the flood of popular literature into the American market?
- How do modern critics of such popular media as the Internet propose to deal with perceived "debasing" material? How effective do you think the American Tract Society's strategy might be today?

Among women who were seeking meaning through their writing, Margaret Fuller was the leading transcendentalist. After demonstrating her own equality by editing the transcendentalist magazine *The Dial* as well as serving as chief literary critic for the *New York Tribune*, Fuller advocated for women's rights in her *Woman in the Nineteenth Century* (1845).

But the most popular women writers of the day were those who were most successful at communicating the sentimentalized role for the new genteel woman. Lydia Sigourney was one of the first American women to carve out an independent living as a writer. Catharine Beecher was another writer who enjoyed enormous success for her practical advice guides aimed at making women more effective homemakers. The novels of female writers such as Susan Warner were among the most popular books published in the first half of the nineteenth century.

Other authors joined Sigourney and Warner in pushing American literature in Romantic directions. James Fenimore Cooper helped to popularize American themes and scenes. Even before Emerson's "American Scholar," Cooper had launched a new sort of American novel and hero. Cooper's *The Pioneers* (1823) was the first of five novels featuring Natty Bumppo, a frontiersman whose rough-hewn virtues were beloved by Romantics and popularly associated with the American frontier.

George Bancroft did for American history what novelists like Cooper did for American literature. Bancroft set out in 1834 to capture the history of the United States from its first settlement, a story that eventually filled ten volumes when he completed it in 1874. Focusing on strong leaders who carried out God's design by bringing liberty into the world, Bancroft made clear that the Jacksonian qualities of individualism, self-sufficiency, and a passionate love of liberty were the essence of the American character. Bancroft's history became the definitive work of its kind, influencing generations of American students and scholars in their interpretations of the nation's past.

The drive to celebrate American scenes and the young nation's uniqueness also influenced the visual arts during this period. Neoclassicism, which emphasized the simple, logical lines found in Greek and Roman art, dominated the art scene at first. After 1825, however, classical scenes were gradually being replaced by American ones. Englishman Thomas Cole came to the United States in 1818 hoping to find a romantic paradise. Cole was disappointed by the neoclassical art scene in Philadelphia, but eventually found the paradise he was seeking in the Hudson River valley. There he began painting romantically exaggerated renderings of the landscape. The refreshing naturalness and Americanness of Cole's paintings attracted a large following, and other artists took up

This 1827 painting by Thomas Cole, capturing a scene from James Fenimore Cooper's *Last of the Mohicans*, illustrates the Romantic mood during the early nineteenth century. In line with artistic romanticism, nature dwarfs all else. Even a large Indian camp seems insignificant in size, lost in an exaggerated image of the mountains in the Hudson River region of New York.

the style. This group of landscapists is known as the **Hudson River school**, after the area where most of them painted.

The paintings of George Caleb Bingham exemplify another movement in American art that reflected the temper of the time. Bingham was born in Virginia and educated for a time in Pennsylvania before he went west to Missouri. There he painted realistic pictures of common people engaged in everyday activities. The flatboat men, marketplace-dwellers, and electioneering politicians in Bingham's paintings were artistic testimony to the emerging democratic style of America in the Jacksonian period (see illustrations on pages 239 and 245).

Culture and Resistance Among Workers

Most genteel people in the antebellum era would have denied that working people had a "culture." But the increasing number of urban workers crafted a viable culture that suited their living and working conditions and was distinct from the genteel culture of their supervisors.

□ **Hudson River school** The first native school of landscape painting in the United States (1825–1875); it attracted artists rebelling against the neoclassical tradition.

minstrel show A variety show in which white actors made up as blacks presented jokes, songs, dances, and comic skits.

Wretched living conditions and dispiriting poverty encouraged working-class people in northern cities to choose social and cultural outlets that were very different from those of upper- and middle-class Americans. Offering temporary relief from unpleasant conditions, drinking was the social distraction of choice. Whiskey and gin were cheap and available during the 1820s and 1830s as western farmers used the new roads and canals to ship distilled spirits to urban markets. In the 1830s, consumers could purchase a gallon of whiskey for 25 cents.

Even activities that did not center on drinking tended to involve it. While genteel and middle-class people remained in their private homes reading Sigourney or Cooper, working people attended popular theaters cheering entertainments designed to appeal to their less polished tastes. **Minstrel shows** featured fast-paced music and raucous comedy. To put the audience in the proper mood, theater owners sold cheap drinks in the lobby or in basement pubs. Alcohol was also sold at sporting events that drew large working-class audiences—bare-knuckle boxing contests, for instance, where the fighting was seldom confined to the boxing ring.

Stinging from their low status in the urbanizing and industrializing society, angry about living in hovels, and freed from inhibitions by hours of drinking, otherwise rational workingmen often pummeled one another to let off steam. And in working-class neighborhoods, where police forces were small, fistfights often turned into brawls and then into riots pitting Protestants against Catholics, immigrants against the native-born, and whites against blacks.

Working-class women experienced the same dull but dangerous working conditions and dismal living circumstances as working-class men, but their lives were even harder. Single women were particularly bad off. They were paid significantly less than men but had to pay as much and sometimes more for living quarters, food, and clothing. Marriage could reduce a woman's personal expenses—but at a cost. While men congregated in the barbershop or candy store drinking and socializing during their leisure hours, married women were stuck in tiny apartments caring for children and doing household chores.

In view of their grim working and living conditions, it is not surprising that some manufacturing workers protested their situations and embraced increasingly active strategies for dealing with them. The first organized labor strike in America took place in 1806, when a group of journeymen shoemakers stopped work to protest the hiring of unskilled workers to perform some tasks that higher-paid journeymen and apprentices had been doing. The strike failed when a New York court declared the shoemakers' actions illegal, but in the years to come many other journeymen's groups would try the same tactic, often with some success.

Unlike the British Luddites (see page 217), journeymen simply asked for decent wages and working conditions and some role in decision making. Throughout the industrializing cities of the Northeast and the smaller manufacturing centers of the West, journeymen banded together in **trade unions**: assemblies of skilled workers grouped by specific occupation. During the 1830s, trade unions from neighboring towns merged with one another to form the beginnings of a national trade union movement. In this way, house carpenters, shoemakers, and other craft workers established national unions through which they attempted to enforce uniform wage standards in their industries. In 1834 journeymen's organizations from a number of industries joined to form the **National Trades' Union**, the first labor organization in the nation's history to represent many different crafts.

Not surprisingly, factory owners, bankers, and others who had a vested interest in keeping labor cheap used every device available to prevent unions from succeeding. Employers formed manufacturing associations to resist union activity and used the courts to keep organized labor from disrupting business. Despite such efforts, a number of strikes affected American industries during the 1830s. In 1834 and again in 1836, women working in the textile mills in Lowell, Massachusetts, closed down production in the face of wage reductions and rising boardinghouse rates. Such demonstrations of power by workers frightened manufacturers, and gradually employers replaced native-born women in the factories with immigrants, who were less liable to organize successfully and, more important, less likely to win approval from sympathetic judges or consumers.

Still, workers won some small victories in the battle to organize. A symbolic breakthrough came in 1842 when the Massachusetts Supreme Court decided in the case of *Commonwealth v. Hunt* that Boston's journeymen boot makers were within their rights to organize "in such manner as best to subserve their own interests" and to call strikes, formalizing an attitude courts had been acting on for some time.

Though never as violent as those of the Luddites, not all labor protests were peaceful. In 1828, for example, immigrant weavers protested the pitiful wages paid by Alexander Knox, New York City's leading textile employer. Storming Knox's home to demand higher pay, the weavers invaded and vandalized his house and beat Knox's son and a cordon of police guards. The rioters then marched to the garret and basement homes of weavers who had refused to join the protest and destroyed their looms.

Culture and Resistance Among Slaves

Like their northern counterparts, slaves fashioned for themselves a culture that helped them to survive and to maintain their humanity under dehumanizing conditions. Traces of an enduring African heritage were visible in slaves' clothing, entertainment, and folkways. Often the plain garments that masters provided were upgraded with colorful headscarves and other decorations similar to ornaments worn in Africa. Hairstyles often resembled those characteristic of African tribes. Music, dancing, and other forms of public entertainment and celebration also showed strong African roots. Musical instruments were copies of traditional ones, modified only by the use of New World materials. And stories that were told around the stoves at night were a New World adaptation of African **trickster tales**. Other links to Africa abounded. Healers among the slaves used African ceremonies, Christian rituals, and both imported and native herbs to effect cures. Taken together, these survivals and adaptations of African traditions provided a strong base underlying a solid African American culture.

Abiding family ties helped to make this cultural continuity possible. Slave families endured despite kinship ties made fragile by their highly precarious life: anyone might be sold at any time. In this insecure environment, another African legacy, the concept of fictive kinship (see page 12), contributed to family stability by turning the whole community of slaves into a vast network of aunts and uncles.

Within families, the separation of work along age and gender lines followed traditional patterns. Slave women, when not laboring at the assigned tasks of plantation work, generally performed domestic duties and tended children, while the men hunted, fished,

trade union A labor organization whose members work in a specific trade or craft.

□ **National Trades' Union** The first national association of trade unions in the United States; it was formed in 1834.

□ *Commonwealth v. Hunt* Significant symbolic decision by the Massachusetts Supreme Court asserting that unionization was legal in that state.

trickster tales Stories that feature as a central character a clever figure who uses his wits and instincts to adapt to changing times; a survivor, the trickster is used by traditional societies, including African cultures, to teach important cultural lessons.

The Problem with Legal History: The Significance of *Commonwealth v. Hunt*

When prominent historian and economist Edwin E. Witte looked at historians' interpretations of early labor decisions, he came to a shocking conclusion: the historians were wrong. Historians, he wrote, had usually concluded that the courts were antagonistic to the working classes because they ruled that "combinations of workmen to raise their wages, shorten hours and compel the employment of their own members" were unlawful conspiracies, and that it took the decision in *Commonwealth v. Hunt* (1842) to turn the situation around. But, Witte argued, "[t]his interpretation of the early American labor cases will not stand the test of an examination of the original sources."

Instead, what Witte discovered was that in the preponderance of antebellum labor cases, the only expressions of hostility to labor were statements made in passing by judges and prosecutors that, as he put it, "have been mistaken for established legal doctrines." Where the actual law was concerned, labor activities as such were never illegal in the United States and therefore *Commonwealth v. Hunt* made no legal difference. Yet historians continued, and still continue, to call *Commonwealth v. Hunt* a legal turning point.

How could such a profound misunderstanding have happened? Are there processes in legal proceedings that historians might not be aware of? Are there some sources historians might not know about? That seems to be the case here. Historians did not realize that everything said in a courtroom is not a legal opinion; expressions of purely personal opinion are not legally binding. In addition, the cases that Witte researched were what are called "unpublished decisions" or "unreported opinions," which were not published in any official case reporter. This failure to report some cases was common during the early nineteenth century when court reporting was still a very primitive art. Nevertheless, the decisions and reasoning in these cases were every bit as binding as any other case. Historians simply did not know where to look and, as noted, even when they found obscure cases they read them wrong.

One other question about sources also arises: Do historians and lawyers consult the same authorities when interpreting the significance of legal cases? Clearly they do not. Witte's groundbreaking article was published in 1926 in the *Yale Law Journal,* a legal review with an intended audience of lawyers and law students rather than in a publication like the *Journal of American History*, aimed at historians and history students. So historians did not know about Witte's piece. Again, they simply did not know where to look.

Historians are usually experts—but not necessarily in everything and rarely in such a specialized field as law or medicine. This means it is always wise for historians to acknowledge their lack of expertise and to consult people in those fields before coming to conclusions. It is also why readers should look closely at the sources a historian has used in assessing legal and other technically specialized records.

Slave artisans often fashioned beautiful and functional items that incorporated both European and African design motifs, creating a unique material culture in the American South. A potter, now known as Dave Drake, crafted enormous jars that he inscribed with original poetry. Slave women often used needlework as a means of self-expression, as exemplified by this Star of Bethlehem quilt, crafted by a slave in Texas known only as Aunt Peggy. (l) McKissick Museum, The University of South Carolinia; (r) Cincinnati Art Museum/The Bridgeman Art Library

did carpentry, and performed other "manly" tasks. Children were likely to help out by tending family gardens and doing other light work until they were old enough to join their parents in the fields or learn skilled trades.

Slaves' religion, like family structure, was another means for preserving unique African American traits. Though slaves often were designated as Baptists or Methodists, the Christianity they practiced differed in significant ways from that of their white neighbors. Slave preachers untrained in theology often merged Christian and African religious figures, creating unique African American religious symbols. Ceremonies too combined African practices such as group dancing with Christian prayer. The merging of African musical forms with Christian lyrics gave rise to a new form of Christian music: the "Negro spiritual."

Unlike workers in the North, who at least had some legal protections and civil rights, slaves had nothing but their own wits to protect them against a society that classed them as disposable personal property. Slaves were skilled at the use of passive resistance. The importance of passive resistance was evident in the folk tales and songs that circulated among slaves, through which clever strategies for getting extra food, clothing, and other supplies were passed on from generation to generation. Slaves often stole food, not because they were hungry but because its unexplainable

disappearance flustered their masters. Farm animals also disappeared mysteriously, tools broke in puzzling ways, people fell ill from unknown diseases, and workers got lost on the way to fields—all these events were subtle signs of slaves' discontent. Slaves also used flattery and trickery, convincing whites that slave-initiated improvements were really the master's idea.

Not all slave resistance was passive. Perhaps the most common form of active resistance was running away (see Map 12.1). The number of slaves who escaped may never be known, though some estimate that an average of about a thousand made their way to freedom each year. But running away was always a dangerous gamble. One former slave recalled, "No man who has never been placed in such a situation can comprehend the thousand obstacles thrown in the way of the flying slave."

The most frightening form of slave resistance was open and armed revolt. The most serious and violent of these uprisings was the work of a black preacher, Nat Turner. After years of planning and organization,

◻ **"Negro spiritual"** A religious folk music originated by African Americans, often expressing a longing for deliverance from the constraints and hardships of their lives.

passive resistance Resistance by nonviolent methods.

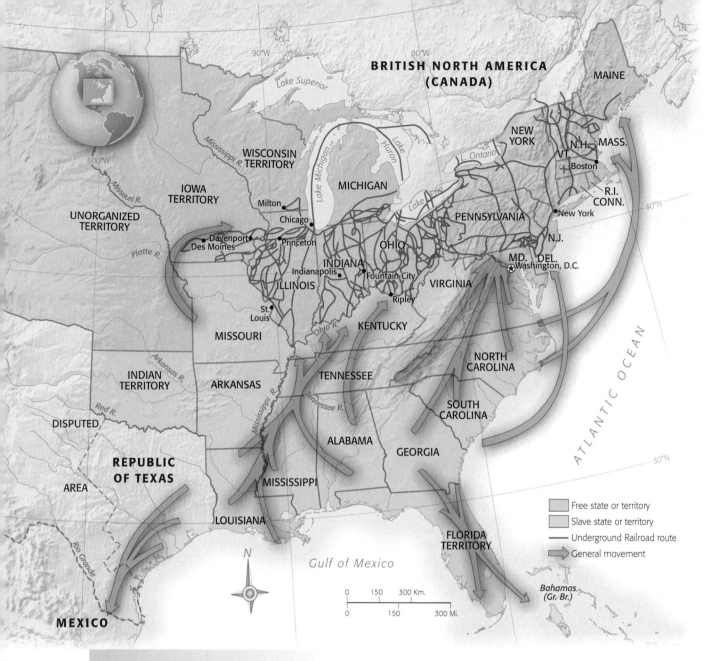

MAP 12.1 Escaping from Slavery
Running away was one of the most prominent forms of slave resistance during the antebellum period. Success often depended on help from African Americans who had already gained their freedom and from sympathetic whites. Beginning in the 1820s an informal and secret network called the Underground Railroad provided escape routes for slaves who were daring enough to risk all for freedom. The routes shown here are based on documentary evidence, but the network's secrecy makes it impossible to know if they are drawn entirely accurately. © Cengage Learning.

in 1831 Turner led a force of about seventy slaves in a predawn raid against the slaveholding households in Southampton County, Virginia. It took four days for white forces to stop the uprising; Turner and sixteen of his followers were finally captured and executed.

In the wake of Nat Turner's Rebellion, fear of slave revolts reached paranoid levels in the South, especially in areas where slaves greatly outnumbered whites. After seeing a play depicting a slave insurrection, Mary Boykin Chesnut gave expression to the fear that plagued whites in the slave South: "What a thrill of terror ran through me as those yellow and black brutes came jumping over the parapets! Their faces were like so many of the same sort at home. . . . How long would they resist the seductive and irresistible call: 'Rise, kill, and be free!'"

Frightened and often outnumbered, whites felt justified in imposing stringent restrictions and using harsh methods to enforce them. In most areas, free African Americans were denied the right to own guns, buy liquor, hold public assemblies, testify in court, and vote. Slaves were forbidden to own any private

No pictures of famed slave revolt leader Nat Turner are known to exist, but this imagined scene shows how Turner might have met with his fellow conspirators. White southerners lived in terror of such scenes and passed severe laws designed to prevent them.

The Granger Collection, New York.

property, to attend unsupervised worship services, and to learn reading and writing.

Experimental Efforts to Regain Community

To many of all classes, society seemed to be spinning out of control as modernization rearranged basic lifestyles. Some religious groups and social thinkers tried to ward off the excesses of Jacksonian individualism by forming utopian communities that experimented with various living arrangements and ideological commitments. Others sought to reinvigorate more traditional forms of religious life.

A wealthy Welsh industrialist, Robert Owen, began one of the earliest experiments along these lines. In 1825 he purchased a tract of land in Indiana called New Harmony. Believing that the solution to poverty in modern society was to collect the unemployed into self-contained and self-supporting villages, Owen opened a textile factory in which ownership was held communally by the workers and decisions were made by group consensus. Even though the community instituted innovations like an eight-hour workday, cultural activities for workers, and the nation's first school offering equal education to boys and girls, New Harmony did not succeed. Owen and his son, Robert Dale Owen, were outspoken critics of organized religion and joined their close associate Frances (Fanny) Wright in advocating radical causes. These leanings made the Owenites unpopular with more traditional

Americans, and when their mill experienced economic hardship in 1827, New Harmony collapsed.

A more famous experiment, Brook Farm, had its origin in the transcendentalist movement. The brainchild of George Ripley, Brook Farm was designed to "prepare a society of liberal, intelligent and cultivated persons, whose relations with each other would permit a more wholesome and simple life than can be led amidst the pressure of our competitive institutions." To carry out this enterprise, Ripley set up a joint-stock company. Most of the stockholders were transcendentalist celebrities such as Nathaniel Hawthorne and Ralph Waldo Emerson, but they disappointed Ripley by failing to invest their time and labor, merely dropping in from time to time. In 1844 Ripley adopted a new constitution that drew upon French utopian socialist Charles Fourier for inspiration. Ripley emphasized community self-sufficiency, the equal sharing of earnings among members of the community, and the periodic redistribution of tasks and status to prevent boredom and elitism. With this new disciplined ideology in place, Brook Farm began to appeal to serious artisans and farmers, but a disastrous fire in 1845 cut the experiment short. Other Fourierist communities were also founded during this period— nearly a hundred such organizations sprang up from Massachusetts to Michigan and southward into Texas.

Unlike Fourierist communities, some communal experiments were grounded in religious beliefs. The Oneida Community, established in central New York in 1848, for example, reflected the notions of its

utopian Ideal; refers to the reformist belief that a perfect society can be created on Earth and that a particular group or leader has the knowledge to actually create such a society.

◻ **New Harmony** Utopian community that Robert Owen established in Indiana in 1825; economic problems and discord among members led to its failure two years later.

Frances (Fanny) Wright Infamous nineteenth-century woman who advocated what at the time were considered radical causes, including racial equality, equality for women, birth control, and open sexuality.

◻ **Brook Farm** An experimental farm based on cooperative living; established in 1841, it first attracted transcendentalists and then serious farmers before fire destroyed it in 1845.

socialist Someone who advocates for the common ownership of manufacturing, farming, and other forms of production so that they benefit society rather than produce individual or corporate profits.

◻ **Charles Fourier** French utopian socialist theorist who argued that people were capable of living in perfect harmony under the right conditions, which included communal life, socialist economics, and republican government.

◻ **Oneida Community** A religious community established in central New York in 1848; its members shared property, practiced group marriage, and reared children under communal care.

As the nation underwent wrenching economic and social changes, many sought radical solutions for the rising anxieties they were experiencing. Religious, socialist, and a variety of other experimental communities dotted the landscape. In one, the Oneida Community, everything was done collectively, including marriage: all men and women were considered to be married to each other. Children who were born in the commune were raised in common by all of the adults and, as this early nineteenth-century etching shows, were often at the center of community life.

founder, John Humphrey Noyes. Though educated in theology at Andover and Yale, Noyes could find no church willing to ordain him because of his strange belief that his followers could escape sin through faith in God, communal living, and group marriage. Unlike Brook Farm and New Harmony, the Oneida Community was very successful financially, establishing thriving logging, farming, and manufacturing businesses. It was finally dissolved as the result of local pressures directed at the "free love" practiced by its members.

Economically successful communes were also operated by the **Shakers**. Free love never disturbed their settlements: Shakers practiced absolute celibacy. Founded in Britain in 1770 and then transported to America in 1774, the sect grew slowly at first, but in the excitement of the early nineteenth century, it expanded at a more vigorous rate. By 1826 eighteen Shaker communities

had been planted in eight states and were home to as many as six thousand followers. The Shaker communities succeeded by pursuing farming activities and the manufacture and sale of furniture and handcrafts admired for their design and workmanship. Like most such experiments, the Shaker movement went into decline after 1860, though vestiges of it remain operative today.

By far the most successful of these experimental communities was the Mormons (see pages 268–269). Beginning in 1831 Joseph Smith Jr. had a series of revelations calling for the creation of what would be called the **United Order**, under which church members consecrated all of their property to the church. The objective, according to Smith, was to make "every man equal according to his family, according to his circumstances and his wants and needs." The church measured off plots of various sizes, up to 40 acres, and assigned them to families. Thus a man who consecrated a lot of property and had a large family might receive a grant of 40 acres, but a man with no family or a small one might receive only 10. The size of a land grant determined the extent to which the recipient was obligated to support community efforts. When the church ordered the construction of irrigation systems or other public works, a man who had been granted 40 acres had to provide four times the amount of labor as one who had been granted 10 acres. And if the allocation produced more than

☐ **Shakers** A mid-eighteenth-century offshoot of the Quakers; founded in England by Mother Ann Lee, Shakers engaged in spirited worship, including dancing and rhythmic shaking, hence their name, and practiced communal living and strict celibacy.

☐ **United Order** A semi-socialistic plan enunciated by Joseph Smith Jr. in 1831 whereby Mormons donated all of their property to the church and the church redistributed it on the basis of need.

the individual family actually needed, all surpluses were to be turned over to the church, from which the needs of the poor were to be supplied. Also, not unlike Christian socialist Noyes, Smith received a revelation permitting plural marriage. These practices were a large part of the reason for the persecution of the Mormons and their flight to Utah, where they increasingly formalized the dictates of the United Order.

A Second Great Awakening

While some were drawn to transcendentalism and a handful chose to follow revolutionary communitarian leaders, others sought solace within existing, mainstream denominations. Beginning in the 1790s both theologians and popular preachers sought to create a new Protestant creed that would maintain the notion of Christian community in an atmosphere of increasing individualism and competition. Disturbed by perceptions of rising secularism and declining church memberships, Protestant activists like Joseph Tracy crafted a new evangelical movement that they hoped would launch a second Great Awakening (see page 88).

Mirroring tendencies in the political and economic realms, Protestant thinking during the opening decades of the nineteenth century emphasized the role of the individual. One young Yale theologian, Nathaniel Taylor, created a new theology that was entirely consistent with the prevailing secular creed of individualism. According to this new doctrine, God offers salvation to all, but it is the individual's responsibility to seek it. Thus the individual has "free will" to choose or not choose salvation. Taylor's ideas struck a responsive chord in a restless and expanding America. Hundreds of ordained ministers, licensed preachers, and lay exhorters carried the message of individual empowerment to an anxious populace.

Unlike Calvinist Puritanism, which characterized women as the weaker sex, the new evangelicalism stressed women's spiritual equality with—and even spiritual superiority to—men. Not surprisingly, young women generally were the first to respond to the new message. The most effective preachers of the day turned women into agents spreading the word to their husbands, brothers, and children.

Charles Grandison Finney stood out among a new generation of preachers. A former schoolteacher and lawyer, Finney experienced a soul-shattering religious conversion in 1821. Declaring that "the Lord Jesus Christ" had retained him "to plead his cause," Finney performed on the pulpit as a spirited attorney

With two wives and several children to help share the burden of work, this relatively prosperous Mormon settler was in a good position to do well, even after the self-exile of the church to the near-desert environment of Utah. Sensitive to disapproval from more traditional Christians, families like this tended to associate exclusively with other Mormons and pressured outsiders to leave as quickly as possible.

might argue a case in court. Seating those most likely to be converted on a special "anxious bench," Finney focused on them as a lawyer might a jury. The result was likely to be dramatic. Many of the targeted people fainted, jerked, or cried out in hysteria. Such drama brought Finney enormous publicity, which he and an army of imitators used to gain access to communities all over the West and Northeast. The result was a nearly continuous season of religious revival. The Second Great Awakening spread from rural community to rural community like a wildfire until, in the late 1830s, Finney carried the fire into Boston and New York City.

The new revivals led to the breakdown of traditional church organizations and the creation of various Christian denominations. Congregationalists, Presbyterians, Baptists, and Methodists split into groups who supported the new theology and those who clung to more traditional notions. In the face of such fragmentation—and competition—all denominations

□ **Joseph Tracy** Early nineteenth-century minister and author often credited with creating the term "Great Awakening" and an influential figure in promoting a Second Great Awakening in antebellum America.

lay exhorter A church member who preaches but is not an ordained minister.

□ **Charles Grandison Finney** Lawyer turned evangelical preacher, he was one of the most influential and successful religious figures during the Second Great Awakening.

□ **Second Great Awakening** An upsurge in religious fervor that began around 1800 and was characterized by revival meetings.

Revival meetings were remarkable affairs. Often lasting several days, they drew huge crowds who might listen to as many as forty preachers in around-the-clock sessions. The impact on the audience frequently was dramatic: one attendee at a New York revival commented that there were "loud ejaculations of prayer . . . some struck with terror . . . others, trembling weeping and crying out . . . fainting and swooning away."

became concerned about state/church relations. In fact, those most fervent in their Christian beliefs joined deists and other Enlightenment-influenced thinkers in arguing steadfastly for even more stringent separation of church and state. Under such pressure, in 1838 Massachusetts became the last state to abolish its legally established church. Disestablishment, in turn, added to the spirit of competition as individual congregations vied for voluntary contributions to keep their churches alive.

Even though religious conversion had become an individual matter and competition over parishioners a genuine concern, revivalists did not ignore the idea of community. "I know this is all algebra to those who

□ **Christian benevolence movement** Early nineteenth-century movement based on a tenet in some Christian theology that the essence of God is self-sacrificing love and that the ultimate duty for Christians is to perform acts of kindness with no expectation of reward in return.

have never felt it," Finney said. "But to those who have experienced the agony of wrestling, prevailing prayer, for the conversion of a soul, you may depend on it, that soul . . . appears as dear as a child is to the mother who brought it forth with pain." This intimate connection forged bonds of mutual responsibility, giving a generation of isolated individuals a common starting point for joint action.

The Middle Class and Moral Reform

The missionary activism that accompanied the Second Great Awakening dovetailed with a reforming inclination among genteel and middle-class Americans. The Christian benevolence movement gave rise to hundreds of voluntary societies ranging from maternal associations designed to improve child rearing to political lobby groups aiming at outlawing alcohol, Sunday mail delivery, and other perceived evils. Such activism drew reformers together in common causes and led to deep friendships and a shared sense of commitment—antidotes to the alienation and loneliness common in the competitive world of the early nineteenth century.

The new theology reinforced the reforming impulse by emphasizing that even the most depraved might be saved if proper means were applied. This idea had immediate application in the realm of crime and punishment. Reformers characterized criminals not as evil but as lost and in need of divine guidance. In Auburn, New York, an experimental prison attempted to put inmates on the path to renewal by combining hard work, discipline, and solitude. Mental illness underwent a similar change in definition. Rather than viewing the mentally ill as possessed agents of evil, reformers now spoke of them as lost souls in need of help. Dorothea Dix, a young, compassionate, reform-minded teacher, advocated publicly funded asylums for the insane. For the balance of the century, Dix toured the country pleading the cause of the mentally ill, succeeding in winning both private and public support for mental health systems.

A hundred other targets for reform joined prisons and asylums on the agenda of middle-class Christian activists. Embracing the Puritan tradition of strict observance of the Sabbath, newly awakened Christians insisted on stopping mail delivery and demanded that canals be closed on Sundays. Some joined Bible and tract societies that distributed Christian literature; others founded Sunday schools or operated domestic missions devoted to winning either the irreligious or the wrongly religious (as Roman Catholics were perceived to be) to the new covenant of the Second Great Awakening.

Many white-collar reformers acted in earnest and were genuinely interested in forging new social welfare systems. A number of their programs, however, seemed more like social control because they tried to force people to conform to a middle-class standard of behavior. Immigrants who chose to cling to familiar ways were suspected of disloyalty. This aspect of benevolent reform was particularly prominent in two important movements: public education and the temperance movement.

Before the War of 1812, most Americans believed that education was the family's or the church's responsibility and did not require children to attend school. But as the complexity of economic, political, and cultural life increased during the opening decades of the nineteenth century, Horace Mann and other champions of education pushed states to introduce formal public schooling. Like his contemporary Charles G. Finney, Mann was trained as a lawyer, but unlike Finney, he believed that ignorance, not sin, lay at the heart of the nation's problems. When Massachusetts made Mann the superintendent of a statewide board of education, he immediately extended the school year to a minimum of six months

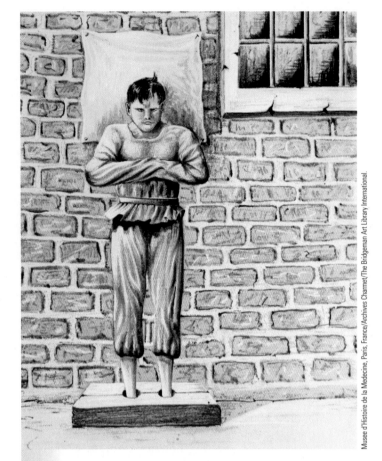

Mistreatment of Insane Young Boy Reporting on conditions for treatment of the insane, humanitarian activist Dorothea Dix told the Massachusetts state legislature in 1843: "I tell what I have seen. . . . Insane persons confined within the Commonwealth, in cages, closets, cellars, stalls, pens! Chained, naked, beaten with rods, and lashed into obedience!" This illustration, from a contemporary French publication, gives some sense of what Dix saw and how the insane were regarded throughout the Western world before reforms began in the mid-nineteenth century.

and gradually replaced the traditional curriculum, rooted in the classics of ancient Roman and Greek learning, with courses like arithmetic, practical geography, and physical science.

But Mann and other reformers were interested in more than "knowledge"; they were equally concerned

▫ **Dorothea Dix** Philanthropist, reformer, and educator who was a pioneer in the movement for specialized treatment of the mentally ill.

irreligious Hostile or indifferent to religion.

▫ **temperance movement** Effort to instill temperance, moderation, or abstinence in the consumption of alcoholic drinks.

▫ **Horace Mann** Educator who called for publicly funded education for all children and was head of the first public board of education in the United States.

Street fights between American-born laborers and immigrants became common during the 1830s and 1840s as immigrants became more visible in American cities and insisted on clinging to their own ethnic ways. Often these erupted into full-blown riots, as in the case depicted here, which took place in Philadelphia in 1844 when the state militia was called in to quell the violence.

that new immigrants and the children of the urban poor be trained in Protestant values and middle-class habits. Thus the books used in public schools emphasized virtues such as promptness, discipline, and obedience to authority. In Philadelphia and other cities where Roman Catholic immigrants concentrated, Catholic parents resisted such cultural pressure on their children. They supported the establishment of parochial schools—a development that aggravated the strain between native-born Protestants and immigrant Catholics.

Another source of such tension was a crusade by awakened Protestants against alcohol. Drinking alcohol had always been common in America but before the early nineteenth century was not broadly perceived as a social problem. During the 1820s and 1830s, however, two key factors contributed to a new, more ominous perception. One was the increasing visibility of drinking and drunkenness, as populations became more concentrated in cities. For example, officials bemoaned public drinking in Rochester, New York, a fast-growing Erie Canal port town where anyone with a few cents could get a glass of whiskey at grocery stores, either of two candy stores, barbershops, or even private homes. The second factor was alcohol's economic impact in a new and more complex

parochial school A school supported by a church parish; in the United States, the term usually refers to a Catholic school.

□ American Colonization Society Organization founded in 1817 to end slavery gradually by assisting individual slaveowners to liberate their slaves and then transporting them to Africa.

world of work. Factory owners and managers recognized that workers who drank often and heavily threatened the quantity and quality of production (and profits). Owners and supervisors alike thus rallied around the temperance movement. By promoting temperance, these reformers believed they could clean up the worst aspects of city life and turn the raucous lower classes into clean-living, self-controlled, peaceful workers.

The institution of slavery also became a hot topic among the nation's reborn Christians. Although some people had always had doubts about the morality of slavery, little organized opposition to it appeared before the American Revolution. By the end of the Revolution, only Georgia and South Carolina continued to allow the importation of slaves, while Massachusetts specifically prohibited slavery altogether and Pennsylvania had begun to phase it out. By the mid-1780s, most states, including those in the South, had active antislavery societies. In 1807, when Congress voted to outlaw permanently the importation of slaves in the following year, little was said in defense of slavery as an institution.

Public feeling about slavery during these years is reflected in the rise of the American Colonization Society, founded in 1817. This society was rooted in economic pragmatism, humanitarian concern for slaves' well-being, and white supremacy. Such ideas prompted the organization to propose that if slave owners emancipated their slaves, or if funds could be raised to purchase their freedom, the freed slaves should immediately be shipped to Africa.

Most preachers active in the Second Great Awakening supported the idea of colonization, but a few individuals pressed for more radical reforms. The most vocal leader among the antislavery forces during the early nineteenth century was William Lloyd Garrison. In 1831 he founded the nation's first prominent abolitionist newspaper, *The Liberator*. In it he advocated immediate emancipation for African Americans, with no compensation for slaveholders. In the following year, Garrison founded the New England Anti-Slavery Society and then, in 1833, the national American Anti-Slavery Society.

At first, Garrison stood alone. Some Christian reformers joined his cause, but the majority held back. In eastern cities, workers lived in dread of either enslaved or free blacks flooding in, lowering wages, and destroying job security. In all regions, white supremacists argued that Garrison's strategy would eventually lead to blacks mixing with the white population, a possibility they found extremely distasteful. Thus most whites detested the notion of immediate emancipation, and radical abolitionists at this early date were almost universally ignored or, worse, attacked when they denounced slavery. Still, support for the movement gradually grew. In 1836 petitions flooded into Congress demanding an end to the slave trade in Washington, D.C. Not ready to engage in an action quite so controversial, Congress passed a **gag rule** that automatically **tabled** any petition to Congress that addressed the abolition of slavery.

Many evangelical women became active in the antislavery cause. Moved by their activism, in 1840 Garrison proposed that a woman be elected to the executive committee of the American Anti-Slavery Society. But later that year, when Elizabeth Cady Stanton and other women went to the first World Anti-Slavery Convention in London, British antislavery advocates refused to seat them.

One prominent female abolitionist, Angelina Grimké, gave voice to her contemporaries' frustration at such treatment: "Are we aliens, because we are women? . . . Have women no country—no interests staked in public weal [welfare]—no liabilities in the common peril—no partnership in a nation's guilt and shame?" In that same year, her sister Sarah went further, writing a powerful indictment against the treatment of women in America and a call for equality. In *Letters on the Equality of the Sexes and the Condition of Woman,* Sarah proclaimed, "The page of history teems with woman's wrongs . . . and it is wet with woman's tears." Women must, she said, "arise in all the majesty of moral power . . . and plant themselves, side by side, on the platform of human rights, with man, to whom they were designed to be companions, equals and helpers in every good word and work." Like Sarah Grimké, many other women backed away from male-dominated causes and began advancing their own cause, as illustrated in 1848, when Lucretia Mott and Elizabeth Cady Stanton called concerned women to Seneca Falls.

THE WHIG ALTERNATIVE TO JACKSONIAN DEMOCRACY

☆ What did Jackson's opponents hope to accomplish when they built their coalition to oppose the Democrats? How successful were they?

☆ What cultural factors helped contribute to the particular composition and policy interests of the Whigs?

The fundamental structural changes that led to social and cultural transformations had an enormous impact on politics as well. Although Andrew Jackson was quite possibly the most popular president since George Washington, not all Americans agreed with his philosophy, policies, or political style. Men like Henry Clay and Daniel Webster, who inherited the crumbling structure of Jefferson's Republican Party, continually opposed Jackson in and out of Congress but seemed unable to overcome sectional differences to challenge Jackson's and Van Buren's cohesive Democratic Party. Gradually, however, anger over Jackson's policies and anxiety about change forged cooperation among the disenchanted, who coalesced into a new national party.

The End of the Old Party Structure

The last full year of Jackson's first term in office, 1832, was a landmark year in the nation's political history. In the course of that single year, the Seminoles declared war on the United States, Jackson declared war on the Second Bank, South Carolina declared war on the binding power of the Constitution, and the Cherokees waged a continuing war in the courts to hold on to their lands. The presidential election that year reflected the air of political crisis.

Henry Clay had started the Bank War to rally Jackson's opponents. The problem was that Jackson's enemies were deeply divided among themselves. Clay opposed Jackson because the president refused to support the American System and used every tool at his disposal to attack Clay's economic policies. Southern politicians like Calhoun, however, feared and hated Clay's nationalistic policies as much as they did Jackson's assertions of federal power. And political outsiders like the Antimasons distrusted all political organizations. The 1832 election campaign underscored these divisions.

The Antimasons kicked off the anti-Jackson free-for-all in September 1831 when they held the nation's first nominating convention in Baltimore. Party co-founder Thurlow Weed's skillful political manipulation had pulled in a wide range of people who were disgusted with what Jefferson had called "political party tricks," and the convention drew a broad constituency. Using all his charm and influence, Weed cajoled the convention into nominating William Wirt, a respected lawyer from Maryland, as its presidential candidate.

Antimasons fully expected that when the Republicans met in convention later in the year, they would rubber-stamp the Antimasonic nomination and present a united front against Jackson. But the

gag rule A rule that limits or prevents debate on an issue.

tabled Action by a legislative body (Congress, for example) to postpone debate on an issue until a positive vote removes the topic from the table.

Republicans, fearful of the Antimasons' odd combination of **machine politics** and antiparty paranoia, nominated Clay as their standard-bearer. The Republicans then issued the country's first formal **party platform**, a ringing document supporting Clay's economic ideas and attacking Jackson's use of the **spoils system**.

Even having two anti-Jackson parties in the running did not satisfy some. Distrustful of the Antimasons and put off by Clay's nationalist philosophy, southerners in both parties refused to support any of the candidates. They finally backed nullification advocate John Floyd of Virginia.

Lack of unity contributed to disaster for Jackson's opponents. Wirt and Floyd received votes that might have gone to Clay. But even if Clay had gotten those votes, Jackson's popularity and the political machinery that he and Van Buren controlled would have given him the victory. The president was reelected with a total of 219 electoral votes to Clay's 49, Wirt's 7, and Floyd's 11. Jackson's party lost five seats in the Senate but gained six in the House of Representatives. Despite unsettling changes in the land and continuing political chaos, the people still wanted the hero of New Orleans as their leader.

The New Political Coalition

If one lesson emerged clearly from the election of 1832, it was that Jackson's opponents needed to pull together if they expected to challenge the growing power of "King Andrew." Adopting names used by political organizations in Great Britain, Clay and his associates began calling Jackson supporters Tories—supporters of the king—and calling themselves Whigs. The antimonarchical label stuck, and the new party formed in 1834 was called the **Whig Party**.

The Whigs eventually absorbed all the major factions that opposed Jackson. At the heart of the party were Clay supporters: advocates of strong government and the American System in economics. The nullifiers in the South, however, quickly came around with Calhoun's growing awareness that Jackson was perhaps more dangerous to his constituents' interests

BORN TO COMMAND.

OF VETO MEMORY.

HAD I BEEN CONSULTED.

KING ANDREW THE FIRST.

Library of Congress Prints & Photographs Division, LC-USZC4-12983.

Calling themselves Whigs after the English political party that opposed royal authority, Henry Clay, John C. Calhoun, and Daniel Webster joined forces to oppose what they characterized as Andrew Jackson's kingly use of power. This lithograph from 1834 depicting Jackson in royal dress stepping on the Constitution expresses their view quite vividly.

than was Clay. The Antimasons joined because of their disgust at Jackson's use of patronage and back-alley politics—not to mention the fact that he was a Mason—overcoming their distrust of Clay's party philosophy. A final major group to rally to the Whigs were evangelicals who disapproved of Jackson's personal lifestyle, his views on slavery, his Indian policy, and his refusal to involve government in their moral causes.

The congressional elections in 1834 provided the first test for the new coalition. In this first electoral contest, the Whigs won nearly 40 percent of the seats in the House of Representatives and more than 48 percent in the Senate. Clearly cooperation was paying off.

Van Buren in the White House

Jackson had seemed to be a tower of strength when he was first elected to the presidency in 1828, but by the end of his second term, he was nearly 70 years old and plagued by various ailments. Old Hickory decided to follow Washington's example and not run for a third term. Instead, Jackson used all the power and patronage at his command to ensure that Martin Van Buren, his most consistent loyalist, would win the presidential nomination at the Democratic Party convention.

machine politics The aggressive use of influence, favors, and trade-offs by a political organization, or "machine," to mobilize support among its followers.

party platform A formal statement of the principles, policies, and promises on which a political party bases its appeal to the public.

spoils system System associated with American politics in which a political party, after winning an election, gives government jobs to its supporters as a reward for working toward victory.

Whig Party Political party started in 1834 as an anti-Jackson coalition, charging "King Andrew" with executive tyranny.

Van Buren was a skilled organizer whose ability to create unlikely political alliances had earned him the nickname "the Little Magician." Throughout Jackson's first term, Van Buren had headed the Kitchen Cabinet and increasingly became Jackson's chief political henchman. In 1832 Jackson had repaid his loyalty by making him vice president, with the intention of launching him into the presidency.

Meanwhile, Clay and his Whig associates were hatching a plot to deny the election to the Democrats. Instead of holding a convention and thrashing out a platform, the Whigs let each region's party organization nominate its own candidates. Whig leaders hoped a large number of candidates would confuse voters and throw the election into the House of Representatives, where skillful political management and Van Buren's unpopularity might unseat the Democrats. As a result, four **favorite sons** ran on the Whig ticket. Daniel Webster of Massachusetts represented the Northeast. Hugh Lawson White, a Tennessean and former Jackson supporter, ran for the Southwest. South Carolina nullifier W. P. Mangum represented the South. William Henry Harrison, former governor of Indiana Territory, was tapped to represent the Northwest.

Weed underestimated the Democrats' hold on the minds of the voters. Van Buren captured 765,483 popular votes—more than Jackson had won in the previous election—but his performance in the Electoral College was significantly weaker than Jackson's had been. Van Buren squeaked by with a winning margin of less than 1 percent, but it was enough to foil Weed's plot to send the election to the House of Representatives.

It became clear from the beginning that Van Buren's presidency would be a troubled one. As soon as he assumed office, the nation was hit by another terrible financial crisis. The **Panic of 1837** was a direct outcome of the Bank War and Jackson's money policies, but it was Van Buren who would take the blame. The crisis had begun with Nicholas Biddle's manipulation of credit and interest rates in an effort to discredit Jackson and have the Second Bank rechartered in spite of the president's veto. Jackson had added to the problem by removing paper money and credit from the economy in an effort to win support from hard-money advocates. Arguing that he wanted to end "the monopoly of the public lands in the hands of speculators and capitalists," Jackson had issued the **Specie Circular** on August 15, 1836. From that day forward payment for public land had to be made in specie.

This austerity policy had the same impact in 1836 as it had in 1819: the national economy collapsed. By May 1837, New York banks were no longer accepting any paper currency, and soon all banks had adopted the policy of accepting specie only. Unable to pay back or collect loans, buy raw materials, or conduct any other sort of commerce, hundreds of businesses, plantations, farms, factories, canals, and other enterprises spiraled into bankruptcy. More than a third of the population was thrown out of work, and people who were fortunate enough to keep their jobs found their pay reduced by as much as 50 percent. Fledgling industries and labor organizations were cast into disarray, and the nation sank into both an economic and an emotional depression.

As credit continued to collapse through 1838 and 1839, President Van Buren tried to address the problems. First, he extended Jackson's hard-money policy, which caused the economy to contract further. Next, in an effort to keep the government solvent, Van Buren cut federal spending to the bone, shrinking the money supply even more. Then, to replace the stabilizing influence lost when the Second Bank was destroyed, he created a national treasury system endowed with many of the powers formerly wielded by the bank. The new regional treasury offices accepted only specie in payment for federal obligations and used that specie to pay federal expenses and debts. As a result, specie was sucked out of local banks and local economies. While fiscally sound by the wisdom of the day, austerity only made matters worse for the average person and drove the last nail into Van Buren's political coffin.

The Log Cabin and Hard Cider Campaign of 1840

The Whigs had learned their lesson in the election of 1836: only a unified party could possibly destroy the political machine built by Jackson and Van Buren. As the nation sank into depression, the Whigs determined to use whatever means were necessary to break the Democrats' grip on the voters and were prepared to line up behind a single candidate.

Once again, Henry Clay hoped to be the party's nominee, but Thurlow Weed convinced the party that William Henry Harrison would have a better chance in the election. For Harrison's running mate, the party chose **John Tyler**, a Virginia senator who had bolted from Jackson's Democratic Party during the Bank War. Weed clearly hoped that the

favorite son A candidate nominated for office by delegates from his or her own region or state.

◻ Panic of 1837 An economic collapse that came as the result of Andrew Jackson's fiscal policies and led to an extended national economic depression.

◻ Specie Circular Order issued by President Jackson in 1836 stating that the federal government would accept only specie—gold and silver—as payment for public land; one of the causes of the Panic of 1837.

John Tyler Virginia senator who left the Democratic Party after conflicts with Andrew Jackson; he was elected vice president in 1840 and became president when William Henry Harrison died in office.

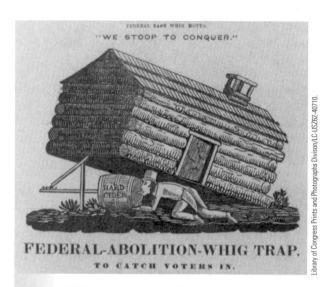

This anti-Whig cartoon suggests that the 1840 log cabin and hard cider campaign for William Henry Harrison was merely a trap set by "bank-parlor, Ruffle-shirt, silk-stocking" elites to capture the votes of the "industrious and laboring classes, of our citizens, of both town and country." Of course, such propaganda failed: Harrison won In an electoral landslide.

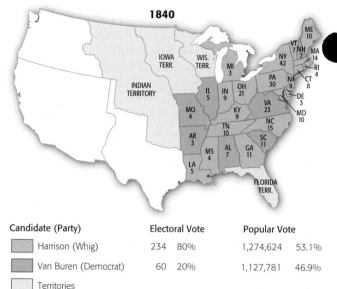

Candidate (Party)	Electoral Vote		Popular Vote	
Harrison (Whig)	234	80%	1,274,624	53.1%
Van Buren (Democrat)	60	20%	1,127,781	46.9%
Territories				

MAP 12.2 Election of 1840

Although the difference in popular votes between William Henry Harrison and Martin Van Buren was small in the election of 1840, Harrison won a landslide victory in the Electoral College. This map shows why. After floundering through several elections, the Whig Party was finally able to organize a national coalition, giving it solid victories in all of the most populous regions of the country. Only the Far West, which was still sparsely settled, voted as a block for Van Buren. © Cengage Learning.

Virginian would draw votes from the planter South while Harrison carried the West and North.

Although the economy was in bad shape, the Whig campaign avoided addressing any serious issues. Instead, the Whigs launched a smear campaign against Van Buren. Although he was the son of a lowly tavern keeper, the Whig press portrayed him as an aristocrat whose expensive tastes were signs of dangerous excess during an economic depression. Harrison really was an aristocrat, but the Whigs played on the Romantic themes so popular among their genteel and middle-class constituents by characterizing him as a simple frontiersman—a Natty Bumppo—who had risen to greatness through his own efforts. Whig claims were so extravagant that the Democratic press soon satirized Harrison in political cartoons showing a rustic hick swilling hard cider. The satire backfired. Whig newspapers and speechmakers seized on the image and sold Harrison, the longtime political insider, as a simple man of the people.

Van Buren had little with which to retaliate. Harrison had a distinguished political and military career behind him. Tyler, too, was well respected. And Van Buren had simply not done a good job of addressing the nation's pressing economic needs. Voters cried out for change and Van Buren could not offer them one. The combination of political dissatisfaction and campaign hype resulted in the biggest voter turnout to that time in American history: nearly twice as many voters came to the polls in 1840 as had voted in 1836. And while Harrison won only 53 percent of the popular vote, Weed's successful political manipulations earned the Whigs nearly 80 percent of the electoral votes, sweeping the Democrats out of the White House (see Map 12.2).

THE TRIUMPH OF MANIFEST DESTINY

☆ What forces in American life contributed to the concept of manifest destiny?

☆ To what extent did the actions taken by American settlers in Oregon and Texas reflect the ideal of manifest destiny?

The key to Harrison's success was the Whig Party's skillful manipulation of the former general's reputation as a frontiersman and popular advocate for westward expansion. With politics bogged down in debates over tariffs, public finance, and dozens of other practical, if boring, policy matters, the nationalistic appeal of seizing and occupying the West brought an air of excitement to public discourse. It was this allure that helped to draw out the thousands of new voters in 1840 and would provide a new basis for political cooperation and contention in the years to come.

The Rise of Manifest Destiny

The new spirit that came to life in American politics and rhetoric in the years after 1840 found expression in a single phrase: manifest destiny. During the antebellum period, romantic nationalism, land hunger, and evangelicalism shaped a new and powerful commitment to westward expansion. As the American Board of Commissioners for Foreign Missions noted in its annual report for 1827, "The tide of emigration is rolling westward so rapidly, that it must speedily surmount every barrier, till it reaches every habitable part of this continent." The power of this force led many to conclude that the westward movement was not just an economic process but was part of a divine plan for North America and the world.

Not surprisingly, the earliest and most aggressive proponents of expansion were Christian missionary organizations, whose many magazines, newsletters, and reports were the first to give it formal voice. Politicians, however, were not far behind. Democratic war-horse and expansion advocate Thomas Hart Benton of Missouri borrowed both the tone and content of missionary rhetoric in his speeches promoting generous land policies, territorial acquisition, and even overseas expansion. In 1825, for example, Benton argued in favor of American colonization of the Pacific coast and eventually of Asia.

Expansion to the North and West

One major complication standing in the way of the nation's perceived manifest destiny was that other countries still owned large parts of the continent. The continued presence of the British, for example, proved to be a constant source of irritation. During the War of 1812, the War Hawks had advocated conquering Canada and pushing the British from the continent altogether. Although events thwarted this ambition, many continued to push for that objective by either legal or extralegal means.

One source of dispute between the United States and Great Britain was the Oregon Question. The vast Oregon tract had been claimed at one time or another by Spain, Russia, France, England, and the United States (see Map 12.3). By the 1820s, only England and the United States continued to contest for its ownership. At the close of the War of 1812, the two countries had been unable to settle their claims, and in 1818 they had agreed to joint occupation of Oregon for ten years. They extended this arrangement indefinitely in 1827, with the proviso that either country could end it with one year's notice.

Oregon's status as neither British nor American presented its occupants with an unstable situation. One early incident occurred in 1841 when a wealthy pioneer died and because the Oregon Country had

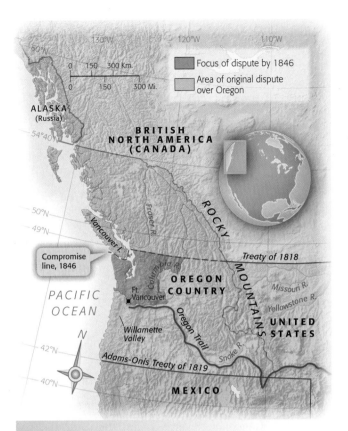

MAP 12.3 Oregon Territory
This map shows the changing boundaries and shifting possession of the Oregon Country. As a result of Polk's aggressive stance and economic pressures, Britain ceded all land south of the 49th parallel to the United States in 1846. © Cengage Learning.

no laws, no guidelines existed on who was entitled to inherit his property. Settlers finally created a **probate court**, instructing it to follow the statutes of the state of New York, and appointed a committee to frame a constitution and draft a basic code of laws. Opposition from the British put an end to this early effort at self-rule, but the movement continued. Two years later, Americans began agitating again, this time because of wolves preying on their livestock. They held a series of "Wolf Meetings" in 1843 to discuss joint protection and resolved to create a civil government. Although

☐ **Oregon Question** The question of the national ownership of the Pacific Northwest; the United States and England renegotiated the boundary in 1846, establishing it at 49° north latitude.

proviso A clause making a qualification, condition, or restriction in a document.

probate court A court that establishes the validity of wills and administers the estates of people who have died.

In the Wider World

Russian Imperial Expansion

As the United States pushed westward toward the Pacific, Russia was expanding its borders southward toward the Mediterranean. And like the United States, the Russians faced serious resistance from indigenous tribes and neighboring nations. Beginning in the 1820s and lasting for over thirty years, tribal groups in the Caucasus Mountains fought a protracted guerrilla war, killing thousands of Russian soldiers yearly. Despite such drastic losses, vast superiority in numbers and technology finally brought victory to the Russians in the late 1850s, and places like Dagestan, Chechnya, and Ossetia were grafted onto the growing empire. Like contemporary Americans, Russians were sure that they were participating in an exceptional mission, a manifest destiny, and when it was over the Tsar's forces declared pride in having "civilized" and "domesticated" a savage frontier. Ironically, throughout the United States, newspapers and magazines condemned Russian aggression, ignoring the amazing parallels between that behavior and their own.

---

the British tried to prevent it, the assembly passed the **First Organic Laws of Oregon** on July 5, 1843, making Oregon an independent republic in all but name. Independence, however, was not the settlers' long-term goal. The document's preamble announced that the code of laws would continue in force "until such time as the United States of America extend their jurisdiction over us."

Revolution in Texas

Similar problems faced American settlers who had taken up residence in Spain's, then Mexico's territories in the Southwest. Although the Spanish and then the Mexican government had invited Anglo-Americans to settle in the region, these pioneers generally ignored Mexican customs and disregarded Mexican law. This was particularly the case after 1829, when Mexico began attaching duties to trade items moving between the region and the neighboring United States. Mexico also abolished importing slaves. Bad

feelings grew over the years, but the distant and politically unstable Mexican government could do little to enforce laws and customs. In addition, despite the friction between cultures in Texas, many Tejanos were disturbed by the corruption and political instability in Mexico City and were as eager as their Texan counterparts to participate in the United States' thriving cotton market.

Assuming responsibility for forging a peaceful settlement, Stephen F. Austin went to Mexico City in 1833. While Austin was there, **Antonio López de Santa Anna** seized power. Although he had supported Mexico's republican constitution, adopted in 1824, Santa Anna had since come to the conclusion that Mexico was not ready for democracy. Upon assuming power, he suspended the constitution, dismissed Congress, and set himself up as the self-declared "Napoleon of the West."

Throughout Mexico, citizens who had anticipated democracy were outraged by Santa Anna's actions. To the south, in Yucatán and elsewhere, provinces openly rebelled. The same potential existed along the northern frontier as well. Trying to avoid an open break, Austin met with Santa Anna in 1834 and presented several petitions advocating reforms and greater self-government in Texas, but Santa Anna made it clear that he intended to exert his authority over the region. On his arrival back in Texas in 1835, Austin declared, "War is our only recourse."

Mexican officials, viewing the unrest in Texas as rebellion against their authority, issued arrest warrants for all the Texas troublemakers they could identify and **deployed** troops to San Antonio. Austin immediately sent out word for Texans to arm themselves. The

---

□ **First Organic Laws of Oregon** A constitution adopted by American settlers in the Oregon Country on July 5, 1843, establishing a government independent from Great Britain and requesting annexation by the United States.

□ **Antonio López de Santa Anna** Mexican general who was president of Mexico when he led an attack on the Alamo in 1836; he again led Mexico during its war with the United States in 1846–1848.

deploy To position military resources (troops, artillery, equipment) in preparation for action.

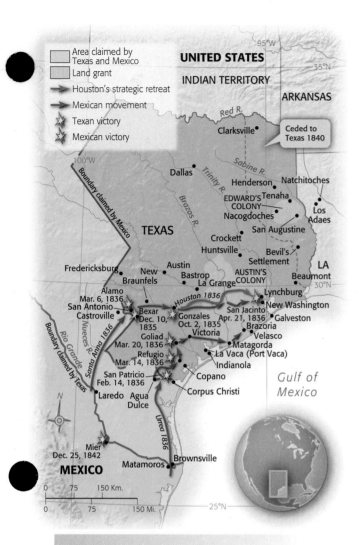

MAP 12.4 Texas Revolution
This map shows troop movements and the major battles in the Texas Revolution, as well as the conflicting boundary claims made by Texans and the Mexican government. The Battle of San Jacinto and the Treaty of Velasco ended the war, but the conflicting land claims continued when Mexico repudiated the treaty. © Cengage Learning.

Texas Revolution started quickly thereafter when the little town of Gonzales refused to surrender a cannon to Mexican officials on September 29, 1835.

Angered by the rebellion, Santa Anna personally led the Mexican army into Texas, arriving in San Antonio on February 23, 1836 (see Map 12.4). Knowing that Santa Anna was on his way, Texas militia commander William Travis moved his troops into the **Alamo**. On March 6 Santa Anna ordered an all-out assault and despite staggering casualties was able to capture the former mission. Most of the post's defenders were killed in the assault, and Santa Anna executed

those who survived the battle. While Travis struggled at the Alamo, General **Sam Houston** was busy rounding up troops for a more general war against the invading Santa Anna.

Despite the loss at the Alamo, Texans continued to underestimate Santa Anna's strength and his resolve to put down the rebellion. After a series of defeats, however, the Texans scored a stunning victory on April 21 at the San Jacinto River and captured Santa Anna. In exchange for his release, in May 1836 Santa Anna signed the **Treaty of Velasco**, officially recognizing Texas's independence and acknowledging the Rio Grande as the border between Texas and Mexico.

As in Oregon, many leaders in Texas hoped their actions would lead to swift annexation by the United States. In 1838 Houston, by then president of the Republic of Texas, invited the United States to annex Texas. Because all of Texas lay below the Missouri Compromise line (see Map 10.1, page 235), John Quincy Adams, now a Whig member of the House of Representatives, **filibustered** for three weeks against the acquisition of such a massive block of potential slave territory. Seeking to avoid national controversy, Congress refused to ratify the annexation treaty.

The Politics of Manifest Destiny

Although Adams was typical of one wing of the Whig coalition, he certainly did not speak for the majority of Whigs on the topic of national expansion. The party of manufacturing, revivalism, and social reform inclined naturally toward the blending of political, economic, and religious evangelicalism that was manifest destiny. William Henry Harrison himself, the united party's first national candidate, was a colorful figure in American westward expansion (see Chapter 10), and his political campaign in 1840 celebrated the simple virtues of frontier life. When Harrison died soon after taking office in 1841, his vice president, John Tyler, picked up the torch of American expansionism.

▫ **Texas Revolution** A revolt by American colonists in Texas against Mexican rule; it began in 1835 and ended with the establishment of the Republic of Texas in 1836.

▫ **Alamo** A fortified Franciscan mission at San Antonio, where Santa Anna's forces wiped out rebellious Texas defenders in 1836.

▫ **Sam Houston** American general and politician who fought in the struggle for Texas's independence from Mexico and became president of the Republic of Texas.

▫ **Treaty of Velasco** Treaty that Santa Anna signed in May 1836 after his capture at the San Jacinto River; it recognized the Republic of Texas, but the Mexican congress later rejected it.

filibuster To use obstructionist tactics, especially prolonged speechmaking, to delay legislative action.

This "Liberty" flag was carried by the Texan army during the battle against Santa Anna's Mexican troops at San Jacinto. It was crafted by the ladies of Newport, Kentucky in support of the cause of Texas independence and entrusted to Kentucky volunteers who ventured to Texas to fight in the revolution.

Tyler was a less typical Whig than even Adams. A Virginian and a states' rights advocate, he had been a staunch Democrat until the nullification crisis, when he bolted the party to protest Jackson's strong assertion of federal power (see page 249). As president, Tyler seemed still to be more Democrat than Whig. Although he had objected to Jackson's use of presidential power, like Old Hickory, Tyler as president was unyielding where ideology was concerned. He vetoed high protective tariffs, internal improvement bills, and attempts to revive the Second Bank of the United States. Tyler's refusal to promote Whig economic policies led to a general crisis in government in 1843, when his entire cabinet resigned over his veto of a bank bill.

Tyler did share his party's desire for expansion, however. He assigned his secretary of state, Daniel Webster, to negotiate a treaty with Britain to settle

□ **Webster-Ashburton Treaty** 1842 treaty that established the present border between Canada and northeastern Maine.

disputes over the Canadian border. The resulting **Webster-Ashburton Treaty** (1842) gave a large chunk of Lower Canada to the United States and finalized the nation's northeastern border. In that same year, Tyler also adopted an aggressive stance on the Oregon Question by appointing Elijah White, one of the organizers of the Wolf Meetings, as the federal Indian agent for the region, undercutting British authority.

Tyler also pushed a forceful policy toward Texas. In 1842 Sam Houston repeated his invitation for the United States to annex Texas, only to be rebuffed by Secretary of State Webster, a New Englander who shared Adams's views. When Webster resigned with the other cabinet officers in 1843, however, Tyler replaced him with fellow Virginian Abel P. Upshur, who immediately reopened the matter of Texas annexation.

Negotiations between Houston's representatives and Tyler's secretary of state—Upshur at first, then, after Upshur's death, John C. Calhoun—led to a treaty of annexation on April 11, 1844. In line with the Treaty of Velasco, the annexation document named

This campaign banner celebrating the Democratic candidacy of James K. Polk and George M. Dallas subtly conveys the party's platform. Surrounding Polk's picture are twenty-five stars, one for each state in the Union. Outside the corner box, a twenty-sixth star stands for Texas, which Polk promised to annex.

the Rio Grande as the southern boundary of Texas. Annexation remained a major arguing point between proslavery and antislavery forces, however, and the treaty failed ratification in the Senate. The issue of Texas annexation then joined the Oregon Question as a major campaign issue in the presidential election of 1844.

This put the two leading political figures of the day, Democrat Martin Van Buren and Whig Henry Clay, in an uncomfortable position. Van Buren was on record as opposing the extension of slavery and was therefore against the annexation of Texas. Clay, the architect of the American System, was opposed to any form of uncontrolled expansion, especially if it meant fanning sectional tensions, and he too opposed immediate annexation of Texas. Approaching the election, both issued statements to the effect that they would back annexation only with Mexico's consent.

Clay's somewhat ambiguous stance on expansion contrasted sharply with Tyler's efforts to advance the cause of manifest destiny. However, President Tyler's constant refusal to support the larger Whig political agenda led the party to nominate Clay anyway. Van Buren was not so lucky. The strong southern wing of the Democratic Party was so put off by Van Buren's position on slavery that it blocked him, securing the nomination of Tennessee congressman James K. Polk.

The Democrats based their platform on the issues surrounding Oregon and Texas. They implied that the regions rightfully belonged to the United States, stating "that the *re-occupation* of Oregon and the *reannexation* of Texas at the earliest practicable period are great American measures." Polk vowed to stand up to the British by claiming the entire Oregon Country up to 54°40′ north latitude and to defend the territorial claims of Texas. For his part, Clay continued to waffle on expansionism, emphasizing economic policies instead.

The election demonstrated the people's commitment to manifest destiny. Clay was a national figure, well respected and regarded as one of the nation's leading statesmen, whereas Polk was barely known outside Tennessee. Still, Polk polled forty thousand more popular votes than Clay and garnered sixty-five more electoral votes. Seeing the election as a political barometer, outgoing president Tyler prepared a special message to Congress in December 1844

◻ **James K. Polk** Tennessee congressman who was a leader of the Democratic Party and the dark-horse winner of the presidential campaign in 1844.

proposing a **joint resolution** annexing Texas. Many congressmen who had opposed annexation could not ignore the clear mandate given to manifest destiny in the presidential election, and the bill to annex Texas passed in February 1845.

Holding to the position he had taken prior to the election, in his annual message for 1845, Polk asked Congress to end the joint occupation of Oregon. Referring to the largely forgotten Monroe Doctrine, the president insisted that no nation other than the United States should be permitted to occupy any part of North America and urged Congress to assert exclusive control over the Oregon Country even if doing so meant war.

Neither the United States nor Britain intended to go to war over Oregon. The only issue—where the border would be—was a matter for the bargaining table, not the battlefield. Recalling the rhetoric that had gotten him elected, Polk insisted on 54°40′. The British lobbied for the Columbia River as the boundary, but their position softened quickly. The fur trade along the Columbia was in rapid decline and had become unprofitable by the early 1840s. As a result, in the spring of 1846, the British foreign secretary offered Polk a compromise boundary at the 49th parallel. The Senate recommended that Polk accept the offer, and a treaty settling the Oregon Question was ratified on June 15, 1846.

joint resolution A formal statement adopted by both houses of Congress and subject to approval by the president; if approved, it has the force of law.

Individual Voices

ELIZABETH CADY STANTON

The "Declaration of Sentiments," Seneca Falls Women's Rights Convention, 1848

At the 1848 Women's Rights Convention held in Seneca Falls, New York, Elizabeth Cady Stanton wrote a "Declaration of Sentiments" that was presented to the three hundred male and female delegates who attended. The document presented an overview of Stanton's and Lucretia Mott's views on the conditions for women. A second document presented eleven specific resolutions relating to equality under the law, rights to control property, and other prominent gender issues, including a demand for woman suffrage. The official minutes of the convention specify that all eleven "were finally passed by a large majority."

Bettmann/Corbis.

① The wording of this portion of the "Declaration of Sentiments" should sound familiar; can you identify what document this language was based on? What rhetorical purpose was served by basing this document on that one?

② What, exactly, is Stanton calling for here? Is it simply extended rights for women or something much more comprehensive?

③ In order for the document to fit here, a list of specific complaints about women's treatment by men has been omitted. A transcription of the official minutes of the convention which contains the full text of both the *Declaration of Sentiments* and *Resolutions* is available at http://ecssba .rutgers.edu/docs/seneca .html.

④ A Whig newspaper called the declaration "the most shocking and unnatural event ever recorded in the history of womanity." Why do you think this document was received so harshly?

When, in the course of human events, it becomes necessary for one portion of the family of man to assume among the people of the earth a position different from that which they have hitherto occupied, but one to which the laws of nature and of nature's God entitle them, a decent respect to the opinions of mankind requires that they should declare the causes that impel them to such a course.

We hold these truths to be self-evident: that all men and women are created equal; that they are endowed by their Creator with certain inalienable rights; that among these are life, liberty, and the pursuit of happiness; that to secure these rights governments are instituted, deriving their just powers from the consent of the governed. Whenever any form of government becomes destructive of these ends, it is the right of those who suffer from it to refuse allegiance to it, and to insist upon the institution of a new government, laying its foundation on such principles, and organizing its powers in such form, as to them shall seem most likely to effect their safety and happiness. **①** Prudence, indeed, will dictate that governments long established should not be changed for light and transient causes; and accordingly all experience hath shown that mankind are more disposed to suffer, while evils are sufferable, than to right themselves by abolishing the forms to which they are accustomed. But when a long train of abuses and usurpations, pursuing invariably the same object, evinces a design to reduce them under absolute despotism, it is their duty to throw off such government, and to provide new guards for their future security. Such has been the patient sufferance of the women under this government, and such is now the necessity which constrains them to demand the equal station to which they are entitled. **②**

The history of mankind is a history of repeated injuries and usurpations on the part of man toward woman, having in direct object the establishment of an absolute tyranny over her. To prove this, let facts be submitted to a candid world. . . . **③**

Now, in view of this entire disfranchisement of one-half the people of this country, their social and religious degradation—in view of the unjust laws above mentioned, and because women do feel themselves aggrieved, oppressed, and fraudulently deprived of their most sacred rights, we insist that they have immediate admission to all the rights and privileges which belong to them as citizens of the United States. **④**

Study Tools

SUMMARY

Americans responded in many different ways to the unsettling changes that had been taking place as the nation modernized and expanded. Different economic classes responded by creating their own cultures and by adopting specific strategies for dealing with anxiety. Some chose violent protest, some passive resistance. Some looked to heaven for solutions and others to earthly utopias. And out of this complex swirl, something entirely new and unexpected emerged: a new America, on its way to being socially, politically, intellectually, and culturally modern.

A new generation emerged that grasped greedily at the opportunities offered by new economic and cultural arrangements. Literacy grew as never before in the nation's history and with it a thirst for new knowledge. Book publishers, magazine editors, and charitable societies competed to meet this new demand for information and entertainment. And this group of young readers sought to express itself not only in literature, but in politics as well. As expanding media made more people aware of issues taking place nationwide, they were drawn into politics as never before. In the presidential election of 1840 almost two and a half million men cast ballots, more than a million more than had voted four years earlier.

In that election, William Henry Harrison, a man who had become a national figure by fighting against Indian sovereignty and for westward expansion, swept a new sentiment into national politics. Increasingly Americans came to believe that the West would provide the solutions to the problems ushered in by new conditions. In the short term, this notion led to an exciting race by Americans toward the Pacific. But different visions about how the West would solve the nation's problems soon added to the ever-growing air of crisis.

CHRONOLOGY
Modernization and Rising Stress

1821	Charles G. Finney experiences a religious conversion
1823	James Fenimore Cooper's *The Pioneers*
1825	Thomas Cole begins Hudson River school of painting
	Robert Owen establishes community at New Harmony, Indiana
1826	Shakers have eighteen communities in the United States
1831	Nat Turner's Rebellion
	William Lloyd Garrison begins publishing *The Liberator*
	Joseph Smith Jr.'s revelations concerning marriage and property
1832	Jackson reelected
1833	Lydia Sigourney publishes bestsellers *Letters to Young Ladies* and *How to Be Happy*
	George Bancroft publishes volume 1 of his American history
	Formation of National Trades' Union
	Formation of Whig Party
1835	Texas Revolution begins
1836	Congress passes the gag rule
	Martin Van Buren elected president
1837	Horace Mann heads first public board of education
	Panic of 1837
	Ralph Waldo Emerson's "American Scholar" speech
	Senate rejects annexation of Texas
1838	Emerson articulates transcendentalism
	Sarah Grimké publishes *Letters on the Equality of the Sexes and the Condition of Women*
1840	Log cabin campaign
	William Henry Harrison elected president
1841	Brook Farm established
	Death of President Harrison; John Tyler becomes president
1842	*Commonwealth v. Hunt*
1843	Dorothea Dix advocates state-funded insane asylums
	Oregon adopts First Organic Laws
1844	James K. Polk elected president
1845	United States annexes Texas
	Term "manifest destiny" coined
1846	Oregon boundary established
1848	Seneca Falls Women's Rights Convention

Study Tools

FOCUS QUESTIONS

If you have mastered this chapter, you should be able to answer these questions and to explain the terms that follow the questions.

1. How did developments in American arts and letters reflect the spirit of change during the Jacksonian era?

2. To what extent did international forces influence American cultural expressions?

3. What did Jackson's opponents hope to accomplish when they built their coalition to oppose the Democrats? How successful were they?

4. What cultural factors helped contribute to the particular composition and policy interests of the Whigs?

5. What forces in American life contributed to the concept of manifest destiny?

6. To what extent did the actions taken by American settlers in Oregon and Texas reflect the ideal of manifest destiny?

KEY TERMS

Lucretia Mott   *p. 281*
William Lloyd Garrison   *p. 281*
romanticism   *p. 282*
Ralph Waldo Emerson   *p. 282*
transcendentalism   *p. 282*
Henry David Thoreau   *p. 282*
Hudson River school   *p. 284*
National Trades' Union   *p. 285*
Commonwealth v. Hunt   *p. 285*
"Negro spiritual"   *p. 287*
New Harmony   *p. 289*
Brook Farm   *p. 289*
Charles Fourier   *p. 289*
Oneida Community   *p. 289*

Shakers   *p. 290*
United Order   *p. 290*
Joseph Tracy   *p. 291*
Charles Grandison Finney   *p. 291*
Second Great Awakening   *p. 291*
Christian benevolence movement   *p. 292*
Dorothea Dix   *p. 293*
temperance movement   *p. 293*
Horace Mann   *p. 293*
American Colonization Society   *p. 294*
spoils system   *p. 296*
Whig Party   *p. 296*

Panic of 1837   *p. 297*
Specie Circular   *p. 297*
Oregon Question   *p. 299*
First Organic Laws of Oregon   *p. 300*
Antonio López de Santa Anna   *p. 300*
Texas Revolution   *p. 301*
Alamo   *p. 301*
Sam Houston   *p. 301*
Treaty of Velasco   *p. 301*
Webster-Ashburton Treaty   *p. 302*
James K. Polk   *p. 303*

SUGGESTED RESOURCES

Donna M. Campbell. "Domestic or Sentimental Fiction, 1820–1865," http://public.wsu.edu/~campbelld/amlit/domestic.htm. An excellent site created by a literary scholar. Discusses many of the leading sentimental writers and has links to their works.

National Archives. "The Struggle for Democracy: Trade Unionism," http://www.nationalarchives.gov.uk/pathways/citizenship/struggle_democracy/trade_unionism.htm. This site covers the whole of the nineteenth century but includes information and documents from the earliest days of union organization in the antebellum period.

National Geographic Education. "The Underground Railroad," http://education.nationalgeographic.com/education/multimedia/interactive/the-underground-railroad/?ar_a=1. An interactive educational site featuring a simulation retracing the experience of runaway slaves, biographies of many key players, maps of various escape routes, and interesting facts and images.

National Park Service. "Shaker Historical Trail," http://www.nps.gov/nr/travel/shaker/index.htm. An informative site with links to other Shaker sites, an excellent introduction to the Shakers, and an extensive bibliography.

National Park Service. "Women's Rights National Historical Park," http://www.nps.gov/wori/historyculture/elizabeth-cady-stanton.htm. This site centers on the Elizabeth Cady Stanton house museum, but contains a great deal of information and links about the early women's rights movement in general.

Public Broadcasting Service. "Nat Turner's Rebellion, 1831," http://www.pbs.org/wgbh/aia/part3/3p1518.html. A brief history of the rebellion with links to a number of primary sources.

13

Sectional Conflict and Shattered Union, 1840–1860

INDIVIDUAL CHOICES

Frederick Douglass

In 1838, Frederick Douglass, a slave living in Baltimore, decided that he would try to escape. This was no sudden impulse; Douglass had been thinking about freedom for most of his life. As a young boy he told his white friends, "You will be free as soon as you are twenty-one, *but I am a slave for life!*" And he had tried once before to make his way to freedom, but was captured and returned to his owner. Though his master threatened to sell him to a cotton plantation in Alabama, Douglass's intelligence and skills were worth more in Baltimore: he was made an apprentice at the local shipyard, eventually becoming a master ship caulker. His productivity earned him a lot of freedom: he made his own contracts, set his own work schedule, and collected his own earnings. "I was now of some importance to my master," Douglass recalled. "I was bringing him from six to seven dollars per week." But he also remembered his liberty. "I have observed this in my experience of slavery," Douglass commented, "that whenever my

National Portrait Gallery, Smithsonian Institution/Art Resource, NY

condition was improved, instead of its increasing my contentment, it only increased my desire to be free."

Using a wide network of personal connections, Douglass raised money and secured forged documents that entitled him to pass unmolested through slave territory. On September 3, Douglass disguised himself as a merchant sailor and made his way northward, arriving in New York City early on the morning of September 4. Although he had a couple of close calls, Douglass's escape had succeeded.

Douglass now was free, but the promised land of the nonslave North proved disappointing. Moving to the town of New Bedford, Massachusetts, where he hoped to earn a living in the boatyards, Douglass found that "such was the strength of prejudice against color, among the white caulkers, that they refused to work with me, and of course I could get no employment." For three years he was forced to do odd jobs to keep himself and his wife alive. "There was no work too hard—none too dirty," he recalled. Despite this decline in status and earnings, Douglass never regretted his choice of freedom, and when he attended an antislavery conference in Nantucket, Douglass stood to speak about his experiences. When famed abolitionist William Lloyd Garrison heard Douglass, he was so moved that he offered to support Douglass as a lecturer in the antislavery cause. Having experienced both slavery in the South and racial discrimination in the North, Douglass chose to speak out for the cause of racial equality for the next fifty years. (See this chapter's Individual Voices feature for an example of his speaking style.)

Though not a politician, Frederick Douglass certainly was not immune to the political wrangling going on around him. Like many Americans, Douglass's life was in a state of constant upheaval as politicians engaged in abstract power games that had all-too-real consequences.

Struggles over tariffs, coinage, internal improvements, public land policy, and dozens of other practical issues intersected in complicated ways with the overinflated egos of power-hungry politicians to create an air of political contention and national crisis. And in the midst of it all, a war with neighboring Mexico brought even more contention and a huge tract of new land into the mix, land that seemed veined with gold, adding greed to the equation. Then strong-willed men such as Jefferson Davis and Stephen A. Douglas threw more fuel on the fire as they fought over the best—that is, most profitable and politically advantageous—route for a transcontinental railroad that would tie this new wealth to the rest of the nation. The halls of Congress rang with debate, denunciation, and even physical violence.

Tangled in it all lurked an institution that Frederick Douglass knew all too well: slavery. In a changing society rife with the problems of expansion, immigration, industrialization, and urbanization, political leaders tried either to seek compromise or to ignore the slavery question altogether. In reality, they could do neither. As the confrontation between northern and southern societies peaked, many people wanted peace and favored reconciliation. Ultimately, however, both sides rejected compromise, leading to America's most destructive and deadly war.

NEW POLITICAL OPTIONS

☆ How did the politicization of slavery in the 1840s begin to move the nation toward crisis?

☆ How did the war with Mexico and its outcomes influence politics?

The presidential elections in 1840 and 1844 had put American expansion at the heart of political debate. While all could affirm the existence of manifest destiny, there was significant disagreement about exactly what form it should take. The political system held together during these years, but the successes enjoyed by third-party challenges were evidence that significant problems churned under the surface. It was clear to many that the nation's political system was not

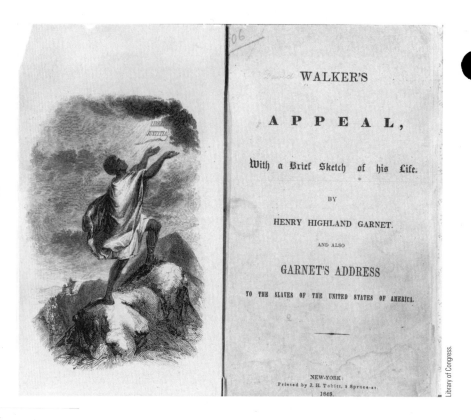

While white abolitionists such as William Lloyd Garrison crafted moral arguments against slavery, African Americans were making a much more direct and emotional appeal. This 1848 publication contained a copy of David Walker's 1829 *Appeal to the Coloured Citizens of the World*, a call for free and enslaved people to rise up, along with a biography of Walker by another noted African American abolitionist Henry Highland Garnet with his appeal to slaves to act for their freedom.

meeting their economic and ideological needs, and they began looking for new options.

Politicizing Slavery in the 1840s

Antislavery sentiments were still not widespread among the American people during the 1840s. However, abolitionist voices were getting more politically insistent. Despite strong and sometimes violent opposition, the abolition movement had continued to grow, especially among the privileged and educated classes in the Northeast.

But the leading voice among the abolitionists, William Lloyd Garrison, consistently alienated his followers. Calling the Constitution "a covenant with death and an agreement with hell," Garrison burned a copy of it, telling his followers, "so perish all compromises with tyranny," and he urged them to have no dealings with a government that permitted so great an evil as slavery. Citing the reluctance of most organized churches to condemn slavery outright, Garrison urged his followers to break with them as well. He also offended many of his white evangelical supporters by associating with and supporting free black advocates of abolition.

◘ **Sojourner Truth** Abolitionist and feminist who was freed from slavery in 1827 and became a leading preacher against slavery and for the rights of women.

During the 1830s, even moderates within the abolition movement had celebrated Frederick Douglass, Sojourner Truth, and other African American abolitionists, welcoming them as members of the American Anti-Slavery Society. But more insistent black voices frightened white abolitionists. African American abolitionist David Walker cried, "The whites want slaves, and want us for their slaves, but some of them will curse the day they ever saw us." Walker advocated that African Americans should "kill or be killed." Another black spokesman, Henry Highland Garnet, proclaimed, "Strike for your lives and liberties. . . . Rather die freemen than live to be slaves."

Garrison's sentiments mobilized some, but most of his followers were more conservative. In 1840 this and other controversial issues caused many of those moderates to bolt from Garrison's American Anti-Slavery Society to form the more temperate American and Foreign Anti-Slavery Society. This new group forged strong ties with mainstream politicians and church leaders who, while opposed to any extension of slavery and sympathetic to moderate abolitionist proposals, had been relatively silent because of Garrison's perceived radicalism.

Efforts by moderate antislavery supporters meshed with the political aspirations of both those who opposed slavery's expansion primarily for political and economic reasons and those who were motivated by purely ethical concerns. Moderates in 1840 challenged both Whig and Democratic ambivalence by forming the Liberty Party.

Specifically disavowing Garrison's drastic aims, Liberty Party leaders argued that slavery would eventually die on its own if it could be confined geographically. In addition, the Liberty Party called for the abolition of slavery in Washington, D.C., and in all the territories where it already existed. Though certainly more popular than Garrison's appeals, this moderate message drew little open political support: in 1840 Liberty Party presidential candidate James G. Birney garnered only about 7,000 votes. But in 1844, when he again ran on the Liberty Party ticket, he won 62,000 popular votes. Clearly a moderate antislavery position was becoming more acceptable.

Opting for War with Mexico

With the Oregon agreement and the annexation of Texas in place, the nation's border issues were now settled from Congress's point of view, but Mexico had a completely different outlook. Mexico had never ratified the Treaty of Velasco ending the Texas Revolution, so Texas's southern border remained in dispute. President Polk wanted a war with Mexico to unify his party and hopefully give the Democrats an electoral edge based on patriotism. Seeking to push Mexico into a fight, the president dispatched John Slidell to Mexico City late in 1845, instructing him to pressure the Mexicans to sell New Mexico and California, in addition to accepting the Rio Grande as the border with Texas. At the same time, Polk dispatched American troops to Louisiana, ready to strike if Mexico resisted Slidell's offers. He also notified Americans in California that if war broke out the Pacific fleet would seize California ports and support an insurrection against Mexican authority.

Nervous but bristling over what seemed to be preparations for war, the Mexican government refused to receive Slidell. Polk then ordered Zachary Taylor to lead troops from New Orleans toward the Rio Grande. Shortly thereafter, an American military party led by John C. Frémont entered California's Salinas Valley. Reaching an end to its patience, on April 22, 1846, Mexico proclaimed that its territory had been violated and declared war. Two days later, Mexican troops engaged a detachment of Taylor's army at Matamoros on the Rio Grande, killing eleven and capturing the rest. When news of the battle reached Washington, Polk immediately called for war. Although the nation was far from united on the issue, Congress agreed on May 13, 1846 (see Map 13.1).

The outbreak of war disturbed many Americans. In New England protest ran high. It was not expansion as such that troubled northeasterners, but the potential that annexing so much land south of the Missouri Compromise line would expand slavery and embolden southern political agendas. Since the Missouri Compromise, some northerners had come to believe that a slaveholding oligarchy controlled life and politics in the South. Abolitionists warned that this "Slave Power" sought to expand its reach until it controlled every aspect of American life. Many viewed Congress's adoption of the gag rule in 1836 and the drive to annex Texas as evidence of the Slave Power's influence.

Serious political combat began in August 1846 when David Wilmot, a Democratic representative from Pennsylvania, proposed an amendment to the war appropriations bill that "neither slavery nor involuntary servitude shall ever exist" in any territory gained in the War with Mexico. The Wilmot Proviso twice passed in the House of Representatives but both times failed in the Senate, where equal state representation gave the South a stronger position. The House finally decided in April to appropriate money for the war without stipulating whether or not slavery would be permitted.

While all this political infighting was going on in Washington, D.C., a real war was going on in the Southwest (see Map 13.1). In California, American settlers rallied in open rebellion in the Sacramento Valley and declared independence in June 1846. They crafted a flag depicting a grizzly bear and announced the birth of the Bear Flag Republic. Frémont's force rushed to join the Bear Flag rebels, and when the little army arrived in Monterey on July 19, they found that the Pacific fleet had already acted on Polk's orders and seized the city. The Mexican forces were in full flight southward.

To round out the greater southwestern strategy, on May 15 Polk ordered Colonel Stephen Kearny to invade New Mexico. After leading his men across 800 miles of desert to Santa Fe, Kearny found a less-than-hostile enemy. Members of the interracial upper class of Santa Fe had already expressed interest in joining the United States and given the opportunity, they surrendered without firing a shot.

□ **Liberty Party** The first antislavery political party; it was formed in Albany, New York, in 1840.

□ **Zachary Taylor** American general whose defeat of Santa Anna at Buena Vista in 1847 made him a national hero and the Whig choice for president in 1848.

□ **John C. Frémont** Explorer, soldier, and politician who explored and mapped much of the American West and Northwest; he later ran unsuccessfully for president.

oligarchy A small group of people or families who hold power.

□ **Wilmot Proviso** An 1846 measure that would have closed any territory acquired from Mexico to slavery; it was defeated in the Senate.

Within a short time, all of the New Mexico region and California were securely in the hands of U.S. forces. In Texas, however, Zachary Taylor faced more serious opposition. Marching across the Rio Grande, Taylor headed for the regional capital of Monterrey, capturing the city in September 1846. Because of his military successes, Taylor became a political threat to Polk within the party. In an attempt to undermine Taylor's political appeal, Polk turned the war effort over to **Winfield Scott**, ordering him to gather an army, drawing men from Taylor's and other forces, and sail to Veracruz. From there the army was to move inland to take Mexico City (see Map 13.1).

Planning to crush Taylor's remaining force and then wheel around to attack Scott, General Santa Anna and his numerically superior army encountered

Taylor at Buena Vista in February 1847. Tired and dispirited from a forced march across the desert, the Mexican army was in no shape to fight, but Santa Anna ordered an attack anyway. Tactically speaking, the **Battle of Buena Vista** was a draw, but it was a strategic victory for the Americans: Taylor's fresher troops stalled Santa Anna's forces, permitting Scott's army to capture Veracruz on March 9. Marching and fighting their way to Mexico City, Scott's force captured it on September 13, 1847.

With Mexico City, all of Texas, New Mexico, and California in American hands, the direction of treaty talks should have been fairly predictable. Scott's enormous success, however, caused the Mexican government's collapse, leaving no one to negotiate with. The Mexican government eventually elected a new president, and finally, on February 2, 1848, the Mexican

MAP 13.1 The Southwest and the Mexican War

When the United States acquired Texas, it inherited the Texans' boundary disputes with Mexico. This map shows the outcome: war with Mexico in 1846 and the acquisition of the disputed territories in Texas as well as most of Arizona, New Mexico, and California through the Treaty of Guadalupe Hidalgo. © Cengage Learning.

An American private, Samuel E. Chamberlain, made this drawing of the Battle of Buena Vista. Present at the battle, Chamberlain watched as Mexican forces overran an artillery emplacement. The Americans eventually turned the tide, and the battle came out a draw. Even so, troops under Santa Anna were forced to retreat into the Mexican interior, spoiling the general's hope for a quick and easy victory against the invading Americans.

San Jacinto Museum of History Association.

delegation signed the **Treaty of Guadalupe Hidalgo**, granting the United States all the territory between the Nueces River and the Rio Grande and between there and the Pacific. In exchange, American envoy Nicholas Trist agreed that the United States would pay Mexico $15 million and would pay any **war reparations** owed to Americans.

Polk was very angry when he heard the terms of the treaty, believing that the sweeping American victory justified annexing all of Mexico. In Congress, however, many antislavery voices protested bringing so much potential slave territory into the Union. Others opposed the annexation because they feared that Mexico's largely Roman Catholic population might be a threat to Protestant institutions in the United States. Still others, many of whom had opposed the war to begin with, had moral objections to taking any territory by force. Perhaps more convincing than any of these arguments, however, was that the war had cost a lot of money, and congressmen were unwilling to allocate more if peace was within reach. With these considerations in mind, the Senate approved the treaty by a vote of 38 to 14.

No sooner had California been acquired than its value increased significantly. In 1848 a group of laborers digging a millrace for John Sutter in northern California found flakes and then chunks of gold.

Despite efforts to suppress the news, by September, information had reached the East that the light work of panning for gold in California could yield $50 a day, two months' wages for an average northern workingman. In 1849 more than a hundred thousand **forty-niners** took up residence in California. And the question of getting that gold back to financial centers in the East would almost immediately become another political controversy.

□ **Winfield Scott** Virginia soldier and statesman who led troops in the War of 1812 and the War with Mexico; he was still serving as a general at the start of the Civil War.

□ **Battle of Buena Vista** Battle in February 1847 during which U.S. troops led by Zachary Taylor forced Santa Anna's forces to withdraw into the interior of Mexico.

□ **Treaty of Guadalupe Hidalgo** Treaty (1848) in which Mexico gave up Texas above the Rio Grande and ceded New Mexico and California to the United States in return for $15 million.

war reparations Payments made to settle damage and injury claims resulting from a war; usually paid by the losing side.

□ **forty-niners** Prospectors who streamed into California in 1849 after the discovery of gold in the Sierra foothills in 1848.

The Election of 1848

The American victory in the War with Mexico was an enormous shot in the arm for American nationalism and manifest destiny, but it also brought the divisive issue of slavery back into mainstream politics.

Suffering ill health, Polk chose not to run for a second term in 1848, leaving the Democrats scrambling for a candidate. They chose Lewis Cass of Michigan—a longtime moderate on slavery issues—as their presidential candidate and balanced the ticket with General William Butler of Kentucky. The Whigs hoped to ride a wave of nationalism following the War with Mexico by running military hero Zachary Taylor, a Louisianan and a slaveholder, for president and moderate New Yorker Millard Fillmore for vice president. Not satisfied with either party's candidates, a number of antislavery advocates banded together to launch yet another third party, the **Free-Soil Party**, and promoted Martin Van Buren as its candidate. Adopting the slogan "free soil, free speech, free labor,

☐ **Free-Soil Party** Successor to the Liberty Party, launched in Buffalo, New York, in 1848; fielded presidential candidates in 1848 and 1852.

and free men," this new coalition avoided taking a radical stand on the issue of slavery itself but was firm about excluding slavery from the territories. When all the votes were counted, Taylor came out the winner with Cass a very close second, but the Free-Soilers netted nearly 10 percent of all votes cast.

Disaffected Voices and Political Dissent

It did not take long after the election of 1848 for cracks in the system to become more prominent. In an effort to compete with Democrats in northeastern cities, the Whigs had tried to win Catholic and immigrant voters away from the rival party. The strategy backfired. Not only did the Whigs not attract large numbers of immigrants, they also alienated two core groups among their existing supporters: artisans, who saw immigrants as the main source of their economic and social woes, and Protestant evangelicals, to whom Roman Catholic Irish and German immigrants symbolized all that was threatening to the American republic. Whig leaders could do little to address these voters' immediate concerns, and increasing numbers left the Whig Party to form state and local coalitions more in tune with their hopes and fears.

One of the most prominent of these locally oriented groups was an anti-Catholic, anti-immigrant group that

Milwaukee County Historical Society.

Convinced that slavery and other sectional issues were blinding Americans to the true dangers stemming from uncontrolled immigration and foreign influence, the Know-Nothing Party ran Millard Fillmore for president in 1856. Banners like this one warned Americans and solicited their votes. Fillmore succeeded in getting 21 percent of the popular vote.

sprung up in New York but soon spread nationally. Bearing close ties, in terms of both leadership and attitudes, to the Antimasons, this loosely knit political network grafted xenophobic views onto strong antiparty sentiments, alleging wholesale voter fraud and government corruption by both major parties. They insisted that debates over slavery were being advanced by both Northern and Southern elites to divert ordinary Americans from the real issues of immigration, loss of job security, urban crowding and violence, and political corruption. Seeking to protect their members from this elite conspiracy, leaders told them to say "I know nothing" if they were questioned about the organization or its political intrigues, hence their name: the Know-Nothings. Increasingly after 1848, these secretive groups became more public and more vocal, promoting a twenty-one-year naturalization period, a ban against naturalized citizens holding public office, and the use of the Protestant Bible in public schools. As future president Rutherford B. Hayes noted, these people were expressing a "general disgust with the powers that be."

NEW POLITICAL REALITIES IN THE 1850S

☆ *What new political options affected the political system during the 1850s? In what ways?*

☆ *In what ways did economic developments such as railroads contribute to political instability?*

As a new decade dawned, developments during the previous ten years continued to destabilize politics as the overinflated egos of power-hungry politicians mixed with very real structural issues to create a new set of political realities in a hothouse environment being increasingly fired up by debates over slavery. The fate of the nation hung in the balance as various interests vied for control and pushed the country ever closer to crisis.

The Politics of Compromise

While dissidents of various types attacked the political parties from outside, problems raised by national expansion were continuing to erode party unity from within. Immediately after Zachary Taylor's election in 1848, California's future became a new divisive issue.

California presented a peculiar political problem. Once word reached the rest of the nation that California was rich with gold, politicians immediately began grasping for control over the newly acquired territory. Although large parts of the area lay below the 36°30′ line that the Missouri Compromise had set for slavery expansion, that legislation had applied only to territory acquired in the Louisiana Purchase, and the failure of Congress to pass Wilmot's Proviso left the question of slavery in the new territories wide open.

Having been primarily responsible for crafting the Missouri Compromise, Henry Clay took it upon himself to find a solution and proposed a complex omnibus bill to the Senate on January 20, 1850. California would enter the Union as a free state, but the slavery question would be left to popular sovereignty in all other territories acquired through the Treaty of Guadalupe Hidalgo. The bill also directed Texas to drop a continuing border dispute with New Mexico in exchange for federal assumption of Texas's public debt. Then, to appease abolitionists, Clay called for an end to the slave trade in Washington, D.C., and balanced that with a clause popular with southerners: a new, more effective fugitive slave law.

Though Clay was trying to please all sectional interests, the omnibus bill satisfied no one; Congress debated it without resolution for seven months. Finally, in July 1850, Clay's proposals were defeated. The 73-year-old political veteran left the capital tired and dispirited, but Stephen A. Douglas of Illinois set himself to the task of reviving the compromise. Using practical economic arguments and backroom political arm twisting, Douglas proposed each component of Clay's omnibus package as a separate bill, steering it forward toward a comprehensive compromise. Finally, in September, Congress passed the Compromise of 1850 (see Map 13.2).

The Compromise of 1850 did little to relieve underlying regional differences and only aggravated political dissent. That slaveowners could pursue runaway slaves into northern states and return them into bondage brought slavery too close to home for many northerners. Throughout the 1850s, both white and African American activists like Harriet Tubman

---

xenophobic Fearful of or hateful toward foreigners or those seen as being different.

□ **Know-Nothings** Members of anti-Catholic, anti-immigrant organizations who eventually formed themselves into a national political party.

omnibus bill A piece of legislation with many parts.

□ **popular sovereignty** In the debate over slavery, the principle that the citizens of each state should determine, by popular vote, whether to permit slavery.

□ **fugitive slave law** Law providing for the return of escaped slaves to their owners.

□ **Stephen A. Douglas** Illinois senator who tried to reconcile northern and southern differences over slavery through the Compromise of 1850 and the Kansas-Nebraska Act.

□ **Compromise of 1850** Plan intended to reconcile North and South on the issue of slavery; it recognized the principle of popular sovereignty and included a strong fugitive slave law.

□ **Harriet Tubman** One of the most famous and most effective of the many African American "conductors" on the Underground Railroad; she is thought to have been personally responsible for leading at least three hundred slaves into freedom.

sought to evade the law by conducting escaped slaves to Canada through a covert network of hiding places called the **Underground Railroad** (see Map 12.1, page 288). Southerners, too, had no reason to celebrate the admission of another nonslave state, further draining their power in Congress, while gaining no positive protection for slavery in either the territories or at home. Still, the compromise created a brief respite from the slavery-extension question at a time when the nation's attention increasingly needed to focus on other major changes in national life.

A Changing Political Economy

In the years following the Compromise of 1850, American economic and territorial growth continued to play a destabilizing role in both national and regional development. Most notably, during the 1850s industrial growth accelerated, further altering the nation's economic structure. By 1860 less than half of all northern workers made a living from agriculture as northern industry became more concentrated. Steam began to replace water as the primary power source, and factories were no longer limited to locations along rivers. The use of interchangeable parts became more sophisticated and intricate. In 1851, for example, Isaac Singer devised an assembly line using this technology and began mass-producing sewing machines, fostering a boom in ready-made clothing. As industry expanded, the North became more reliant on the West and South for raw materials and for the food consumed by those working in northeastern factories.

Railroad development stimulated economic and industrial growth. Between 1850 and 1860, the number of miles of track in the United States increased from nine thousand to more than thirty thousand. In 1852 the Michigan Southern Railroad completed the first line into Chicago from the East, and by 1855 that city had become a key transportation hub linking regions farther west with the eastern seaboard. Developing this transportation system was difficult. A lack of bridges and of a standard **rail gauge**—at least twelve different measurements were used—meant that cargoes frequently had to be transferred from one rail line to another. Despite these problems, railroads quickly became an integral part of the expanding American economy. Western farmers who had previously shipped their products downriver to New Orleans now sent them much more rapidly by rail to eastern industrial centers. The availability of reliable transportation induced farmers to cultivate more

MAP 13.2 The Compromise of 1850
The acquisition of Texas and California brought a showdown between North and South over representation in the national government. As this map shows, the Compromise of 1850 permitted Texas and California to be admitted to the Union without seriously undermining the balance of power in the Senate. In the House of Representatives, however, the balance favored the North. © Cengage Learning.

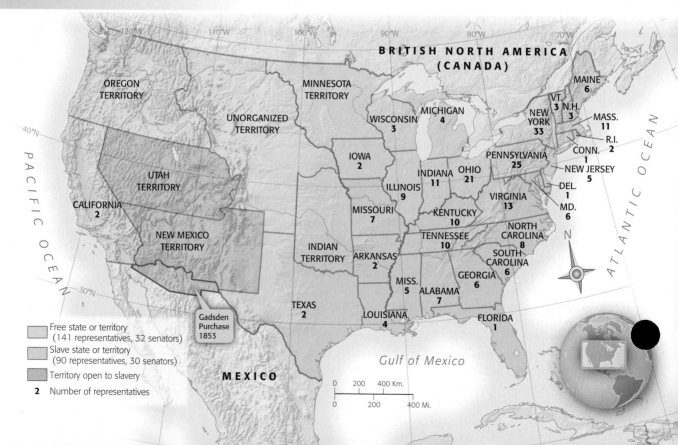

land, and enterprising individuals started up related businesses such as warehouses and grain elevators, simplifying storage and loading along railroad lines. Mining boomed, particularly the iron industry; the railroads not only transported ore but also became a prime consumer.

Building a railroad required huge sums of money. In populous areas, where passenger and freight traffic was heavy, the promise of a quick and profitable return on investment allowed railroads to raise sufficient capital by selling company stock. In sparsely settled regions, however, where investment returns were much slower, state and local governments loaned money directly to rail companies, financed them indirectly by purchasing stock, or extended state tax exemptions. The most crucial aid to railroads, however, was federal land grants.

The federal government, which owned vast amounts of unsettled territory, gave land to railroad developers who then leased or sold plots along the proposed route to finance construction. In 1850 Stephen A. Douglas netted a 2.6-million-acre land grant to Illinois, Mississippi, and Alabama for a railroad between Chicago and Mobile. Congress also invested heavily in plans for a transcontinental railroad and on March 4, 1853, appropriated $150,000 to survey potential routes across the continent.

While Americans were enjoying the rail boom, crop failures throughout Europe were creating new markets for American produce. During the 1850s, the price of grain rose sharply in world markets. Railroads allowed western farmers to ship directly to eastern seaports and on to Europe. Meanwhile, technological advances in farming equipment enabled American farmers to harvest enough grain to meet world demand. Using the steel plow devised in 1837 by John Deere, farmers could cultivate more acres with greater ease. The mechanical reaper invented in 1831 by Cyrus McCormick allowed a single operator to harvest as much as fourteen field hands could. The combination of greater production potential and speedy transportation prompted westerners to increase farm size and concentrate on cash crops. The outcome of these developments was a vast increase in the economic and political power of the West.

Western grain markets provided the foodstuffs for American industrialization, but, as noted in Chapter 11, Europe provided much of the labor. Total immigration to the United States exceeded 100,000 for the first time in 1848, and in 1851, 221,000 people migrated to the United States from Ireland alone. In 1852 the number of German immigrants reached 145,000. Many of these newcomers were not trained in skilled crafts and wound up settling in the industrial urban centers of the Northeast, where they could find work in the factories.

This combination of changes set the stage for political crisis. Liberalized suffrage rules transformed naturalized immigrants into voters, and both parties courted them, adding their interests to the political pot. Meanwhile, a mechanized textile industry, hungry for southern fiber, lent vitality to the continued growth of the cotton kingdom and the slave labor system that gave it life. Northern political leaders visualized an industrial nation based on free labor, but that view ran counter to the southern elites' ideals of agrarian capitalism based on slavery. In the West, most continued to believe in the Jeffersonian ideal of an agricultural nation of small and medium-size farms and could not accept either industrial or cotton capitalism as positive developments.

Political Instability and the Election of 1852

Dynamic economic progress improved material life throughout the nation, but it also raised serious questions about what course progress should take. As one clear-sighted northern minister pointed out in 1852, the debate was not about whether America should pursue progress but about "different kinds and methods of progress." Contradictory visions of national destiny were about to cause the breakdown of the existing party system.

Slavery seemed to loom behind every debate, but most Americans, even southerners, had no personal investment in the institution. Two-thirds of southerners owned no slaves, tolerating the institution but having only fleeting contact with the great plantations and their peculiar labor system. Northerners, too, were largely indifferent. Men like young Illinois state congressman Abraham Lincoln believed the

□ **Underground Railroad** The secret network of northerners who helped fugitive slaves escape to Canada or to safe areas in free states.

rail gauge The distance between train tracks.

grain elevator A building equipped with mechanical lifting devices and used for storing grain.

□ **John Deere** American industrialist who pioneered the manufacture of steel plows especially suited for working hard-packed prairie soil.

□ **Cyrus McCormick** Virginia inventor and manufacturer who developed and mass-produced the McCormick reaper, a machine that harvested grain.

agrarian capitalism A system of agriculture based on the efficient, specialized production of crops intended to generate profits rather than subsistence.

□ **Abraham Lincoln** Illinois lawyer and politician who, in a losing senatorial campaign in 1858, argued against popular sovereignty in debates with Stephen Douglas; he was elected president in 1860.

New technologies responded to but also drove an economic revolution in the United States during the decades just prior to the Civil War. Power looms in the Northeast, cotton gins in the South, and farming machinery in the West increased productivity and launched the emergence of a national capitalist economy. The complicated intersection between economies is illustrated by this engraving of farm implement inventor Cyrus McCormick showing both his inventions and the enormous factory needed to manufacture them.

institution was wrong but were not inclined to do anything about it. What mattered to these people was not slavery but autonomy—control over local affairs and over their own lives.

The slavery question challenged notions of autonomy in both the North and the South. In their widely disseminated rhetoric, abolitionists expanded the specter of the Slave Power conspiracy, especially

▫ **Harriet Beecher Stowe** American novelist and abolitionist whose novel *Uncle Tom's Cabin* fanned antislavery sentiment in the North.

▫ **conscience Whigs** Members of the Whig Party who supported moderate abolitionism, as opposed to cotton Whigs, members who opposed abolitionism.

▫ **James Buchanan** Pennsylvania senator who was elected president in 1856 after gaining the Democratic nomination as a compromise candidate.

▫ **Franklin Pierce** New Hampshire lawyer and Democratic politician nominated as a compromise candidate and elected president in 1852.

in the aftermath of the Compromise of 1850. Growing numbers perceived this conspiracy as intent on imposing southern ways and installing southern elites or their sympathizers in seats of power in every section of the nation. Whether farmers in Illinois or artisans in Pennsylvania, common people stood ready to resist a southern takeover of local institutions. Likewise, common people in the South feared interference from outsiders in view of the ever more vigorous antisouthern crusade by northern activists.

After the Compromise of 1850 momentarily eased regional fears, sectional tensions flamed anew in 1852 with the publication of *Uncle Tom's Cabin* by **Harriet Beecher Stowe**. Stowe portrayed the darkest inhumanities of southern slavery in the first American novel to include African Americans as central characters. *Uncle Tom's Cabin* sold three hundred thousand copies in its first year. Adapted for the stage, it became one of the most popular plays of the period. The book stirred public opinion and breathed new life into antislavery sentiments, leading Free-Soilers and so-called **conscience Whigs** to renew their efforts to limit or end slavery. When these activists saw that the Whig

Harriet Beecher Stowe's *Uncle Tom's Cabin* was the first American novel that featured African American characters in prominent roles. It was issued in various editions and, as this store advertisement makes clear, it sold in enormous numbers. Note the different purchasing options, including both inexpensive paperback copies, a lavish bound "Superb Illustrated Edition," and an edition in German.

Party was incapable of addressing the slavery question in any effective way, they began to look for other political options.

Superficially, the Whigs seemed well organized and surprisingly unified as a new presidential election approached in 1852. Zachary Taylor had died in office in July 1850, and they nominated General Winfield Scott, Taylor's rival for fame in the War with Mexico. The Democrats remained divided through forty-nine ballots, unable to decide among Lewis Cass of Michigan, Stephen A. Douglas of Illinois, and James Buchanan of Pennsylvania. They finally settled on the virtually unknown Franklin Pierce of New Hampshire, who pledged to uphold the Compromise of 1850 and keep slavery out of politics. This promise was enough to bring Martin Van Buren back to the Democrats, and he brought many Free-Soilers back with him. Many others, though, abandoned Van Buren and joined forces with conscience Whigs.

Scott was a national figure and a distinguished military hero, but Pierce gathered 254 electoral votes to Scott's 42, exposing the disarray in the Whig Party. Splits between "cotton" and "conscience" groups splintered Whig unity, and regional tension escalated as Free-Soil rhetoric clashed with calls for extending slavery. Confrontations between Catholics and Protestants and between native-born and immigrant laborers caused bitter animosity. In the North, where immigration, industrialization, and antislavery sentiment were most prevalent and economic friction most

This crudely drawn cartoon savagely satirizes the positions taken by the Democratic Party in its 1852 presidential platform, depicting candidate Franklin Pierce bowing down before a slaveholder who is saying "Save the Union, And with the 'meanest' Yankee grease Smear the hinges of your knees And in 'silence' pray for peace" while the Devil looks on. The cartoon's title makes its purpose clear, asking "Freemen of America, how long will you be ledd [sic] by such Leaders."

pronounced, massive numbers of voters, believing the Whigs incapable of addressing current problems, deserted the party.

Increasing Tension Under Pierce

The Democratic Party and Franklin Pierce also felt the pressures of a changing electorate. Pierce was part of the Young America Movement, which, as a whole, tried to ignore the slavery issue, advocating romantic and aggressive nationalism, manifest destiny, and republican revolutions throughout the Americas. In line with the Young America agenda, Pierce emphasized expansion; choosing a route for a transcontinental railroad became the keystone in his agenda for the nation.

Southerners knew that a railroad based in the South would channel the flow of gold from California through their region and would also allow new settlement and cotton agriculture to spread beyond the waterways that had proved necessary for expansion so far. Eventually the new territories would become states, increasing the South's national political power.

That model of development was totally unacceptable to several groups: to northern evangelicals, who viewed slavery as a moral blight on the nation; to Free-Soil advocates, who believed the spread of slavery would degrade white workers; and to northern manufacturers, who wanted to maintain dominance in Congress to ensure continued economic protection. In May 1853, only two months after assuming office, Pierce inflamed all of these groups by sending James Gadsden, a southern railroad developer, to Mexico to purchase a strip of land lying below the southern border of the New Mexico Territory. Any rail line built westward from a southern city to California would have to cross that land, and Pierce and his southern supporters wanted to make sure it was part of the United States. The Gadsden Purchase (see Map 13.2), signed on December 30, 1853, added 29,640 square miles of land to the

United States for a cost of $10 million. It also finalized the southwestern border of the United States.

The Gadsden Purchase prompted proponents of a southern route for the transcontinental railroad, led by Secretary of War Jefferson Davis, to push for government sponsorship of the project. Having invested his own money in more northerly rail development, Illinois senator Stephen A. Douglas blocked Davis's efforts and pushed for a route westward from his home town of Chicago. But this route would have to pass through Indian Territory that was not open to rail development. To rectify this problem, Douglas introduced a bill on January 4, 1854, calling for the incorporation of the entire northern half of Indian Territory into a new federal entity called Nebraska.

Douglas knew that he would need both northern and southern support to get his bill through Congress, and he sought to silence possible opposition by proposing that the slavery question in the territory be left to popular sovereignty—let the voters of Nebraska decide. When southerners pointed out that the proposed territory was above the Missouri Compromise line and that Congress might prohibit popular sovereignty from functioning, Douglas responded that the Compromise of 1850 superseded the 1820 Missouri Compromise. But to calm southerners he finally supported an amendment to his original bill dividing the territory in half—Nebraska in the north and Kansas in the south (see Map 13.3). The amended legislation—called the Kansas-Nebraska Act—rested on the assumption that popular sovereignty would lead to slavery in Kansas and free labor in Nebraska.

TOWARD A HOUSE DIVIDED

☆ *How did various political coalitions react to the Kansas-Nebraska Act?*

☆ *What was the effect of these reactions on the national political climate?*

Once again slavery threatened national political stability. In the North, opponents of the bill formed local coalitions to defeat it. On January 24, 1854, a group of antislavery politicians including Salmon P. Chase, Gerrit Smith, Joshua Giddings, and Charles Sumner published "The Appeal of the Independent Democrats in Congress, to the People of the United States." They called the bill an "atrocious plot" to make Nebraska a "dreary region of despotism, inhabited by masters and slaves." On February 28, opponents of the Kansas-Nebraska bill met in Ripon, Wisconsin, and recommended the formation of a new political party. Similar meetings took place in several northern states as opposition to the bill grew. In the wake of these meetings, the existing party system collapsed and a new one arose to replace it.

□ **Young America Movement** A political movement popular among young voters during the 1840s and early 1850s, advocating free-market capitalism, national expansionism, and American patriotism.

□ **Gadsden Purchase** A strip of land in present-day Arizona and New Mexico that the United States bought from Mexico in 1853 to secure a southern route for a transcontinental railroad.

□ **Jefferson Davis** Secretary of war under Franklin Pierce; he later became president of the Confederacy.

□ **Kansas-Nebraska Act** An 1854 law creating the Kansas and Nebraska territories and allowing residents to decide whether to allow slavery within their borders.

□ **Charles Sumner** Co-founder of the Republican Party and a strong advocate for abolition and racial equality; he was brutally beaten by a southern congressman in 1856 after delivering a speech attacking the South.

MAP 13.3 The Kansas-Nebraska Act
This map shows Stephen Douglas's proposed compromise organizing the vast territory separating the settled northern United States from California and Oregon. Designed in part to win profitable rail connections for Douglas's home district in Illinois, the Kansas-Nebraska Act stirred a political crisis by repealing the Missouri Compromise and replacing it with popular sovereignty. © Cengage Learning.

A Shattered Compromise

Despite this strong opposition, Douglas and Pierce rallied support for the Kansas-Nebraska Act. On May 26, 1854, after gaining approval in the House of Representatives, the bill passed the Senate, and Pierce soon signed it into law. Passage of the act crystallized northern antislavery sentiment. As Senator William Seward of New York vowed, "We will engage in competition for the virgin soil of Kansas, and God give the victory to the side which is stronger in numbers as it is in right."

Antislavery forces, however, remained divided into at least three major groups. The Free-Soil contingent opposed any extension of slavery but did not necessarily favor abolishing the institution. The other two groups—Garrisonians and evangelicals—wanted immediate abolition but disagreed on many particulars. William Lloyd Garrison and his followers believed that slavery was the primary evil facing the nation, while evangelicals agreed that slavery was evil, but believed it was one among many vices undermining the virtuous republic. All three groups constantly agitated against slavery and what they perceived as southern control of national politics. They weakened the Democratic Party's strength in the North but could not bring themselves to align behind a single opposition party.

Actions perceived as further evidence of the Slave Power conspiracy also undermined Democratic unity. Private armies invaded territories in Latin America and the Caribbean, which many in the North concluded were Slave Power efforts. In this atmosphere, President Pierce unintentionally destabilized the Democratic Party and the nation by pushing for the purchase of Cuba from Spain. When the Spanish refused, three of Pierce's European ministers met in Ostend, Belgium, in October 1854, and secretly drafted a justification for taking Cuba by force. When the so-called Ostend Manifesto became public in 1855, many northerners were convinced that Pierce and the Democratic Party were in league with the Slave Power to expand slavery. These perceptions stirred antislavery anxieties and fueled the growth of the newly formed anti-Democratic coalitions.

☐ **Ostend Manifesto** Declaration by American foreign ministers in 1854 that if Spain refused to sell Cuba, the United States might be justified in taking it by force.

Federal officials often found themselves in an awkward position as civil war threatened in Kansas during the 1850s. Here, Colonel Edwin Vose Sumner, commander of Fort Leavenworth and an opponent of slavery, acts upon orders from the proslavery territorial government to break up an antislavery convention in Topeka in 1856. Sumner prevented the meeting from convening, but refused to disarm the conventioneers, winning three cheers from the assembled crowd.

The Kansas State Historical Society.

Bleeding Kansas

Meanwhile, political friction was about to ignite Kansas. In April 1854, abolitionist Eli Thayer of Worcester, Massachusetts, organized the New England Emigrant Aid Society to encourage antislavery supporters to move to Kansas. They reasoned that flooding a region subject to popular sovereignty with right-minded residents could effectively "save" it from slavery. This group eventually sent two thousand armed settlers to Kansas, founding Lawrence and other communities. With similar designs, proslavery southerners, particularly those in Missouri, also encouraged settlement in the territory. Like their northern counterparts, these southerners came armed and ready to fight for their cause.

President Pierce appointed governors in both Kansas and Nebraska and instructed them to organize elections for territorial legislatures. As proslavery and antislavery settlers vied for control of Kansas, the region became a testing ground for popular sovereignty. When the vote came on March 30, 1855, a large contingent of armed slavery supporters from Missouri crossed into Kansas and cast ballots for proslavery candidates. According to later Senate investigations, 60 percent of the votes cast were illegal. These unlawful ballots gave proslavery supporters a large majority in the Kansas legislature. They promptly expelled all abolitionist legislators and enacted the Kansas Code—a group of laws meant to drive all antislavery forces out of the territory. Antislavery advocates responded by organizing their own free-state government and drawing up an alternative constitution, which they submitted to the voters.

Bloodshed soon followed. Attempting to bring the conflict to conclusion, proslavery territorial judge Samuel LeCompte called a grand jury of slavery supporters that indicted members of the free-state government for treason and sent a **posse** of about eight hundred men to Lawrence. There they "arrested" the antislavery forces and sacked the town. The violence did not end there. Hearing news of the "Sack of Lawrence," John Brown, an antislavery activist, murdered five proslavery men living along the Pottawatomie River south of Lawrence. This "Pottawatomie Massacre" triggered a series of episodes in which more than two hundred men were killed.

The Kansas issue also led to violence in Congress. During the debates over the admission of the territory, Massachusetts senator Charles Sumner made insulting remarks about South Carolina's 60-year-old senator Andrew Butler. Butler was out of town, but Butler's nephew, Representative Preston Brooks, accosted Sumner and beat him nearly to death with a cane. Though **censured** by the House of Representatives, Brooks was overwhelmingly reelected by his home district and openly praised for his actions—he received canes as gifts from admirers all over the South.

Meanwhile the presidential election of 1856 was approaching. The Pierce administration's actions, southern expansionism, and the Kansas-Nebraska controversy swelled the ranks of dissenters like those

posse A group of citizens deputized by a court or peace officer to assist in law enforcement.

☐ John Brown Abolitionist who fought proslavery settlers in Kansas in 1855; he was hanged for treason after seizing the U.S. arsenal at Harpers Ferry in 1859 as part of an effort to liberate southern slaves.

censure To issue an official rebuke, as by a legislature to one of its members.

who had convened in Ripon. Now formally calling themselves the **Republican Party**, these northern and western groups began actively seeking support. Immigration also remained a major issue, but the Know-Nothings, despite their success at the local and state levels, split over slavery at their initial national convention in 1855; many then joined Republican coalitions. John C. Frémont, a moderate abolitionist who had achieved fame as the "liberator of California," won the Republican nomination. For their part, the Democrats rejected both Pierce and Douglas and nominated James Buchanan from Pennsylvania, selecting John C. Breckinridge of Kentucky as Buchanan's running mate to balance the ticket between North and South.

The election became a contest for party survival rather than a national referendum on slavery. Buchanan received 45 percent of the popular vote and 163 electoral votes. Frémont finished second with 33 percent of the popular vote and 114 electoral votes. Know-Nothing Millard Fillmore received 21 percent of the popular vote but only 8 electoral votes. Frémont's surprisingly narrow margin of defeat demonstrated the appeal of the newly formed Republican coalition to northern voters. The Know-Nothings disappeared and never again attempted to organize nationally.

Bringing Slavery Home to the North

On March 4, 1857, James Buchanan became president of the United States. The 65-year-old Pennsylvanian had begun his political career in Congress in 1821 and owed much of his success to southern support. His election came at a time when the nation needed strong leadership, but Buchanan seemed unable to provide it. His attempt to preserve the politics of avoidance only strengthened extremism in both the North and the South. **Regionalism** colored all political issues, and every debate became a contest between competing social, political, and economic ideologies.

Though Buchanan's shortcomings contributed to the rising crisis, an event occurred within days of his inauguration that sent shock waves through the already troubled nation. **Dred Scott**, a slave once owned by army surgeon John Emerson, sued for his freedom. Scott's attorney argued that between 1831 and 1833, Emerson had taken Scott with him during various military postings to areas where the Missouri Compromise banned slavery, making Scott a free man. When, after nearly six years in the Missouri courts, the state supreme court rejected this argument in 1852, Scott, with the help of abolitionist lawyers, appealed to the United States Supreme Court. In a 7-to-2 decision, the Court ruled against Scott. Chief Justice Roger B. Taney, formerly a member of Andrew Jackson's Kitchen Cabinet and a stalwart Democrat, argued that in the eyes of the law slaves were not people but property; as such, they could not be citizens of the United States and

had no right to petition the Court. Taney then ignited a political powder keg by ruling that Congress had no constitutional authority to limit slavery in federal territories, thereby declaring the Missouri Compromise unconstitutional.

While southerners generally celebrated the decision, antislavery forces and northern evangelical leaders called the *Dred Scott* decision a mockery of justice and a crime against a "higher law." Some radical abolitionists argued that the North should separate from the Union. Others suggested impeaching the Supreme Court. Already incensed by events in Kansas, antislavery leaders predicted that the next move by the Slave Power conspiracy would be to get the Supreme Court to strike down antislavery laws in northern states.

Meanwhile, the Kansas issue still burned. That very few slaveholders actually moved into the territory

☐ **Republican Party** Political party formed in 1854 that opposed the extension of slavery into the western territories.

regionalism Loyalty to the interests of a particular region of the country.

☐ **Dred Scott** Slave who sued for his liberty in the Missouri courts, arguing that four years on free soil had made him free; the Supreme Court's 1857 ruling against him negated the Missouri Compromise.

Kingdom of Heavenly Peace

In 1851, a visionary leader named Hung Hsiu-ch'üan founded a movement in China called the Tàipíng Tian Guó, or the Kingdom of Heavenly Peace. Based on half-understood Christian tenets and other imported ideas, Hung set out to reform Chinese society by eliminating class distinctions, granting women social and economic equality with men and eliminating foot-binding (a crippling practice that prevented the growth of girls' feet), and instituting land reform that would distribute land equally to all. This message appealed greatly to the poorer classes, and the Tàipíng movement grew rapidly, alarming landowners and the ruling Qing Dynasty. In 1853 Hung and a militant army of peasants captured the southern capital of Nanjing and focused on controlling China's western territories and the central Yangtze valley. Already in disarray from foreign conflicts, the Qing Dynasty met the Tàipíng's challenge with as much force as it could muster. By the time Hung died and the movement dissipated in 1864, it is estimated that nearly 30 million Chinese had died in the conflict to create the Kingdom of Heavenly Peace.

did nothing to deter proslavery leaders, who met in Lecompton, Kansas, in June 1857 to draft a state constitution favoring slavery. When the Lecompton constitution was submitted for voters' approval, antislavery forces protested by refusing to vote, so it was easily ratified. But when it was revealed that more than two thousand nonresidents had voted illegally, both Republicans and northern Democrats in Congress roundly denounced it. The statehood bill passed the Senate, but the House of Representatives rejected it. The Lecompton constitution came back to Kansas for another vote. This time Free-Soilers participated in the election and defeated the proposed constitution. Kansas remained a territory.

Growing Friction and Expanding Violence

Both the Kansas controversy and the *Dred Scott* decision undermined the Democratic commitment to popular sovereignty. Entertaining presidential ambitions, party leader Stephen Douglas sought a solution that might win him both northern and southern support in a run for that office in 1860. He got his opportunity in a debate with his 1858 Republican rival for the

U.S. Senate, Abraham Lincoln. Born on the Kentucky frontier in 1809, Lincoln had accompanied his family from one failed farm to another, picking up schooling in Indiana and Illinois as opportunities arose. As a young man he worked odd jobs—farm worker, ferryman, surveyor, and store clerk. He was eventually elected to the Illinois legislature and began a serious study of law. A strong Whig, Lincoln followed Henry Clay's economic philosophy and steered a middle course between the "cotton" and "conscience" wings of the Whig Party. Lincoln acknowledged that slavery was evil but contended that it was the unavoidable consequence of black racial inferiority. The only way to get rid of the evil, he believed, was to prevent its expansion into the territories, forcing it to die out naturally. Douglas's position favoring popular sovereignty flew in the face of Lincoln's designs and so, at a debate in Freeport, Illinois, Lincoln asked Douglas to explain how the people of a territory could exclude slavery in light of the *Dred Scott* ruling. Douglas's reply became known as the Freeport Doctrine. Slavery, he said, needed the protection of "local police regulations." In any territory, citizens opposed to slavery could elect representatives who would "by unfriendly legislation" prevent the introduction of slavery. This, then, would become Douglas's solution as he approached the 1860 election.

Northern activists utterly rejected Douglas's compromise and increasingly called for a violent response to the Slave Power, and in 1857 John Brown came east to oblige them. He convinced several prominent antislavery leaders to finance a daring plan to raise an army of slaves in an all-out insurrection against their masters. Brown and a small party of followers attacked the federal arsenal at Harpers Ferry, Virginia, on October 16, 1859, attempting to seize weapons. The arsenal proved an easy target, but no slaves joined the

◻ **Lecompton constitution** State constitution written for Kansas in 1857 at a convention dominated by proslavery forces; it would have allowed slavery, but Kansas voters rejected it.

◻ **Freeport Doctrine** Stephen Douglas's belief, stated at Freeport, Illinois, that a territory could exclude slavery by writing local laws or regulations that made slavery impossible to enforce.

◻ **Harpers Ferry** Town in present-day West Virginia and site of the U.S. arsenal that John Brown briefly seized in 1859.

What Shall We Say About John Brown?

It is virtually impossible to be neutral about John Brown. As Dennis E. Frye, the chief historian at Harpers Ferry National Historical Park, wrote: "Americans do not deliberate John Brown. Instead, we 'feel' his enduring legacy . . . Saint or Madman? Murderer or Liberator? Devil or Martyr? Terrorist or Freedom Fighter? John Brown is not what we think, but what we feel." This presents a particular problem for historians: What shall we say about John Brown?

Turning to the primary documents does not really help. If we listen to the voices of leading literary figures from that time we learn that we should regard him, in the words of Louisa May Alcott, as "St. John the Just." Ralph Waldo Emerson echoed the same sentiment, calling Brown "a pure idealist of artless goodness." How different this was from the position taken by Virginia assemblyman James L. Kemper, who stated "All Virginia [will] stand forth as one man and say to fanaticism, whenever you advance a hostile foot upon our soil, we will welcome you with bloody hands and hospitable graves." Or the *Charleston Mercury*, which editorialized, "The day of compromise is passed. The South must control her own destinies or perish." Or even the northern *Chicago Press and Tribune*, which declared him "as mad as a March hare."

"Mad" or not, we simply cannot dismiss John Brown as the leader of some demented cult. Over the more than 150 years since Brown's raid, much has come to light, not so much about Brown himself, but about larger forces that were at work. For example, over the two years prior to the raid itself, Brown had multiple meetings with leading reform figures, the so-called "Secret Six"—Thomas Wentworth Higginson, Samuel Gridley Howe, Theodore Parker, Franklin Benjamin Sanborn, Gerrit Smith, and George Luther Stearns—who helped to organize and finance the raid. While all of these men were dedicated abolitionists, and despite Smith's self-commitment to an insane asylum to avoid prosecution for his role in the affair, none of them were madmen. Of course, how much they knew about the full extent of Brown's intentions—his plan to establish an independent state with himself as commander in chief, for example—remains unknown, but they certainly did not shy away from the idea of violence in the cause of antislavery.

But what may be even more telling is what historians have learned about the people who actually accompanied Brown on his raid. As historian Tony Horwitz has noted, his followers included farmers, artisans, lawyers, poets, Jewish shopkeepers, former slaves, and free blacks who, like the Secret Six, appear to have been rational players driven to extreme action by an unflagging commitment to "destroying an institution they felt violated the nation's founding promise of liberty and equality for all."

Characters like John Brown always present a dilemma. He clearly was, as William Henry Harrison described Tecumseh, "one of those uncommon geniuses who spring up occasionally to produce revolutions and overturn the established order of things." We might, like Henry David Thoreau, ask "Is it not possible that an individual may be right and a government wrong? Are laws to be enforced simply because they were made?" and let Brown off the hook. Or does this give free rein to any person with a strong ideological commitment to whatever cause to commit whatever acts seem justified at the time? This is not a dilemma that historians can solve; we can only lay out the facts and encourage you to reach your own conclusions.

John Steuart Curry/Kansas State Historical Society.

John Brown.

uprising. Local citizens surrounded the arsenal, firing on Brown and his followers until federal troops commanded by **Robert E. Lee** arrived. On October 18, Lee's forces battered down the barricaded entrance and arrested Brown. He was tried, convicted of treason, and hanged on December 2, 1859.

Brown's raid on Harpers Ferry captured the imagination of radical abolitionists. Republican leaders denounced it, but other northerners proclaimed Brown a martyr. Church bells tolled in many northern cities on the day of his execution. Such reactions caused many appalled southerners—even very moderate ones—to seriously consider **secession**. In Alabama, Mississippi, and Florida, state legislatures resolved that a Republican victory in the upcoming presidential election would provide sufficient justification for such action.

THE DIVIDED NATION

☆ *In what ways was the presidential election in 1860 an outcome of the realignment of the party system during the 1850s?*

☆ *Why did the election results have the political effects that they did?*

The Republicans were a new phenomenon on the American political scene: a purely regional political party. Rather than making any attempt to forge a national coalition, the party drew its strength and ideas almost entirely from the North. The Republican platform—"Free Soil, Free Labor, and Free Men"—stressed the defilement of white labor by slavery and contended that the Slave Power conspiracy was eroding the rights of free whites everywhere. By taking up a cry against "Rum, Romanism, and Slavery," the Republicans drew former Know-Nothings and temperance advocates into their ranks. The Democrats hoped to maintain a national coalition, but as the nation approached a new presidential election, their hopes began to fade.

The Dominance of Regionalism

During the Buchanan administration, Democrats found it increasingly difficult to achieve national party unity. Facing Republican pressure in their own states, northern Democrats realized that any concession to southern Democratic demands for extending or protecting slavery would cost them votes at home. In April 1860, as the party convened in Charleston, South Carolina, each side was ready to do battle for its political life.

The fight began when northern supporters of Stephen A. Douglas championed a popular sovereignty position. Southern radicals demanded a plank calling for the legal protection of slavery in the territories. After heated debates, neither side would compromise. When the delegates finally voted, the Douglas forces carried the day. Disgusted delegates from eight southern states walked out of the convention. Shocked, the remaining delegates adjourned; they would reconvene in Baltimore in June. Most southern delegates boycotted the Baltimore proceedings, and Douglas easily won the Democratic presidential nomination with moderate southerner Herschel V. Johnson of Georgia as his running mate. Hoping to attract moderate voters from both the North and the South, the party's final platform supported popular sovereignty and emphasized allegiance to the Union.

The southern Democratic contingent met one week later, also in Baltimore, and nominated Vice President John C. Breckinridge of Kentucky as its presidential candidate and Joseph Lane of Oregon as his running mate. The southern Democrats' platform vowed support for the Union but called for federal protection of slavery in the territories and guaranteed preservation of slavery where it already existed.

In May 1860, a group of former Whigs and Know-Nothings along with some disaffected Democrats convened in Baltimore and formed the **Constitutional Union Party**. They nominated John Bell, a former southern Know-Nothing and wealthy slaveholder from Tennessee, and Edward Everett of Massachusetts, a former Whig leader, as his running mate. Hoping to resurrect the politics of compromise, the party resolved to take no stand on the sectional controversy and pledged to uphold the Constitution.

Having lost most of its moderates to the Constitutional Union coalition and having virtually no southerners in its ranks to start with, the Republican convention faced few ideological divisions, but personality conflicts were rife. The front-runner for the Republican nomination appeared to be William Seward of New York. A former Whig and longtime New York politician, Seward had actively opposed any extension of slavery during the early 1850s but had switched to the popular-sovereignty position during the Kansas controversy. Several other Republican favorites—Salmon P. Chase of Ohio, Simon Cameron of Pennsylvania, and Edward Bates of Missouri—agreed with Seward's position but sought the nomination for themselves. Eventually, however, Abraham Lincoln emerged as Seward's major competition.

□ **Robert E. Lee** A Virginian with a distinguished career in the U.S. Army who later assumed command of the Confederate army in Virginia during most of the Civil War.

secession Withdrawal from the nation.

□ **Constitutional Union Party** Political party that organized on the eve of the Civil War with no platform other than preservation of the Constitution, the Union, and the law.

THE POLITICAL QUADRILLE
Music by Dred Scott

[LC-USZ62-14827]/Library of Congress Prints and Photographs Division.

Capturing the racial and political tensions in the country at the time, this cartoon illustrates how the *Dred Scott* case set the agenda for the presidential election of 1860. Here Scott provides the music as each of the four presidential candidates dances with a partner who symbolizes his perceived political orientation. John C. Breckinridge (upper left) dances with fellow southern Democrat James Buchanan, illustrating his alignment with southern proslavery hard-liners. John H. Bell (lower right) dances with a Native American, symbolizing his nativist Know-Nothing affiliations, suggesting avoidance of the slavery issue. Meanwhile, Stephen A. Douglas (lower left) escorts a disheveled Irishman, suggesting his alignment with northeastern urban interests including immigrants and other "undesirables." Finally, Abraham Lincoln (upper right) is seen with an African American woman, an obvious reference to his party's perceived abolitionist leanings.

Many delegates considered Seward too radical and his campaign manager, Thurlow Weed (see page 240, 295), was perceived by many as a corrupt opportunist. Lincoln, in contrast, had a reputation for integrity and had not seriously alienated any of the Republican factions. He won the nomination on the third ballot.

The Election of 1860

The 1860 presidential campaign began as several separate contests. Lincoln and Douglas competed for northern votes; the Republicans were not even on the ballot in the Deep South. Douglas proclaimed himself the only national candidate but received most of his support from northerners who feared the consequences of a Republican victory. By the same token, Breckinridge and the southern Democrats expected no support in the North. Bell and the Constitutional Unionists attempted to campaign in both regions but attracted mostly southern voters anxious to stave off disunion.

Slavery and sectionalism were the key issues. Even moderate southerners started to believe that the

Republicans intended to crush their way of life and to enslave southern whites economically while freeing southern blacks. Northern qualms were aroused as well when the pro-Democrat *New York Herald* contended that the election of Lincoln would bring "hundreds of thousands" of slaves north to compete with whites for jobs, resulting in "African amalgamation with the fair daughters of the Anglo-Saxon, Celtic, and Teutonic races."

Seeking to counter such scare tactics, national Republican leaders forged a platform that advocated limits on slavery's expansion but contained no planks seeking an end to slavery in areas where it already existed. They also called for higher tariffs (to appeal to northern industrialists) and for internal improvements and public lands legislation (to appeal to westerners). Particularly in the Midwest, party leaders

Deep South The region of the South farthest from the North, usually said to include the states of Alabama, Florida, Georgia, Louisiana, Mississippi, and South Carolina.

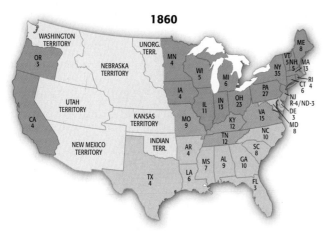

1860

Candidate (Party)	Electoral Vote		Popular Vote	
Lincoln (Republican)	180	59.4%	1,865,593	39.8%
Douglas (Northern Democrat)	12	3.9%	1,382,713	29.5%
Breckinridge (Southern Democrat)	72	23.8%	848,356	18.1%
Bell (Constitutional Union)	39	12.9%	592,906	12.6%
Territories, no returns				

MAP 13.4 Election of 1860

The election of 1860 confirmed the worst fears expressed by concerned Union supporters during the 1850s: changes in the nation's population made it possible for one section to dominate national politics. As this map shows, the Republican and southern Democratic parties virtually split the nation, and the Republicans were able to seize the presidency. © Cengage Learning.

worked hard to portray themselves as "the white man's party." These tactics alienated a few abolitionists but persuaded many northerners and westerners to support the party.

On November 6, 1860, Abraham Lincoln was elected president of the United States with 180 electoral votes—a clear majority—but only 40 percent of the popular vote. Lincoln carried all the northern states, California, and Oregon (see Map 13.4). Douglas finished second with 29 percent of the popular vote but just 12 electoral votes. He won only Missouri. Bell won the 39 electoral votes of Virginia, Kentucky, and Tennessee. Breckinridge, as expected, carried the

□ **John J. Crittenden** Kentucky senator who made an unsuccessful attempt to prevent the Civil War by proposing a series of constitutional amendments protecting slavery south of the Missouri Compromise line.

fire-eaters A nickname given to southerners who were particularly vocal and active in supporting secession.

Deep South but tallied only 72 electoral votes and 18 percent of the popular vote nationwide. For the first time in American history, a purely regional party held the presidency. The Republicans, who had made no effort to win votes in the South, also swept congressional races in the North and secured a large majority in the House of Representatives for the upcoming term.

The First Wave of Secession

After the Republican victory, southern sentiment for secession snowballed, especially in the Deep South. The Republicans were a "party founded on a single sentiment," stated the *Richmond Examiner:* "hatred of African slavery." The *New Orleans Delta* agreed, calling the Republicans "essentially a revolutionary party." But this party now controlled the national government. To a growing number of southerners, the Republican victory was proof that secession was the only alternative to political domination. Most Republicans did not believe that the South would actually leave the Union: Seward had ridiculed threats of secession and Lincoln believed that the "people of the South" had "too much sense" to launch an "attempt to ruin the government." During the campaign, he had promised "no interference by the government, with slaves or slavery within the states," and he continued to urge moderation.

In a last-ditch attempt at compromise, John J. Crittenden proposed a block of constitutional amendments on December 18, 1860. These called for extending the Missouri Compromise line westward across the continent, forbidding slavery north of the line, and protecting slavery to the south; maintaining the interstate slave trade; and requiring federal compensation to slaveowners who were unable to recover fugitive slaves from northern states. Surprisingly, this plan appealed to some northerners, especially businessmen who feared that secession would cause a major depression. Lincoln warned, however, that such a plan would "lose us everything we gained by the election." The Senate defeated Crittenden's proposal by a vote of 25 to 23.

Meanwhile, on December 20, 1860, delegates in South Carolina met to consider seceding from the Union. South Carolina had long been a hotbed of resistance to federal authority, and state officials determined to take action to protect slavery before the newly elected Republican administration came to power. Amid general jubilation, South Carolina delegates voted unanimously to dissolve their ties with the United States. Just as the fire-eaters hoped, other southern states followed. During January 1861, delegates convened in Mississippi, Florida, Alabama, Georgia, and Louisiana and voted to secede (see Map 13.5). Meanwhile in Texas, which had been holding back, secessionists rejected unionist pleas from

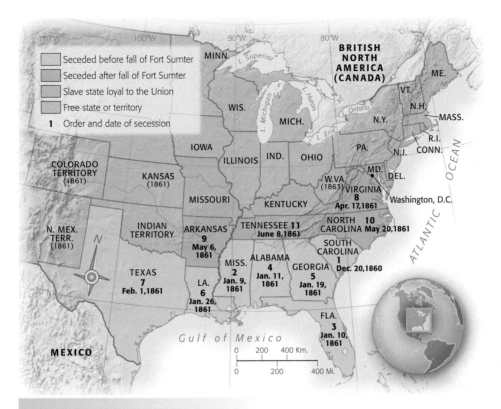

Legend:
- Seceded before fall of Fort Sumter
- Seceded after fall of Fort Sumter
- Slave state loyal to the Union
- Free state or territory
- 1 Order and date of secession

MAP 13.5 Secession
This map shows the breakup of the Union begun by South Carolina's secession in December 1860. The Cotton Belt followed South Carolina's lead in January, and the rest of the Confederate states joined them later in the spring of 1861. Free states then aligned to oppose southern secession, while the border states and inland territories were caught in the middle. © Cengage Learning.

Governor Sam Houston and opted to join neighboring Louisiana in rebellion. The Confederacy now numbered seven states.

On February 4, 1861, delegates from the seven seceding states and from several states still considering secession met in Montgomery, Alabama, and formed the **Confederate States of America**. During the several weeks that followed, the provisional congress drafted a constitution, and the Confederate states ratified it on March 11, 1861.

The Confederate constitution emphasized the "sovereign and independent character" of the states and guaranteed the protection of slavery in any new territories acquired. It allowed tariffs solely for the purpose of raising government revenue and prohibited government funding of internal improvements. It also limited the president and vice president to a single six-year term. A cabinet composed of six executive department heads rounded out the executive branch. In all other respects, the Confederate government was identical to that in the United States. In fact, the U.S. Constitution was acknowledged as the supreme law in the Confederacy except in those particulars where it conflicted with provisions in the Confederate Constitution.

Responses to Disunion

Even as late as March 1861, a significant number of southerners did not favor secession. John Bell and Stephen Douglas together had received more than 50 percent of southern votes in 1860, winning support from southerners who desired compromise. These "plain folk" joined together with some large planters, who stood to suffer economic loss from disunion, in calls for moderation and compromise. And the border states, which were less invested in cotton and had numerous ties with the North, were not strongly inclined toward secession. In February, Virginia had

□ **Confederate States of America** Political entity formed by the seceding states of South Carolina, Georgia, Florida, Alabama, Mississippi, Texas, and Louisiana in February 1861; Virginia, Arkansas, Tennessee, and North Carolina joined later.

called for a peace conference to meet in Washington in an effort to forestall hostilities, but this attempt, like Crittenden's effort, also failed to hold the Union together.

The division in southern sentiments was a major stumbling block to the election of a Confederate president. Many moderate delegates to the constitutional convention refused to support fire-eaters, believing them to be equally responsible with the Republicans for initiating the crisis. The convention remained deadlocked until two pro-secession Virginia attendees nominated Mississippi moderate Jefferson Davis as a compromise candidate.

Davis appeared to be the ideal choice. A West Point graduate, he served during the War with Mexico, was elected to the Senate soon afterward, then left the Senate in 1851 to run unsuccessfully for governor in Mississippi. After serving as secretary of war under Franklin Pierce, he returned to the Senate in 1857. Although Davis had long championed southern interests and owned many slaves, he was no romantic fire-eater. When he had fought for a southern route for a transcontinental railroad, he believed that it would benefit the South economically, but he also felt that it would tie the whole nation more firmly together. Like many of his contemporaries, however, Davis had become increasingly alarmed by the prospect of declining southern political power. Immediately after Mississippi's declaration of secession, Davis resigned his Senate seat and threw in with the Confederacy.

To moderates like Davis, the presidential election of 1860 was simply a forceful demonstration that unless the South took a strong stand against outside interference, the region would no longer be able to control its own internal affairs. The initial northward tilt in the Senate created by California's admission in 1850 had been aggravated in 1858 by the admission of Minnesota and by Oregon's statehood in 1859. Southerners, Davis believed, needed to act in concert to convince northerners to either leave the South alone or face the region's withdrawal from the nation.

Elected provisional president of the Confederate States of America unanimously on February 9, 1861, Davis addressed the cheering crowds in Montgomery a week later and set forth the Confederate position: "The time for compromise has now passed," he said. "The South is determined to maintain her position, and make all who oppose her smell Southern powder and feel Southern steel." In his inaugural address several days later, he stressed a desire for peace but reiterated that the "courage and patriotism of the Confederate States" would be "found equal to any measure of defense which honor and security may require."

A few months before being nominated by the Republican Party as its presidential candidate, Abraham Lincoln permitted Illinois artist Leonard Volk to cast the future president's face in plaster. Preserved for all these years, this casting and the many reproductions that have been struck from it remain the most accurate picture we have of Lincoln before the secession crisis tore the nation apart. Captured in time, we can see the noble and serious man whose unflinching determination saw the nation through its worst historical crisis. As the many hundreds of photographs and other images of Lincoln during his presidency attest, he would never look this young and confident again.

Northern Democrats and Republicans alike watched developments in the South with dismay. President Buchanan argued that secession had no constitutional validity and that any state leaving the Union did so unlawfully, but he also asserted that the federal government had no constitutional power to "coerce a State" to remain in the Union. He blamed the crisis on "incessant and violent agitation on the slavery question," chiding northerners for disregarding fugitive slave laws and calling for a constitutional amendment protecting slavery.

Waiting to assume the office he had just won, Lincoln wrestled with the twin problems of what he would do about secession and slavery. On one hand, he directly opposed Buchanan's position, stating that "My opinion is that no state can, in any way, lawfully get out of the Union, without the consent of the others." But he was more moderate where slavery was concerned, writing to reassure southerners that a Republican administration would not "directly or indirectly, interfere with their slaves, or with them, about their slaves."

Before he could do anything else, Lincoln first had to unite his party. In an attempt to appease all the Republican factions, he chose his cabinet with great care. His vice president, Hannibal Hamlin of Maine, had supported Lincoln but was also a friend of William Seward and had been chosen to balance the ticket factionally. Lincoln continued this balancing act with cabinet appointments for his four main rivals for nomination. Seward received the job of secretary of state. Edward Bates of Missouri became attorney general and Simon Cameron of Pennsylvania secretary of war. Salmon P. Chase of Ohio became secretary of the Treasury. Despite Lincoln's evenhandedness, his political balancing act was not easy to maintain: Chase and Seward, for instance, had a long history of political infighting and hated each other.

THE NATION DISSOLVED

☆ *What problems confronted Abraham Lincoln and Jefferson Davis in March 1861?*

☆ *How did their actions contribute to the escalating national crisis?*

Abraham Lincoln was inaugurated on March 4, 1861. In his inaugural address he repeated themes that he had been stressing since the election: no interference with slavery in states where it existed, no extension of slavery into the territories, and no tolerance of secession. Lincoln believed that the nation remained unbroken, and he pledged to see "that the laws of the Union be faithfully executed in all the States." This policy, he continued, necessitated "no bloodshed or violence, and there shall be none, unless it is forced upon the national authority." If war came, he argued, it would be over secession, not slavery, for the federal government had a duty to maintain the Union by any means, including force.

Lincoln, Sumter, and War

Lincoln's first presidential address drew mixed reactions. Most Republicans found it firm and reasonable, applauding its tone. Union advocates in both the North and the South thought the speech held promise for the future. Even former rival Stephen Douglas stated, "I am with him." Moderate southerners commended Lincoln's "temperance and conservatism" and believed the speech was all "any reasonable Southern man" could have expected. Confederates and their sympathizers, however, branded the speech a "Declaration of War."

But war was brewing even before Lincoln assumed office. In December 1860, South Carolina officials ordered the state militia to seize two federal forts—Fort Moultrie and Castle Pinckney—and the federal arsenal at Charleston. In response, Major Robert Anderson

In this vivid engraving, South Carolina shore batteries under the command of P. G. T. Beauregard shell Fort Sumter, the last federal stronghold in Charleston Harbor, on the night of April 12, 1861. Curious and excited civilians look on from their rooftops, never suspecting the horrors that would be the outcome of this rash action.

Picture Research Consultants & Archives.

moved all federal troops from Charleston to **Fort Sumter**, an island stronghold in Charleston Harbor. The Confederate congress demanded that President Buchanan remove all federal troops from the sovereign territory of the Confederacy. Despite his sympathy for the southern cause, Buchanan announced that Fort Sumter would be defended "against all hostile attacks, from whatever quarter." On January 9, 1861, a Charleston Harbor **battery** fired on a supply ship as it attempted to reach the fort. Buchanan denounced the action but did nothing.

Immediately after taking office in March, Lincoln received a report from Fort Sumter that supplies were running low. Under great pressure from northern public opinion to do something, he responded cleverly. He informed South Carolina governor Francis Pickens of his peaceful intention to send unarmed boats carrying food and supplies to the besieged fort.

☐ **Fort Sumter** Fort at the mouth of the harbor of Charleston, South Carolina, scene of the opening engagement of the Civil War in April 1861.

battery An army artillery unit, usually supplied with heavy guns.

Lincoln thus placed the Confederacy in a no-win position: allow the fort to be resupplied or fire on an unarmed ship, which would be sufficiently dishonorable to justify stronger federal action. After studying the situation, Confederate officials determined to beat Lincoln to the punch. President Davis ordered the Confederate commander at Charleston, General P. G. T. Beauregard, to demand the evacuation of Sumter and, if the federals refused, to "proceed, in such a manner as you may determine, to reduce it." On April 11, while the supply ships were still on their way, Beauregard called on Anderson to surrender. When Anderson rejected the ultimatum, shore batteries opened fire. After a thirty-four-hour artillery battle, Anderson surrendered. Neither side had inflicted casualties on the other, but civil war had officially begun.

Across the North, newspapers contrasted the president's resolute but restrained policy with the violent aggression of the Confederates, and the public rallied behind the Union cause. In New York City, where southern sympathizers had once vehemently criticized abolitionist actions, a million people attended a Union rally. Even northern Democrats rallied behind the Republican president, hearkening to Stephen Douglas's statement that "there can be no neutrals in this war, only patriots—or traitors." Spurred by the public outcry and confident of support, Lincoln called for seventy-five thousand militiamen to be mobilized "to maintain the honor, the integrity, and the existence of our National Union, and the perpetuity of popular government." Northern states responded immediately and enthusiastically. Across the Upper South and the border regions, however, the call to arms meant that a decision had to be made: whether to continue in the Union or join the Confederacy.

Choosing Sides in Virginia

The need for southern unity in the face of what he saw as northern aggression pushed Jefferson Davis to employ a combination of political finesse and force to create a solid southern alignment. He selected his cabinet with this in mind, choosing one cabinet member from each state except his own Mississippi and appointing men of varying degrees of radicalism. But unity among the seven seceding states was only one of Davis's worries. A more pressing concern was alignment among the eight slave states that remained in the Union. These states were critical, for they contained more than half of the entire southern population (two-thirds of its white population), possessed most of the South's industrial capacity, produced most

of its food, and raised more than half of its horses. In addition, many experienced and able military leaders lived in these states. If the Confederacy was to have any chance of survival, the human and physical resources of the whole South were essential.

It was not Davis's appeal for solidarity but Lincoln's call to mobilize the militia that won most of the other slave states for the Confederate cause. In Virginia, Governor John Letcher refused to honor Lincoln's demand for troops, and on April 17 a special convention declared for secession. Voters in Virginia overwhelmingly ratified this decision in a popular referendum on May 23. By then Letcher had offered Richmond as a site for the new nation's capital. The Confederate congress accepted the offer in order to strengthen ties with Virginia.

Not all Virginians were flattered at becoming the seat for the Confederacy. Residents of the western portion of the state had strong Union ties and long-standing political differences with their neighbors east of the Allegheny Mountains. Forty-six counties called mass Unionist meetings to protest the state's secession, and in a June convention at Wheeling, they elected their own governor, Francis H. Pierpoint, and drew up a constitution. In May 1862 the West Virginia legislature convened and requested admission to the United States.

For many individuals in the Upper South, the decision to support the Confederacy was not an easy one. Virginian Robert E. Lee, for example, was deeply devoted to the Union. A West Point graduate and career officer in the U.S. Army, he had a distinguished record in the War with Mexico and as superintendent of West Point. General Winfield Scott, commander of the Union forces, called Lee "the best soldier I ever saw in the field." Recognizing his military skill, Lincoln offered Lee field command of the Union armies, but the Virginian refused, deciding that he should serve his native state instead. Lee agonized over the decision but told a friend, "I cannot raise my hand against my birthplace, my home, my children." He resigned his U.S. Army commission in April 1861. When he informed Scott, a personal friend and fellow Virginian, of his decision, Scott replied, "You have made the greatest mistake of your life, but I feared it would be so." Scott chose to remain loyal to the Union.

A Second Wave of Secession

Influenced by Virginia, three other states joined the Confederacy. Arkansas had voted against secession in March, hoping that bloodshed might be averted, but when Lincoln called for militia units, Governor Henry M. Rector answered, "None will be furnished. The demand is only adding insult to injury." The state then called a second convention and on May 6 seceded from the Union. North Carolinians had

□ **Richmond** Port city on the James River in Virginia; already the state capital, it became the capital of the Confederacy.

It Matters Today

Ex Parte Merryman

On May 25, 1861, a Maryland state militiaman named John Merryman was arrested by federal troops and charged with treason as the result of alleged pro-Confederate activities. Merryman's attorney immediately filed for a writ of habeas corpus demanding that the government show just cause for detaining him. General George Cadwalader, the commander of the fort where Merryman was being held, responded that by order of the president of the United States, he had suspended Merryman's habeas corpus rights. In a lengthy legal opinion, Chief Justice Roger Taney ruled that because the section of the Constitution stating that "The privilege of the Writ of Habeas Corpus" may be suspended "in Cases of Rebellion or Invasion" was in Article I, which enumerates the powers of Congress, that only Congress, and not the president or a military officer, could suspend habeas corpus. Today the question of whether, or under what circumstances, limitations on habeas corpus protections can be applied to both citizens and noncitizens is a particularly important issue in the struggle against both foreign and domestic terrorism, and a number of recent cases have had to review *Ex Parte Merryman* as these questions have arisen.

- Does it seem as though Taney's decision was the right one under the circumstances? How might you argue against it?
- Take a look at a recent military detention case (*Hamdi v. Rumsfeld* or perhaps *Hamdan v. Rumsfeld*) and analyze to what extent that decision parallels *Ex Parte Merryman*.

---

also hoped for compromise, but moderates turned secessionist when Secretary of War Simon Cameron **requisitioned** "two regiments of militia for immediate service" against the Confederacy. Governor John W. Ellis replied, "I regard the levy of troops made by this administration for the purpose of subjugating the states of the South [to be] in violation of the Constitution and a gross usurpation of power." North Carolina seceded on May 20.

Tennessee, the eleventh and final state to join the Confederacy, was the home of many moderates, including John Bell, the Constitutional Union candidate in 1860. Eastern residents favored the Union, but those in the west favored the Confederacy. The state's voters at first rejected disunion overwhelmingly, but after the fighting began, Governor Isham C. Harris and the state legislature initiated military ties with the Confederacy, forcing another vote on the issue. Western voters carried the election, approving the agreement and seceding from the Union on June 8. East Tennesseans, who remained loyal Unionists, tried to divide the state much as West Virginians had done, but Davis ordered Confederate troops to occupy the region, thwarting the effort.

Trouble in the Border States

Four slave states remained in the Union, and the start of hostilities brought political and military confrontation in three of the four. Delaware quietly stayed in the Union. Voters there had favored Breckinridge in 1860, but the majority of voters disapproved of secession, and few of the state's citizens owned slaves. Maryland, Missouri, and Kentucky, however, each contained large, vocal secessionist factions and appeared poised to bolt to the Confederacy.

Maryland was particularly vital to the Union, for it enclosed Washington, D.C., on the three sides not bordered by Virginia. Maryland's significance became apparent on April 6, 1861, when a Massachusetts regiment responding to Lincoln's call for troops passed through Baltimore on the way to the capital. A mob confronted the soldiers, attacking them with bricks, bottles, and pistols. The soldiers returned fire. When the violence subsided, twelve Baltimore residents and four soldiers lay dead, and dozens more were wounded. Secessionists reacted violently, destroying railroad bridges to keep additional northern troops out of the state. In effect, Washington, D.C., was cut off from the North.

Lincoln and General Scott ordered the military occupation of Baltimore and declared **martial law**, much as Davis had done in eastern Tennessee. The

---

requisition To demand for military use.

martial law Temporary rule by military authorities, imposed on a civilian population in time of war or when civil authority has broken down.

Building momentum toward civil war severely tested loyalties in the United States. In border regions of the South, places like Virginia and Tennessee, many remained loyal to the Union and tried to stop the outbreak of violence. Northern border states were equally torn. In April 1861, a mob in Baltimore rioted in response to federal troops marching through the city on their way to the nation's capital. As shown in this illustration, bricks and rocks, then bullets and bayonets, expressed the anger and frustration besetting a nation in crisis.

The Granger Collection.

state legislature finally met and voted to remain neutral. Lincoln then instructed the army to arrest suspected southern sympathizers and hold them without formal hearings or charges. With southern sympathizers suppressed, new state elections were held. The new legislature, overwhelmingly Unionist, voted against secession.

Kentucky had important economic ties to the South but was strongly nationalistic. The governor refused to honor Lincoln's call for troops, but the state legislature voted to remain neutral. Both the North and the South honored that neutrality. Kentucky's own militia, however, split into two factions, and the state became a leading example of bloody fighting among members of the same family.

In Missouri, Governor Claiborne F. Jackson, a former proslavery activist in Kansas, pushed for secession, arguing that Missourians were bound together "in one brotherhood with the States of the South." When Unionists frustrated the secession movement, Jackson's forces seized the federal arsenal at Liberty and wrote to Jefferson Davis requesting artillery to support an assault on the arsenal at St. Louis. Union sympathizers, however, fielded their own forces and fought Jackson at every turn. Rioting broke out in St. Louis as civilians clashed with soldiers, and mob violence marred the nights. Jackson's secessionist movement sent representatives to the Confederate congress in Richmond, but Union forces maintained nominal control of the state and drove prosouthern leaders into exile.

FREDERICK DOUGLASS
What to the Slave Is the Fourth of July?

Oppositional language and shocking rhetoric played a leading role in the twentieth-century civil rights movement. Examining historical documents reveals that this was not a new phenomenon. Credible because of his own experience, Frederick Douglass became a very effective speaker for the abolition cause—often by shocking audiences. The following passage, from an 1852 Fourth of July address to the Ladies' Anti-Slavery Society of Rochester, illustrates Douglass's use of such rhetoric.

National Portrait Gallery, Smithsonian Institution/Art Resource, NY.

❶ To whom is Douglass referring here? Who did he consider his constituency to be?

❷ What is Douglass's point in denying connection to the holiday about which he had been invited to speak?

❸ Douglass is quoting here from Psalm 137, which he had recited in full earlier in the speech. This psalm, which relates to the fall of Israel, is cited again when Douglass discusses the fate of nations that defy God. What point was Douglass making in citing this psalm?

Fellow-citizens, pardon me, allow me to ask, why am I called upon to speak here to-day? What have I, or those I represent, to do with your national independence? ❶ Are the great principles of political freedom and of natural justice, embodied in that Declaration of Independence, extended to us? and am I, therefore, called upon to bring out humble offering to the national altar, and to confess the benefits and express devout gratitude for the blessings resulting from your independence to us? . . .

But such is not the state of the case. I say it with a sad sense of the disparity between us. I am not included within the pale of this glorious anniversary! Your high independence only reveals the immeasurable distance between us. The blessings in which you, this day, rejoice, are not enjoyed in common. The rich inheritance of justice, liberty, prosperity and independence, bequeathed by your fathers, is shared by you, not by me. The sunlight that brought life and healing to you, has brought stripes and death to me. This Fourth [of] July is *yours*, not *mine*. . . . ❷

Fellow-citizens; above your national, tumultuous joy, I hear the mournful wail of millions! whose chains, heavy and grievous yesterday, are, to-day, rendered more intolerable by the jubilee shouts that reach them. If I do forget, if I do not faithfully remember those bleeding children of sorrow this day, "may my right hand forget her cunning, and may my tongue cleave to the roof of my mouth!" ❸ To forget them, to pass lightly over their wrongs, and to chime in with the popular theme, would be treason most scandalous and shocking, and would make me a reproach before God and the world.

Study Tools

SUMMARY

Throughout the 1840s, slavery became increasingly politicized. The War with Mexico that began in 1846 raised, and then the Compromise of 1850 failed to alleviate, regional tension and debates. The Whig Party, strained by fragmentation among its factions, disintegrated, and two completely new groups—the Know-Nothings and the Republicans—competed to replace it. A series of events—including the Kansas-Nebraska Act and the *Dred Scott* decision—intensified regional polarization, and radicals on both sides fanned the flames of sectional rivalry. Even the Democratic Party could not hold together, splitting into northern and southern wings. By 1859, the young Republican Party, committed to restricting slavery's expansion, seemed poised to gain control of the federal government. Fearing that the loss of political power would doom their way of life, southerners recoiled in terror. Neither side felt it could afford to back down.

With the election of Abraham Lincoln in 1860, seven southern states withdrew from the Union. Last-minute efforts at compromise failed, and on April 12, 1861, five weeks after Lincoln's inauguration, Confederate forces fired on federal troops at Fort Sumter in Charleston Harbor. Lincoln believed that he had to call the nation to arms, and this move forced wavering states to choose sides. Internal divisions in Virginia, Tennessee, Maryland, Kentucky, and Missouri brought further violence and military action. Before summer, a second wave of secession finally solidified the lineup and established the boundary lines between the two competing societies. The stakes were set, the division was complete: the nation was poised for the bloodiest war in its history.

CHRONOLOGY
Toward a Shattered Union

1840	Formation of the Free-Soil Party
1846	War with Mexico begins
1848	Treaty of Guadalupe Hidalgo
	Zachary Taylor elected president
	Immigration to United States exceeds 100,000
1850	Compromise of 1850
	Zachary Taylor dies; Millard Fillmore becomes president
1852	First railroad line completed to Chicago
	Harriet Beecher Stowe's *Uncle Tom's Cabin*
	Franklin Pierce elected president
	Whig Party collapses
	Know-Nothing Party emerges
1853	Gadsden Purchase

1854	Republican Party formed
	Kansas-Nebraska Act
	Ostend Manifesto
1855	Proslavery posse sacks Lawrence, Kansas
1856	James Buchanan elected president
1857	*Dred Scott* decision
1858	Lincoln-Douglas debates
1859	John Brown's raid on Harpers Ferry
1860	Abraham Lincoln elected president
	Crittenden compromise fails
1861	Confederate States of America formed
	Fort Sumter shelled

Study Tools

FOCUS QUESTIONS

If you have mastered this chapter, you should be able to answer these questions and to explain the terms that follow the questions.

1. How did the politicization of slavery in the 1840s begin to move the nation toward crisis?

2. How did the war with Mexico and its outcomes influence politics?

3. What new political options affected the political system during the 1850s? In what ways?

4. In what ways did economic developments such as railroads contribute to political instability?

5. How did various political coalitions react to the Kansas-Nebraska Act?

6. What was the effect of these reactions on the national political climate?

7. In what ways was the presidential election in 1860 an outcome of the realignment of the party system during the 1850s?

8. Why did the election results have the political effects that they did?

9. What problems confronted Abraham Lincoln and Jefferson Davis in March 1861?

10. How did their actions contribute to the escalating national crisis?

KEY TERMS

Sojourner Truth p. 310
Liberty Party p. 311
Zachary Taylor p. 311
John C. Frémont p. 311
Wilmot Proviso p. 311
Winfield Scott p. 312
Battle of Buena Vista p. 312
Treaty of Guadalupe Hidalgo p. 313
forty-niners p. 313
Free-Soil Party p. 314
Know-Nothings p. 315
popular sovereignty p. 315
fugitive slave law p. 315
Stephen A. Douglas p. 315
Compromise of 1850 p. 315

Harriet Tubman p. 315
Underground Railroad p. 316
John Deere p. 317
Cyrus McCormick p. 317
Abraham Lincoln p. 317
Harriet Beecher Stowe p. 318
conscience Whigs p. 318
James Buchanan p. 319
Franklin Pierce p. 319
Young America Movement p. 320
Gadsden Purchase p. 320
Jefferson Davis p. 320
Kansas-Nebraska Act p. 320

Charles Sumner p. 320
Ostend Manifesto p. 321
John Brown p. 322
Republican Party p. 323
Dred Scott p. 323
Lecompton constitution p. 324
Freeport Doctrine p. 324
Harpers Ferry p. 324
Robert E. Lee p. 326
Constitutional Union Party p. 326
John J. Crittenden p. 328
Confederate States of America p. 329
Fort Sumter p. 331
Richmond p. 332

SUGGESTED RESOURCES

Library of Congress. "Primary Documents in American History: Compromise of 1850," http://www.loc.gov/rr/program/bib/ourdocs/Compromise1850.html. A rich collection of documents relating to this political development and surrounding events.

Library of Congress. "Primary Documents in American History: *Dred Scott v. Sandford*," http://www.loc.gov/rr/program/bib/ourdocs/DredScott.html. Another rich collection from the Library of Congress.

National Park Service. "Fort Sumter National Monument," http://www.nps.gov/fosu/index.htm. A very nice site for learning about the fort and the famous first battle of the Civil War.

National Park Service. "Frederick Douglass National Historic Site," http://www.nps.gov/frdo/index.htm. Centering on the Frederick Douglass house, this site has many resources relating to him and the abolition movement.

Northern Illinois University. "The Mexican-American War," http://dig.lib.niu.edu/mexicanwar/about.html. An informative site with primary sources and other useful tools.

14

A Violent Choice: Civil War, 1861–1865

INDIVIDUAL CHOICES

Mary Ashton Rice Livermore

Mary Ashton Rice grew up in the heady atmosphere that permeated antebellum Boston, and she joined many of her contemporaries in adopting a commitment to individual improvement and universal reform. She attended several schools in Boston and finally took a job as a teacher to support herself while attending the Female Seminary in Charlestown, Massachusetts. After graduation, she took a position as a resident teacher on a Virginia plantation, where she saw slavery firsthand and hated it. After three years in the South, Rice made a choice to devote the balance of her life to reform. Returning to Massachusetts, she became active in Boston-area reform movements and met Universalist minister and reform editor Daniel P. Livermore, whom she married in 1845. Over the next ten years, she and Daniel contributed regularly to local reform newspapers and magazines and worked in various and increasingly activist organizations.

With the passage of the Kansas-Nebraska Act, the Livermores decided to move to Kansas in 1857 to add their voices and votes to the struggle to keep Kansas a free state. But when they arrived in Chicago, their daughter became ill and the family decided to halt its journey. Still burning with reform fever, they founded a magazine, *The New Covenant*, to bring New England–style activist journalism to the Midwest.

When war broke out in 1861, Mary immediately formed a female society devoted to "the relief of sick and wounded soldiers, and for the care of

Mary A. Livermore

Library of Congress.

soldiers' families." Gathering a number of like-minded women into a tight organization, she and her lieutenants traveled to cities throughout the Midwest, even into hotly contested Missouri, gathering medical supplies and morale-raising cartons filled with homemade food, personal care items, and often, encouraging notes from sympathetic women addressed to anonymous soldiers in the field.

Over the next two years, women throughout the Midwest who had formed similar organizations began to coordinate their efforts and link their societies together. In 1863 these various societies finally merged into the Northwestern Sanitary Commission, a major arm of the national U.S. Sanitary Commission, with Livermore at its head. In that same year, she launched a four-month-long effort to raise money and educate the public about the deplorable health conditions in army camps, raising over $70,000. Her success led communities around the country to begin giving formal recognition to female relief organizations and to their leaders as effective executives.

Reflecting on popular writings about women, Livermore commented, "One would suppose in reading them that women possess but one class of physical organs, and that these are always diseased. Such teaching is pestiferous, and tends to cause and perpetuate the very evils it professes to remedy." Never shy about sharing her views with men—whether military camp commanders whose ignorance of public health matters endangered soldiers' lives or politicians who were slow to fund relief efforts—Livermore resolved after the war to work toward gaining for women the recognition that their efforts during the war had proved they deserved (see the Individual Voices feature at the end of this chapter). As a feminist editor and activist, Livermore spent the rest of her life laboring for justice.

The outbreak of war between the states shocked many in the already troubled nation. Lying in a sickbed in Boston, Mary Livermore's father declared that he would rather die than see the nation divided. But for his daughter, this was a moment of triumph and opportunity. For years she and her husband had worked to bring about the end of slavery, and now it appeared that a revolution was at hand.

Many shared the perception that this was a revolutionary moment, but uncertainty accompanied the excitement. The South would find it more and more difficult to withstand the superior manpower and resources controlled by the Union. And the North would suffer frustrations of its own as President Lincoln's generals let opportunity after opportunity slip by. In desperation, Lincoln would finally redefine the war by issuing the Emancipation Proclamation. From that point forward, hopes for a peaceful resolution evaporated: both sides would demand total victory or total destruction.

The war would affect many people in many different ways. For some, like Mary Livermore, it would afford great opportunities for advancement. For others,

it would be a long, torturous ordeal. But one thing was true for everyone and for the nation at large: nothing would be the same after the conflagration was over.

THE POLITICS OF WAR

☆ *What problems did Abraham Lincoln and Jefferson Davis face as they led their respective nations into war?*

☆ *How did each chief executive deal with those problems?*

Running the war posed complex problems for both Abraham Lincoln and Jefferson Davis. At the outset, neither side had the experience, soldiers, or supplies to wage an effective war, and foreign diplomacy and international trade were vital to both. But perhaps the biggest challenge confronting both Davis and Lincoln was internal politics. Lincoln had to contend not only with northern Democrats and southern sympathizers but also with divisions in his own party. Davis also faced internal political problems. The Confederate

Library of Congress Prints and Photographs Division [LC-DIG-ppmsca-37010]

Library of Congress.

"It is easy to understand how men catch the contagion of war," Mary Ashton Rice Livermore asserted. Many on both sides certainly caught it during the opening days of the Civil War. This Union soldier *(left)* and Confederate cavalryman *(right)* volunteered for service and obviously were eager to fight. Such enthusiasm seldom lasted long as days and weeks of boredom, often accompanied by disease and punctuated by brief but heated battles, caused enormous anxiety that eroded the fighting spirit.

constitution guaranteed a great deal of autonomy to the Confederate states, and each state had a different opinion about war strategy and national objectives.

Union Policies and Objectives

Abraham Lincoln took the oath of office in March 1861, but Congress did not convene until July. In effect, Lincoln ruled by executive proclamation for three months, vastly expanding the wartime powers of the presidency.

Having assumed nearly absolute authority, Lincoln faced the need to rebuild an army in disarray. When hostilities broke out, the Union had only sixteen thousand men in uniform, and nearly one-third of the officers resigned to support the Confederacy. What military leadership remained was aged: seven of the

eight heads of army bureaus had been in the service since the War of 1812, including General in Chief Winfield Scott, who was 74 years old. Only two Union officers had ever commanded a **brigade**, and both were in their seventies. Weapons were old, and supplies were low. On May 3, Lincoln exceeded his constitutional authority by calling for regular army recruits to meet the crisis without a Congressional declaration of war. "Whether strictly legal or not," he asserted, such actions were based on "a popular demand, and a public necessity."

Lincoln had also ordered a naval blockade of the Confederate states, which became an integral part of the Union strategy devised by the aged Winfield Scott. Scott ordered that the blockade of southern ports be combined with a strong Union thrust down the Mississippi River, the primary artery in the South's transportation system. This strategy would break the southern economy and split the Confederacy into two isolated parts. Like many northerners, Scott believed that economic pressure would bring southern moderates forward to negotiate a settlement. A war-fevered northern press ridiculed what it called the **anaconda plan**.

When Congress finally convened on July 4, 1861, Lincoln explained his actions and reminded congressmen that he had neither the constitutional

brigade A military unit consisting of two or more regiments and composed of between fifteen hundred and thirty-five hundred men.

☐ **anaconda plan** Winfield Scott's plan (named after a snake that smothers prey in its coils) to blockade southern ports and take control of the Mississippi River, thus splitting the Confederacy, cutting off southern trade, and causing an economic collapse.

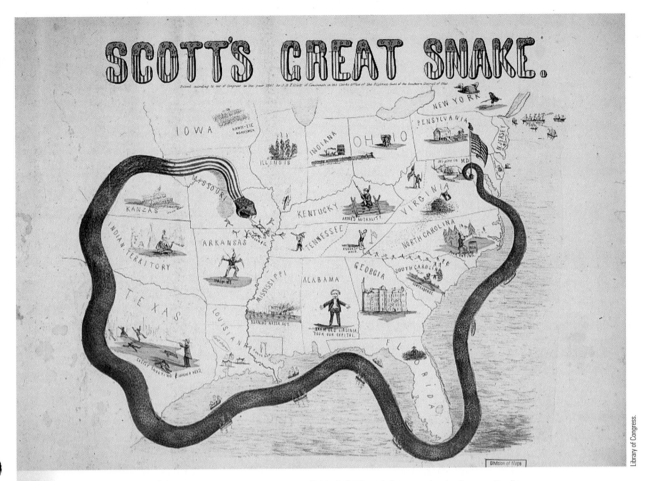

SCOTT'S GREAT SNAKE.

Though many northerners thought it was too passive, General Winfield Scott's "anaconda plan" was actually very well conceived. As this 1861 lithograph shows, Scott called for a naval blockade of the South and seizure of the Mississippi River, shutting down transportation routes to ruin the Confederate economy. Scott retired at the end of the war's first year, but his plan continued to shape the Union's overall strategy.

authority to abolish slavery nor any intention of doing so. Rebellion, not slavery, had caused the crisis and the seceding states must be brought back into the Union, regardless of the cost. "Our popular government has been called an experiment," he argued, and the point to be settled now was "its successful maintenance against a formidable internal attempt to overthrow it." Both houses of Congress passed resolutions validating Lincoln's earlier actions.

This seemingly unified front did not last. Viewing vengeance as the correct objective, **Radical Republicans** in Congress growled, "If their whole country must be laid waste, and made a desert, in order to save this union, so let it be." They pressed for and passed a series of confiscation acts that inflicted severe penalties against individuals in rebellion. Treason was punishable by death, and anyone aiding the Confederacy was to be punished with imprisonment, attachment of property, and confiscation of slaves. All persons living in the eleven seceding states, whether loyal to the Union or not, were declared enemies of the Union and subject to the provisions of the law.

The Radicals splintered any consensus Lincoln might have achieved in his own party, and northern Democrats railed against his accumulation of power. To keep an unruly Congress from undermining his efforts, Lincoln shaped early Union strategy to appease all factions and used military appointments to smooth political feathers. His attitudes frequently enraged radical abolitionists, but Lincoln maintained his calm in the face of their criticism and merely reinforced his intentions. "What I do about slavery and the colored race," he stated in 1862, "I do because it helps to save the Union; and what I forbear, I forbear because I do not believe it would help to save the Union."

Nevertheless, Lincoln had far greater physical and human resources at his command than did the

□ **Radical Republicans** Republican faction that tried to limit presidential power and enhance congressional authority during the Civil War; Radicals opposed moderation toward the South or any toleration of slavery.

TABLE 14.1 Comparison of Union and Confederate Resources

	UNION (23 STATES)	CONFEDERACY (11 STATES)
Total population	20,700,000	9,105,000[a]
Manufacturing establishments	110,000	18,000
Manufacturing workers	1,300,000	110,000
Miles of railroad	21,973	9,283
Troop strength (est.)	2,100,000	850,000

Source: Data from *Battles and Leaders of the Civil War* (1884–1888; reprinted ed., 1956).
[a]Includes 3,654,000 blacks, most of them slaves and not available for military duty.

Confederates (see Table 14.1). The Union was home to more than twice as many people as the Confederacy, had vastly superior manufacturing and transportation systems, and enjoyed almost a monopoly in banking and foreign exchange. Lincoln also had a well-established government structure and formal diplomatic relations with other nations of the world. Still, these advantages could not help the war effort unless properly harnessed.

Confederate Policies and Objectives

At the start of the war, the Confederacy had no army, no navy, no war supplies, no government structure, no foreign alliances, and a political situation as ragged as the Union's. Each Confederate state had its own ideas about the best way to conduct the war. After the attack on Fort Sumter, amassing supplies, troops, ships, and war materials was the main task for Davis and his cabinet. Politics, however, influenced southern choices about where to field armies and who would

direct them, how to run a war without offending state leaders, and how to pursue foreign diplomacy.

The Union naval blockade posed an immediate problem. The Confederacy had no navy and no capacity to build naval ships. But it did have the extremely resourceful Stephen Mallory as secretary of the navy. Under Mallory's direction, southern coastal defenders converted river steamboats, tugboats, and revenue cutters into harbor patrol gunboats, and they developed and placed explosive mines at the entrances to southern harbors.

Confederates pinned their main hope of winning the war on the army. Fighting for honor was praiseworthy behavior in the South, and southerners strongly believed they could "lick the Yankees" despite their disadvantage in manpower and resources. Thousands volunteered before the Confederate war department was even organized. By the time Lincoln issued his call for seventy-five thousand militiamen, the Confederates already had sixty thousand men in uniform.

Despite this rush of fighting men, the South faced major handicaps. Even with the addition of the four Upper South states (Virginia, North Carolina, Tennessee, and Arkansas), as of 1860, the South built only 4 percent of all locomotives and only 3 percent of all firearms manufactured in the United States. The North produced almost all of the country's cloth, pig iron, boots, and shoes. Early in the war, the South could produce enough food but lacked the means to transport it where it was needed.

The miracle worker in charge of supplying southern troops with weapons and ammunition was Josiah Gorgas, who became chief of ordnance in April 1861. Gorgas purchased arms from Europe while his ordnance officers bought or stole copper pots and tubing to make percussion caps, bronze church bells to make cannon, and lead weights to make bullets. He built factories and foundries to manufacture small arms. But despite his extraordinary skill, he could not supply all of the Confederate troops. When the Confederate congress authorized the enlistment of four hundred thousand additional volunteers in 1861, the war department had to turn away more than half of the enlistees because it lacked equipment for them.

Internal politics also plagued the Davis administration. First, he alienated his high-spirited populace by advocating a defensive war in the belief the Union would give up if the war was made too costly. As one southern editor put it, the "idea of waiting for blows, instead of inflicting them is altogether unsuited to the genius of our people." But even a defensive posture proved hard to maintain. Despite the shortage of arms, state governors hoarded weapons seized from federal arsenals for their own state militias and demanded that their states' borders be protected, spreading troops dangerously thin.

revenue cutter A small, lightly armed boat used by government customs agents to apprehend merchant ships violating customs laws.

pig iron Crude iron, direct from a blast furnace, that is cast into rectangular molds called pigs in preparation for conversion into steel, cast iron, or wrought iron.

ordnance Weapons, ammunition, and other military equipment.

percussion cap A thin metal cap containing an explosive compound, needed to fire the guns used in the Civil War.

The Diplomatic Front

Perhaps the biggest challenge facing the Confederacy was gaining international recognition and foreign aid. The primary focus of Confederate foreign policy was Great Britain. For years, the South had been exporting huge amounts of cotton to Britain, and many southerners felt that formal recognition of Confederate independence would immediately follow secession. Political and economic realities as well as ethical issues doomed them to disappointment. After all, the Union was still an important player in international affairs, and the British were not going to risk offending the emerging industrial power without good cause. Also, many English voters were morally opposed to slavery and would have objected to an open alliance with the slaveholding Confederacy. On May 13, 1861, Queen Victoria proclaimed official neutrality but granted **belligerent status** to the South.

The British pronouncement set the tone for other European responses and was much less than southerners had hoped for. But Britain's rejection of Lincoln's position that the conflict was a rebellion against duly authorized government was also a blow to the North. Lincoln could do little but accept British neutrality. In November 1861, however, an incident at sea nearly scuttled British-Union relations. James Murray Mason, the newly appointed Confederate emissary to London, and John Slidell, the Confederate minister to France, were traveling to their posts aboard the *Trent*, a British merchant ship bound for London. After the *Trent* left Havana, the U.S. warship *San Jacinto* stopped the British ship. Mason, Slidell, and their staffs were removed from the *Trent* and taken to Boston as prisoners of war.

Northerners celebrated the action, but the British viewed the *Trent* affair as aggression against a neutral government, a violation of international law, and an affront to their national honor. Lincoln ordered the release of the prisoners and apologized to the British, handling the incident so adroitly that the public outcry was largely forgotten when Mason and Slidell arrived in London.

The Union's First Attack

Like most southerners, northerners were confident that military action would bring the war to a quick end. General Irvin McDowell made the first move when his troops crossed into Virginia. McDowell's troops, though high-spirited, were poorly trained and undisciplined. They ambled along as if they were on a country outing, allowing P. G. T. Beauregard enough time to position his troops in defense of a vital rail center near Manassas Junction along a creek called Bull Run (see Map 14.1).

McDowell attacked on Sunday, July 21, and maintained the offensive most of the day. He seemed poised to overrun the Confederates until southern reinforcements under Thomas J. Jackson stalled

TABLE 14.2   Battle of Bull Run, July 21, 1861

	UNION ARMY	CONFEDERATE ARMY
Commanders	Irvin McDowell	P. G. T. Beauregard
Troop strength	17,676	18,053
Killed	460	387
Wounded	1,124	1,582
Captured	1,312	13
Total losses	2,896	1,982

Source: Data from *Battles and Leaders of the Civil War* (1884–1888; reprinted ed., 1956).

the Union advance. Jackson's unflinching stand at Bull Run earned him the nickname "Stonewall," and under intense cannon fire, Union troops panicked and began fleeing into a throng of northern spectators who had brought picnic lunches and settled in to watch the battle. Thoroughly humiliated before a hometown crowd, Union soldiers retreated toward Washington. Jefferson Davis immediately ordered the invasion of the Union capital, but the Confederates were also in disarray and made no attempt to pursue the fleeing Union forces (see Table 14.2).

This battle profoundly affected both sides. In the South, the victory stirred confidence that the war would be short and victory complete. Northerners, disillusioned and embarrassed, pledged that no similar retreats would occur. Lincoln removed McDowell from command and appointed George B. McClellan,

belligerent status Recognition that a participant in a conflict is a nation engaged in warfare rather than a rebel against a legally constituted government; full diplomatic recognition is one possible outcome.

▫ **Bull Run** A creek in Virginia not far from Washington, D.C., where Confederate soldiers forced federal troops to retreat in the first major battle of the Civil War, fought in July 1861.

▫ **Thomas J. Jackson** Confederate general nicknamed "Stonewall"; he commanded troops at both battles of Bull Run and was mortally wounded by his own soldiers at Chancellorsville in 1863.

▫ **George B. McClellan** U.S. general tapped by Lincoln to organize the Army of the Potomac; a skillful organizer but slow and indecisive as a field commander. He replaced Winfield Scott, who retired at the end of 1861, as general in chief of Union forces.

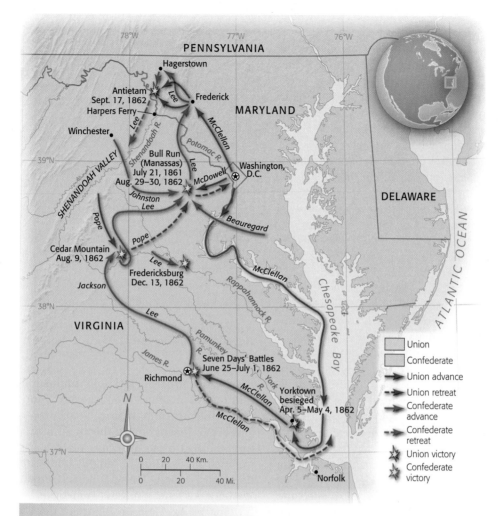

MAP 14.1 Union Offensives into Virginia, 1861–1862
This map shows two failed Union attempts to invade Virginia: the Battle of Bull Run (July 1861) and the Peninsular Campaign (August 1862). Confederate victories embarrassed the richer and more populous Union. The map also shows the Battle of Antietam (September 1862), in which the Union army under General George McClellan finally defeated Confederate troops under Robert E. Lee. © Cengage Learning.

ordering the creation of the **Army of the Potomac** to defend the capital from Confederate attack and spearhead any offensives into Virginia. Lincoln also replaced Secretary of War Simon Cameron with Edwin Stanton, a politician and lawyer from Pennsylvania.

General McClellan's strengths were in organization and discipline. Both were sorely needed. Before Bull Run, the largely unsupervised raw recruits in army camps received no military instruction. Under McClellan, months of training turned the 185,000-man army into a well-drilled and efficient unit. Calls to attack Richmond began anew, but

McClellan, seemingly in no hurry for battle, continued to drill the troops and remained in the capital.

FROM BULL RUN TO ANTIETAM

☆ *How did military action during the opening years of the war affect the people's perceptions of the war in the North and South?*

☆ *Why did Lincoln issue the Emancipation Proclamation when and in the way he did? What types of responses did it elicit?*

Reorganizing the military and forming the Army of the Potomac did not accomplish Lincoln's goal of toppling the Confederacy quickly and bringing the rebellious South back into the Union. In the second year of the war, frustration followed frustration as

☐ **Army of the Potomac** Army created to guard the U.S. capital after the Battle of Bull Run in 1861; it became the main Union army in the East.

Mexican Americans in the Civil War

Probably no event in American history has been studied, researched, and written about more than the Civil War. But when historian Jerry D. Thompson examined the story more closely, he realized that part of it was still missing. In a narrative of black and white Americans, where were the brown Americans? That is, why were the history books so silent about the role of Mexican Americans in this great struggle over slavery, secession, and union?

Thanks to Thompson, we now know that nearly ten thousand men of Mexican descent served as soldiers in the Civil War, constituting about half of the estimated twenty thousand men of Hispanic background who fought. About half of these were recruited in New Mexico, with smaller numbers coming from California and between three thousand and four thousand from Texas. At least twenty-five hundred Texans of Mexican descent joined the Confederate army. Many fought in various battles along the border with Mexico, a hotly contested region that itself is highly understudied. Another significant contingent was part of the company formed by Henry Hopkins Sibley that marched on Union forces in New Mexico, where they fought against other Hispanics on the Union side. But some belonged to a brigade under the command of John Bell Hood that was active in almost all of the major battles that took place in Virginia.

Another one thousand or so Tejanos also joined the Union army. Some of these were members of Adrian J. Vidal's Partisan Rangers, a guerilla band that raided Confederate positions along the Rio Grande from Mexico. Most, however, served in the Texas Union Army, which was formed originally by Unionist Texas refugees in New Orleans late in 1862. In 1863 these forces were active in campaigns in Louisiana and then, in October of that year, participated in a series of battles along the Rio Grande, at which time more Tejanos were recruited, forming an almost exclusively Mexican American Second Regiment of Texas Cavalry.

Why had history been so silent about the role of Mexican Americans for so long? Thompson suggests that one reason was that Mexican American motives for fighting in the war were fundamentally different than the motives of other Americans. In Texas, Mexican Americans collectively owned only sixty slaves when the war broke out, and most had no interest in the "peculiar institution." Often their participation was rooted in local political conflicts or even family feuds. But is this enough to answer the question? Historians know that such personal issues often influenced decisions about which side to fight for. In the end it seems to come down to the fact that the national narrative about the Civil War continues to be in black and white; adding brown somehow seems inconsistent and disturbing. But historians need to get over their reticence about broadening the palette and painting a more colorfully inclusive narrative not just of the Civil War, but of our history generally.

BIVOUAC OF CONFEDERATE TROOPS ON THE LAS MORAS, TEXAS, WITH STOLEN U. S. WAGONS, ETC.—Sketched by a Member of the Corps.—[See Page 381.]

Harpers Weekly, June 15, 1861/Picture Research Consultants & Archives.

Mexican American Confederate soldiers with captured Union equipment camped on Las Moras Creek in Texas.

Angered by years of systematic mistreatment at the hands of federal authorities, many Native Americans in Indian Territory were eager to enlist for service with the Confederacy. Confederate president Jefferson Davis chose his Indian agents carefully to take advantage of this much-needed source of aid. As this daguerreotype illustrates, Davis's diplomacy was highly successful; many young Indians flocked to Confederate recruitment rallies to join the army.

Wisconsin Historical Society.

Confederate forces continued to outwit and outfight numerically superior and better-equipped federal troops. After Bull Run it was clear that the war would be neither short nor glorious.

The War in the West

While the war in the East slid into inactivity, events in the West seemed almost as futile for the Union forces. In the border state of Missouri, the conflict rapidly degenerated into guerrilla warfare. Confederate William Quantrill's Raiders matched atrocities committed by Unionist guerrilla units called Jayhawkers. Union officials seemed unable to stop the ambushes, arson,

□ **Ulysses S. Grant** U.S. general who, after a series of victories in the Mississippi Valley, became general in chief of the Union army in 1864; he later became president of the United States.

theft, and murder, and Missouri remained a lawless battleground throughout the war.

Both the United States and the Confederacy coveted the western territories nearly as much as they did the border states. In 1861 Confederate Henry Hopkins Sibley recruited thirty-seven hundred Texans and marched into New Mexico, defeating a Union force at Valverde, but his losses were high. Needing provisions to continue the operation, he sent units to raid abandoned Union storehouses at Albuquerque and Santa Fe, but withdrawing federal troops had burned whatever supplies they could not carry. The small Confederate force at Santa Fe encountered a much larger federal force and won a miraculous victory, but the effort left the Confederates destitute of supplies. Under constant attack, the starving Confederate detachment evaded Union troops and retreated back into Texas.

Confederate leaders sought alliances with several Indian tribes in the newly settled Indian Territory south of Kansas. Many of the residents there had endured the Trail of Tears (see page 248) and had no love for the Union. If these Indian tribes aligned with the Confederacy, they not only could supply troops but might also form a buffer between Union forces in Kansas and the thinly spread Confederate defenses west of the Mississippi.

President Davis appointed General Albert Pike, an Arkansas lawyer who had represented the Creeks in their battle against removal in the 1830s, as special commissioner for the Indian Territory in March 1861. Pike negotiated with several tribes and on October 7 signed a treaty with members of the Cherokee, Choctaw, Creek, Chickasaw, and Seminole tribes that granted the Indians more nearly equal status—at least on paper—than any previous federal treaty, and it guaranteed that Indians would be asked to fight only to defend their own territory.

Struggle for the Mississippi

Union efforts in the west were dictated largely by Scott's anaconda plan as **Ulysses S. Grant** moved against southern strongholds in the Mississippi Valley in 1862. On February 6, he took Fort Henry along the Tennessee River and ten days later captured Fort Donelson on the Cumberland River near Nashville, Tennessee (see Map 14.2). In this one swift stroke, Grant successfully penetrated Confederate western defenses and brought Kentucky and most of Tennessee under federal control.

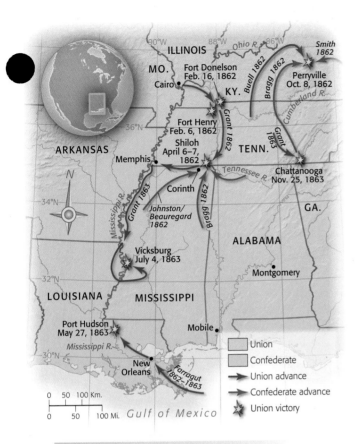

MAP 14.2 The War in the West, 1862–1863

This map illustrates the anaconda plan at work. The Union navy closed southern harbors, while Grant's troops worked to seal the northern end of the Mississippi River. © Cengage Learning.

TABLE 14.3 **Battle of Shiloh, April 6–7, 1862**

	UNION ARMY	CONFEDERATE ARMY
Commanders	William Tecumseh Sherman	Albert Sidney Johnston (killed)
	Ulysses S. Grant	P. G. T. Beauregard
Troop strength	75,000	44,000
Killed	1,754	1,723
Wounded	8,408	8,012
Captured, missing	2,885	959
Total losses	13,047	10,694

Source: Data from *Battles and Leaders of the Civil War* (1884–1888; reprinted ed., 1956).

Confederate general Albert Sidney Johnston finally reorganized the retreating southern troops while Grant was waiting for reinforcements. Early on April 6, to Grant's surprise, Johnston attacked at Pittsburg Landing, Tennessee, near a small country meetinghouse called Shiloh Church. Some Union forces under General William Tecumseh Sherman were driven back, but the Confederate attack soon lost momentum as Union defenses stiffened. The Battle of Shiloh raged until midafternoon. When Johnston was mortally wounded, General Beauregard took command and by day's end believed the enemy defeated. But Union reinforcements arrived during the night, and the next morning Grant counterattacked, pushing the Confederates back.

The losses on both sides were staggering (see Table 14.3). The Battle of Shiloh made the reality of war apparent to everyone but made a particularly strong impression on the common soldier. After Shiloh, one Confederate wrote: "Death in every awful form, if it really be death, is a pleasant sight in comparison to the fearfully and mortally wounded." Few people foresaw that the horrible carnage at Shiloh was but a taste of what was to come.

Farther south, Admiral David G. Farragut led a fleet of U.S. Navy gunboats against New Orleans, the commercial and banking center of the South, and on April 25 forced the city's surrender. Farragut then sailed up the Mississippi, hoping to take the well-fortified city of Vicksburg, Mississippi. He scored several victories, but at Port Hudson, Louisiana, the combination of Confederate defenses and shallow water forced him to halt. Meanwhile, on June 6, Union gunboats destroyed a Confederate fleet at Memphis, Tennessee, and brought the upper Mississippi under Union control. Vicksburg remained the only major obstacle to Union control over the entire river (see Map 14.2).

☐ **William Tecumseh Sherman** U.S. general who supported Grant in the West; later captured Atlanta, Georgia, and led a destructive march to the Atlantic coast.

☐ **Battle of Shiloh** Battle in Tennessee in April 1862 that ended with an unpursued Confederate withdrawal; both sides suffered heavy casualties for the first time, but neither side gained ground.

☐ **Vicksburg** City that was key to control of the Mississippi River, held by the Confederates until mid-1863.

Desperate to break the grip of the Union anaconda, the Confederate navy converted the captured Union ship U.S.S. *Merrimac* into the ironclad C.S.S. *Virginia*. Virtually immune to any weapon carried by Union frigates, the *Virginia* dominated the sea-lanes out of Norfolk Harbor. The Union navy eventually completed construction of its own ironclad, the U.S.S. *Monitor*, which defeated the *Virginia* in a dramatic sea battle, eliminating that weapon from the Confederate arsenal.

Lee's Aggressive Defense of Virginia

The anaconda plan was well on its way to cutting the Confederacy in two, but the general public in the North thought that the path to real victory led to Richmond, capital of the Confederacy. Confederates, too, realized that Richmond would be an important prize for the North and took dramatic steps to keep their capital city out of enemy hands.

In an effort to skirt Confederate defenses, when General McClellan finally acted, he executed a surprise move by transporting the entire Army of the Potomac by ship to Fort Monroe, Virginia, to attack Richmond from the south. Initiating what would be called the Peninsular Campaign, the army marched up the peninsula between the York and James Rivers (see Map 14.1). In typical fashion, McClellan

▫ Peninsular Campaign McClellan's attempt in the spring and summer of 1862 to capture Richmond by advancing up the peninsula between the James and York Rivers; Confederate forces under Robert E. Lee drove his troops back.

proceeded cautiously. The outnumbered Confederate forces took advantage of his indecision and twice slipped away, retreating toward Richmond while McClellan followed. Hoping to overcome the odds by surprising his Union opponent, General Joseph E. Johnston, commander of the Confederate Army of Northern Virginia, wheeled about and attacked at Seven Pines on May 31. Though the battle was indecisive—both sides claimed victory—it halted McClellan's progress and disabled Johnston, who was seriously wounded.

With McClellan stalled, Confederate stalwart Stonewall Jackson staged a brilliant diversionary thrust down the Shenandoah Valley toward Washington. In thirty days, he and his "foot cavalry" marched 350 miles, defeated three Union armies in five battles, captured and sent back to Richmond a fortune in provisions and equipment, inflicted twice as many casualties as they received, and confused and immobilized Union forces in the region.

Meanwhile, McClellan was marking time near Richmond waiting for reinforcements. With Johnston wounded, Davis had been forced to replace him, choosing Robert E. Lee. Daring, bold, and tactically aggressive, Lee enjoyed combat, pushed his troops to the maximum, and was well liked by those serving under him. He had an uncanny ability to read the character of his opponents, predict their maneuvers, and exploit their mistakes. It now fell to Lee to deal with the invading Yankees. In a move that became typical of his generalship, Lee split his forces and attacked from all sides over a seven-day period in August, forcing McClellan into a defensive position. The Peninsular Campaign was over. The self-promoting Union general had been beaten in part by his own indecisiveness.

Fed up with McClellan, Lincoln ordered the Army of the Potomac back to Washington and gave command to General John Pope, who soon encountered Lee's army again at the Manassas rail line on August 30. The Confederates pretended to retreat, and when Pope followed, Lee soundly defeated Lincoln's new general in the Second Battle of Bull Run. Thoroughly disappointed with Pope's performance, but lacking any other viable replacement, Lincoln once again named McClellan commander of the Army of the Potomac.

Lee's Invasion of Maryland

Feeling confident after the second victory at Bull Run, Lee devised a bold offensive against Maryland. On September 4, he crossed the Potomac, formulating an intricate offensive by dividing his army into three separate attack wings. But someone was careless—Union soldiers found a copy of Lee's detailed instructions wrapped around some cigars at an abandoned Confederate campsite. If McClellan had acted swiftly on this intelligence, he could have crushed Lee's army piece by piece, but he waited sixteen hours before advancing. By then, Lee had learned of the missing orders and quickly withdrew. Lee reunited some of his forces at Sharpsburg, Maryland, around Antietam Creek (see Map 14.1). There, on September 17, the Army of the Potomac and the Army of Northern Virginia engaged in the bloodiest single-day battle of the Civil War.

The casualties in this one battle were more than double those suffered in the War of 1812 and the War with Mexico combined. "The air was full of the hiss of bullets and the hurtle of grapeshot," one Union soldier said, and "the whole landscape turned red." The bitter fighting exhausted both armies. After a day of rest, Lee retreated across the Potomac. Stonewall Jackson, covering Lee's retreat, soundly thrashed a force that McClellan sent in pursuit. But for the first time, General Lee experienced defeat.

Although Lee's offensive had been thwarted, Lincoln was not pleased with the performance of his army and its leadership. He felt that McClellan could have destroyed Lee's forces if he had attacked earlier or, failing that, had pursued the fleeing Confederate army. He fired McClellan again, this time for good, and placed Ambrose E. Burnside in command.

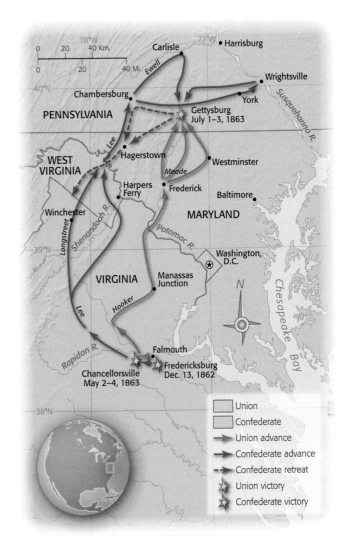

MAP 14.3 Fredericksburg, Chancellorsville, and Gettysburg
This map shows the campaigns that took place during the winter of 1862 and spring of 1863, culminating in the Battle of Gettysburg (July 1863). General Meade's victory at Gettysburg may have been the critical turning point of the war. © Cengage Learning.

Burnside moved his forces to the east bank of the Rappahannock River overlooking Fredericksburg, Virginia (see Map 14.3), where he delayed for almost

◻ **Second Battle of Bull Run** Union defeat near Bull Run in August 1862; Union troops led by John Pope were outmaneuvered by Lee.

◻ **Antietam Creek** Site of a battle that occurred in September 1862 when Lee's forces invaded Maryland; both sides suffered heavy losses, and Lee retreated into Virginia.

◻ **Fredericksburg** Site in Virginia of a Union defeat in December 1862 that demonstrated the incompetence of the new Union commander, Ambrose E. Burnside.

three weeks. Lee used the time to fortify the heights west of the city with men and artillery. On December 13, in one of the worst mistakes of the war, Burnside ordered a day-long frontal assault. The results were devastating. Federal troops, mowed down from the heights, suffered tremendous casualties, and once again the Army of the Potomac retreated to Washington.

Diplomacy and the Politics of Emancipation

Lee's victories carried heavy casualties, and with its ability to supply and deploy troops rapidly diminishing, the Confederacy desperately needed British aid, but nothing seemed to shake Britain's commitment to neutrality. Britain possessed a surplus of cotton and did not need southern supplies, neutralizing the South's only economic lever and frustrating Davis's diplomatic goals. Radical Republicans were also frustrated. No aspect of the war was going as they had expected. They had hoped that the Union army would defeat the South in short order. Instead the war effort was dragging on. More important from the Radicals' point of view, nothing was being done about slavery.

Politically astute as always, Lincoln acted to appease the Radical Republicans, foster popular support in the North for the war effort, and increase favorable sentiment for the Union cause abroad. During the summer of 1862, he drafted a proclamation freeing the slaves in the Confederacy and submitted it to his cabinet. Cabinet members advised that he postpone announcing the policy until after the Union had achieved a military victory. On September 22, five days after the Battle of Antietam, Lincoln unveiled the Emancipation Proclamation, which would abolish slavery in the states "in rebellion" on January 1, 1863.

Although the Emancipation Proclamation was a major step toward ending slavery, it actually freed no slaves. The proclamation applied only to slavery in areas controlled by the Confederacy, not in any area controlled by the Union. Some found this exception troubling, but the president's reasoning was sound. He could not afford to alienate the four slave states that had remained in the Union, nor could he commit any manpower to enforce emancipation in the areas that had been captured from the Confederacy.

Lincoln made emancipation entirely conditional on a Union military victory, a gambit designed to force critics of the war, whether in the United States or Great Britain, to rally behind his cause.

Whether or not it was successful as a humanitarian action, issuing the Emancipation Proclamation at the time he did and in the form he did was a profoundly successful political step for Lincoln. Although a handful of northern Democrats and a few Union military leaders called it an "absurd proclamation of a political coward," more joined Frederick Douglass in proclaiming, "We shout for joy that we live to record this righteous decree." Meanwhile, in Britain, most applauded the document and rallied against recognition of the Confederacy.

Still, Lincoln's new general in chief, Henry Halleck, was chilled by the document. As he explained to Grant, the "character of the war has very much changed within the last year. There is now no possible hope of reconciliation." The war was now about slavery as well as secession, and the Emancipation Proclamation committed the Union to conquering the enemy. As Lincoln told one member of his cabinet, the war would now be "one of subjugation."

THE HUMAN DIMENSIONS OF THE WAR

☆ How did the burdens of war affect society in the North and the South?

☆ How did individuals and governments in both regions respond to those burdens?

The Civil War imposed tremendous stress on American society. As the men marched off to battle, women faced the task of caring for families and property alone. As casualties increased, the number of voluntary enlistments decreased, and both sides searched for ways to find replacements for dead and wounded soldiers. The armies constantly demanded not only weapons and ammunition but also food, clothing, and hardware. Government spending was enormous, and inflation soared. Society in both North and South changed to meet an array of hardships as individuals facing unfamiliar conditions attempted to carry on their lives amid the war's devastation.

Instituting the Draft

By the end of 1862, heavy casualties, massive desertion, and declining enlistments had depleted both armies. Although the North had a much larger population to draw from, its enlistments sagged with its

□ **Emancipation Proclamation** Lincoln's order abolishing slavery as of January 1, 1863, in states "in rebellion" but not in border territories still loyal to the Union.

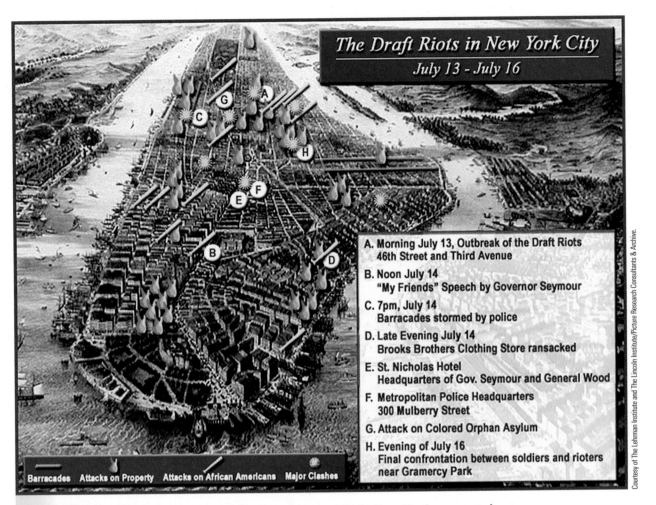

The Draft Riots in New York City
July 13 - July 16

A. Morning July 13, Outbreak of the Draft Riots
46th Street and Third Avenue

B. Noon July 14
"My Friends" Speech by Governor Seymour

C. 7pm, July 14
Barracades stormed by police

D. Late Evening July 14
Brooks Brothers Clothing Store ransacked

E. St. Nicholas Hotel
Headquarters of Gov. Seymour and General Wood

F. Metropolitan Police Headquarters
300 Mulberry Street

G. Attack on Colored Orphan Asylum

H. Evening of July 16
Final confrontation between soldiers and rioters
near Gramercy Park

Barracades   Attacks on Property   Attacks on African Americans   Major Clashes

Angered by the fact that rich men were virtually exempt from the draft, frightened by the prospect of job competition from freed southern slaves, and frustrated by the lack of resolution on the battlefield, workingmen took to the streets in New York City during the summer of 1863 to protest against the war. Well-dressed men, African Americans, and leading war advocates were the main targets of mob violence during three nights of uncontrolled rioting. As this illustration shows, the violence was not confined to any one part of the city.

military fortunes during 1862. More than a hundred thousand Union soldiers were absent without official leave. Most volunteers had enlisted in 1861 for limited terms, which would soon expire. Calling on state militias netted few replacements because the Democrats, who made tremendous political gains at the state level in 1862, at times refused to cooperate. To bypass state officials and ensure enough manpower, Congress passed the Conscription Act in March 1863. In effect, the law made all single men between the ages of 20 and 45 and married men between 20 and 35 eligible for service. Government agents collected names in a house-to-house survey, and draftees were selected by lottery.

The conscription law did offer "escape routes." Drafted men could avoid military service by providing—that is, hiring—an "acceptable substitute"

or by paying a $300 fee to purchase an exemption. The burden of service thus fell on farmers and urban workers who were already suffering from high taxation and inflation caused by the war. Added to that was workers' fear that multitudes of former slaves freed by the Emancipation Proclamation would pour into the already crowded job market, further lowering the value of their labor. Overall, the urban poor felt a sense of alienation, which exploded in the summer of 1863 in New York, where antidraft rioting erupted across city.

□ **Conscription Act** Law passed by Congress in 1863 that established a draft but allowed wealthy people to escape it by hiring a substitute or paying the government a $300 fee.

The trouble started on July 13 when armed demonstrators protesting unfair draft laws engaged in a spree of violence. During three nights of rioting, white workingmen beat many African Americans and lynched six. The Colored Orphan Asylum and several homes owned by blacks were burned. Mobs ransacked businesses owned by African Americans and by people who employed them. Irish men and women and members of other groups that seemed to threaten job security also felt the mob's fury. The rioters also expressed their frustration against Republican spokesmen and officials. Republican journalist Horace Greeley was hanged in effigy, and the homes of other prominent Republicans and abolitionists were vandalized. Protesting draft exemptions for the rich, rioters also set upon well-dressed strangers on the streets. After four days of chaos, federal troops put down the riot. Fearful of future violence, the city council of New York City voted to pay the $300 exemption fee for all poor draftees who chose not to serve in the army.

The Confederacy also instituted a draft after the first wave of enlistments dried up. Conscription in the South, as in the North, met with considerable resentment. Believing that plantations were necessary to the war effort and that slaves would not work unless directly overseen by masters, in 1862 Confederate officials passed the Twenty Negro Law, which exempted planters owning twenty or more slaves from military service. Like the exemptions in the North, the southern policy fostered the feeling that the poor were going off to fight while the rich stayed safely at home. The law was modified in 1863, requiring exempted planters to pay $500, and in 1864, the number of slaves required to earn an exemption was lowered to fifteen. Nevertheless, resentment continued to smolder.

□ **Horace Greeley** Journalist and politician who helped found the Republican Party; his newspaper, the *New York Tribune,* was known for its antislavery stance.

hanged in effigy To hang, as if on a gallows, a crude likeness or dummy—an effigy—representing a hated person.

□ **Twenty Negro Law** Confederate law that exempted planters owning twenty or more slaves from the draft on the grounds that overseeing farm labor done by slaves was necessary to the war effort.

□ **Homestead Act** Law passed by Congress in 1862 that promised ownership of 160 acres of public land to any citizen or would-be citizen who lived on and cultivated the land for five years.

□ **greenbacks** Paper money issued by the Union; it was not backed by gold.

Wartime Economy in the North and South

Despite enormous economic stress, Northern industry and population actually grew during the Civil War. Operating in cooperation with government, manufacturing experienced a boom. Manufacturers of war supplies benefited from government contracts. Textiles and shoemaking boomed as new labor-saving devices improved efficiency and increased production. Congress stimulated economic growth by means of subsidies and land grants to support a transcontinental railroad, higher tariffs to aid manufacturing, and land grants that states could use to finance higher education. In 1862 Congress passed the Homestead Act to make land available to more farmers. The law granted 160 acres of the public domain in the West to anyone who lived on, and improved, the land for five years.

Of course, the economic picture was not entirely positive. The Union found itself resorting to financial tricks to keep the economy afloat. Facing a cash-flow emergency in 1862, Congress passed the Legal Tender Act, authorizing Treasury Secretary Salmon Chase to issue $431 million in paper money, known as greenbacks, that was backed not by gold but only by the government's commitment to redeem the bills. Financial support also came through selling bonds. In the fall of 1862, Philadelphia banker Jay Cooke started a bond drive. More than $2 billion worth of government bonds were sold, most of them paid for in greenbacks. These emergency measures helped the Union survive the financial pressures created by the war, but the combination of bond issues and unbacked currency set up a highly unstable situation that came back to haunt Republicans after the war.

The South, an agrarian society, began the war without an industrial base. Here the government intervened more directly in the economy, offering generous loans to new or existing companies that would produce war materials. Josiah Gorgas started government-owned production plants in Alabama, Georgia, and South Carolina. These innovative programs, however, could not compensate for inadequate prewar industrialization.

The supply of money was also a severe problem in the South. Like the North, the South tried to ease cash-flow problems by printing paper money, eventually issuing more than $1 billion in unbacked currency. The outcome was runaway inflation. By the time the war ended, southerners were paying more than $400 for a barrel of flour.

Southern industrial shortcomings severely handicapped the army. Many Confederate soldiers were barefoot because shoes were in such short supply. Ordnance was always in demand. Northern plants could produce more than five thousand muskets a day; Confederate production never exceeded three hundred. The most serious shortage, however, was food. Although the South was an agricultural region, most of its productive acreage was devoted to cotton, tobacco, and other inedible crops. Corn and rice were the primary food products, but supplies were continually reduced by military campaigns and Union occupation of farmlands. Hog production suffered from the same disruptions, and while Southern cattle were abundant, most were range stock grown for hides and tallow rather than for food. Hunger became a miserable part of daily life for the Confederate armies.

Civilians in the South suffered from the same shortages as the army. Because of prewar shipping patterns, the few rail lines that crossed the Confederacy ran north and south. Distribution of goods became almost impossible as invading Union forces cut rail lines and disrupted production. The flow of cattle, horses, and food from the West diminished when Union forces gained control of the Mississippi. Imported goods had to evade the Union naval blockade. Southern society, cut off from the outside world, consumed its existing resources and found no way to obtain more.

Women in Two Nations at War

Because the South had fewer men than the North to send to war, a larger proportion of southern families were left in the care of women. Some women successfully supported their families. Others struggled in complete poverty amid the ravages of war. One woman wrote to the Confederacy's secretary of war, pleading that he "discharge" her husband so that "he might do his children some good" rather than leaving them "to suffer." Some disregarded the authorities. "Desert again, Jake," one shouted to her husband, who was being drafted for the second time. Most southern women, however, supported the war effort. Women became responsible for much of the South's agricultural and industrial production, overseeing crops and laboring in the fields, working in factories, managing estates, and operating businesses while, in most cases, also running the household—and waiting for the dreaded message that a husband or child would not return from the front. As one southern soldier wrote, women bore "the greatest burden of this horrid war."

Women in the North served in much the same capacity as their southern counterparts. They maintained families and homes alone, working to provide income and raise children. Although they did not face the shortages and ravages of battle that made life so hard for southern women, they did work in factories, run family businesses, teach school, and supply soldiers. Many served in managerial capacities or as writers and civil servants. Even before the war ended, northern women were going south to educate former slaves and help them find a place in American society. Like Mary Livermore, women assumed new roles that helped prepare them for greater involvement in social and political life after the war.

Women from both South and North actively participated in the war itself. Many women on both sides served as scouts, couriers, and spies; and more than four hundred disguised themselves as men and served as active soldiers until they were discovered. General William S. Rosecrans expressed dismay when one of his sergeants was delivered of "a bouncing baby boy," which was, the general complained, "in violation of all military regulations." Army camps frequently included officers' wives, female employees, camp followers, and women who came to help in whatever way they could.

Free Blacks, Slaves, and War

The Civil War marked a revolution for African Americans, but change was not always for the better. At first, many free blacks attempted to enlist in the Union army but were turned away. In 1861 General Benjamin F. Butler began using runaway slaves, called *contrabands*, as laborers. Several other northern commanders quickly adopted the practice. As the number of contrabands increased, however, the Union grappled with problems of housing and feeding them.

In the summer of 1862, Congress authorized the acceptance of "persons of African descent" into the armed forces, but enlistment remained low. After the Emancipation Proclamation, Union officials actively recruited former slaves, raising troops from among the freedmen and forming them into regiments known as the U.S. Colored Troops. Some northern state governments sought free blacks to fill state draft quotas; agents offered generous bonuses to those who signed up. By the end of the war, about 180,000 African Americans had enlisted in northern armies; by 1865, almost two-thirds of Union troops in the Mississippi Valley were black.

At first, African American regiments were used as laborers rather than being allowed to fight. But several black regiments, when finally allowed into battle, performed so well that they won grudging respect. These men fought in 449 battles in every theater of the war and had a casualty rate 35 percent higher than that of white soldiers. Still, army officials discriminated against African American soldiers in a variety of ways. Units were segregated, and until 1864, blacks were paid less than whites. All black regiments had white commanders; only one hundred African Americans were commissioned as officers. And Confederates

Women served in many different capacities during the Civil War. An unknown number of them actually dressed as men to join the fighting. Frances Clayton was one of the few documented cases of such Civil War gender-bending.

violently resented the Union's use of these troops: African American soldiers suffered atrocities because some Confederate leaders refused to take black prisoners. In all, about sixty-eight thousand black Union soldiers were killed or wounded in battle, and twenty-one were awarded the Congressional Medal of Honor.

The war effort in the South relied heavily on the slave population, mostly as producers of food and as military laborers. Slaves constituted more than half of the workforce in armament plants and military hospitals. Though crucial to the southern war effort, slaves suffered more than other southerners in the face of food shortages and other privations. And after Lincoln issued the Emancipation Proclamation, fears of slave revolts prompted whites to institute harsh

security procedures. Hungry and even less free than usual, slaves became the greatest unsung casualties of the war.

Life and Death at the Front

Many volunteers on both sides in the Civil War had romantic notions about military service. Most were disappointed. Life as a common soldier was anything but glorious. Letters and diaries written by soldiers tell of long periods of doing nothing in overcrowded camps, interrupted only by furious spells of dangerous action.

Though life in camp was tedious, it could be nearly as dangerous as time spent on the battlefield. Problems with supplying safe drinking water and disposing of waste constantly plagued military leaders. Diseases such as dysentery and **typhoid fever** frequently swept through unsanitary camps. And in the overcrowded conditions that often prevailed, smallpox and other contagious diseases passed rapidly from person to person. At times, as many as a quarter of the uninjured people in camps were disabled by one or another of these ailments.

Lacking in resources, organization, and expertise, the South did little to upgrade camp conditions. In the North, however, women like Mary Livermore drew on the organizational skills they had gained as antebellum reformers and created voluntary organizations to address the problem. As the small local relief societies gradually merged into regional organizations, President Lincoln in June 1861 responded to their concerns by creating the **United States Sanitary Commission**, a government agency responsible for advising the military on public health issues and investigating sanitary problems. "The Sanitary," as it was called, put hundreds of nurses into the field, providing much-needed relief for overburdened military doctors.

Nurses on both sides showed bravery and devotion. Often working under fire at the front and with almost no medical supplies, these volunteers nursed sick and wounded soldiers, watched as they died not

typhoid fever An infectious disease transmitted through contact with contaminated water, milk, or food; causes severe intestinal distress and high fever.

☐ **United States Sanitary Commission** Government commission established by Abraham Lincoln to improve public health conditions in military camps and hospitals.

COME AND JOIN US BROTHERS.

PUBLISHED BY THE SUPERVISORY COMMITTEE FOR RECRUITING COLORED REGIMENTS
1210 CHESTNUT ST. PHILADELPHIA.

Kean Collection/Getty Images.

Eager to fill constantly depleting army ranks, Union officials appealed to African Americans to volunteer for military service. This recruiting poster, which bore the legend "Come Join Us, Brothers," presents a glorified vision of what conditions were like for black units. One accurate detail is that the only officer in the scene is white; in fact, hardly any African Americans were permitted to command troops during the Civil War.

In the Wider World

The Geneva Convention

While war was devastating the lives of Americans, a Swiss businessman, Henry Dunant, was in the midst of organizing to address similar devastation worldwide. Having witnessed the Battle of Solferino in 1859, in which over twenty-three thousand French and Austrian troops were wounded, Dunant devoted himself to protecting the rights of the wounded and prisoners of war. In 1863 Dunant brought together a so-called "committee of five," which called for an international convention in Geneva, Switzerland. Delegates from fourteen nations attended this first Geneva Convention and signed accords calling for the protection of wounded soldiers and for medical personnel in the field. They devised an internationally recognized symbol to identify those under protection—a red cross on a field of white. In the years to come, dozens of nations would sign and expand the Geneva Convention, and in 1876 Dunant's "committee of five" was renamed the International Committee of the Red Cross, the name it still bears today.

only from their wounds but also from infection and disease, and offered as much comfort and help as they could. Clara Barton, known as the "Angel of the Battlefield," recalled "speaking to and feeding with my own hands each soldier" as she attempted to nurse them back to health. The numbers of wounded who filled the hospital tents was unprecedented, largely because of technological innovations in weaponry that had taken place during the antebellum period. New rifled muskets had many times the range of the old smoothbore weapons used during earlier wars—the effective range of the Springfield rifle used by many Union soldiers was 400 yards, and a stray bullet could still kill a man at 1,000 yards. Rifled artillery also added to the casualty count, as did exploding artillery shells, which sent deadly shrapnel ripping through lines of men. Many surgeons at the front lines could do little more than amputate limbs to save lives. Hospitals, understaffed and lacking supplies and medicines, frequently became breeding grounds for disease. The war exacted a tremendous emotional toll on everyone, even on those who escaped physical injury. As one veteran

□ **Clara Barton** Organizer of a volunteer service to aid sick and wounded Civil War soldiers; she later founded the American branch of the Red Cross.

rifled Having a series of spiral grooves inside the barrel of a gun that cause the projectile to spin, giving it greater range and accuracy.

□ **Andersonville** Confederate prisoner of war camp in northern Georgia where some fourteen thousand Union prisoners died of disease and malnutrition.

put it, soldiers had seen "so many new forms of death" and "so many frightful and novel kinds of mutilation."

Conditions were even worse in prison camps. Throughout much of the war, an agreement provided for prisoner exchanges, but that did not prevent overcrowding and unsanitary conditions. And as the war dragged on, the exchange system stopped working effectively. Also, late in the war, Union commanders suspended all prisoner exchanges in hopes of depriving the South of much-needed replacement soldiers.

The most notorious of the Civil War prison camps was Andersonville, in northern Georgia, where thousands of Union captives languished in an open stockade with only a small creek for water and virtually no sanitary facilities. Without enough food to feed its own armies and civilian population, the Confederacy could allocate little food for its overcrowded prison camps. Designed to house ten thousand men, Andersonville held more than thirty-three thousand prisoners during the summer of 1864. As many as one hundred men died of disease and malnutrition within its walls each day; estimates put the death toll at that one prison at nearly fourteen thousand over the course of the war.

Even death itself came to be redefined, as 8 percent of the white male population in the United States between the ages of 13 and 43 died in such a short time and in such grisly ways. People at the front reported being numbed by the horror. One army surgeon reported, "I pass over the putrefying bodies of the dead . . . and feel as . . . unconcerned as though they were two hundred pigs." Nor was distance any insulation from the horrors of death.

The new art of photography brought graphic images of the gruesome carnage directly into the nation's parlors. "Death does not seem half so terrible as it did long ago," one Texas woman reported. "We have grown used to it."

WAGING TOTAL WAR

☆ *What factors contributed to the Union's adoption of a total war strategy after 1863?*

☆ *Was total war justifiable in light of the human and property damage it inflicted and the overall consequences it achieved? Why or why not?*

As northerners anticipated the presidential election of 1864, Lincoln faced severe challenges on several fronts. The losses to Lee and Jackson in Virginia and the failure to catch Lee at Antietam had eroded public support. Many northerners resented the war, conscription, and abolitionism. Others feared Lincoln's powerful central government.

Northern Democrats advocated a peace platform and turned to George B. McClellan, Lincoln's ousted general, as a potential presidential candidate. Lincoln also faced a challenge from within his own party. Radical Republicans, who felt he was too soft on the South and unfit to run the war, began planning a campaign to win power. They championed the candidacy of John C. Frémont, who had become an ardent advocate of the complete abolition of slavery.

Lincoln's Generals and Southern Successes

The surest way for Lincoln to stop his political opponents was through military success. After Burnside's disaster at Fredericksburg, Lincoln demoted him and elevated General Joseph Hooker. Despite Hooker's reputation for bravery in battle—his nickname was "Fighting Joe"—Lee soundly defeated his forces at Chancellorsville in May 1863 (see Map 14.3 and Table 14.4). After Hooker had maneuvered Lee into a corner, Stonewall Jackson unleashed a vicious attack, and according to one of his subordinates Fighting Joe simply "lost his nerve." Hooker resigned, and Lincoln replaced him with General George E. Meade.

▫ **Chancellorsville** Site in Virginia where in May 1863 Confederate troops led by Lee defeated a much larger Union force.

Library of Congress.

In 1862, photographer Mathew Brady put on a public display of battlefield scenes in his New York gallery that brought the war home to civilians as nothing had before. The *New York Times* proclaimed: "Mr. Brady has done something to bring home to us the terrible reality and earnestness of war. If he has not brought bodies and laid them on our dooryard and along the streets, he has done something very like it."

Chancellorsville was a devastating loss for the North, but it was perhaps more devastating for the Confederates. After he led the charge that unnerved Hooker, Jackson's own men mistakenly shot him as he rode back toward his camp in the darkness. Doctors amputated Jackson's arm in an attempt to save his life. "He has lost his left arm," moaned Lee, "but I have lost my right." Eight days later, Jackson died of pneumonia.

Despite that loss, at a meeting of Confederate leaders in Richmond, Lee proposed another major invasion of the North, arguing that such a maneuver would allow the Confederates to gather supplies and might encourage the northern peace movement, revitalize the prospects of foreign recognition, and perhaps capture the Union capital. Confederate leaders agreed and approved Lee's plan.

The Army of Northern Virginia met only weak opposition as it crossed the Potomac River (see Map 14.3). In Maryland and Pennsylvania the troops seized livestock, supplies, food, clothing, and shoes. Learning that a Union contingent was in the area of Gettysburg, Pennsylvania, and believing them to be weaker than they were, on June 29 Lee moved to engage the Federals. Meade, whose Army of the Potomac had been trailing Lee's army as it marched north from Chancellorsville, immediately dispatched a detachment to reinforce Gettysburg. On the following day, the two armies began a furious three-day battle.

Arriving in force on July 1, Meade took up an almost impregnable defensive position on the hills along Cemetery Ridge. The Confederates hammered both ends of the Union line but could gain no ground. On the third day, Lee ordered a major assault on the middle of the Union position. Eleven brigades, more than thirteen thousand men, led by fresh troops under Major General George E. Pickett, tried to cross open ground and take the hills held by Meade, while Major J. E. B. "Jeb" Stuart's cavalry attacked from the east. Lee made few strategic mistakes during the war, but Pickett's charge was foolhardy. Meade's forces drove off the attack. The whole field was "dotted with our soldiers," wrote one Confederate officer. Losses on both sides were high (see Table 14.5), but Confederate casualties exceeded twenty-eight thousand men, more than half of Lee's army. Lee retreated, his invasion of the North a failure.

On the heels of this major victory for the North came news from Mississippi that after a seven-week siege, Vicksburg had fallen to Grant on July 4

(see Map 14.2). Then on July 9, Port Hudson, the last Confederate garrison on the Mississippi, also surrendered. The "Father of Waters," said Lincoln, "again goes unvexed to the sea."

Despite jubilation over the recent victories, Lincoln and the North remained frustrated. After Gettysburg, Lincoln waited for word of Lee's capture, believing it would signal the end of the rebellion. But like McClellan, Meade failed to pursue the retreating Confederates. When the president learned of Lee's escape, he said in disbelief, "Our Army held the war in the hollow of their hand and they would not close it."

Disappointment in Tennessee also soon marred the celebration over Gettysburg and Vicksburg. Union general William S. Rosecrans had taken the rail center of Chattanooga, but on September 18, Braxton Bragg's forces attacked Rosecrans at Chickamauga Creek. Rosecrans scurried back to refuge in Chattanooga, leaving troops in place to cover his retreat. This force, under the command of George H. Thomas, delayed the Confederate offensive and, in the words of one veteran, "saved the army from defeat and rout." Bragg nonetheless was able to follow and laid siege to Chattanooga from the heights overlooking the city.

With Lee and his army intact and Rosecrans pinned down in Tennessee, the war, which in July had appeared to be so nearly over, was, in Lincoln's words, "prolonged indefinitely." Lincoln needed a new kind of general.

□ **Gettysburg** Site in Pennsylvania where in July 1863 Union forces under General George Meade defeated Lee's Confederate forces, turning back Lee's invasion of the North.

TABLE 14.4 **Battle of Chancellorsville, May 1–4, 1863**

	UNION ARMY	CONFEDERATE ARMY
Commanders	Joseph Hooker	Robert E. Lee
Troop strength	75,000	50,000
Killed	1,606	1,665
Wounded	9,762	9,081
Captured, missing	5,919	2,018
Total losses	17,287	12,764

Source: Data from *Battles and Leaders of the Civil War* (1884–1888; reprinted ed., 1956).

At Gettysburg, a series of battles like the one shown here—this one on the last day of the fighting—cost Confederate General Robert E. Lee more than half of his entire army and forced his retreat into Virginia.

Grant, Sherman, and the Invention of Total War

Among the available choices, Grant had shown the kind of persistence and boldness Lincoln thought necessary. Lincoln placed him in charge of all Union forces in the West on October 16. Grant immediately replaced Rosecrans with the more intrepid and decisive Thomas. Sherman's troops joined Thomas under Grant's command on November 14. This united force rid the mountains above Chattanooga of Confederate strongholds and drove Bragg's forces out of southern Tennessee. Confederate forces also withdrew from Knoxville in December, leaving the state under Union control.

While fighting raged in Tennessee, Lincoln took a break from his duties in the White House to participate in the dedication of a national cemetery at the site where, just months before, the Battle of Gettysburg had taken the lives of thousands. In the speech he delivered on November 19, 1863, Lincoln dedicated not only the cemetery but the war effort itself to the fallen soldiers, and also to a principle. "Fourscore and seven years ago," Lincoln said, "our fathers brought forth on this continent a new nation, conceived in liberty and dedicated to the proposition that all men are created equal." The Gettysburg Address was circulated in

TABLE 14.5   Battle of Gettysburg, July 1–3, 1863

	UNION ARMY	CONFEDERATE ARMY
Commanders	George E. Meade	Robert E. Lee
Troop strength	75,000	50,000
Killed	3,155	3,903
Wounded	14,529	18,735
Captured, missing	5,365	5,425
Total losses	23,049	28,063

Source: Data from *Battles and Leaders of the Civil War* (1884–1888; reprinted ed., 1956).

▪ **Gettysburg Address** A speech given by Abraham Lincoln on November 19, 1863, dedicating a national cemetery in Gettysburg, Pennsylvania; it expressed Lincoln's maturing view of the war and its purpose.

It Matters Today

The Gettysburg Address

When the Civil War began, Lincoln made it clear that defending the Constitution was his only objective. But when he spoke on the Gettysburg battlefield two years later, commemorating the deaths of the thousands who fell there, he gave voice to a broader vision and a more noble goal. In that speech, Lincoln referenced the Declaration of Independence, *not* the Constitution, transforming Thomas Jefferson's stirring announcement of the Enlightenment principle that "all men are created equal" into the central element in the great American struggle. We seldom take political speeches very seriously these days, but this one changed the conception of the Constitution itself. After Lincoln's death, Congress enacted the Fourteenth Amendment, transforming Jefferson's—and Lincoln's—statement of principle into the law of the land. To this day—well more than "fourscore and seven years" since Lincoln's famous speech—"we hold this truth to be self-evident" in principle and in law through the Constitution Lincoln envisioned in that speech.

- What does the Gettysburg Address reflect about popular attitudes toward the war following the Battle of Gettysburg? Given what you know about the era, what do you think explains the speech's impact?
- In what significant ways did the principles stated by Lincoln at Gettysburg modify the nation's understanding of the Constitution? How has this understanding manifested itself in legislation and landmark legal cases in recent years?

the media and galvanized many Americans who had come to doubt the war's purpose.

Delighted with Grant's successes in Tennessee, Lincoln promoted him again on March 10, 1864, this time to general in chief. Grant immediately left his command in the West to prepare an all-out attack on Lee and Virginia, authorizing Sherman to pursue a campaign into Georgia.

In Grant and Sherman, Lincoln had found what he needed. On the surface, neither seemed a likely candidate for a major role in the Union army. Both were West Point graduates but left the army after the War with Mexico to seek their fortunes. Neither had succeeded in civilian life: Grant was a binge drinker who had accomplished little, and Sherman had failed as a banker and a lawyer. Despite their checkered

pasts, these two men invented a new type of warfare that eventually brought the South to its knees. Grant and Sherman were willing to wage **total war** to destroy the South's will.

One of Grant's first acts was to cut the supply of Confederate soldiers by suspending prisoner of war exchanges. He understood that one outcome of this policy would be slow death by starvation for Union prisoners, but he reasoned that victory was his primary goal and that suffering and death were unavoidable in war. Throughout the remainder of the war, this single-mindedness pushed Grant to make decisions that cost tens of thousands of lives on both sides.

On May 4, Grant and Meade moved toward Richmond and Robert E. Lee. The next day, Union and Confederate armies collided in a tangle of woods called The Wilderness, near Chancellorsville (see Map 14.4). Two days of bloody fighting followed. Grant decided to skirt Lee's troops and head for Richmond, but Lee anticipated the maneuver and blocked Grant's route at Spotsylvania. Twelve days of fighting ensued. Grant again attempted to move around Lee, and again Lee anticipated him. On June 1, the two armies met at Cold Harbor, Virginia. After each side had consolidated its position,

□ **total war** War waged with little regard for the welfare of troops on either side or for enemy civilians; the objective is to destroy both the human and the economic resources of the enemy.

□ **Cold Harbor** Site at which Grant ordered a doomed assault on Lee's center that cost enormous Union casualties; one of a series of battles in the spring of 1864 in which Grant, accepting unspeakable carnage, tried to maneuver his army past Lee's.

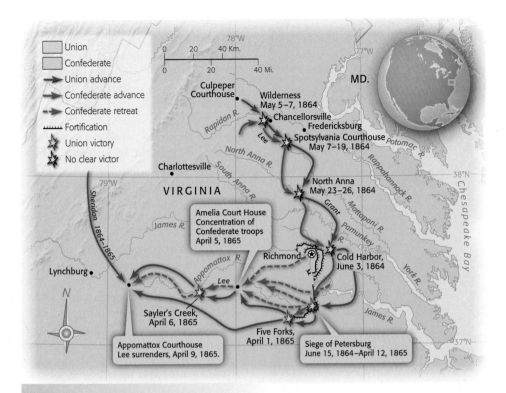

MAP 14.4 The Final Virginia Campaign, 1864–1865
This map shows the series of battles during the late spring of 1864 in which Grant's army suffered staggering casualties but finally drove Lee into retreat. After holding out for months behind heavy fortifications in Petersburg, Lee made a daring attempt to escape in April 1865 but was headed off by General Philip Sheridan's troops. Grant quickly closed in on the greatly weakened Confederate army, forcing Lee's surrender. © Cengage Learning.

Grant ordered a series of frontal attacks against the entrenched Confederates on June 3. Lee's veteran troops waited patiently in perhaps the best position they had ever defended, while Union soldiers expecting to die marched toward them. The assault failed amid unspeakable slaughter.

One southerner described Grant's assaults as "inexplicable and incredible butchery." Many of the young federal attackers at Cold Harbor had pinned their names on their shirts in the hope that their shattered bodies might be identified after the battle. Casualties on both sides at Spotsylvania and Cold Harbor were staggering, but Union losses were unimaginably horrible. As one Confederate officer put it, "We have met a man, this time, who either does not know when he is whipped, or who cares not if he loses his whole army." During the three encounters, Grant lost a total of sixty thousand troops, more than Lee's entire army. Said Lee, "This is not war, this is murder." But Grant's seeming wantonness was calculated, for the Confederates lost more than twenty-five thousand troops. And Grant knew, as did Lee, that the Union could afford the losses but the Confederacy could not.

After Cold Harbor, Grant steered the Union army toward Petersburg, south of Richmond, to try to take the vital rail center and cut off the southern capital. But Lee rapidly shifted his troops again, beat back Grant's advance, and occupied Petersburg. Grant bitterly regretted this failure, feeling that he could have ended the war. Instead, the campaign settled into a siege that neither side wanted.

The Election of 1864 and Sherman's March to the Sea

Lincoln was under fire from two directions. On May 31, 1864, the Republicans met in Cleveland and dumped him from the ticket, officially nominating John C. Frémont as their presidential candidate. Lincoln supporters, who began calling themselves the Union Party, held their nominating convention in June and nominated Lincoln. To attract Democrats who still favored fighting for a clear victory, Union Party

Disliked by most of his fellow officers because of his coarse behavior and binge drinking, Ulysses S. Grant had the right combination of daring, unconventionality, and ruthlessness to wear down Robert E. Lee's forces in Virginia and finally defeat the Confederate army.

delegates dumped Republican Vice President Hannibal Hamlin and chose Andrew Johnson, a southern Democrat, as Lincoln's running mate. Then, in August, the Democratic National Convention met at Chicago. The Democrats pulled together many Copperheads and other northerners who were so upset by the heavy casualties that they were determined to stop the war, even at the cost of allowing slavery to continue. The Democrats selected McClellan as their presidential candidate and included a peace plank in their platform. Thus Lincoln sat squarely in the middle between one group that castigated him for pursuing the war and another group that rebuked him for failing to pursue it vigorously enough.

◻ **Andrew Johnson** Tennessee senator who became Lincoln's running mate in 1864 and who succeeded to the presidency after Lincoln's assassination.

◻ **Copperheads** Derogatory term (the name of a poisonous snake) applied to northerners who supported the South during the Civil War.

Jefferson Davis's administration also faced serious criticism as deprivation and military losses mounted. In an effort to solve their mutual problems, Lincoln and Confederate vice president Alexander H. Stephens had conversations about negotiating a settlement. Lincoln stated his terms: reunion, abolition, and amnesty for Confederates. Stephens balked, pointing out that "amnesty" applied to criminals and that the South had "committed no crime." The only possible outcomes of the war for the South, he concluded, were independence or extermination, even if it meant enduring the sight of "every Southern plantation sacked and every Southern city in flames." The words proved prophetic.

Grant had instructed Sherman "to get into the interior of the enemy's country as far as you can, inflicting all the damage you can against their war resources." Sherman responded with a vengeance. Slowly and skillfully his army advanced southward from Tennessee toward Atlanta, one of the South's few remaining industrial centers (see Map 14.5). Confederate general Joseph E. Johnston repeatedly retreated to keep Sherman from annihilating his army. President Davis then replaced Johnston with John Bell Hood, who vowed to take the offensive. Hood attacked, but Sherman inflicted such serious casualties that Hood had to retreat to Atlanta.

For days Sherman shelled Atlanta and wrought havoc in the surrounding countryside. When a last-ditch southern attack failed, Hood evacuated the city on September 1. Sherman's victory caused tremendous despair among Confederates but gave great momentum to Lincoln's reelection campaign. Also boosting Lincoln's reelection efforts was General Philip Sheridan's campaign in the Shenandoah Valley, an important source of food for Lee's army. Adopting the same sort of devastating tactics that Sherman used so successfully, Sheridan's men lived off the land and destroyed both military and civilian supplies whenever possible. Accepting high casualties, Sheridan drove Confederate forces from the region in October, laying waste to much of Lee's food supply in the process.

These victories proved the decisive factor in the election of 1864. Sherman's and Sheridan's successes defused McClellan's argument that Lincoln was not competent to direct the Union's military fortunes and quelled much antiwar sentiment in the North. Equally discredited, the Radical Republican platform and the Frémont candidacy disappeared before election day. When the votes were counted, Lincoln learned that he had defeated McClellan—by half a million popular votes and by a landslide margin of 212 to 21 in the Electoral College.

Meanwhile, Sherman grew bored with the occupation of Atlanta and posed a bold plan to Grant. He wanted to ignore Hood and go on the offensive, cutting "a swath through to the sea." "I can make

Georgia howl," he promised. Despite some misgivings, Grant agreed and convinced Lincoln.

A week after the election, Sherman began preparing for his 300-mile March to the Sea (see Map 14.5). His intentions were clear. "We are not only fighting hostile armies, but a hostile people," he stated. By devastating the countryside and destroying the South's ability to conduct war, he intended to break down southerners' will to resist. "We cannot change the hearts of those people of the South," he concluded, but we can "make them so sick of war that generations would pass away before they would again appeal to it." With that, he set out on his march to the coastal town of Savannah, leaving Atlanta in ruins. His troops plundered and looted farms and towns on the way, foraging for food and supplies. Sherman entered Savannah unopposed on December 21.

The March to the Sea completed, Sherman turned north. In South Carolina, the first state to secede and fire shots, Sherman's troops took special delight in ravaging the countryside. When they reached Columbia, flames engulfed the city. With the state capital in flames, Confederate forces in South Carolina abandoned their posts, moving north to join with Joseph E. Johnston's army in an effort to stop Sherman from crossing North Carolina and joining Grant in Virginia. Union forces quickly moved into abandoned southern strongholds, including Charleston, where Major Robert Anderson, who had commanded Fort Sumter in April 1861, returned to raise the Union flag over the fort that he had surrendered four years earlier.

The End of Lee and Lincoln

Under increasing pressure from Sherman, the Confederacy's military situation was deteriorating rapidly. In a last-ditch effort to keep the Confederacy alive, Lee advised Davis to evacuate Richmond—the army intended to withdraw from besieged Petersburg and abandon the capital, moving west as rapidly as possible toward Lynchburg (see Map 14.4). From there Lee hoped to use surviving rail lines to move his troops south to join with Johnston's force in North Carolina. The unified armies might then halt Sherman's advance and wheel around to deal with Grant.

Suffering none of his predecessors' indecisiveness, Grant ordered an immediate assault as Lee's forces retreated from Petersburg. Lee had little ammunition,

> ◻ **March to the Sea** Sherman's march through Georgia from Atlanta to Savannah in late 1864, during which Union soldiers carried out orders to destroy everything in their path.

MAP 14.5 Sherman's Campaign in the South
This map shows how William Tecumseh Sherman's troops slashed through the South, destroying both civilian and military targets and reducing the South's will to continue the war. © Cengage Learning.

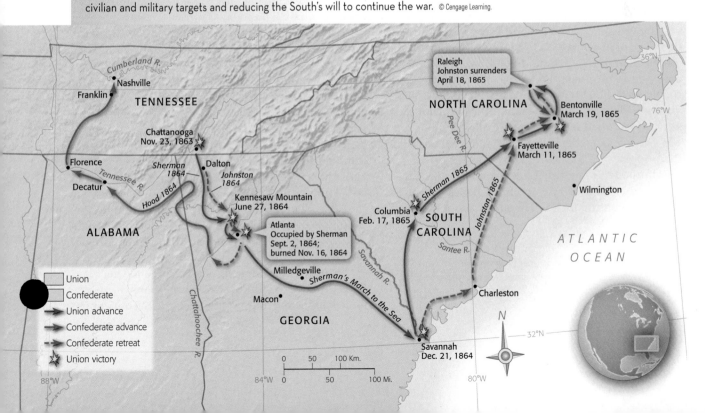

The nation's mood shifted from celebration to shock when it learned that President Lincoln had fallen to an assassin's bullet. His funeral provided an occasion for the entire country to mourn, not only his death but also the deaths of hundreds of thousands of Americans who had fallen in the Civil War. This funeral procession through the streets of Washington, D.C. was the first of many as his body wound its way across the country by train toward its eventual burial in Illinois.

almost no food, and only thirty-five thousand men. As they retreated westward, hundreds of southern soldiers collapsed from hunger and exhaustion. On April 9, Sheridan's Army of the Shenandoah arrived, cutting off Lee's retreat. Union forces now surrounded Lee's broken army. Saying, "There is nothing left for me to do but go and see General Grant," Lee sent a note offering surrender.

The two generals met at a private home in the little village of Appomattox Courthouse, Virginia. Grant offered generous terms, allowing Confederate officers and men to go home "so long as they observe their paroles and the laws in force where they reside." This guaranteed them immunity from prosecution for treason and became the model for surrender. Grant sent the starving Confederates rations and let them keep their horses.

On the following day, Lincoln addressed a crowd outside the White House about his hopes and plans for rebuilding the nation. He talked about the need

□ **John Wilkes Booth** Actor and southern sympathizer who on April 14, 1865, five days after Lee's surrender, fatally shot President Lincoln at Ford's Theater in Washington.

for flexibility in pulling the nation back together after the long and bitter conflict. In December 1863, he had issued a Proclamation of Amnesty and Reconstruction offering pardons to any Confederates who would take a loyalty oath. After his reelection in 1864, Lincoln had begun to plan for the Confederacy's eventual surrender, and he pushed for a constitutional ban on slavery, which passed on January 31, 1865.

With victory at hand and a peace plan in place, on April 14, after an exhausting day in conference with Grant and his cabinet, Lincoln chose to relax by attending a play at Ford's Theater in Washington. At about ten o'clock, John Wilkes Booth, an actor and a southern sympathizer, entered the president's box and shot him. Meanwhile, one of Booth's accomplices entered the home of Secretary of State Seward, who was bedridden as a result of a carriage accident, and stabbed him several times before being driven out. Another accomplice was supposed to assassinate Vice President Johnson but apparently lost his nerve. Although the conspiracy had failed, one of its main objectives succeeded: the following morning, Lincoln died of his wound.

Even though Lincoln was dead and Lee had fallen, the war continued. Joseph E. Johnston, whose forces succeeded in preventing Sherman from joining

Grant, did not surrender until April 18. And although most of his forces had been defeated, Jefferson Davis remained in hiding and called for guerrilla warfare and continued resistance. But one by one, the Confederate officers surrendered to their Union opponents. On May 10, Davis was captured near Irwinville, Georgia. Andrew Johnson, who had assumed the presidency upon Lincoln's death, issued a statement to the American people that armed rebellion against legitimate authority could be considered "virtually at an end." The last battle of the Civil War was fought by predominantly Mexican American soldiers on May 12 and 13 at Palmito Ranch in South Texas.

The price of victory was high for both the winner and the loser. More than 350,000 Union soldiers had been killed in action. No exact figures exist for the Confederacy, but southern casualties probably equaled or exceeded those of the Union. The war had wrecked the economy of the South. Union military campaigns had wiped out most southern rail lines, destroyed the South's manufacturing capacity, and severely reduced agricultural productivity. Both sides had faced rising inflation during the war, but the Confederacy's actions to supply troops and keep the war effort going had bled the South of most of its resources and money. Secession had been defeated, but reunion remained a distant and difficult objective.

Individual Voices

MARY ASHTON RICE LIVERMORE

Women and the War Effort

When the Civil War broke out, women in both the North and South rallied in support of the war effort. An unknown number actually dressed up as men to enter the ranks as combat soldiers. Others carried on volunteer work, both at home and in the field, becoming fundraisers, nurses, and public health advocates. Mary Livermore spent most of the war as a soldiers' relief worker. She urged other women to act on their patriotism by becoming involved in ways that would draw on the particular skills and affinities that nineteenth-century Americans believed belonged exclusively to women. After the war, she wrote a book recounting her experiences and presenting her perspectives. The following excerpt it taken from that 1888 publication.

Library of Congress.

❶ How does Livermore characterize the differences between men and women in terms of their response to the appeals of war? What does this reflect about general attitudes toward gender in mid-nineteenth-century America?

❷ What is Livermore suggesting here about the role of women during wartime? Does she portray this role as inferior, superior, or equal to that played by men?

❸ In light of this eloquent description of women's efforts during the war, what would Livermore probably suggest about appropriate peacetime employment for women? Would you characterize this as a "feminist" or a "traditionalist" statement? What leads you to this conclusion?

It is easy to understand how men catch the contagion of war, especially when they feel their quarrel to be just. One can comprehend how, fired with enthusiasm, and inspired by martial music, they march to the cannon's mouth, where the iron hail rains heaviest, and the ranks are mowed down like grain in harvest. But for women to send forth their husbands, sons, brothers and lovers to the fearful chances of the battle-field, knowing well the risks they run,—this involves exquisite suffering and calls for another kind of heroism. . . . **❶**

The number of women who actually bore arms and served in the ranks during the war was greater than is supposed. . . . Such service was not the noblest that women rendered the country during its four year's struggle for life, and no one can regret that these soldier women were exceptional and rare. It is better to heal a wound than to make one. And it is to the honor of American women, not that they led hosts to the deadly charge, and battled amid contending armies, but that they confronted the horrid aspects of war with mighty life and earnestness. **❷** They kept up their own courage and that of their households. They became ministering angels to their countrymen who periled health and life for the nation. They sent the love and impulses of home into the extended ranks of the army, through the unceasing correspondence they maintained with "the boys in blue." They planned largely, and toiled untiringly, and with steady persistence to the end, that the horrors of the battle-field might be mitigated, and the hospitals abound in needed comforts. **❸**

Study Tools

SUMMARY

Both the Union and the Confederacy entered the war in 1861 with glowing hopes. Jefferson Davis pursued a defensive strategy, certain that northerners would soon tire of war and let the South withdraw from the Union. Abraham Lincoln countered by using the superior human, economic, and natural resources of the North to strangle the South into submission. But both leaders became increasingly frustrated during the first year of the war.

For Lincoln, the greatest frustration was military leadership. Beginning with the first Battle of Bull Run, Union forces seemed unable to win any major battles. Although Union forces under Ulysses S. Grant's command scored victories in the Mississippi Valley, the Federals were stalemated. Robert E. Lee and Thomas "Stonewall" Jackson seemed able to defeat any Union general that Lincoln sent to oppose them.

The war's nature and direction changed after the fall of 1862, however. Lee invaded Maryland and was defeated at Antietam. Despite this crushing loss, Union generals still failed to capture Lee or to subdue Confederate forces in Virginia. Still angered by military blundering, political attacks, and popular unrest, Lincoln issued the Emancipation Proclamation in an effort to undermine southern efforts and unify northern ones. After the proclamation, the only option for either side was total victory or total defeat.

After further reversals in the spring of 1863, Union forces turned the tide in the war by defeating Lee's army at Gettysburg and taking Vicksburg to gain full control of the Mississippi. With an election drawing near, Lincoln spurred his generals to deal the death blow to the Confederacy, and two in particular rose to the occasion. During the last half of 1864, William Tecumseh Sherman wreaked havoc, making Georgia "howl." And Grant, in a wanton display of disregard for human life, drove Lee into a defensive corner. In November, buoyed by Sherman's victories in Georgia, Lincoln was reelected.

Suffering was not confined to those at the front. Governments in both the North and the South had to dig deep into depleting economic resources to keep the war effort going. Inflation plagued both nations, and common people faced hunger, disease, and lawlessness. Riots broke out in major cities, including New York. But throughout the country many people responded heroically to their own privations and to suffering at the front. Women such as Clara Barton and Mary Livermore faced up to epidemics, enemy gunfire, and gender bias to institute public health standards and bring solace to suffering civilians and soldiers alike.

As hope dwindled for the South in the spring of 1865, Lee made a final desperate effort to keep the flagging Confederacy alive, racing to unify the last surviving remnants of the once-proud southern army. But Grant closed a net of steel around Lee's troops, forcing surrender. Lincoln immediately promoted a gentle policy for reunion, but his assassination ended this effort. The saintly American hero was gone, leaving a southern Democrat—Andrew Johnson—as president and a nation reeling in shock. The war was over, but the issues were still unresolved.

CHRONOLOGY
War Between the States

1861	Lincoln takes office and runs Union by executive authority until July
	Fort Sumter falls
	Battle of Bull Run
	McClellan organizes the Union army
1862	Grant's victories in Mississippi Valley
	Battle of Shiloh
	U.S. Navy captures New Orleans
	Peninsular Campaign
	Battle of Antietam
	African Americans permitted in Union army
1863	Emancipation Proclamation takes effect
	Union enacts conscription
	Battle of Chancellorsville and death of Stonewall Jackson
	Union victories at Gettysburg and Vicksburg
	Draft riots in New York City
1864	Grant invades Virginia
	Sherman captures Atlanta
	Lincoln reelected
	Sherman's March to the Sea
1865	Lee abandons Petersburg and Richmond
	Lee surrenders at Appomattox Courthouse
	Lincoln proposes a gentle reconstruction policy
	Lincoln assassinated

Study Tools

FOCUS QUESTIONS

If you have mastered this chapter, you should be able to answer these questions and to explain the terms that follow the questions.

1. What problems did Abraham Lincoln and Jefferson Davis face as they led their respective nations into war?

2. How did each chief executive deal with those problems?

3. How did military action during the opening years of the war affect the people's perceptions of the war in the North and South?

4. Why did Lincoln issue the Emancipation Proclamation when and in the way he did? What types of responses did it elicit?

5. How did the burdens of war affect society in the North and the South?

6. How did individuals and governments in both regions respond to those burdens?

7. What factors contributed to the Union's adoption of a total war strategy after 1863?

8. Was total war justifiable in light of the human and property damage it inflicted and the overall consequences it achieved? Why or why not?

KEY TERMS

anaconda plan   p. 340

Radical Republicans   p. 341

Bull Run   p. 343

Thomas J. Jackson   p. 343

George B. McClellan   p. 343

Army of the Potomac   p. 344

Ulysses S. Grant   p. 346

William Tecumseh Sherman   p. 347

Battle of Shiloh   p. 347

Vicksburg   p. 347

Peninsular Campaign   p. 348

Second Battle of Bull Run   p. 349

Antietam Creek   p. 349

Fredericksburg   p. 349

Emancipation Proclamation   p. 350

Conscription Act   p. 351

Horace Greeley   p. 352

Twenty Negro Law   p. 352

Homestead Act   p. 352

greenbacks   p. 352

United States Sanitary
    Commission   p. 355

Clara Barton   p. 356

Andersonville   p. 356

Chancellorsville   p. 357

Gettysburg   p. 358

Gettysburg Address   p. 359

total war   p. 360

Cold Harbor   p. 360

Andrew Johnson   p. 362

Copperheads   p. 362

March to the Sea   p. 363

John Wilkes Booth   p. 364

SUGGESTED RESOURCES

Library of Congress. "Selected Civil War Photographs," http://memory.loc.gov/ammem/cwphtml/cwphome.html. This collection provides an excellent introduction to visual images of the Civil War, the first war in history to be extensively photographed.

National Archives at the City of New York. "The Union Blockade: Lincoln's Proclamations," http://www.archives.gov/nyc/education/blockade.html. Presents primary documents concerning the Union blockade of the Confederacy with critical thinking questions and links to related "Teachable Texts" in the archives.

National Park Service. "American Battlefield Protection Program," http://www.nps.gov/hps/abpp/civil.htm. An index page with links to all of the National Park Service battlefield sites.

National Park Service. "The Civil War," http://www.nps.gov/civilwar/index.htm. The National Park Service maintains hundreds of Civil War sites: battlefields, trails, house museums, etc. This website provides a general introduction to the war and has many other interesting features.

15

Reconstruction: High Hopes and Shattered Dreams, 1865–1877

INDIVIDUAL CHOICES

Joseph Rainey

On December 12, 1870, Joseph Rainey became the first African American to serve in the House of Representatives. Rainey had come a long way since he was born into slavery in 1832 in Georgetown, South Carolina. Growing up, he had a relatively privileged life compared to most slaves. His father, also a slave, was a barber, and as the law required, he kept part of what he earned. Rainey's father eventually saved enough to buy freedom for his family.

Rainey learned the barber's skills from his father, but his trade was interrupted by the Civil War. The Confederate Army put him to work building fortifications, then crewing on a blockade runner (a ship that carried goods through the Union navy's blockade from Bermuda, the closest British port). Rainey and his wife, Susan, managed to escape to Bermuda, where slavery was illegal. There he resumed his trade as a barber, and Susan opened a dress shop. They saved their earnings and returned to South Carolina at the end of the war with considerable savings.

Rainey soon chose to enter Republican politics. He held several party offices and appointed positions before winning elections to the state constitutional convention in 1868, to the state legislature in 1870, and later that same year to the U.S. House of

Library of Congress.

Representatives. He was reelected to Congress in 1872 with no opposition. In 1874 and 1876, however, when he ran for reelection, he faced increasing, and increasingly violent, opposition—even threats to his life—but he won both times. By then, it took courage for a black man to run for office in many parts of the South. In some places, African American candidates were assassinated by those seeking to restore white supremacy. In most places, black candidates and voters faced intimidation or violence. Defeated in 1878 as Reconstruction was collapsing throughout the South, Rainey left office in early 1879.

As a member of the House of Representatives, Rainey spoke forcefully in support of the Ku Klux Klan Act of 1871; an excerpt appears in the Individual Voices feature at the end of this chapter. The act was intended to use federal authority to end the reign of terror against African Americans that was being carried out by the Klan and similar organizations. He also worked tirelessly for the passage of the Civil Rights bill, and was especially committed to desegregating public schools. In his speech to Congress in support of the bill, he vividly described the widespread segregation in many aspects of southern life. The bill passed in early 1875, but without provisions on school segregation or equality for segregated schools. Rainey's efforts were not limited to matters affecting African Americans. He also supported legislation to grant amnesty to many former Confederates, seeing it as a balance to the Civil Rights Act, and he opposed efforts to restrict immigration from China.

Rainey was not the only African American who escaped to freedom while the war was raging. That experience was repeated time and time again, with many variations, all across the South. Those many individual decisions were made legal by the Emancipation Proclamation, enforced by the presence of Union armies, and made permanent by the Thirteenth Amendment to the Constitution. Like Rainey, African Americans often had their own ideas about what they wanted most from freedom.

After four long, bloody years of civil war, Union armies had smashed across the South, leaving wreckage in their wake: shelled buildings, ravaged farms, twisted railroad tracks. Slavery—the dominant economic and social institution in many parts of the South—collapsed. As white southerners grieved for their dead and were dismayed by their ravaged countryside, many were also deeply troubled by the **emancipation** of 4 million slaves. The end of slavery forced southerners of both races to develop new social, economic, and political patterns. The years following the war were a time of physical rebuilding throughout the South, but historians use the term **Reconstruction** to refer primarily to the rebuilding of the federal union and to the political, economic, and social changes that came to the South. Reconstruction involved some of the most momentous questions in American history: How was the defeated South to be treated? What was to be the future of the former slaves? Should key decisions be made by the federal government or in state capitols and county courthouses throughout the South? Which branch of the government was to establish policies? What would happen to those who had supported the Confederacy? Thousands of voices across the nation proposed very different answers.

As the dominant Republicans turned their attention from waging war to reconstructing the Union, they wrote into law and the Constitution new definitions of the Union itself. They also defined the rights of the **freed people** and the terms on which the South might rejoin the Union. And they permanently changed the definition of American citizenship.

emancipation Release from slavery.

◻ **Reconstruction** Term applied by historians to the years 1865–1877, when the Union was restored after the Civil War; important changes were made to the federal Constitution, and relations between the races were transformed in the South.

freed people Former slaves; *freed people* is the term used by historians to refer to former slaves, whether male or female.

Most white southerners disliked the new rules emerging from Washington, and some resisted. Disagreement over the future of the South and the status of the former slaves led to conflict between the president and Congress. A temporary result of this conflict was a more powerful Congress and a less powerful executive. A lasting outcome of these events was a significant increase in the authority of the federal government and new limits on local and state governments.

Reconstruction significantly changed many aspects of southern life. In the end, however, Reconstruction failed to fulfill many African Americans' hopes for their lives as free people.

PRESIDENTIAL RECONSTRUCTION

☆ *What did Presidents Lincoln and Johnson seek to accomplish for the South? How did white southerners respond to those efforts?*

On New Year's Day, 1863, the Emancipation Proclamation took effect. At the time, however, the proclamation did not affect any slaves because it abolished slavery only in territory under Confederate control and was, therefore, unenforceable. But every advance of a Union army after January 1, 1863, brought emancipation to the slaves of the Confederacy.

Republican War Aims

For **Abraham Lincoln** and the Republican Party, freedom for the slaves became a central concern partly because **abolitionists** were influential within the party. During its 1860 electoral campaign, the Republican Party had promised only to prohibit slavery in the territories, and Lincoln initially defined the war as one to maintain the Union. Some leading Republicans, however, wanted to abolish slavery everywhere. As Union troops moved into the South, some slaves simply walked away from their owners. Many sought safety with the Union army. Soon former slaves became Union soldiers as well. Abolitionists throughout the North—including **Frederick Douglass**, an escaped slave and an important leader of the abolition movement—now argued that emancipation would be meaningless unless the government guaranteed the civil and political rights of the former slaves. Thus some Republicans expanded their definition of war objectives to include abolishing slavery, extending citizenship for the former slaves, and guaranteeing the equality of all citizens before the law. At the time, these were extreme views on abolition and equal rights, and the people who held them were called **Radical Republicans**, or simply Radicals.

Thaddeus Stevens, 73 years old in 1865, was the leading Radical in the House of Representatives. He

Thaddeus Stevens, seen here at the height of his power, was the leader of the Radical Republicans in the House of Representatives. He died in 1868. He requested that he be buried in a cemetery that did not discriminate on the basis of race.

had made a successful career as a Pennsylvania lawyer and iron manufacturer before winning election to Congress in 1858. Born with a clubfoot, he identified with those outside the social mainstream. He became a compelling spokesman for abolition and an uncompromising advocate of equal rights for African Americans. A masterful parliamentarian, he was known for his honesty and sarcastic wit. From the beginning of the war, Stevens urged that the slaves not only be freed but also be armed to fight the Confederacy.

◻ **Abraham Lincoln** (1809–1865) Sixteenth president of the United States, who presided over the Union during the Civil War, issued the Emancipation Proclamation, initiated Reconstruction, and was assassinated shortly after beginning his second term as president.

abolitionist Individual who condemns slavery as morally wrong and seeks to abolish (eliminate) slavery.

◻ **Frederick Douglass** (c. 1818–1895) Escaped slave who became a leader of the abolition movement and later an important African American leader and Republican politician.

◻ **Radical Republicans** Group within the Republican Party during the Civil War and Reconstruction that advocated for abolition of slavery, citizenship for the former slaves, and sweeping alteration of the South.

By the end of the war, some 180,000 African Americans, the great majority of them freedmen, had served in the Union army and a few thousand in the Union navy. Many more worked for the army as laborers.

Charles Sumner of Massachusetts, a prominent Radical in the Senate, had argued for **racial integration** of Massachusetts schools in 1849 and won election to the U.S. Senate in 1851. The Senate's foremost champion of abolition, he suffered a severe beating in 1856 because of an antislavery speech. After emancipation, Sumner, like Stevens, fought for full political and civil rights for the freed people.

Stevens, Sumner, and other Radicals opposed slavery both on moral grounds and because they believed free labor was more productive. Slaves worked to escape punishment, they argued, but free workers worked to benefit themselves. Eliminating slavery and instituting a free-labor system, they claimed, would benefit everyone by increasing the nation's productivity. In this view, free labor not only contributed centrally to the dynamism of the North's economy, but was crucial to democracy itself. "The middling classes who own the soil, and work it with their own hands," Stevens once proclaimed, "are the main support of every free government."

Not all Republicans agreed with the Radicals. All Republicans objected to slavery, but not all Republicans were abolitionists. Similarly, not all Republicans wanted to extend full citizenship rights to the former slaves. Some favored rapid restoration of the South to the Union so that the federal government could concentrate on stimulating the nation's economy and developing the West. Such Republicans are usually referred to as **moderates**.

Lincoln's Approach to Reconstruction: "With Malice Toward None"

After the Emancipation Proclamation, President Lincoln and the congressional Radicals agreed that abolition of slavery had to be a condition for the return of the South to the Union. Major differences soon appeared, however, over other terms for reunion and the roles of the president and Congress in establishing those

racial integration Equal opportunities to participate in a society or organization by people of different racial groups; the absence of race-based barriers to full and equal participation.

moderates People whose views are midway between two extreme positions; in this case, Republicans who favored some reforms but not all the Radicals' proposals.

pardon Governmental directive canceling punishment for a person or people who have committed a crime.

amnesty General pardon granted by a government, especially for political offenses.

suffrage The right to vote.

terms. In his second inaugural address, a month before his death, Lincoln defined the task facing the nation:

> With malice toward none; with charity for all; with firmness in the right, as God gives us to see the right, let us strive on to finish the work we are in: to bind up the nation's wounds; to care for him who shall have borne the battle, and for his widow and orphan, to do all which may achieve and cherish a just and lasting peace among ourselves, and with all nations.

Lincoln began to rebuild the Union on the basis of these principles. As soon as Union armies occupied portions of southern states, he appointed temporary military governors for those regions and tried to restore civil government as quickly as possible.

Drawing on the president's constitutional power to issue **pardons** (Article II, Section 2), Lincoln issued a Proclamation of **Amnesty** and Reconstruction in December 1863. Called the "Ten Percent Plan," it promised a full pardon and restoration of rights to those who swore their loyalty to the Union and accepted the abolition of slavery. Only high-ranking Confederate leaders were not eligible. Once those who had taken the oath in a state amounted to 10 percent of the votes cast by that state in the 1860 election, the pardoned voters were to write a new state constitution that abolished slavery, elect state officials, and resume self-government.

Some Radicals considered Lincoln's approach too lenient. When they tried to set more stringent standards, Lincoln blocked them, fearing their plan would slow restoration of civil government and perhaps lengthen the war.

Under Lincoln's Ten Percent Plan, new state governments were established in Arkansas, Louisiana, and Tennessee during 1864 and early 1865. In Louisiana, the new government denied voting rights to men who were one-quarter or more black. Radicals complained, but Lincoln urged patience, suggesting the reconstructed government in Louisiana was "as the egg to the fowl, and we shall sooner have the fowl by hatching the egg than by smashing it." Radicals, however, concluded that freed people were unlikely to receive equitable treatment from state governments formed under the Ten Percent Plan. Some moderates agreed and moved toward the Radicals' position that only **suffrage** could protect the freedmen's rights and that only federal action could guarantee black suffrage.

Abolishing Slavery Forever: The Thirteenth Amendment

Amid questions about the rights of freed people, congressional Republicans prepared for the final destruction of slavery. The Emancipation Proclamation had been a wartime measure, justified partly by military necessity. It never applied in Union states. State legislatures or conventions abolished slavery in West

These Union soldiers and officers in 1865 are administering the oath of allegiance to the United States to white southerners as part of the process of restoring civil government in the South.

Virginia, Maryland, Missouri, and the reconstructed state of Tennessee. In early 1865, slavery remained legal in Delaware and Kentucky, and prewar state laws—which might or might not be valid—permitted slavery in the states that had seceded. To destroy slavery forever, Congress in January 1865 approved the Thirteenth Amendment, which read simply, "Neither slavery nor involuntary servitude, except as a punishment for crime whereof the party shall have been duly convicted, shall exist within the United States, or any place subject to their jurisdiction."

The Constitution requires any amendment to be ratified by three-fourths of the states—then twenty-seven of thirty-six states. By December 1865, only nineteen of the twenty-five Union states had ratified the amendment. The measure passed, however, when eight of the reconstructed southern states approved it. In the end, therefore, the abolition of slavery hinged on action by reconstructed state governments in the South.

Andrew Johnson and Reconstruction

In April 1865, shortly after the surrender of the main Confederate army, Lincoln was assassinated by a supporter of the Confederacy. Vice President Andrew Johnson became president. Johnson had never had an opportunity to attend school and spent his early life struggling against poverty. As a young man in Tennessee, he worked as a tailor, then turned to politics. His wife, Eliza McCardle Johnson, tutored him in reading, writing, and arithmetic. A Democrat, Johnson was elected to Congress and later as governor before winning election to the U.S. Senate in 1857. His political support came primarily from small-scale farmers and working people. The state's elite of plantation owners usually opposed him. Johnson, in turn, resented their wealth and power, and blamed them for secession and the Civil War.

◻ **Thirteenth Amendment** Constitutional amendment, ratified in 1865, that abolished slavery in the United States and its territories.

◻ **Andrew Johnson** (1808–1875) Seventeenth president of the United States; elected vice president in 1864, became president after Lincoln's assassination, and was impeached, but not removed from the presidency.

In the Wider World

Abolition of Slavery Around the World

By abolishing slavery, the United States followed the lead of most of the nations of Europe and Latin America. Slavery had existed throughout human history, but in the eighteenth century, Enlightenment thinkers began to criticize slavery as violating human rights. At the same time, some religious groups, notably the Quakers, began to work for abolition. The following list summarizes general patterns in the abolition of slavery around the world; space does not permit listing all nations.

Though illegal, chattel slavery still exists in parts of Africa and the Middle East, notably Mauritania and Sudan. In other places, people work in conditions approaching slavery, through forced prostitution, debt bondage, and forced-labor camps.

1587	Slave trade abolished in Japan
1772	Slavery abolished in England and Wales
1794	Slavery abolished in France
1807	British navy begins operations to end the international slave trade
1808	United States prohibits importation of slaves
1820s	Slavery abolished in most Spanish-speaking Latin American nations
1833	Slavery abolished within the British Empire
1848	Slavery abolished within the French Empire
1861	Abolition of serfdom in Russia
1863	Emancipation Proclamation (United States); slavery abolished within the Dutch Empire
1865	Thirteenth Amendment (United States)
1876	Slavery abolished within the Ottoman Empire
1888	Slavery abolished in Brazil
1910	Slavery abolished in China
1926	Thirty-five nations sign a Convention to Suppress the Slave Trade and Slavery
1948	United Nations adopts the Universal Declaration of Human Rights, including calls to abolish slavery and the slave trade
1962	Slavery abolished in Saudi Arabia

Johnson was the only southern senator who rejected the Confederacy. Early in the war, Union forces captured Nashville, the capital of Tennessee, and Lincoln appointed Johnson as military governor. Johnson dealt harshly with Tennessee secessionists, especially wealthy planters. Radical Republicans approved. Johnson was elected vice president in 1864, receiving the nomination in part because Lincoln wanted to appeal to Democrats and Unionists in border states.

chattel slavery Condition in which one person is legally defined as the personal property of another person.

states' rights Political position favoring limitation of the federal government's power and maximum self-government by individual states.

empower To increase the power or authority of some person or group.

When Johnson became president, Radicals hoped he would join their efforts to transform the South. Johnson, however, was strongly committed to states' rights and opposed the Radicals' objective of a powerful federal government. "White men alone must manage the South," Johnson announced, although he recommended limited political roles for the freedmen. Self-righteous and uncompromising, Johnson saw the major task of Reconstruction as empowering the region's white middle class and excluding wealthy planters from power.

Like Lincoln, Johnson relied on the president's constitutional power to grant pardons. He wanted a quick restoration of the southern states to the Union and granted amnesty to most former Confederates who pledged loyalty to the Union and support for emancipation. In one of his last actions as president, he granted full pardon and amnesty to all southern rebels—unlike Lincoln who exempted high-ranking

Before emancipation, slaves typically made their own clothing or received the used outfits of their owners and overseers. With emancipation, freed people with an income could afford to dress more fashionably. The Harry Stevens family probably put on their best clothes for a visit to the photographer in 1866.

Confederates from his pardons—although the Fourteenth Amendment (discussed later in this chapter) prevented him from restoring their right to hold office.

Johnson appointed **provisional** civilian governors for the southern states not already reconstructed. He instructed them to reconstitute state government and to call constitutional conventions of delegates elected by pardoned voters. Some provisional governors, however, appointed former Confederates to state and local offices, outraging those who expected Reconstruction to bring to power loyal Unionists committed to a new southern society.

The Southern Response: Minimal Compliance

Johnson expected the state constitutional conventions to abolish slavery, ratify the Thirteenth Amendment, renounce secession, and **repudiate** their state's war debts. The states were then to hold elections and resume their places in the Union. State conventions during the summer of 1865 usually complied with these requirements, some grudgingly. Every state, however, rejected black suffrage.

By April 1866, a year after the close of the war, all the southern states had fulfilled Johnson's requirements for rejoining the Union and had elected legislators, governors, and members of Congress. Johnson had hoped for the emergence of new political leaders in the South but was dismayed at the number of rich planters and former Confederate officials who won elections.

Most white southerners, however, viewed Johnson as their protector, standing between them and the Radicals. His support for states' rights and his opposition to federal determination of voting rights led white southerners to expect that they would shape the transition from slavery to freedom—that they, and not Congress, would define the status of the former slaves.

FREEDOM AND THE LEGACY OF SLAVERY

☆ *What seem to have been the leading objectives among freed people as they explored their new opportunities?*

☆ *How do the differing responses of freed people and southern whites show different understandings of the significance of emancipation?*

As state conventions wrote new constitutions, African Americans throughout the South set about creating new, free lives for themselves. In the antebellum South, all slaves and most free African Americans had led lives tightly constrained by law and custom. They were permitted few social organizations of their own. Not surprisingly, the central theme of the black response to emancipation was a desire for freedom from white control, for **autonomy** as individuals and as a community. The prospect of autonomy touched every aspect of life—family, churches, schools, newspapers, and a host of other social institutions. From this ferment of freedom came new, black institutions that provided

provisional Temporary.
repudiate The act of rejecting the validity or authority of something; to refuse to pay.
autonomy Control of one's own affairs.

the basis for southern African American communities. At the same time, the economic life of the South had been shattered by the Civil War and was being transformed by emancipation. Thus white southerners also faced drastic economic and social change.

Defining the Meaning of Freedom

At the most basic level, freedom came every time an individual slave stopped working for a master and claimed the right to be free. Thus freedom did not come to all slaves at the same time or in the same way. For some, freedom came before the Emancipation Proclamation when they walked away from their owners, crossed into Union-held territory, and asserted their liberty. Toward the end of the war, as civil authority broke down throughout much of the South, many slaves declared their freedom and left the site of their bondage. Some left for good, but many remained nearby, though with a new understanding of their relationship to their former masters. For some, freedom did not come until ratification of the Thirteenth Amendment.

Across the South, the approach of Yankee troops set off a joyous celebration—called a Jubilee—among those who knew their enslavement was ending. As one Virginia woman remembered, "Such rejoicing and shouting you never heard in your life." Once the celebrating was over, however, the freed people had to decide how best to use their freedom.

The freed people expressed their new status in many ways. Some chose new names to symbolize their new beginning. Many freed people changed their style of dress, discarding the cheap clothing provided to slaves. Some acquired guns. A significant benefit of freedom was the ability to travel without a pass and without being checked by the patrollers who had enforced the pass system.

Many freed people took this new opportunity to travel. Some felt they had to leave the site of their enslavement to experience full freedom. One freed man later recalled that he refused to work for his last owner, not because he had anything against him but because he wanted "to take my freedom." A freed woman said, "If I stay here I'll never know I'm free." Most traveled only short distances, to find work or land to farm, to

seek family members separated from them by slavery, or for other well-defined reasons.

The towns and cities of the South attracted some freed people. The presence of Union troops and federal officials promised protection from the random violence against freed people that occurred in rural areas. In March 1865, Congress created the Freedmen's Bureau to assist the freed people in their transition to freedom. In cities and towns, this agency offered assistance with finding work and necessities. Cities and towns also held black churches, newly established schools, and other social institutions, some begun by free blacks before the war. Some African Americans came to towns and cities looking for work. Little housing was available, however, so freed people often crowded into hastily built shanties. Sanitation was poor and disease a common scourge. Such conditions improved only very slowly.

Creating Communities

During Reconstruction, African Americans created their own communities with their own social institutions, beginning with family ties. Joyful families were sometimes reunited after years of separation caused by the sale of a spouse or children. Other people spent years searching for lost family members.

The new freedom to conduct religious services without white supervision was especially important. Churches quickly became the most prominent social organizations in African American communities. Churches were, in fact, among the very first social institutions that African Americans fully controlled. During Reconstruction, black denominations grew rapidly in the South, including the African Methodist Episcopal, African Methodist Episcopal Zion, and several Baptist groups (all founded before the Civil War). Black ministers helped congregation members adjust to the changes that freedom brought, and ministers often became key leaders within developing African American communities.

Throughout the cities and towns of the South, African Americans created schools. Setting up a school, said one, was "the first proof" of independence. Many new schools were for both children and adults, because laws had prohibited education for slaves. The desire to learn was widespread and intense. One freedman in Georgia wrote to a friend: "The Lord has sent books and teachers. We must not hesitate a moment, but go on and learn all we can."

When African Americans set up schools, they faced severe shortages of teachers, books, and schoolrooms—everything but students. As abolitionists and northern reformers tried to assist the transition from slavery to freedom, many of them also focused on education. The Freedmen's Bureau played an important role in organizing and equipping schools. Freedmen's

patrollers During the era of slavery, white guards who made the rounds of rural roads to make certain that slaves were not moving about the countryside without written permission from their masters.

pass system Laws that forbade slaves to travel without written authorization from their owners.

◻ **Freedmen's Bureau** Agency established in 1865 to aid former slaves in their transition to freedom, especially by administering relief and sponsoring education.

Faith Memorial Church, seen here in a photo from 1915, was built by the Rev. Mr. Guerry during reconstruction. The location was not specified in the book where the photograph originally appeared.

Aid Societies sprang up in most northern cities and, along with northern churches, collected funds and supplies for the freed people. Teachers—mostly white women, often from New England, and often acting on religious impulses—came from the North. Northern aid societies and church organizations, together with the Freedmen's Bureau, established schools to train black teachers. Some of those schools evolved into black colleges. By 1870, the Freedmen's Bureau supervised more than four thousand schools, with more than nine thousand teachers and 247,000 students. Still, in 1870, only one-tenth of school-age black children were in school.

African Americans created other social institutions in addition to churches and schools, including fraternal orders, benevolent societies, and newspapers. By 1866, the South had ten black newspapers, led by the *New Orleans Tribune*. These newspapers played important roles in shaping African American communities.

In politics, African Americans' first objective was recognition of their equal rights as citizens. Frederick Douglass insisted, "Slavery is not abolished until the black man has the ballot." In 1865, political conventions of African Americans attracted hundreds of leaders of the emerging black communities. They called for equality and voting rights, and pointed to black contributions in the American Revolution and the Civil War as evidence of patriotism and devotion. They also appealed to the nation's republican traditions, in particular the Declaration of Independence and its dictum that "all men are created equal."

Land and Labor in the Postwar South

Few white southerners welcomed the end of slavery. Only a few former slave owners provided financial assistance to their former slaves, and some tried to keep their slaves from learning of their freedom.

Many freed people looked to Union troops for assistance. When General William T. Sherman led his victorious army through Georgia in the closing months of the war, thousands of African American men, women, and children claimed their freedom and followed in the Yankees' wake. Their leaders told Sherman that they wanted to "reap the fruit of our own labor." In January 1865, Sherman issued Special Field Order No. 15, setting aside the Sea Islands and land along the South Carolina coast for freed families. Each family, he specified, was to receive 40 acres and the loan of an army mule. By June, the area had filled with forty thousand freed people settled on 400,000 acres of "Sherman land."

Sherman's action encouraged African Americans to expect that the federal government would redistribute land throughout the South. "Forty acres and a mule" became a rallying cry. Only land, Thaddeus Stevens proclaimed, would give freed people control of their own labor. "If we do not furnish them with homesteads," Stevens said, "we had better left them in bondage."

By the end of the war, the Freedmen's Bureau controlled some 850,000 acres of land abandoned by former owners or confiscated from Confederate leaders. In July 1865, General Oliver O. Howard, head of the bureau, directed that this land be divided into 40-acre plots to be given to freed people. However, President Johnson ordered Howard to halt land redistribution and to return to its former owners land already handed over. Johnson's order displaced thousands of African Americans who had already taken their 40 acres. Those who had expected land of their

fraternal order A men's organization, often with a ceremonial initiation, that typically provided rudimentary life insurance.

benevolent society Organization dedicated to some charitable purpose.

land redistribution Division of land held by large landowners into smaller plots that are turned over to landless people.

During Reconstruction, freed people gave a high priority to schools, often with the assistance of the Freedmen's Bureau and northern missionary societies. This teacher and her barefoot pupils were photographed in the 1870s, in Petersburg, Virginia. In such schools, one teacher typically taught grades 1 through 8.

Clayton Lewis, William L. Clements Library, University of Michigan.

own felt betrayed. One later recalled that they had expected "a heap from freedom dey didn't git."

The Freedmen's Bureau also assisted white refugees. In a few places, white recipients of aid outnumbered the freed blacks. Many southern whites had never owned slaves, and now feared they would have to compete with the freed people for farmland or wage labor. Like the freed people, many southern whites lacked the means to farm on their own. When the Confederate government collapsed, Confederate money became worthless. This sudden reduction in the amount of money in circulation, together with the failure of southern banks and the devastation of the southern economy, meant that the entire region was short of capital.

Sharecropping slowly emerged across much of the South, derived from the central realities of southern agriculture. Much of the land was in large holdings, but the landowners had no one to work it. Capital was scarce. Many landowners lacked cash to hire farm workers. Many families, both black and white, wanted their own farm but had no land, no supplies, and no money. Under sharecropping, an individual—usually a family head—signed a contract with a landowner to rent land as home and farm, paying a share of the

harvest as rent. The landlord's share might amount to half or more of the crop if the landlord provided mules, tools, seed, and fertilizer as well as land. Many landowners thought that sharecropping encouraged tenants to be productive, to get as much value as possible from their shares of the crop.

Southern farmers—black or white, sharecroppers or owners of small plots—often found themselves in debt to a local merchant who advanced supplies on credit. In return for credit, the merchant required a lien (a legal claim) on the growing crop. Many landlords ran stores that they required their tenants to patronize. Often the share paid as rent and the debt owed the store exceeded the value of the entire harvest. Furthermore, many rental contracts and crop liens were automatically renewed if all debts were not paid at the end of a year. Thus, in spite of their efforts to achieve greater control over their lives and labor, many southern farm families, black and white alike, found themselves trapped by sharecropping and debt. Still, sharecropping gave freed people more control over their daily lives than had slavery.

Landlords could exercise political as well as economic power over their tenants. Until the 1890s, voting was an open process, and any observer could see how an individual voted (as illustrated on page 385). Thus, when a landlord or merchant advocated a particular candidate, the unspoken message was often an implicit threat to cut off credit at the store or to evict a sharecropper if he did not vote accordingly. Such forms of economic coercion could undercut voting rights.

The White South: Confronting Change

The Civil War and the end of slavery transformed the lives of white southerners as well as black southerners.

capital Money, especially the money invested in a commercial enterprise.

sharecropping System for renting farmland in which tenant farmers—the sharecroppers—give landlords a share of their crops, rather than cash, as rent.

crop lien Legal claim to a farmer's crop, similar to a mortgage, based on the use of crops as collateral for extension of credit by a merchant.

coercion Use of threats or force to compel action.

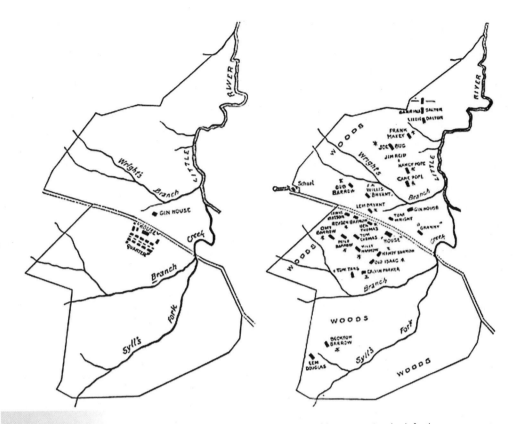

David C. Barrow, Jr., "A Georgia Plantation," *Scribner's Monthly*, vol. 21 issue 5 March 1881.

These maps of a plantation in Georgia appeared in *Scribner's Monthly* in 1881. On the left, the pre-war plantation, had one center for plantation activities—the owner's house, the slave quarters, and the various buildings for work and storage. The map on the right shows the same plantation in 1881, with a large number of small, family farms operated by sharecroppers.

For some, the changes were nearly as profound as those experienced by freed people. Savings vanished. Some homes and other buildings were destroyed. Thousands left the South.

Before the war, few white southerners had owned slaves, and very few owned large numbers. Distrust or even hostility had always existed between the privileged planter families and the many whites who farmed small plots. Some regions populated by small-scale farmers had resisted secession, and some welcomed the Union victory and supported the Republicans during Reconstruction. Some southerners also welcomed the prospect of the economic transformation that northern capital might bring.

Most white southerners, however, shared what one North Carolinian described in 1866 as "the bitterest hatred toward the North." Even people with no attachment to slavery detested the Yankees who so profoundly changed their lives. During the early phases of Reconstruction, most white southerners apparently expected that, except for slavery, things would soon be put back much as they had been before the war. For many, the "lost cause" of the Confederacy came to symbolize their defense of their prewar lives, not an attempt to break up the nation or protect slavery.

In late 1865 and 1866, the newly organized state legislatures passed **black codes** defining the new legal status of African Americans. These regulations varied from state to state, but every state placed significant restrictions on black people. Various black codes required African Americans to have an annual employment contract, limited them to agricultural work, forbade them from moving about the countryside without permission, restricted their ownership of land, and provided for forced labor by those guilty of **vagrancy**—which usually meant anyone without a job. Taken together, the black codes represented an effort by white southerners to define a legally subordinate place for African Americans and significantly restrict their new freedom.

black codes Laws passed by the southern states after the Civil War limiting the civil rights of freed people and defining their status as subordinate to whites.

vagrancy Legal condition of having no fixed place of residence or means of support.

Planning the contemplated murder of John Campbell in North Carolina (engraving), English School, (19th century)/Private Collection/© Look and Learn/Rosenberg Collection/The Bridgeman Art Library.

THE KU-KLUX-KLAN AGAIN.—PLANNING THE CONTEMPLATED MURDER OF JOHN CAMPBELL, IN NORTH CAROLINA.

In this picture, the artist has portrayed a Republican leader, white grocer John Campbell, pleading for mercy from a group of bizarrely dressed Klansmen in Moore County, North Carolina, on August 10, 1871. The Klansmen flogged Moore before releasing him. Curiously, the artist depicted Campbell as an African American.

the national leader was called the grand wizard. Klan members covered their faces with hoods, wore white robes, and rode horses draped in white as they set out to intimidate black Republicans and their white allies. Klan members also attacked less politically prominent people, whipping African Americans accused of not showing sufficient deference to whites, and nightriders burned black churches and schools. By such tactics, the Klan devastated Republican organizations in many communities.

CONGRESSIAL RECONSTRUCTION

☆ *Why did congressional Republicans take control over Reconstruction policy? How successful were they?*

☆ *How did the Fourteenth and Fifteenth Amendments change the nature of the federal union?*

The black codes, violence against freed people, and the failure of southern authorities to stem the violence turned northern opinion against President Johnson's lenient approach to Reconstruction. Increasing numbers of moderate Republicans accepted the Radicals' arguments that the freed people required greater federal protection, and congressional Republicans moved to take control of Reconstruction. When stubborn and uncompromising Andrew Johnson ran up against stubborn and uncompromising Thaddeus Stevens, the nation faced a constitutional crisis.

Challenging Presidential Reconstruction: The Civil Rights Act of 1866

In December 1865, the Thirty-Ninth Congress (elected in 1864) met for the first time. Republicans outnumbered Democrats by more than three to one. President Johnson proclaimed Reconstruction complete and the Union restored, but few Republicans agreed. Events in the South had convinced most moderate Republicans of the need to protect free labor in the South and establish basic rights for freed people. Most also agreed that Congress could withhold representation from the South until reconstructed state governments met these conditions.

On the first day of the Thirty-ninth Congress, moderate Republicans joined Radicals to exclude newly elected congressmen from the South. Citing Article I, Section 5, of the Constitution (which makes each house of Congress the judge of the qualifications of its members), Republicans set up a Joint Committee on Reconstruction to evaluate whether electees from southern states were entitled sit in Congress. In the meantime, the former Confederate states had no representation in Congress.

Some white southerners used violence to coerce freed people into accepting a subordinate status. Violence and terror became closely associated with the Ku Klux Klan, a secret organization formed in 1866 and led by a former Confederate general. The turn to terror suggests that Klan members felt themselves largely powerless through normal politics, and used terror to create a climate of fear among their opponents. Most Klan members were small-scale farmers and workers, but the leaders were often prominent within their own communities—one Freedmen's Bureau agent observed, "The most respectable citizens are engaged in it." Klan groups existed throughout the South, but operated with little central control. Their major goals were to restore white supremacy and to destroy the Republican Party. Other, like-minded organizations also formed and adopted similar tactics.

Klan members were called ghouls. Officers included cyclops, night-hawks, and grand dragons, and

◻ **Ku Klux Klan** Secret society organized in the South after the Civil War to restore white supremacy by means of violence and intimidation.

white supremacy Racist belief that whites are inherently superior to other races and entitled to rule over them.

Congressional Republicans also moved to provide more assistance to the freed people. Moderates and Radicals approved a bill extending the Freedmen's Bureau and giving it more authority against racial discrimination. When Johnson vetoed it, Congress passed a slightly revised version. Republicans also produced a civil rights bill, a far-reaching measure extending citizenship to African Americans and guaranteeing certain rights to all citizens. Johnson vetoed both the civil rights bill and the revised Freedmen's Bureau bill, but Congress passed both over his veto. With creation of the Joint Committee on Reconstruction and passage of the Civil Rights and Freedmen's Bureau acts, Congress took control of Reconstruction.

For the first time, the Civil Rights Act of 1866 defined all persons born in the United States (except Indians not taxed) as citizens and listed certain rights of all citizens, including the right to testify in court, own property, make contracts, bring lawsuits, and enjoy "full and equal benefit of all laws." It restricted state authority on the grounds that the rights of national citizenship took precedence over state actions. The law expanded federal powers in unprecedented ways and challenged traditional concepts of states' rights. Though the law applied to all citizens, its most immediate consequence was to benefit African Americans.

Debate in Congress focused on the freed people. Some supporters saw the Civil Rights Act as a way to secure freed people's basic rights. For other Republicans, the bill carried broader implications because it empowered the federal government to force states to abide by the principle of equality before the law. They applauded its redefinition of federal-state relations. Senator Lot Morrill of Maine described it as "absolutely revolutionary" but added, "Are we not in the midst of a revolution?"

When President Johnson vetoed the bill, he argued that it violated states' rights. He may have hoped to generate enough political support to elect a conservative Congress in 1866 and to win the presidency in 1868. He probably expected his veto to turn voters against the Radicals. Instead, the veto led most moderate Republicans to abandon hope of cooperating with him. In April 1866, when Congress passed the Civil Rights Act over Johnson's veto, it was the first time that Congress had overridden a presidential veto of major legislation.

Defining Citizenship: The Fourteenth Amendment

Leading Republicans worried that the Civil Rights Act could be amended or repealed by a later Congress or declared unconstitutional by the Supreme Court. Only a constitutional amendment, they concluded, could permanently safeguard the freed people's rights as citizens.

The Fourteenth Amendment began as a Radical proposal for a constitutional guarantee of equality before the law. However, the final wording—the longest of any amendment—resulted from many compromises. Section 1 of the amendment defined American citizenship in much the same way as the Civil Rights Act of 1866, then specified that

> No State shall make or enforce any law which shall abridge the privileges or immunities of citizens of the United States; nor shall any State deprive any person of life, liberty, or property, without due process of law; nor deny to any person within its jurisdiction the equal protection of the laws.

The Constitution and Bill of Rights prohibit federal interference with basic civil rights. The Fourteenth Amendment extends this protection against action by state governments.

The amendment was vague on some points. For example, it penalized states that did not enfranchise African Americans by reducing their congressional representation, but it did not specifically guarantee to African Americans the right to vote.

Not everyone approved of the final wording. Charles Sumner condemned the provision that permitted a state to deny suffrage to male citizens if it accepted a penalty. Woman suffrage advocates, led by Elizabeth Cady Stanton and Susan B. Anthony, complained that the amendment, for the first time, introduced the word *male* into the Constitution in connection with voting rights.

Despite such concerns, Congress approved the Fourteenth Amendment by a straight party vote and sent it to the states for ratification. Tennessee promptly ratified the amendment, became the first reconstructed state government to be recognized by Congress, and was exempted from most later Reconstruction legislation.

Although Congress adjourned in the summer of 1866, the nation's attention remained fixed on Reconstruction. In May and July, in Memphis and New Orleans, bloody riots aimed at

---

civil rights Rights, privileges, and protections that are part of citizenship.

◻ **Fourteenth Amendment** Constitutional amendment, ratified in 1868, defining American citizenship and rights and restricting state authority and the political activities of former Confederates.

enfranchise To grant the right to vote to an individual or group.

◻ **Elizabeth Cady Stanton** Founder and leader of the American woman suffrage movement from 1848 (Seneca Falls Convention) until her death in 1902.

◻ **Susan B. Anthony** Tireless campaigner for woman suffrage and close associate of Elizabeth Cady Stanton.

The Fourteenth Amendment

The Fourteenth Amendment is one of the most important sources of Americans' civil rights, next to the Bill of Rights (the first ten amendments). One key provision in the Fourteenth Amendment is the definition of American citizenship. Previously, the Constitution did not address that question. The Fourteenth Amendment cleared up any confusion about who was, and who was not, a citizen.

The amendment also specifies that no state could abridge the liberties of a citizen "without due process of law." Until this time, the Constitution and the Bill of Rights restricted action by the *federal* government to restrict individual liberties. The Supreme Court has interpreted the Fourteenth Amendment to mean that the restrictions placed on the federal government by the First Amendment also limit state governments—that no *state* government may abridge freedom of speech, press, assembly, and religion.

The Supreme Court continues to interpret the Fourteenth Amendment when it is presented with new cases involving state restrictions on the rights of citizens. For example, in *Roe v. Wade* (1973), the Supreme Court cited the due process clause among other provisions of the Constitution to conclude that state laws may not prevent women from having abortions. In *Lawrence v. Texas* (2003), the Court cited the Fourteenth Amendment to conclude that states may not punish adults for engaging in consensual sexual activities. Current arguments over same-sex marriage often focus on the equal-protection clause of the Fourteenth Amendment.

- Look up the Fourteenth Amendment in the back of this book. How does the Fourteenth Amendment define citizenship? Using an online newspaper, can you find recent proposals to change the definition of American citizenship?
- What current political issues might lead to court cases in which the Fourteenth Amendment is likely to be invoked?

African Americans turned more moderates against Johnson's Reconstruction policies. Some interpreted congressional elections that fall as a referendum on Reconstruction and the Fourteenth Amendment, pitting Johnson against the Radicals. Republicans swept the 1866 elections, outnumbering Democrats 143 to 49 in the new House of Representatives, and 42 to 11 in the Senate. Lyman Trumbull, senator from Illinois and a leading moderate, voiced the consensus of congressional Republicans: Congress should now "hurl from power the disloyal element" in the South.

Radicals in Control

As congressional Radicals struggled with President Johnson over control of Reconstruction, it became clear that the Fourteenth Amendment might fall short of ratification. Rejection by ten states could prevent its acceptance. By March 1867, the amendment had been rejected by twelve states—Delaware, Kentucky, and all former Confederate states except Tennessee. Moderate Republicans who had expected the Fourteenth Amendment to be the final

Reconstruction measure now became receptive to other proposals by the Radicals.

On March 2, 1867, Congress overrode Johnson's veto of the Military Reconstruction Act, which divided the Confederate states (except Tennessee) into five military districts. Each district was to be governed by a military commander authorized by Congress to use military force to protect life and property. These ten states were to elect delegates and hold constitutional conventions, and all adult male citizens were to vote, except former Confederates who were barred from office under the proposed Fourteenth Amendment. The constitutional conventions were then to create new state governments that permitted black suffrage, and the new governments were to ratify the Fourteenth Amendment. Congress would then evaluate whether those state governments were ready to regain representation in Congress.

Congress had wrested a major degree of control over Reconstruction from the president, but it was not finished. The Command of the Army Act specified that the president could issue military orders only through the General of the Army—Ulysses S. Grant,

Tickets such as these were in high demand, for they permitted the holder to watch the proceedings as the Radical leaders presented their evidence to justify removing Andrew Johnson from the presidency.

Library of Congress.

considered an ally of Congress—and that the General of the Army could not be removed without Senate permission. Congress thereby blocked Johnson from direct communication with military commanders in the South. The Tenure of Office Act specified that officials appointed with the Senate's consent were to remain in office until the Senate approved a successor, thereby preventing Johnson from removing federal officials who opposed his policies. Johnson understood both measures as invasions of presidential authority.

Early in 1867, some Radicals began to consider impeaching President Johnson. The Constitution (Article I, Sections 2 and 3) gives the House of Representatives exclusive power to **impeach** the president—that is, to charge the chief executive with misconduct. The Constitution specifies that the Senate shall hold a trial on those charges, with the chief justice of the Supreme Court presiding. If found guilty by a two-thirds vote of the Senate, the president is removed from office.

When Johnson directly challenged Congress over the Tenure of Office Act by removing Edwin Stanton as secretary of war, Johnson's opponents now claimed he had violated the law. When the House Judiciary Committee failed to bring impeachment charges, the Joint Committee on Reconstruction, led by Thaddeus Stevens, took over. On February 24, 1868, the House adopted eleven articles, or charges, nearly all based on the Stanton affair. The actual reasons the Radicals wanted Johnson removed were clear to all: they disliked him and his actions.

To convict Johnson and remove him from the presidency required a two-thirds vote by the Senate. Johnson's defenders argued he had done nothing to warrant impeachment. The Radicals' legal case was weak, but they urged senators to vote on whether they wished Johnson to remain as president. Some moderates, fearing the precedent of removing a president

for such flimsy reasons, joined with Democrats to defeat the Radicals. The vote was 35 in favor of conviction and 19 against, one vote short of the required two-thirds. By this tiny margin, Congress endorsed the principle that it should not remove the president from office simply because members of Congress disagree with or dislike the president.

Political Terrorism and the Election of 1868

The Radicals' failure to unseat Johnson left him with less than a year remaining in office. As the election approached, the Republicans nominated Ulysses S. Grant for president. A war hero, popular throughout the North, Grant committed himself to the congressional view of Reconstruction. The Democrats nominated Horatio Seymour, a former governor of New York, and denounced Reconstruction.

In the South, the campaign stirred up fierce activity by the Ku Klux Klan and similar groups. **Terrorists** assassinated an Arkansas congressman, three members of the South Carolina legislature, and several other Republican leaders. Throughout the South, mobs attacked Republican offices and meetings, and sometimes attacked any black person they could find. Such coercion had its intended effect at the ballot box.

Despite such violence, many Americans may have anticipated a calmer political future. In June 1868 Congress had readmitted seven southern states that met the requirements of congressional Reconstruction.

impeach To charge a public official with improper, usually criminal, conduct.

terrorists Those who use threats and violence to achieve ideological or political goals.

TOWARD A MORE PERFECT UNION

Constitutional Revolution

Senator Lot Morrill described what they were doing as "revolutionary," and historians have agreed that the constitutional changes of the Civil War and Reconstruction were a constitutional revolution or even "the second American revolution." Before the Civil War, some Americans had argued that the Union was voluntary and states could secede or nullify federal laws. Now it was clear that the United States was one nation, indivisible—and that secession constituted insurrection and would be met by force.

Defenders of slavery had long argued that Congress had no constitutional authority to limit, much less abolish, slavery. The Thirteenth Amendment changed that forever.

Previously, states had their own definitions of citizenship, and the *Dred Scott* decision of the U.S. Supreme Court (1857) stated that African Americans could not be citizens. The Fourteenth Amendment now defined an American citizenship that took precedence over state definitions and significantly limited state authority. The Fifteenth Amendment similarly limited state authority over voter eligibility.

Overall, the constitutional revolution of the Civil War and Reconstruction significantly enhanced federal authority at the expense of the states.

In July, the secretary of state declared the Fourteenth Amendment ratified. In November, Grant easily won the presidency, carrying twenty-six of the thirty-four states and 53 percent of the vote.

Voting Rights and Civil Rights

With Grant in the White House, Radical Republicans moved to secure voting rights for all African Americans. The states still defined voting rights. Congress had required southern states to enfranchise black males as the price of readmission to the Union, but only seven northern states had taken that step. Further, any state that had enfranchised African Americans

□ **Fifteenth Amendment** Constitutional amendment, ratified in 1870, that prohibited states from denying the right to vote because of a person's race or because a person had been a slave.

disfranchisement Taking away the right to vote.

nativity Place of birth.

discrimination Denial of equal treatment based on prejudice or bias.

could change its law at any time. In addition to the principled arguments of Douglass and other Radicals, many Republicans concluded that they needed to guarantee black suffrage in the South if they were to continue to win presidential elections and enjoy majorities in Congress.

To secure suffrage rights for all African Americans, Congress approved the **Fifteenth Amendment** in February 1869. The amendment prohibited both federal and state governments from restricting the right to vote because of "race, color, or previous condition of servitude." Like the Fourteenth Amendment, the Fifteenth marked a compromise between moderates and Radicals. Some African American leaders argued for language guaranteeing voting rights to all male citizens, because prohibiting some grounds for **disfranchisement** might imply the legitimacy of other grounds. Some Radicals tried, unsuccessfully, to add "**nativity**, property, education, or religious beliefs" to the prohibited grounds. Democrats condemned the Fifteenth Amendment as a "revolutionary" attack on states' authority to define voting rights.

Elizabeth Cady Stanton, Susan B. Anthony, and other advocates of woman suffrage opposed the amendment because it ignored restrictions based on sex. For nearly twenty years, efforts to secure women's rights and black rights had marched together. Once black male suffrage came under discussion, however, this alliance began to fracture. The break was eventually papered over, but the wounds never completely healed.

Despite such opposition, within thirteen months the proposed amendment received the approval of enough states to take effect. Success came in part because Republicans, who might otherwise have been reluctant to impose black suffrage in the North, concluded that the future success of their party required black suffrage in the South.

The Fifteenth Amendment did not reduce the violence—especially at election time—that had become almost routine in the South. When Klan activity escalated in the elections of 1870, southern Republicans looked to Washington for support. In 1870 and 1871, Congress adopted several Enforcement Acts—often called the Ku Klux Klan Acts—to enforce the Fourteenth and Fifteenth Amendments.

Despite obstacles, the prosecution of Klansmen began in 1871. Across the South hundreds were indicted, and many were convicted. In South Carolina, President Grant declared martial law. By 1872, federal intervention had broken much of the strength of the Klan.

Congress passed one final Reconstruction measure. Charles Sumner introduced a bill prohibiting **discrimination** in 1870 and in each subsequent session of Congress until his death in 1874. On his deathbed, Sumner urged his visitors to "take care of the civil-rights bill," begging them, "Don't let it fail."

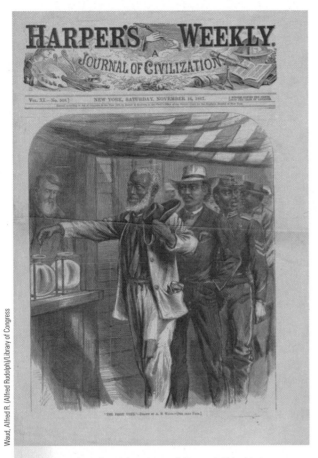

This engraving, from the cover of *Harper's Weekly* in November 1867, shows black men lined up to vote. The artist has shown first an older workingman, with his tools in his pocket; next a well-dressed, younger man, probably a city-dweller and perhaps a leader in the emerging black community; next a Union soldier. Voters received a ballot (a "party ticket") from a party campaigner and deposited that ballot in a ballot box, in full sight of all. Voting was not secret until much later.

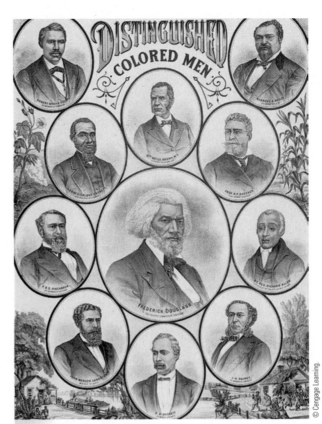

This lithograph from 1883 depicts African American men, most of whom had leading roles in Black Reconstruction: Frederick Douglass is in the center. Joseph Rainey is in the lower right.

Approved after Sumner's death, the **Civil Rights Act of 1875** prohibited racial discrimination in the selection of juries and in public transportation and **public accommodations**.

BLACK RECONSTRUCTION

☆ *What major groups made up the Republican Party in the South during Reconstruction? Compare their reasons for being Republicans, their relative sizes, and their objectives.*

☆ *What were the most lasting results of the Republican state administrations?*

Congressional Reconstruction set the stage for new developments at state and local levels throughout the South. African Americans never completely controlled any state government but did form a significant element in the governments of several states. The time when African Americans participated prominently in state and local politics is usually called **Black Reconstruction**. It began with efforts by African Americans to take part in politics as early as 1865 and lasted for more than a decade. A few African Americans continued to hold elective office in the South after 1877, but by then they could do little to bring about significant political change. Map 15.1 indicates the proportion of African Americans in each of the southern states, and also the years when each state was under a Reconstruction state government.

☐ **Civil Rights Act of 1875** Law passed by Congress in 1875 prohibiting racial discrimination in selection of juries and in businesses open to the general public.

public accommodations Hotels, bars and restaurants, theaters, and other places set up to do business with anyone who can pay the price of admission.

☐ **Black Reconstruction** The period of Reconstruction when African Americans took an active role in state and local government.

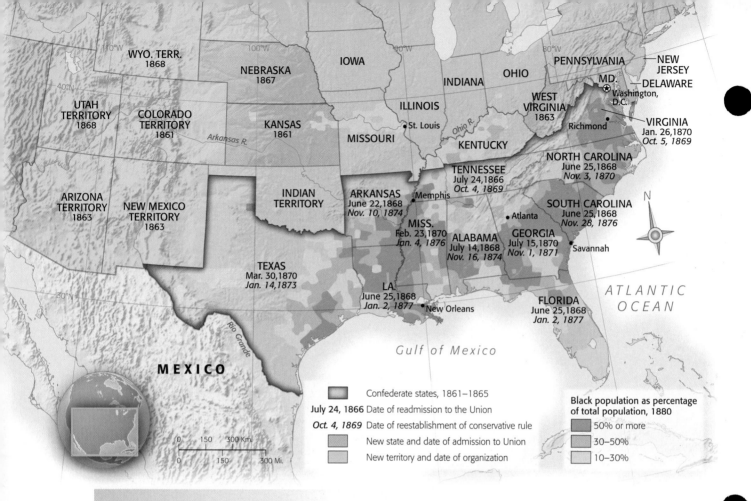

MAP 15.1 African American Population and the Duration of Reconstruction
This map shows the proportion of African Americans in the South and the dates when each former Confederate state was under a Reconstruction state government. Does the map suggest any relationship between the proportion of a state's population that was African American and the time that the state spent under a Reconstruction state government? © Cengage Learning.

The Republican Party in the South

Nearly all African Americans who participated in politics did so as Republicans, and they formed the majority of the Republican Party in the South. Nearly all black Republicans were new to politics, and they often braved considerable personal danger by participating in a party that many white southerners equated with the conquering Yankees.

Suffrage made politics centrally important for African American communities. The state constitutional conventions that met in 1868 included 265 black delegates, but only in Louisiana and South Carolina were half or more of the delegates black. With suffrage established, southern Republicans began to elect African Americans to public office. Between 1869 and 1877, fourteen black men (including Joseph Rainey) served in the national House of Representatives, and Mississippi sent two African Americans to the U.S. Senate.

Across the South, six African Americans served as lieutenant governors, and one of them, P. B. S. Pinchback, succeeded briefly to the governorship of

Louisiana. More than six hundred black men served in southern state legislatures, but only in South Carolina did African Americans ever have a majority in the state legislature. Elsewhere they formed part of a Republican majority but rarely held key legislative positions. Only in South Carolina and Mississippi did legislatures elect black presiding officers. Although politically inexperienced, most African Americans who held office during Reconstruction had some education. Of the eighteen who served in statewide offices, all but three are known to have been born free. P. B. S. Pinchback, for example, was educated in Ohio and served in the army as a captain before entering politics in Louisiana. Most black politicians first achieved prominence through service with the army, the Freedmen's Bureau, the new schools, or the religious and civic organizations of black communities.

Republicans gained power in southern states only by attracting some white voters. These white Republicans are usually remembered by the names fastened on them by their political opponents: "carpetbaggers" and "scalawags." Both groups included idealists who

Bags made of carpeting, like this one, were inexpensive luggage. Southern opponents of Reconstruction fastened the label "carpetbaggers" on northerners who came south to participate in Reconstruction, suggesting that they were cheap opportunists. Collection of Picture Research Consultants and Archives.

hoped to create a new southern society, but both also included opportunists expecting to exploit politics for personal gain.

Southern Democrats applied the term carpetbagger to northern Republicans who came to the South after the war, regarding them as second-rate schemers—outsiders with their belongings packed in a cheap carpet bag. In fact, most northerners who came south were well-educated men and women from middle-class backgrounds. Most men had served in the Union army and moved south before blacks could vote. They included lawyers, newspaper editors, and investors in agricultural land, as well as teachers in the new schools, or agents of the Freedmen's Bureau, and most hoped to transform the South by creating new institutions based on northern models, especially free labor and free public schools. Few in number, transplanted northerners nonetheless took leading roles in state constitutional conventions and state legislatures. Some were also prominent advocates of economic modernization.

Southern Democrats reserved their greatest contempt for those they called scalawags, slang for someone unscrupulous and worthless. Scalawags were white southerners who became Republicans. They included many southern Unionists, who had opposed secession, and others who thought the Republicans offered the best hope for economic recovery. Scalawags included merchants, artisans, and professionals who favored a modernized South. Others were small-scale farmers who saw Reconstruction as a way to end political domination by the plantation owners.

The freedmen, white newcomers from the North, and white southerners who made up the Republican Party in the South hoped to inject new ideas into that region. They tried to modernize state and local governments and make the postwar South more like the North. They repealed outdated laws and established or expanded schools, hospitals, orphanages, and penitentiaries.

Creating Public Education, Fighting Discrimination, and Building Railroads

Free public education was perhaps the most enduring legacy of Black Reconstruction, because Reconstruction constitutions required tax-supported public schools. Implementation, however, was expensive and proceeded slowly. By the mid-1870s, only half of southern children attended public schools.

In creating public schools, Reconstruction state governments faced a central question: Would white and black children attend the same schools? Many African Americans favored racially integrated schools. Southern white leaders, including many southern white Republicans, argued that integration would destroy the fledgling public school system by driving whites away. In the end, no state required school integration. Southern states also created separate black normal schools (to train schoolteachers) and colleges. On balance, most blacks probably agreed with Frederick Douglass that separate schools were "infinitely superior" to no public education at all. Some found other reasons to accept segregated schools—separate black schools gave a larger role to black parents, and they hired black teachers and administrators.

Creating and operating two educational systems, one white and one black, was costly, and funds were always limited. Black schools almost always received fewer dollars per student than white schools. Despite their accomplishments, the segregated schools institutionalized discrimination.

Reconstruction state governments moved toward protection of equal rights in other areas. Southern Republicans often wrote into their new state constitutions prohibitions against discrimination and protections for civil rights. Some Reconstruction state

carpetbagger Derogatory term for the northerners who came to the South after the Civil War to take part in Reconstruction.

scalawag Derogatory term for white southerners who aligned themselves with the Republican Party during Reconstruction.

segregated Separated on account of race or class, such as the separation of blacks from whites in most southern school systems.

governments enacted laws guaranteeing equal access to public transportation and public accommodations. Elsewhere, efforts to pass equal access laws foundered on the opposition of southern white Republicans, who often joined Democrats to favor segregation. Such conflicts pointed up the internal divisions within the southern Republican Party. Even when equal access laws were passed, they were often not enforced.

Republicans everywhere—North, South, and West—sought to use government authority to encourage economic growth and development. Promoting economic development often meant encouraging railroad construction. In the South, as elsewhere, some state governments granted land to railroads, or lent them money, or committed the state's credit to underwrite bonds for construction. Sometimes they subsidized railroads without planning adequately or determining whether companies were financially sound. Some projects failed as companies squandered funds without building rail lines. During the 1870s, only 7,000 miles of new track were laid in the South, compared with 45,000 miles elsewhere in the nation. Even that was a considerable accomplishment for the South, given its dismal economic situation.

Railroad companies and other corporations sometimes sought favorable treatment by bribing public officials. All too many officeholders—South, North, and West—accepted their offers. Given the excessive favoritism that most public officials showed to corporations, revelations and allegations of corruption became common from New York to Mississippi to California.

Southern politics proved especially ripe for corruption as government responsibilities expanded rapidly and created new opportunities for scoundrels. Too many Reconstruction officials—white and black—saw politics as a way to improve their own finances. One South Carolina legislator bluntly described his attitude toward electing a U.S. senator: "I was pretty hard up, and I did not care who the candidate was if I got two hundred dollars." Corruption was usually nonpartisan, but it seemed more prominent among Republicans because they held the most important offices.

William Mahone, shown here at about the time he served in the U.S. Senate from Virginia, had been a railroad developer in Virginia before the Civil War. A major general in the Confederate army, he again became head of a railroad company after the war. He organized a political coalition of African Americans, white Republicans, and conservative Democrats that took control of state government and elected Mahone to the U.S. Senate, where he usually caucused with the Republicans.

Library of Congress Prints and Photographs Division[LC-BH832- 2462].

THE END OF RECONSTRUCTION

☆ *What major factors brought about the end of Reconstruction? Evaluate their relative significance.*

From the beginning, most white southerners resisted the new order that the conquering Yankees imposed on them. Initially, resistance took the form of black codes and the Klan. Later, some southern opponents of Reconstruction developed new strategies, but terror remained an important instrument of resistance.

The "New Departure" and the 1872 Presidential Election

By 1869, some leading southern Democrats had abandoned their resistance to change, deciding instead to accept some Reconstruction measures and African American suffrage. At the same time, they also tried to secure restoration of political rights for former Confederates. Behind this New Departure for southern Democrats lay the belief that continued resistance

equal access Right of any person to make the same use of a public facility, such as streetcars, as any other person.

underwrite To assume financial responsibility for; here, to guarantee the purchase of bonds.

▫ **New Departure** Strategy adopted by some leading southern Democrats of cooperating with some Reconstruction measures in the hope of winning compromises favorable to their party.

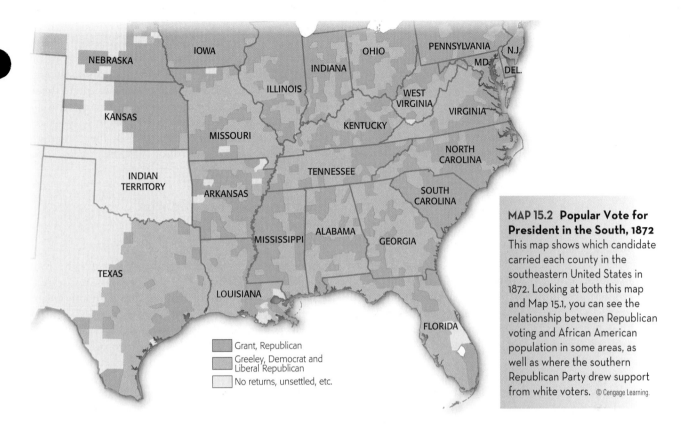

MAP 15.2 **Popular Vote for President in the South, 1872** This map shows which candidate carried each county in the southeastern United States in 1872. Looking at both this map and Map 15.1, you can see the relationship between Republican voting and African American population in some areas, as well as where the southern Republican Party drew support from white voters. © Cengage Learning.

Grant, Republican

Greeley, Democrat and Liberal Republican

No returns, unsettled, etc.

would only cause more regional turmoil and prolong federal intervention.

Sometimes southern Democrats supported conservative Republicans for state and local offices instead of members of their own party, hoping to defuse concern in Washington and dilute Radical influence in state government. This strategy appeared first in Virginia, where William Mahone forged a broad political **coalition** that accepted black suffrage and in 1869 elected as governor a northern-born banker and moderate Republican. Virginia thereby avoided Radical Republican rule.

Coalitions of Democrats and moderate Republicans won in Tennessee in 1869 and in Missouri in 1870. Elsewhere leading Democrats grudgingly accepted black suffrage but attacked Republicans for raising taxes, increasing state spending, and being corrupt. Such campaigns brought a positive response from many taxpayers because southern tax rates had risen significantly to support the new schools, railroad subsidies, and other modernizing programs. Several victories by so-called **Redeemers** and New Departure Democrats in the early 1870s also coincided with renewed terrorist activity aimed at Republicans. The worst single incident occurred in 1873. A group of armed freedmen fortified the town of Colfax, Louisiana, to hold off Democrats who were planning to seize the county government. After a three-week siege, well-armed whites overcame the black defenders and killed 280 African Americans. Leading

Democrats rarely endorsed such bloodshed, but they reaped political advantages from it.

The New Departure movement coincided with a nationwide division within the Republican Party. The Liberal Republican movement attracted moderates, concerned that the Radicals had gone too far. Others opposed Grant on issues unrelated to Reconstruction, especially growing evidence of corruption.

Horace Greeley, editor of the *New York Daily Tribune,* won the Liberal nomination for president in 1872. An opponent of slavery before the Civil War, Greeley had given strong support to the Fourteenth and Fifteenth Amendments. But he had sometimes taken puzzling positions, including a willingness to let the South secede. One political observer described him as "honest, but . . . conceited, fussy, and foolish." Greeley had long ripped the Democrats in his newspaper columns, but the Democrats nonetheless nominated him in an effort to defeat Grant. Grant won convincingly, carrying 56 percent of the vote and winning every northern state and ten of the sixteen southern and border states (see Map 15.2).

coalition An alliance, especially a temporary one of different people or groups.

◻ **Redeemers** Southern Democrats who hoped to bring the Democratic Party back into power and to suppress Black Reconstruction.

The Politics of Terror: The "Mississippi Plan"

By 1872, nearly all southern whites had abandoned the Republicans, and Black Reconstruction had ended in several states. African Americans, however, maintained their Republican loyalties. As Democrats worked to unite southern whites behind their banner of white supremacy, the South polarized politically along racial lines. Elections in 1874 proved disastrous for Republicans: Democrats won more than two-thirds of the South's seats in the House of Representatives and "redeemed" several more states.

Terrorism against black Republicans and their remaining white allies played a role in some Democratic victories in 1874. Where the Klan had worn disguises and ridden at night, by 1874 Democrats often formed rifle companies, put on red-flannel shirts, and marched and drilled in public. In some areas, armed whites prevented African Americans from voting or terrorized prominent Republicans, especially African American Republicans.

Republicans in 1874 lost support in the North because of scandals within the Grant administration and because a major economic depression was producing high unemployment. In the 1874 elections, Democrats won control of the House of Representatives for the first time since the 1850s and could block any new Reconstruction proposals.

During 1875 in Mississippi, political violence reached such levels that the use of terror to overthrow Reconstruction became known as the Mississippi Plan. Democratic rifle clubs broke up Republican meetings and attacked Republican leaders. One black Mississippian described the election as "the most violent time we have ever seen." When Mississippi's carpetbagger governor, Adelbert Ames, requested federal help, President Grant declined. Grant feared that the southern Reconstruction governments had become so discredited that further federal military intervention might endanger the election prospects of Republican candidates in the North.

---

depression Period of economic contraction, characterized by decreasing business activity, falling prices, and high unemployment.

◻ Mississippi Plan Use of threats, violence, and lynching by Mississippi Democrats in 1875 to intimidate Republicans and bring the Democratic Party to power.

◻ Rutherford B. Hayes (1822–1893) Seventeenth president of the United States; Ohio governor and former Union general, president when Reconstruction ended.

◻ Compromise of 1877 Name applied by historians to discussions around the disputed presidential election of 1876; in the end, Republicans gained the presidency, and southern Democrats received some concessions.

Democrats swept the Mississippi elections, winning four-fifths of the state legislature. When the legislature convened, it impeached and removed from office Alexander Davis, the black Republican lieutenant governor, on grounds no more serious than those brought against Andrew Johnson. Facing similar action, Governor Ames resigned and left the state. Ames had foreseen the result during the campaign when he wrote, "A revolution has taken place—by force of arms."

The Troubled Presidential Election of 1876

In 1876, on the centennial of American independence, the nation stumbled through a deeply troubled—and potentially dangerous—presidential election. As revelations of corruption in the Grant administration multiplied, both parties sought candidates known for their integrity. The Democrats nominated Samuel J. Tilden, governor of New York, who had fought political corruption in New York City. The Republicans selected Rutherford B. Hayes, a Civil War general and governor of Ohio. During the campaign in the South, intimidation of Republicans, both black and white, continued in many places.

Early election reports indicated a victory for Tilden (see Map 15.3). In addition to the border states and South, he also carried New York, New Jersey, and Indiana. Tilden received 51 percent of the popular vote versus 48 percent for Hayes.

State Republican officials still controlled the counting and reporting of ballots in South Carolina, Florida, and Louisiana. Charging voting fraud, Republican election boards in those states rejected enough ballots so that the official count gave Hayes narrow majorities and thus a one-vote margin of victory in the Electoral College. Crying fraud in return, Democratic officials in those states submitted their own versions of the vote count. Angry Democrats vowed to see Tilden inaugurated, by force if necessary. Some Democratic newspapers ran headlines that read "Tilden or War."

For the first time, Congress faced the problem of disputed electoral votes that could decide the outcome of an election. To resolve the challenges, Congress created a commission of five senators, five representatives, and five Supreme Court justices. The Republicans had a one-vote majority on the commission.

As commission hearings droned on through January and into February 1877, informal discussions took place among leading Republicans and Democrats. The result has been called the Compromise of 1877.

Southern Democrats demanded an end to federal intervention in southern politics but insisted on federal subsidies for railroad construction and waterways in the South. And they wanted one of their own

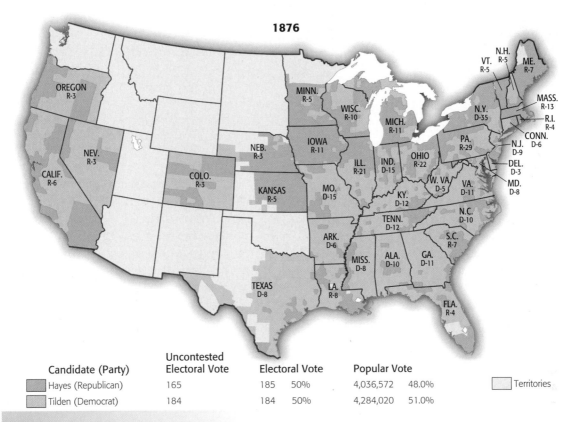

1876

Candidate (Party)	Uncontested Electoral Vote	Electoral Vote		Popular Vote	
Hayes (Republican)	165	185	50%	4,036,572	48.0%
Tilden (Democrat)	184	184	50%	4,284,020	51.0%

Territories

MAP 15.3 Election of 1876
The end of Black Reconstruction in the South combined with Democratic gains in the North to give a popular majority to Samuel Tilden, the Democratic candidate. The disputed electoral vote was ultimately resolved in favor of Rutherford B. Hayes, the Republican. © Cengage Learning.

as postmaster general because that office held the key to most federal patronage. In return, southern Democrats seemed willing to abandon Tilden's claim to the White House. The Compromise of 1877, however, was never set down in one place or agreed to by all parties.

By a straight party vote, the commission confirmed the election of Hayes. Soon after his inauguration, the new president ordered the last of the federal troops withdrawn from the South. The era of a powerful federal government pledged to protect "equality before the law" for all citizens was over. The last three Republican state governments fell in 1877, giving the Democrats, the party of white supremacy, control in every southern state. One Radical journal bitterly concluded that African Americans had been forced "to relinquish the artificial right to vote for the natural right to live." In parts of the South thereafter, election fraud and violence became routine. A Mississippi judge acknowledged in 1890 that "since 1875 . . . we have been preserving the ascendancy of the white people by . . . stuffing ballot boxes, committing perjury and here and there in the state carrying the elections by fraud and violence."

Reconstruction was over. The Civil War was more than ten years in the past. Many moderate Republicans had hoped that the Fourteenth and Fifteenth Amendments and the Civil Rights Act would guarantee black rights without a continuing federal presence in the South. Southern Democrats persistently argued—on paltry evidence—that carpetbaggers and scalawags were all corrupt, that they manipulated black voters, that African American officeholders were ignorant and illiterate, and that southern Democrats wanted only honest self-government. The truth of the situation made little difference.

Northern Democrats had always opposed Reconstruction and readily adopted the southern Democrats' version of reality. Such portrayals found growing acceptance among other northerners too, for many had shown their own racial bias when they resisted black suffrage and kept their public schools segregated. In 1875, when Grant refused to use federal troops to protect black rights, he declared that "the whole public are tired out with these . . . outbreaks in the South." He was quoted widely and with approval throughout the North. In addition, a major depression in the mid-1870s, unemployment and labor disputes,

A Deeper Understanding of History

When Historians Disagree

The Civil War and Reconstruction, like the American Revolution, form a dividing point in American history, a time when Americans made important and long-lasting choices about their future. Such dividing points attract historians, who seek to understand such momentous decisions. But historians don't always agree about the meaning of such important events.

When historians approach a research project, they often begin with questions that they seek to answer by examining primary sources. The most typical primary sources are documents—things written by people who participated in or observed the event being studied. Though historians' questions begin with the basic facts—who, what, when, where—they almost always include the more difficult questions of causation and motivation: Why did events unfold as they did? What motivated individuals and groups to make the decisions they made? While historians tend to agree on the facts, they may disagree on causation and motivation, because those questions require judgments about the meaning of documents, the resolution of conflicting sources, and the relative importance of documents. Historians must also decide what weight to give to the views of those on differing sides of an issue; for example, how much weight to give to the perspectives of black leaders of Reconstruction compared to those of their white opponents. Though historians seek to be objective and to understand the past on its own terms, they may unconsciously view the past through the biases and prejudices of their own time.

The history of Reconstruction provides examples. After 1877, southern whites held up Reconstruction as a failure. William A. Dunning endorsed that interpretation in *Reconstruction: Political & Economic, 1865–1877*, published in 1907, and his conclusions dominated the thinking of most white historians for a generation. Early black historians disagreed. George Washington Williams, a Union army veteran, had earlier written a two-volume history of African Americans that appeared in 1882. *Black Reconstruction in America,* by W. E. B. Du Bois, which appeared in 1935, challenged Dunning's assumptions and conclusions. Both presented fully the role of African Americans in Reconstruction and pointed to the accomplishments of Reconstruction state governments and black leaders. Beginning in the 1940s and continuing into the 1960s, as the racial attitudes of many white Americans were challenged and often changed by the civil rights movement (covered in Chapters 25 and 26), white historians increasingly questioned Dunning's views and began to give more attention to the perspectives of the African Americans who had taken part in Reconstruction. Historians today recognize that Reconstruction produced significant changes in southern life and in the life of the nation, and that Reconstruction collapsed partly because of internal flaws, partly because of divisions within the Republican Party, and partly because of the political terrorism unleashed in the South and the refusal of the North to commit the force required to protect the constitutional rights of African Americans.

Butler Library, Columbia University in the City of New York.

William Archibald Dunning taught in the history department of Columbia University from 1886 to his death in 1922, and was honored by the presidency of the American Historical Association in 1913 and the presidency of the American Political Science Association in 1921.

Schomburg Center/Art Resource, NY.

W. E. B. Du Bois combined the life of a scholar with that of an activist for black rights. From 1910 to 1933, in addition to his scholarly writing, he also edited *The Crisis,* the monthly magazine of the National Association for the Advancement of Colored People. *Black Reconstruction* was published in 1935, shortly after he returned to college teaching.

the growth of industry, the emergence of big business, and the development of the West focused the attention of many Americans, including many members of Congress, on economic issues.

Some Republicans, to be certain, kept the faith of their abolitionist and Radical forebears and hoped the federal government might again protect black rights. But though Republicans routinely condemned violations of black rights after 1877, few Republicans showed much interest in using federal power to prevent such outrages.

After Reconstruction

After 1877, southern Democrats moved to establish new systems of politics and race relations. They worked to reduce taxes, dismantle Reconstruction legislation and agencies, and eliminate meaningful black participation in politics. They also began the process of turning the South into a one-party region, a situation that reached its fullest development around 1900 and persisted through the 1950s.

Voting and officeholding by African Americans did not cease in 1877, but without federal enforcement of black rights, the threat of violence and the potential for economic retaliation by landlords and merchants sharply reduced meaningful political involvement. Efforts to mobilize black voters posed dangers to candidates and voters, and many black political leaders concluded that their political survival depended on favors from influential white Republicans or even from Democratic leaders. The public schools survived, segregated and underfunded, but nonetheless presenting important opportunities. Many Reconstruction-era laws remained on the books, and for a time many theaters, bars, restaurants, hotels, streetcars, and railroads continued to serve African Americans without discrimination. White supremacy had been established by force of arms, however, and blacks exercised their rights at the sufferance of the dominant whites.

After 1877, Reconstruction was held up as a failure. Although far from accurate, the southern whites' version of Reconstruction—that conniving carpetbaggers and scalawags had manipulated ignorant freedmen—appealed to many white Americans throughout the nation, and it gained widespread acceptance among many novelists, journalists, and historians. Thomas Dixon's popular novel *The Clansman* (1905) inspired the highly influential film *The Birth of a Nation* (1915). Historically inaccurate and luridly racist, the book and the movie portrayed Klan members as heroes who rescued the white South, and especially white southern women, from domination and debauchery at the hands of depraved freedmen and carpetbaggers. (For the response of historians, see the A Deeper Understanding of History feature.)

Today we recognize that Reconstruction produced many positive changes both in the South and elsewhere. The creation of public schools was among the important changes in southern life produced by the Reconstruction state governments. The Fourteenth and Fifteenth Amendments eventually provided the constitutional leverage to restore the principle of equality before the law that so concerned the Radicals.

Individual Voices

CONGRESSMAN JOSEPH RAINEY,
from a Speech Supporting the Ku Klux Klan Act

In the House of Representatives, Joseph Rainey was a consistent defender of African Americans and a strong proponent for federal protection for all those southerners who were attacked because they were Republicans. These are excerpts from his speech in support of the Ku Klux Klan act.

Library of Congress.

❶ Where does Rainey fix the blame for the crimes he describes?

❷ How does Rainey respond to arguments that military rule has no place in a republic? How does he indicate that he is not just appealing for protection of African Americans?

❸ How does Rainey define the problem as one that goes to the very center of what it means to be an American?

A remedy is needed to meet the evil now existing in most of the southern States, but especially in that one which I have the honor to represent in part, the State of South Carolina. The enormity of the crimes constantly perpetrated there finds no parallel in the history of this Republic in her very darkest days. . . . The prevailing spirit of the Southron [white southerner] is either to rule or to ruin. Voters must perforce succumb to their wishes or else risk life itself. . . . **❶**

Daily reports come to us of men throughout the country being whipped; of school-houses for colored children being closed, and of parties being driven from their houses and their families. . . . The law affords no protection for life and property in this county, and the sooner the country knows it and finds a remedy for it, the better it will be. Better a thousand times the rule of the bayonet than the humiliating lash of the Ku Klux and the murderous bullet of the midnight assassin. . . . This protection is equally desired for those loyal whites . . . who are now undergoing persecution simply on account of their activity in carrying out Union principles and loyal sentiments in the South. . . . **❷**

In the dawn of our freedom our young Republic was widely recognized and proudly proclaimed to the world the refuge, the safe asylum of the oppressed of all lands. Shall it be said that at this day, through mere indifference and culpable neglect, this grand boast of ours is become a mere form of words, an utter fraud? I earnestly hope not! And yet, if we stand with folded arms and idle hands, while the cries of our oppressed brethren sound in our ears, what will it be but a proof to all men that we are utterly unfit for our glorious mission, unworthy of our noble privileges, as the greatest of republics, the champions of freedom for all men? **❸**

Study Tools

SUMMARY

At the end of the Civil War, the nation faced difficult choices regarding the restoration of the defeated South and the future of the freed people. Committed to ending slavery, President Lincoln nevertheless chose a lenient approach to restoring states to the Union, partly to persuade southerners to abandon the Confederacy and accept emancipation. When Johnson became president, he took an even more lenient approach.

The end of slavery brought new opportunities for African Americans, whether or not they had been slaves. Taking advantage of the opportunities that freedom opened, they tried to create independent lives for themselves, and they developed social institutions that helped to define black communities. Because few managed to acquire land of their own, most became either sharecroppers or wage laborers. White southerners also experienced economic dislocation, and many also became sharecroppers. Most white southerners expected to keep African Americans in a subordinate role and initially used black codes and violence toward that end.

In reaction against the black codes and violence, Congress took control of Reconstruction and passed the Civil Rights Act of 1866, the Fourteenth Amendment, and the Reconstruction Acts of 1867. An attempt to remove Johnson from the presidency was unsuccessful.

Additional federal Reconstruction measures included the Fifteenth Amendment, laws against the Ku Klux Klan, and the Civil Rights Act of 1875. Several of these measures strengthened the federal government at the expense of the states.

Enfranchised freedmen, white and black northerners who moved to the South, and some southern whites created a southern Republican Party that governed most southern states for a time. The most lasting contribution of these state governments was the creation of public school systems. Like government officials elsewhere, however, some southern politicians fell prey to corruption.

In the late 1860s, many southern Democrats chose a "New Departure": they grudgingly accepted some features of Reconstruction and sought to recapture control of state governments. By the mid-1870s, however, southern politics turned almost solely on race. The 1876 presidential election was very close and hotly disputed. In the end, Hayes took office and ended Reconstruction. Without federal protection for their civil rights, African Americans faced terrorism, violence, and even death if they challenged their subordinate role. With the end of Reconstruction, the South entered an era of white supremacy in politics and government, the economy, and social relations.

CHRONOLOGY
Reconstruction

1863	Emancipation Proclamation
1864	Lincoln reelected
1865	Freedmen's Bureau created
	Civil War ends
	Andrew Johnson becomes president
	Thirteenth Amendment (abolishing slavery) ratified
1866	Ku Klux Klan formed
	Congress takes control over Reconstruction
1867	Military Reconstruction Act
1868	Impeachment and acquittal of President Johnson
	Fourteenth Amendment (defining citizenship) ratified
	Grant elected president
1869–1870	Victories of "New Departure" Democrats in some southern states
1870	Fifteenth Amendment (guaranteeing voting rights) ratified
1870–1871	Ku Klux Klan Acts
1872	Grant reelected
1875	Civil Rights Act of 1875
	Mississippi Plan ends Reconstruction in Mississippi
1876	Disputed presidential election
1877	Compromise of 1877; Hayes becomes president
	End of Reconstruction

Study Tools

FOCUS QUESTIONS

If you have mastered this chapter, you should be able to answer these questions and to explain the terms that follow the questions.

1. What did Presidents Lincoln and Johnson seek to accomplish for the South? How did white southerners respond to those efforts?

2. What seem to have been the leading objectives among freed people as they explored their new opportunities?

3. How do the differing responses of freed people and southern whites show different understandings of the significance of emancipation?

4. Why did congressional Republicans take control over Reconstruction policy? How successful were they?

5. How did the Fourteenth and Fifteenth Amendments change the nature of the federal union?

6. What major groups made up the Republican Party in the South during Reconstruction? Compare their reasons for being Republicans, their relative sizes, and their objectives.

7. What were the most lasting results of the Republican state administrations?

8. What major factors brought about the end of Reconstruction? Evaluate their relative significance.

KEY TERMS

Reconstruction *p. 370*

Abraham Lincoln *p. 371*

Frederick Douglass *p. 371*

Radical Republicans *p. 371*

Thirteenth Amendment *p. 373*

Andrew Johnson *p. 373*

Freedmen's Bureau *p. 376*

Ku Klux Klan *p. 380*

Fourteenth Amendment *p. 381*

Elizabeth Cady Stanton *p. 381*

Susan B. Anthony *p. 381*

Fifteenth Amendment *p. 384*

Civil Rights Act of 1875 *p. 385*

Black Reconstruction *p. 385*

New Departure *p. 388*

Redeemers *p. 389*

Mississippi Plan *p. 390*

Rutherford B. Hayes *p. 390*

Compromise of 1877 *p. 390*

SUGGESTED RESOURCES

W. E. B. Du Bois. *Black Reconstruction in America* (1935; reprint ed., Oxford University Press, 2007). This 2007 edition of Du Bois's classic includes an introduction that places Du Bois's work into the context of work by subsequent historians.

Eric Foner. *Reconstruction: America's Unfinished Revolution, 1863–1877* (1988; reprint ed., Harper, 2002). Still the standard account after nearly a quarter century; thorough and detailed (700-plus pages).

Gilder Lehrman Institute of American History. "Reconstruction," http://www.gilderlehrman.org/history-by-era/civil-war-and-reconstruction-1861-1877/reconstruction. Includes essays by prominent historians, primary sources, and suggestions for additional reading.

Michael Perman. *Emancipation and Reconstruction*, 2nd ed. (Harlan Davidson, 2003). A good, brief, and well-written introduction to the topics.

Public Broadcasting System. "Reconstruction: The Second Civil War," *The American Experience*, http://www.pbs.org/wgbh/amex/reconstruction/index.html. A large collection of primary sources and photographs, intended to accompany the PBS program of the same name. The film itself is not available online.

Documents

Declaration of Independence in Congress, July 4, 1776

When, in the course of human events, it becomes necessary for one people to dissolve the political bonds which have connected them with another, and to assume, among the powers of the earth, the separate and equal station to which the laws of nature and of nature's God entitle them, a decent respect to the opinions of mankind requires that they should declare the causes which impel them to the separation.

We hold these truths to be self-evident: That all men are created equal; that they are endowed by their Creator with certain unalienable rights; that among these are life, liberty, and the pursuit of happiness; that, to secure these rights, governments are instituted among men, deriving their just powers from the consent of the governed; that whenever any form of government becomes destructive of these ends, it is the right of the people to alter or to abolish it, and to institute new government, laying its foundation on such principles, and organizing its powers in such form, as to them shall seem most likely to effect their safety and happiness. Prudence, indeed, will dictate that governments long established should not be changed for light and transient causes; and accordingly all experience hath shown that mankind are more disposed to suffer, while evils are sufferable, than to right themselves by abolishing the forms to which they are accustomed. But when a long train of abuses and usurpations, pursuing invariably the same object, evinces a design to reduce them under absolute despotism, it is their right, it is their duty, to throw off such government, and to provide new guards for their future security. Such has been the patient sufferance of these colonies; and such is now the necessity which constrains them to alter their former systems of government. The history of the present King of Great Britain is a history of repeated injuries and usurpations, all having in direct object the establishment of an absolute tyranny over these states. To prove this, let facts be submitted to a candid world.

He has refused his assent to laws, the most wholesome and necessary for the public good.

He has forbidden his governors to pass laws of immediate and pressing importance, unless suspended in their operation till his assent should be obtained; and, when so suspended, he has utterly neglected to attend to them.

He has refused to pass other laws for the accommodation of large districts of people, unless those people would relinquish the right of representation in the legislature, a right inestimable to them, and formidable to tyrants only.

He has called together legislative bodies at places unusual, uncomfortable, and distant from the depository of their public records, for the sole purpose of fatiguing them into compliance with his measures.

He has dissolved representative houses repeatedly, for opposing, with manly firmness, his invasions on the rights of the people.

He has refused for a long time, after such dissolutions, to cause others to be elected; whereby the legislative powers, incapable of annihilation, have returned to the people at large for their exercise; the state remaining, in the mean time, exposed to all the dangers of invasions from without and convulsions within.

He has endeavored to prevent the population of these states; for that purpose obstructing the laws for naturalization of foreigners; refusing to pass others to encourage their migration hither, and raising the conditions of new appropriations of lands.

He has obstructed the administration of justice, by refusing his assent to laws for establishing judiciary powers.

He has made judges dependent on his will alone, for the tenure of their offices, and the amount and payment of their salaries.

He has erected a multitude of new offices, and sent hither swarms of officers to harass our people and eat out their substance.

He has kept among us, in times of peace, standing armies, without the consent of our legislatures.

He has affected to render the military independent of, and superior to, the civil power.

He has combined with others to subject us to a jurisdiction foreign to our constitution, and unacknowledged by our laws, giving his assent to their acts of pretended legislation:

For quartering large bodies of armed troops among us;

For protecting them, by a mock trial, from punishment for any murders which they should commit on the inhabitants of these states;

For cutting off our trade with all parts of the world;

For imposing taxes on us without our consent;

For depriving us, in many cases, of the benefits of trial by jury;

For transporting us beyond seas, to be tried for pretended offenses;

For abolishing the free system of English laws in a neighboring province, establishing therein an arbitrary government, and enlarging its boundaries, so as to render it at once an example and fit instrument for introducing the same absolute rule into these colonies;

For taking away our charters, abolishing our most valuable laws, and altering fundamentally the forms of our governments;

For suspending our own legislatures, and declaring themselves invested with power to legislate for us in all cases whatsoever.

He has abdicated government here, by declaring us out of his protection and waging war against us.

He has plundered our seas, ravaged our coasts, burned our towns, and destroyed the lives of our people.

He is at this time transporting large armies of foreign mercenaries to complete the works of death, desolation, and tyranny already begun with circumstances of cruelty and perfidy scarcely paralleled in the most barbarous ages, and totally unworthy the head of a civilized nation.

He has constrained our fellow-citizens, taken captive on the high seas, to bear arms against their country, to become the executioners of their friends and brethren, or to fall themselves by their hands.

He has excited domestic insurrection among us, and has endeavored to bring on the inhabitants of our frontiers the merciless Indian savages, whose known rule of warfare is an undistinguished destruction of all ages, sexes, and conditions.

In every stage of these oppressions we have petitioned for redress in the most humble terms; our repeated petitions have been answered only by repeated injury. A prince, whose character is thus marked by every act which may define a tyrant, is unfit to be the ruler of a free people.

Nor have we been wanting in our attentions to our British brethren. We have warned them, from time to time, of attempts by their legislature to extend an unwarrantable jurisdiction over us. We have reminded them of the circumstances of our emigration and settlement here. We have appealed to their native justice and magnanimity; and we have conjured them, by the ties of our common kindred, to disavow these usurpations, which would inevitably interrupt our connections and correspondence. They, too, have been deaf to the voice of justice and of consanguinity. We must, therefore, acquiesce in the necessity which denounces our separation, and hold them, as we hold the rest of mankind, enemies in war, in peace friends.

We, therefore, the representatives of the United States of America, in General Congress assembled, appealing to the Supreme Judge of the world for the rectitude of our intentions, do, in the name and by the authority of the good people of these colonies, solemnly publish and declare, that these United Colonies are, and of right ought to be, FREE AND INDEPENDENT STATES; that they are absolved from all allegiance to the British crown, and that all political connection between them and the state of Great Britain is, and ought to be, totally dissolved; and that, as free and independent states, they have full power to levy war, conclude peace, contract alliances, establish commerce, and do all other acts and things which independent states may of right do. And for the support of this declaration, with a firm reliance on the protection of Divine Providence, we mutually pledge to each other our lives, our fortunes, and our sacred honor.

JOHN HANCOCK
and fifty-five others

Articles of Confederation

Whereas the Delegates of the United States of America in Congress assembled did on the fifteenth day of November in the Year of our Lord One Thousand Seven Hundred and Seventy seven, and in the Second Year of the Independence of America agree to certain articles of Confederation and perpetual Union between the States of Newhampshire, Massachusetts-bay, Rhodeisland and Providence Plantations, Connecticut, New-York, New-Jersey, Pennsylvania, Delaware, Maryland, Virginia, North-Carolina, South-Carolina and Georgia in the Words following, viz. "Articles of Confederation and perpetual Union between the states of Newhampshire, Massachusetts-bay, Rhodeisland and Providence Plantations, Connecticut, New-York, New-Jersey, Pennsylvania, Delaware, Maryland, Virginia, North-Carolina, South-Carolina and Georgia.

Article I The Stile of this confederacy shall be "The United States of America."

Article II Each state retains its sovereignty, freedom and independence, and every Power, Jurisdiction and right, which is not by this confederation expressly delegated to the United States, in Congress assembled.

Article III The said states hereby severally enter into a firm league of friendship with each other, for their common defence, the security of their Liberties, and their mutual and general welfare, binding themselves to assist each other, against all force offered to, or attacks made upon them, or any of them, on account of religion, sovereignty, trade, or any other pretence whatever.

Article IV The better to secure and perpetuate mutual friendship and intercourse among the people of the different states in this union, the free inhabitants of each of these states, paupers, vagabonds and fugitives from Justice excepted, shall be entitled to all privileges and immunities of free citizens in the several states; and the people of each state shall have free ingress and regress to and from any other state, and shall enjoy therein all the privileges of trade and commerce, subject to the same duties, impositions and restrictions as the inhabitants thereof respectively, provided that such restriction shall not extend so far as to prevent the removal of property imported into any state, to any other state of which the Owner is an inhabitant; provided also that no imposition, duties or restriction shall be laid by any state, on the property of the united states, or either of them.

If any Person guilty of, or charged with treason, felony, or other high misdemeanor in any state, shall flee from Justice, and be found in any of the united states, he shall upon demand of the Governor or executive power, of the state from which he fled, be delivered up and removed to the state having jurisdiction of his offence.

Full faith and credit shall be given in each of these states to the records, acts and judicial proceedings of the courts and magistrates of every other state.

Article V For the more convenient management of the general interests of the united states, delegates shall be annually appointed in such manner as the legislature of each state shall direct, to meet in Congress on the first Monday in November, in every year, with a power reserved to each state, to recall its delegates, or any of them, at any time within the year, and to send others in their stead, for the remainder of the Year.

No state shall be represented in Congress by less than two, nor by more than seven Members; and no person shall be capable of being a delegate for more than three years in any term of six years; nor shall any person, being a delegate, be capable of holding any office under the united states, for which he, or another for his benefit receives any salary, fees or emolument of any kind.

Each state shall maintain its own delegates in a meeting of the states, and while they act as members of the committee of the states.

In determining questions in the united states, in Congress assembled, each state shall have one vote.

Freedom of speech and debate in Congress shall not be impeached or questioned in any Court, or place out of Congress, and the members of congress shall be protected in their persons from arrests and imprisonments, during the time of their going to and from, and attendance on congress, except for treason, felony, or breach of the peace.

Article VI No state without the Consent of the united states in congress assembled, shall send any embassy to, or receive any embassy from, or enter into any conference, agreement, or alliance or treaty with any King, prince or state; nor shall any person holding any office of profit or trust under the united states, or any of them, accept of any present, emolument, office or title of any kind whatever from any king, prince or foreign state; nor shall the united states in congress assembled, or any of them, grant any title of nobility.

No two or more states shall enter into any treaty, confederation or alliance whatever between them, without the consent of the united states in congress assembled, specifying accurately the purposes for which the same is to be entered into, and how long it shall continue.

No state shall lay any imposts or duties, which may interfere with any stipulations in treaties, entered into by the united states in congress assembled, with any king, prince or state, in pursuance of any treaties already proposed by congress, to the courts of France and Spain.

No vessels of war shall be kept up in time of peace by any state, except such number only, as shall be deemed necessary by the united states in congress assembled, for the defence of such state, or its trade; nor shall any body of forces be kept up by any state, in time of peace, except such number only, as in the judgment of the united states, in congress assembled, shall be deemed requisite to garrison the forts necessary for the defence of such state; but every state shall always keep up a well regulated and disciplined militia, sufficiently armed and accoutred, and shall provide and constantly have ready for use, in public stores, a due number of field pieces and tents, and a proper quantity of arms, ammunition and camp equipage.

No state shall engage in any war without the consent of the united states in congress assembled, unless such state be actually invaded by enemies, or shall have received certain advice of a resolution being formed by some nation of Indians to invade such state, and the danger is so imminent as not to admit of a delay, till the united states in congress assembled can be consulted: nor shall any state grant commissions to any ships or vessels of war, nor letters of marque or reprisal, except it be after a declaration of war by the united states in congress assembled, and then only against the kingdom or state and the subjects thereof, against which war has been so declared, and under such regulations as shall be established by the united states in congress assembled, unless such state be infested by pirates, in which case vessels of war may be fitted out for that occasion, and kept so long as the danger shall continue, or until the united states in congress assembled shall determine otherwise.

Article VII When land-forces are raised by any state for the common defence, all officers of or under the rank of colonel, shall be appointed by the legislature of each state respectively by whom such forces shall be raised, or in such manner as such state shall direct, and all vacancies shall be filled up by the state which first made the appointment.

Article VIII All charges of war, and all other expences that shall be incurred for the common defence or general welfare, and allowed by the united states in congress assembled, shall be defrayed out of a common treasury, which shall be supplied by the several states, in proportion to the value of all land within each state, granted to or surveyed for any Person, as such land and the buildings and improvements thereon shall be estimated according to such mode as the united states in congress assembled, shall from time to time direct and appoint. The taxes for paying that proportion shall be laid and levied by the authority and direction of the legislatures of the several states within the time agreed upon by the united states in congress assembled.

Article IX The united states in congress assembled, shall have the sole and exclusive right and power of determining on peace and war, except in the cases mentioned in the sixth article—of sending and receiving ambassadors—entering into treaties and alliances, provided that no treaty of commerce shall be made whereby the legislative power of the respective states shall be restrained from imposing such imposts and duties on foreigners, as their own people are subjected to, or from prohibiting the exportation or importation of any species of goods or commodities whatsoever—of establishing rules for deciding in all cases, what captures on land or water shall be legal, and in what manner prizes taken by land or naval forces in the service of the united states shall be divided or appropriated.—of granting letters of marque and reprisal in times of peace—appointing courts for the trial of piracies and felonies committed on the high seas and establishing courts for receiving and determining finally appeals in all cases of captures, provided that no member of congress shall be appointed a judge of any of the said courts.

The united states in congress assembled shall also be the last resort on appeal in all disputes and differences now subsisting or that hereafter may arise between two or more states concerning boundary, jurisdiction or any other cause whatever; which authority shall always be exercised in the manner following. Whenever the legislative or executive authority or lawful agent of any state in controversy with another shall present a petition to congress, stating the matter in question and praying for a hearing, notice thereof shall be given by order of congress to the legislative or executive authority of the other state in controversy, and a day assigned for the appearance of the parties by their lawful agents, who shall then be directed to appoint by joint consent, commissioners or judges to constitute a court for hearing and determining the matter in question: but if they cannot agree, congress shall name three persons out of each of the united states, and from the list of such persons each party shall alternately strike out one, the petitioners beginning, until the number shall be reduced to thirteen; and from that number not less than seven, nor more than nine names as congress shall direct, shall in the presence of congress be drawn out by lot, and the persons whose names shall be so drawn or any five of them, shall be commissioners or judges, to hear and finally determine the controversy, so always as a major part of the judges who shall hear the cause shall agree in the determination: and if either party shall neglect to attend at the day appointed, without shewing reasons, which congress shall judge sufficient, or being present shall refuse to strike, the congress shall proceed to nominate three persons out of each state, and the secretary of congress shall strike in behalf of such party absent or refusing; and the judgment and sentence of the court to be appointed, in the manner before prescribed, shall be final and conclusive; and if any of the parties shall refuse to submit to the authority of such court, or to appear to defend their claim or cause, the court shall nevertheless proceed to pronounce sentence, or judgment, which shall in like manner be final and decisive, the judgment or sentence and other proceedings being in either case transmitted to congress, and lodged among the acts of congress for the security of the parties concerned: provided that every commissioner, before he sits in judgment, shall take an oath to be administered by one of the judges of the supreme or superior court of the state, where the cause shall be tried, "well and truly to hear and determine the matter in question, according to the best of his judgment, without favour, affection or hope of reward:" provided also that no state shall be deprived of territory for the benefit of the united states.

All controversies concerning the private right of soil claimed under different grants of two or more states, whose jurisdictions as they may respect such lands, and the states which passed such grants are adjusted, the said grants or either of them being at the same time claimed to have originated antecedent to such settlement of jurisdiction, shall on the petition of either party to the congress of the united states, be finally determined as near as may be in the same manner as is before prescribed for deciding disputes respecting territorial jurisdiction between different states.

The united states in congress assembled shall also have the sole and exclusive right and power of regulating the alloy and value of coin struck by their own authority, or by that of the respective states—fixing the standard of weights and measures throughout the united states.—regulating the trade and managing all affairs with the Indians, not members of any of the states, provided that the legislative right of any state within its own limits be not infringed or violated—establishing and regulating post-offices from one state to another, throughout all the united states, and exacting such postage on the papers passing thro' the same as may be requisite to defray the expences of the said office—appointing all officers of the land forces, in the service of the united states, excepting regimental officers.—appointing all the officers of the naval forces, and commissioning all officers whatever in the service of the united states—making rules for the government and regulation of the said land and naval forces, and directing their operations.

The united states in congress assembled shall have authority to appoint a committee, to sit in the recess of congress, to be denominated "A Committee of the States," and to consist of one delegate from each state; and to appoint such other committees and civil officers as may be necessary for managing the general affairs of the united states under their direction—to appoint one of their number to preside, provided that no person be allowed to serve in the office of president more than one year in any term of three years; to ascertain the necessary sums of Money to be raised for the service of the united states, and to appropriate and apply the same for defraying the public expences—to borrow money, or emit bills on the credit of the united states, transmitting every half year to the respective states an account of the sums of money so borrowed or emitted,—to build and equip a navy—to agree upon the number of land forces, and to make requisitions from each state for its quota, in proportion to the number of white inhabitants in such state; which requisition shall be binding, and thereupon the legislature of each state shall appoint the regimental officers, raise the men and cloath, arm and equip them in a soldier like manner, at the expence of the united states, and the officers and men so cloathed, armed and equipped shall march to the place appointed, and within the time agreed on by the united states in congress assembled: But if the united states in congress assembled shall, on consideration of circumstances judge proper that any state should not raise men, or should raise a smaller number than its quota, and that any other state should raise a greater number of men than the quota thereof, such extra number shall be raised, officered, cloathed, armed and equipped in the same manner as the quota of such state, unless the legislature of such state shall judge that such extra number cannot be safely spared out of the same, in which case they shall raise, officer, cloath, arm and equip as many of such extra number as they judge can be safely spared. And the officers and men so cloathed, armed and equipped, shall march to the place appointed, and within the time agreed on by the united states in congress assembled.

The united states in congress assembled shall never engage in a war, nor grant letters of marque and reprisal in time of peace, nor enter into any treaties or alliances, nor coin money, nor regulate the value thereof, nor ascertain the sums and expences necessary for the defence and welfare of the united states, or any of them, nor emit bills, nor borrow money on the credit of the united states, nor appropriate money, nor agree upon the number of vessels of war, to be built or purchased, or the number of land or sea forces to be raised, nor appoint a commander in chief of the army or navy, unless nine states assent to the same: nor shall a question on any other point, except for adjourning from day to day be determined, unless by the votes of a majority of the united states in congress assembled.

The congress of the united states shall have power to adjourn to any time within the year, and to any place within the united states, so that no period of adjournment be for a longer duration than the space of six Months, and shall publish the Journal of their proceedings monthly, except such parts thereof relating to treaties, alliances or military operations as in their judgment require secresy; and the yeas and nays of the delegates of each state on any question shall be entered on the Journal, when it is desired by any delegate; and the delegates of a state, or any of them, at his or their request shall be furnished with a transcript of the said Journal, except such parts as are above excepted, to lay before the legislatures of the several states.

Article X The committee of the states, or any nine of them, shall be authorised to execute, in the recess of congress, such of the powers of congress as the united states in congress assembled, by the consent of nine states, shall from time to time think expedient to vest them with; provided that no power be delegated to the said committee, for the exercise of which, by the articles of confederation, the voice of nine states in the congress of the united states assembled is requisite.

Article XI Canada acceding to this confederation, and joining in the measures of the united states, shall be admitted into, and entitled to all the advantages of this union: but no other colony shall be admitted into the same, unless such admission be agreed to by nine states.

Article XII All bills of credit emitted, monies borrowed and debts contracted by, or under the authority of congress, before the assembling of the united states, in pursuance of the present confederation, shall be deemed and considered as a charge against the united states, for payment and satisfaction whereof the said united states, and the public faith are hereby solemnly pledged.

Article XIII Every state shall abide by the determinations of the united states in congress assembled, on all questions which by this confederation are submitted to them. And the Articles of this confederation shall be inviolably observed by every state, and the union shall be perpetual; nor shall any alteration at any time hereafter be made in any of them; unless such alteration be agreed to in a congress of the united states, and be afterwards confirmed by the legislatures of every state.

AND WHEREAS it hath pleased the Great Governor of the World to incline the hearts of the legislatures we respectively represent in congress, to approve of, and to authorize us to ratify the said articles of confederation and perpetual union. Know Ye that we the undersigned delegates, by virtue of the power and authority to us given for that purpose, do by these presents, in the name and in behalf of our respective constituents, fully and entirely ratify and confirm each and every of the said articles of confederation and perpetual union, and all and singular the matters and things therein contained: And we do further solemnly plight and engage the faith of our respective constitutents, that they shall abide by the determinations of the united states in congress assembled, on all questions, which by the said confederation are submitted to them. And that the articles thereof shall be inviolably observed by the states we respectively represent, and that the union shall be perpetual. In Witness whereof we have hereunto set our hands in Congress. Done at Philadelphia in the state of Pennsylvania the ninth Day of July in the Year of our Lord one Thousand seven Hundred and Seventy-eight, and in the third year of the independence of America.

Constitution of the United States of America and Amendments*

Preamble

We the people of the United States, in order to form a more perfect union, establish justice, insure domestic tranquillity, provide for the common defense, promote the general welfare, and secure the blessings of liberty to ourselves and our posterity, do ordain and establish this Constitution for the United States of America.

Article I

Section 1 All legislative powers herein granted shall be vested in a Congress of the United States, which shall consist of a Senate and a House of Representatives.

Section 2 The House of Representatives shall be composed of members chosen every second year by the people of the several States, and the electors in each State shall have the qualifications requisite for electors of the most numerous branch of the State Legislature.

No person shall be a Representative who shall not have attained to the age of twenty-five years, and been seven years a citizen of the United States, and who shall not, when elected, be an inhabitant of that State in which he shall be chosen.

Representatives and direct taxes shall be apportioned among the several States which may be included within this Union, according to their respective numbers, *which shall be determined by adding to the whole number of free persons, including those bound to service for a term of years and excluding Indians not taxed, three-fifths of all other persons.* The actual enumeration shall be made within three years after the first meeting of the Congress of the United States, and within every subsequent term of ten years, in such manner as they shall by law direct. The number of Representatives shall not exceed one for every thirty thousand, but each State shall have at least one Representative; *and until such enumeration shall be made, the State of New Hampshire shall be entitled to choose three, Massachusetts eight, Rhode Island and Providence Plantations one, Connecticut five, New York six, New Jersey four, Pennsylvania eight, Delaware one, Maryland six, Virginia ten, North Carolina five, South Carolina five, and Georgia three.*

When vacancies happen in the representation from any State, the Executive authority thereof shall issue writs of election to fill such vacancies.

The House of Representatives shall choose their Speaker and other officers; and shall have the sole power of impeachment.

Section 3 The Senate of the United States shall be composed of two Senators from each State, *chosen by the legislature thereof,* for six years; and each Senator shall have one vote.

Immediately after they shall be assembled in consequence of the first election, they shall be divided as equally as may be into three classes. The seats of the Senators of the first class shall be vacated at the expiration of the second year, of the second class at the expiration of the fourth year, and of the third class at the expiration of the sixth year, so that one-third may be chosen every second year; *and if vacancies happen by resignation or otherwise, during the recess of the legislature of any State, the Executive thereof may make temporary appointments until the next meeting of the legislature, which shall then fill such vacancies.*

No person shall be a Senator who shall not have attained to the age of thirty years, and been nine years a citizen of the United States, and who shall not, when elected, be an inhabitant of that State for which he shall be chosen.

The Vice-President of the United States shall be President of the Senate, but shall have no vote, unless they be equally divided.

The Senate shall choose their other officers, and also a President *pro tempore,* in the absence of the Vice-President, or when he shall exercise the office of President of the United States.

The Senate shall have the sole power to try all impeachments. When sitting for that purpose, they shall be on oath or affirmation. When the President of the United States is tried, the Chief Justice shall preside: and no person shall be convicted with-out the concurrence of two thirds of the members present.

Judgment in cases of impeachment shall not extend further than to removal from the office, and disqualification to hold and enjoy any office of honor, trust or profit under the United States: but the party convicted shall nevertheless be liable and subject to indictment, trial, judgment and punishment, according to law.

Section 4 The times, places and manner of holding elections for Senators and Representatives shall be prescribed in each State by the legislature thereof; but the Congress may at any time by law make or alter such regulations, except as to the places of choosing Senators.

The Congress shall assemble at least once in every year, and such meeting *shall be on the first Monday in December, unless they shall by law appoint a different day.*

Section 5 Each house shall be the judge of the elections, returns and qualifications of its own members, and a majority of each shall constitute a quorum to do business; but a smaller number may adjourn from day to day, and may be authorized to compel the attendance of absent members, in such manner, and under such penalties, as each house may provide.

Each house may determine the rules of its proceedings, punish its members for disorderly behavior, and with the concurrence of two-thirds, expel a member. Each house shall keep a journal of its proceedings, and

---

* Passages no longer in effect are printed in italic type.

from time to time publish the same, excepting such parts as may in their judgment require secrecy; and the yeas and nays of the members of either house on any question shall, at the desire of one-fifth of those present, be entered on the journal.

Neither house, during the session of Congress, shall, without the consent of the other, adjourn for more than three days, nor to any other place than that in which the two houses shall be sitting.

Section 6 The Senators and Representatives shall receive a compensation for their services, to be ascertained by law and paid out of the treasury of the United States. They shall in all cases except treason, felony and breach of the peace, be privileged from arrest during their attendance at the session of their respective houses, and in going to and returning from the same; and for any speech or debate in either house, they shall not be questioned in any other place.

No Senator or Representative shall, during the time for which he was elected, be appointed to any civil office under the authority of the United States, which shall have been created, or the emoluments whereof shall have been increased, during such time; and no person holding any office under the United States shall be a member of either house during his continuance in office.

Section 7 All bills for raising revenue shall originate in the House of Representatives; but the Senate may propose or concur with amendments as on other bills.

Every bill which shall have passed the House of Representatives and the Senate, shall, before it become a law, be presented to the President of the United States; if he approve he shall sign it, but if not he shall return it with objections to that house in which it originated, who shall enter the objections at large on their journal, and proceed to reconsider it. If after such reconsideration two-thirds of that house shall agree to pass the bill, it shall be sent, together with the objections, to the other house, by which it shall likewise be reconsidered, and, if approved by two-thirds of that house, it shall become a law. But in all such cases the votes of both houses shall be determined by yeas and nays, and the names of the persons voting for and against the bill shall be entered on the journal of each house respectively. If any bill shall not be returned by the President within ten days (Sundays excepted) after it shall have been presented to him, the same shall be a law, in like manner as if he had signed it, unless the Congress by their adjournment prevent its return, in which case it shall not be a law.

Every order, resolution, or vote to which the concurrence of the Senate and House of Representatives may be necessary (except on a question of adjournment) shall be presented to the President of the United States; and before the same shall take effect, shall be approved by him, or being disapproved by him, shall be repassed by two-thirds of the Senate and House of Representatives, according to the rules and limitations prescribed in the case of a bill.

Section 8 The Congress shall have power

To lay and collect taxes, duties, imposts, and excises, to pay the debts and provide for the common defense and general welfare of the United States; but all duties, imposts and excises shall be uniform throughout the United States;

To borrow money on the credit of the United States;

To regulate commerce with foreign nations, and among the several States, and with the Indian tribes;

To establish an uniform rule of naturalization, and uniform laws on the subject of bankruptcies throughout the United States;

To coin money, regulate the value thereof, and of foreign coin, and fix the standard of weights and measures;

To provide for the punishment of counterfeiting the securities and current coin of the United States;

To establish post offices and post roads;

To promote the progress of science and useful arts by securing for limited times to authors and inventors the exclusive right to their respective writings and discoveries;

To constitute tribunals inferior to the Supreme Court;

To define and punish piracies and felonies committed on the high seas and offenses against the law of nations;

To declare war, grant letters of marque and reprisal, and make rules concerning captures on land and water;

To raise and support armies, but no appropriation of money to that use shall be for a longer term than two years;

To provide and maintain a navy;

To make rules for the government and regulation of the land and naval forces;

To provide for calling forth the militia to execute the laws of the Union, suppress insurrections, and repel invasions;

To provide for organizing, arming, and disciplining the militia, and for governing such part of them as may be employed in the service of the United States, reserving to the States respectively the appointment of the officers, and the authority of training the militia according to the discipline prescribed by Congress;

To exercise exclusive legislation in all cases whatsoever, over such district (not exceeding ten miles square) as may, by cession of particular States, and the acceptance of Congress, become the seat of government of the United States, and to exercise like authority over all places purchased by the consent of the legislature of the State, in which the same shall be, for erection of forts, magazines, arsenals, dockyards, and other needful buildings;—and

To make all laws which shall be necessary and proper for carrying into execution the foregoing powers, and all other powers vested by this Constitution in the government of the United States, or in any department or officer there of.

Section 9 The migration or importation of such persons as any of the States now existing shall think proper to admit shall not be prohibited by the Congress prior to the year 1808; but a tax or duty may be imposed on such importation, not exceeding $10 for each person.

The privilege of the writ of habeas corpus shall not be suspended, unless when in cases of rebellion or invasion the public safety may require it.

No bill of attainder or ex post facto law shall be passed.

No capitation, or other direct, tax shall be laid, unless in proportion to the census or enumeration herein before directed to be taken.

No tax or duty shall be laid on articles exported from any State.

No preference shall be given by any regulation of commerce or revenue to the ports of one State over those of another; nor shall vessels bound to, or from, one State, be obliged to enter, clear, or pay duties in another.

No money shall be drawn from the treasury, but in consequence of appropriations made by law; and a regular statement and account of the receipts and expenditures of all public money shall be published from time to time.

No title of nobility shall be granted by the United States: and no person holding any office of profit or trust under them, shall, without the consent of the Congress, accept of any present, emolument, office, or title, of any kind whatever, from any king, prince, or foreign state.

Section 10 No State shall enter into any treaty, alliance, or confederation; grant letters of marque and reprisal; coin money; emit bills of credit; make anything but gold and silver coin a tender in payment of debts; pass any bill of attainder, ex post facto law, or law impairing the obligation of contracts, or grant any title of nobility.

No State shall, without the consent of Congress, lay any imposts or duties on imports or exports, except what may be absolutely necessary for executing its inspection laws: and the net produce of all duties and imposts, laid by any State on imports or exports, shall be for the use of the treasury of the United States; and all such laws shall be subject to the revision and control of the Congress.

No State shall, without the consent of Congress, lay any duty of tonnage, keep troops or ships of war in time of peace, enter into any agreement or compact with another State, or with a foreign power, or engage in war, unless actually invaded, or in such imminent danger as will not admit of delay.

Article II

Section 1 The executive power shall be vested in a President of the United States of America. He shall hold his office during the term of four years, and, together with the Vice-President, chosen for the same term, be elected as follows:

Each State shall appoint, in such manner as the legislature thereof may direct, a number of electors, equal to the whole number of Senators and Representatives to which the State may be entitled in the Congress; but no Senator or Representative, or person holding an office of trust or profit under the United States, shall be appointed an elector.

The electors shall meet in their respective States, and vote by ballot for two persons, of whom one at least shall not be an inhabitant of the same State with themselves. And they shall make a list of all the persons voted for, and of the number of votes for each; which list they shall sign and certify, and transmit sealed to the seat of government of the United States, directed to the President of the Senate. The President of the Senate shall, in the presence of the Senate and House of Representatives, open all the certificates, and the votes shall then be counted. The person having the greatest number of votes shall be the President, if such number be a majority of the whole number of electors appointed; and if there be more than one who have such majority, and have an equal number of votes, then the House of Representatives shall immediately choose by ballot one of them for President; and if no person have a majority, then from the five highest on the list said house shall in like manner choose the President. But in choosing the President the votes shall be taken by States, the representation from each State having one vote; a quorum for this purpose shall consist of a member or members from two-thirds of the States, and a majority of all the States shall be necessary to a choice. In every case, after the choice of the President, the person having the greatest number of votes of the electors shall be the Vice-President. But if there should remain two or more who have equal votes, the Senate shall choose from them by ballot the Vice-President.

The Congress may determine the time of choosing the electors and the day on which they shall give their votes; which day shall be the same throughout the United States.

No person except a natural-born citizen, *or a citizen of the United States at the time of the adoption of this Constitution,* shall be eligible to the office of President; neither shall any person be eligible to that office who shall not have attained to the age of thirty-five years, and been fourteen years a resident within the United States.

In cases of the removal of the President from office or of his death, resignation, or inability to discharge the powers and duties of the said office, the same shall devolve on the Vice-President, and the Congress may by law provide for the case of removal, death, resignation, or inability, both of the President and Vice-President, declaring what officer shall then act as President, and such officer shall act accordingly, until the disability be removed, or a President shall be elected.

The President shall, at stated times, receive for his services a compensation, which shall neither be increased nor diminished during the period for which he shall have been elected, and he shall not receive within that period any other emolument from the United States, or any of them.

Before he enter on the execution of his office, he shall take the following oath or affirmation:—"I do solemnly swear (or affirm) that I will faithfully execute the office of the President of the United States, and will to the best of my ability preserve, protect and defend the Constitution of the United States."

Section 2 The President shall be commander in chief of the army and navy of the United States, and of the militia of the several States, when called into the actual service of the United States; he may require the opinion, in writing, of the principal officer in each of the executive departments, upon any subject relating to the duties of their respective offices, and he shall have power to grant reprieves and pardons for offenses against the United States, except in cases of impeachment.

He shall have power, by and with the advice and consent of the Senate, to make treaties, provided two-thirds of the Senators present concur; and he shall nominate, and by and with the advice and consent of the Senate, shall appoint ambassadors, other public ministers and consuls, judges of the Supreme Court, and all other officers of the United States, whose appointments are not herein otherwise provided for, and which shall be established by law: but Congress may by law vest the appointment of such inferior officers, as they think proper, in the President alone, in the courts of law, or in the heads of departments.

The President shall have power to fill up all vacancies that may happen during the recess of the Senate, by granting commissions which shall expire at the end of their next session.

Section 3 He shall from time to time give to the Congress information of the state of the Union, and recommend to their consideration such measures as he shall judge necessary and expedient; he may, on extraordinary occasions, convene both houses, or either of them, and in case of disagreement between them, with respect to the time of adjournment, he may adjourn them to such time as he shall think proper; he shall receive ambassadors and other public ministers; he shall take care that the laws be faithfully executed, and shall commission all the officers of the United States.

Section 4 The President, Vice-President and all civil officers of the United States shall be removed from office on impeachment for, and on conviction of, treason, bribery, or other high crimes and misdemeanors.

Article III

Section 1 The judicial power of the United States shall be vested in one Supreme Court, and in such inferior courts as the Congress may from time to time ordain and establish. The judges, both of the Supreme and inferior courts, shall hold their offices during good behavior, and shall, at stated times, receive for their services a compensation which shall not be diminished during their continuance in office.

Section 2 The judicial power shall extend to all cases, in law and equity, arising under this Constitution, the laws of the United States, and treaties made, or which shall be made, under their authority;—to all cases affecting ambassadors, other public ministers and consuls;—to

all cases of admiralty and maritime jurisdiction;—to controversies to which the United States shall be a party;—to controversies between two or more States;—*between a State and citizens of another State;*—between citizens of different States;—between citizens of the same State claiming lands under grants of different States, and between a State, or the citizens thereof, and foreign states, citizens or subjects.

In all cases affecting ambassadors, other public ministers and consuls, and those in which a State shall be party, the Supreme Court shall have original jurisdiction. In all the other cases before mentioned, the Supreme Court shall have appellate jurisdiction, both as to law and fact, with such exceptions, and under such regulations, as the Congress shall make.

The trial of all crimes, except in cases of impeachment, shall be by jury; and such trial shall be held in the State where said crimes shall have been committed; but when not committed within any State, the trial shall be at such place or places as the Congress may by law have directed.

Section 3 Treason against the United States shall consist only in levying war against them, or in adhering to their enemies, giving them aid and comfort. No person shall be convicted of treason unless on the testimony of two witnesses to the same overt act, or on confession in open court.

The Congress shall have power to declare the punishment of treason, but no attainder of treason shall work corruption of blood, or forfeiture except during the life of the person attainted.

Article IV

Section 1 Full faith and credit shall be given in each State to the public acts, records, and judicial proceedings of every other State. And the Congress may by general laws prescribe the manner in which such acts, records, and proceedings shall be proved, and the effect thereof.

Section 2 The citizens of each State shall be entitled to all privileges and immunities of citizens in the several States.

A person charged in any State with treason, felony, or other crime, who shall flee from justice, and be found in another State, shall on demand of the executive authority of the State from which he fled, be delivered up, to be removed to the State having jurisdiction of the crime.

No person held to service or labor in one State, under the laws thereof, escaping into another, shall, in consequence of any law or regulation therein, be discharged from such service or labor, but shall be delivered up on claim of the party to whom such service or labor may be due.

Section 3 New States may be admitted by the Congress into this Union; but no new State shall be formed or erected within the jurisdiction of any other State; nor any State be formed by the junction of two or more States, or parts of States, without the consent of the legislatures of the States concerned as well as of the Congress.

The Congress shall have power to dispose of and make all needful rules and regulations respecting the territory or other property belonging to the United States; and nothing in this Constitution shall be so construed as to prejudice any claims of the United States, or of any particular State.

Section 4 The United States shall guarantee to every State in this Union a republican form of government, and shall protect each of them against invasion; and on application of the legislature, or of the executive (when the legislature cannot be convened), against domestic violence.

Article V

The Congress, whenever two-thirds of both houses shall deem it necessary, shall propose amendments to this Constitution, or, on the application of the legislatures of two-thirds of the several States, shall call a convention for proposing amendments, which, in either case, shall be valid to all intents and purposes, as part of this Constitution, when ratified by the legislatures of three fourths of the several States, or by conventions in three-fourths thereof, as the one or the other mode of ratification may be proposed by the Congress; provided *that no amendments which may be made prior to the year one thousand eight hundred and eight shall in any manner affect the first and fourth clauses in the ninth section of the first article;* and that no State, without its consent, shall be deprived of its equal suffrage in the Senate.

Article VI

All debts contracted and engagements entered into, before the adoption of this Constitution, shall be as valid against the United States under this Constitution, as under the Confederation.

This Constitution, and the laws of the United States which shall be made in pursuance thereof; and all treaties made, or which shall be made, under the authority of the United States, shall be the supreme law of the land; and the judges in every State shall be bound thereby, anything in the Constitution or laws of any State to the contrary notwithstanding.

The Senators and Representatives before mentioned, and the members of the several State legislatures, and all executive and judicial officers, both of the United States and of the several States, shall be bound by oath or affirmation to support this Constitution; but no religious test shall ever be required as a qualification to any office or public trust under the United States.

Article VII

The ratification of the conventions of nine States shall be sufficient for the establishment of this Constitution between the States so ratifying the same.

Done in Convention by the unanimous consent of the States present, the seventeenth day of September in the year of our Lord one thousand seven hundred and eighty-seven and of the Independence of the United States of America the twelfth. In witness whereof we have hereunto subscribed our names.

GEORGE WASHINGTON
and thirty-seven others

Amendments to the Constitution*

Amendment I

Congress shall make no law respecting an establishment of religion, or prohibiting the free exercise thereof; or abridging the freedom of speech, or of the press; or the right of the people peaceably to assemble, and to petition the government for a redress of grievances.

Amendment II

A well-regulated militia being necessary to the security of a free State, the right of the people to keep and bear arms shall not be infringed.

Amendment III

No soldier shall, in time of peace, be quartered in any house without the consent of the owner, nor in time of war, but in a manner to be prescribed by law.

Amendment IV

The right of the people to be secure in their persons, houses, papers, and effects, against unreasonable searches and seizures, shall not be violated, and no warrants shall issue but upon probable cause, supported by oath or affirmation, and particularly describing the place to be searched, and the persons or things to be seized.

Amendment V

No person shall be held to answer for a capital, or otherwise infamous crime, unless on a presentment or indictment of a grand jury, except in cases arising in the land or naval forces, or in the militia, when in actual service in time of war or public danger; nor shall any person be subject for the same offense to be twice put in jeopardy of life or limb; nor shall be compelled in any criminal case to be a witness against himself, nor be deprived of life, liberty, or property, without due process of law; nor shall private property be taken for public use without just compensation.

---

* The first 10 amendments (the Bill of Rights) were adopted in 1791.

Amendment VI

In all criminal prosecutions, the accused shall enjoy the right to a speedy and public trial, by an impartial jury of the State and district wherein the crime shall have been committed, which district shall have been previously ascertained by law, and to be informed of the nature and cause of the accusation; to be confronted with the witnesses against him; to have compulsory process for obtaining witnesses in his favor, and to have the assistance of counsel for his defense.

Amendment VII

In suits at common law, where the value in controversy shall exceed twenty dollars, the right of trial by jury shall be preserved, and no fact tried by a jury shall be otherwise reexamined in any court of the United States, than according to the rules of the common law.

Amendment VIII

Excessive bail shall not be required, nor excessive fines imposed, nor cruel and unusual punishments inflicted.

Amendment IX

The enumeration in the Constitution, of certain rights, shall not be construed to deny or disparage others retained by the people.

Amendment X

The powers not delegated to the United States by the Constitution, nor prohibited by it to the States, are reserved to the States respectively, or to the people.

Amendment XI

[Adopted 1798]

The judicial power of the United States shall not be construed to extend to any suit in law or equity, commenced or prosecuted against one of the United States by citizens of another State, or by citizens or subjects of any foreign state.

Amendment XII

[Adopted 1804]

The electors shall meet in their respective States, and vote by ballot for President and Vice-President, one of whom, at least, shall not be an inhabitant of the same State with themselves; they shall name in their ballots the person voted for as President, and in distinct ballots the person voted for as Vice-President, and they shall make distinct lists of all persons voted for as President, and of all persons voted for as Vice-President, and of the number of votes for each, which lists they shall sign and certify, and transmit sealed to the seat of government of the United States, directed to the President of the Senate;—the President of the Senate shall, in the presence of the Senate and House of Representatives, open all the certificates and the votes shall then be counted;—the person having the greatest number of votes for President shall be the President, if such number be a majority of the whole number of electors appointed; and if no person have such majority, then from the persons having the highest numbers not exceeding three on the list of those voted for as President, the House of Representatives shall choose immediately, by ballot, the President. But in choosing the President, the votes shall be taken by States, the representation from each State having one vote; a quorum for this purpose shall consist of a member or members from two-thirds of the States, and a majority of all the States shall be necessary to a choice. And if the House of Representatives shall not choose a President whenever the right of choice shall devolve upon them, before the fourth day of March next following, then the Vice-President shall act as President, as in the case of the death or other constitutional disability of the President.

The person having the greatest number of votes as Vice-President shall be the Vice-President, if such number be a majority of the whole number of electors appointed; and if no person have a majority, then from the two highest numbers on the list the Senate shall choose the Vice-President; a quorum for the purpose shall consist of two-thirds of the whole number of Senators, and a majority of the whole number shall be necessary to a choice. But no person constitutionally ineligible to the office of President shall be eligible to that of Vice-President of the United States.

Amendment XIII

[Adopted 1865]

Section 1 Neither slavery nor involuntary servitude, except as a punishment for crime whereof the party shall have been duly convicted, shall exist within the United States, or any place subject to their jurisdiction.

Section 2 Congress shall have power to enforce this article by appropriate legislation.

Amendment XIV

[Adopted 1868]

Section 1 All persons born or naturalized in the United States, and subject to the jurisdiction thereof, are citizens of the United States and of the State wherein they reside. No State shall make or enforce any law which shall abridge the privileges or immunities of citizens of the United States; nor shall any State deprive any person of life, liberty, or property, without due process of law; nor deny to any person within its jurisdiction the equal protection of the laws.

Section 2 Representatives shall be apportioned among the several States according to their respective numbers, counting the whole number of persons in each State, excluding Indians not taxed. But when the right to vote at any election for the choice of Electors for President and Vice-President of the United States, Representatives in Congress, the executive and judicial officers of a State, or the members of the legislature thereof, is denied to any of the male inhabitants of such State, being twenty-one years of age and citizens of the United States, or in any way abridged, except for participation in rebellion, or other crime, the basis of representation therein shall be reduced in the proportion which the number of such male citizens shall bear to the whole number of male citizens twenty-one years of age in such State.

Section 3 No person shall be a Senator or Representative in Congress, or Elector of President and Vice-President, or hold any office, civil or military, under the United States, or under any State, who, having previously taken an oath, as a member of Congress, or as an officer of the United States, or as a member of any State legislature, or as an executive or judicial officer of any State, to support the Constitution of the United States, shall have engaged in insurrection or rebellion against the same, or given aid or comfort to the enemies thereof. Congress may, by a vote of two-thirds of each house, remove such disability.

Section 4 The validity of the public debt of the United States, authorized by law, including debts incurred for payment of pensions and bounties for services in suppressing insurrection or rebellion, shall not be questioned. But neither the United States nor any State shall assume or pay any debt or obligation incurred in aid of insurrection or rebellion against the United States, or any claim for the loss or emancipation of any slave; but all such debts, obligations, and claims shall be held illegal and void.

Section 5 The Congress shall have power to enforce, by appropriate legislation, the provisions of this article.

Amendment XV

[Adopted 1870]

Section 1 The right of citizens of the United States to vote shall not be denied or abridged by the United States or by any State on account of race, color, or previous condition of servitude.

Section 2 The Congress shall have power to enforce this article by appropriate legislation.

Amendment XVI

[Adopted 1913]

The Congress shall have power to lay and collect taxes on incomes, from whatever source derived, without apportionment among the several States, and without regard to any census or enumeration.

Amendment XVII

[Adopted 1913]

Section 1 The Senate of the United States shall be composed of two Senators from each State, elected by the people thereof, for six years; and each Senator shall

have one vote. The electors in each State shall have the qualifications requisite for electors of [voters for] the most numerous branch of the State legislatures.

Section 2 When vacancies happen in the representation of any State in the Senate, the executive authority of such State shall issue writs of election to fill such vacancies: Provided, that the Legislature of any State may empower the executive thereof to make temporary appointments until the people fill the vacancies by election as the Legislature may direct.

Section 3 This amendment shall not be so construed as to affect the election or term of any Senator chosen before it becomes valid as part of the Constitution.

Amendment XVIII

[Adopted 1919; Repealed 1933]

Section 1 After one year from the ratification of this article the manufacture, sale, or transportation of intoxicating liquors within, the importation thereof into, or the exportation thereof from the United States and all territory subject to the jurisdiction thereof, for beverage purposes, is hereby prohibited.

Section 2 The Congress and the several States shall have concurrent power to enforce this article by appropriate legislation.

Section 3 This article shall be inoperative unless it shall have been ratified as an amendment to the Constitution by the legislatures of the several States, as provided by the Constitution, within seven years from the date of the submission thereof to the States by the Congress.

Amendment XIX

[Adopted 1920]

Section 1 The right of citizens of the United States to vote shall not be denied or abridged by the United States or by any State on account of sex.

Section 2 The Congress shall have power to enforce this article by appropriate legislation.

Amendment XX

[Adopted 1933]

Section 1 The terms of the President and Vice-President shall end at noon on the 20th day of January, and the terms of Senators and Representatives at noon on the 3rd day of January, of the years in which such terms would have ended if this article had not been ratified; and the terms of their successors shall then begin.

Section 2 The Congress shall assemble at least once in every year, and such meeting shall begin at noon on the 3d day of January, unless they shall by law appoint a different day.

Section 3 If, at the time fixed for the beginning of the term of the President, the President-elect shall have died, the Vice-President-elect shall become President. If a President shall not have been chosen before the time fixed for the beginning of his term, or if the President-elect shall have failed to qualify, then the Vice-President-elect shall act as President until a President shall have qualified; and the Congress may by law provide for the case wherein neither a President-elect nor a Vice-President-elect shall have qualified, declaring who shall then act as President, or the manner in which one who is to act shall be selected, and such persons shall act accordingly until a President or Vice-President shall have qualified.

Section 4 The Congress may by law provide for the case of the death of any of the persons from whom the House of Representatives may choose a President whenever the right of choice shall have devolved upon them, and for the case of the death of any of the persons from whom the Senate may choose a Vice-President whenever the right of choice shall have devolved upon them.

Section 5 Sections 1 and 2 shall take effect on the 15th day of October following the ratification of this article.

Section 6 This article shall be inoperative unless it shall have been ratified as an amendment to the Constitution by the Legislatures of three-fourths of the several States within seven years from the date of its submission.

Amendment XXI

[Adopted 1933]

Section 1 The eighteenth article of amendment to the Constitution of the United States is hereby repealed.

Section 2 The transportation or importation into any State, Territory, or Possession of the United States for delivery or use therein of intoxicating liquors, in violation of the laws thereof, is hereby prohibited.

Section 3 This article shall be inoperative unless it shall have been ratified as an amendment to the Constitution by conventions in the several States, as provided in the Constitution, within seven years from the date of submission thereof to the States by the Congress.

Amendment XXII

[Adopted 1951]

Section 1 No person shall be elected to the office of President more than twice, and no person who has held the office of President, or acted as President, for more than two years of a term to which some other person was elected President shall be elected to the office of President more than once. But this article shall not apply to any person holding the office of President when this article was proposed by the Congress, and shall not prevent any person who may be holding the office of President, or acting as President, during the term within which this article becomes operative from holding the office of President or acting as President during the remainder of such term.

Section 2 This article shall be inoperative unless it shall have been ratified as an amendment to the Constitution by the legislatures of three-fourths of the several States within seven years from the date of its submission to the States by the Congress.

Amendment XXIII

[Adopted 1961]

Section 1 The District constituting the seat of Government of the United States shall appoint in such manner as the Congress may direct:

A number of electors of President and Vice-President equal to the whole number of Senators and Representatives in Congress to which the District would be entitled if it were a State, but in no event more than the least populous State; they shall be in addition to those appointed by the States, but they shall be considered for the purposes of the election of President and Vice-President, to be electors appointed by a State; and they shall meet in the District and perform such duties as provided by the twelfth article of amendment.

Section 2 The Congress shall have the power to enforce this article by appropriate legislation.

Amendment XXIV

[Adopted 1964]

Section 1 The right of citizens of the United States to vote in any primary or other election for President or Vice-President, for electors for President or Vice-President, or for Senator or Representative in Congress, shall not be denied or abridged by the United States or any State by reason of failure to pay any poll tax or other tax.

Section 2 The Congress shall have the power to enforce this article by appropriate legislation.

Amendment XXV

[Adopted 1967]

Section 1 In case of the removal of the President from office or of his death or resignation, the Vice-President shall become President.

Section 2 Whenever there is a vacancy in the office of the Vice-President, the President shall nominate a Vice-President who shall take office upon confirmation by a majority vote of both Houses of Congress.

Section 3 Whenever the President transmits to the President pro tempore of the Senate and the Speaker of the House of Representatives his written declaration that he is unable to discharge the powers and duties of his office, and until he transmits to them a written declaration to the contrary, such powers and duties shall be discharged by the Vice-President as Acting President.

Section 4 Whenever the Vice-President and a majority of either the principal officers of the executive departments or of such other body as Congress may by law provide, transmit to the President pro tempore of the Senate and the Speaker of the House of Representatives their written declaration that the President is unable to discharge the powers and duties of his office, the Vice-President shall immediately assume the powers and duties of the office as Acting President.

Thereafter, when the President transmits to the President pro tempore of the Senate and the Speaker of the House of Representatives his written declaration that no inability exists, he shall resume the powers and duties of his office unless the Vice-President and a majority of either the principal officers of the executive department[s] or of such other body as Congress may by law provide, transmit within four days to the President pro tempore of the Senate and the Speaker of the House of Representatives their written declaration that the President is unable to discharge the powers and duties of his office. Thereupon Congress shall decide the issue, assembling within forty-eight hours for that purpose if not in session. If the Congress, within twenty-one days after receipt of the latter written declaration, or, if Congress is not in session, within twenty-one days after Congress is required to assemble, determines by two-thirds vote of both Houses that the President is unable to discharge the powers and duties of his office,

the Vice-President shall continue to discharge the same as Acting President; otherwise, the President shall resume the powers and duties of his office.

Amendment XXVI

[Adopted 1971]

Section 1 The right of citizens of the United States, who are eighteen years of age or older, to vote shall not be denied or abridged by the United States or by any State on account of age.

Section 2 The Congress shall have power to enforce this article by appropriate legislation.

Amendment XXVII

[Adopted 1992]

No law, varying the compensation for the services of the Senators and Representatives, shall take effect, until an election of Representatives shall have intervened.

Presidential Elections

Year	Number of States	Candidates	Parties	Popular Vote	% of Popular Vote	Electoral Vote	% Voter Participation[a]
1789	11	**George Washington**	No party			69	
		John Adams	designations			34	
		Other candidates				35	
1792	15	**George Washington**	No party			132	
		John Adams	designations			77	
		George Clinton				50	
		Other candidates				5	
1796	16	**John Adams**	Federalist			71	
		Thomas Jefferson	Democratic Republican			68	
		Thomas Pinckney	Federalist			59	
		Aaron Burr	Democratic Republican			30	
		Other candidates				48	
1800	16	**Thomas Jefferson**	Democratic Republican			73	
		Aaron Burr	Democratic Republican			73	
		John Adams	Federalist			65	
		Charles C. Pinckney	Federalist			64	
		John Jay	Federalist			1	
1804	17	**Thomas Jefferson**	Democratic Republican			162	
		Charles C. Pinckney	Federalist			14	
1808	17	**James Madison**	Democratic Republican			122	
		Charles C. Pinckney	Federalist			47	
		George Clinton	Democratic Republican			6	
1812	18	**James Madison**	Democratic Republican			128	
		DeWitt Clinton	Federalist			89	
1816	19	**James Monroe**	Democratic Republican			183	
		Rufus King	Federalist			34	
1820	24	**James Monroe**	Democratic Republican			231	
		John Quincy Adams	Independent Republican			1	

Year	Number of States	Candidates	Parties	Popular Vote	% of Popular Vote	Electoral Vote	% Voter Participation[a]
1824	24	**John Quincy Adams**	Democratic Republican	108,740	30.5	84	26.9
		Andrew Jackson	Democratic Republican	153,544	43.1	99	
		Henry Clay	Democratic Republican	47,136	13.2	37	
		William H. Crawford	Democratic Republican	46,618	13.1	41	
1828	24	**Andrew Jackson**	Democratic Republican	647,286	56.0	178	57.6
		John Quincy Adams	National Republican	508,064	44.0	83	
1832	24	**Andrew Jackson**	Democratic Republican	688,242	54.5	219	55.4
		Henry Clay	National Republican	473,462	37.5	49	
		William Wirt	Anti-Masonic	101,051	8.0	7	
		John Floyd	Democratic			11	
1836	26	**Martin Van Buren**	Democratic	765,483	50.9	170	57.8
		William H. Harrison	Whig			73	
		Hugh L. White	Whig			26	
		Daniel Webster	Whig	739,795	49.1	14	
		W. P. Mangum	Whig			11	
1840	26	**William H. Harrison**	Whig	1,274,624	53.1	234	80.2
		Martin Van Buren	Democratic	1,127,781	46.9	60	
1844	26	**James K. Polk**	Democratic	1,338,464	49.6	170	78.9
		Henry Clay	Whig	1,300,097	48.1	105	
		James G. Birney	Liberty	62,300	2.3		
1848	30	**Zachary Taylor**	Whig	1,360,967	47.4	163	72.7
		Lewis Cass	Democratic	1,222,342	42.5	127	
		Martin Van Buren	Free-Soil	291,263	10.1		
1852	31	**Franklin Pierce**	Democratic	1,601,117	50.9	254	69.6
		Winfield Scott	Whig	1,385,453	44.1	42	
		John P. Hale	Free-Soil	155,825	5		
1856	31	**James Buchanan**	Democratic	1,832,955	45.3	174	78.9
		John C. Frémont	Republican	1,339,932	33.1	114	
		Millard Fillmore	American	871,731	21.6	8	
1860	33	**Abraham Lincoln**	Republican	1,865,593	39.8	180	81.2
		Stephen A. Douglas	Democratic	1,382,713	29.5	12	
		John C. Breckinridge	Democratic	848,356	18.1	72	
		John Bell	Constitutional Union	592,906	12.6	39	
1864	36	**Abraham Lincoln**	Republican	2,206,938	55.0	212	73.8
		George B. McClellan	Democratic	1,803,787	45.0	21	
1868	37	**Ulysses S. Grant**	Republican	3,013,421	52.7	214	78.1
		Horatio Seymour	Democratic	2,706,829	47.3	80	

Year	Number of States	Candidates	Parties	Popular Vote	% of Popular Vote	Electoral Vote	% Voter Participation[a]
1872	37	**Ulysses S. Grant**	Republican	3,596,745	55.6	286[b]	71.3
		Horace Greeley	Democratic	2,843,446	43.9		
1876	38	**Rutherford B. Hayes**	Republican	4,036,572	48.0	185	81.8
		Samuel J. Tilden	Democratic	4,284,020	51.0	184	
1880	38	**James A. Garfield**	Republican	4,453,295	48.5	214	79.4
		Winfield S. Hancock	Democratic	4,414,082	48.1	155	
		James B. Weaver	Greenback-Labor	308,578	3.4		
1884	38	**Grover Cleveland**	Democratic	4,879,507	48.5	219	77.5
		James G. Blaine	Republican	4,850,293	48.2	182	
		Benjamin F. Butler	Greenback-Labor	175,370	1.8		
		John P. St. John	Prohibition	150,369	1.5		
1888	38	**Benjamin Harrison**	Republican	5,477,129	47.9	233	79.3
		Grover Cleveland	Democratic	5,537,857	48.6	168	
		Clinton B. Fisk	Prohibition	249,506	2.2		
		Anson J. Streeter	Union Labor	146,935	1.3		
1892	44	**Grover Cleveland**	Democratic	5,555,426	46.1	277	74.7
		Benjamin Harrison	Republican	5,182,690	43.0	145	
		James B. Weaver	People's	1,029,846	8.5	22	
		John Bidwell	Prohibition	264,133	2.2		
1896	45	**William McKinley**	Republican	7,102,246	51.1	271	79.3
		William J. Bryan	Democratic	6,492,559	47.7	176	
1900	45	**William McKinley**	Republican	7,218,491	51.7	292	73.2
		William J. Bryan	Democratic; Populist	6,356,734	45.5	155	
		John C. Wooley	Prohibition	208,914	1.5		
1904	45	**Theodore Roosevelt**	Republican	7,628,461	57.4	336	65.2
		Alton B. Parker	Democratic	5,084,223	37.6	140	
		Eugene V. Debs	Socialist	402,283	3.0		
		Silas C. Swallow	Prohibition	258,536	1.9		
1908	46	**William H. Taft**	Republican	7,675,320	51.6	321	65.4
		William J. Bryan	Democratic	6,412,294	43.1	162	
		Eugene V. Debs	Socialist	420,793	2.8		
		Eugene W. Chafin	Prohibition	253,840	1.7		
1912	48	**Woodrow Wilson**	Democratic	6,296,547	41.9	435	58.8
		Theodore Roosevelt	Progressive	4,118,571	27.4	88	
		William H. Taft	Republican	3,486,720	23.2	8	
		Eugene V. Debs	Socialist	900,672	6.0		
		Eugene W. Chafin	Prohibition	206,275	1.4		
1916	48	**Woodrow Wilson**	Democratic	9,127,695	49.4	277	61.6
		Charles E. Hughes	Republican	8,533,507	46.2	254	
		A. L. Benson	Socialist	585,113	3.2		
		J. Frank Hanly	Prohibition	220,506	1.2		

Year	Number of States	Candidates	Parties	Popular Vote	% of Popular Vote	Electoral Vote	% Voter Participation[a]
1920	48	**Warren G. Harding**	Republican	16,143,407	60.4	404	49.2
		James M. Cox	Democratic	9,130,328	34.2	127	
		Eugene V. Debs	Socialist	919,799	3.4		
		P. P. Christensen	Farmer-Labor	265,411	1.0		
1924	48	**Calvin Coolidge**	Republican	15,718,211	54.0	382	48.9
		John W. Davis	Democratic	8,385,283	28.8	136	
		Robert M. La Follette	Progressive	4,831,289	16.6	13	
1928	48	**Herbert C. Hoover**	Republican	21,391,993	58.2	444	56.9
		Alfred E. Smith	Democratic	15,016,169	40.9	87	
1932	48	**Franklin D. Roosevelt**	Democratic	22,809,638	57.4	472	56.9
		Herbert C. Hoover	Republican	15,758,901	39.7	59	
		Norman Thomas	Socialist	881,951	2.2		
1936	48	**Franklin D. Roosevelt**	Democratic	27,752,869	60.8	523	61.0
		Alfred M. Landon	Republican	16,674,665	36.5	8	
		William Lemke	Union	882,479	1.9		
1940	48	**Franklin D. Roosevelt**	Democratic	27,307,819	54.8	449	62.5
		Wendell L. Wilkie	Republican	22,321,018	44.8	82	
1944	48	**Franklin D. Roosevelt**	Democratic	25,606,585	53.5	432	55.9
		Thomas E. Dewey	Republican	22,014,745	46.0	99	
1948	48	**Harry S Truman**	Democratic	24,105,695	49.5	303	53.0
		Thomas E. Dewey	Republican	21,969,170	45.1	189	
		J. Strom Thurmond	States' Rights	1,169,021	2.4	39	
		Henry A. Wallace	Progressive	1,156,103	2.4		
1952	48	**Dwight D. Eisenhower**	Republican	33,936,234	55.1	442	63.3
		Adlai E. Stevenson	Democratic	27,314,992	44.4	89	
1956	48	**Dwight D. Eisenhower**	Republican	35,590,472	57.6	457	60.6
		Adlai E. Stevenson	Democratic	26,022,752	42.1	73	
1960	50	**John F. Kennedy**	Democratic	34,226,731	49.7	303	62.8
		Richard M. Nixon	Republican	34,108,157	49.5	219	
1964	50	**Lyndon B. Johnson**	Democratic	43,129,566	61.1	486	61.7
		Barry M. Goldwater	Republican	27,178,188	38.5	52	
1968	50	**Richard M. Nixon**	Republican	31,710,470	43.4	301	60.6
		Hubert H. Humphrey	Democratic	30,898,055	42.7	191	
		George C. Wallace	American Independent	9,446,167	13.5	46	
1972	50	**Richard M. Nixon**	Republican	47,169,911	60.7	520	55.2
		George S. McGovern	Democratic	29,170,383	37.5	17	
		John G. Schmitz	American	1,099,482	1.4		
1976	50	**Jimmy Carter**	Democratic	40,830,763	50.1	297	53.5
		Gerald R. Ford	Republican	39,147,793	48.0	240	

Year	Number of States	Candidates	Parties	Popular Vote	% of Popular Vote	Electoral Vote	% Voter Participation[a]
1980	50	**Ronald Reagan**	Republican	43,899,248	50.8	489	52.6
		Jimmy Carter	Democratic	35,481,432	41.0	49	
		John B. Anderson	Independent	5,719,437	6.6	0	
		Ed Clark	Libertarian	920,859	1.1	0	
1984	50	**Ronald Reagan**	Republican	54,455,075	58.8	525	53.1
		Walter Mondale	Democratic	37,577,185	40.6	13	
1988	50	**George Bush**	Republican	48,901,046	53.4	426	50.2
		Michael Dukakis	Democratic	41,809,030	45.6	111[c]	
1992	50	**Bill Clinton**	Democratic	44,908,233	43.0	370	55.0
		George Bush	Republican	39,102,282	37.4	168	
		Ross Perot	Independent	19,741,048	18.9	0	
1996	50	**Bill Clinton**	Democratic	47,401,054	49.2	379	49.0
		Robert Dole	Republican	39,197,350	40.7	159	
		Ross Perot	Independent	8,085,285	8.4	0	
		Ralph Nader	Green	684,871	0.7	0	
2000	50	**George W. Bush**	Republican	50,465,169	47.79	271	50.7
		Albert Gore, Jr.	Democratic	50,996,062	49.4	266[d]	
		Ralph Nader	Green	2,529,871	2.40	0	
2004	50	**George W. Bush**	Republican	62,040,610	51	286	60.7
		John F. Kerry	Democratic	59,028,109	48	252	
		Ralph Nader	Independent	463,653	1	0	
2008	50	**Barack Obama**	Democratic	69,498,459	52.9	365	61.7
		John McCain	Republican	59,948,283	45.7	173	
2012	50	**Barack Obama**	Democratic	65,455,010	51	332	58.2
		Mitt Romney	Republican	60,771,703	47	206	

Candidates receiving less than 1 percent of the popular vote have been omitted. Thus the percentage of popular vote given for any election year may not total 100 percent.

Before the passage of the Twelfth Amendment in 1804, the Electoral College voted for two presidential candidates; the runner-up became vice president.

Before 1824, most presidential electors were chosen by state legislatures, not by popular vote.

[a]Percent of voting-age population casting ballots (eligible voters).
[b]Greeley died shortly after the election; the electors supporting him then divided their votes among minor candidates.
[c]One elector from West Virginia cast her Electoral College presidential ballot for Lloyd Bentsen, the Democratic Party's vice-presidential candidate.
[d]One elector from the District of Columbia abstained.

Index

American Indians *(continued)*
(illus.); removal to Far West, 270; Revolution and, 122, 124, 127, 137, 137 (illus.), 139; as serfs, 32; as slaves, 67; in Southeast, 38–39; in Spanish colonies, 25–26, 28, 29, 32; spirituality of, 17–18; Tecumseh and, 202–203, 208, 209 (map); trade with, 12, 16, 17, 41–42; treaties with, 173, 174, 198, 246; warfare and, 38; War of 1812 and, 210–211, 213, 215. *See also* Indian policy; specific battles and treaties; specific groups and leaders

American Prohibitory Act, 118

American Revenue Act, 104

American Revolution, 126, 170; African Americans in, 120, 122, 122 (illus.), 124, 139; battle for Boston, 127–128; in Carolinas, 129; chronology, 149; diplomacy during, 133–134, 136; economy during, 136; events leading to, 56, 101, 121; first years of, 127–133; Indians and, 122, 124, 127, 137, 137 (illus.), 139; Jackson and, 239; loyalists and, 120, 122, 124, 127, 129, 139, 140, 143, 144; military camps in, 133; Northern Campaign, 130 (map); rights after, 142; slavery and, 144–147; South, 138–139, 138 (map); western land claims after, 142 (map), 155 (map); women and, 143–144, 149

"American Scholar, The" (Emerson), 282

American System (Clay), **228**–229, 232, 236, 251, 296, 303

American Tract Society, 266, 276, 283

America(s): European and Indian settlements in, 31 (map); European empires in, 16–21; imperial wars in, 91–93; as New World, 19–20; origins of, 3–6; Russian frontier in, 36; Spain and, 15–16, 27, 28–29. *See also* Colonies and colonization; Expansion and expansionism; New World; specific countries and regions, 31

Ames, Adelbert, 390

Ames, Fisher, 185, 191–192

Amish: in Pennsylvania, 66

Amnesty, 128; Andrew Johnson and, 374

Anaconda plan, 340, 341 (illus.), 347 (map), 348

Anasazi Indians, 11, 11 (illus.)

Anderson, Robert, 331, 332

Andersonville prison camp, **356**

Andros, Edmund, 62, 63

Anglicans, 51, 57, 142; in Connecticut, 88. *See also* Church of England

Animals: Columbian Exchange and, **18**; migration of, 3. *See also* specific animals

Annapolis conference, 160

Anne of Austria, 35

Annexation, 273; of Texas, 301, 302, 303, 304, 311

Annuities, 209

Antebellum period: immigration during, 261 (map); manifest destiny in, 299; in South, **254**–259. *See also* South; specific issues

Anthony, Susan B., 381, 384

Antietam Creek, Battle of, 349

Antifederalists, 152, **164,** 165, 165 (map), 166, 176

Antimasonic Party, 240, 241

Antimasons, 295, 296, **296**

Antislavery movement, 146, 309, 310–311, 310 (illus.), 338; Kansas-Nebraska Act and, 320, 321. *See also* Abolition; Slaves and slavery

Antislavery societies, 294

Anti-Slavery Society (Britain), 236, 294

Apache Indians, 11, 40, 42

Appalachian Mountains: settlement to west of, 104. *See also* Proclamation Line

"Appeal of the Independent Democrats in Congress…, The," 320

Appomattox Courthouse, Lee's surrender at, 364

Apprentices, 82, 260, 264, 266

Arabella (ship), 58

Arabian Peninsula, 3

Arab world: Muslims and, 3; slave trade and, 3

Arapaho Indians, 40

Archaeological digs: Jamestown, 53 (illus.)

Arikara Indians, 39

Aristocracy: of planters, 255–256

Arkansas, 219, 332, 372

Armed forces: American Indians in, 122, 124, 127, 137, 139; in American Revolution, 128–129, 132 (illus.); in Civil War, 340, 340 (illus.), 359–361; in War of 1812, 210, 211, 212, 213. *See also* Draft (military); Soldiers; Wars and warfare; specific battles and wars

Army of Northern Virginia, 349, 358

Army of the Potomac, 348, 349; creation of, **344**

Army of the Shenandoah, 364

Arnold, Benedict, 127, 129, 132, 139

Arrohateck Indians, 52

Articles of Confederation, 152, **154,** 161, 176; diplomacy under, 157–158; document, A3–A6; ratification of, 154. *See also* Constitution (U.S.)

Articles of Constitution

Artisans: Revolution and, 122; slave, **259,** 287, 287 (illus.); women, 83 (illus.)

Art(s): Neoclassicism in, 283. *See also* specific arts and artists

Ascetics: Franciscans as, **37**

Ashley, William Henry, 268, 278

Asia: colonies in, 233; trade with, 15–16

Assassinations: of Lincoln, 364, 367

Assemblies: colonial, and English view of, 91. *See also* Legislature; specific assemblies

Assembly: right of, 142

Astor, John Jacob, 217

Astrolabe, 15, 15 (illus.)

Atlanta: in Civil War, 362

Atlantic Ocean region, 3; change in, 6–8

Atlantic slave trade: Western Africa and, 20, 20 (map)

Attucks, Crispus, 111

Auburn prison system, 293

Austin, Moses, 219

Austin, Stephen F., 219, 300

Austria: imperial warfare and, 93

Authority: of colonial governors, 90

Autonomy, 375

Awakening: new evangelicalism and, 194–195. *See also* Great Awakening

Azores, 13

Aztecs, 11, 28, 36

Bache, Sarah, 126

Backcountry, 75, 78, 85, 164; life in, 83; post-Revolution depression and, 158; Regulator movement in, 85–86; Revolution and, 123, 129, 139; violence in, 85

Bacon, Nathaniel, 48–49, 48 (illus.), 65, 66, 73; "Manifesto Concerning the Troubles in Virginia, 1676," 70; "The Manifesto of the People," 49

Bacon's Rebellion, 48–49, 56, 85

Bahamas, 15

Balance of payments: Jefferson and, **192**

Baltimore: Catholics in, 55–56; Civil War in, 333, 334 (illus.); in War of 1812, 214–215

Home manufacturing, 261–262
Homestead Act, 352
Hood, John Bell, 345, 362
Hooker, Joseph, 357, 358
Hooker, Thomas, 60
Hopewell Treaties, 158
Hopi Indians, 36, 40
Horses: on Plains, 40, 40
    (illus.), 41–42, 41 (map)
Horseshoe Bend, Battle of, 215
Hospitals: during Civil War, 356
House of Burgesses, 54, 54 (illus.)
House of Representatives, 161;
    1800 election and, 184; first
    African American to serve
    in, 369–370, 369 (illus.).
    See also Congress (U.S.)
House of Trade (Spain), 32
House slaves, 259
Housing: of American Indians, 11, 11
    (illus.); for blue-collar Americans,
    264; of British soldiers at colonial
    expense, 96; for immigrants,
    264; in Massachusetts Bay, 59;
    of slaves, 257, 258 (illus.)
Houston, Sam, 301, 302
Howard, Oliver O., 377
Howe, Richard, 129, 130, 131
Howe, Samuel Gridley, 325
Howe, William, 128, 129, 130, 131
Hudson, Henry, 32
Hudson Bay, 93
Hudson River region, 32,
    33, 33 (illus.), 81
Hudson River school, 284
"Humanus" (Thomas Paine), 122
Hume, David, 86
Hunger, 367; during Civil War, 353
Hunter, Robert, 85
Hunter-gatherers: climate and, 9;
    Indians as, 8, 11, 38; political
    organization among, 12
Hunting: horses and, 40, 40 (illus.);
    by Plains Indians, 39, 40, 40 (illus.)
Huron Confederacy, 93 (map)
Huron Indians, 16, 34, 39,
    102; French and, 92
Hutchinson, Anne, 60, 72
Hutchinson, Thomas, 106, 107, 113
Hutchinson, William, 60
Hydrology, 9

Ice Age: Great Ice Age, 3, 39;
    Little Ice Age, 7, 39
Iceland, 3, 6
"I Hear America Singing"
    (Longfellow), 282
Illinois, 217, 234; statehood for, 157

Immigrants and immigration:
    backcountry and, 83; during
    eighteenth century, 75; in
    industrial workforce, 317;
    manufacturing cities and, 263; to
    Middle Colonies, 82; origin and
    settlement of (1820-1850), 260, 261
    (map); in Pennsylvania, 66; slaves
    as involuntary, 80–81. *See also* Slaves
    and slavery; Westward movement;
    specific locations and groups
Impeach, 187
Impeachment: of Andrew Johnson,
    383, 383 (illus.); of Pickering, 187
Implied power, 170
Import duties, 104
Import taxes: colonial trade
    and, 77. *See also* Taxation
Impressment, 136, 205,
    205 (illus.), 206
Indentured servants, 57, 68, 76,
    79. *See also* Slaves and slavery
Independence: diplomatic, 133–134;
    movement toward, 119–120;
    recognition of, 134, 136
Independence Hall,
    Philadelphia, 118 (illus.)
India: England and, 137
Indiana, 217, 234; statehood for, 157
Indian policy: of Harrison,
    223; of Jackson, 213, 246;
    Tecumseh on, 223
Indian Removal Act (1830),
    246, 246 (map)
Indians. *See* American Indians
Indian Springs, Treaty of, 245
Indian Territory, 248, 320, 346
Indigenous peoples, 1–2, 4–5,
    8, 10–12; migrations of, 3–5.
    See also American Indians
Indigo, 74, 75, 76
Individualism: transcendentalism
    and, 282, 283
Industrial economy:
    immigrants and, 264
Industrialization: interchangeable
    parts and, 316; workers and, 285.
    See also Factories; Manufacturing
Inequities, 169
Infant depravity, 267
Inflation, 30; during Civil War,
    352, 367; in Revolution, 136
Influence peddling, 238
Inner light: of Quakers, 66
Insane asylums, 293, 293 (illus.)
Installment loans, 233
Installments, 232
Insubordination, 89
Insurrection, 122

Intellectual thought:
    Enlightenment and, 86–87;
    Romanticism and, 282–284;
    Transcendentalism and, 282
Interchangeable parts, 262, 316
Intermountain Plateau: Indians of, 11
Internal taxes, 188
International affairs. *See*
    Diplomacy; Foreign policy
International Committee of
    the Red Cross, 356
International relations: Monroe
    Doctrine and, 232. *See*
    also Foreign policy
Interposition, 182
Interstate commerce, 230
Intolerable Acts, 113–114,
    115, 116, 134
Invasion line: in colonies, 76
Investment: in canal building, 275; in
    railroads, 317. *See also* Speculators
Ireland: English colonization in, 29;
    Henry VIII and, 29; immigrants
    from, 75, 260, 317; linen industry
    in, 76; rebellions in, 158
Iron and iron industry: in sub-
    Saharan Africa, 13
Iron industry: railroads and, 317
Iroquois Confederacy, 93 (map)
Iroquois Indians, 61; economic
    and social patterns of, 8, 10;
    in French and Indian War, 96;
    imperial wars and, 93; Revolution
    and, 122, 127, 131, 132
Iroquois League, 39; English and, 92
Irreligious, 293
Isabella (Spain). *See* Ferdinand
    and Isabella (Spain)
Islam, 3; African trade with, 3;
    Reconquista and, 7; scientific and
    mathematical knowledge and, 87;
    western Europe and, 7 (map)
Itinerant preachers, **88**

Jackson, Andrew, 240, 251, 323;
    Bank of the United States and,
    243, 244 (illus.), 251; cabinet
    of, 242; Creek Indians and, 213,
    246; 1824 election and, 236; 1828
    election and, 241, 241 (map),
    242 (illus.); Florida border and,
    231–232; inauguration of, 241;
    Indians and, 245–249, 251; as
    "King Andrew," 239, 241, 243, 296,
    296 (illus.); monetary policies
    of, 243, 244; nullification crisis
    and, 249, 251; retrenchment and,
    241–242, 243; War of 1812 and,

A Brief Primary Reader
for U.S. History

Volume 1

EDITOR: Michael Bellesiles
Emory University

CENGAGE
Learning™

Australia • Brazil • Japan • Korea • Mexico • Singapore • Spain • United Kingdom • United States

U.S. History, Volume 1
Table of Contents

The Colonial Period (to 1763)

The Revolutionary Period (1763-1789)

Early Republic (1789-1835)

The Crisis of The Union (1836-1861)

Vespucci's First Voyage
(1497)

AMERIGO VESPUCCI

Another Italian seaman working for the Spanish monarchs, Amerigo Vespucci had a much keener understanding of where he was than did his immediate predecessor, Christopher Columbus. Vespucci worked for the company in Seville that fitted out Columbus's first voyage west, and he spent the next several years arranging backing for his own expedition. Vespucci touched the mainland of South America in 1497, and seemed to understand rather quickly that he was not in Asia. It was Vespucci's account of his journeys, published in Florence in 1505, that popularized Western exploration and led the German geographer Waldseemüller to attach the name America to these new lands. Vespucci wrote the following letter to Pier Soderini, the Gonfalonier of the Venetian Republic.

Questions to Consider

- Why did Vespucci take sides in a dispute among different tribes?
- What was the primary source of profit for this expedition?

...[We] made towards the land, and before we reached it, had sight of a great number of people who were going along the shore, by which we were much rejoiced: and we observed that they were a naked race. They shewed themselves to stand in fear of us. I believe (it was) because they saw us clothed and of other appearance (than their own). They all withdrew to a hill, and for whatsoever signals we made to them of peace and of friendliness, they would not come to parley with us.... [W]e put to land with the boats, and sprang on shore full 40 men in good trim. And still the land's people appeared shy of converse with us, and we were unable to encourage them so much as to make them come to speak with us. And this day we laboured so greatly in giving them of our wares, such as rattles and mirrors, beads, spalline, and other trifles, that some of them took confidence and came to discourse with us. And after having made good friends with them, the night coming on, we took our leave of them and returned to the ships.

...The next day when the dawn appeared we saw that there were infinite numbers of people upon the beach, and they had their women and children with them.... And before we reached the land, many of them jumped into the sea and came swimming to receive us...for they are very great swimmers, with as much confidence as if they had for a long time been acquainted with us; and we were pleased with this their confidence. For so much as we learned of their manner of life and customs, it was that they go entirely naked, as well the men as the women....

They are of medium stature, very well proportioned. Their flesh is of a colour that verges into red like a lion's mane; and I believe that if they went clothed, they would be as white as we. They have not any hair upon the body, except the hair of the head which is long and black and especially in the women, whom it renders handsome. In aspect they are not very good-looking, because they have broad faces, so that they would seem Tartar-like. They let no hair grow on their eyebrows, nor

Source: Charles W. Eliot, ed., *American Historical Documents, 1000–1904* (New York, 1910), pp. 30–46.

on their eyelids, nor elsewhere, except the hair of the head: for they hold hairiness to be a filthy thing. They are very light footed in walking and in running, as well the men as the women; so that a woman recks nothing of running a league or two, as many times we saw them do. And herein they have a very great advantage over us Christians. They swim (with an expertness) beyond all belief, and the women better than the men: for we have many times found and seen them swimming two leagues out at sea without anything to rest upon....

These people have neither King, nor Lord, nor do they yield obedience to any one, for they live in their own liberty.... Amongst those people we did not learn that they had any law, nor can they be called Moors nor Jews, and (they are) worse than pagans: because we did not observe that they offered any sacrifice. Nor even had they a house of prayer. Their manner of living I judge to be Epicurean: their dwellings are in common, and their houses (are) made in the style of huts, but strongly made, and constructed with very large trees, and covered over with palm-leaves, secure against storms and winds: and in some places (they are) of so great breadth and length, that in one single house we found there were 600 souls. And we saw a village of only thirteen houses where there were four thousand souls....

Their riches consist of birds' plumes of many colours, or of rosaries which they make from fishbones, or of white or green stones which they put in their cheeks and in their lips and ears, and of many other things which we in no wise value they use to trade, they neither buy nor sell. In fine, they live and are contented with that which nature gives them. The wealth that we enjoy in this our Europe and elsewhere, such as gold, jewels, pearls, and other riches, they hold as nothing. And although they have them in their own lands, they do not labour to obtain them, nor do they value them. They are liberal in giving, for it is rarely they deny you anything: and on the other hand, liberal in asking, when they shew themselves your friends....

And (now) desiring to depart upon our voyage, they made complaint to us how at certain times of the year there came from over the sea to this their land, a race of people very cruel, and enemies of theirs; and (who) by means of treachery or of violence slew many of them, and ate them; and some they made captives, and carried them away to their houses, or country: and how they could scarcely contrive to defend themselves from them, making signs to us that (those) were an island-people and lived out in the sea about a hundred leagues away. And so piteously did they tell us this that we believed them. And we promised to avenge them of so much wrong. And they remained overjoyed herewith....

At the end of the seven days we came upon the islands, which were many, some (of them) inhabited, and others deserted. And we anchored at one of them: where we saw a numerous people who called it Iti....We made for land: where we found (assembled) about 400 men, and many women, and all naked... They...seemed right warlike men; for they were armed with their weapons, which are bows, arrows, and lances and most of them had square wooden targets; and bore them in such wise that they did not impede the drawing of the bow. And when we had come with our boats to about a bowshot of the land, they all sprang into the water to shoot their arrows at us and to prevent us from leaping upon shore.... And so much did they persist in preventing us from landing, that we were compelled to play with our artillery. And when they heard the explosion, and saw one of them fall dead, they all drew back to the land....

And having armed ourselves as best we could, we advanced towards the shore, and they sought not to hinder us from landing, I believe from fear of the cannons. And we jumped on land, 57 men in four squadrons, each one (consisting of) a captain and his company and we came to blows with them. And after a long battle (in which) many of them (were) slain, we put them to flight, and pursued them to a village having made about 250 of them captives, and we burnt the village, and returned to our ships with victory and 250 prisoners, leaving many of them dead and wounded, and of ours there were no more than one killed, and 222 captive slaves. And reached the port of Calis (Cadiz) on the 15th day of October, 1498, where we were well received and sold our slaves. Such is what befell me, most noteworthy, in this my first voyage.

2

The Exploration of California (1602)

SEBASTIAN VIZCAINO

In the 1590s English attacks on Spanish ships in the Pacific convinced the Viceroy of New Spain of the need to establish a settlement along the California coast. Sebastian Vizcaino, a successful merchant in the Mexico-to-Philippines trade, was commissioned to undertake this enterprise. His first effort failed in the face of Indian resistance. Vizcaino set off in May 1602 from Acapulco with three ships under his command. This journey resulted in the first Spanish knowledge of Monterey Bay, which was to become a major target for future settlement. Based on their explorations of the Sea of Cortez, as they called the Gulf of Mexico, the Spanish thought California was a giant island. Vizcaino's diary, excerpted below, was first published in Madrid in 1882.

Questions to Consider

- How did Vizcaino perceive the Indians and their culture?
- Why did Vizcaino attach a Spanish and sacred name to every physical feature?

Departure from the Bay of the Eleven Thousand Virgins

We sailed...on Sunday, the 20th of [October], from the Bay of the Eleven Thousand Virgins.... The next day Captain Peguero and Ensign Juan Francisco, with some soldiers, went on shore with orders to search diligently for water and to treat well the Indians who were on the beach. When they arrived on the land they made wells near the sea and found plenty of good water. More than a hundred Indian warriors came to the place with their bows and arrows and with clubs for throwing. These Indians were very insolent, to the extent of drawing their bows and picking up stones to throw at us. Without taking notice of them except to make signs of

peace, the captain and ensign embarked, and having come on board reported to the general what had happened.

The next day Captain Peguero, Ensign Pasqual de Alarcon, and the chief pilot, Francisco Bolanos, went ashore to take water. To them the general gave orders to treat the Indians well and to deal with them with great care and prudence.... Arriving on land we found a multitude of Indians arrayed for battle, and although, on our part, we gave them to understand that we intended to do them no harm, but to get water,...the Indians... tried to prevent the taking of water and to take from us the bottles and barrels. This made it necessary to fire three arquebus shots at them; whereupon, with the noise of the powder and someone's crying at the death of some of the others, they fled with great outcries; but at the end of two hours a multitude of Indians returned...holding councils among themselves, apparently, as to what they should do, and then, with arms in hand, they came toward us, who to them seemed few,

Source: Herbert Eugene Bolton, ed., *Spanish Exploration in the Southwest 1542–1706* (New York, 1916), pp. 76–78, 80–88, 91–92.

with their women and children, bows and arrows. Ensign Pasqual de Alarcon went out to meet them, telling them by signs that they must be quiet, and that they should be friends. Thereupon the Indians said they would do so upon condition that we would not fire any more arquebuses at them, which appeared to them many. They gave a female dog as a hostage…At midnight…the general ordered us to set sail. This bay was named San Simon y San Judas.[1]

….Thereupon we continued our voyage, skirting along the coast until the 24th of the month, which was the eve of the feast of the glorious Santa Catalina, when we discovered three large islands. We approached them with difficulty because of a head-wind, and arrived at the middle one, which is more than twenty-five leagues around.[2]

On the 27th…a multitude of Indians came out in canoes of cedar and pine, made of planks very well joined and calked, each one with eight oars and with fourteen or fifteen Indians, who looked like galley-slaves. They came alongside without the least fear and came on board our ships, mooring their own. They showed great pleasure at seeing us, telling us by signs that we must land, and guiding us like pilots to the anchorage. The general received them kindly and gave them some presents, especially to the boys….

The people go dressed in seal skins, the women especially covering their loins, and their faces show them to be modest; but the men are thieves, for anything they saw unguarded they took. They are a people given to trade and traffic and are fond of barter, for in return for old clothes they would give the soldiers skins, shells, nets, thread, and very well twisted ropes, these in great quantities and resembling linen. They have dogs like those in Castile.

…The general went inland to see the opposite coast. He found on the way a level prairie, very well cleared, where the Indians were assembled to worship an idol which was there. It resembled a demon, having two horns, no head, a dog at its feet, and many children painted all around it. The Indians told the general not to go near it, but he approached it…and made a cross, and placed the name of Jesus on the head of the demon, telling the Indians that that was good, and from heaven, but that the idol was the devil. At this the Indians marvelled, and they will readily renounce it and receive our Holy Faith, for apparently they have good intellects and are friendly and desirous of our friendship….

…We left this said island of Santa Catalina… December 1st…. [W]e went on skirting the coast, and on Monday…we sighted two other large islands.

---

[1] Colnett Bay.
[2] Santa Catalina Island.

Passing between the first and the mainland, a canoe came out to us with two Indian fishermen, who had a great quantity of fish, rowing so swiftly that they seemed to fly. They came alongside without saying a word to us and went twice around us with so great speed that it seemed impossible; this finished, they came aft, bowing their heads in the way of courtesy. The general ordered that they be given a cloth, with bread. They received it, and gave in return the fish they had, without any pay…. After they had gone five Indians came in another canoe, so well constructed and built that since Noah's Ark a finer and lighter vessel with timbers better made has not been seen. Four men rowed, with an old man in the centre, [singing] as in a *mitote* of the Indians of New Spain, and the others responding to him. Before coming alongside they stopped and he saluted us three times, making many ceremonious gestures with his head and body…. Only the old man spoke, he saying by signs that we must go to his land, where they would give us much food and water, for there was a river. He gave us a flask of it which he had brought…. This Indian made himself so well understood by signs that he lacked nothing but ability to speak our language. He came to say that as a pledge of the truth of what he said one of us should get into his canoe and go to his land, and that he would remain on board ship with us as a hostage.

…It was agreed that the Indians should depart, being given to understand by signs that next day we would go to their land; but such were the efforts of this Indian to get us to go to it that as a greater inducement he said he would give to each one of us ten women to sleep with. This Indian was so intelligent that he appeared to be not a barbarian but a person of great understanding. We showed him lead, tin, and plates of silver. He sounded them with his finger and said that the silver was good but the others not….

We arrived…at this port of Monterey, on the 16th of…December, at seven o'clock in the evening. The next day the general ordered Ensign Alarcon to go ashore, with orders to make a hut where mass could be said and to see if there was water, and what the country was like. He found that there was fresh water, and a great oak near the shore, where he made the hut and arbor to say mass. The…rest of the men landed at once; and mass having been said and the day having cleared, there having been much fog, we found ourselves to be in the best port that could be desired, for besides being sheltered from all the winds, it has many pines for masts and yards, and live oaks and white oaks, and water in great quantity, all near the shore. The land is fertile, with a climate and soil like those of Castile…. The land is thickly populated with numberless Indians, of whom a great many came several times to our camp. They appeared to be a gentle and peaceable people.

They said by signs that inland there are many settlements....

In view of the fact that we had so many sick...and that the supplies were becoming exhausted,...it seemed to the general impossible to complete the exploration this time without a new supply of men and provisions; and he therefore at once called a conference...to consider what should be done for the best service of his Majesty. It was decided that the admiral's ship should return as a messenger to the viceroy of New Spain with a copy of the records of the discoveries as far as this place....

The Mayflower Compact (1620)

WILLIAM BRADFORD AND OTHERS

The Pilgrims, Protestant separatists who took seriously the injunction to have no communion with sinners, left the Netherlands in 1620 bound originally for the Chesapeake. After a hard journey aboard the Mayflower, the Pilgrims decided to settle in New England instead. Before going ashore at Plymouth, the Pilgrims entered into the following compact—"the first foundation of their governmente in this place," as their governor, William Bradford, put it. Bradford noted that the compact was necessary as there were many aboard the Mayflower who "would use their owne libertie; for none had power to command them." These nonseparatists posed a threat to the religious and social unity of the colony, and Bradford hoped that the compact would provide the means of keeping them in check. The document was signed by 41 of the Mayflower's 102 passengers.

Questions to Consider

- What would the role of nonsignatories be under the compact's government?
- What is the compact's stated goal?

In the name of God, Amen. We whose names are under-written, the loyall subjects of our dread sovereign Lord, King James, by the grace of God, of Great Britaine, Franc, and Ireland kind, defender of the faith, etc., haveing undertaken, for the glorie of God, and advancement of the Christian faith, and honour of our king and countrie, a voyage to plant the first colonie in the Northerne parts of Virginia, doe by these presents solemnly and mutualy in the presence of God, and one of another, covenant and combine our selves togeather into a civill body politick, for our better ordering and preservation and furtherance of the ends aforesaid; and by vertue hearof to enacte, constitute, and frame such just and equall laws, ordinances, acts, constitutions, and offices, from time to time, as shall be thought most meete and convenient for the generall good of the Colonie, unto which we promise all due submission and obedience. In witnes wherof we have hereunder subscribed our names at Cap-Codd the 11. of November, in the year of the raigne of our soveraigne lord, King James, of England, France, and Ireland the eighteenth, and of Scotland the fiftie fourth. Ano: Dom. 1620....

Source: William T. Davis, ed., *Bradford's History of Plymouth Plantation, 1606–1646* (New York, 1908), p. 107.

4

The De Leon Expeditions to Texas (1689)

D A M I A N   M A S S A N E T

In 1684 the Spanish learned that la Salle had entered the Gulf of Mexico intending to establish a French colony at the mouth of the Mississippi. The government in Mexico sent Alonso de Leon, the governor of Coahuila province, to destroy this effort. On his first expedition, de Leon discovered that la Salle had missed Louisiana and lost at least two of his ships on the coast of Texas. De Leon spent the next several years searching for errant Frenchmen in territory claimed by France. He was accompanied on his fourth and fifth expeditions by Father Damian Massanet, who wrote the following account. On the last of these journeys, Massanet established a pair of missions near the Neches River, thus beginning the Spanish settlement of Texas.

Questions to Consider

- Why were the Spanish so intent on finding a few stranded Frenchmen?
- Why did Father Massanet feel that a mass was sound preparation for a military operation?

At this time I was living at the Mission Caldera, in the province of Coahuila, whither I had gone with the intention of seeing whether I could make investigations and obtain information about the interior of the country to the north and northeast, on account of facts gathered from a letter now in my possession, which had been given in Madrid to our Father Fray Antonio Linaz. This letter treats of what the blessed Mother Maria de Jesus de Agreda[1] made known in her convent to the father custodian of New Mexico, Fray Alonso de Benavides. And the blessed Mother tells of having been frequently to New Mexico and to the Gran Quivira, adding that eastward from the Gran Quivira are situated the kingdoms of Ticlas, Theas, and Caburcol.... Because of this information,...together with the fact of my call to the ministry for the conversion of the heathen, I had come over and dwelt in the missions of Coahuila, and learning that His Excellency was taking steps to open up the interior, to lead to the discovery of the bay of Espiritu Santo,[2] and to find out whether any Frenchmen were there, I endeavored to learn from the Indians coming from the interior whether they knew where there dwelt men white like the Spaniards. And in time I learned that there were indeed some....

Just at this time there arrived another Indian, of the Quems nation, and he told me that he had been even in the very houses of the French; there were many of them, he said, including women; they were well armed, and

Source: Herbert Eugene Bolton, ed., *Spanish Exploration in the Southwest 1542–1706* (New York, 1916), pp. 354–364, 367, 369, 372–375.

[1] Maria de Jesus de Agreda was a Spanish nun who had out-of-body experiences in which she converted masses of Indians in North America.—*Ed.*

[2] On the Gulf Coast of Texas.—*Ed.*

had some very large firearms (which were the pieces of ordnance). On my asking whether he were well acquainted with the country, he said that, if I wished, he would take me to the place without any risk, that there we should also find priests like myself, and that already the people were sowing maize and other crops....

We left Coahuila on the twenty-sixth of March in the year 1689, and went as far as the Rio del Norte, which, in the said province of Coahuila, is called the Rio Grande.... On the morning of the next day Captain Alonso de Leon asked me what we should do in order to ascertain the number of Frenchmen and the condition of things in their village. With regard to this there were various opinions, mine being that, since we had with us the Quems Indian who was well acquainted with the country, we should all have a mass sung in honor of the Blessed Virgin of Guadalupe that very morning, at the very place in which we were; also that when we should succeed in reaching the dwellings of the Frenchmen we should have another mass celebrated, in honor of Saint Anthony of Padua. All consented very readily to this, and, soon, at about nine o'clock in the morning, the mass to the Virgin was sung....

We started the next morning, and three leagues off we found the village of the Frenchmen on the bank of the stream.... [We] found six houses, not very large, built with poles plastered with mud, and roofed over with buffalo hides, another larger house where pigs were fattened, and a wooden fort made from the hulk of a wrecked vessel. The fort had one lower room which was used as a chapel for saying mass, and...an upper story serving for a store-house, wherein we found some six loads of iron,...also eight small guns and three swivels made of iron, the largest pieces being for a charge of about six pounds of shot. The pieces and one swivel were buried, and Captain Alonso de Leon carried off two of the swivels. There was a great lot of shattered weapons, broken by the Indians—firelocks, carbines, cutlasses—but they had not left the cannon, only one being found. We found two unburied bodies, which I interred, setting up a cross over the grave. There were many torn-up books, and many dead pigs.

...I myself set fire to the fort, and as there was a high wind—the wood, by the way, was from the sloop brought by the Frenchmen, which had sunk on entering the bay—in half an hour the fort was in ashes. This was at the hour of noon; afterwards we went down to the coast of the bay...[S]ome of the soldiers...said that they wished to bathe, in order to be able to tell that they had bathed in the sea, this being esteemed so remarkable a thing that they carried away flasks of seawater which later, in their own country of Monterey, it was held a great favor to try and to taste, because it was seawater....

Our company reached the San Marcos River, and came upon the Indians of the rancheria Emat,...and these Indians said that further along there were other Indians, and with them two Frenchmen. Leon, remaining with a few soldiers, sent for them and they came. The one was named Pedro Muni, a Creole, from the city of Paris, the other Pedro Talo, a Creole, from New France; these had firelocks, a sack of powder, and shot, more than twenty reales of the lowest value, in silver, Spanish money, and eighty gold eight-dollar doubloons, French money. After the doubloons had been passed from hand to hand, there were only thirty-nine left. One of the two Frenchmen mentioned, P. Muni, must have been about twenty years old; the other, Pedro Talo, eleven or twelve.

5

The Salem Witchcraft Trials (1692)

THOMAS BRATTLE

In 1692 a witchcraft hysteria swept through the town of Salem, Massachusetts. The crisis began with some teenage girls complaining of mysterious pains and convulsions. The local minister, Samuel Parris, fed the crisis by encouraging the girls to make accusations of witchcraft against other members of the community. A special court was created to hear these cases, and it sentenced many people to death, executing twenty alleged witches before the governor put a halt to the trials. Thomas Brattle, a prominent local merchant, supplied the following description to an unknown British minister.

Questions to Consider

- Why would Parris want to discover witchcraft in his town?
- What flaws did Brattle find in the court's procedures?

Reverend Sir,

...First, as to the method which the Salem justices do that in their examinations, it is truly this: A warrant being issued out to apprehend the persons that are charged and complained of by the afflicted children, as they are called; said present. The justices ask the apprehended why they afflict those poor children; to which the apprehended answer, they do not afflict them. The justices order the apprehended to look upon the said children, which accordingly they do; and at the time of that look...the afflicted are cast into a fit. The afflicted persons then declare and affirm, that the apprehended persons, though of never so good repute, are forthwith committed to prison, on suspicion for witchcraft. One of the Salem justices...saw reason to change his opinion of Mr. Alden, because that at the time he touched the poor child, the poor child came out of her fit. I suppose

his Honour never made the experiment, whether there was not as much virtue in his own hand as there was in Mr. Alden's, to cure by a touch....

I cannot but condemn this method of the justices, of making this touch of the hand a rule to discover witchcraft; because I am fully persuaded that it is sorcery, and a superstitious method, and that which we have no rule for, either from reason or religion....

Secondly, with respect to the confessors, as they are improperly called, or such as confess themselves to be witches...there are now about fifty of them in prison; many of which I have again and again seen and heard; and I cannot but tell you, that my faith is strong concerning them, that they are deluded, imposed upon, and under the influence of some evil spirit; and therefore unfit to be evidences either against themselves, or any one else....

These confessors, as they are called, do very often contradict themselves, as inconsistently as is usual for any crazed, distempered person to do.... The judges themselves have, at some times, taken these confessors

Source: *Collections of the Massachusetts Historical Society* (Boston, 1798), pp. 61–79.

in flat lies, or contradictions, even in the courts; by reason of which, one would have thought, that the judges would have frowned upon the said confessors, discarded them, and not minded one tittle of an thing that they said: but instead thereof, as sure as we are men, the judges vindicate these confessors, and solve their contradictions, by proclaiming, that the devil takes away their memory, and imposes upon their brain....

It is true, that over and above the evidences of the afflicted persons, there are many evidences brought in, against the prisoner at the bar; either that he was at a witch meeting, or that he performed things which could not be done by an ordinary natural power; or that she sold butter to a sailor which proving bad at sea; and the seamen exclaiming against her, she appeared, and soon after there was a storm, or the like. But what if there were ten thousand evidences of this nature; how do they prove the matter of indictment....

As to the late executions, I shall only tell you, that in the opinion of many unprejudiced, considerate and considerable spectators, some of the condemned went out of the world not only with as great protestations, but also with as good shews of innocency, as men could do.

They protested their innocency as in the presence of the great God, whom forthwith they were to appear before: they wished, and declared their wish, that their blood might be the last innocent blood shed upon that account.... Nineteen persons have now been executed, and one pressed to death for a mute: seven more are condemned; two of which are reprieved, because they pretend their being with child....

These afflicted persons do say, and often have declared it, that they can see spectres when their eyes are shut, as well as when they are open...I am sure they lie, at least speak safely, if they say so; for the thing, in nature, is an utter impossibility. It is true, they may strongly fancy, or have things represented to their imagination, when their eyes are shut; and I think this is all which ought to be allowed to these blind, nonsensical girls; and if our officers and courts have apprehended, imprisoned, condemned, and executed our guiltless neighbours, certainly our error is great, and we shall rue it in the conclusion....

6

Justice for the Indians (1700)

S A M U E L   S E W A L L

Few Puritans found it easy to extend Christian mercy to New England's Indians. One of the few sincere Puritans on this issue was the prominent judge Samuel Sewall. In this letter to Sir William Ashhurst, Sewall expresses his doubts with current policies and suggests that more missionaries should come from among the Indians themselves.

Questions to Consider

- Why did the people of Massachusetts have so much trouble getting along with the Indians?
- What would the consequences of Sewall's suggestions have been, had they been followed?

May 3, 1700

Honble. Sir, — The last Fall, I had notice of my being entrusted with a share in managing the Indian Affairs, And presently upon it, the Commissioners[1] were pleasd to appoint me their Secretary. As I account it an honor to be thus employed; so according to my mean ability, I shall endeavour faithfully to serve the Corporation and Commissioners, as I shall receive Instructions from them.

I have met with an Observation of some grave Divines, that ordinarily when God intends Good to a Nation, He is pleasd to make use of some of themselves, to be instrumental in conveying of that Good unto them. Now God has furnished several of the Indians with considerable abilities for the Work of the Ministry, and Teaching School, And therefore I am apt to believe, that if the Indians so qualified, were more taken notice of in suitable Rewards, it would conduce very much to the propagation of the Gospel among them. Besides the Content they might have in a provision of necessary Food and Raiment, the Respect and honor of it, would quicken their Industry, and allure others to take pains in fitting themselves for a fruitfull discharge of those Offices.

One thing more, I would crave leave to suggest, We have a very long and grievous War with the Eastern Indians, and it is of great Concernment to His Majs. Interests here that a peace be concluded with them upon firm and sure foundations. Which in my poor opinion cannot well be, while our Articles of Accord with them remain so very General as they doe. I should think it requisite that convenient Tracts of land should be set out to them; and that by plain and natural Boundaries, as much as may be; as Lakes, Rivers, Mountains, Rocks, Upon which for any English man to encroach, should be account a Crime. Except this be done I fear their own Jealousies, and the French Friers will persuade them, that the English, as they encrease, and think they want more room, will never leave till they have crouded them quite out of all their Lands. And it will be a vain attempt for us to offer Heaven to them, if they take up prejudices against us, as if we did grudge them a Living upon their own Earth....

Source: *Collections of the Massachusetts Historical Society* (Boston, 1886), sixth series, 1: pp. 231–233.
[1] Of the Society for Propagating the Gospel Among the Indians.—*Ed.*

7

Sinners in the Hands of an Angry God (1741)

JONATHAN EDWARDS

When Jonathan Edwards came to Enfield, Connecticut, to deliver the following sermon in July 1741, the Great Awakening was sweeping the North American colonies with religious enthusiasm. Edwards was the minister in Northampton, Massachusetts, a position he had inherited from his grandfather, the renowned Solomon Stoddard. Though well known throughout New England, Edwards's did not travel widely. In an era when the same minister preached sermon after sermon for decades without a break, a visiting minister tended to generate excitement. Edwards knocked them off their feet. The power of the sermon was instantly recognized, and it was published the same year.

Questions to Consider

- What hope is there of salvation?
- Why is God angry?

Deut. xxxii. 35—Their foot shall slide in due time.—

In this verse is threatened the vengeance of God on the wicked unbelieving Israelites, who were God's visible people, and who lived under the means of grace; but who, notwithstanding all God's wonderful works towards them, remained…void of counsel, having no understanding in them….

The observation from the words that I would now insist upon is this.—"There is nothing that keeps wicked men at any one moment out of hell, but the mere pleasure of God"…. The truth of this observation may appear by the following considerations.

1. There is no want of power in God to cast wicked men into hell at any moment. Men's hands cannot be strong when God rises up. The strongest have no power to resist him, nor can any deliver out of his hands…. We find it easy to tread on and crush a worm that we see crawling on the earth; so it is easy for us to cut or singe a slender thread that any thing hangs by: thus easy is it for God, when he pleases, to cast his enemies down to hell. What are we, that we should think to stand before him, at whose rebuke the earth trembles, and before whom the rocks are thrown down?

2. They deserve to be cast into hell; so that divine justice never stands in the way, it makes no objection against God's using his power at any moment to destroy them. Yea, on the contrary, justice calls aloud for an infinite punishment of their sins….

3. They are already under a sentence of condemnation to hell. They do not only justly deserve to be cast down thither, but the sentence of the law of God, that eternal and immutable rule of righteousness that God has fixed between him and mankind, is gone out against them, and stands against them; so that they are bound over already to hell….

4. They are now the objects of that very same anger and wrath of God, that is expressed in the torments of hell. And the reason why they do not go down to hell at each moment, is not because God, in whose power they are, is not then very angry with them…. Yea, God is a

Source: *The Works of President Edwards* (10 vols.; New York, 1830), 7: pp. 163–177.

great deal more angry with great numbers that are now on earth: yea, doubtless, with many that are now in this congregation, who it may be are at ease, than he is with many of those who are now in the flames of hell.

So that it is not because God is unmindful of their wickedness, and does not resent it, that he does not let loose his hand and cut them off. God is not altogether such an one as themselves, though they may imagine him to be so. The wrath of God burns against them, their damnation does not slumber; the pit is prepared, the fire is made ready, the furnace is now hot, ready to receive them; the flames do now rage and glow. The glittering sword is whet, and held over them, and the pit hath opened its mouth under them....

But the foolish children of men miserably delude themselves in their own schemes, and in confidence in their own strength and wisdom; they trust to nothing but a shadow.... God has laid himself under no obligation, by any promise to keep any natural man out of hell one moment. God certainly has made no promises either of eternal life, or of any deliverance or preservation from eternal death, but what are contained in the covenant of grace, the promises that are given in Christ, in whom all the promises are yea and amen....

...That world of misery that lake of burning brimstone, is extended abroad under you. There is the dreadful pit of the glowing flames of the wrath of God; there is hell's wide gaping mouth open; and you have nothing to stand upon, nor anything to take hold of; there is nothing between you and hell but the air; it is only the power and mere pleasure of God that holds you up....

Your wickedness makes you as it were heavy as lead, and to tend downwards with great weight and pressure towards hell; and if God should let you go, you would immediately sink and swiftly descend and plunge into the bottomless gulf, and your healthy constitution, and your own care and prudence, and best contrivance, and all your righteousness, would have no more influence to uphold you and keep you out of hell, than a spider's web would have to stop a fallen rock. Were it not for the sovereign pleasure of God, the earth would not bear you one moment; for you are a burden to it; the creation groans with you....

The God that holds you over the pit of hell, much as one holds a spider, or some loathsome insect over the fire, abhors you, and is dreadfully provoked: his wrath towards you burns like fire; he looks upon you as worthy of nothing else, but to be cast into the fire; he is of purer eyes than to bear to have you in his sight; you are ten thousand times more abominable in his eyes, than the most hateful venomous serpent is in ours. You have offended him infinitely...and yet it is nothing but his hand that holds you from falling into the fire every moment. It is to be ascribed to nothing else, that you did not go to hell the last night; that you was suffered to awake again in this world, after you closed your eyes to sleep. And there is no other reason to be given, why you have not dropped into hell since you arose in the morning, but that God's hand has held you up. There is no other reason to be given why you have not gone to hell, since you have sat here in the house of God, provoking his pure eyes by your sinful wicked manner of attending his solemn worship. Yea, there is nothing else that is to be given as a reason why you do not this very moment drop down into hell.

...There is reason to think, that there are many in this congregation now hearing this discourse, that will actually be the subjects of this very misery to all eternity. We know not who they are, or in what seats they sit, or what thoughts they now have.... If we knew who it was, what an awful sight would it be to see such a person!...And it would be no wonder if some persons, that now sit here, in some seats of this meeting-house, in health, quiet and secure, should be there before tomorrow morning. Those of you that finally continue in a natural condition, that shall keep out of hell longest will be there in a little time! your damnation does not slumber; it will come swiftly, and, in all probability, very suddenly upon many of you. You have reason to wonder that you are not already in hell.

...Therefore, let every one that is out of Christ, now awake and fly from the wrath to come. The wrath of Almighty God is now undoubtedly hanging over a great part of this congregation: Let every one fly out of Sodom: "Haste and escape for your lives, look not behind you, escape to the mountain, lest you be consumed."

8

Resolutions of the Stamp Act Congress (1765)

THE STAMP ACT CONGRESS

George Grenville, the British Prime Minister in 1765, thought that he had partially solved England's revenue problems with the Stamp Act. By requiring the American colonists to pay a few cents for every kind of document and paper-work, from wedding certificates to pamphlets opposing the Stamp Act, this new tax would finally make the colonies pay for their own protection. Many colonists felt otherwise, insisting that only their representatives could pass taxes. Since there were no American representatives in Parliament, the implication seemed to be that Parliament could not tax America. In October 1765 representatives from nine of the colonies met in New York as the Stamp Act Congress, issuing the following set of resolutions.

Questions to Consider

- Did these Americans object to the Stamp Acts because of the cost?
- By the logic of these resolutions, could Parliament pass any legislation relative to the American colonies?

The members of this Congress, sincerely devoted, with the warmest sentiments of affection and duty to His Majesty's Person and Government, inviolably attached to the present happy establishment of the Protestant succession, and with minds deeply impressed by a sense of the present and impending misfortunes of the British colonies on this continent; having considered as maturely as time will permit the circumstances of the said colonies, esteem it our indispensable duty to make the following declarations of our humble opinion, respecting the most essential rights and liberties of the colonists, and of the grievances under which they labour, by reason of several late Acts of Parliament.

1. That His Majesty's subjects in these colonies, owe the same allegiance to the Crown of Great-Britain, that is owing from his subjects born within the realm, and all due subordination to that august body the Parliament of Great-Britain.

2. That His Majesty's liege subjects in these colonies, are entitled to all the inherent rights and liberties of his natural born subjects within the kingdom of Great-Britain.

3. That it is inseparably essential to the freedom of a people, and the undoubted right of Englishmen, that no taxes be imposed on them, but with their own consent, given personally, or by their representatives.

4. That the people of these colonies are not, and from their local circumstances cannot be, represented in the House of Commons in Great-Britain.

5. That the only representatives of the people of these colonies, are persons chosen therein by themselves, and that no taxes ever have been, or can be constitutionally imposed on them, but by their respective legislatures.

Source: Hezekiah Niles, ed., *Principles and Acts of the Revolution in America* (Philadelphia, 1876), pp. 163.

6. That all supplies to the Crown, being free gifts of the people, it is unreasonable and inconsistent with the principles and spirit of the British Constitution, for the people of Great-Britain to grant to His Majesty the property of the colonists.

7. That trial by jury is the inherent and invaluable right of every British subject in these colonies.

8. That the late Act of Parliament, entitled, An Act for granting and applying certain Stamp Duties, and other Duties, in the British colonies and plantations in America, etc., by imposing taxes on the inhabitants of these colonies, and the said Act, and several other Acts, by extending the jurisdiction of the courts of Admiralty beyond its ancient limits, have a manifest tendency to subvert the rights and liberties of the colonists.

9. That the duties imposed by several late Acts of Parliament, from the peculiar circumstances of these colonies, will be extremely burthensome and grievous; and from the scarcity of specie, the payment of them absolutely impracticable.

10. That as the profits of the trade of these colonies ultimately center in Great-Britain, to pay for the manufactures which they are obliged to take from thence, they eventually contribute very largely to all supplies granted there to the Crown.

11. That the restrictions imposed by several late Acts of Parliament, on the trade of these colonies, will render them unable to purchase the manufactures of Great-Britain.

12. That the increase, prosperity, and happiness of these colonies, depend on the full and free enjoyment of their rights and liberties, and an intercourse with Great-Britain mutually affectionate and advantageous.

13. That it is the right of the British subjects in these colonies, to petition the King, Or either House of Parliament.

Lastly, That it is the indispensable duty of these colonies, to the best of sovereigns, to the mother country, and to themselves, to endeavour by a loyal and dutiful address to his Majesty, and humble applications to both Houses of Parliament, to procure the repeal of the Act for granting and applying certain stamp duties, of all clauses of any other Acts of Parliament, whereby the jurisdiction of the Admiralty is extended as aforesaid, and of the other late Acts for the restriction of American commerce.

9

Jefferson on Slavery (1784)

THOMAS JEFFERSON

Probably no member of the Revolutionary generation agonized over the questions of freedom and slavery more than Thomas Jefferson. Despite all of the moral and intellectual flaws he kept discovering in the institution of slavery, he persisted in owning slaves until his death in 1826. Scholars have long debated the consistency of Jefferson's thought on the issue, without reaching consensus. Probably Jefferson's most sustained justification of slavery came in his *Notes on the State of Virginia*, begun as a response to the specific questions of the French diplomat, the Marquis de Barbe-Marbois. The work became Jefferson's rebuttal to European criticisms of America. Jefferson privately published two hundred copies in Paris in 1784. *Notes on the State of Virginia* was published in the United States in 1794.

Questions to Consider

- What damage does slavery do to the slave owner?
- How can the same man have written "All men are created equal"?

It will probably be asked, Why not retain and incorporate the blacks into the state, and thus save the expense of supplying, by importation of white settlers, the vacancies they will leave? Deep rooted prejudices entertained by the whites; ten thousand recollections, by the blacks, of the injuries they have sustained; new provocations; the real distinctions which nature has made; and many other circumstances, will divide us into parties, and produce convulsions which will probably never end but in the extermination of the one or the other race. To these objections, which are political, may be added others, which are physical and moral.

The first difference which strikes us is that of color…. And is this difference of no importance? Is it not the foundation of a greater or less share of beauty in the two races? Are not the fine mixtures of red and white, the expressions of every passion by greater or less suffusions of color in the one, preferable to that eternal monotony, which reigns in the countenances, that immovable veil of black which covers all the emotions of the other race? Add to these, flowing hair, a more elegant symmetry of form, their own judgment in favor of the whites, declared by their preference of them, as uniformly as is the preference of the Oran-utan for the black women over those of his own species. The circumstance of superior beauty, is thought worthy attention in the propagation of our horses, dogs, and other domestic animals; why not in that of man? Besides those of color, figure, and hair, there are other physical distinctions proving a difference of race. They have less hair on the face and body. They secrete less by the kidneys, and more by the glands of the skin, which gives them a very strong and disagreeable odor. This greater degree of transpiration, renders them more tolerant of heat, and less so of cold, than the whites…. They seem to require less sleep. A black, after hard labor through the day, will be induced by the slightest amusements to sit up till midnight, or later, though knowing he must be out with the first dawn of the morning.

They are at least as brave, and more adventuresome. But this may perhaps proceed from a want of fore-

Source: Andrew A. Lipscomb and Albert Ellery Bergh, eds., *The Writings of Thomas Jefferson* (Washington, D.C., 1904), 2: pp. 191–201, 225–228.

thought, which prevents their seeing a danger till it be present. When present, they do not go through it with more coolness or steadiness than the whites. They are more ardent after their female; but love seems with them to be more an eager desire, than a tender delicate mixture of sentiment and sensation. Their griefs are transient. Those numberless afflictions, which render it doubtful whether heaven has given life to us in mercy or in wrath, are less felt, and sooner forgotten with them. In general, their existence appears to participate more of sensation than reflection. To this must be ascribed their disposition to sleep when abstracted from their diversions, and unemployed in labor. An animal whose body is at rest, and who does not reflect, must be disposed to sleep of course.

...It would be unfair to follow them to Africa for this investigation. We will consider them here, on the same stage with the whites, and where the facts are not apocryphal on which a judgment is to be formed. It will be right to make great allowances for the difference of condition, of education, of conversation, of the sphere in which they move. Many millions of them have been brought to, and born in America. Most of them indeed have been confined to tillage, to their own homes, and their own society; yet many have been so situated, that they might have availed themselves of the conversation of their masters; many have been brought up to the handicraft arts, and from that circumstance have always been associated with the whites....

There must doubtless be an unhappy influence on the manners of our people produced by the existence of slavery among us. The whole commerce between master and slave is a perpetual exercise of the most boisterous passions, the most unremitting despotism on the one part, and degrading submissions on the other. Our children see this, and learn to imitate it; for man is an imitative animal. This quality is the germ of all education in him. From his cradle to his grave he is learning to do what he sees others do. If a parent could find no motive either in his philanthropy or his self-love, for restraining the intemperance of passion towards his slave, it should always be a sufficient one that his child is present. But generally it is not sufficient. The parent storms, the child looks on, catches the lineaments of wrath, puts on the same airs in the circle of smaller slaves, gives a loose to the worst of passions, and thus nursed, educated, and daily exercised in tyranny, cannot but be stamped by it with odious peculiarities. The man must be a prodigy who can retain his manners and morals undepraved by such circumstances.... And can the liberties of a nation be thought secure when we have removed their only firm basis, a conviction in the minds of the people that these liberties are of the gift of God? That they are not to be violated but with his wrath? Indeed I tremble for my country when I reflect that God is just; that his justice cannot sleep for ever; that considering numbers, nature and natural means only, a revolution of the wheel of fortune, an exchange of situation, is among possible events; that it may become probable by supernatural interference! The Almighty has no attribute which can take side with us in such a contest.

10

An African View of the Slave Trade (1789)

O L A U D A H   E Q U I A N O

Born in what is now Nigeria, Olaudah Equiano was kidnapped at the age of eleven. He was then sold several times, until he finally arrived at the coast and was sold across the Atlantic. After some time in Barbados, Equiano was sold to a Virginia planter, who sold him to an officer in the British navy. Equiano traveled widely with his final owner and was included on some expeditions exploring the Arctic. One ship's captain named him Gustavus after a Swedish king, and Equiano had himself baptized as Gustavus Vassa. Along the way, he also learned to read and write English. With the help of a Quaker merchant, Equiano purchased his freedom, then decided to write an autobiography, which was published in London in 1789. As the first African commentary on the Atlantic slave trade, Equiano's book captured public attention, and was reprinted in the United States in 1794.

Questions to Consider

- Does Equiano distinguish between his treatment as a slave in Africa and his treatment as a slave after his arrival at the coast?
- How does Equiano describe his feelings on being torn from his family?

...One day, when all our people were gone out to their works as usual, and only I and my dear sister were left to mind the house, two men and a woman got over our walls, and in a moment seized us both, and, without giving us time to cry out, or make resistance, they stopped our mouths, and ran off with us into the nearest wood. Here they tied our hands, and continued to carry us as far as they could, till night came on, when we reached a small house, where the robbers halted for refreshment, and spent the night. We were then unbound, but were unable to take any food; and, being quite overpowered by fatigue and grief, our only relief

was some sleep, which allayed our misfortune for a short time....

When we went to rest the following night they offered us some victuals; but we refused it; and the only comfort we had was in being in one another's arms all that night, and bathing each other with our tears. But alas! we were soon deprived of even the small comfort of weeping together. The next day proved a day of greater sorrow than I had yet experienced; for my sister and I were then separated, while we lay clasped in each other's arms. It was in vain that we besought them not to part us; she was torn from me, and immediately carried away, while I was left in a state of distraction not to be described. I cried and grieved continually; and for several days I did not eat any thing but what they forced into my mouth.

At length, after many days travelling, during which I had often changed masters, I got into the hands of a

Source: Olaudah Equiano, *The Interesting Narrative of the Life of Olaudah Equiano, or Gustavus Vassa, The African* (2 vols.; London: 1789), 1: pp. 47–51, 65–75.

chieftain, in a very pleasant country. This man had two wives and some children, and they all used me extremely well, and did all they could to comfort me; particularly the first wife, who was something like my mother. Although I was a great many days journey from my father's house, yet these people spoke exactly the same language with us.

…[W]ithout the least previous knowledge, one morning early, while my dear master and companion was still asleep, I was wakened out of my reverie to fresh sorrow, and hurried away even amongst the uncircumcised…. The change I now experienced was as painful as it was sudden and unexpected. It was a change indeed from a state of bliss to a scene which is inexpressible to me, as it discovered to me an element I had never before beheld, and till then had no idea of, and wherein such instances of hardship and cruelty continually occurred as I can never reflect on but with horror.

All the nations and people I had hitherto passed through resembled our own in their manners, customs, and language: but I came at length to a country, the inhabitants of which differed from us in all those particulars. I was very much struck with this difference, especially when I came among a people who did not circumcise, and ate without washing their hands. They cooked also in iron pots, and had European cutlasses and cross bows, which were unknown to us, and fought with their fists among themselves. Their women were not so modest as ours, for they ate, and drank, and slept, with their men. But, above all, I was amazed to see no sacrifices or offerings amongst them. In some of those places the people ornamented themselves with scars, and likewise filed their teeth very sharp. They wanted sometimes to ornament me in the same manner, but I would not suffer them; hoping that I might some time be among a people who did not thus disfigure themselves, as I thought they did.

…I continued to travel, sometimes by land, sometimes by water, through different countries and various nations, till, at the end of six or seven months after I had been kidnapped, I arrived at the sea coast….

The first object which saluted my eyes when I arrived on the coast was the sea, and a slave ship, which was then riding at anchor, and waiting for its cargo. These filled me with astonishment, which was soon converted into terror when I was carried on board. I was immediately handled and tossed up to see if I were sound by some of the crew; and I was now persuaded that I had gotten into a world of bad spirits, and that they were going to kill me. Their complexions too differing so much from ours, their long hair, and the lan-

guage they spoke, (which was very different from any I had ever heard) united to confirm me in this belief. Indeed such were the horrors of my views and fears at the moment, that, if ten thousand worlds had been my own, I would have freely parted with them all to have exchanged my condition with that of the meanest slave in my own country. When I looked round the ship too and saw a large furnace or copper boiling, and a multitude of black people of every description chained together, every one of their countenances expressing dejection and sorrow, I no longer doubted of my fate; and, quite overpowered with horror and anguish, I fell motionless on the deck and fainted….

I now saw myself deprived of all chance of returning to my native country, or even the least glimpse of hope of gaining the shore, which I now considered as friendly; and I even wished for my former slavery in preference to my present situation, which was filled with horrors of every kind, still heightened by my ignorance of what I was to undergo. I was not long suffered to indulge my grief; I was soon put down under the decks, and there I received such a salutation in my nostrils as I had never experienced in my life: so that, with the loathsomeness of the stench, and crying together, I became so sick and low that I was not able to eat, nor had I the least desire to taste any thing. I now wished for the last friend, death, to relieve me; but soon, to my grief, two of the white men offered me eatables; and, on my refusing to eat, one of them held me fast by the hands, and laid me across I think the windlass, and tied my feet, while the other flogged me severely. I had never experienced any thing of the kind before; and although, not being used to the water, I naturally feared that element the first time I saw it, yet nevertheless, could I have got over the nettings, I would have jumped over the side, but I could not; and, besides, the crew used to watch us very closely who were not chained down to the decks, lest we should leap into the water: and I have seen some of these poor African prisoners most severely cut for attempting to do so, and hourly whipped for not eating. This indeed was often the case with myself.

…I feared I should be put to death, the white people looked and acted, as I thought, in so savage a manner; for I had never seen among any people such instances of brutal cruelty; and this not only shewn towards us blacks, but also to some of the whites themselves. One white man in particular I saw, when we were permitted to be on deck, flogged so unmercifully with a large rope near the foremast, that he died in consequence of it; and they tossed him over the side as they would have done a brute. This made me fear these people the more…

11

Farewell Address (1796)

G E O R G E   W A S H I N G T O N

Refusing to consider a third term as president, George Washington retired grate-fully to Mount Vernon. He left behind for the public this last political testament, his advice for the nation he helped to found, based, he felt, on his long experience in public service. Certainly his own presidency had convinced him that the nation faced a grave danger: internal dissension exacerbated by foreign entangle-ments. Washington had in mind the emerging Jeffersonian opposition to the Federalist government and the division between those who sided with the French in their wars against the monarchical powers led by Britain. Washington based this farewell address on one he had prepared in 1792 since he anticipated serv-ing only a single term as president. He never delivered the address as a speech but had it published in a Philadelphia newspaper in September 1796.

Questions to Consider

- Why did Washington place so much emphasis on neutrality?
- How far did he think the government should go in responding to organized do-mestic opposition to its policies?
- What makes political parties dangerous to a republic?

Friends and Fellow Citizens:...In looking forward to the moment which is intended to terminate the career of my political life, my feelings do not per-mit me to suspend the deep acknowledgment of that debt of gratitude which I owe to my beloved country for the many honors it has conferred upon me; still more for the steadfast confidence with which it has sup-ported me, and for the opportunities I have thence en-joyed of manifesting my inviolable attachment by services faithful and persevering, though in usefulness unequal to my zeal....

Here, perhaps, I ought to stop. But a solicitude for your welfare, which cannot end but with my life, and the apprehension of danger, natural to that solicitude, urge me on an occasion like the present, to offer to your

solemn contemplation and to recommend to your fre-quent review some sentiments which are the result of much reflection, of no inconsiderable observation, and which appear to me all important to the permanency of your felicity as a people....

The unity of government which constitutes you one people is also now dear to you. It is justly so, for it is a main pillar in the edifice of your real independence, the support of your tranquillity at home, your peace abroad, of your safety, of your prosperity, of that very liberty which you so highly prize. But as it is easy to foresee that from different causes and from different quarters much pains will be taken, many artifices em-ployed, to weaken in your minds the conviction of this truth, as this is the point in your political fortress against which the batteries of internal and external ene-mies will be most constantly and actively (though often covertly and insidiously) directed, it is of infinite mo-ment that you should properly estimate the immense value of your national union to your collective and in-

Source: James D. Richardson, *A Compilation of the Messages and Papers of the Presidents* (Washington, D.C., 1896), 1: pp. 213–224.

dividual happiness; that you should cherish a cordial, habitual, and immovable attachment to it; accustoming yourselves to think and speak of it as the palladium of your political safety and prosperity; watching for its preservation with jealous anxiety; discountenancing whatever may suggest even a suspicion that it can in any event be abandoned, and indignantly frowning upon the first dawning of every attempt to alienate any portion of our country from the rest or to enfeeble the sacred ties which now link together the various parts.

…In contemplating the causes which may disturb our union it occurs as a matter of serious concern that any ground should have been furnished for characterizing parties by *geographical* discriminations—*Northern* and *Southern*; *Atlantic* and *Western*—whence designing men may endeavor to excite a belief that there is a real difference of local interests and views. One of the expedients of party to acquire influence within particular districts is to misrepresent the opinions and aims of other districts. You cannot shield yourselves too much against the jealousies and heartburnings which spring from these misrepresentations; they tend to render alien to each other those who ought to be bound together by fraternal affection….

This Government, the offspring of your own choice, uninfluenced and unawed, adopted upon full investigation and mature deliberation, completely free in its principles, in the distribution of its powers, uniting security with energy, and containing within itself a provision for its own amendment, has a just claim to your confidence and your support. Respect for its authority, compliance with its laws, acquiescence in its measures, are duties enjoined by the fundamental maxims of true liberty…. The very idea of the power and the right of the people to establish government presupposes the duty of every individual to obey the established government.

…Let me now take a more comprehensive view, and warn you in the most solemn manner against the baneful effects of the spirit of party generally.

This spirit, unfortunately, is inseparable from our nature, having its root in the strongest passions of the human mind. It exists under different shapes in all governments, more or less stifled, controlled, or repressed; but in those of the popular form it is seen in its greatest rankness and is truly their worst enemy….

It serves always to distract the public councils and enfeeble the public administration. It agitates the community with ill-founded jealousies and false alarms; kindles the animosity of one part against another; foments occasionally riot and insurrection. It opens the door to foreign influence and corruption, which find a facilitated access to the government itself through the channels of party passion. Thus the policy and the will of one country are subjected to the policy and will of another.

There is an opinion that parties in free countries are useful checks upon the administration of government, and serve to keep alive the spirit of liberty. This within certain limits is probably true; and in governments of a monarchical cast patriotism may look with indulgence, if not with favor, upon the spirit of party. But in those of the popular character, in governments purely elective, it is a spirit not to be encouraged. From their natural tendency it is certain there will always be enough of that spirit for every salutary purpose; and there being constant danger of excess, the effort ought to be by force of public opinion to mitigate and assuage it. A fire not to be quenched, it demands a uniform vigilance to prevent its bursting into a flame, lest, instead of warming, it should consume.

As a very important source of strength and security, cherish public credit. One method of preserving it is to use it as sparingly as possible, avoiding occasions of expense by cultivating peace, but remembering also that timely disbursements to prepare for danger frequently prevent much greater disbursements to repel it; avoiding likewise the accumulation of debt, not only by shunning occasions of expense, but by exertions in time of peace to discharge the debts which unavoidable wars have occasioned, not ungenerously throwing upon posterity the burthen which we ourselves ought to bear…. [B]ear in mind that toward the payment of debts there must be revenue; that to have revenue there must be taxes; that no taxes can be devised which are not more or less inconvenient and unpleasant…

In the execution of such a plan nothing is more essential than that permanent, inveterate antipathies against particular nations and passionate attachments for others should be excluded, and that in place of them just and amicable feelings toward all should be cultivated. The nation which indulges toward another an habitual hatred or an habitual fondness is in some degree a slave. It is a slave to its animosity or to its affection, either of which is sufficient to lead it astray from its duty and its interest….

The great rule of conduct for us in regard to foreign nations is, in extending our commercial relations to have with them as little political connection as possible. So far as we have already formed engagements let them be fulfilled with perfect good faith. Here let us stop….

Harmony, liberal intercourse with all nations are recommended by policy, humanity, and interest. But even our commercial policy should hold an equal and impartial hand, neither seeking nor granting exclusive favors or preferences;…diffusing and diversifying by gentle means the streams of commerce, but forcing nothing;… constantly keeping in view that it is folly in one nation to look for disinterested favors from another.... There can be no greater error than to expect or calculate upon real favors from nation to nation. It is an illusion which experience must cure, which a just pride ought to discard....

I anticipate with pleasing expectation that retreat in which I promise myself to realize without alloy the sweet enjoyment of partaking in the midst of my fellow-citizens the benign influence of good laws under a free government—the ever-favorite object of my heart, and the happy reward, as I trust, of our mutual cares, labors and dangers.

GO. WASHINGTON

12

The Monroe Doctrine (1823)

J O H N   Q U I N C Y   A D A M S

What we now call the Monroe Doctrine was, in fact, written by his Secretary of State, John Quincy Adams, and formed part of President Monroe's annual message to Congress on December 2, 1823. Adams sought to ensure the legitimacy of the newly independent republics of Latin America and feared that the European powers would seek to re-establish their empires in the Americas. Monroe's statements had little initial impact and were not drawn upon as an actual doctrine guiding American foreign policy until late in the nineteenth century.

Questions to Consider

- On what basis did Adams and Monroe seek to deny Europe the right to interfere in the affairs of the western hemisphere?
- Did the United States have any collateral right to intervene in European affairs?

At the proposal of the Russian Imperial Government, made through the minister of the Emperor residing here, a full power and instructions have been transmitted to the minister of the United States at St. Petersburg to arrange by amicable negotiation the respective rights and interests of the two nations on the northwest coast of this continent. A similar proposal has been made by His Imperial Majesty to the Government of Great Britain, which has likewise been acceded to. The Government of the United States has been desirous by this friendly proceeding of manifesting the great value which they have invariably attached to the friendship of the Emperor and their solicitude to cultivate the best understanding with his Government. In the discussions to which this interest has given rise and in the arrangements by which they may terminate the occasion has been judged proper for asserting, as a principle in which the rights and interests of the United States are involved, that the American continents, by the free and independent condition which they have assumed and maintain, are henceforth not to be considered as subjects for future colonization by any European powers…

It was stated at the commencement of the last session that a great effort was then making in Spain and Portugal to improve the condition of the people of those countries, and that it appeared to be conducted with extraordinary moderation. It need scarcely be remarked that the results have been so far very different from what was then anticipated. Of events in that quarter of the globe, with which we have so much intercourse and from which we derive our origin, we have always been anxious and interested spectators.

The citizens of the United States cherish sentiments the most friendly in favor of the liberty and happiness of their fellow-men on that side of the Atlantic. In the wars of the European powers in matters relating to themselves we have never taken any part, nor does it comport with our policy to do so. It is only when our rights are invaded or seriously menaced that we resent injuries or make preparation for our defense. With the movements in this hemisphere we are of necessity more immediately connected, and by causes which must be obvious to all enlightened and impartial observers. The

Source: James D. Richardson, ed., *A Compilation of the Messages and Papers of the Presidents, 1787–1897* (Washington, D.C., 1896), 2: pp. 209, 217–219.

political system of the allied powers is essentially different in this respect from that of America. This difference proceeds from that which exists in their respective Governments; and to the defense of our own, which has been achieved by the loss of so much blood and treasure, and matured by the wisdom of their most enlightened citizens, and under which we have enjoyed unexampled felicity, this whole nation is devoted. We owe it, therefore, to candor and to the amicable relations existing between the United States and those powers to declare that we should consider any attempt on their part to extend their system to any portion of this hemisphere as dangerous to our peace and safety. With the existing colonies or dependencies of any European power we have not interfered and shall not interfere. But with the Governments who have declared their independence and maintain it, and whose independence we have, on great consideration and on just principles, acknowledged, we could not view any interposition for the purpose of oppressing them, or controlling in any other manner their destiny, by any European power in any other light than as the manifestation of an unfriendly disposition toward the United States. In the war between those new Governments and Spain we declared our neutrality at the time of their recognition, and to this we have adhered, and shall continue to adhere, provided no change shall occur which, in the judgement of the competent authorities of this Government, shall make a corresponding change on the part of the United States indispensable to their security.

The late events in Spain and Portugal shew that Europe is still unsettled. Of this important fact no stronger proof can be adduced than that the allied powers should have thought it proper, on any principle satisfactory to themselves, to have interposed by force in the internal concerns of Spain. To what extent such interposition may be carried, on the same principle, is a question in which all independent powers whose governments differ from theirs are interested, even those most remote, and surely none of them more so than the United States. Our policy in regard to Europe, which was adopted at an early stage of the wars which have so long agitated that quarter of the globe, nevertheless remains the same, which is, not to interfere in the internal concerns of any of its powers; to consider the government de facto as the legitimate government for us; to cultivate friendly relations with it, and to preserve those relations by a frank, firm, and manly policy, meeting in all instances the just claims of every power, submitting to injuries from none. But in regard to those continents circumstances are eminently and conspicuously different. It is impossible that the allied powers should extend their political system to any portion of either continent without endangering our peace and happiness; nor can anyone believe that our southern brethren, if left to themselves, would adopt it of their own accord. It is equally impossible, therefore, that we should behold such interposition in any form with indifference. If we look to the comparative strength and resources of Spain and those new Governments, and their distance from each other, it must be obvious that she can never subdue them. It is still the true policy of the United States to leave the parties to themselves, in hope that other powers will pursue the same course.

13

The Confessions of Nat Turner (1831)

N A T   T U R N E R

On August 21, 1831 in southeastern Virginia, Nat Turner led seventy fellow slaves in a revolt that sought to end their bondage. The uprising seems to have begun spontaneously. Turner began by killing his owner, Joseph Travis, and Travis's family. By the time the rebellion had been crushed just two days later, the rebels had killed fifty-seven whites. The local whites responded brutally in turn, executing two hundred slaves, many of whom had nothing to do with the uprising. The revolt unnerved Southern whites. Turner and his owner had gotten along well; Turner described Travis as a kind man who had encouraged Turner to learn to read and write and to become a preacher. Turner was hanged with thirteen of his fellow rebels. Turner dictated the following confession to his attorney, Thomas R. Gray.

Questions to Consider

- Why would a trusted slave who had been given an unusual amount of freedom lead a rebellion?
- Was Gray correct in calling these events "the offspring of gloomy fanaticism"?

You have asked me to give a history of the motives which induced me to undertake the late insurrection, as you call it. To do so I must go back to the days of my infancy, and even before I was born.... In my childhood a circumstance occurred which made an indelible impression on my mind, and laid the ground work of that enthusiasm, which has terminated so fatally to many both white and black, and for which I am about to atone at the gallows.... Being at play with other children, when three or four years old, I was telling them something, which my mother overhearing, said it had happened before I was born.

I stuck to my story, however, and related some things which went in her opinion to confirm it—others being called on were greatly astonished, knowing that these things had happened, and caused them to say in my hearing, I surely would be a prophet, as the Lord had shewn me things that had happened before my birth. And my father and mother strengthened me in this my first impression, saying in my presence, I was intended for some great purpose....

My grandmother, who was very religious, and to whom I was much attached—my master, who belonged to the church, and other religious persons who visited the house...noticing the singularity of my manners, I suppose, and my uncommon intelligence for a child, remarked I had too much sense to be raised [a slave], and if I was, I would never be of any service to any one as a slave. To a mind like mine, restless, inquisitive and observant of every thing that was passing, it is easy to suppose that religion was the subject to which it would be directed....

Having soon discovered to be great, I must appear so, and therefore studiously avoided mixing in society, and wrapped myself in mystery, devoting my time to

Source: *The Anglo-African Magazine* 1 (December, 1859), pp. 388–394.

fasting and prayer. By this time, having arrived to man's estate, and hearing the Scriptures commented on at meetings, I was struck with that particular passage which says: "Seek ye the kingdom of Heaven and all things shall be added unto you." I reflected much on this passage, and prayed daily for light on this subject: As I was praying one day at my plough, the spirit spoke to me, saying "Seek ye the kingdom of Heaven and all things shall be added unto you." …And I was greatly astonished, and for two years prayed continually, whenever my duty would permit. And then again I had the same revelation, which fully confirmed me in the impression that I was ordained for some great purpose in the hands of the Almighty.

…Now finding I had arrived to man's estate, and was a slave, and these revelations being made known to me, I began to direct my attention to this great object, to fulfill the purpose for which, by this time, I felt assured I was intended. Knowing the influence I had obtained over the minds of my fellow servants…I now began to prepare them for my purpose, by telling them something was about to happen that would terminate in fulfilling the great promise that had been made to me.

…And about this time I had a vision, and I saw white spirits and black spirits engaged in battle, and the sun was darkened, the thunder rolled in the Heavens, and blood flowed in streams, and I heard a voice saying, "Such is your luck, such you are called to see, and let it come rough or smooth, you must surely bear it."

…And from the first steps of righteousness until the last, was I made perfect; and the Holy Ghost was with me, and said "Behold me as I stand in the Heavens," and I looked and saw the forms of men in different attitudes and there were lights in the sky to which the children of darkness gave other names than what they really were, for they were the lights of the Savior's hands, stretched forth from east to west, even as they were extended on the cross on Calvary for the redemption of sinners. And I wondered greatly at these miracles, and prayed to be informed of a certainty of the meaning thereof, and shortly afterwards, while labor-ing in the field, I discovered drops of blood on the corn, as though it were dew from heaven, and I communicated it to many, both white and black, in the neighborhood…. And now the Holy Ghost had revealed itself to me, and made plain the miracles it had shown me—for as the blood of Christ had been shed on this earth, and had ascended to heaven for the salvation of sinners, and was now returning to earth again in the form of dew,…it was plain to me that the Savior was about to lay down the yoke he had borne for the sins of men, and the great day of judgment was at hand….

And by signs in the heavens that it would make known to me when I should commence the great work…. And on the appearance of the sign, (the eclipse of the sun last February) I should arise and prepare myself, and slay my enemies with their own weapons. And immediately on the sign appearing in the heavens, the seal was removed from my lips, and I communicated the great work laid out for me to do, to four in whom I had the greatest confidence, (Henry, Hark, Nelson and Sam)….

Since the commencement of 1830, I had been living with Mr. Joseph Travis, who was to me a kind master, and placed the greatest confidence in me; in fact, I had no cause to complain of his treatment to me….

Hark got a ladder and set it against the chimney, on which I ascended, and hoisting a window, entered and came down stairs, unbarred the door, and removed the guns from their places. It was then observed that I must spill the first blood. On which, armed with a hatchet, and accompanied by Will, I entered my master's chamber, it being dark, I could not give a death blow, the hatchet glanced from his head, he sprang from the bed and called his wife, it was his last word, Will laid him dead with a blow of his axe, and Mrs. Travis shared the same fate, as she laid in bed. The murder of this family, five in number, was the work of a moment; not one of them awoke; there was a little infant sleeping in a cradle, that was forgotten, until we had left the house and gone some distance, when Henry and Will returned and killed it.

14

The Dangers of Immigration (1835)

SAMUEL F. B. MORSE

Samuel Morse was a man of many accomplishments, a noted painter as well as the inventor of the telegraph. In the 1830s he became convinced that the United States was being overrun by Catholic immigrants who posed a danger to America's democratic institutions. Certain that the United States suffered few flaws, Morse held that the very character of the country would be changed for the worse unless immigration was halted immediately. Or, as Morse asked, "Can one throw mud into pure water and not disturb its clearness?" Morse would later play a key role in the development of the nativist Know Nothing Party, which enjoyed a period of success in the 1850s.

Questions to Consider

- What was the attraction of nativism for so many voters?
- Why, in Morse's view, couldn't Catholics be reliable citizens?

I have shown what are the *Foreign materials* imported into the country, with which the Jesuits can work to accomplish their designs. Let us examine this point a little more minutely. These materials are the *varieties of Foreigners* of the same Creed, the Roman Catholic, over all of whom the Bishops or Vicars General hold, as a matter of course, ecclesiastical rule; and we well know what is the nature of Roman Catholic ecclesiastical rule,—it is the double refined spirit of despotism, which, after arrogating to itself the prerogatives of Deity, and so claiming to bind or loose the *soul* eternally, makes it, in the comparison, but a mere trifle to exercise absolute sway in all that relates to the body. The notorious ignorance in which the great mass of these emigrants have been all their lives sunk, until their minds are dead, makes them but senseless machines; they obey orders mechanically, for it is the habit of their ed-

ucation, in the despotic countries of their birth. And can it be for a moment supposed by any one that by the act of coming to this country, and being naturalized, their darkened intellects can suddenly be illuminated to discern the nice boundary where their *ecclesiastical obedience* to their priests *ends,* and their *civil independence* of them *begins?* The very supposition is absurd. They obey their priests as demigods, from the habit of their whole lives; they have been taught from infancy that their priests are infallible in the greatest matters, and can they, by mere importation to this country, be suddenly imbued with the knowledge that in civil matters their priests may err, and that they are not in these also their infallible guides?…Must not the priests, as a matter almost of *certainty,* control the opinions of their ignorant flock in civil as well as religious matters? and do they not do it?….

That a change of some kind in the Naturalization Laws is required, seems to be conceded on all sides, but the nature and extent of this change are strangely opposite in character. While some, and doubtless the greater part of the American population, would have them changed with the view of *discouraging* immigration, and

Source: Samuel F. B. Morse, *Imminent Dangers to the United States Through Foreign Immigration* (New York: E. B. Clayton, 1835), pp. 13, 17, 19, 25.

of guarding our institutions from foreign interference, at the point where they are not only assailable, but where they are at this moment actually assailed and greatly endangered; others would have them changed so as to throw down all the barriers which protect us as an independent nation, and extend the right of suffrage, strange as it may seem, with such an unheard of universality of application, as no advocate of the proper and just principles of universal suffrage ever before ventured to dream of; to the extent, in fact, virtually of giving the administration of our government to any and all nations of the world, no matter how barbarous, who choose to take the trouble to exercise it. Instead of guarding with greater vigilance and care our institutions, when attacked, by new defences, these patriots would not only make no resistance, but would actually invite the enemy, by demolishing the fortresses already existing, and yield up the country into his uncontrolled possession.

...The foreigner presents himself at the door, and claims to be admitted into this community, and to *equal* rights with the rest of the family. On what ground? Why, on that of his *natural rights,* as set forth in our Declaration of Independence. He quotes it, and says, "all men are created equal," "they are endowed with certain unalienable rights, among these are life, liberty, and the pursuit of happiness." 'I am a man, and therefore am entitled, according to your own showing, to equality, and my unalienable rights.' Thus the question seems to him unanswerably settled. Let us examine the matter. The first inquiry respects the meaning of these phrases. If there should be any diversity of opinion as to *what they do mean,* there can at least be no difficulty in ascertaining what they *do NOT mean....* It is very clear then that Congress, in the Declaration of Independence, did not mean to allow of *any such construction of that instrument in regard to abstract equality, as should in effect be directly subversive of Independence....* They certainly did not mean by equality *that the minority should be superior or equal to the majority....* These points are clear, and they at once settle the question as to the right of foreigners who come to our shores and demand to be admitted

into the community on *equal* terms, and plead as their warrant the *declared abstract principles of the government.* If we are indeed an independent nation, we surely have a right to regulate all *admission into* the nation....

The arbitrary governments of Europe,—those governments who keep the people in the most abject obedience at the point of the bayonet, with Austria at their head, have combined to attack us in every vulnerable point that the nation exposes to their assault. They are impelled by self-preservation to attempt our destruction,—they must destroy democracy.... If they do not overthrow American liberty, American liberty will overthrow their despotism.... They are acting in accordance with their convictions, and declarations, and they are acting wisely. They have already sent their chains, and oh! to our shame be it spoken, are fastening them upon a sleeping victim. Americans, you are marked for their prey, not by foreign bayonets, but *by weapons surer of effecting the conquest of liberty* than all the munitions of physical combat in the military or naval storehouses of Europe.... Will you be longer deceived by the pensioned Jesuits, who having surrounded your press, are now using it all over the country to stifle the cries of danger, and lull your fears by attributing your alarm to a false cause.... Awake! To your posts!... Fly to protect the vulnerable places of your Constitution and Laws. Place your guards; you will need them, and quickly too.—And first, shut your gates. Shut the open gates.... Will you despise the cry of danger? Well, be it so.... Open wide your doors. Yes, throw down your walls. Invite, nay allure, your enemies. Enlarge your almshouses and your prisons; be not sparing of your money; complain not of the outrages in your streets, nor the burden of your taxes. You will be repaid in praises of your toleration and liberality....

[Y]our country is filling with a noble foreign population, all friends of liberty, all undoubted Democrats, taught in the school of Democratic Europe,...selected with the greatest care by Austria's Democratic Emperor, and Rome's Democratic Pope.... Democracy is safe with such keepers. The country is in no danger. Sleep on.

15

Texas Invades New Mexico (1841)

M A N U E L   A R M I J O

The 1830s was a time of political turmoil in the Southwest. In Texas, settlers from the United States revolted against Mexican sovereignty and declared an independent state. In New Mexico, the Chimayo Rebellion threatened Mexican control over its other northern states. In 1837 General Manuel Armijo put down the uprising in New Mexico and executed its leaders. As governor of New Mexico for the last decade of Mexican rule, Armijo's primary problem remained the repeated efforts of Texas to invade his state. In 1841 an expedition of Texans under General McLeod invaded New Mexico. In the following proclamation, Governor Armijo calls on his citizens to resist the invaders. Armijo defeated the Texans, taking the entire force prisoner in October 1841.

Questions to Consider

- Why would anyone within New Mexico welcome the invasion by the Texans?
- Was Armijo justified in warning that the New Mexicans were endangered by the loss of their religion and property?

The Governor and Commandant General of New Mexico to Its Inhabitants.

Fellow Patriots:—The ever accredited mildness that in all epochs and circumstances has characterized the benignity of the Mexican government, which, as a guide, has ever been followed by the one who addresses you, from the time he was given the honor of governing you, as governor and commanding general of this department, well satisfied of the docility of all and each of its inhabitants, he does not for a moment hesitate to address you (to the effect) that if there be one or several (among you) who, seduced with or deceived by coaxing words have without foresight effected any compromise

assuring those governing Texas that they will be in their favor in the present struggle with Mexico;... provided that at present, and from today on, they accredit their patriotism, adhesion, loyalty and fidelity to our legitimate and paternal government of the Mexican republic to which we have the honor of belonging; in the name of the same, and upon my word of honor, the corresponding pardon is solemnly hereof promised without fear of the least damage being inflicted on you on account of such a deed, and without the least impairment to the nationality and patriotism to which you are creditors by a thousand titles as the patrimony of loyalty bequeathed to you as a heritage by your ancestors.

Yes, my dear fellow citizens and fellow patriots, it is not to be feared and much less believed, that, with the danger of losing your religion, your country, and your property, you would hesitate for a single moment to place yourselves under the shadow of and around your

Source: Benjamin M. Read, *Illustrated History of New Mexico* (Santa Fe, 1912), pp. 402–403.

national flag, and that, facing all the dangers, and exaggerated perils, we, the New Mexicans (despite the plots of those rivals and traitors, the Texans, and their followers) shall display our valor and earn the laurels which shall be displayed on a level with and parallel to those of the most warlike nations on earth. This I promise you, and with this, your fellow citizen and chief drinks to your health.

MANUEL ARMIJO,
SANTA FE, N. M., SEPT. 18, 1841.

16

Workers and Immigrants (1845)

VOICE OF INDUSTRY

The following condemnation of immigration was published in the *Voice of Industry*, a workers' newspaper published in Fitchburg, Massachusetts. Appearing on October 9, 1845, under the title, "Progress of Monopoly," this article saw mass immigration as a threat to the prosperity and rights of American labor.

Questions to Consider

• Who, in the workers' view, was responsible for this threat?

• What solutions were available to American workers?

We copy the following item from the Lowell Journal. "Two hundred workmen from England arrived at the Iron Works at Danville, Penn., where they are to be employed."

The above few lines contain an important lesson for every workingman and woman in America, they clearly exhibit to the unbiased, investigating and reflecting mind, the onward rapid strides of the great, deep-rooted inhuman monster system of capital against labor, which is fast devouring every tangible and valuable right that belongs to the working classes of this country, as moral, physical and intellectual beings, capable of filling the land with an abundance, and generating peaceful industry, virtue and happiness.... The democratic republican capital of this country, which has been so amply fortified against foreign despotic capital by the suffrages of American workingmen ("all for their especial benefit;") says there are not enough "free, independent and well paid" workingmen and women in this country; consequently foreign operatives and workmen must be imported—no tariff on these! no, no, it wont do to protect the capital of American working-men and women (their labor) against foreign competition! for this would be anti-republican. But, "protect the rich capitalist and he will take care of the laborer."

Now the capitalists of the Danville Iron works wish to protect themselves against these "disorderly strikes," by importing a surplus of help; the Lowell capitalists entertain the same republican idea of self protection, the Pittsburg and Alleghany city capitalists, whose sympathies, (if they have any,) have been recently appealed to, wish to secure themselves against "turn-outs" by creating a numerous poor and dependant populace. Isolated capital everywhere and in all ages protects itself by the poverty, ignorance, and servility of a surplus population, who will submit to its base requirements—hence the democratic or Whig capital of the United States is striving to fill the country with foreign workmen—English workmen, whose abject condition in their own country has made them tame, submissive and "peaceable, orderly citizens;" that is, work fourteen and sixteen hours per day, for what capital sees fit to give them, and if it is not enough to provide them a comfortable house to shelter their wives and children and furnish them with decent food and clothes, why, they must live in cellars, go hungry and ragged!—and for this state of things, capitalists are not answerable. O! no— "they (the laborers) aint obliged to take it—they are free to go when they please!"

Source: John R. Commons et al., eds., *A Documentary History of American Industrial Society* (Cleveland, Ohio, 1910), 7: pp. 88–89.

17

Manifest Destiny (1845)

J O H N   O ' S U L L I V A N

Few phrases have so perfectly summarized popular political attitudes as did "Manifest Destiny." The belief that God intended for the United States to spread its political power over the entire continent dominated the United States for much of the nineteenth century, most particularly within the Democratic Party. John O'Sullivan, editor of *The United States Magazine and Democratic Review*, was an influential Democrat and expansionist. The following editorial not only gave a name to what many Americans already felt, but also accelerated demands for the annexation of Texas. O'Sullivan repeated these arguments later that year in demanding all of the Oregon territory.

Questions to Consider

- Why did O'Sullivan feel justified in insisting that debate end on the annexation of Texas?
- What right did the Republic of Mexico have to this territory?
- What role did slavery play in the question of annexation?

It is time now for opposition to the Annexation of Texas to cease, all further agitation of the waters of bitterness and strife, at least in connexion with this question…It is time for the common duty of Patriotism to the Country to succeed;—or if this claim will not be recognized, it is at least time for common sense to acquiesce with decent grace in the inevitable and the irrevocable.

Texas is now ours. Already, before these words are written, her Convention has undoubtedly ratified the acceptance, by her Congress, of our proffered invitation into the Union; and made the requisite changes in her already republican form of constitution to adopt it to its future federal relations. Her star and her stripe may already be said to have taken their place in the glorious blazon of our common nationality; and the sweep of our eagle's wing already includes within its circuit the wide extent of her fair and fertile land….

Source: John O'Sullivan, "Annexation," *The United States Magazine and Democratic Review* 17 (July and Aug. 1845), pp. 5–10.

Why, were other reasoning wanting, in favor of now elevating this question of the reception of Texas into the Union, out of the lower region of our past party dissensions, up to its proper level of a high and broad nationality, it surely is to be found, found abundantly, in the manner in which other nations have undertaken to intrude themselves into it, between us and the proper parties to the case, in a spirit of hostile interference against us, for the avowed object of thwarting our policy and hampering our power, limiting our greatness and checking the fulfillment of our manifest destiny to overspread the continent allotted by Providence for the free development of our yearly multiplying millions. This we have seen done by England, our old rival and enemy; and by France, strangely coupled with her against us….

It is wholly untrue, and unjust to ourselves, the pretence that the Annexation has been a measure of spoliation, unrightful and unrighteous—of military conquest under forms of peace and law—of territorial aggrandizement at the expense of justice, and justice due by a double sanctity to the weak. This view of the question is wholly unfounded, and has been before so amply refuted in these pages, as well as in a thousand other modes, that we shall not again dwell upon it. The independence of Texas was complete and absolute. It was an independence, not only in fact but of right. No obligation of duty towards Mexico tended in the least degree to restrain our right to effect the desired recovery of the fair province once our own—whatever motives of policy might have prompted a more deferential consideration of her feelings and her pride, as involved in the question. If Texas became peopled with an American population, it was by no contrivance of our government, but on the express invitation of that of Mexico herself; accompanied with such guaranties of State independence, and the maintenance of a federal system analogous to our own, as constituted a compact fully justifying the strongest measures of redress on the part of those afterwards deceived in this guaranty, and sought to be enslaved under the yoke imposed by its violation. She was released, rightfully and absolutely released, from all Mexican allegiance, or duty of cohesion to the Mexican political body, by the acts and fault of Mexico herself, and Mexico alone. There never was a clearer case….

Nor is there any just foundation for the charge that Annexation is a great pro-slavery measure—calculated to increase and perpetuate that institution. Slavery had nothing to do with it. Opinions were and are greatly divided, both at the North and South, as to the influence to be exerted by it on Slavery and the Slave States. That it will tend to facilitate and hasten the disappearance of Slavery from all the northern tier of the present Slave States, cannot surely admit of serious question. The greater value in Texas of the slave labor now employed in those States, must soon produce the effect of draining off that labor southwardly, by the same unvarying law that bids water descend the slope that invites it. Every new Slave State in Texas will make at least one Free State from among those in which that institution now exists—to say nothing of those portions of Texas on which slavery cannot spring and grow—to say nothing of the far more rapid growth of new States in the free West and Northwest, as these fine regions are overspread by the emigration fast flowing over them from Europe, as well as from the Northern and or Eastern States of the Union as it exists. On the other hand, it is undeniably much gained for the cause of the eventual voluntary abolition of slavery, that it should have been thus drained off towards the only outlet which appeared to furnish much probability of it the ultimate disappearance of the negro race from our borders. The Spanish-Indian-American populations of Mexico, Central America and South America, afford the only receptacle capable of absorbing that race whenever we shall be prepared to slough it off—to emancipate it from slavery, and (simultaneously necessary) to remove it from the midst of our own. Themselves already of mixed and confused blood, and free from the "prejudices" which among us so insuperably forbid the social amalgamation which can alone elevate the Negro race out of a virtually servile degradation even though legally free, the regions occupied by those populations must strongly attract the black race in that direction; and as soon as the destined hour of emancipation shall arrive, will relieve the question of one of its worst difficulties, if not absolutely the greatest.

…[T]here is a great deal of Annexation yet to take place, within the life of the present generation, along the whole line of our northern border. Texas has been absorbed into the Union in the inevitable fulfilment of the general law which is rolling our population westward, the connexion of which with that ratio of growth in population which is destined within a hundred years to swell our numbers to the enormous population of *two hundred and fifty millions* (if not more), is too evident to leave us in doubt of the manifest design of Providence in regard to the occupation of this continent. It was disintegrated from Mexico in the natural course of events, by a process perfectly legitimate on its own part, blameless on ours; and in which all the censures due to wrong, perfidy and folly, rest on Mexico alone. And possessed as it was by a population which was in truth but a colonial detachment from our own, and which was still bound by myriad ties of the very heartstrings to its old relations, domestic and political, their incorporation into the Union was not only inevitable, but the most natural, right and proper thing in the world—and it is only astonishing that there should be any among ourselves to say it nay.

18

Declaration of Sentiments (1848)

SENECA FALLS CONVENTION

A bold extension of the logic and wording of Jefferson's Declaration of Independence to women, the Declaration of Sentiments shocked Victorian America with its challenge to accepted gender relations. The Declaration was the product of the Seneca Falls Convention organized by Lucretia Mott and Elizabeth Cady Stanton. Already famous as Abolitionists, Mott and Stanton felt that the same logic that drove the American Revolution and the antislavery crusade should extend equality to women. The Declaration was approved by the convention on July 20, 1848. A second convention in August laid the organizational groundwork for this first women's movement.

Questions to Consider

- Why were so many of their contemporaries, even among the Abolitionists, deeply disturbed by the Declaration?

- How could an Abolitionist consistently oppose slavery but favor the continuation of women's inferior status?

When, in the course of human events, it becomes necessary for one portion of the family of man to assume among the people of the earth a position different from that which they have hitherto occupied, but one to which the laws of nature and of nature's God entitle them, a decent respect to the opinions of mankind requires that they should declare the causes that impel them to such a course.

We hold these truths to be self-evident: that all men and women are created equal; that they are endowed by their Creator with certain inalienable rights; that among these are life, liberty, and the pursuit of happiness; that to secure these rights governments are instituted, deriving their just powers from the consent of the governed. Whenever any form of government becomes destructive of these ends, it is the right of those who suffer from it to refuse allegiance to it, and to insist upon the institution of a new government, laying its foundation on such principles, and organizing its powers in such form, as to them shall seem most likely to effect their safety and happiness.... Such has been the patient sufferance of the women under this government, and such is now the necessity which constrains them to demand the equal station to which they are entitled.

The history of mankind is a history of repeated injuries and usurpations on the part of man toward

Source: Elizabeth Cady Stanton, Susan B. Anthony, and Matilda Joslyn Gage, eds., *History of Woman Suffrage* (New York, 1881), 1: pp. 70–71.

woman, having in direct object the establishment of an absolute tyranny over her. To prove this, let facts be submitted to a candid world.

He has never permitted her to exercise her inalienable right to the elective franchise.

He has compelled her to submit to laws, in the formation of which she had no voice.

He has withheld from her rights which are given to the most ignorant and degraded men—both natives and foreigners.

Having deprived her of this first right of a citizen, the elective franchise, thereby leaving her without representation in the halls of legislation, he has oppressed her on all sides.

He has made her, if married, in the eye of the law, civilly dead.

He has taken from her all right in property, even to the wages she earns.

...In the covenant of marriage, she is compelled to promise obedience to her husband, he becoming, to all intents and purposes, her master—the law giving him power to deprive her of her liberty, and to administer chastisement....

After depriving her of all rights as a married woman, if single, and the owner of property, he has taxed her to support a government which recognizes her only when her property can be made profitable to it.

He has monopolized nearly all the profitable employments, and from those she is permitted to follow, she receives but a scanty remuneration. He closes against her all the avenues to wealth and distinction which he considers most honorable to himself....

He has denied her the facilities for obtaining a thorough education, all colleges being closed against her.

He allows her in Church, as well as State, but a subordinate position, claiming Apostolic authority for her exclusion from the ministry and, with some exceptions, from any public participation in the affairs of the Church.

He has created a false public sentiment by giving to the world a different code of morals for men and women, by which moral delinquencies which exclude women from society, are not only tolerated, but deemed of little account in man.

He has usurped the prerogative of Jehovah himself, claiming it as his right to assign for her a sphere of action, when that belongs to her conscience and to her God.

He has endeavored, in every way that he could, to destroy her confidence in her own powers, to lessen her self-respect, and to make her willing to lead a dependent and abject life.

Now, in view of this entire disfranchisement of one-half the people of this country, their social and religious degradation—in view of the unjust laws above mentioned, and because women do feel themselves aggrieved, oppressed, and fraudulently deprived of their most sacred rights, we insist that they have immediate admission to the rights and privileges which belong to them as citizens of the United States.

In entering upon the great work before us, we anticipate no small amount of misconception, misrepresentation, and ridicule; but we shall use every instrumentality within our power to effect our object....

19

My Bondage and My Freedom (1855)

F R E D E R I C K   D O U G L A S S

One of thousands of slaves to steal himself and escape to freedom, Frederick Douglass triumphed over his former masters in becoming the most articulate opponent of slavery. A dynamic speaker and brilliant polemicist, Douglass devoted his life to battling the twin evils of slavery and racism. He published three versions of his autobiography, the first in 1845. *My Bondage and My Freedom* was the most complete exploration of his experience of slavery.

Questions to Consider

- What is the importance for Douglass of his opening observation that slaves lack a family history?
- Why were slave owners so terrified by the idea of an educated slave?

In regard to the *time* of my birth, I cannot be as definite as I have been respecting the *place*. Nor, indeed, can I impart much knowledge concerning my parents. Genealogical trees do not flourish among slaves. A person of some consequence here in the north, sometimes designated *father,* is literally abolished in slave law and slave practice. It is only once in a while that an exception is found to this statement. I never met with a slave who could tell me how old he was. Few slave-mothers know anything of the months of the year, nor of the days of the month. They keep no family records, with marriages, births, and deaths. They measure the ages of their children by spring time, winter time, harvest time, planting time, and the like; but these soon become undistinguishable and forgotten. Like other slaves, I cannot tell how old I am. This destitution was among my earliest troubles. I learned when I grew up, that my master—and this is the case with masters generally—allowed no questions to be put to him, by which a slave might learn his age. Such questions

deemed evidence of impatience, and even of impudent curiosity. From certain events, however, the dates of which I have since learned, I suppose myself to have been born about the year 1817....

The practice of separating children from their mother, and hiring the latter out at distances too great to admit of their meeting, except at long intervals, is a marked feature of the cruelty and barbarity of the slave system. But it is in harmony with the grand aim of slavery, which, always and everywhere, is to reduce man to a level with the brute. It is a successful method of obliterating from the mind and heart of the slave, all just ideas of the sacredness of *the family,* as an institution.

...My poor mother, like many other slave-women, had many *children,* but NO FAMILY!

...I say nothing of *father,* for he is shrouded in a mystery I have never been able to penetrate. Slavery does away with fathers, as it does away with families. Slavery has no use for either fathers or families, and its laws do not recognize their existence in the social arrangements of the plantation. When they *do* exist, they are not the outgrowths of slavery, but are antagonistic to that system. The order of civilization is reversed here. The name of the child is not expected to be

Source: Frederick Douglass, *My Bondage and My Freedom* (New York, 1855), pp. 34–37, 142–147.

that of its father, and his condition does not necessarily affect that of the child…. He may be a *freeman;* and yet his child may be a *chattel.* He may be white, glorying in the purity of his Anglo-Saxon blood; and his child may be ranked with the blackest slaves. Indeed, he *may* be, and often *is,* master and father to the same child. He can be father without being a husband, and may sell his child without incurring reproach, if the child be by a woman in whose veins courses one thirty-second part of African blood. My father was a white man, or nearly white. It was sometimes whispered that my master was my father.

…[T]he fact remains, in all its glaring odiousness, that, by the laws of slavery, children, in all cases, are reduced to the condition of their mothers. This arrangement admits of the greatest license to brutal slaveholders, and their profligate sons, brothers, relations and friends, and gives to the pleasure of sin, the additional attraction of profit. A whole volume might be written on this single feature of slavery, as I have observed it. One might imagine, that the children of such connections, would fare better, in the hands of their masters, than other slaves.

The rule is quite the other way; and a very little reflection will satisfy the reader that such is the case. A man who will enslave his own blood, may not be safely relied on for magnanimity. Men do not love those who remind them of their sins unless they have a mind to repent—and the mulatto child's face is a standing accusation against him who is master and father to the child. What is still worse, perhaps, such a child is a constant offense to the wife. She hates its very presence, and when a slaveholding woman hates, she wants not means to give that hate telling effect. Women—white women, I mean—are IDOLS at the south, not WIVES, for the slave women are preferred in many instances; and if these *idols* but nod, or lift a finger, woe to the poor victim: kicks, cuffs and stripes are sure to follow.

Masters are frequently compelled to sell this class of their slaves, out of deference to the feelings of their white wives; and shocking and scandalous as it may seem for a man to sell his own blood to the traffickers in human flesh, it is often an act of humanity toward the slave-child to be thus removed from his merciless tormentors….

Ignorance is a high virtue in a human chattel; and as the master studies to keep the slave ignorant, the slave is cunning enough to make the master think he succeeds….

The frequent hearing of my mistress reading the bible, for she often read aloud when her husband was absent, soon awakened my curiosity in respect to this *mystery* of reading, and roused in me the desire to learn. Having no fear of my kind mistress before my eyes, (she had then given me no reason to fear) I frankly asked her to teach me to read; and, without hesitation, the dear woman began the task, and very soon, by her assistance, I was master of the alphabet, and could spell words of three or four letters. My mistress seemed almost as proud of my progress, as if I had been her own child; and, supposing that her husband would be as well pleased, she made no secret of what she was doing for me. Indeed, she exultingly told him of the aptness of her pupil, of her intention to persevere in teaching me, and of the duty which she felt it to teach me, at least to read *the bible….*

Master Hugh was amazed at the simplicity of his spouse, and, probably for the first time, he unfolded to her the true philosophy of slavery, and the peculiar rules necessary to be observed by masters and mistresses, in the management of their human chattels. Mr. Auld promptly forbade continuance of her instruction; telling her, in the first place, that the thing itself was unlawful; that it was also unsafe, and could only lead to mischief. To use his own words, further, he said,…"he should know nothing but the will of his master, and learn to obey it." "If you teach that nigger—speaking of myself—how to read the bible, there will be no keeping him;" "it would forever unfit him for the duties of a slave….If you learn him now to read, he'll want to know how to write; and, this accomplished, he'll be running away with himself."

Such was the tenor of Master Hugh's oracular exposition of the true philosophy of training a human chattel; and it must be confessed that he very clearly comprehended the nature and the requirements of the relation of master and slave. His discourse was the first decidedly anti-slavery lecture to which it had been my lot to listen. Mrs. Auld evidently felt the force of his remarks; and, like an obedient wife, began to shape her course in the direction indicated by her husband.

The effect of his words, *on me,* was neither slight nor transitory. His iron sentences—cold and harsh—sunk deep into my heart, and stirred up not only my feelings into a sort of rebellion, but awakened within me a slumbering train of vital thought. It was a new and special revelation, dispelling a painful mystery, against which my youthful understanding had struggled, and struggled in vain, to wit: the *white* man's power to perpetuate the enslavement of the *black* man. "Very well," thought I; "knowledge unfits a child to be a slave." I instinctively assented to the proposition; and from that moment I understood the direct pathway from slavery to freedom….

Cotton Is King (1858)

J A M E S   H .   H A M M O N D

On the level of personal conduct, it is difficult to discover a more vile individual in the antebellum Senate than James Hammond. Yet this former governor of South Carolina was one of the most effective advocates for the Southern position in the years just before the war. The following speech was delivered in the Senate on March 4, 1858, in support of the admission of Kansas as a slave state under the Lecompton Constitution. Kansas was divided in these years by the principle of popular sovereignty, which allowed the inhabitants of a territory to determine their government. Supporters and opponents of slavery poured into Kansas to determine its future. An entirely pro-slavery convention held at Lecompton in 1857 crafted a constitution that would make slavery perpetual in Kansas. Even the author of popular sovereignty, Stephen Douglas, was appalled, and the Democratic party was on the point of dissolution.

Questions to Consider

- Is Hammond anticipating the Civil War?
- Is his self-confidence justified?
- What is a mudsill, and why does every society need one?

...As I am disposed to see this question settled as soon as possible, and am perfectly willing to have a final and conclusive settlement now,...I think it not improper that I should attempt to bring the North and South face to face, and see what resources each of us might have in the contingency of separate organizations.

If we never acquire another foot of territory for the South, look at her. Eight hundred and fifty thousand square miles. As large as Great Britain, France, Austria, Prussia and Spain. Is not that territory enough to make an empire that shall rule the world? With the finest soil, the most delightful climate, whose staple productions none of those great countries can grow, we have three thousand miles of continental sea shore line so indented with bays and crowded with islands, that, when their shore lines are added, we have twelve thousand miles....

But, in this territory lies the great valley of the Mississippi, now the real, and soon to be the acknowledged seat of the empire of the world....

On this fine territory we have a population four times as large as that with which these colonies separated from the mother country, and a hundred, I might say a thousand fold stronger....Upon our muster-rolls we have a million of men. In a defensive war, upon an emergency, every one of them would be available. At any time, the South can raise, equip, and maintain in the field, a larger army than any Power of the earth can send against her, and an army of soldiers—men brought up on horseback, with guns in their hands....

But if there were no other reason why we should never have war, would any sane nation make war on cotton? Without firing a gun, without drawing a sword, should they make war on us we could bring the whole world to our feet. The South is perfectly competent to go on, one, two, or three years without planting a seed of cotton. I believe that if she was to plant but half her cotton, for three years to come, it would be an immense

Source: *Selections from the Letters and Speeches of the Hon. James H. Hammond, of South Carolina* (New York, 1866), pp. 301–322.

advantage to her. I am not so sure but that after three years' entire abstinence she would come out stronger than ever she was before, and better prepared to enter afresh upon her great career of enterprise. What would happen if no cotton was furnished for three years? I will not stop to depict what everyone can imagine, but this is certain: England would topple headlong and carry the whole civilized world with her, save the South. No, you dare not make war on cotton. No power on earth dares to make war upon it. Cotton *is* king.

...Who can doubt, that has looked at recent events, that cotton is supreme? When the abuse of credit had destroyed credit and annihilated confidence; when thousands of the strongest commercial houses in the world were coming down, and hundreds of millions of dollars of supposed property evaporating in thin air;[1] when you came to a dead lock, and revolutions were threatened, what brought you up? Fortunately for you it was the commencement of the cotton season, and we have poured in upon you one million six hundred thousand bales of cotton just at the crisis to save you from destruction....

But, sir, the greatest strength of the South arises from the harmony of her political and social institutions. This harmony gives her a frame of society, the best in the world, and an extent of political freedom, combined with entire security, such as no other people ever enjoyed upon the face of the earth....

In all social systems there must be a class to do the menial duties, to perform the drudgery of life. That is, a class requiring but a low order of intellect and but little skill. Its requisites are vigor, docility, fidelity. Such a class you must have, or you would not have that other class which leads progress, civilization, and refinement. It constitutes the very mud-sill of society and of political government; and you might as well attempt to build a house in the air, as to build either the one or the other, except on this mud-sill. Fortunately for the South, she found a race adapted to that purpose to her hand.... We use them for our purpose, and call them slaves. We found them slaves by the common "consent of mankind," which, according to Cicero, *"lex naturae est."*[2]

...The Senator from New York said yesterday that the whole world had abolished slavery. Aye, the *name*, but not the *thing*; all the powers of the earth cannot abolish that. God only can do it when he repeals the *fiat*, "the poor ye always have with you".... The difference between us is, that our slaves are hired for life and well compensated; there is no starvation, no begging, no want of employment among our people, and not too much employment either. Yours are hired by the day, not cared for, and scantily compensated.... We do not think that whites should be slaves either by law or necessity. Our slaves are black, of another and inferior race. The status in which we have placed them is an elevation. They are elevated from the condition in which God first created them, by being made our slaves.... They are happy, content, unaspiring, and utterly incapable, from intellectual weakness, ever to give us any trouble by their aspirations. Yours are white, of your own race.... Our slaves do not vote. We give them no political power. Yours do vote, and...if they knew the tremendous secret, that the ballot-box is stronger than "an army with banners," and could combine, where would you be? Your society would be reconstructed, your government overthrown, your property divided.... You have been making war upon us to our very hearthstones. How would you like for us to send lecturers and agitators North, to teach these people this, to aid in combining, and to lead them?...

---

[1] Hammond is referring to the Panic of 1857.—*Ed.*

[2] "Is the law of nature."—*Ed.*

The Lincoln–Douglas Debates (1858)

ABRAHAM LINCOLN and STEPHEN DOUGLAS

No debate has so captivated America as that between Abraham Lincoln and Stephen Douglas in their epic campaign for the United States Senate. Their exchanges were widely reported in the Northern press; the Southern newspapers largely ignored the contest, being equally disgusted with each man. Since the legislature selected senators at that time, the Democratic victory in the Illinois state elections sent Douglas back to the Senate. Douglas had been the acknowledged leader of the Democratic Party in Congress and thought that he had resolved the great sectional dispute over the issue of slavery with his proposal of popular sovereignty. In brief, the inhabitants of each territory were to determine the nature of their government and institutions. Unfortunately for Douglas, the first test of this principle, which overturned the Missouri Compromise of 1820, came in Kansas and led to years of bloodshed and the Lecompton Constitution. The latter document was the product of an entirely pro-slavery convention, and Douglas refused to support it, alienating the Southern leadership. In 1860 Douglas would gain the nomination of a divided Democratic Party, facing a Southern Democratic candidate, as well as the nominee of the new antislavery Republican Party, Abraham Lincoln. This version of the debates is taken from the original transcriptions, complete with crowd reaction.

Questions to Consider

- Why was the future of slavery in the territories so important to most people at this time?
- How did the recent Dred Scott decision affect this election?
- Why does Douglas keep referring to Lincoln's opposition to the Mexican War?
- Was Lincoln a racist?

Douglas at Ottawa

...Mr. Lincoln served with me in the Legislature in 1836, when we both retired, and he subsided, or became sub-merged, and he was lost sight of as a public man for some years. In 1846, when Wilmot introduced his celebrated proviso, and the Abolition tornado swept over the country, Lincoln again turned up as a member of Congress from the Sangamon district.... Whilst in Congress, he distinguished himself by his opposition to the Mexican war, taking the side of the common enemy against his own country; ["that's true"] and when he re-

Source: Edwin Erle Sparks, ed., *Collections of the Illinois State Historical Library* (Springfield, 1908), 3: pp. 91–97, 100–110, 267–269, 352–353.

turned home he found that the indignation of the people followed him everywhere, and he was again submerged, or obliged to retire into private life, forgotten by his former friends. ["And will be again."] He came up again in 1854, just in time to make this Abolition or Black Republican platform, in company with Giddings, Lovejoy, Chase, and Fred Douglass, for the Republican party to stand upon. [Laughter, "Hit him again," etc.]

…Having formed this new party for the benefit of deserters from Whiggery, and deserters from Democracy, and having laid down the Abolition platform which I have read, Lincoln now takes his stand and proclaims his Abolition doctrines. Let me read a part of them. In his speech at Springfield to the Convention which nominated him for the Senate, he said:—

"In my opinion it will not cease until a crisis shall have been reached and passed. 'A house divided against itself cannot stand.' I believe this Government *cannot endure permanently half Slave and half Free.* I do not expect the Union to be dissolved,—I do not expect the house to fall; *but I do expect it will cease to be divided.* It will become all one thing, or all the other. Either the opponents of slavery *will arrest the further spread of it,* and place it where the public mind shall rest, in the belief *that it is in the course of ultimate extinction,* or its advocates *will push it forward till it shall become alike lawful in all the States,*—old as well as new, North as well as South."

["Good," "good," and cheers.]

I am delighted to hear you Black Republicans say "good." [Laughter and cheers.] I have no doubt that doctrine expresses your sentiments ["Hit them again," "that's it."], and I will prove to you now, if you will listen to me, that it is revolutionary, and destructive of the existence of this Government…. Mr. Lincoln, in the extract from which I have read, says that this Government cannot endure permanently in the same condition in which it was made by its framers,—divided into Free and Slave States…. Why can it not exist divided into Free and Slave States? Washington, Jefferson, Franklin, Madison, Hamilton, Jay, and the great men of that day, made this government divided into Free States and Slave States, and left each State perfectly free to do as it pleased on the subject of slavery. ["Right, right."] Why can it not exist on the same principles on which our fathers made it? ["It can."] They knew when they framed the Constitution that in a country as wide and broad as this, with such a variety of climate, production, and interest, the people necessarily required different laws and institutions in different localities. They knew that the laws and regulations which would suit the granite hills of New Hampshire would be unsuited to the rice plantations of South Carolina, ["Right, right."] and they therefore provided that each State should retain its own Legislature and its own sovereignty, with the full and complete power to do as it pleased within its own limits, in all that was local and not national. [Applause.]

One of the reserved rights of the States was the right to regulate the relations between master and servant, on the slavery question. At the time the Constitution was framed there were thirteen States in the Union, twelve of which were slaveholding States and one a Free State. Suppose this doctrine of uniformity preached by Mr. Lincoln, that the States should all be Free or all be Slave had prevailed, and what would have been the result? Of course, the twelve slaveholding States would have overruled the one Free State, and slavery would have been fastened by a Constitutional provision on every inch of the American Republic, instead of being left, as our fathers wisely left it, to each State to decide for itself. ["Good, good," and "three cheers for Douglas."] Here I assert that uniformity in the local laws and institutions of the different States is neither possible or desirable. If uniformity had been adopted when the Government was established, it must inevitably have been the uniformity of slavery everywhere, or else the uniformity of negro citizenship and negro equality everywhere.

We are told by Lincoln that he is utterly opposed to the Dred Scott decision, and will not submit to it, for the reason that he says it deprives the negro of the rights and privileges of citizenship. [Laughter and applause.] That is the first and main reason which he assigns for his warfare on the Supreme Court of the United States and its decision. I ask you, are you in favor of conferring upon the negro the rights and privileges of citizenship? ["No, no."] Do you desire to strike out of our State Constitution that clause which keeps slaves and free negroes out of the State, and allows the free negroes to flow in, ["Never."] and cover your prairies with black settlements? Do you desire to turn this beautiful State into a free negro colony, ["No, no."] in order that when Missouri abolishes slavery she can send one hundred thousand emancipated slaves into Illinois, to become citizens and voters, on an equality with yourselves? ["Never," "no."] If you desire negro citizenship, if you desire to allow them to come into the State and settle with the white man, if you desire them to vote on an equality with yourselves, and to make them eligible to office, to serve on juries, and to adjudge your rights, then support Mr. Lincoln and the Black Republican party, who are in favor of the citizenship of the negro. ["Never, never."] For one, I am opposed to negro citizenship in any and every form. [Cheers.] I believe this Government was made on the white basis. ["Good."] I believe it was made by white men, for the benefit of white men and their posterity forever, and I am in favor of confining citizenship to white men, men of European birth and descent, instead of conferring it upon negroes,

Indians, and other inferior races. ["Good for you." "Douglas forever."]

Mr. Lincoln, following the example and lead of all the little Abolition orators, who go around and lecture in the basements of schools and churches, reads from the Declaration of Independence that all men were created equal, and then asks, How can you deprive a negro of that equality which God and the Declaration of Independence award to him? He and they maintain that negro equality is guaranteed by the laws of God, and that it is asserted in the Declaration of Independence. If they think so, of course they have a right to say so, and so vote. I do not question Mr. Lincoln's conscientious belief that the negro was made his equal, and hence is his brother; [laughter] but for my own part, I do not regard the negro as my equal, and positively deny that he is my brother, or any kin to me whatever. ["Never," "Hit him again," and cheers.]

...Now I do not believe that the Almighty ever intended the negro to be the equal of the white man. ["Never, never."] If he did, he has been a long time demonstrating the fact. [Cheers.] For thousands of years the negro has been a race upon the earth, and during all that time, in all latitudes and climates, wherever he has wandered or been taken, he has been inferior to the race which he has there met. He belongs to an inferior race and must always occupy an inferior position. ["Good," "that's so," etc.] I do not hold that because the negro is our inferior that therefore he ought to be a slave. By no means can such a conclusion be drawn from what I have said. On the contrary, I hold that humanity and Christianity both require that the negro shall have and enjoy every right, every privilege, and every immunity consistent with the safety of the society in which he lives. ["That's so."] On that point, I presume, there can be no diversity of opinion. You and I are bound to extend to our inferior and dependent beings every right, every privilege, every facility and immunity consistent with the public good.

The question then arises, What rights and privileges are consistent with the public good? This is a question which each State and each Territory must decide for itself. Illinois has decided it for herself. We have provided that the negro shall not be a slave, and we have also provided that he shall not be a citizen, but protect him in his civil rights, in his life, his person and his property, only depriving him of all political rights whatsoever, and refusing to put him on an equality with the white man. ["Good."] That policy of Illinois is satisfactory to the Democratic party and to me; and if it were to the Republicans, there would then be no question upon the subject. But the Republicans say that he ought to be made a citizen, and when he becomes a citizen he becomes your equal, with all your rights and privileges. ["He never shall."] They assert the Dred Scott decision to be monstrous because it denies that the negro is or can be a citizen under the Constitution. Now, I hold that Illinois had a right to abolish and prohibit slavery as she did, and I hold that Kentucky has the same right to continue and protect slavery,...and that each and every State of this Union is a sovereign power, with the right to do as it pleases upon this question of slavery, and upon all its domestic institutions.

Lincoln at Ottawa

...I will say here, while upon this subject, that I have no purpose, directly or indirectly, to interfere with the institution of slavery in the States where it exists. I believe I have no lawful right to do so, and I have no inclination to do so. I have no purpose to introduce political and social equality between the white and the black races. There is a physical difference between the two which, in my judgment, will probably forever forbid their living together upon the footing of perfect equality; and inasmuch as it becomes a necessity that there must be a difference, I, as well as Judge Douglas, am in favor of the race to which I belong having the superior position. I have never said anything to the contrary, but I hold that, notwithstanding all this, there is no reason in the world why the negro is not entitled to all the natural rights enumerated in the Declaration of Independence,—the right to life, liberty, and the pursuit of happiness. [Loud cheers.] I hold that he is as much entitled to these as the white man. I agree with Judge Douglas he is not my equal in many respects,—certainly not in color, perhaps not in moral or intellectual endowment. But in the right to eat the bread, without the leave of anybody else, which his own hand earns, he is my equal, and the equal of Judge Douglas, and the equal of every living man. [Great applause.]

...I leave it to you to say whether, in the history of our Government, this institution of slavery has not always failed to be a bond of union, and, on the contrary, been an apple of discord and an element of division in the house. [Cries of "yes, yes," and applause.] I ask you to consider whether, so long as the moral constitution of men's minds shall continue to be the same, after this generation and assemblage shall sink into the grave, and another race shall arise, with the same moral and intellectual development we have,—whether, if that institution is standing in the same irritating position in which it now is, it will not continue an element of division? [Cries of "Yes, yes."] If so, then I have a right to say that, in regard to this question, the Union is a house divided against itself; and when the Judge reminds me that I have often said to him that the institution of slavery has existed for eighty years in some States, and yet it does not exist in some others, I agree to the fact, and I account for it by looking at the position in which our fathers originally placed it,—restricting it from the new Territories where it had not gone, and legislating to cut off its source by the abrogation of the slave-trade, thus putting the seal of legislation *against its spread.*

The public mind *did* rest in the belief that it was in the course of ultimate extinction. [Cries of "Yes, yes."] But lately, I think—and in this I charge nothing on the Judge's motives—lately, I think, that he, and those acting with him, have placed that institution on a new basis, which looks to the *perpetuity and nationalization of slavery.* [Loud cheers.] And while it is placed upon this new basis, I say, and I have said that I believe we shall not have peace upon the question until the opponents of slavery arrest the further spread of it, and place it where the public mind shall rest in the belief that it is in the course of ultimate extinction; or, on the other hand, that its advocates will push it forward until it shall become alike lawful in all the States, old as well as new, North as well as South. Now, I believe if we could arrest the spread, and place it where Washington and Jefferson and Madison placed it, it would be in the course of ultimate extinction, and the public mind would, as for eighty years past, believe that it was in the course of ultimate extinction. The crisis would be past, and the institution might be let alone for a hundred years, if it should live so long, in the States where it exists; yet it would be going out of existence in the way best for both the black and the white races. [Great cheering.]…

Lincoln at Charleston

…While I was at the hotel to-day, an elderly gentleman called upon me to know whether I was really in favor of producing a perfect equality between the negroes and white people. [Great laughter.] While I had not proposed to myself on this occasion to say much on that subject, yet as the question was asked me, I thought I would occupy perhaps five minutes in saying something in regard to it. I will say, then, that I am not, nor ever have been, in favor of bringing about in any way the social and political equality of the white and black races; [applause] that I am not, nor ever have been, in favor of making voters or jurors of negroes, nor of qualifying them to hold office, nor to intermarry with white people; and I will say, in addition to this, that there is a physical difference between the white and black races which I believe will forever forbid the two races living together on terms of social and political

equality. And inasmuch as they cannot so live, while they do remain together there must be the position of superior and inferior, and I as much as any other man am in favor of having the superior position assigned to the white race.

I say upon this occasion: I do not perceive that because the white man is to have the superior position the negro should be denied everything. I do not understand that because I do not want a negro woman for a slave I must necessarily want her for a wife. [Cheers and laughter.] My understanding is that I can just let her alone. I am now in my fiftieth year, and I certainly never have had a black woman for either a slave or a wife.…

Lincoln at Galesburg

…But there is still a difference, I think, between Judge Douglas and the Republicans in this…. Judge Douglas declares that if any community want slavery, they have a right to have it. He can say that logically, if he says that there is no wrong in slavery; but if you admit that there is a wrong in it, he cannot logically say that anybody has a right to do wrong. He insists that, upon the score of equality, the owners of slaves and owners of property—of horses and every other sort of property—should be alike, and hold them alike in a new Territory. That is perfectly logical if the two species of property are alike and are equally founded in right. But if you admit that one of them is wrong, you cannot institute any equality between right and wrong. And from this difference of sentiment,—the belief on the part of one that the institution is wrong, and a policy springing from that belief which looks to the arrest of the enlargement of that wrong; and this other sentiment, that it is no wrong, and a policy sprung from that sentiment, which will tolerate no idea of preventing the wrong from growing larger, and looks to there never being an end of it through all the existence of things,—arises the real difference between Judge Douglas and his friends on the one hand, and the Republicans on the other.

Now, I confess myself as belonging to that class in the country who contemplate slavery as a moral, social, and political evil, having due regard for its actual existence amongst us and the difficulties of getting rid of it in any satisfactory way, and to all the constitutional obligations which have been thrown about it; but, nevertheless, desire a policy that looks to the prevention of it as a wrong, and looks hopefully to the time when as a wrong it may come to an end. [Great applause.]…